About the Author

Joseph Phillips, PMP, Project+, CTT+, is the Director of Education for Instructing.com. He has managed and consulted on projects for industries including technical, pharmaceutical, manufacturing, and architectural, among others. Joseph has served as a project management consultant for organizations creating project offices, maturity models, and best-practice standardization.

As a leader in adult education, Joseph has taught organizations about information technology project management, risk management, and how to successfully implement project management methodologies, as well as many other courses. He has taught at Columbia College, the University of Chicago, Ball State University, and for corporate clients like IU Health, the State of Indiana, and Chase Bank. A Certified Technical Trainer, Joseph has instructed more than 12,000 professionals and has contributed as an author or editor to more than 35 books on technology, careers, and project management.

Joseph is a member of the Project Management Institute and is active in local project management chapters. He has spoken on project management, project management certifications, and project methodologies at numerous trade shows, PMI chapter meetings, and employee conferences in the United States and in Europe. When not writing, teaching, or consulting, Joseph can be found behind a camera or on the working end of a fly rod. You can contact him through www.instructing.com.

About the Technical Editor

James A. Ward, principal consultant with James A. Ward & Associates, Inc., manages a practice specializing in information technology project management, business systems analysis, technical writing, and PMO implementation. His services are highly sought after for interim IT management and implementation of quality and process improvement initiatives. His seminars and workshops in project management, PMP exam preparation, quality improvement, requirements definition, project risk management, and Microsoft Project are always well attended and highly recommended by his clients. He is a frequent speaker at IT and project management conferences and has written numerous articles for professional journals.

He holds an MBA in finance from the University of Chicago, and bachelor's degrees in economics and mathematics from the University of Minnesota. He is a PMP-certified project manager. He resides in Richmond, Virginia, and can be reached via e-mail at soozward@earthlink.net.

ALL ■ IN ■ ONE

CAPM®/PMP

Project Management
Certification

EXAM GUIDE
Third Edition

ALL ▪ IN ▪ ONE

CAPM®/PMP®
Project Management
Certification

EXAM GUIDE
Third Edition

Joseph Phillips

New York • Chicago • San Francisco
Athens • London • Madrid • Mexico City • Milan
New Delhi • Singapore • Sydney • Toronto

Cataloging-in-Publication Data is on file with the Library of Congress

CAPM®/PMP® Project Management Certification All-in-One Exam Guide, Third Edition

1234567890 DOC DOC 109876543

ISBN: Book p/n 978-0-07-177602-8 and CD p/n 978-0-07-177603-5
of set 978-0-07-177604-2

MHID: Book p/n 0-07-177602-8 and CD p/n 0-07-177603-6
of set 0-07-177604-4

Sponsoring Editor *Timothy Green*	**Technical Editor** *James A. Ward*	**Composition** *EuroDesign—Peter F. Hancik*
Associate Editor *Stephanie Evans*	**Copy Editor** *Mike McGee*	**Illustration** *Howie Severson*
Editorial Supervisor *Jody McKenzie*	**Proofreader** *Nancy Bell*	**Art Director, Cover** *Jeff Weeks*
Project Editor *Rachel Gunn*	**Indexer** *James Minkin*	
Acquisitions Coordinator *Mary Demery*	**Production Supervisor** *James Kussow*	

For my sweetheart, Natalie.

CONTENTS AT A GLANCE

CONTENTS

ACKNOWLEDGMENTS

More than once, I've said that I'm the luckiest guy in the room. I get to write and talk for a living—what could be better than that? I'm so grateful for the opportunity to write, and I must thank the wonderful group of people at McGraw-Hill for their belief in me to write yet another book on project management. Thank you to Tim Green, my good friend and editor, for his guidance, patience, and confidence. Thank you to Stephanie Evans and Mary Demery—two wonderful people. Thank you both for keeping me organized, focused, and consistent. Thank you to James Ward, the accurate and persistent technical editor, for all of his hard work. Thanks to Mike McGee for helping me be a better writer, and to Rachel Gunn for helping me be a better project manager. And thank you to Peter Hancik who took my scribbles and created all the artwork in this book.

I would also like to thank the hundreds of people who have attended my PMP Boot Camps and project management courses over the past years. Your questions and conversations have helped me create this book and will help thousands of others earn their PMI certifications. A big thank you to my friend Kerry Kuehn and his team at Sedona Learning. Thanks also to my friends Fred and Carin McBroom, Jim Chambers, Lamont Hatcher, Jonathan Acosta, Don Kunhle, Jo and Andy Diaczyk, Greg and Mary Huebner, Greg Kirkland, and Gareth Hancock. Finally, I must thank my parents Don and Virginia Phillips and my fine brothers Steve, Mark, Sam, and Ben.

INTRODUCTION

This book is divided into two major sections. Part I, which consists of Chapters 1, 2, and 3, discusses the broad overview of project management and how it pertains to the Certified Associate in Project Management (CAPM) and the Project Management Professional (PMP) examinations. Part II contains Chapters 4 through 14, which detail each of the ten knowledge areas and the PMI Code of Ethics and Professional Conduct.

If you are just beginning your PMP or CAPM quest, you should read the first section immediately, as it will help you build a strong foundation for your exam. If you already have a strong foundation in project management and need specific information on the knowledge areas, then move on to the second section. You'll find this section specific to the exam knowledge areas that will help you—gulp—pass the PMI examination.

The book is designed so that you can read the chapters in any order you like. However, if you examine the *Guide to the Project Management Body of Knowledge* (PMBOK), you'll notice that the order of information presented is the same as the order of information in this book. In other words, you can read a chapter of the PMBOK and then read a more detailed explanation in this book. This book is a guide to the guide.

PMP Exam Readiness Checklist

Exam Domain and Exam Percentage	Chapter #
Initiating the Project: 13%	
Complete a project assessment	1, 3, 4
Define the high-level scope	1, 3, 4, 5
Identify and perform stakeholder analysis	1, 2, 3, 4, 5, 10, 13
Develop the project charter	1, 3, 4
Obtain project charter approval	1, 3, 4
Planning the Project: 24%	
Define and record requirements, constraints, and assumptions	4, 5, 6, 7, 10
Create the Work Breakdown Structure (WBS)	4, 5
Create a budget plan	4, 7
Develop the project schedule and timeline	4, 6
Create the human resource management plan	4, 9
Create the communications plan	4, 10
Develop the project's procurement management plan	4, 12
Establish the project's quality management plan	4, 8
Define the change management plan	4, 5
Create the project risk management plan	4, 11
Present the project management plan to the key stakeholders	4, 5, 10, 13

Exam Domain and Exam Percentage	Chapter #
Host the project kickoff meeting	1, 4
Executing the Project: 30%	
Manage project resources for project execution	5, 6, 7, 9, 13
Enforce the quality management plan	4, 8
Implement approved changes as directed by the change management plan	4, 5, 6, 7, 8, 10, 11, 12
Execute the risk management plan to manage and respond to risk events	4, 11
Develop the project team through mentoring, coaching, and motivation	4, 9, 10, 13
Monitoring and Controlling the Project: 25%	
Measure project performance	5, 6, 7, 8, 10, 11
Verify and manage changes to the project	4, 5, 6, 7, 8, 9, 10, 11, 12
Ensure that project deliverables conform to quality standards	4, 5, 8
Monitor all risks and update the risk register	4, 5, 11
Review corrective actions and assess issues	4, 5, 8, 10
Manage project communications to ensure stakeholder engagement	4, 10, 13
Closing the Project: 8%	
Obtain final acceptance for the project	4, 5, 10
Perform operational transfer of the project deliverables	4, 5, 13
Ensure financial, legal, and administrative closure	4, 5, 7, 10
Create and distribute the final project report	4, 5, 10, 13
Archive and retain project records	10
Measure customer satisfaction	1, 3, 4, 8, 9, 10

CAPM Exam Readiness Checklist

Exam Objective	Chapter #
The Project Management Processes for a Project (15%)	3
Project Integration Management (12%)	4
Project Scope Management (11%)	5
Project Time Management (12%)	6
Project Cost Management (7%)	7
Project Quality Management (6%)	8
Project Human Resources Management (8%)	9
Project Communications Management (6%)	10
Project Risk Management (9%)	11
Project Procurement Management (7%)	12
Project Stakeholder Management (7%)	13

PART I

Project Management Foundation

Preparing for the Exam

In this chapter, you will
- Learn to qualify for the PMP and the CAPM certification
- Learn PMP and CAPM exam details
- Create a strategy to pass your project management certification exam
- Learn all about the PMBOK
- Understand details on projects, project management, and operations
- Know how to be a successful project manager
- Work with programs and project management offices
- Qualify for your exam

This is a book on how to pass the Project Management Professional (PMP) and the Certified Associate in Project Management (CAPM) exams.

If you're looking for a book on how to do project management, look elsewhere. If you're looking for a book on how projects—good projects—should operate, this book isn't for you. If you're looking for a primer on project management, move along. Plenty of excellent books are available that can help you reach those goals.

But if you're looking for a definitive book on how to pass your project management certification examination, this is the book for you. It will clearly, quickly, and fully explain how to pass your certification exam the first time. And then you can get back to your life. After all, the exams aren't fun, and I'm certain you have more important things to do than spend more time than necessary to pass an exam.

 VIDEO For a more detailed explanation, watch the *Passing Your Project Management Certification Exam* video now.

What this book will do for you:

- Help you see the PMP and CAPM exam objectives in detail
- Allow you to watch me field various questions and subjects. Throughout this book, I'll reference videos that I've created to help with the more in-depth topics. Watch 'em and learn!
- Help focus your efforts only on exam objectives

- Tell you how to pass the PMP or CAPM exam—not just take the exam
- Offer you "roadmaps" for each chapter's content
- Give you over 800 practice questions (fun!)
- Make your life more exciting(!)

This first chapter covers many things that will help you prepare for and pass your project management certification exam.

Not everyone can take the PMP or the CAPM exam—you have to qualify first. I think this is great. We, and soon you, don't need the market flooded with the "paper certifications" that other industries have experienced. This certification is special—it proves that the certified professional has documented project management experience and education, and has passed a tough, rigorous exam. If it were easy, everyone would do it.

NOTE As this book covers the PMP and the CAPM examinations, sometimes I'll hop from details on one exam to details on the other. Don't worry—these exams overlap so much that these awkward moments will be few and far between. Besides, if the information I'm sharing doesn't relate to you, yawn, stretch, and then move along to the information that does. I won't hold it against you.

All About the PMP Exam

To become a PMP, you need the following (check out Figure 1-1; it's pretty):

- A bachelor's degree or the global equivalent, and 36 non-overlapping months of project management experience totaling 4,500 hours of project management activities within the last eight years.

  Or:

- A high school diploma, associate's degree, or the global equivalent, and 60 non-overlapping months of project management experience totaling 7,500 hours of project management tasks within the last eight years.

- Regardless of your degree, you will need 35 contact hours of project management education. (Ahem—I teach project management classes for companies around the world, including an Exam Boot Camp that satisfies this requirement. E-mail me for details at pmpcapm@projectseminars.com.) Here are the PMI (Project Management Institute)-approved methods for accruing the project management education contact hours:

  - Courses offered by PMI-registered education providers.

  - University or college project management courses.

PMP Candidate: Choose the appropriate path

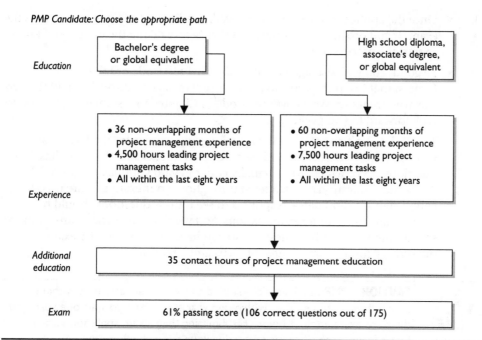

Figure 1-1   The PMP candidate must qualify to take the examination.

- Courses offered by PMI component organizations.
- Courses offered through your organization.
- Distance learning education companies if they offer an end-of-course assessment.
- Courses offered by training companies.
- No, the PMI chapter meetings and self-study don't count. (Darn! Just reading this book won't satisfy your project management education hours.)
- Extensive review of your application. Every application will pass through a review period. If your application needs an audit, you'll be notified via e-mail.
- Audit! Not every application is audited, but if your application is selected for an audit, you'll have to provide documentation of your experience, education, and verification of the projects you've worked on. It's fun, fun, fun. Oh, and the PMI can even audit you after you've "earned" your certification. (Yikes! Here's where honesty is the best policy.)
- Applicants must provide contact information on all projects listed on their PMP exam application. In the past, applicants did not have to provide project contact information unless their application was audited. Now each applicant has to provide project contact information as part of the exam process.

- Once the application has been approved, candidates have one year to pass the exam. If you procrastinate and wait a year before taking the exam, you'll have to start the process over.

- Be good. You will also agree to abide by the PMP Code of Ethics and Professional Conduct. You can get your very own copy through the PMI's web site: www.pmi.org. We'll cover this code in Chapter 14—something for you to look forward to (no peeking!).

- The PMI doesn't reveal what the actual passing score is for the PMP exam— you'll only receive a pass or fail score for the entire exam. The exam has 200 questions, 25 of which don't actually count toward your passing score. These 25 "seeded" questions are scattered throughout your exam and are used to collect stats on candidates' responses to see if these questions should be incorporated into future examinations. You won't know if you're answering a seeded question or a live question, so you have to answer all the exam questions with the same degree of focus and attention.

 CAUTION PMP candidates are limited to three exam attempts within one year. If they fail three times within one year, they'll have to wait one year after the third exam attempt before resubmitting their exam application again. Don't focus on this—focus on passing your exam the first time.

The PMP exam will test you on your experience and knowledge in five different areas, as Table 1-1 shows. You'll have to provide specifics on tasks completed in each knowledge area on your PMP examination application. The following domain specifics and their related exam percentages are correct as of this writing. I strongly encourage you to double-check these specifics at www.pmi.org. It's possible they've changed since this writing.

All About the CAPM Exam

The CAPM exam also has requirements to qualify to take it—and to pass it. This part is just a bit different from the PMP exam objectives. The Project Management Institute (PMI), the fine folks who govern these certifications, have not provided the same level of exam details as they have for the PMP as of this writing. Don't flip out; the requirements are lighter and the exam required score is lower—and this book will prepare you for CAPM success. Figure 1-2 demonstrates the following CAPM examination details:

- A high school diploma, global equivalent, or better (basically, if you graduated from high school, you're on your way).

    And either:

- A whopping 1,500 hours or more as a project team member. You'll have to document what you did on your projects through the PMI's Experience Verification Form—and that's one form per project. The PMI is a stickler that

Exam Domain	Domain Tasks	Percentage of Exam
Initiating the Project	Complete a project assessment Define the high-level scope Identify stakeholders and perform stakeholder analysis Identify and document high-level risks, assumptions, and constraints Develop the project charter Obtain project charter approval	13 percent
Planning the Project	Define and record detailed requirements, constraints, and assumptions Create the work breakdown structure (WBS) Create a budget plan Develop the project schedule and timeline Create the human resource management plan Create the communications plan Develop the project's procurement management plan Establish the project's quality management plan Define the change management plan Create the project risk management plan Present the project management plan to the key stakeholders Host the project kickoff meeting	24 percent
Executing the Project	Obtain and manage project resources for project execution Execute the project tasks while distributing information and managing stakeholder expectations Enforce the quality management plan Implement approved changes as directed by the change management plan Execute the risk management plan to manage and respond to risk events Develop the project team through mentoring, coaching, and motivation	30 percent
Monitoring and Controlling the Project	Measure project performance Verify and manage changes to the project Ensure project deliverables conform to quality standards Monitor all risks and update the risk register Review corrective actions and assess issues Manage project communications to ensure stakeholder engagement	25 percent
Closing the Project	Obtain final acceptance for the project Perform an operational transfer of the project deliverables Ensure financial, legal, and administrative project closure Create and distribute the final project report Document lessons learned Archive and retain project records Measure customer satisfaction	8 percent
TOTAL		100 percent

Table 1-1 Test Objectives for the PMP Examination

Figure 1-2
How to qualify
for the CAPM
examination

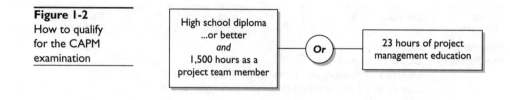

your projects be projects, not operations. A project has a definite beginning and a definite ending—ongoing endeavors do not count.

Or:

- Complete 23 hours of project management education, which you'll document on the PMI's Project Management Education Form. (The PMI really loves these formal documents, don't they?) Here's the cool thing: There's no time limit on when to complete this project management education, as long as you can prove it. Note that the class has to be completed prior to completing the CAPM application (finish your class and then finish the CAPM application). (Ahem—I teach project management classes for companies around the world, including an Exam Boot Camp that satisfies this requirement. E-mail me for details: cs@instructing.com.) Here are the PMI-approved methods for accruing the project management education hours:
  - Courses offered by PMI-registered education providers.
  - University or college project management courses.
  - Courses offered by PMI component organizations.
  - Courses offered through your organization.
  - Distance learning education companies if they offer an end-of-course assessment.
  - Courses offered by training companies.
  - No, the PMI chapter meetings and self-study don't count. (Darn! Just reading this book won't satisfy your project management education hours.)
- As with the PMP candidates, your CAPM application could be audited. If your application is selected for an audit, you'll have to provide documentation of your experience, education, and proof of the projects you worked on.
- Once your application has been approved, you have one year to pass the exam. If you procrastinate and don't take the exam before a year is out, you'll have to start the process over.
- CAPM candidates must also agree to abide by the PMI's Code of Ethics and Professional Conduct. You can get your very own copy through the PMI's web site at www.pmi.org. We'll cover this code in Chapter 13—something for you to look forward to (no peeking!).

CAUTION Once you're a CAPM, you're a CAPM for up to five years. At the end of the five years, you can move on to the PMP certification, take the CAPM examination again, or choose not to renew your title. Ideally, you'll have accrued enough project management experience to sit for the PMP exam.

The CAPM exam has 150 test questions, 15 of which are considered "pretest" questions that don't count toward or against your passing score. Despite the term "pretest," these questions are seeded throughout the exam to test their worthiness for future exam questions. They don't count against you, but you won't know if you're answering a live question or a pretest question. Either way, you'll have three hours to complete the CAPM exam.

The CAPM exam objectives don't go into the same level of detail as the PMP certification does. Our pals at the PMI have painted the CAPM objectives with some very broad strokes—which may be a good thing. Table 1-2 provides a breakdown on the CAPM objectives (double-check www.pmi.org to confirm that these objectives are still valid).

Money and Your Exam

These exams aren't free, and you don't want to waste your hard-earned cash by failing the exam. Focus on passing the exam on your first shot. But just in case some of your colleagues ask, I've included the retake fees. You can, and should, confirm the costs I've listed here with the PMI through their web site. They've changed fees in the past, and you don't want your exam fees to dig into your beer and pizza cash:

- Join the PMI: $119 (join the PMI first because it lowers your exam fee by a few bucks; if you join your local PMI chapter, as you should, there will be an additional chapter fee, usually around $25.)

Exam Objective	Percentage of Exam
The Project Management Processes for a Project	15 percent (approximately 23 questions)
Project Integration Management	12 percent (approximately 18 questions)
Project Scope Management	11 percent (approximately 17 questions)
Project Time Management	12 percent (approximately 18 questions)
Project Cost Management	7 percent (approximately 11 questions)
Project Quality Management	6 percent (approximately 9 questions)
Project Human Resources Management	8 percent (approximately 12 questions)
Project Communications Management	6 percent (approximately 9 questions)
Project Risk Management	9 percent (approximately 14 questions)
Project Procurement Management	7 percent (approximately 11 questions)
Project Stakeholder Management	7 percent (approximately 11 questions)

Table 1-2 The CAPM Exam Objectives

- The PMP exam for a PMI member: $405
- The PMP exam for a non-PMI member: $555
- The PMP re-exam for a PMI member: $275
- The PMP re-exam for a non-PMI member: $375
- CAPM exam for a PMI member: $225
- CAPM exam for a non-PMI member: $300
- CAPM re-exam for a PMI member: $150
- CAPM re-exam for a non-PMI member: $200

Passing the Exam

Let's face the facts: This isn't much fun. Learning is hard work. The PMI's book, *A Guide to the Project Management Body of Knowledge*, 5th edition (which I'll just call the *PMBOK* from now on, thank you), reads like the literary equivalent of a sleeping pill. You don't want this process to last any longer than necessary, and your goal should be—it better be—to pass your certification exam on your first attempt. So don't simply think of "taking the exam." Instead, focus on "passing your exam," so you can get back to your real life.

Just as your projects have plans, you need a plan for how to study, how to prepare, and then how to pass the exam. You can relax on this part—I've done most of the work for you.

 EXAM COACH   I'm not knocking the PMBOK—really! It's a fine reference book and it's what your PMI exam is based on. The book is written, edited, and reviewed by hundreds of volunteer project managers. These are good people who've invested their life into the book. Thank you to them for their hard work and contribution to the project management community. Having said that, know that it's a tough book to actually sit and read. Use it as a reference point for your exam prep.

Creating Your Study Strategy

I'll be your study buddy. You need a realistic timeline and a realistic expectation for studying to pass your exam. You can create whatever strategy you like, but here's my recommended approach to passing your exam. This book has 14 chapters and two appendixes. Each chapter in my book corresponds directly with the PMBOK—except I'm goofy and the PMBOK is boring. Chapter 14, while it doesn't relate directly to the PMBOK, deals with the PMI's Code of Ethics and Professional Conduct. Appendix A explains every project management document mentioned directly in the PMBOK. Appendix B is the summary of all the stuff you absolutely must know to pass your exam. The glossary is a glossary—all the terms I use in this book (yeah, all of them).

VIDEO For a more detailed explanation, watch the *How to Use This Book* video now.

Throughout this book, you'll see an icon that looks like this one. It means that you should download the digital content or use your e-reader and watch a video of me discussing the key concepts for that chapter. Sometimes I'll include more than one video per chapter, depending on the topic. I recommend that you watch the chapter video before moving on to the next chapter. The videos are usually short, and I'm providing some good stuff. These are packed with information, I promise—no sales pitches.

At the end of each chapter, you'll find key terms. Get a stack of index cards and make flashcards of the key terms. It's not that tricky to make yourself a set of flashcards: write the term on one side of the card in big, fat letters. On the other side of the index card, write the definition. The idea is that you'll "flash" through these every day as you plow through this beast of a book—it'll help you keep the early chapters fresh in your mind as you happily move toward the end of this fine piece of literature. Look at the name of the term and define the term aloud; flip the card over and make certain you're correct.

At the end of each chapter, you'll find 20 practice exam questions. These questions test your comprehension of the chapter. I've written these questions to be tougher than what you'll likely encounter on the live exam. My logic is that if you can answer my questions, you can answer the PMI's questions, too. In the digital content, you'll find a Microsoft Excel spreadsheet titled "Exam Scores"—you can see it in Figure 1-3. Enter your chapter scores in the spreadsheet, and you can track which chapters you need more work in and focus your study time accordingly.

DIGITAL CONTENT For a more detailed explanation, check out the Exam Scores spreadsheet to track how you are performing on a chapter-by-chapter basis.

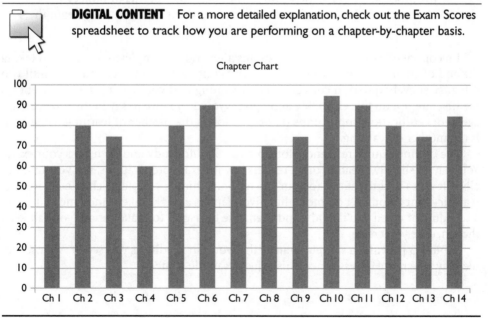

Figure 1-3 You can track your chapter scores to focus your studying accordingly.

In the Total Tester Premium test engine that comes with this book, there are 750 total CAPM and PMP practice exam questions. You can customize your practice exams by domain or by chapter, and you can even select how many questions you want included and how much time you have to complete it. Check out Appendix C for more information about how the Total Tester Premium test engine works. There are three pools of practice questions for you:

- **PMP Practice Exam Questions**   There are over 400 practice exam questions in this pool that emulate those you'll find on the actual PMP exam. If you choose take a PMP practice exam, it will pull 200 questions from the pool, weighted with the same balance you'll find on the actual PMP exam, and you'll have four hours to complete it. If you're going for your CAPM, you can still use these questions as practice, as most of the project management concepts are the same.

- **CAPM Practice Exam Questions**   There are over 300 practice exam questions in this pool that emulate those you'll find on the actual CAPM exam. If you're a PMP candidate, don't dismiss these questions. While the 150-question CAPM practice exam is shorter in length at 3 hours, the questions can be a good review of the project management principles for your exam, too.

- **Process Review Quiz**   This 200-question quiz is good for both CAPMs and PMPs. It is, however, a bit different than the practice exam questions you'll find in the CAPM and PMP pool of questions. This exam only quizzes you on the processes, inputs, tools and techniques, and outputs of project management. It's a tough review quiz, but it will help you really learn the 47 processes of project management and their components.

I recommend you complete these exams after you've completed reading and taking the end-of-chapter exams in this book. Keep taking each exam over and over until you can answer every question correctly. (I'm assuming that you won't get 100 percent on the first attempt on this exam. My apologies if you do.) I love to say in my project management certification boot camps that repetition is the mother of learning. Repetition is the mother of learning.

I've outlined quick references for how you should study and then pass your exam. You may be slightly ahead of other readers in your exam preparations, so I've intentionally left dates and timelines to your discretion. I think a couple of chapters a week is realistic—but I wouldn't do more than five chapters a week. Take some time and create a schedule of when you'll study, and then take measures to make certain you can keep the schedule you create.

Table 1-3 provides a sample strategy that you can modify as you see fit. Your schedule may take more or less time—this is just a sample strategy.

Day	Chapters	Activities
Day 1	1	Complete chapter exam. Create and review flashcards.
Day 2	2	Complete chapter exam. Create and review flashcards.
Day 3	3	Complete chapter exam. Create and review flashcards.
Day 4		Review first three chapter exams. Memorize flashcards.
Day 5		Watch chapter videos again. Review flashcards.
Day 6	4	Complete chapter exam. Create and review flashcards.
Day 7	5	Complete chapter exam. Create and review flashcards.
Day 8	6	Complete chapter exam. Create and review flashcards.
Day 9		Review Chapters 4, 5, and 6. Review chapter exams to date. Review flashcards. Watch videos from Chapters 4, 5, and 6.
Day 10	7	Complete chapter exam. Create and review flashcards.
Day 11		Review chapter exams to date. Review flashcards. Watch videos from Chapter 7. Practice formulas from Chapters 6 and 7.
Day 12	8	Complete chapter exam. Create and review flashcards.
Day 13	9	Complete chapter exam. Create and review flashcards.
Day 14	10	Complete chapter exam. Create and review flashcards.
Day 15		Review chapter exams to date. Review flashcards. Practice formulas from Chapters 6 and 7.
Day 16	11	Complete chapter exam. Create and review flashcards.
Day 17	12	Complete chapter exam. Create and review flashcards.
Day 18	13	Complete chapter exam. Create and review flashcards.

Table 1-3 A Sample Study Strategy

Day	Chapters	Activities
Day 19	14	Complete chapter exam. Create and review flashcards. Download Code of Ethics and Professional Conduct from www.pmi.org.
Day 20		Review Chapters 11, 12, 13, and 14 exams. Review key terms to date. Watch Chapters 11, 12, 13, and 14 videos.
Day 21		Complete a PMP Practice Exam. Keep taking PMP Practice Exams until you get a perfect score.
Day 22		Review key terms. Watch chapter videos.
Day 23	Appendix A	Confirm familiarity with project management documents.
Day 24	Appendix B	Confirm knowledge of key project management topics. Review flashcards.
Day 25		Complete a CAPM Practice Exam. Keep taking CAPM Practice Exams until you get a perfect score.
Day 26		Review flashcards. Review chapter exams.
Day 27		Complete the Process Review Quiz.
Day 28		Pass the project management exam. Gloat to peers. Send e-mail to cs@instructing.com with comments on this book and how it helped you pass your exam.

Table 1-3 A Sample Study Strategy *(continued)*

What Your Exam Is Based On

Your project management exam is based on the PMI's publication *A Guide to the Project Management Body of Knowledge.* This is commonly called the PMBOK (pronounced PIM-bach), and that's how I'll refer to it from now on. I'm not looking to pick fights or be critical, but the PMBOK is drier than wheat toast. It's not an easy read, a fun read, or, much of the time, a complete read.

The PMBOK doesn't aim to define all of the avenues of project management in great detail. Rather, it tries to provide a general overview of the good practices of project management. The PMBOK defines the generally accepted project management practices that are most widely utilized. The funny thing about the PMBOK—it's not the project management body of knowledge, it's a *guide* to the project management body of knowledge. Everything you need to know about project management isn't in that book—but most of the things are. You'll need experience and other sources of exam preparation (like this book), along with constant effort to pass the PMP and the CAPM exams.

One of my favorite lines from the PMBOK comes from section 1.1: "Good practice does not mean that the knowledge described should always be applied uniformly on all projects." I love this quote, because it's a fancy way of saying, "Calm down. You don't have to do every freaking process, activity, and system within this book—just determine the processes that are best for your project and then do them correctly."

 EXAM TIP   Your exam, however, will quiz you on all of the processes, systems, and documents identified by the PMBOK, because all of these characteristics are appropriate for projects, but probably not appropriate for every project you'll manage.

When you join the PMI, you'll get an online-based copy of the PMBOK as part of your membership, or you can plunk down a few bucks at your favorite bookstore (or through the PMI's web site) and get a printed version of the book today. As of this writing, I think the online version of the PMBOK is clunky, hard to read, and it prints tiny—hopefully your access will be better than mine. I gave up and bought the printed version. I recommend you have a copy of the PMBOK for several reasons:

- Your exam is based on the PMBOK. As much as I'd like for your exam to be based on just my writings, it isn't. The PMBOK is what your exam is based on, so you should always reference that book along with the one you're reading now.

- This book is based on the PMBOK. Okay, I gave myself an out in the preceding paragraph, but truthfully, I've worked very hard for my book to be in sync with the PMBOK. I'll occasionally reference the PMBOK as we move through the chapters, but you can always double-check my facts, questions, and figures with the PMBOK if you really want to.

- The PMBOK, as dry as it may be, is an excellent book to have in your project management arsenal. It defines processes, systems, and documents that you'll likely encounter in your project management endeavors.

- Having a copy of the PMBOK on your desk strikes fear and awe into your uncertified colleagues. Well, maybe just the ones from Carlisle, Pennsylvania.

EXAM COACH   Throughout this book, I'll pop into my coaching mode. Like right now. Do you really need to read the PMBOK to pass the exam? That's a tough question and I get it a bunch. For some people, no, they don't need to. For others, yes, they do. I've made a genuine effort to write for the exam objectives so you can study this book instead of the PMBOK. I do believe, however, that you should have a copy of the PMBOK as a handy reference for your exam prep. The PMBOK is not an easy or fun read, but it can help support your exam efforts.

What Is a Project?

You're a project manager, so you've probably got a good idea of what a project is already. I'm hoping. The PMBOK defines a project as "a temporary endeavor to create a unique product, service, or result." Projects, like good stories, have a definite beginning and a definite end. A project is over when the product, service, or result is created, the scope is fulfilled, and the customer has accepted the end result. Or, in not so pleasant times, it's over when it becomes evident that the project won't be able to create the desired product, service, or result for whatever reason (skills, cost, time, and so on).

Temping a Project

Some project managers get hung up on the idea of a project being temporary. After all, some projects can last for years or decades—but they don't last forever. Projects are *temporary* in that they have a definite ending somewhere in the future. Projects—at least, most projects—create something that will last for some time, usually longer than the project team or longer than the time it took to complete the project itself. Consider a project to build a house, create a park, or develop a software application. These deliverables will be utilized for some time. In other words, the project ends, but the benefits and deliverables of the project continue.

Notice I said that project deliverables usually last longer than the project itself. For some special projects, this isn't true—such as for a project to host a trade show, an event, or a fantastic party. Once the event is over, the project is also over.

"Temporary" can also refer to the market window status. Remember the Internet dot-com boom? It was definitely temporary. I'm sure in your business you can identify examples of market windows that were temporary. Project teams are also examples of temporary structures: the team comes together, does the work of the project, and then once the project is over, so is the project team.

Defining a Project's Uniqueness

Ready for a horrible joke? How do you catch a unique rabbit? Unique up on him. (As in, "You sneak up on him." My son loved this joke when he was eight ... not so much anymore.) The point of the joke is that a project should be unique from the rest of your organization's operations. Consider the creation of a new car. The designing, drafting, modeling, and the creative process of creating a new car could be a project. The manufacturing of the automobile, however, typically isn't a project—that's operations. Unique things that a project can create include:

- Products such as software
- Products that are components for other projects, such as the blueprints for a new warehouse
- A new service that will be integrated into your organization's functions, such as a help desk or an Internet application
- A feasibility study, research and development outcomes, or trend analysis

Progressively Elaborating a Project

Progressive elaboration is a process that all projects move through. The project manager and the project team start very broadly—typically with a project's concepts—and then the concept is refined with details, studies, and discussion until a project *scope statement* is formed. The scope statement may pass through additional steps to continue to refine the project's objectives.

Did you ever read any of the Sherlock Holmes stories? Holmes would create a very broad theory of the mystery's solution and then, through a scientific approach and deductive reasoning, narrow his theory over and over until he finally solved the case. He started very broad and then narrowed his hypothesis. This is one example of progressive elaboration, although Sir Arthur Conan Doyle never called it that. Basically, progressive elaboration means that you start with a very broad concept and then, through steady progressions, you gather more detail to clarify the concept your project centers on. Figure 1-4 is a simple example of progressive elaboration with a project to create a new home.

Why Do Projects?

Projects are typically endeavors that don't fall into an organization's normal operations. Basically, projects are chunks of work that need to be completed, but the work doesn't necessarily fall into any predefined function of an organization, such as accounting or sales.

Projects can also be managed by organizations that complete projects all the time for other organizations. Consider an IT consulting company that swoops into company after company to install and configure new networks, servers, or computer software. Or consider an architectural firm that designs buildings for other companies. Or think of practically any service-based business, and you'll find a performing organization that completes projects for other entities.

Figure I-4
Progressive elaboration means progressing through steady, incremental steps.

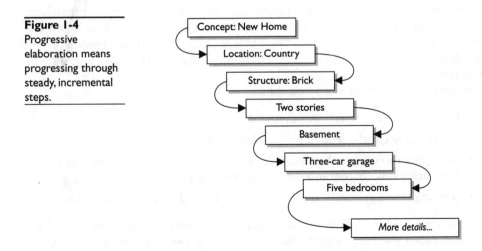

Organizations that treat practically every undertaking as a project are likely participating in management by projects. This means they operate by relying heavily on project management principles to complete their work. This isn't unusual in consulting agencies, construction firms, or IT shops—they exist through management by projects.

Projects are most likely undertaken for any of the following reasons:

- **Opportunity** The market demand may call for a project to create a new product, service, or solution.

- **Organizational needs** I bet you can identify some needs within your company that would make dandy projects: upgrading computers, training your staff, changing the menu in the company cafeteria. Usually, organizational needs focus on reducing costs or increasing revenue, and sometimes both (bonus!).

- **Customers** Your customers have things that they want you to create for them. Sometimes these requests develop into projects.

- **Technology** Technology seems to change and advance daily, and this often spurs new projects to keep up with or ahead of competitors. Know any IT gurus out there managing technical projects?

- **Legal requirements** Laws and regulations can give rise to new projects. Publicly traded companies have been required to secure their IT data in compliance with the Sarbanes–Oxley Act. Health-care organizations must adhere to HIPAA (Health Insurance Portability and Accountability Act of 1996) requirements. And U.S. companies have been working with OSHA requirements for years and years. Initial conformance to these requirements often creates new projects.

What Is Project Management?

You know what projects are, so what's project management? I can hear you sighing and saying, "It's just the management of a project." And I'd concur, but your exam will likely need a more robust definition. The PMBOK defines *project management* as "the application of knowledge, skills, tools, and techniques to project activities to meet project requirements."

Managing a project centers on four things:

- Identifying your project's requirements

- Establishing clearly defined project objectives

- Managing project stakeholders by adapting your plans and approaches to keep those folks happy and the project moving along

- Keeping scope, schedule, costs, risk, resources, and quality all in balance

This last point really defines the Iron Triangle of Project Management. Sometimes this is also called the Triple Constraints of Project Management. Figure 1-5 demon-

Figure 1-5
The Iron Triangle of
Project Management
comprises time, cost,
and scope.

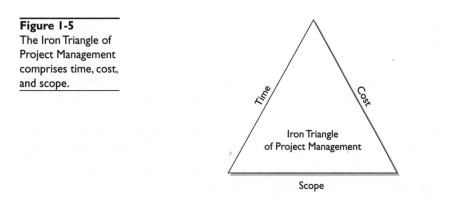

strates the Iron Triangle's concept: All three sides must remain in balance, or the project's quality or other facets will suffer. It's not rocket science: If your scope is enormous but your budget and/or schedule is puny, your project will likely suffer or even fail. Chapters 5, 6, and 7 in this book (and in the PMBOK) focus on these three constraints of scope, time, and cost, so you'll see the Iron Triangle at least three more times.

Back to the PMBOK

I follow the PMBOK section by section throughout this book. Of course, I take the PMBOK and expound on it just a bit—I hope you like it. This section reflects the PMBOK's navel-gazing. For some reason, the authors of the PMBOK interject a logical discussion on project management with a pondering on how their book is organized. Okay. You won't be tested on this specifically, but it's helpful to know as you organize your thoughts and study strategy. So here's the scoop on the PMBOK contents and how this book treats them:

- Chapter 1: The "Introduction" sets the tone and paints the big picture of what the PMBOK can do for you. It's breezy and gets you moving into the book, kind of like this chapter.

- Chapter 2: "Organizational Influences and Project Life Cycle" discusses the environment where projects happen. The project life cycle describes the phases a project moves through from start to completion.

- Chapter 3: "Project Management Processes for a Project." It discusses the 47 project management processes and the five process groups they live within. It's meaty, and we'll discuss it in depth in Chapter 3 of this book.

Section 3: "The Project Management Knowledge Areas" has ten chapters, and each knowledge area gets its own chapter in the PMBOK. Here's a brief overview of each chapter:

- Chapter 4: "Project Integration Management" defines how each knowledge area is affected by the control and outcome of the other knowledge areas. Project integration management is the gears of project management.

- Chapter 5: "Project Scope Management" defines how a project manager should create, monitor, control, and complete the project scope.

- Chapter 6: "Project Time Management" defines how the project manager should estimate the project duration, create the schedule, do some fancy math problems with time, and control and react to all aspects of managing the project schedule.

- Chapter 7: "Project Cost Management" focuses on the project budget and how it is estimated, spent, audited, and controlled through the project. Cha-ching!

- Chapter 8: "Project Quality Management" centers on defining and adhering to the quality expectations of the project stakeholders. We'll examine a whole bunch of charts that measure quality within a project.

- Chapter 9: "Project Human Resources Management" delves into the methods to organize, lead, and manage your project team. We'll also discuss some philosophies and human resource theories.

- Chapter 10: "Project Communications Management" is all about how a project manager should gather, create, and disperse project information. The basic theme for this chapter is who needs what information, when they need it, and in what modality.

- Chapter 11: "Project Risk Management" describes how you, your project team, and other experts will identify, analyze, and plan responses to risks within your project. We'll cover risk matrixes, contingency reserves, and ways to track risks within your project.

- Chapter 12: "Project Procurement Management" is all about buying the products and services your project may need to be successful. Procurement management includes obtaining acquisitions, selecting sellers, and creating contracts. Get your wallet ready.

- Chapter 13: "Project Stakeholder Management" defines the (new to PMBOK, 5th Edition) stakeholder management planning, executing, and controlling processes. Once you've identified the stakeholders, in project initiation, you'll create a plan to keep the stakeholder in control throughout the project.

- Chapter 14, in this book, doesn't correspond directly to the PMBOK, but correlates to the PMI's Code of Ethics and Professional Conduct. I'll explain how you can answer these questions directly and accurately for your exam. Keep in mind that agreement to abide by the Code of Ethics and Professional Conduct for both the PMP and the CAPM candidates is required, and you'll have several exam questions on ethics and on adhering to the PMI's professional code. I'm certain you'll do fine.

Being a Project Expert

You can take a project management class and not be an expert in project management. You can even be a PMP or a CAPM and not be a good project manager. Sorry, but it's true. To be an expert in project management, you need to rely on more than just the tools, techniques, and other mechanics of project management. You'll need five things:

- *A Guide to the Project Management Body of Knowledge*
- Expertise in your application area and an understanding of the relevant standards and regulations
- An understanding of the environment in which your project takes place
- General management knowledge and skills
- The ability to deal with people (your interpersonal skills)

These five attributes and how they interact with one another are depicted in Figure 1-6. The goal of this book is to help you pass your certification exam, but I'm certain the goal of passing the exam is to help you advance your career and become a better, more valuable project manager. With that thought process, it's easy to see how these skills are interdependent. Let's take a quick look at each of these project management attributes.

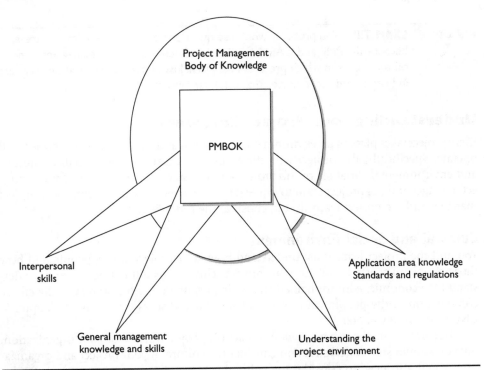

Figure 1-6   The project management areas of expertise overlap one another.

Using the Project Management Body of Knowledge

Yep, back to the PMBOK. (Technically, the Project Management Body of Knowledge is the wealth of information that is available to the project management community.) As far as your exam is concerned, *A Guide to the Project Management Body of Knowledge* is what's important.

Working with Your Application Area

An application area is your area of expertise, whether it be construction, manufacturing, sales, technology, or something else. And an application can get even more specific if we break down an organization into more detail: functional departments, technical domains, management arenas, and even industry groups, like automotive, health care, and so on. An application area is simply the area of expertise with which the project interacts.

Most, if not all, application areas have specific standards and regulations that the project management team must consider as they plan their work and implement their project plan. A *standard* is a generally accepted guideline for your industry, whereas a *regulation* is a rule that your industry must follow, or risk fines and penalties. I like to say that standards are optional and regulations are not. No one ever went to jail because they didn't follow a standard. Plenty of people have visited the big house for not following regulations.

 EXAM TIP You probably won't see questions on specific application areas, because the PMP and CAPM certifications focus on project management, not on the arenas in which projects take place. Just know that application areas are industries and technologies that can host projects.

Understanding Your Project Environment

Every project takes place in an environment—a location and culture where the project will operate. Specifically, the project will affect and be affected by the social, economic, and environmental variables of the project environment. It's paramount for the project manager and the project team to understand the project environment. Every project manager and the project team should consider the following.

Cultural and Social Environment

You and the project team must understand how your project affects people and how those people may affect you and your project. This means it'll behoove you to understand the economic, educational, ethical, religious, demographic, and even the ethnic composition of the people your project affects. We'll discuss this more in Chapter 9, Chapter 13, and Chapter 14.

Your project may not have a wide impact on people outside of your organization, but you should still understand and consider the culture of your project and organization. You'll also need to consider the cultural achievability of your project, the stakeholders within your organization, their political power, and the project manager's autonomy over the project.

International and Political Environment

If your project spans the globe, you and the project team will need to consider the international and local laws of where your project will operate and how the conditions of the project may vary based on where the work is being completed. You'll also need to consider fun things like differences in languages, time zones, and holidays; travel issues; non-collocated teams; and the headaches associated with video and teleconferences.

NOTE "Non-collocated" is just another way to describe virtual teams or project teams that aren't located in one geographical spot.

Physical Environment

If your project will change the landscape or physical structure of a building, you'll need to consider the ecology, geography, and the environmental concerns, laws, and risks that are associated with these changes. Consider a project to build a bridge over a wetland area—there will definitely be ecological, geographical, and environmental concerns to deal with. (I'd worry about alligators, too.)

Relying on General Management Skills

To be a project manager, you have to be a manager. This means you're focused on one important thing: key results. And how do you get results? You'll rely on:

- Accounting skills
- Procurement
- Sales and marketing
- Contracting abilities
- Manufacturing and distribution principles
- Organization and logistics
- Strategic, tactical, and operational planning
- Leverage of the organizational structure and the organizational behavior
- Administration of your project team, reasonable compensation, rewards and recognition, and career paths
- Health and safety standards and regulations
- Using IT to your advantage

If you come from a business background, you'll have an edge on your project management exam. Much of project management is based on management skills, and you can rely, to some extent, on your experience to help answer exam questions. A word of caution, however: The exam is based first upon the PMBOK and then on your skills. Answer your questions according to the PMBOK first. In most organizations, however, the project manager needs three things to be successful:

- **Knowledge** Understanding the business environment and how project management operates.

- **Performance** Understanding the business and project management is great, but the project manager must get things done. Apply the knowledge you know to get the results you want.

- **Personal** Your personality, character, likeability, and effectiveness all contribute to how well the project manager accomplishes the project objective. I believe that people want to work with people they like. It's always better to have someone want to work for you, the project manager, than someone who has to work for you.

Dealing with People

As a project manager, you have to interact with people—lots of people. You need interpersonal skills to work with, motivate, lead, and manage other people. Specifically, you'll need the following interpersonal skills:

- **The ability to effectively communicate** Communication is the core of project management and will likely take up most of your time.

- **A knack for influencing the organization** This is simply the ability to get things done. (Wink, wink—I am hinting at politics, power, negotiations, and trade-offs.)

- **A penchant for leading** Project managers are leaders, not followers. You need to be able to lead the project team, stakeholders, and even vendors toward the vision of the project.

- **Motivating people** Can you energize and excite people about your project? You need to.

- **Negotiating and managing conflicts** A good project manager has the ability to negotiate, lead negotiations, and resolve conflicts in the best interest of the project.

- **Solving problems** Projects are often full of problems that you'll need to figure out. Want to know a secret? Your project management certification exam is just one example you can apply problem solving to. The questions are tricky, and you'll have to use some brain power to deduce the right choice.

Many of these interpersonal skills also overlap with general management skills. Management is all about getting key results; it's about getting things done. Leadership, something good project managers have, is about aligning people, directing people, and motivating people to do their work with passion.

Examining the Project Management Context

Projects typically fall under some umbrella within an organization: project portfolio management, project offices, or programs. The project management context describes all the different scenarios where a project may reside.

Your real-life organization may have one, all, or even none of these descriptions—don't sweat it. For your exam, however, you'll need to be familiar with these different organizational situations and how each one affects the project and the project manager.

Working with Programs

A program is a collection of related projects organized to gain benefits from the projects that wouldn't be realized if the projects were managed independently. Consider a program of building a skyscraper. There could be lots of projects within the skyscraper program: structure, elevators, electrical, plumbing, and tons more.

If each project were managed independently, a lot of work would have to be duplicated within the construction of the new skyscraper. But by creating a program, you can save time and effort by managing projects collectively. For example, the electrician, the telephone installer, and the network engineer can pool their resources to pull the electrical cables, telephone cables, and network cables all at once.

The point to take away from this discussion on programs is that projects are usually contributing one major deliverable and can work together to save time, effort, and dollars.

Opening Your Portfolio

Project portfolio management is the selection, management, and collection of projects within an organization. Unlike a program, the projects may not be directly related, but they contribute to the organization's overall strategic plan. For example, a construction company may have a collection of projects in which some are high-profile projects that could change a city skyline, and other projects are minor, such as the construction of a small garage or home.

The portfolio of projects defines the rules for selecting, maintaining, and even funding the projects within an organization. We all know that a company usually has only so much money to invest in the projects it selects. Project portfolio management defines the projects that should be selected based on need, risk and reward, return on investment, and practically any other issues an organization identifies.

Unfortunately, or fortunately, depending on how you look at it, project managers aren't usually directly involved in project portfolio management. This activity is generally reserved for senior management, because they decide which projects best propel an organization's mission, purpose, and strategy. Project managers inherit upper management's vision and then manage the projects they've been assigned.

Working with Subprojects

A subproject is just a project that's been lopped off from a larger project. For example, a project to build a new house may create a subproject for all of the home automation, home theater, and home network installation. The subproject is managed as its own project, but has constraints and requirements within the confines of the larger project to create the new home. Other examples of subprojects include:

- **A single phase within a project life cycle**   A good example is the phases of construction on a new home: permits, excavation, foundation, framing, and so on. Each phase could be a subproject.

- **Human resource skill sets**   Consider all of the work that plumbers, electricians, carpenters, and other skilled workers can do. The related work of each professional could form a subproject.

- **Specialized technology, materials, or activities**   The installation of a new type of siding for our home construction project could be considered a subproject, where we'd use a team of specialists to manage and complete the subproject.

Working with Project Management Offices

A project management office, often just called a PMO, oversees all of the projects and supports all of the project managers within an organization. PMOs can be organized to manage all projects within an organization, within departments, or even by the nature of the project work, such as IT versus marketing. Sometimes a project management office might be called a "project office" or a "program office."

Most PMOs support the project manager and the project team through software, training, templates, standardized policies, and procedures. PMOs often coordinate communications across projects, offer mentoring to project managers, and help resolve issues between project team members, project managers, and stakeholders. Project managers working with a PMO typically report to a chief project officer or program officer, depending on the organizational structure.

Chapter Summary

You're done with Chapter 1. Congrats!

In this chapter, we talked about what it takes to be a Project Management Professional (PMP) and what it takes to be a Certified Associate in Project Management (CAPM). Which one are you geared for? Depending on which certification you're going to achieve, you'll create a strategy on how you'll use this book, your time, and the PMBOK to pass the examination.

You'll need to know the 47 management processes and how these processes map to the nine knowledge areas of project management. This book discusses clearly and in detail these project management processes and knowledge areas you'll need to be familiar with to pass your certification exam. And don't forget that the Process Review Quiz will quiz you on all of the moving parts of the project processes.

I also discussed what a project is—and is not. You now know that a project is a short-term endeavor to create a unique product or service. Projects are created for any number of reasons, from marketplace demand to solving a problem within an organization.

Projects, regardless of why they were created, move through a progressive elaboration to provide accurate and complete descriptions of their goals and objectives. Recall that progressive elaboration typically starts with a broad synopsis of a project's goals, and through rounds of discussion, analysis, and brainstorming, the characteristics of a project become more detailed until, finally, the project vision is created.

A project manager must understand the environment and circumstances that the project will operate in. The locale, culture, and conditions surrounding the project can affect the project success as much as the project manager's ability to lead and manage the facets of the project and the project team. If a project management office exists, it can provide training and support for the project manager to effectively lead the project team to complete the project work.

Your next step in your certification quest is to create flashcards on the key terms and then to complete the 20-question exam. When you're done with the exam, fire up the Exam Scores spreadsheet and record your chapter score. Keep moving!

Key Terms

A Guide to the Project Management Body of Knowledge (PMBOK)   The PMI publication that defines widely accepted project management practices. The CAPM and the PMP exam are based on this book.

Application areas   The areas of expertise, industry, or function where a project is centered. Examples of application areas include architecture, IT, health care, and manufacturing.

Certified Associate in Project Management (CAPM)   A person who has slightly less project management experience than a PMP, but who has qualified for and then passed the CAPM examination.

Cultural and social environment   Defines how a project affects people and how those people may affect the project. Cultural and social environments include the economic, educational, ethical, religious, demographic, and ethnic composition of the people affected by the project.

Deliverable   A product, service, or result created by a project. Projects can have multiple deliverables.

General management skills   These include the application of accounting, procurement, sales and marketing, contracting, manufacturing, logistics, strategic planning, human resource management, standards and regulations, and information technology.

International and political environment   The consideration of the local and international laws, languages, communication challenges, time zone differences, and other non-collocated issues that affect a project's ability to progress.

Interpersonal skills   The ability to interact, lead, motivate, and manage people.

Iron Triangle of Project Management   A triangle with the characteristics of time, cost, and scope. Time, cost, and scope each constitute one side of the triangle; if any side of the Iron Triangle is not in balance with the other sides, the project will suffer. The Iron Triangle of Project Management is also known as the Triple Constraints of Project Management, as all projects are constrained by time, cost, and scope.

Physical environment   The physical structure and surroundings that affect a project's work.

Program   A collection of related projects working in unison toward a common deliverable.

Progressive elaboration   The process of gathering project details. This process uses deductive reasoning, logic, and a series of information-gathering techniques to identify details about a project, product, or solution.

Project   A temporary endeavor to create a unique product, service, or result. The end result of a project is also called a deliverable.

Project environment   The location and culture of the environment where the project work will reside. The project environment includes the social, economic, and environmental variables the project must work with or around.

Project Management Institute (PMI)   An organization of project management professionals from around the world, supporting and promoting the careers, values, and concerns of project managers.

Project management office (PMO)   A central office that oversees all projects within an organization or within a functional department. A PMO supports the project manager through software, training, templates, policies, communication, dispute resolution, and other services.

Project Management Professional (PMP)   A person who has proven project management experience and has qualified for and then passed the PMP examination.

Project portfolio management   The management and selection of projects that support an organization's vision and mission. It is the balance of project priority, risk, reward, and return on investment. This is a senior management process.

Subprojects   A smaller project managed within a larger, parent project. Subprojects are often contracted work whose deliverable allows the larger project to progress.

Triple Constraints of Project Management   Also known as the Iron Triangle. This theory posits that time, cost, and scope are three constraints that every project has.

Questions

1. You'll need to recognize project management terms and be able to apply them in your CAPM or PMP examination. A series of activities to create a unique product or service by a specific date is best described as which one of the following?

    A. A program

    B. An operation

    C. A project

    D. A subproject

2. Ben is a new employee in your organization and he's been assigned to your project team. Ben doesn't understand why he is on your project team because he thinks everything is part of the organization's day-to-day operations. Which of the following is likely to be part of an operation?

    A. Providing electricity to a community

    B. Designing an electrical grid for a new community

    C. Building a new dam as a source of electricity

    D. Informing the public about changes at the electrical company

3. You are the project manager of the HBH Project to install 40 new servers for your company network. You recommend, as part of your project planning, using progressive elaboration. Some of the project team members are confused on this concept. Of the following, which one is the best example of progressive elaboration?

    A. It is the process of decomposing the work into small, manageable tasks.

    B. It is the process of taking a project from concept to completion.

    C. It is the process of taking a project concept to a project budget.

    D. It is the process of identifying the business needs of a potential project.

4. Your organization would like to create a new product based on market research. This new product will be created by a project. This is an example of which one of the following reasons to launch a new project?

    A. Organizational need

    B. Customer request

    C. Market demand

    D. Legal requirement

5. Your organization utilizes projects, programs, and portfolios. Some of the project team members are confused on what a program is. A program is which one of the following?

    A. A very large, complex project

  B. A collection of small projects with a common goal

  C. A collection of projects with a common objective.

  D. A collection of subprojects with a common customer

6. Sam and Sarah are in a heated discussion over a new program in the organization. They are trying to determine who will make the tactical decisions in the projects within the program. Who manages programs?

  A. Management

  B. Project sponsors

  C. Project managers

  D. Program managers

7. You have an excellent idea for a new project that can increase productivity by 20 percent in your organization. Management, however, declines to approve the proposed project because too many resources are already devoted to other projects. You have just experienced what?

  A. Parametric modeling

  B. Management by exception

  C. Project portfolio management

  D. Management reserve

8. While the project manager must balance risks, resources, and other aspects of the project, one of the fundamental concepts is the Iron Triangle. Of the following, which is not part of the Iron Triangle?

  A. Quality.

  B. Time

  C. Scope

  D. Cost

9. Holly is a new project manager and she's working toward her CAPM certification. She is having some trouble understanding which processes she should implement in her new project based on the available processes in the PMBOK Guide. Of the following, which statement is correct?

  A. A project manager must use every process identified within the PMBOK on every project.

  B. A project must use every tool and technique as identified within the PMBOK on every project.

  C. A project manager must use the most appropriate processes on every project.

  D. A project manager must agree that he will use all of the project management tools and techniques on every project.

10. Projects are temporary endeavors to create a unique product, service, or result. Which one of the following does not relate to the concept of "temporary" in project management?

     A. The project team

     B. The market window status on which the project is capitalizing

     C. The project deliverable ╱

     D. The project manager

11. Harold is the project manager of the JHG Project for his company and he's meeting with the key stakeholders to describe the deliverables of the project that will be implemented. Hanna, one of the stakeholders, is confused on why Harold talks about results of the project that aren't necessarily implemented. As an example, Harold says that a project creates a unique product, service, or result. Which one of the following is a result?

     A. A new piece of software

     B. A new airplane

     C. A feasibility study ⸝

     D. A call center

12. You are the project manager of the GHY Project for your company and you're working with the key project stakeholders to define the requirements of the project. One of the stakeholders mentions that there are industry standards, but there are also regulations for the project to consider. What is the difference between a standard and a regulation?

     A. A standard is optional; regulations are not. ⟍

     B. A standard is not optional; a regulation may be.

     C. A standard is rarely optional; regulations are never optional.

     D. A standard is a guideline; a regulation is a request.

13. A project manager needs five areas of expertise to be successful. Which one is not one of the five areas of expertise?

     A. Application area knowledge

     B. An understanding of the project environment

     C. PMP or CAPM certification ⟍

     D. Interpersonal skills

14. Project managers must be aware of the political and social environments that the project operates within. These environments can affect the project's ability to operate, can limit working hours, or cause embarrassment when the project manager assumes other cultures are the same as hers. Which one of the following is not a characteristic of a project's cultural and social environment?

     A. Economics ╱

    B. Time zone differences

    C. Demographics

    D. Ethics

15. You are the project manager of the KHGT Project, which will span four countries around the world. You will need to consider all of the following characteristics of the international and political environment except for which one?

    A. International, national, regional, and local laws

    B. Customs

    C. Customers

    D. Holidays

16. Project managers need interpersonal skills, such as likeability, to help get the project work done. The project manager needs interpersonal skills to be effective in any organization and project. Which one of the following is not an example of an interpersonal skill?

    A. Financial management and accounting

    B. Influencing the organization

    C. Motivating people

    D. Problem solving

17. Jane is a senior project manager in your company. Wally is a new project manager who is working toward his CAPM certification. Jane decides that Wally would be a good candidate to manage a subproject in the organization. Brenda, the project sponsor, isn't certain what Jane means by a subproject. What is a subproject?

    A. It is a smaller project that supports a parent project.

    B. It is a project that is performing below expectations.

    C. It is a project that has been experiencing project spin-off.

    D. It is the delegation of a project phase.

18. Erin is a new project manager who is working toward her CAPM. She has been assigned a small project in her organization, but she feels that she could use some additional training, coaching, and mentoring. Where will a project manager most likely get project management mentoring?

    A. Project Management International

    B. The American Society for Quality

    C. The project management office

    D. Subject matter experts

19. Project managers and functional managers need to be able to recognize a condition that is best suited for a project, and a condition that is an operation within an entity. Which one of the following is an example of operations?

   A. Creating a new community park

   B. Designing a new car

   C. Sending monthly invoices to an organization's 25,000 customers

   D. Removing an old server and replacing it with a newer one

20. When considering the selection of projects to be initiated, project portfolio management considers all of the following except for which one?

   A. Risk/reward categories

   B. Lines of business

   C. The project manager's experience

   D. General types of projects

Questions and Answers

1. You'll need to recognize project management terms and be able to apply them in your CAPM or PMP examination. A series of activities to create a unique product or service by a specific date is best described as which one of the following?

   A. A program

   B. An operation

   C. A project

   D. A subproject

   C. A project is a temporary endeavor to create a unique product, service, or result. Deadlines and cost constraints are tied to the project. A is incorrect because programs are a collection of projects working toward a common cause. B is incorrect because operations are ongoing activities of an organization. D, a subproject, describes a project that is part of and supports a larger project, so it is also incorrect.

2. Ben is a new employee in your organization and he's been assigned to your project team. Ben doesn't understand why he is on your project team because he thinks everything is part of the organization's day-to-day operations. Which of the following is likely to be part of an operation?

   A. Providing electricity to a community

   B. Designing an electrical grid for a new community

   C. Building a new dam as a source of electricity

   D. Informing the public about changes at the electrical company

A. Providing electricity to a community is the best example of operations because it is an ongoing activity. B, C, and D are all examples of projects, as they are temporary and create a unique product, service, or result.

3. You are the project manager of the HBH Project to install 40 new servers for your company network. You recommend, as part of your project planning, using progressive elaboration. Some of the project team members are confused on this concept. Of the following, which one is the best example of progressive elaboration?

   A. It is the process of decomposing the work into small, manageable tasks.

   B. It is the process of taking a project from concept to completion.

   C. It is the process of taking a project concept to a project budget.

   D. It is the process of identifying the business needs of a potential project.

   B. According to the PMBOK, progressive elaboration means developing in steps and then continuing by increments. Choice A describes the process of breaking down the project scope into the task list. C is not a valid choice for this question. D is part of determining if a project should be chartered and thus is not the best answer for this question.

4. Your organization would like to create a new product based on market research. This new product will be created by a project. This is an example of which one of the following reasons to launch a new project?

   A. Organizational need

   B. Customer request

   C. Market demand

   D. Legal requirement

   C. Projects can be created for a number of reasons, and this example supports the market demand choice. A, an organizational need, is a project to satisfy an internal need. B is incorrect because no specific customer asked for this new product. D is incorrect because there is no legal requirement to create the new product.

5. Your organization utilizes projects, programs, and portfolios. Some of the project team members are confused on what a program is. A program is which one of the following?

   A. A very large, complex project

   B. A collection of small projects with a common goal

   C. A collection of projects with a common objective

   D. A collection of subprojects with a common customer

   C. A program is a collection of projects working together to gain benefits by managing the projects as a group rather than on an individual basis. A, B, and

D are not attributes of programs because projects within a program neither are necessarily small nor are they subprojects.

6. Sam and Sarah are in a heated discussion over a new program in the organization. They are trying to determine who will make the tactical decisions in the projects within the program. Who manages programs?

   A. Management

   B. Project sponsors

   C. Project managers

   D. Program managers

   D. Programs are managed by program managers. A, B, and C are incorrect choices.

7. You have an excellent idea for a new project that can increase productivity by 20 percent in your organization. Management, however, declines to approve the proposed project because too many resources are already devoted to other projects. You have just experienced what?

   A. Parametric modeling

   B. Management by exception

   C. Project portfolio management

   D. Management reserve

   C. Project portfolio management is the management, selection, and assignment of projects that support an organization's business objectives. A, B, and D are not valid answers.

8. While the project manager must balance risks, resources, and other aspects of the project, one of the fundamental concepts is the Iron Triangle. Of the following, which is not part of the Iron Triangle?

   A. Quality

   B. Time

   C. Scope

   D. Cost

   A. Quality, while important, is not part of the Iron Triangle of Project Management. B, C, and D make up the Iron Triangle.

9. Holly is a new project manager and she's working toward her CAPM certification. She is having some trouble understanding which processes she should implement in her new project based on the available processes in the PMBOK Guide. Of the following, which statement is correct?

   A. A project manager must use every process identified within the PMBOK on every project.

B. A project must use every tool and technique as identified within the PMBOK on every project.

C. A project manager must use the most appropriate processes on every project.

D. A project manager must agree that he will use all of the project management tools and techniques on every project.

C. A project manager does not have to use all of the processes within the PMBOK, only the most appropriate. A, B, and D are incorrect statements because the project manager does not use every process or tool and technique within the PMBOK.

10. Projects are temporary endeavors to create a unique product, service, or result. Which one of the following does not relate to the concept of "temporary" in project management?

A. The project team

B. The market window status on which the project is capitalizing

C. The project deliverable

D. The project manager

C. Most projects create a deliverable that will outlive the project itself. A, B, and D are incorrect because these attributes are temporary in nature.

11. Harold is the project manager of the JHG Project for his company and he's meeting with the key stakeholders to describe the deliverables of the project that will be implemented. Hanna, one of the stakeholders, is confused on why Harold talks about results of the project that aren't necessarily implemented. As an example, Harold says that a project creates a unique product, service, or result. Which one of the following is a result?

A. A new piece of software

B. A new airplane

C. A feasibility study

D. A call center

C. The PMBOK classifies the concept of creating feasibility as a result. A, B, and D describe products and services.

12. You are the project manager of the GHY Project for your company and you're working with the key project stakeholders to define the requirements of the project. One of the stakeholders mentions that there are industry standards, but there are also regulations for the project to consider. What is the difference between a standard and a regulation?

A. A standard is optional; regulations are not.

B. A standard is not optional; a regulation may be.

C. A standard is rarely optional; regulations are never optional.

D. A standard is a guideline; a regulation is a request.

A. This is the best choice because standards are optional while regulations are not. B, C, and D do not accurately describe the difference between standards and regulations.

13. A project manager needs five areas of expertise to be successful. Which one is not one of the five areas of expertise?

A. Application area knowledge

B. An understanding of the project environment

C. PMP or CAPM certification

D. Interpersonal skills

C. Believe it or not, you don't have to be a PMP or a CAPM to be a successful project manager. A, B, and D are valid characteristics of a project manager.

14. Project managers must be aware of the political and social environments that the project operates within. These environments can affect the project's ability to operate, can limit working hours, or cause embarrassment when the project manager assumes other cultures are the same as hers. Which one of the following is not a characteristic of a project's cultural and social environment?

A. Economics

B. Time zone differences

C. Demographics

D. Ethics

B. Time zone differences are not part of the cultural and social environment, but are part of the international and political environment. A, C, and D are part of the cultural and social environment.

15. You are the project manager of the KHGT Project, which will span four countries around the world. You will need to consider all of the following characteristics of the international and political environment except for which one?

A. International, national, regional, and local laws

B. Customs

C. Customers

D. Holidays

C. Customers are not part of the international and political environment. A, B, and D are part of this environment.

16. Project managers need interpersonal skills, such as likeability, to help get the project work done. The project manager needs interpersonal skills to be effective in any organization and project. Which one of the following is not an example of an interpersonal skill?

    A. Financial management and accounting

    B. Influencing the organization

    C. Motivating people

    D. Problem solving

    A. Financial management and accounting is not an interpersonal skill. B, C, and D are examples of interpersonal skills, so these choices are invalid for this question.

17. Jane is a senior project manager in your company. Wally is a new project manager who is working toward his CAPM certification. Jane decides that Wally would be a good candidate to manage a subproject in the organization. Brenda, the project sponsor, isn't certain what Jane means by a subproject. What is a subproject?

    A. It is a smaller project that supports a parent project.

    B. It is a project that is performing below expectations.

    C. It is a project that has been experiencing project spin-off.

    D. It is the delegation of a project phase.

    A. A subproject is a project that is typically smaller than the original that supports a parent project. B, C, and D do not accurately describe a subproject.

18. Erin is a new project manager who is working toward her CAPM. She has been assigned a small project in her organization, but she feels that she could use some additional training, coaching, and mentoring. Where will a project manager most likely get project management mentoring?

    A. Project Management International

    B. The American Society for Quality

    C. The project management office

    D. Subject matter experts

    C. Project managers will most likely receive mentoring from the project management office. A is not a valid choice. B is not a valid choice because ASQ does not provide mentoring for project managers. D is not the best choice for the question because the PMBOK specifically identifies the PMO as a source for mentoring.

19. Project managers and functional managers need to be able to recognize a condition that is best suited for a project, and a condition that is an operation within an entity. Which one of the following is an example of operations?

A. Creating a new community park

B. Designing a new car

C. Sending monthly invoices to an organization's 25,000 customers

D. Removing an old server and replacing it with a newer one

> C. This is the best example of operations because the answer implies that this work is done every month. A, B, and D are all unique endeavors that may be done once or just occasionally, but are not part of ongoing operations.

20. When considering the selection of projects to be initiated, project portfolio management considers all of the following except for which one?

A. Risk/reward categories

B. Lines of business

C. The project manager's experience

D. General types of projects

> C. While the experience of the project manager is likely considered during the assignment of projects, it is not considered during project portfolio management. A, the risk and reward of the project is considered. B and D, the lines of business and the general types of projects, are also considered as part of project portfolio management.

Managing a Project

In this chapter, you will
- Learn how a project moves through phases
- Discover how to work with project stakeholders
- Understand how different organizations operate
- Learn the types of organizational structures and their characteristics

You've got lots of work to do as a project manager: meetings, planning, coordination, leading the project team, and ensuring that the project work is done according to the project plan. You're with the project all the way, from the get-go to the final closure report. You work with project stakeholders to gather requirements, keep them posted on the progress, and manage their influence over the project as much as possible. It's an ongoing job that ends just after the project work does.

While your job as the project manager centers on getting the project work done, we know that it's really more than just doing the project work. Logistics and problem solving cling to the project like socks to a wool skirt. That's what you'll learn in this chapter (no, not about socks).

 VIDEO For a more detailed explanation, watch the *Working Through a Project's Life Cycle* video now.

Identifying the Project Life Cycle

Projects are born, they live, and then they die. Morbid, isn't it? But that simple metaphor of being born, living, and dying is exactly what the Project Management Institute (PMI) calls the duration of a project: the project life cycle. A project life cycle is the project from start to finish. Every project in the world has its own life cycle. Consider any project you've ever worked on, whether it was in construction, manufacturing, or information technology. Every project was born (initiated), lived (planned, executed, monitored, and controlled), and then died (closed). That's the project life cycle.

If we were to visit a technology guru and check out his projects, they'd have a different life cycle from what a construction company's projects might have. Every project life cycle is unique to the nature of the work being completed.

EXAM TIP Because every project has its own life cycle, regardless of the application area, it's tough for PMI to ask specific questions on this subject. You'll likely encounter questions about what a project life cycle is, but not on the activities that would take place in a project's life cycle.

Examining a Project Life Cycle

A project is an uncertain business, and the larger the project, the more uncertainty. For this reason, among others, projects are broken down into smaller, more manageable phases. A project phase allows a project manager to see the project as a whole and yet still focus on completing the project one phase at a time.

A life cycle is almost always comprised of multiple phases. You can most often identify a project life cycle by the phases that exist within the project. A construction project may, for example, move through these phases:

- Research
- Pre-construction
- Site work
- Foundation
- Framing
- Rough-in
- Interior finishes
- Exterior finishes
- Landscaping

The end result of a phase generally creates a project deliverable and allows the project to move toward its completion. Check out the preceding list. Just because a phase has been completed does not necessarily mean that the next phase can automatically begin. A *phase-end review* is needed to determine that the phase has met all of its obligations, and then to authorize the initiation of the subsequent phase. A phase-end review is also known as a phase exit, phase gate, or a kill point.

 EXAM TIP You might also know the end of a project phase as a decision gate, stage gate, or kill point. A kill point is an ideal opportunity to "kill" a project at the end of a phase.

Imagine a construction project to build a new sports complex for your city. The foundation of the entire sports complex may not need to be 100 percent complete for the framing of the building to begin. The framing could begin as long as the risk associated with starting this phase of the project was acceptable. The practice of overlapping phases is called *fast tracking* (we'll see this again in Chapter 6 in a discussion on project time management). While fast tracking does save project time, it can increase project risk.

EXAM TIP Fast tracking is an example of schedule compression, as it allows project phases to overlap. Fast tracking can, however, increase project risk. Fast tracking is not the same as lead time, which is the negative time between project activities. Some project managers do a type of fast tracking by adding *lead time* to activities on the critical path. Technically, fast tracking allows entire phases to overlap, whereas lead time allows activities to overlap.

In most organizations, regardless of the project manager's experience, management wants to see proof of progress, evidence of work completed, and good news of how well the project is moving. *Phases* are an ideal method of keeping management informed of the project progression. The following illustration depicts a project moving from conception to completion. At the end of each phase is some deliverable that the project manager can show to management and customers.

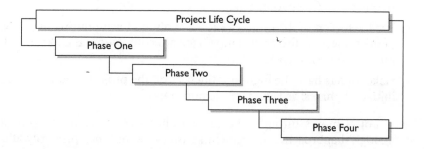

Some projects use an iterative relationship. These special projects are great for endeavors where there's a fair amount of uncertainty surrounding the project's longevity or technology, or the market conditions are shifting. These projects only plan for one phase of a project at a time, and the next phase of the project is planned while the current phase of the project is being executed. This approach allows the project manager and the organization to adapt to circumstances, create usable benefits in each phase, and maximize resource utilization across the organization.

A predictive life cycle, more commonly called a plan-driven or waterfall approach, is a life cycle that "predicts" the work that will happen in each phase of the project. Through a series of waterfalls, where the outputs of one phase allow the next phase to begin, the project moves through a defined approach in each phase. Each phase in this approach usually requires different resources and skills, so the project team may be large, but may not necessarily all work on the project together other than the scope definition activities. Changes to the scope are more tightly controlled in this plan-driven approach than in other project management approaches.

While the predictive life cycle approach seems tightly controlled, the adaptive approach can seem like change is encouraged. You might also know the adaptive approach as the agile method to project management. Change does happen often in the adaptive approach because there's an expectation for change and the project's stakeholders are actively involved in the entire project. Adaptive projects move through iterations of planning and execution (usually in two to four weeks), alternating from planning and communicating to the project team executing the project plan.

Project Life Cycle Characteristics

Because every project in the world is unique, it's impossible to say exactly what must happen in every phase of the project life cycle. There are, however, characteristics of every project life cycle that are universal:

- Phases are typically sequential and the completion of a phase allows subsequent phases to begin.

- Project costs and staffing requirements are generally low at the project beginning phases, while costs and resources are highest in the project intermediate phases. As the project moves toward completion, the cost and resource requirements generally wane.

- The likelihood of the project's success is always lowest during the early phases of the project. As the project moves toward completion, the likelihood of the project's success increases.

- Stakeholders have the highest influences on the project product during the initiating phases, as Figure 2-1 demonstrates.

Every project moves through phases, and phases compose the project life cycle. Phases are logical approaches to segmenting the work, but they primarily allow management, an organization, or a project manager to have better control over the work done in each phase. Each phase within a project determines:

- The work that will happen in that phase
- The deliverables that will be created as a result of that phase
- How the phase deliverables will be reviewed, approved, and validated
- The needed resources for that phase
- How that phase will be approved to allow successor phases to launch

Comparing Project Life Cycles and Product Life Cycles

There must be some distinction between the project life cycle and the product life cycle. We've covered the project life cycle—the accumulation of phases from start to completion within a project—but what is a product life cycle?

A product life cycle is the whole life of the product the project has created. If your company had a brilliant idea to create a new piece of software, initiated and managed a project to create the software, and then implemented the software, that would be most of the product life cycle. The remainder of the product life cycle is the usage and support of the software until someday, sadly, the software is determined to be out-of-date and retired from your organization. The product life cycle is the whole gosh-darn span of time, from concept to project to usage to retirement.

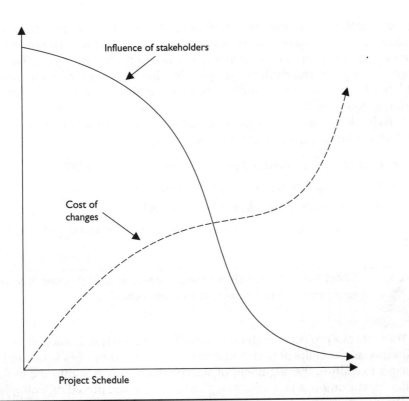

Figure 2-1 Stakeholder influence wanes as the project moves toward completion. Cost due to changes increases as the project moves toward completion.

Meeting the Project Stakeholders

Stakeholders are those fine folks and organizations who are involved in the project or who will be affected by its outcome—in other words, people, groups, businesses, customers, and communities that have a vested interest in the project. If you're a project manager who is working with a senior project manager, or if you are assisting the project manager, you are a stakeholder as well. One of the first project management processes you'll do is to identify the project stakeholders—something that's essential for stakeholder management throughout the project. If you overlook stakeholders, they'll be offended, but more likely you'll be missing out on key information you'll need for project planning and execution.

Stakeholders may like, love, or hate your project. Consider an organization that is hosting a project to move all their workers to a common word processing application. Everyone within this organization must now use the same word processing application. Your job, as the project manager, is to see that it happens.

Within your project, you've got stakeholders who like the project; they favor the project deliverable. Other stakeholders love the project—they cannot wait for all of the organization to use the same application for word processing. These people are considered positive stakeholders. And, sigh, there are those stakeholders who hate your project and want to do everything they can to make your project fail. Yep, these people are negative stakeholders. It's possible that you may have some neutral stakeholders who can affect your project, but they're indifferent to what your project is aiming to accomplish.

Stakeholders, especially negative stakeholders, may try to influence the project itself. This can be attempted in many ways:

- Political capital leveraged to change the project deliverable
- Change requests to alter the project deliverable
- Scope addendums to add to the project deliverable
- Sabotage, through physical acts or rumors, gossip, and negative influence

EXAM TIP Any stakeholder who is opposed to, is threatened by, or wants your project to just go away is a negative stakeholder.

Your role as a project manager is to identify and align stakeholders, and to ascertain their expectations of the project. You may lead the project or work with another project manager to confirm the alignment of stakeholder priorities within the project. Stakeholder identification is not always as clear-cut as in the preceding example. Because stakeholders are defined as people who are affected by the outcome of your project, external customers may be stakeholders in your project, too.

Consider a company that is implementing a frequent-customer discount project. External customers will use a card that tracks their purchases and that gives them discounts on certain items they buy. Is the customer in this instance a stakeholder? What if the customer doesn't want to use the card? Is she still a stakeholder?

Stakeholders can go by many different names: internal and external customers, project owners, financiers, contractors, family members, government regulatory agencies, communities, cities, citizens, project team members, and more. The classification of stakeholders into categories is not as important as realizing and understanding stakeholders' concerns and expectations. However, the identification and classification of stakeholders does allow the project manager to deliver effective and timely communications to the appropriate stakeholders.

NOTE In high-profile projects, where stakeholders will conflict over the project purpose, deliverables, cost, and schedule, the project manager may want to use the Delphi Technique to gain anonymous consensus among stakeholders. The Delphi Technique allows stakeholders to offer opinions and input without fear of retribution from management, by using rounds of anonymous surveys to find a consensus among the key project stakeholders.

Key Project Stakeholders

Beyond those stakeholders affected by the project deliverable are key stakeholders on every project. Let's meet them:

- **Project manager** The project manager is the person—which could also be you, the Certified Associate in Project Management (CAPM) or Project Management Professional (PMP)—who is accountable for managing the project. He or she guides the team through the project phases to completion.

- **Customer/user** The customer is the person or group that will use the project deliverable. In some instances, a project may have many different customers. Consider a book publisher for children. The bookstores distribute the children's book; the adults pay for the book; the children read the book. There is also some consideration given to the user versus the customer. The user uses the product; the customer pays for it. A stakeholder can be both a user and a customer.

- **Functional management** Functional management consists of the managers of the administration or functional units of an organization. They have their own staff, are part of ongoing operations, and may lend resources to your project. Often it's the functional management that employs the people responsible for completing the project work.

- **Project team members** The project team is the collection of individuals who will, hopefully, work together to ensure the success of the project. The project manager works with the project team to guide, schedule, and oversee the project work. The project team completes the project work.

- **Sponsor** The sponsor authorizes the project. This person or group ensures that the project manager has the necessary resources, including monies, to get the work done. The project sponsor is someone within the performing organization who has the power to authorize and sanction the project work, and who is ultimately responsible for the project's success. Ideally, project sponsors shield the project manager from attacks, scope changes, and authority challenges.

- **Sellers and business partners** These are people who may not be directly affected by the project's product, but their interaction with the organization can influence a project. Sellers and business partners are the vendors, suppliers, and contractors for your project.

- **PMO** The project management office (PMO) is considered a stakeholder of the project it oversees. If an organization does not have a PMO, then this stakeholder, of course, doesn't exist. The PMO provides project management support, templates, and training, and helps direct the project management activities of the organization.

- **Portfolio managers** This entity is a high-level committee or board within the organization that decides which projects and programs the organization should invest in. The board will review each proposed endeavor, evaluating its cost, benefits, return on investment, and other project characteristics to determine if the project is worthy for the organization to pursue. This board may also be known as the portfolio review board.

- **Program managers** Program managers lead programs for the organization. A program is a collection of projects that are working in concert to create benefits for the organization that the organization could not realize by managing the projects as individual efforts. All projects that reside in a program automatically include the program manager as a stakeholder in their project.

- **Operations management** "Operations" describes the typically ongoing, day-to-day activities at the core function of an organization. Operations management is slightly different from functional management; operations deal with the saleable goods and services at the heart of the organization's overall purpose.

Managing Stakeholder Expectations

Have you ever had an experience that didn't live up to your expectations? Not much fun, is it? With project management and the large number of stakeholders, it's easy to see how some stakeholders' expectations won't be realistic due to cost, schedule, or feasibility. A project manager must find solutions to create win-win scenarios between stakeholders.

 EXAM TIP If you want to manage stakeholders' expectations, you have to know who they are first. Identify the stakeholders, and then you can identify their requirements. Once the expectations for a project are identified, get them on paper! Nothing beats documentation.

Managing Expectations in Action

Consider a project to implement new customer relationship management (CRM) software. This project has three primary stakeholders with differing expectations:

- The sales director primarily wants a technical solution that will ensure fast output of order placements, proposals, and customer contact information—regardless of the cost.

- The marketing director primarily wants a technical solution that can track call volume, customer sales history, and trends with the least cost to implement.

- The IT director wants a technical solution that will fan into the existing network topology, have considerable ease of use, and be reliable—without costing more than 20 percent of his budget for ongoing support.

In this scenario, the project manager will have to work with each of the stakeholders to determine a winning solution that satisfies all of the project requirements while addressing the stakeholders' demands. The project manager assistant and the project manager may interview these stakeholders to rank their priorities, along with required and optional results for the project deliverables.

Specifically, the solution for the conflict of stakeholders is to satisfy the needs of the customer first. Customer needs, or the business need of why the project was initiated, should guide the project through its life cycle. Once the project scope is aligned with the customer's needs, the project manager may work to satisfy the differing expectations of the stakeholders.

Identifying the Organizational Influences

Projects happen within organizations, and in most instances, the organization is larger than the project. This means that your project has to answer to someone, some department, or even a customer of the organization. As much as I'd like to call all of the shots on all the projects I manage, and I'm sure you wish the same, we both know we have to answer to someone within our organization. The people that project managers answer to are the influencers within an organization.

 EXAM TIP *Cultural norms* describe the culture and the styles of an organization. Cultural norms, such as work ethics, hours, view of authority, and shared values, can affect how the project is managed. It's important for the project manager to know what the cultural norms are and to operate accordingly.

How a project is influenced is largely based on the type of organization that the project is occurring within. Project-centric organizations fall under two big umbrellas:

- *Organizations that exist primarily to perform projects for others.* Think of architects, IT consulting firms, engineering firms, consultants, and just about any other agency that completes work for others on a contract basis. (This is what I do as a writer and corporate educator.)

- *Organizations that use management by projects to manage their business.* These organizations manage their work through their project management system. An IT department, for example, may treat an upgrade of all their network servers as a project. A manufacturer may treat a customer's job as a project. In the traditional sense, these activities are part of their operations, but because there's a definite beginning and ending to that specific work, they're taking advantage of a project management system they've adapted or created.

You also have to consider the maturity of the organization where the project is being hosted. A large internal organization that's been established for years will likely have a more detailed project management system than a startup entrepreneurial company. The standards, regulations, culture, and procedures influence how the project should be managed, how the project manager will lead and discipline the project team, the reporting relationships, and the flow of communications that will take place. Consider the cultural components within an organization:

- Defined values, beliefs, and expectations of the project work

- Policies and procedures, both within the organization and external to the organization (consider the policies that govern the banking industry, for example)

- Defined authority for the project manager and over the project managers

- Defined working hours and work ethics of the project team, project manager, and management

Completing Projects in Different Organizational Structures

Organizations are structured into one of six models, the organizational structure of which will affect the project in some aspect. In particular, the organizational structure will set the level of authority, the level of autonomy, and the reporting structure that the project manager can expect to have within the project. Figure 2-2 shows the level of authority for the project manager and the functional manager in each of the organizational structures. The organizational structures include:

- Functional
- Weak matrix
- Balanced matrix
- Strong matrix
- Projectized
- Composite

NOTE Understanding the type of organizational structure you're working in will help you be a better project manager.

Functional Organizations

Functional organizations are entities that have clear divisions regarding business units and their associated responsibilities. For example, a functional organization may have an accounting department, manufacturing department, research and development department, marketing department, and so on. Each department works as a separate entity within the organization, and each employee works in a department unique to their area of expertise. In these classical organizations, there is a clear relationship between an employee and a specific functional manager.

Figure 2-2
The organizational structure determines the authority that the project manager and functional manager will have

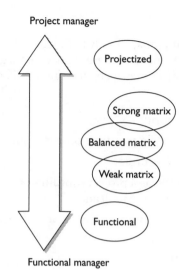

Functional organizations do complete projects, but these projects are specific to the function of the department that the project falls into. For example, the IT department could implement new software for the finance department. The role of the IT department is separate from the finance department, but the need for coordination between the two would be evident. Communication between departments flows through functional managers down to the project team. Project managers in functional organizations have the following attributes:

- Little power
- Little autonomy
- Report directly to a functional manager
- May be known as a project coordinator, project expeditor, project administrator, or team leader (or project scapegoat)
- Project role is part time
- Project team is part time
- Little or no administrative staff to expedite the project management activities

Matrix Structures

Matrix structures are organizations that blend departmental duties and employees together on a common project. These structures allow for project team members from multiple departments to work toward the project completion. In these instances, the project team members have more than one boss. Depending on the number of projects a team member is participating in, she may have to report to multiple project managers as well as to her functional manager.

Weak Matrix

Weak matrix structures map closely to functional structures. The project team may come from different departments, but the project manager reports directly to a specific functional manager. Project managers in weak matrix organizations have the following attributes:

- Limited authority
- Management of a part-time project team
- Part-time project role
- May be known as a project coordinator, project expeditor, project administrator, or team leader
- May have part-time administrative staff to help expedite the project

Balanced Matrix

A balanced matrix structure has many of the same attributes as a weak matrix, but the project manager has more time and power regarding the project. A balanced matrix still has time-accountability issues for all the project team members, because their functional managers will want reports on their time within the project. Project managers in a balanced matrix have the following attributes:

- Reasonable authority
- May manage a part-time project team
- Have a full-time role as a project manager
- May have part-time administrative staff to help expedite the project

Strong Matrix

A strong matrix equates to a strong project manager. In this type of organization, many of the same attributes for the project team exist, but the project manager gains power when it comes to project work. The project team may also have more time available for the project, even though the members may come from multiple departments within the organization. Project managers in a strong matrix have the following attributes:

- A reasonable-to-high level of power
- Management of a part-time to nearly full-time project team
- Have a full-time role as a project manager
- Have a full-time administrative staff to help expedite the project

Projectized Structure

The projectized structure is at the pinnacle of project management structures. This organizational type groups employees, collocated or not, by activities on a particular project. The project manager in a projectized structure may have complete, or very close to complete, power over the project team. Project managers in a projectized structure enjoy a high level of autonomy over their projects, but also have a higher level of responsibility regarding the project's success.

Project managers in a projectized structure have the following attributes:

- High-to-complete level of authority over the project team
- Work full-time on the project with his or her team (though there may be some slight variation)
- Have a full-time administrative staff to help expedite the project

Composite Organizations

On paper, all of these organizational structures look great. In reality, few companies map to only one of these structures all of the time. For example, a company using the functional model may create a special project consisting of talent from many different departments. Such project teams report directly to a project manager and will work on a high-priority project for its duration. These entities are called *composite* organizations because they may be a blend of multiple organizational types.

Table 2-1 summarizes the most common organizational structures and their attributes.

Managing Project Teams

Depending on which organizational structure you're operating within will also determine the type of project team you're managing. As you might guess, in a projectized structure, you'll have a full-time project team, sometimes called a dedicated project team. In a functional or matrix environment, you'll likely have a part-time team. When

	Project Manager's Authority	Project Manager's Role	Resources on Project	Budget Control	Project Administrative Staff
Projectized	High	Full-time	High to total	Project manager	Full-time
Strong Matrix	Moderate to high	Full-time	Moderate to high	Project manager	Full-time
Balanced Matrix	Low to moderate	Full-time	Low to moderate	Project manager and functional management	Part-time
Weak Matrix	Limited	Part-time	Limited	Functional management	Part-time
Functional	Little	Part-time	Little	Functional management	Part-time

Table 2-1 Organizational Structures and Their Influence on Project Managers

you're working with project team members that float from project to project, as in a matrix environment, you'll have to coordinate with the other project managers, the functional managers, and even the project team members about your project plans and need for resources.

Project teams in a functional, matrix, or projectized organizational structure often utilize contract-based workers to help achieve the project scope. These contractors are individuals who are represented by third parties or consulting agencies. When you're working with companies that have been hired to help and become part of the project team, you've created a partnership among your company and the vendor's company. This partnership is ruled by the contract and may conflict with the project manager's approach, style, and project governance. You can alleviate much of the strain in a partnership by clearly communicating expectations of the entire project team and determining as early as possible if the contractors have issues with the way the project team will be managed.

In today's electronic-based world, it's more and more common to work with virtual teams. Virtual teams use web-collaboration software to host meetings, to share electronic workspaces, and to allow employees to work remotely. This, of course, saves on travel expenses, allows utilization of talented workers from all areas of an organization, and permits easier communications than just telephone conversations and e-mail. Virtual teams do face additional problems that need to be addressed: time zone differences, language barriers, technology reliability, and cultural differences.

Working with Your PMO

Recall that a PMO is a schmancy club where all the project managers get together for cigars and martinis. Not really—I just wanted to see if you were paying attention. The PMO coordinates the activities of all the project managers. Its primary goal is to create a uniform approach on how projects operate within the organization. PMOs can exist in any structure, but are most commonly used in matrix structures and in projectized environments.

The role of the PMO is typically to support the project management in the form of providing templates, project management software, training, leadership, and even granting authority for the project's existence. Often, the PMO provides the administrative support a project manager can expect in a projectized environment.

Here's the big caveat with PMOs: Project team members in a projectized environment are traditionally working on one project at a time. A PMO, however, may elect to share project team members among projects if it best serves the organization. So basically, there's no hard-and-fast rule for the assignment of project team members to an individual project if they are reporting to the PMO rather than directly to the project manager. For your CAPM or PMP exam, keep this in mind: The project managers report to the PMO, and the PMO may exercise its authority over the project managers' control of the project team.

Defining a Project Management System

A project management system is a collection of tools, resources, a project management methodology, and defined procedures a project manager uses to complete a project. Project management is typically defined for the organization, and the collection of tools and resources is considered the project management system—it's the approach to managing projects within an organization.

Your project management plan defines how your project will work with and utilize the project management system on which your organization relies. Of course, you don't have to have a project management system, but most companies do. A project management system will vary based on the project's application area, organizational structure, and the project complexity.

If an organization is using a PMO, the PMO will likely control and dictate the functions of the project management system. For your CAPM or PMP exam, know that a project management system defines the processes and procedures a project manager is to follow to complete a project.

Chapter Summary

Studying for your project management exam can be its own project. You have a sense already where this project is going: to earn your certification. Sooner or later, your certification project will end, and you'll move on to other goals. Projects are the same way. They have a life of their own, and it's called the project life cycle.

Every project, regardless of the application area, follows its own logical path from initiation to closure. Within the project life cycle, phases allow the project to move toward completion. At the end of a phase, the project should create some deliverable or condition that allows the next phase to begin. Sometimes, depending on the associated risk, phases are allowed to begin even when previous phases are not completed. This is called fast tracking.

A project has the most uncertainty of finishing successfully at the beginning because it's a long, long way from completion. As a project moves closer to completion, the likelihood of project success increases, because the completion of phases moves the project closer to completing the project objectives. Also, at the start of the project, stakeholders have the highest influence on the project's deliverables. This means they can easily pick and choose, and change their minds over and over because nothing has been created yet. When the project begins to create deliverables and move toward closure, it becomes increasingly difficult for stakeholders to change their minds on what the project deliverable should be. Stakeholders can still change their mind (and they often do), but it'll usually cost more time and money the later they wait to announce changes to the project requirements.

Speaking of stakeholders (the folks who have a vested interested in the outcome of a project), it's up to the project team to define all of the stakeholders within a project. If the project team fails to identify a key stakeholder, trouble and risk can ensue. Recall that stakeholders can also be classified as positive, neutral, or negative, depending on their position on the project's purpose and the desired project deliverable.

The organizational structure can help the project team identify the stakeholders, and the organizational structure also identifies the project manager's authority. This authority ranks from low to high in the following order of organizational structures: functional, weak matrix, balanced matrix, strong matrix, projectized.

Project management offices support the project manager by providing software, templates, training, and often administrative staffing.

For your exam, pay special attention to the attributes of a project life cycle and its phases. You'll also want to zoom in on the organizational structures and their characteristics. You'll likely encounter questions in which you, as the project manager, will need to respond to a scenario. The response will be determined by the organizational structure within which the project manager is operating.

Key Terms

Adaptive life cycle   This is a project life cycle that anticipates many changes to the project scope and demands highly involved project stakeholders. Because change happens often, change control is managed tightly by the project manager. This approach is also known as the agile project management methodology.

Balanced matrix structure   An organization where organizational resources are pooled into one project team, but the functional managers and the project managers share the project power.

Composite structure   An organization that creates a blend of the functional, matrix, and projectized structures.

Customer/user   The person(s) who will pay for and use the project's deliverables.

Deliverable   A verifiable, measurable product or service created by a phase and/or a project.

Functional structure   An organization that is divided into functions, and each employee has one clear functional manager. Each department acts independently of the other departments. A project manager in this structure has little to no power and may be called a project coordinator.

Influencers   Persons who can positively or negatively influence a project's ongoing activities and/or the project's likelihood of success.

Kill point   The review of a phase to determine if it accomplished its requirements. A kill point signals an opportunity to kill the project if it should not continue.

Negative stakeholder   A stakeholder who does not want a project to succeed. He or she may try to negatively influence the project and help it fail.

Performing organization   The organization whose employees or members are most directly involved in the project work.

Phase   The logical division of a project based on the work or deliverable completed within that phase. Common examples include the phases within construction, software development, or manufacturing.

Phase exit   The review of a phase to determine if it accomplished its requirements. It signals the exiting of one phase and the entering of another.

Phase gate   The review of a phase to determine if it accomplished its requirements. Like a phase exit, a phase gate shows the qualifications to move from one phase to another.

Phase-end review   The review of a phase to determine if it accomplished its requirements. A phase-end review is also called a phase exit, a phase gate, and a kill point.

Positive stakeholder   A stakeholder who wants a project to exist and succeed. He or she may try to positively influence the project and help it succeed.

Predictive life cycle   A predictive life cycle, also called a plan-driven approach, is a life cycle that "predicts" the work that will happen in each phase of the project. The project plan, time, cost, and scope are defined early in the project and predict what is to happen in the project.

Product life cycle   The life cycle of the product a project creates. For example, a project can create a piece of software; the software then has its own life cycle until it becomes defunct.

Project life cycle   The collection of phases from the start of a project to its completion.

Project management office (PMO)   A business unit that centralizes the operations and procedures of all projects within the organization. The PMO supports the project manager through software, templates, and administrative support. A PMO can exist in any organizational structure, but it is most common in matrix and projectized structures.

Project management system   The defined set of rules, policies, and procedures that a project manager follows and utilizes to complete the project.

Project stakeholder   Anyone who has a vested interest in a project's operation and/or its outcome.

Projectized structure   An organization that assigns a project team to one project for the duration of the project life cycle. The project manager has high-to-almost-complete project power.

Strong matrix structure   An organization where organizational resources are pooled into one project team, but the functional managers have less project power than the project manager.

Weak matrix structure   An organization where organizational resources are pooled into one project team, but the functional managers have more project power than the project manager.

Case Study

Managing Projects from Start to Completion

This case study examines the project process and the phases a project moves through to reach its conclusion. The Riverside Community Park Project was an endeavor to create a 140-acre community recreation park alongside the White River. The project, led by Thomas Stanford and assisted by Jan Steinberg, included many deliverables for the community, including:

- A walkway along the river, connecting restaurants and neighborhoods
- Hiking trails
- Baseball and soccer fields
- Water access points
- Picnic areas
- Children's playgrounds
- An indoor swimming facility
- Parking areas

Examining the Project Deliverables

The first phase the project moved through was in-depth planning and development. The project scope was broken down into four major categories:

- River-related deliverables, such as docks and fishing areas
- Structural-related deliverables, such as the indoor swimming facility
- Environment-related deliverables, such as the hiking trails
- Common areas, such as the picnic and parking areas

Each of these deliverables was broken down into components that could, in turn, be broken down into exact deliverables for the project. For example, the indoor swimming facility included the excavation of the grounds for the building, the construction of the building, and the construction of the indoor swimming pool.

Each deliverable was broken down to ensure that all of the required components were included in the project plan. Each category of deliverables went through a similar process to ensure that all of the deliverables were accounted for and that the project plans were complete. Stanford and Steinberg worked with a large project team that specialized in different disciplines within the project work.

For example, Holly Johnson of EQHN Engineering served as team lead for the river-related deliverables. Johnson has years of experience in construction projects dealing with lakes, rivers, and manufactured waterways. Her expert judgment contributed to the development of the plan and the breaking down of the work.

Don Streeping of RHD Architecture and Construction helped Stanford develop the requirements, features, and components of the indoor swimming facility. RHD architects designed the building and swimming facilities for the project and helped map out the timeline for a feasible completion and successful opening day.

Grey Jansen with the Department of Natural Resources and Marci Koening with the Department of Urban Planning worked with Stanford to create several different hiking trails and a pedway along the riverfront. The elaborate trail system offers trails ranging from challenging hikes to pleasant strolls. In addition, the pedway allows visitors to walk through more than 50 acres along the river and to visit restaurants, shopping centers, and other commercial ventures within the park. Without Jansen's and Koening's expertise, the project would not have been a success.

Finally, John Anderson led the team responsible for the common areas. The children's playgrounds are topnotch, and there is ample parking and access to the park. In addition, Anderson's team created soccer fields and two Little League baseball diamonds.

Examining the Project Phases

When the project was launched, the 140-acre tract was a marshy, brush-filled plot of land that was mostly inaccessible to the general public. For this undertaking to be successful, the project had to move through several phases. Many of the deliverables, such as the parking areas and maintenance roads, had to be created first in order to allow the equipment and workers to access the sites throughout the park.

Phase One

The first phase of the project was in-depth planning. Stanford and Steinberg worked with each of the team leaders and other experts to coordinate the activities to create the deliverables in a timely fashion. To maximize the return on investment, the project's plan called for immediate deliverables for the public.

The planning phase of the project resulted in:

- The project plan and subsidiary plans, such as cost, risk, and scope management plans
- Design specifications for each of the major deliverables
- A schedule that allowed for the deliverables to work in tandem and for them to support one another throughout the project plan
- The creation of a work authorization system
- Continued community buy-in for the project

Phase Two

Once the project's plan and coordination between teams was realized, John Anderson's crew went to work on Phase Two of the project: creating accessibility. This phase of the project became known as the "Rough-In" phase because roads, parking, and preparation of the park were needed immediately. This phase resulted in:

- Access roads throughout the park

- Entry roads to the park at several points throughout the city

- Junction roads that allowed easy access for construction equipment to be stored on-site for the project's duration

Phase Three

Phase Three of the project allowed each team to begin its work independently, with an eye toward common delivery dates. For example, Johnson and Jansen had expertise in separate deliverables: the water access points and the trails throughout the park. The project plan called for trails along the river and through the woods, which would be built by Johnson's crew. In tandem with creating the hiking trails, Johnson's team went to work on the river pedway. At several points along the river pedway, trails from the woods would connect to the paved surface. These two deliverables were timed so that both teams would work together on connecting the nature trails with the river pedway. In addition, caution had to be taken to preserve the environment in the woods and in the water.

Streeping's primary responsibility was the creation of the indoor swimming facility. This deliverable required excavation, the digging and creation of the indoor swimming pool, and the construction of the facility to house the indoor swimming pool. Streeping had to coordinate the construction with Anderson, as the swimming pool needed the largest parking area in the compound. Stanford and Steinberg worked with each team leader to facilitate a common schedule for each of the deliverables.

This phase saw its first completed deliverable for the project: A children's playground was opened near the park entrance that the public could begin using immediately. The playground can easily host up to 75 children at once and has parking for up to 50 cars. In addition, a picnic shelter was opened adjacent to the playground. Because of the proximity of the park and playground to nearby shops and restaurants, this deliverable was well-received by the community, and the public began enjoying the facilities immediately.

Other deliverables in the phase included:

- Restroom facilities installed at several points throughout the park

- Excavation of several water access points

- Excavation for the swimming facility

- Clearing and leveling for the soccer and baseball fields

Phase Four

Phase Four of the project focused on creating more usable deliverables for the general public. The focus was on the hiking trails throughout the park and on partial completion of the river pedway. The hiking trails required brush to be removed, some trees to be removed, and the land to be graded for passable hiking. The pedway was initially formed as a concrete path that would be blacktopped once it was connected throughout the park. Like the hiking trails, the pedway required the removal of brush and trees while considering the environmental preservation of the river.

Jansen's and Anderson's teams worked together to clear the pedway, remove the brush along the riverbank, and preserve the older trees to create a stunning walk along the river. To create maximum deliverables, the pedway was implemented at opposite ends of the 50-acre trail, with plans to be connected at acre 25. This allowed the public to enjoy the deliverables in increments from either end of the park.

This phase created these deliverables:

- Seven of the ten hiking trails in the system were cleared and opened for public usage.

- A total of 30 acres of the river pedway were completed (15 acres on both ends of the pedway).

- The swimming pool was excavated and the concrete body of the pool was installed.

Phase Five

Phase Five of the project was perhaps the most exciting, as it completed several deliverables:

- The remaining three of the hiking trails were completed. These trails included bridges over small creeks that feed into the White River.

- The remaining 20 acres of the river pedway were excavated and completed with the concrete pour. People can now walk or ride their bikes the entire 50-acre length alongside the river.

- The soccer and baseball facilities were installed, which included restrooms, concession stands, bleachers, fences, and dugouts. The fields were also seeded and fertilized, and will be officially open for public use next spring when the grass is healthy.

Phase Six

Phase Six of the project was the longest, but most satisfying. This phase focused on the completion of the indoor swimming facility. The structure includes two Olympic-size swimming pools, diving boards, locker rooms, sauna and steam facilities, and a restaurant. The building is situated on a hill that overlooks the river pedway—it is the crown jewel of the park. The facility was completed as planned and was opened to the public.

This phase also included:

- The completion of blacktopping the 50-acre pedway along the river
- The closing and sodding of the temporary construction equipment corral
- Installing the remaining playgrounds and picnic areas throughout the park
- Opening the water access points, including a commercial dock for fishers and boaters
- The official opening of the soccer and baseball fields

Controlling Project Changes

Throughout the project, the public had many requests for changes to the project scope. The project scope was quite large, and the project budget had limited room for additional changes without requesting additional funds.

When changes were proposed, such as the addition of tennis courts to the common areas, they were considered for validity, cost, risk, and the impact on the project scope. A change control board, which Stanford initiated, considered the proposed changes and then approved or declined the changes based on predetermined metrics such as time, cost, and overall change to the original project scope.

When the project was initiated, a public meeting was held to gather input from the community on the deliverables they would most like to see in the park. At this point of the project, the stakeholders—the community at large—had a great opportunity to voice their opinions on what the park should and should not include. Once a consensus was created for the park deliverables and a scope was created, it became challenging for anyone to add to it.

Some changes, however, proved valuable and were added to project deliverables. For example, the commercial fishing and boating dock within the park was a viable opportunity for a local businessperson to provide a service for boaters and the community at no cost to the project. Koening and Johnson worked with the business to ensure that it met the city codes, safety regulations, and fit within the scheme and overall effect of the project.

Other changes, such as the tennis courts, were declined. While there very well may be many tennis players in the community, this request was denied for several reasons:

- The city already supports many tennis courts in the community.
- A private tennis club is in the vicinity of the park, and they protested the addition of the tennis courts, as this would be an economic blow to their business.
- No tennis players had requested the courts at any of the public meetings discussing the creation of the park.

Changes, especially in a project of this size, had to be tracked and documented. Any changes that were approved or declined were cataloged for reference against future change requests that may have entered the project.

Questions

1. There is a difference between the project, the project life cycle, the project schedule, and the overall project objective. At the core of these terms is the project life cycle. The project life cycle comprises which of the following?

   A. Phases

   B. Milestones

   C. Estimates

   D. Activities

2. Marci Koening, the project manager for the ERP Project, is about to complete the project phase review. The completion of a project phase is also known as which of the following?

   A. Lessons learned

   B. The kill point

   C. Earned value management

   D. Conditional advancement

3. You are the project manager of the GHY Project for your organization. You have been tasked with creating new software for your web site which must also be available to users on mobile devices. There are several deliverables that must be documented for this project. Which of the following best describes a project deliverable?

   A. The resources used by the project to complete the necessary work

   B. The resources exported from the project as a result of the project work

   C. The end result of a project planning session

   D. A verifiable, measurable work product

4. As the project manager, you must work with your project team to identify the project and the project phases within the project schedule. This identification helps to communicate expectations and outcomes of the project work. The compilation of all the phases within a project equates to the

   _____.

   A. Project life cycle

   B. Product life cycle

   C. Project completion

   D. Project processes

5. Projects move through a logical progression from the initiation to the project closure. It's important to understand the fluctuation of costs, schedules, resources, and risks within the logical progression of the project life cycle. Which of the following describes the early stages of a project?

   A. High costs and high demands for resources

   B. A high demand for change

   C. A high demand for project team time

   D. Low costs and low demands for resources

6. Management has asked you to help them identify the points of the project where the risk of failure is highest and lowest. As a general rule, at which point is the risk of failure the lowest, but the consequence of failure the highest?

   A. During the early stages.

   B. During the middle stages.

   C. During the final stages.

   D. The risk of failure is even across all project phases.

7. Project team members are most likely to work full-time on a project in which of the following organizational structures?

   A. Functional

   B. Weak matrix

   C. Strong matrix

   D. Projectized

8. Marcy is the project manager of the GQD Project for her organization. She is working with Stan, the project sponsor, and they are identifying the most likely phases for this type of project work. Why would an organization divide a project into phases?

   A. To provide better management and control of the project

   B. To identify the work that will likely happen within a phase of the project

   C. To identify the resources necessary to complete a phase of the project

   D. To define the cash-flow requirements within each phase of the project

9. You are the project manager for your organization. Gary, a new project team member, approaches you because he's confused about the concept of the project life cycle. If you were explaining the project life cycle to Gary, you could say that all of the following are true statements about the project life cycle except for which one?

   A. The project life cycle defines the work to be done in each phase of the project.

B. The project life cycle defines the deliverables that each phase will create.

C. The project life cycle defines who is involved in each phase.

D. The project life cycle defines how much each phase will cost.

10. You are the project manager of a new project. When is the likelihood of failing to achieve the objectives the highest within your project?

   A. There is not enough information provided to know for certain.

   B. At the start of the project.

   C. At the end of the project.

   D. During the intermediate phases of the project.

11. You are the project manager for your organization and a new project has just been initiated. You know it is important to identify stakeholders and their attitudes toward the project as early as possible in the project life cycle. Which one of the following is an example of a positive stakeholder?

   A. The comptroller within your organization

   B. A customer who is eager for your project's deliverable

   C. An environmental group that has claims against your project

   D. A union

12. You know that there are positive, negative, and neutral stakeholders in your project. And based on your influence, stakeholders' attitudes toward the project can change. You want to work with the project team to ensure that all of the project stakeholders have been identified as part of the project initiation. None of the following are key project stakeholders except for which one?

   A. Union

   B. Sellers

   C. Technical interface

   D. Inspector

13. You are a project manager acting in a functional organization. The functional manager and you disagree about several deliverables the project will be creating. The functional manager insists that you begin the project work now. What must you do?

   A. Begin work.

   B. Resolve all of the issues with the functional manager before you begin working.

   C. Continue planning because you are the project manager.

   D. Begin work as long as the issues don't affect the project deliverables.

14. You are a project manager working under a PMO. Your project resources are shared among several projects. To whom will the project team members report?

    A. The project manager of each project

    B. The functional managers

    C. The PMO

    D. The project manager of their primary project

15. You are the project manager for your organization and you're working with the project team to explain the approach of the project life cycle and how you'll be managing proposed changes to the project scope. As a general rule, at what point in the project may stakeholders most cost-effectively recommend changes to the project deliverable?

    A. Before the project charter is created

    B. At the start of the project

    C. During the intermediate phases

    D. During the final phase of the project

16. Beth is the project manager for her organization and she's just received word that the organization has decided to kill a project. When is this decision most likely made?

    A. At the end of a phase

    B. At the start of a phase

    C. When the project is not meeting its financial requirements

    D. When technology has superseded some of the technology used within the project

17. Nancy is a project manager for the NHG Corporation. She has identified several positive stakeholders for her construction project and a few negative stakeholders. Nancy and the project team have been meeting regularly with the positive stakeholders but have not met with the negative stakeholders. What can happen if Nancy ignores negative stakeholders?

    A. Her project will likely succeed without any objections.

    B. Her project may suffer poor political capital from the negative stakeholders.

    C. Her project will risk failure to bring the project to a successful end.

    D. The negative stakeholders will not have an opportunity to communicate with the project manager.

18. Don is the project manager for his organization. In this project, his team will be comprised of local workers and workers from Scotland, India, and Belgium. Don knows that he needs to consider the working hours, culture,

and expectations of this virtual team in order to manage it successfully. All of the following are cultural attributes of an organization except for which one?

A. Policies and procedures

B. Work ethics

C. View of authority relationships

D. Experience of the project management team

19. You are a new project manager for your organization. Management has asked you to begin creating a project management plan with your project team based on a recently initiated project. The project management plan defines which one of the following?

A. Who the project manager will be

B. How the project manager will use the project management system

C. When the project team will be assembled and released

D. How the deliverable will be shipped to the customer

20. You are the project manager in your organization. Unlike your last job, which used a functional structure, this organization is utilizing a weak matrix. Who has full authority over project funding in a weak matrix?

A. The project manager

B. The functional manager

C. The PMO

D. The project sponsor

Questions and Answers

1. There is a difference between the project, the project life cycle, the project schedule, and the overall project objective. At the core of these terms is the project life cycle. The project life cycle comprises which of the following?

A. Phases

B. Milestones

C. Estimates

D. Activities

A. The project life cycle is comprised of phases. B is incorrect because milestones may exist within the project plan but they do not constitute the project life cycle. C is wrong because estimates are not directly related to the project life cycle. D is incorrect because activities are performed within the phases of the project life cycle, but not the project life cycle itself.

2. Marci Koening, the project manager for the ERP Project, is about to complete the project phase review. The completion of a project phase is also known as which of the following?

   A. Lessons learned

   B. The kill point

   C. Earned value management

   D. Conditional advancement

   > B. The completion of a project phase may also be known as a kill point. Lessons learned is a collection of information and knowledge gained through an experience, typically a phase, within the project, so A is wrong. Earned value management can happen at different times throughout the project, not just at the end of a project phase; therefore, C is wrong. D, conditional advancement, is a term that describes the conditions that must be present for the work to continue on a project. Conditional advancement, however, does not have to happen only at the end of a project phase.

3. You are the project manager of the GHY Project for your organization. You have been tasked with creating a new software for your website which must also be available to mobile users. There are several deliverables that must be documented for this project. Which of the following best describes a project deliverable?

   A. The resources used by the project to complete the necessary work

   B. The resources exported from the project as a result of the project work

   C. The end result of a project planning session

   D. A verifiable, measurable work product

   > D. A deliverable is something that can be verified and measured. A defines the resources in order to create the deliverable. B is an inaccurate statement. C defines how the work and resources will be utilized to create the project deliverable, not the deliverable itself.

4. As the project manager, you must work with your project team to identify the project and the project phases within the project schedule. This identification helps to communicate expectations and outcomes of the project work. The compilation of all the phases within a project equates to the

   _____.

   A. Project life cycle

   B. Product life cycle

   C. Project completion

   D. Project processes

   > A. The project life cycle comprises all of the project phases within a project. B is incorrect because the product life cycle describes how long a product will be

in use after it is created. C and D are incorrect because they do not accurately describe the project life cycle.

5. Projects move through a logical progression from the initiation to the project closure. It's important to understand the fluctuation of costs, schedules, resources, and risks within the logical progression of the project life cycle. Which of the following describes the early stages of a project?

   A. High costs and high demands for resources

   B. A high demand for change

   C. A high demand for project team time

   D. Low costs and low demands for resources

   D. Projects typically have low costs and low demands for resources early in their life cycle. A, B, and C are incorrect statements in regard to projects.

6. Management has asked you to help them identify the points of the project where the risk of failure is highest and lowest. As a general rule, at which point is the risk of failure the lowest, but the consequence of failure the highest?

   A. During the early stages.

   B. During the middle stages.

   C. During the final stages.

   D. The risk of failure is even across all project phases.

   C. As the project moves closer to completion, the likelihood of risk diminishes, but should the project fail, its consequence is the highest because of the time, monies, and effort invested in the project. A, B, and D are incorrect in regard to risk assessment in a project.

7. Project team members are most likely to work full-time on a project in which of the following organizational structures?

   A. Functional

   B. Weak matrix

   C. Strong matrix

   D. Projectized

   D. Projectized structures often have project team members assigned to the project on a full-time basis. A, B, and C are incorrect because these structures have part-time project teams.

8. Marcy is the project manager of the GQD Project for her organization. She is working with Stan, the project sponsor, and they are identifying the most likely phases for this type of project work. Why would an organization divide a project into phases?

   A. To provide better management and control of the project

B. To identify the work that will likely happen within a phase of the project

C. To identify the resources necessary to complete a phase of the project

D. To define the cash-flow requirements within each phase of the project

A. Organizations often divide projects into phases to make the management and control of the project easier and more productive. B and C are incorrect because these statements identify an attribute of a phase, not the reason to create all phases. D is incorrect because this statement is not true for all projects. In addition, cash-flow forecasting is part of planning and is not universal to all project phases.

9. You are the project manager for your organization. Gary, a new project team member, approaches you because he's confused about the concept of the project life cycle. If you were explaining the project life cycle to Gary, you could say that all of the following are true statements about the project life cycle except for which one?

A. The project life cycle defines the work to be done in each phase of the project.

B. The project life cycle defines the deliverables that each phase will create.

C. The project life cycle defines who is involved in each phase.

D. The project life cycle defines how much each phase will cost.

D. The project life cycle does not define how much each phase of the project will cost. The project life cycle does define the work to be done in each phase, the deliverables each phase will create, and the resources needed in each phase, so choices A, B, and C are incorrect.

10. You are the project manager of a new project. When is the likelihood of failing to achieve the objectives the highest within your project?

A. There is not enough information provided to know for certain.

B. At the start of the project.

C. At the end of the project.

D. During the intermediate phases of the project.

B. Projects are most likely to fail at the start of the project. As the project moves closer to the project completion, its odds of finishing successfully increase. A is not an accurate statement. C is incorrect because the project is more likely to finish successfully at the end of the project. D is also incorrect because the intermediate phases show progress toward project completion. The closer the project moves away from its start and toward completion, the higher the odds of success are.

11. You are the project manager for your organization and a new project has just been initiated. You know it is important to identify stakeholders and their

attitudes toward the project as early as possible in the project life cycle. Which one of the following is an example of a positive stakeholder?

A. The comptroller within your organization

B. A customer who is eager for your project's deliverable

C. An environmental group that has claims against your project

D. A union

B. The eager customer is an example of a positive stakeholder. A, the comptroller, is usually an influencer and not a positive or negative stakeholder for most projects. C, the environmental group that has claims against your project, is an example of a negative stakeholder. D, the union, is another example of a project influencer. In this example, the union is neutral, but there are instances when a union could become either a positive or negative stakeholder.

12. You know that there are positive, negative, and neutral stakeholders in your project. And based on your influence, stakeholders' attitudes toward the project can change. You want to work with the project team to ensure that all of the project stakeholders have been identified as part of the project initiation. None of the following are key project stakeholders except for which one?

A. Union

B. Sellers

C. Technical interface

D. Inspector

B. The seller is the only key stakeholder the PMBOK specifically addresses out of those listed in this question. A, the union, and C, the technical interface, could be examples of influencers, but not in every project. D, an inspector, is not a key stakeholder in every project, although an inspector could be considered an influencer if one were involved with your project.

13. You are a project manager acting in a functional organization. The functional manager and you disagree about several deliverables the project will be creating. The functional manager insists that you begin the project work now. What must you do?

A. Begin work.

B. Resolve all of the issues with the functional manager before you begin working.

C. Continue planning because you are the project manager.

D. Begin work as long as the issues don't affect the project deliverables.

A. Because you are working within a functional organization, you have little to no power, and the functional manager has all of the power. You must obey the functional manager and get to work. B, C, and D are all incorrect choices for the project manager in a functional structure.

14. You are a project manager working under a PMO. Your project resources are shared among several projects. To whom will the project team members report?

   A. The project manager of each project

   B. The functional managers

   C. The PMO

   D. The project manager of their primary project

   A. When resources are shared and a PMO exists, the project resources report to the PMO for staff assignments, but they'll report to the project manager of each project they're assigned to. B is correct in a functional structure. C is incorrect because the PMO may be responsible for staff alignment and assignment, but the project team does not report to the PMI. D is not valid.

15. You are the project manager for your organization and you're working with the project team to explain the approach of the project life cycle and how you'll be managing proposed changes to the project scope. As a general rule, at what point in the project may stakeholders most cost-effectively recommend changes to the project deliverable?

   A. Before the project charter is created

   B. At the start of the project

   C. During the intermediate phases

   D. During the final phase of the project

   B. It's easiest and least costly for stakeholders to ask for changes at the start of the project. A is incorrect because changes can easily be requested after the charter is created but before the project work begins. C is not true because changes may affect work that has already been completed. D is absolutely false because these changes may have the highest cost on the project.

16. Beth is the project manager for her organization and she's just received word that the organization has decided to kill a project. When is this decision most likely made?

   A. At the end of a phase

   B. At the start of a phase

   C. When the project is not meeting its financial requirements

   D. When technology has superseded some of the technology used within the project

A. The end of a phase is also known as a kill point. B is inaccurate because projects are most likely killed at the end of a project phase, not at its start. C is incorrect because the most likely answer is A. D is also incorrect because technology may change, but the demand for the project deliverable may not. If technology has changed, the project may elect to upgrade the technology being used to the newer available technology.

17. Nancy is a project manager for the NHG Corporation. She has identified several positive stakeholders for her construction project and a few negative stakeholders. Nancy and the project team have been meeting regularly with the positive stakeholders but have not met with the negative stakeholders. What can happen if Nancy ignores negative stakeholders?

   A. Her project will likely succeed without any objections.

   B. Her project may suffer poor political capital from the negative stakeholders.

   C. Her project will risk failure to bring the project to a successful end.

   D. The negative stakeholders will not have an opportunity to communicate with the project manager.

   C. Nancy cannot simply ignore the negative stakeholders. Their influence on the project may cause the project to fail. Nancy must work with the negative stakeholders to squelch their protests, or consider their demands to ensure compliance or agreement with their issues. A, B, and D are all inaccurate outcomes of ignoring the stakeholders.

18. Don is the project manager for his organization. In this project, his team will be composed of local workers and workers from Scotland, India, and Belgium. Don knows that he needs to consider the working hours, culture, and expectations of this virtual team in order to manage it successfully. All of the following are cultural attributes of an organization except for which one?

   A. Policies and procedures

   B. Work ethics

   C. View of authority relationships

   D. Experience of the project management team

   D. The experience of the project management team is not a cultural attribute of an organization. A, B, and C—the policies and procedures, the work ethics, and the view of authority relationships—are all classic examples of an organization's culture.

19. You are a new project manager for your organization. Management has asked you to begin creating a project management plan with your project team based on a recently initiated project. The project management plan defines which one of the following?

A. Who the project manager will be

B. How the project manager will use the project management system

C. When the project team will be assembled and released

D. How the deliverable will be shipped to the customer

B. The project plan defines how the project management system will be used. A is incorrect. The project charter defines the project manager. C is incorrect because the staffing management plan (see Chapter 9) defines how the project team will be assembled and managed. Technically, the staffing management plan is part of the overall project management plan, but B is the most correct answer presented. D is incorrect because not every project will need to ship a deliverable to a customer.

20. You are the project manager in your organization. Unlike your last job, which used a functional structure, this organization is utilizing a weak matrix. Who has full authority over project funding in a weak matrix?

A. The project manager

B. The functional manager

C. The PMO

D. The project sponsor

B. The functional manager has the power over the project funding, not the project manager. In a weak matrix, the functional manager is likely to be the project sponsor. A, C, and D are all incorrect statements because these do not define the authority of the project manager in a weak matrix structure.

Examining the Project Processes

In this chapter, you will

- Understand how the five project management process groups interact
- Understand the activities of project initiation
- Know how to plan a project
- Learn how a project team executes the project plan
- Explore how a project manager monitors and controls a project
- Study how to close a project

Projects are chockablock with processes. A *process* is a set of actions and activities to achieve a product, result, or service. It's the work of project management to move the work of the project toward the deliverable the project aims to create. As you'll discover in this chapter, there are 47 project management processes that a project manager and the project team use to move a project along. The goal of these processes is to have a successful project, but a project's success is based on more than just leveraging these processes. A successful project depends on four things:

- Using the *appropriate processes* at the *appropriate times*. A project manager must recognize situations within the project that call for different processes and then determine which process or combination of processes is most needed to meet the project objectives.
- Following a *defined project management approach* for execution and project control.
- Developing and implementing a solid *project management plan* that addresses all areas of the project.
- Conforming the project and the project management approach to the *customer requirements and expectations*.
- Balancing the project time, cost, scope, quality, resources, and risks while meeting the project objectives.

Sure, all of this sounds so easy on paper, doesn't it? But project management is not an easy task, and the goal of a certified project manager is to recognize the situations, react to the problems or opportunities, and move the project work toward achieving the customer's requirements. The 47 project management processes are the actions that help any project manager do just that.

This chapter covers the entire project management life cycle. We'll follow the activities that happen in each of the project management process groups, and see what the results of those actions are.

VIDEO For a more detailed explanation, watch the *Moving Through the Project Management Processes* video now.

Exploring the Project Management Processes

Before we get too deep into this chapter, learn this: *You do not have to do every single project management process on every single project.* The project manager and the project team must determine which project management processes are most appropriate for each project. Once the necessary processes have been identified, the project manager and project team must also determine to what extent the processes are needed. The processes are tailored to their project. Larger projects require more detail than smaller ones.

The 47 project management processes have been recognized as good practices for most projects, but they are not a mandate for good practices on all projects. For your Project Management Institute (PMI) examination, however, you'll be tested on all of the project management processes in detail. Yep. Although you may not use all of the project management processes in the real world, the exam will test you on all of the processes as if you do. Why? Because there is, no doubt, more than one way to manage a project. The PMI isn't stubborn enough to say it's our way or no way—that'd be unreasonable.

The approach that the PMI does take, however, is based somewhat on W. Edwards Deming's plan-do-check-act cycle, as Figure 3-1 demonstrates. In Deming's model, adapted by the American Society for Quality (ASQ), the end of one process launches the start of another. For example, the end of the planning process allows the launch of

Figure 3-1
The standard project model is based on Deming's plan-do-check-act cycle.

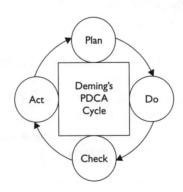

the doing process. Once the work has been completed, you check it. This approach is called the Deming PDCA cycle. If the work checks out, you move right into the acting process.

The project management model, which we'll see throughout this chapter, is a bit more involved than the plan-do-check-act approach. Figure 3-2 demonstrates the big picture of project management:

1. The project starts with *initiating*, where the project manager is assigned.

2. The project moves into *planning* the project work.

3. The results of planning allow the plans to be *executed*.

4. *Monitoring and controlling* processes oversee and overlap the other process groups, and can shift the project back into execution or back to planning.

5. The project moves into *closing* the project or phase.

The components of the model are called the *process groups*. Process groups are collections of the processes you'll be performing in different situations within your project. You've experienced, I'm sure, that projects are initiated, planned, executed, monitored and controlled, and then closed. Distinct actions fit nicely within each one of the process groups—that's the gist of this chapter.

Examining the Process Group Interactions

At first glance, the project management model seems simple. With more study, however, you'll see how complex the interactions between the groups can be. First, project managers realize that there is more than one way to manage a project. Second, these processes and their interactions are the generally accepted best approach to project management. Having said that, there is no hard-and-fast rule as to the order in which processes should occur once the project is in motion. The nature of the project, the scenario, and the experienced conditions, along with the culture and maturity of the organization, will dictate which process is the best process at any given project moment.

Figure 3-2
All projects move through five process groups to reach their completion.

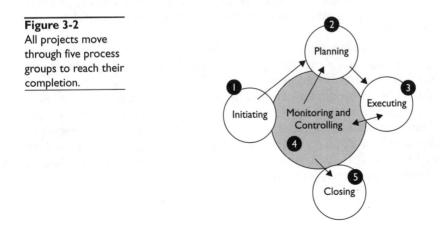

The general consensus, not necessarily the order, of the process groups is as follows:

1. Initiating
2. Planning
3. Executing
4. Monitoring and controlling
5. Closing

The caveat is that a project manager can move between the planning, executing, and monitoring and controlling process groups on an as-needed basis. For example, during project execution, a new risk could be identified. The project manager and project team would then move back into the planning phase to determine how to respond to the new risk, and then they'd continue to monitor and control the project for additional risks.

 EXAM TIP The generally accepted flow of the process groups can also apply to more than just projects. A project manager can use the processes within these groups for each phase of a project.

Choosing the Appropriate Processes

A moment of clarity: There's a bunch of processes in project management. Sure, we've already established that you won't need all these processes for every project you manage, but you can be darned certain you'll need all of the processes to pass your Certified Associate in Project Management (CAPM) or Project Management Professional (PMP) exam. Let's dive in and check out these process groups and all their kids—the 47 project management processes.

You've already learned the five process groups: initiating, planning, executing, monitoring and controlling, and closing. These groups are universal to all projects, from building the pyramids to rolling out the latest, greatest whiz-bang software over your IT network. It doesn't matter; project management is project management. Figure 3-3 captures all of the processes in the most likely order in which they should happen—if they're going to happen (remember, you don't need all of the processes on every project, every single time).

In addition to project management processes, there are also product-oriented processes. These processes are unique to the organization that is creating the product of the project. Product processes are also unique to the type of work required to create the product. Let's put this in the real world. If you're creating a new software application, or building a house, or designing a brochure, there are some processes that are unique to that type of work. In addition, imagine all the different home construction companies in the world. Each company could have similar projects, but their internal product processes and terminology could be unique to each company. The good news is that you won't have to know much about product processes for your CAPM or the PMP exam.

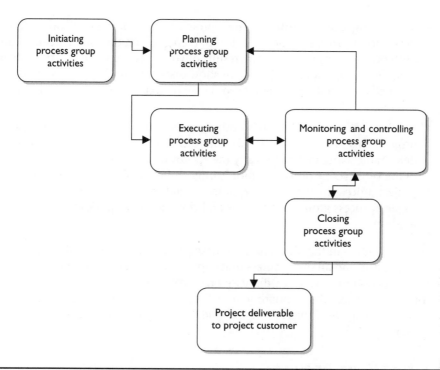

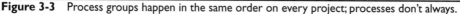

Figure 3-3 Process groups happen in the same order on every project; processes don't always.

Working with Process Groups

Project management is more than just getting the project work done. It's the management, leadership, and execution of the work performed by the project team. (And by execution, I mean the project team executing the project plan, not you executing the team—although that can be tempting at times.) You'll move through some logical activities to get your project moving along. These are the process groups that are universal to project management. Let's take a more detailed look at these process groups and the type of work that will be happening in each:

- **Initiating**   Management and/or your customer is authorizing the project or a project phase to begin.

- **Planning**   You and the key stakeholders are defining and refining the project goals and objectives. Once the project objectives have been defined, you and the key stakeholders will plan on how to reach those objectives.

- **Executing**   Now that you have a project plan, it's time to put the plan into action. You've heard the saying, "Plan your work and now work your plan"? This is the "working your plan" part.

- **Monitoring and controlling**   Your project team is doing the work, but it's up to you to measure and monitor things to ensure that the project team is doing the work as it was planned. The results of your measurements—primarily in cost, time, scope, and quality—will show discrepancies between what was planned and what was experienced. These discrepancies are your project variances.

- **Closing**   Boy, howdy! There's nothing more fun, usually, than closing a project. This process group focuses on formal acceptance of the project's final deliverable. Note that technically the approval of the deliverable is the result of the verify scope process, a monitoring and controlling process. The close project process makes that acceptance formal with a project sign-off. The closing process group also focuses on bringing the project or project phase to a tidy ending.

Now that you've got the big picture on these process groups, let's take that in-depth look at each group and all the business that happens within each one. Each subheading in the five process group sections discussed next covers one of the 47 project management processes. (Thus, the "Initiating Your Project" process group includes two processes: "Developing the Project Charter" and "Identifying the Stakeholders.") Hold your excitement!

Initiating Your Project

The initiating process group starts all the project fun. It contains the formal processes that start a project or a project phase. These initiating processes, which I'll delve into in one moment, are often done outside of the project manager's domain of control. For example, a company's project portfolio management may not include any input from the project managers within their firm. The senior management could choose which projects should be initiated and funded long before the project managers get involved. In other organizations, the project manager may be involved from the project conception all the way through the project closure. As a general rule, the initiation of a project happens, to some extent, without the project manager, but the initiation process group is included as part of the project management life cycle.

 EXAM TIP   Projects are authorized, not the project manager. You do not have a project until you have an approved charter.

The project manager is assigned during initiation, and the inputs from the original project initiator and/or the project sponsor are considered throughout the initiation processes. One of the first activities of the project is to document the project assumptions and constraints. Here's the difference between these two:

- *Assumptions* are things believed to be true but not proven to be. For example, construction projects plan to complete their work during the spring and summer months because of cooperating weather. It's an assumption that the weather will be agreeable for their work during these seasons as opposed to the winter months, although this isn't always true.

- *Constraints* are anything that restricts a project manager's options. For example, a customer must have the project deliverable by a specific date. Or the project cost must not exceed $2 million. Or the software must be compatible with an Oracle database. Usually, any project requirement preceded by "must" is a good sign of a constraint.

Assumptions and constraints are documented in the *project charter*. The project charter officially authorizes the project and is authorized outside of the project boundaries. This means that the charter should come from some entity that is above the project manager and the functional managers involved in the project. Figure 3-4 illustrates this concept. While the project management team may help write the charter, the funding and authorization come from higher up in the organization or from the project customer.

At the start of each project phase, especially on larger projects, it's ideal to repeat the initiating processes for the phase you're about to begin. This helps to ensure that the project remains focused on the business needs the project is to solve. This includes confirming the availability of the needed project resources (cash, people, materials, and equipment). Based on this discovery, the project should be allowed to continue on to the next phase, delayed, or (gulp!) canceled. Another benefit of moving through these initiating processes at the start of each phase is that it allows the performing

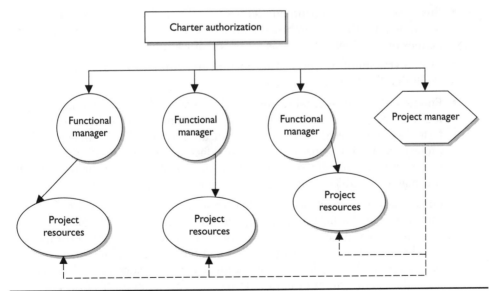

Figure 3-4   Project charters come from outside of the project boundaries.

organization to determine if the original business need that the project was created to solve is still valid; if not, the project can be killed. Yes, killed; remember that the end of a phase is called a project kill point.

When a project or phase is moving through the initiating process group, the project manager needs to include the key stakeholders in the processes. This is a "PMI-ism," but it's also some real-world advice: Including the stakeholders during the initiating phase accomplishes several things for the project:

- It creates shared ownership of the project.

- It ensures deliverable acceptance at project or phase closure.

- It improves stakeholder satisfaction.

- It facilitates communication between the project manager and the stakeholders.

Developing the Project Charter

The project charter is created during the initiating process group. Recall that the project charter authorizes the project or, in a larger project, the charter initiates the project phase. The charter documents the business need, defines the project deliverable, and authorizes the project manager to expend organizational resources. To create the project charter, you'll need the following inputs:

- **Contract**   You won't always need a contract, but if an organization performs projects for other organizations, such as a consulting firm, the contract serves as a key input to creating the project charter.

- **Business case**   This document defines why the project is worthy of the investment for the deliverables the project will bring. The business case defines the cost-benefit analysis for the organization.

- **Project statement of work**   This document defines the product, service, or result that the project will be creating.

- **Enterprise environmental factors**   This is a new term that you'll be seeing lots of throughout the remainder of this book. Enterprise environmental factors are any external or internal organizational factors that can affect project success. Enterprise environmental factors include the culture, organizational structure, resources, the commercial databases the project will use, market conditions, and your project management software.

- **Organizational process assets**   This is another term that you'll see throughout the *PMBOK* and during our time together in this book. "Organizational process assets" is a fancy way of describing how a company does business. It includes the processes and procedures unique to an organization, plans, guidelines, and knowledge bases, such as the lessons learned documentation from past projects and any relevant historical information.

Identifying Stakeholders

Stakeholders are the people and organizations actively involved in the project and the people and organizations that are affected by the project. The process of identifying the project stakeholders should happen early in the project to prevent rework, changing requirements, and new threats to the project success. Stakeholder identification happens throughout the entire project. You don't want to accidentally overlook stakeholders, so at the onset of each project life cycle phase, you and the project team (and sometimes other stakeholders) should pause and determine if all the correct stakeholders are involved and have been identified. If you forget to include a stakeholder, they might cause your project to be delayed, become adverse to your project, and be upset. Always be on the lookout for project stakeholders. In order to do this project management process, you'll need:

1. Project charter

2. Procurement documents

3. Enterprise environmental factors

4. Organizational process assets

The only output of stakeholder identification is the stakeholder register. This is the documentation of all the identified stakeholders, their contact information, and project interests.

 NOTE Stakeholder management is so important in project management that the *PMBOK Guide*, 5ᵗʰ edition has allotted a whole chapter to this project management knowledge area. In this book, it's Chapter 13. You have to identify your stakeholders before you can manage them.

Planning the Project

Projects fail at the beginning and not the end. A project needs effective planning, or it will be doomed. The whole point of the planning process group is to develop the project management plan. The good news is that the entire project plan doesn't have to happen in one session; in fact, planning is an iterative process, and the project manager and the project team return to the planning phase as needed to allow the project to move forward.

Ask any project manager if changes ever happen in their projects, and they'll give you a sad yes (unless they lie). Changes, often the nemesis of a project manager, require the project manager and the project team to revisit these planning processes to consider the impact of the changes on the entire project. This may include, unfortunately, revisiting the initiating processes and making changes to the project charter, although this is a drastic and infrequent event.

One approach to project management that has gained fans in the past few years is *rolling wave planning*. Rolling wave planning, seen in Figure 3-5, entails iterations of

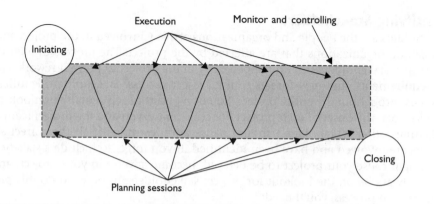

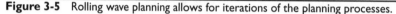

Figure 3-5   Rolling wave planning allows for iterations of the planning processes.

planning throughout the project life cycle. Changes and conditions within the project require the project manager and the project team to revisit the planning processes and then to move on to the project. Rolling wave planning can also be experienced in larger projects, where a project team plans in detail for the immediate work and leaves the future work less planned. As the project approaches each phase, detailed planning takes place, creating iterations, or waves, of planning.

The project manager and the project team should create an environment where stakeholders can participate and contribute to the project planning processes. A project manager wants to use the skills and knowledge of the stakeholders to help define the project scope and the product scope, as well as to ensure that the project work will deliver upon the stakeholders' expectations.

A frequent question from students of my project management classes centers on project management planning. I'm asked, "If planning is so important and iterative, how does a project manager know when the planning process group should end?" Of course, planning cannot, thankfully, continue forever. There must be project boundaries and considerations of the enterprise environmental factors that dictate the amount of time a project team invests in the initial planning and the project work. As a project moves into execution and, by default, monitoring and controlling, the project team can revisit the planning processes as needed to allow the project to continue. For example, if new risks are identified within the project, then additional planning is required to evaluate and respond to the risks.

EXAM TIP   The planning process group has 24 processes. This section contains a brief overview of each of these processes and their inputs and outputs. I recommend that you become familiar with these to the point that you'd recognize the type of work associated with each process, but don't invest too much time memorizing the inputs and outputs of each process.

Developing the Project Management Plan

The project management plan is not one plan, but a collection of subsidiary plans that dictate how the project will operate within that knowledge area. It also defines how the project will operate within planning, executing, monitoring and controlling, and closing process groups. To create the project management plan, you'll need:

- **Project charter**   You need a charter before you can have a project.
- **Enterprise environmental factors**   These are the rules, processes, and procedures the project manager has to abide by.
- **Organizational process assets**   These are the templates, guidelines, software, and historical information that can help the project manager manage the project.
- **Project management processes outputs**   The outputs of the other processes will contribute to the project management plan.

Planning Scope Management

The project management process of planning scope management is the actual creation of the project's scope management plan. This plan, a subsidiary plan of the overall project management plan, defines how the project manager and the project team will go about creating the project, controlling the project, and then validating the scope. Most likely, this plan will be a template from organizational process assets that's adapted to the current project, but this doesn't mean the project manager and team can shortcut this process. Each project is different, so there must be adequate time allotted for the project management plan and its creation. You'll need four inputs to do this process:

- Project management plan
- Project charter
- Enterprise environmental factors
- Organizational process assets

This process creates the scope management plan and the requirement management plan. These two plans work together to direct how the scope is created, controlled and validated—and how the requirements of the project are also identified, controlled, and might be allowed to be changed.

Collecting Requirements

Projects are based on the requirements elicited from the project stakeholders. The project requirements will serve as an input to the project scope statement. The project scope is the work that must be done in order to create the product, service, or result the project aims to deliver. The project manager, the project team, and the stakeholders work together to collect the project requirements. To collect the project requirements, you'll need five inputs:

- Scope management plan
- Requirement management plan
- Stakeholder management plan
- A project charter
- Stakeholder register (a directory of who the stakeholders are, their contact information, and general opinions, concerns, and perceived threats about the project)

The stakeholder register is a directory of all the identified stakeholders. The collect requirements process creates the requirements documentation—a direct result of the requirements elicitation that the project manager, the project team, and the business analyst work to create. This process also creates the requirements documentation and the requirements traceability matrix. These two work together to protect the requirements from change, to ensure that approved changes are reflected throughout the project artifacts, and to track the requirements from identification to fulfillment during project execution.

Defining the Project Scope Statement

Now that the project has a project scope management plan, the project manager, project team, and the key stakeholders can go about defining the actual project scope. The project scope statement serves as a basis for all future project decisions. As part of defining the project scope, these inputs are needed:

- Scope management plan
- Project charter
- Requirements documents
- Organizational process assets

This process group has just two outputs:

- Project scope statement (all the work required to satisfy the project requirements and objectives)
- Project documents updates (based on stakeholder elicitation, the business case, and solutions for the identified problem or opportunity that may need to be updated to reflect any refinements)

DIGITAL CONTENT Processes have three general parts, as you may have noticed: Inputs, Tools and Techniques, and Outputs. PMP and CAPM candidates often call this the ITTO of project management. I've included a nifty PDF document called "Process ITTO Quick Review". It lists all of the processes by knowledge area and the inputs, tools and techniques, and outputs of each process. Enjoy!

Creating the Work Breakdown Structure (WBS)

The WBS is created in the planning process group. This process takes the project scope and breaks it down into smaller, more manageable components. In Chapter 5, we'll discuss the WBS, its purpose, and its creation. To create a WBS, you'll need the following:

- Scope management plan
- Project scope statement
- Documented project requirements
- Enterprise environmental factors
- Organizational process assets

As a result of creating the WBS, the project manager will get some extras, wanted or not:

- Project document updates
- Scope baseline (comprises the scope statement, the WBS, and the WBS dictionary)

EXAM TIP The *scope baseline* is so important for your exam that I'm mentioning it again. The scope baseline comprises the project scope statement, the WBS, and the WBS dictionary. It is a cornerstone to project management. If you're stumped on a question and one of the choices is the scope baseline, go ahead and choose that. It may not always be the best choice, but I'd wager that it predominantly will be.

Plan Schedule Management

The project management process of plan schedule management is the creation of the schedule management plan. This plan, part of the project management plan, defines how the project's schedule is developed, managed, executed, and controlled. Because stakeholders will be so interested in how long the project will take to complete, it's best to take a forward stance on creating and defining the project's schedule. This plan aims to create and analyze a schedule that's feasible for the project team, vendors, and to set stakeholder expectations. To create the schedule management plan, the only output of this process, you'll need four inputs:

- Project management plan
- Project charter

- Enterprise environmental factors
- Organizational process assets

Defining the Project Activities

Once the WBS has been created, the project manager and project team can examine the deliverables and then determine the actual work to create the things the WBS promises. This process is activity definition. To complete this process, you'll need:

- Schedule management plan
- Scope baseline
- Organizational process assets
- Enterprise environmental factors

As a result of defining the project activities, the project team will receive these outputs:

- **Activity list**   This lists the activities the project team will need to complete to create the deliverables defined in the WBS.
- **Activity attributes**   These describe the nature of the activities, needed human resources, materials, risk, and other conditions that may affect the activities.
- **Milestone list**   This shows significant points of progress, and you can only reach milestones by completing the activities in the activity list.

Sequencing the Project Activities

It's a logical progression from defining the project deliverables and the activities needed to create them to putting those activities in a particular order. To sequence the project activities, the project team will need:

- Schedule management plan
- Activity attributes
- Activity list
- Milestone list
- Project scope statement
- Organizational process assets (If you've done work like this before, you likely won't need to reinvent the activity list and sequencing.)
- Enterprise environmental factors

As with the majority of the processes in planning, the output of the processes often includes other project elements that may be needed for later purposes in project planning. Activity sequencing is no different; the outputs of this process are

- Project document updates, which include any activity list updates and activity attribute updates.
- Project schedule network diagrams. These visualize the sequence of activities, and you'll learn more about these in Chapter 6.

Estimating Activity Resources

The project manager needs to know what resources will be required for each of the project activities. To complete this process, you'll need the following inputs:

- Schedule management plan
- Activity attributes
- Activity lists
- Resource calendars (when resources are available; remember, resources are people but also facilities, equipment, and materials)
- Risk register
- Activity cost estimates
- Enterprise environmental factors
- Organizational process assets

Once the project manager has completed estimating the resources, he or she will receive several outputs as a result of this process:

- Activity resource requirements
- Resource breakdown structure
- Project document updates

Estimating the Activity Durations

Once the project manager knows what activities are required and in what order the activities should happen, it's time to estimate how long each activity will take to complete. To create the activity duration estimates, the project manager will need:

- Schedule management plan
- Activity attributes
- Activity list
- Activity resource requirements
- Resource calendars
- Project scope statement
- Risk register
- Resource breakdown structure
- Enterprise environmental factors

- Organizational process assets

While this process primarily creates the duration of each of the project's activities, the project manager may also have activity attribute updates. Outputs include:

- Activity duration estimates
- Project document updates

Developing the Project Schedule

The project schedule is more than just the sum of how long each event will take. The project schedule considers the availability of the project resources, the risks, the attributes of the project activities, and more. Chapter 6 will focus on this process, but for now, here are the inputs required to create the project schedule:

- Schedule management plan
- Activity list
- Activity attributes
- Project schedule network diagrams
- Activity resource requirements
- Resource calendars
- Activity duration estimates (how long the activities take, so you can schedule the appropriate resources for the duration of the activity)
- Project scope statement
- Risk register
- Project staff assignments
- Resource breakdown structure
- Enterprise environmental factors
- Organizational process assets

Based on these inputs to the schedule development, the project team will have six outputs:

- Schedule baseline (your anticipated preview of how the project schedule will develop)
- Project schedule (the calendar that defines when the project will take place, including the working hours, access to the job site, and any other time constraints put on the project)
- Schedule data (includes the milestones, activities, activity attributes, assumptions, and constraints)
- Project calendars

- Project management plan updates
- Project document updates

Plan Cost Estimating

This project management process defines the policies and procedures for the project manager and the project team to plan, manage, execute, and control the project costs within the project. This plan will likely be greatly influenced by existing enterprise environmental factors within the organization. For example, your company probably already has strict cost management guidelines, such as methods for estimating project costs, spending the project budget, and tracking costs within the project. To complete this planning process, you'll need these project elements:

- Project management plan
- Project charter
- Enterprise environmental factors
- Organizational process assets

As you may have guessed, the only output of this project management process is the cost management plan.

Cost Estimating

Projects cost money, and every stakeholder with a checkbook wants to know how much the project will cost. This process focuses on estimating the costs for the project. The following serve as inputs to this process:

- Cost management plan
- Human resource plan (also includes the staffing management plan to describe when resources will be brought onto and released from the project)
- Scope baseline
- Project schedule
- Risk register (database of the project risks and their characteristics, including when the risk events may happen and what their financial impact may be)
- Enterprise environmental factors
- Organizational process assets

The preceding inputs will help the project manager create the following outputs of cost estimating:

- Activity cost estimates (how much the work will cost)
- Basis of the activity cost estimates (information on how you estimated the project costs, including any assumptions made during the estimating process)
- Project document updates

Determining the Project Budget

Once the project manager has created the cost estimate, he or she will aggregate the individual activities and their attributes, such as labor and materials, to create a cost baseline for the project. This process requires several inputs:

- Cost management plan
- Scope baseline
- Activity cost estimates
- Basis of estimates
- Project schedule
- Resource calendars
- Risk register
- Agreements and contracts (if applicable)
- Organizational process assets

The outputs of cost budgeting are

- Cost performance baseline (anticipated expenses for the project mapped to the deliverables of the project)
- Project funding requirements (when the funds will be needed for purchases in the project)
- Project document updates

Planning for Quality

The project manager, the project team, and the key stakeholders will work together to determine how the project will achieve the expected levels of quality within the project. Chapter 8 will discuss quality in detail, but for now, there are several inputs to this quality planning:

- Project management plan
- Stakeholder register
- Risk register
- Requirement documents
- Enterprise environmental factors
- Organizational process assets

As a result of planning for the quality, the project management team will create the following outputs:

- Quality management plan (describes how the organization's quality policies will be implemented)

- Process improvement plan (describes how the processes within the project can be improved)
- Quality metrics (the defined values that you'll measure to prove quality)
- Quality checklists (ideal for repetitive actions to ensure each action is performed the same way each time)
- Project document updates

Planning for Human Resources

Of course, the project will need people to do the work—that's the project team! Chapter 9 discusses human resource planning in detail. This process specifically focuses on creating the human resources plan and defining the project roles, reporting relationships, and responsibilities of the project team members. Here are the required inputs for human resources planning:

- The project management plan
- Activity resource requirements
- Enterprise environmental factors
- Organizational process assets

Once all the planning is completed, the project manager will have one little output:

- Human resource plan

 EXAM TIP   Remember that the autonomy of the project manager must also be considered when planning for human resources. The organizational structure will indicate what level of autonomy the project manager has. Functional structures concede very little power to the project manager, while granting most of the authority to the functional managers. The matrix structures describe the power of the project manager in relation to the functional manager: weak, balanced, or strong. Project managers have the most authority in a projectized environment.

Planning for Project Communications

It's been said that 90 percent of a project manager's time is spent communicating. With that factoid, it's no wonder that the project manager will want to plan to communicate effectively. Here are the required inputs to get this process started:

- Project management plan
- Stakeholder register
- Enterprise environmental factors
- Organizational process assets

There are two outputs of this process:

- Communications management plan
- Project document updates

Communication is always something to discuss. (I will in Chapter 10.)

Planning for Project Risks

The project manager, the project team, and the key stakeholders will plan how to manage risk and the associated risk management activities. We'll cover this process in Chapter 11, but here are the inputs for this process for now:

- Project management plan
- Project charter
- Stakeholder register
- Enterprise environmental factors
- Organizational process assets

This process also has but one output:

- Risk management plan

Identifying the Project Risks

Once the risk management plan has been created, the project management team can go about the process of identifying all the good and naughty risks within the project. To get this fun started, they'll need these inputs:

- Risk management plan (defines how risks will be identified, analyzed, responded to, and monitored throughout the project)
- Cost management plan
- Schedule management plan
- Quality management plan
- Human resource management plan
- Scope baseline
- Activity cost estimates
- Activity duration estimates
- Stakeholder register
- Project documents
- Procurement documents

- Enterprise environmental factors
- Organizational process assets

This process will create the central repository of project risks:

- Risk register

Chapter 11 explains the risk identification process and the risk register in greater detail.

Completing Qualitative Risk Analysis

Qualitative risk analysis is completed in the planning process group and "qualifies" the identified risks for additional study and analysis. Here are the inputs for this process:

- Risk management plan
- Scope baseline
- Risk register
- Enterprise environmental factors
- Organizational process assets

The only outputs of this process are

- Project documents updates

In particular, the identified risks' qualitative attributes should be updated in the risk register.

Completing Quantitative Risk Analysis

This process aims to quantify the risk exposure for the risks in the project. This process is covered in more detail in Chapter 11. Here are the inputs for this process:

- Risk management plan
- Project cost management plan
- Project schedule management plan
- Risk register
- Enterprise environmental factors
- Organizational process assets

Like qualitative analysis, quantitative analysis has but one output:

- Project documents update

Planning the Risk Responses

Okay, the project manager, the project team, and all the key stakeholders have had some serious fun identifying and performing analysis on the project risks. Now it's time to get down to the business of planning the responses to the identified risks. There are only two inputs to the risk response planning process:

- Risk management plan
- Risk register

This process may take some time, and will create two outputs:

- Project management plan updates
- Project documents updates

Planning Procurement Management

When a project manager needs to purchase something for the project, there are usually rules and procedures he or she must follow within the organization. The plan procurement management process defines the allowed approach and identifies potential sellers for the project manager. This process has nine inputs:

- Project management plan
- Requirement documentation
- Risk register
- Activity resource requirements
- Project schedule
- Activity cost estimates
- Stakeholder register
- Enterprise environmental factors
- Organizational process assets

All of these inputs allow the project manager and the project team to consider and evaluate what needs to be purchased, determine what risks may need to be considered, and then to decide how the purchasing will commence. Chapter 12 centers on procurement, but here are the outputs of this process:

- Procurement management plan
- Procurement statement of work
- Procurement documents (things like the Request for Quote, Request for Proposal, Invitation for Bid)
- Source selection criteria (factors that determine which vendor gets the contract; consider things like price, experience, availability, and warranties)

- Make-or-buy decisions (mathematical analysis to determine if better to purchase from a vendor or to create the solution in-house—there's usually more to the decision than just crunching the numbers to see what's the best deal, such as availability of resources, opportunity to learn a new skill, or the headache of dealing with a vendor.)
- Change requests
- Project documents updates

Planning for Stakeholder Management

This project management process plans and identifies appropriate methods to manage, maintain, and engage stakeholders in the project. The project manager wants to balance the involvement, influence, and expectations of the project stakeholders without delaying the project execution, but also assuring quality and meeting the stakeholders' requirement in the project deliverable. This project management process has four inputs:

- Project management plan
- Stakeholder register
- Enterprise environmental factors
- Organizational process assets

There are two outputs of this planning process:

- Stakeholder management plan
- Project documents update

Executing Processes

The executing processes allow the project work to be performed. They include the execution of the project plan, the execution of vendor management, and the management of the project implementation. The project manager works closely with the project team in this process group to ensure that the work is being completed and that the work results are of quality. The project manager also works with vendors to ensure that their procured work is complete, of quality, and meets the obligations of the contracts.

Throughout the project, variances may happen. A *variance* is simply the difference between what was planned and what was experienced. For example, there are cost variances, schedule variances, and even scope variances. When variances happen within a project, the project manager and the project team retreat to the planning process group, analyze the variance, and determine the best method to respond. The response may, in turn, cause the project management plan to be changed, which could, in turn, affect the activities of the execution process group.

This process group is about getting the project work done. You can plan as much as you want, but it's the doing that matters. This process group consumes more of the project budget than any other group because the project team is doing the work, using the materials, and relying on the vendors to deliver upon their contracts. This process group has eight processes.

Directing and Managing Project Work

This is the heart of the project: getting the work done. This process guides, directs, and leads the project team to complete their assignments according to the project management plan. The project team's performance is measured, and that information will serve as input to performance reviews later in the project (Team members be warned!). Here are the inputs for managing and executing the project plan:

- Project management plan
- Approved change requests
- Enterprise environmental factors
- Organizational process assets

The outputs of project execution are

- Deliverables
- Work performance data (how the project activities are performing in comparison to what was planned)
- Change requests
- Project management plan updates
- Project documents updates

Performing Quality Assurance

Quality assurance (QA) is a management process that all projects adhere to within an organization. QA will be discussed in more detail in Chapter 8. Here are the inputs to performing quality assurance:

- Quality management plan
- Process improvement plan
- Quality metrics
- Quality control measurements (different specifications based on the application area)
- Project documents

All of these QA input processes will help the project management team create the following outputs:

- Change requests
- Project management plan updates
- Project documents updates
- Organizational process assets updates

Acquiring the Project Team

The project team doesn't join the project until the execution process group. This is a great example of how the planning process group is an iterative process. The project manager is in planning and then shifts to execution to acquire the project team. Now the project team and the project manager return to planning to create the project management plan. To complete the team acquisition, the following inputs are needed:

- Human resource plan
- Enterprise environmental factors (the rules in your organization on how the project manager is allowed to acquire the project team)
- Organizational process assets

Using these inputs, the project manager creates the following outputs:

- Project staff assignments (your team—handpicked, assigned to the project, or procured for the project duration)
- Resource calendars
- Project management plan updates

Developing the Project Team

Developing the project team is an execution process that seeks to determine and, if necessary, improve, the skill sets of the project team members. This process, which I'll talk about in Chapter 9, also focuses on improving the interaction, communication, and trust of the project team members. You'll need the following inputs to facilitate project team development:

- Human resource plan
- Project staff assignments (training can be part of team development)
- Resource calendars (to schedule the team development activities)

This process creates just two little, but important, outputs:

- Team performance assessments
- Enterprise environmental factors updates

Team performance assessments will help the project manager make decisions on how to better manage and lead the project team members—and to perform future team development exercises.

 EXAM TIP Team development is more than lunch. The PMI likes team development exercises, so think of whitewater rafting trips and team excursions away from the office with the entire project team. However, not all team development exercises involve off-site activities. They can be accomplished in the context of the project work as well.

Managing the Project Team

As a project manager, you'll have to manage the project team. This means you'll need to track your team's performance, provide feedback, resolve issues within the project and team, and make changes so that the team can work better. You'll need six inputs to complete this process:

- Human resource management plan
- Project staff assignments
- Team performance assessments (project manager usually performs some type of performance review of each project team member)
- Issue log
- Work performance reports (may vary from organization to organization; project manager reports how the project team as a whole performed their project duties)
- Organizational process assets

This process creates five outputs:

- Change requests
- Project management plan updates
- Project documents updates
- Enterprise environmental factors updates
- Organizational process assets updates

Manage Communications

Based on the project's communication management plan the project manager and the project team will work together to communicate the most appropriate message, to the correct stakeholders, at the correct time. This is the execution of who needs to know what—and when. The project manager has to disperse information to keep the project stakeholders informed of the project's health, status, and pending actions. This project management process requires four inputs:

- Communications management plan
- Work performance reports
- Enterprise environmental factors
- Organizational process assets

As a result of managing project communications, there are four outputs:

- Project communications
- Project documents updates

- Project management plan updates
- Organizational process assets updates

Conducting Project Procurements

Remember all that fun earlier with procurement? Now the project manager is waiting for those pesky vendors to respond to the procurement documents. To complete this executing process, the project manager will need the following inputs:

- Procurement management plan
- Procurement documents
- Source selection criteria
- Seller proposals
- Project documents
- Make-or-buy decisions
- Procurement statement of work
- Organizational process assets

As a result of this process, the project manager will receive six outputs:

- Selected sellers
- Agreements
- Resource calendars
- Change requests
- Project management plan updates
- Project documents updates

Managing Stakeholder Engagement

The project manager must work closely with the project stakeholders to keep them interested and involved in the project. This project management process aims to help the project team meet the stakeholders' expectations while also keeping expectations in check. You don't want stakeholders hovering over every project activity, but you also don't want them to disappear and ignore their responsibilities to stay involved with certain project decisions. This project management process has four inputs:

- Stakeholder management plan
- Communications management plan
- Change log
- Organizational process assets

The outcomes of this process are:

- Issue log
- Change requests
- Project management plan updates
- Project documents updates
- Organizational process assets updates

Examining the Monitoring and Controlling Process Groups

Wouldn't the project management life be even greater if all of the projects went off without a hitch? If only the project team, the project work, the stakeholders, and the vendors would cooperate. Oh, but we know that projects have to be constantly monitored like a three-year-old in a china shop.

This process group focuses on monitoring the project work for variances, changes, and discrepancies so that corrective action can be used to ensure that the project continues to move toward its successful completion. This means lots of measuring, inspecting, and communicating with the project team to ensure that the project plan is followed, variances to the plan are reported, and responses can be expedited.

This process group also is concerned with changes that may attack the Iron Triangle of Project Management: time, cost, and scope. As changes are allowed into the project, or as changes sneak into a project through scope creep, they must be examined for their overall effect on the project's execution and, ultimately, on the project deliverable. Chapters 5, 6, and 7 will cover scope, time, and cost control, but project managers also have to be concerned with quality control. It doesn't do much good if a project is completed on time and on budget, but the deliverable is full of errors and of poor quality. Chapter 8 will examine quality control in detail. Let's take a quick look at each of the 11 processes within this group.

> **EXAM TIP** While there are 11 processes within the monitoring and controlling process group, it doesn't mean that the project manager needs to use all 11 processes for every project.

Monitoring and Controlling the Project Work

What'd you expect to be doing in the monitor and control process group? This process is the heart of the process group and includes the entire collection of project characteristics, such as time, cost, and quality statistics. Based on the collected statistics, the project manager can measure the project success, identify trends, make forecasts, create project reports, and take actions to improve the project. Here are the inputs for this process:

- Project management plan
- Schedule forecasts

- Cost forecasts
- Validated changes
- Work performance information
- Enterprise environmental factors
- Organizational process assets.

Monitoring and controlling the project work will give the project team four outputs:

- Change requests
- Work performance reports
- Project management plan updates
- Project documents updates

Performing Integrated Change Control

Integrated change control is a process that examines how a change affects all parts of a project. Consider a change to the project scope on a project you've worked on. The change likely affected the project cost, the project schedule, and the expectations of the project quality. The change may also have affected other regions of your project: risk management, communications, human resources, and even procurement. Integrated change control manages the approved changes within a project, how and when the changes may occur, and determines if a change to the project may have already occurred. This process, as fun as it is, happens from project initiation through project closing. There are many inputs for this process:

- Project management plan
- Work performance reports
- Requested changes (should be documented and passed through the change control system)
- Enterprise environmental factors
- Organizational process assets

These inputs and this process will help the project manager and the project team create the following outputs:

- Approved change requests
- Change log
- Project management plan updates
- Project documents updates

Validating the Project Scope

If you were to hire an architectural firm to build your next mansion, you'd periodically visit the house under construction to ensure that the workers and the architects were building according to the plans you provided them. At the end of the project, you'd walk through the home and create a "punch list" of all the things that needed to be changed or repaired according to your agreement. The architectural firm would work with you to ensure that you're happy with the deliverable you asked for and the deliverable they have created for you. This is *scope validation*: the formal acceptance by inspection of the project deliverables. Here are the inputs the project manager needs to facilitate this process with the project customer:

- Project management plan
- Requirements documentation
- Requirements traceability matrix (a table of requirements that records when each requirement was identified, when the requirement should be created, and when the requirement was actually delivered)
- Accepted deliverables
- Work performance data

NOTE It is not the requirements that are created or delivered, it is the deliverable product, service, or result that meets the requirements.

The customer would inspect and then, hopefully, formally accept the project work or provide feedback on what needs to be corrected or changed. Here are the outputs of scope validation:

- Accepted deliverables
- Change requests
- Work performance information
- Project documents updates

Controlling the Project Scope

Once the project scope statement has been created, it is paramount to guard the scope from unauthorized changes and to follow a scope change control system within the project to ensure that any approved changes reflect the changes through cost, time, scope, quality, and the other knowledge areas within the project. Here are the inputs to perform this process:

- Project management plan (You will need the project scope management plan.)
- Requirements documentation

- Requirements traceability matrix (If changes enter the project, you'll need to update this matrix to show the new requirements.)
- Work performance data
- Organizational process assets

The outputs of this massive and not-so-enjoyable process are

- Work performance information
- Change requests
- Project management plan updates
- Project documents updates
- Organizational process asset updates

Controlling the Project Schedule

This process isn't a mystery. It's simply keeping the project on schedule so it finishes on time as planned. When variances happen within the project, the project manager and the project team have to plan for how to respond to these schedule variances. I'll discuss scheduling and schedule control in Chapter 6. For now, here are the inputs for this process:

- Project management plan
- Project schedule
- Work performance data
- Project calendars
- Schedule data
- Organizational process assets

This process creates several outputs:

- Work performance information
- Schedule forecasts
- Change requests
- Project management plan updates
- Organizational process asset updates
- Project documents updates

Controlling the Project Cost

Have you ever noticed that it's usually easier to get more time than money for your projects? Management dreads hearing that a project will cost more due to errors and variances. This process aims to prevent cost overruns and to control the expenses within a project. There are many inputs for this process:

- Project management plan
- Project funding requirements
- Work performance data
- Organizational process assets

Chapter 7 is all about managing project costs, including creating cost estimates and budgets. Here are the outputs of cost control:

- Work performance information
- Cost forecasts (a prediction based on the current project performance of where the project's budget is going to end up)
- Change requests
- Project management plan updates
- Project documents updates
- Organizational process assets updates

Performing Quality Control

Quality control (QC), which is covered in Chapter 8, is all about keeping the mistakes out of the project deliverables—and ultimately away from the customers—before the project is declared finished. QC is considered an inspection-driven process, because that's the primary activity involved with it. Here are the inputs to perform this process:

- Project management plan
- Quality metrics
- Quality checklists
- Work performance data
- Approved change requests
- Deliverables
- Project documents
- Organizational process assets

QC creates many outputs that can help the project manager and the project team improve the project performance and ensure that the project work is completed correctly for the customer. Here are the outputs of QC:

- Quality control measurements
- Validated changes (specifically, validated defect repairs)
- Validated deliverables

- Work performance information
- Change requests
- Project management plan updates
- Project documents updates
- Organizational process assets updates

Controlling Project Communications

Management, your project team, key stakeholders, and the project customer will want the project manager to keep them abreast of the project. This process centers on the project manager understanding what's happening throughout the entire project, being able to retrieve the information as it's needed, and distributing the information to the correct stakeholders as it's needed. There are four inputs to controlling the project communications:

- Project management plan
- Project communications
- Issue log
- Work performance data
- Organizational process assets

As the project manager controls the project communications, there will be four outputs:

- Work performance information
- Change requests
- Project management plan updates
- Project documents updates
- Organizational process assets updates

Controlling Project Risks

A risk is an uncertain event or condition that can affect the project's outcome. Project managers often think of risks as negative events, but that's not always the case. Many risks, such as using a new material, a new vendor, or a new approach to the project work, aren't negative, but have positive outcomes. Chapter 11 will discuss both positive and negative risks in detail. There are four inputs to the risk monitoring and controlling process:

- Project management plan (specifically, the risk management plan)
- Risk register
- Work performance data
- Work performance reports

Risk monitoring and control happens throughout the project's life cycle, not just once. As this process is completed, there will be five outputs:

- Work performance information
- Change requests
- Project management plan updates
- Project documents updates
- Organizational process assets updates

Controlling Procurement

If a project manager has to complete the procurement management process, she will also need to administer the project contracts. This process, which Chapter 12 explores, ensures that the relationship between the buyer and the seller remains intact, reviews how the seller is performing according to the terms of the contract, and works with the seller to ensure they continue to abide by the agreed contractual terms. This process has six inputs:

- Project management plan
- Procurement documents
- Agreements
- Approved change requests
- Work performance reports
- Work performance data

Controlling the project procurement creates five outputs:

- Work performance information
- Change requests. (The contract change control system oversees how changes can enter the contracted work. In addition, the terms of the contract may dictate the costs and allowance for change.)
- Project management plan updates
- Project documents updates
- Organizational process assets updates

Closing the Project

In project management, few things are more rewarding than closing a project. It's extremely satisfying, and sometimes sad, to officially close a project and move along to other challenges. This final project management process group has but two processes, but it's no less important than the other process groups within a project. The goals of closing a project are to officially confirm that all of the needed processes have been completed, that the deliverables have been transferred to the user or organization, and that the project is done.

Project closure also is concerned with the success of the project, and these processes can be used when a project may be canceled before reaching the desired deliverables. If a project has multiple phases, the processes within this group can be used for each phase and at the end of the project.

Closing the Project or Phase

This is the project goal: Close the project and get back to your life. You'll also use these processes to close out a phase. There are just three inputs to project and phase closure:

- Project management plan (should direct the project manager on what internal processes are required to close the project or phase in the organization)
- Accepted deliverables (deliverables that have successfully completed scope validation)
- Organizational process assets

When the project manager closes a project, two outputs are created and completed:

- Final product, service, or result transition (the things your project has created, including the project documents and the deliverables the stakeholders have expected)
- Organizational process assets updates

Closing Procurements

If a project manager has worked with vendors on a project, then there are processes that must be completed prior to project closure to ensure that all of the terms of the contract have been met. This allows the project manager to confirm that the seller has met its obligations and that the project manager's organization has also met the obligations of the contract before the project is closed. Here are the inputs to this process:

- Project management plan (Specifically, you'll need the procurement management plan.)
- Procurement documentation (This means you'll need the contract documentation and any details about the contract closure procedure.)

As a result of performing these activities, there are two outputs of this process:

- Closed procurements
- Organizational process assets updates

Examining How the Processes Interact

The five project management process groups are not unlike the Rubik's Cube toy: What you do in one area affects all the other areas. In project management, the interactions between the processes are somewhat chronological. However, the processes are often iterative and transient, and allow the project management team to shift from process group to process group. The process groups allow for plenty of overlap throughout the project. For example, the extent of the monitoring and controlling processes is directly affected by the planning process group.

You've seen throughout this chapter that the output of one process is often an input to another process. The planning process group is the best example of this axiom; project plans are created and then executed for each knowledge area. As a project moves through its life cycle, the activities of project management—that is, the 47 individual processes—interact, overlap, and share commonalities that allow the project to move forward. Note that in a multiphase project, these processes can be applied to each individual phase and to the project as a whole.

All of these processes are not needed on every single project—only the processes that are relevant to the specific project are needed. For example, a low-priority, simple move-add-change (MAC) project within an organization likely won't need to complete all 47 processes in order for the project to be completed successfully. However, a four-year project to build a skyscraper will likely use all 47 processes.

Constraints within a project are often seen as process inputs. Consider any project you've worked on where management has enforced a project deadline. The deadline is a constraint that may not allow the project team to determine the best completion through normal project planning, but rather by working backward from the deadline. Constraints that serve as inputs to processes can cause additional risks on schedule and quality, can increase project costs, and may even require the project scope to be reduced to hit the project's target preset end date. No fun for anyone!

Chapter Summary

Don't you feel great now that you've seen all of the project management processes, the process groups where they live, and how all these processes interact with one another? Your PMI examination is all about project management, and project management is, of course, all about the processes needed to complete the project. Projects move through a project management life cycle of initiating, planning, executing, monitoring and controlling, and, ultimately, closing. Table 3-1 is a quick summary of each project management process group and the processes you'll find in each group. I'll cover all of these in detail through the remainder of this book:

Project Management Processes	Corresponding Chapter
Initiating process group—2 processes	
Develop project charter	4: Project Integration Management
Identify stakeholders	13: Project Stakeholder Management
Planning process group—24 processes	
Develop project management plan	4: Project Integration Management
Plan scope management	5: Project Scope Management
Collect requirements	5: Project Scope Management
Define scope	5: Project Scope Management
Create WBS	5: Project Scope Management
Plan schedule management	6: Project Time Management
Define activities	6: Project Time Management
Sequence activities	6: Project Time Management
Estimate activity resources	6: Project Time Management
Estimate activity duration	6: Project Time Management
Develop schedule	6: Project Time Management
Plan cost management	7: Project Cost Management
Estimate project costs	7: Project Cost Management
Determine project budget	7: Project Cost Management
Plan quality management	8: Project Quality Management
Plan human resource management	9: Project Human Resource Management
Plan communications management	10: Project Communications Management
Plan project risk management	11: Project Risk Management
Identify project risks	11: Project Risk Management
Perform qualitative risks	11: Project Risk Management
Perform quantitative risks	11: Project Risk Management
Plan risk responses	11: Project Risk Management
Plan procurement management	12: Project Procurement Management
Plan stakeholder management	13: Project Stakeholder Management
Executing Process Group—8 processes	
Direct and manage project work	4: Project Integration Management
Perform QA	8: Project Quality Management
Acquire the project team	9: Project Human Resource Management
Develop project team	9: Project Human Resource Management
Manage project team	9: Project Human Resource Management

Table 3-1   The 47 Project Management Processes across Five Process Groups

Project Management Processes	Corresponding Chapter
Manage communications	10: Project Communications Management
Conduct procurements	12: Project Procurement Management
Manage stakeholder engagement	13: Project Stakeholder Management
Monitoring and Controlling—11 processes	
Monitor and control the project work	4: Project Integration Management
Perform integrated change control	4: Project Integration Management
Validate scope	5: Project Scope Management
Control the project scope	5: Project Scope Management
Control the project schedule	6: Project Time Management
Control the project costs	7: Project Cost Management
Perform quality control	8: Project Quality Management
Control project communications	10: Project Communications Management
Control project risks	11: Project Risk Management
Conduct procurements	12: Project Procurement Management
Control stakeholder engagement	13: Project Stakeholder Management
Closing Processes—2 processes	
Close the project or phase	4: Project Integration Management
Close procurement	12: Project Procurement Management

Table 3-1   The 47 Project Management Processes across Five Process Groups *(continued)*

The project management processes span the entire project, which means that not only do the processes live inside of the process groups we've covered here, but also the activities of the processes can be lumped into one of the ten knowledge areas of project management. Part II of this book deals with the project management knowledge areas.

Processes interact based on the situations within the project. Not all of these processes will interact on every project, and not every process is needed on every single project. Your CAPM or PMP examination will test you, however, on all of these processes, since it's possible for a project to use all 47 project management processes.

Key Terms

Assumption   A belief that may or may not be true within a project. Weather is an example of an assumption in construction projects.

Change request   A documented request to add to or remove from the project scope. A change request may be initiated to change an organizational process asset, such as a template or a form.

Closing process group   The project management process group that contains the activities to close out a project and project contracts.

Constraint   A condition, rule, or procedure that restricts a project manager's options. A project deadline is an example of a constraint.

Corrective action   A corrective action brings project work back into alignment with the project plan. A corrective action may also address a process that is producing errors.

Cost baseline   The aggregation of the project deliverables and their associated costs. The difference between the cost estimates and the actual cost of the project identifies the cost variance.

Defect repair   The activity to repair a defect within the project.

Deming's PDCA cycle   Standard project management is based on Deming's plan-do-check-act cycle, which describes the logical progression of project management duties.

Enterprise environmental factors   Any external or internal organizational factors that can affect project success. Enterprise environmental factors include the culture, organizational structure, resources and commercial databases the project will use, market conditions, and your project management software.

Executing process group   The project management process group that provides the activities to carry out the project management plan to complete the project work.

Initiating process group   The project management process group that allows a project to be chartered and authorized.

Issue log   A record of the issue, its characteristics, the issue owner, and a target date for resolving the issue.

Manage project team   The project manager must, according to enterprise environmental factors, manage the project team to ensure that they are completing their work assignments with quality and according to plan.

Manage stakeholder expectations   This process is based on what the stakeholders expect from the project and on project communications from the project manager.

Monitoring and controlling process group   The project management process group oversees, measures, and tracks project performance.

Organizational process assets   The methodology an organization uses to perform its business, as well as the guidelines, procedures, and knowledge bases, such as the lessons learned documentation from past projects and any relevant historical information.

Planning process group   The project management process group that creates the project management plan to execute, monitor and control, and close the project.

Preventive action   A risk-related action that avoids risk within the project. A workaround to a problem within your project is an example of a preventive action.

Process   A set of integrated activities to create a product, result, or service. Project management processes allow the project to move toward completion.

Product process   A process that is unique to the type of work creating the product of the project. Product processes can also be unique to the performing organization of the project.

Project calendar   The calendar that documents when the project work can occur.

Project charter   A document that comes from outside of the project boundaries and authorizes the existence of a project.

Project deliverable   The output of the project.

Project scope statement   The project scope defines the project, the project deliverables, product requirements, project boundaries, acceptance procedures, and scope control.

Resource calendar   The calendar that documents which project resources are available for the project work.

Risk register   A central repository of the project risks and their attributes.

Risk   An uncertain event or condition that can have a negative or positive impact on the project.

Rolling wave planning   Iterations of planning throughout the project life cycle.

Schedule baseline   The expected timeline of the project. The difference between the planned schedule and the experience schedule reveals schedule variances within the project.

Scope baseline   The sum of the project deliverables. The project scope statement, the WBS, and the WBS dictionary are called the project scope baseline. The differences between the WBS and what is created is a scope variance.

Stakeholder   A person or group that is affected by the project or that may affect the group. Stakeholders can be positive, negative, or neutral in their attitude toward the project success.

Stakeholder engagement   The project manager and project team aim to keep the project stakeholders engaged and involved in the project to ensure that decisions, approvals, and communications are maintained as defined in the stakeholder management plan and the stakeholder management strategy.

WBS dictionary   A document that defines every identified element of the WBS.

Work breakdown structure (WBS)   A breakdown of the project scope.

Work-around   An immediate response to a negative risk within the project. This is an example of a corrective action.

Questions

1. Yolanda is the project manager of the Data Migration Project for her organization. As the project manager Yolanda should identify which project management processes are most appropriate for this type of project. What is a project process?

   A. The creation of a product

   B. The progressive elaboration resulting in a product

   C. A series of actions that bring about a product, result, or service

   D. A series of actions that allow the project to move from concept to deliverable

2. There are five project management process groups that allow projects to move from start to completion. Which one of the following is NOT one of the project management process groups?

   A. Initiating

   B. Planning

   C. Communicating

   D. Closing

3. Of the following, which is the logical order of the project management processes?

   A. Initiating, planning, monitoring and controlling, executing, closing

   B. Initiating, planning, executing, monitoring and controlling, closing

   C. Planning, initiating, monitoring and controlling, executing, closing

   D. Planning, initiating, executing, closing, monitoring and closing

4. You are the project manager of the GRT Construction Project. Your project team announces how they are happy to be done with project planning. You inform the team, however, that you and they will likely be returning to project planning throughout the project. This ongoing process of project planning is also known as _____.

   A. Constant integration planning

   B. Rolling wave planning

   C. Continuous planning

   D. Phase gates

5. You are the project manager for the AQA Project. You would like to include several of the customers in the project planning sessions. Your project leader would like to know why the stakeholders should be involved since your project team will be determining the best method to reach the project objectives. You should include the stakeholders because _____.

A. It generates goodwill between the project team and the stakeholders.

B. It allows the stakeholders to see the project manager as the authority of the project.

C. It allows the project team to meet the stakeholders and express their concerns regarding project constraints.

D. It allows the project team to leverage the skills and knowledge of the stakeholders to develop the project plan.

6. You are the project manager of a new mobile application project for a client. You have requested that several of the stakeholders participate in the initiation of the project. Why is this important?

A. It improves the probability of shared ownership.

B. It allows for scope constraints.

C. It prevents scope creep.

D. It allows for effective communications.

7. You are coaching several new project managers in your organization about the project management life cycle and the purpose of each group. There is some confusion, however, about the actual purpose of the project management planning process group. What is the primary purpose of the planning process group?

A. To initiate the project work

B. To determine the project cost

C. To determine the Iron Triangle of Project Management

D. To develop the project management plan

8. Beth is the project customer for a home construction project. The project is likely to be awarded to your company's design firm, but there are still some questions regarding the proposal your company has offered to Beth. Robert, your manager, wants you to be the project manager on this project even though it technically hasn't been awarded to your company. When is a project manager typically selected?

A. Planning phase

B. Executing phase

C. Initiation phase

D. When the project charter is approved

9. Gary is teaching a group of project managers about the PMP and the *PMBOK Guide*. Gary wants to clearly communicate what project management is according to the *PMBOK Guide*. Which one of the following statements best describes what project management is?

   A. Project management is the application of knowledge, skills, tools, and techniques to project team members to meet project requirements.

   B. Project management is the application of knowledge, skills, tools, and techniques to project activities to meet project requirements.

   C. Project management is the collection of the project management processes used on every project.

   D. Project management is the application of the project management processes that are used on every project.

10. In order for a project to be successful, there must be four conditions. Which one of the following is not a condition required for project success?

   A. The project team must select the appropriate processes to meet the project objectives.

   B. The project team must select applicable knowledge areas in order to meet the project objectives.

   C. The project team must comply with requirements to meet stakeholder needs, wants, and expectations.

   D. The project team must balance the competing demands of scope, time, cost, quality, resources, and risk to create a quality product.

11. When a project manager and a project team choose the processes that they deem applicable to their project, this is called what?

   A. Tailoring

   B. Faulty project management

   C. Functional project management

   D. Rolling wave planning

12. Ron is the project manager of a new project and he's eager to meet the project team to get the project planned and the work moving. However, he's confused as to when he will actually acquire the team. In which process group will the project team be acquired?

   A. Initiating

   B. Planning

   C. Executing

   D. Monitoring and controlling

13. You are the project manager of a new project. You have worked with management to identify several initial assumptions and constraints for your project. Where will these items be documented?

   A. Project management plan

   B. Project scope statement

    C. Project charter

    D. Risk management plan

14. Ben is the project manager for his company. A customer has requested a new website and asked that Ben serve as the project manager since he's done great work in the past for her company. Based on this information, when does a project become officially authorized?

    A. When the project charter is written

    B. When the project is funded

    C. When the project team is assembled

    D. When the project charter is approved

15. You are the project manager of a new project to construct a children's playground in your community. The project is being funded by a private donor, but they expect you to manage the project with the fullest attention. When does the vast majority of a project's budget get expended?

    A. During the planning process group activities

    B. During the execution process group activities

    C. During the initiation process group activities

    D. During the procurement process group activities

16. You have identified a negative risk within your project and would like to implement a work-around to the risk. A work-around is an example of what?

    A. A corrective action

    B. A defect repair

    C. Preventive action

    D. Poor project management

17. You are working on a new high-profile project. Management has asked that you pause the project at the end of each project phase to communicate with them about the work and the project progress, and provide cost and schedule forecasts. Which process group can provide feedback between project phases?

    A. Planning

    B. Executing

    C. Monitoring and controlling

    D. Closing

18. You are the project manager of an IT upgrade project for a health care client. The client demands perfection in the project's product because of the lives your project's product will affect. Which process aims to eliminate causes of unsatisfactory performance?

    A. Scope definition

    B. Scope validation

    C. Quality control

    D. Cost control

19. Mick is the project manager of the CHA Design Project. The project has been performing poorly on both costs and schedule. The customer has become very aggravated with the project problems and has decided to cancel the project. Which process must happen next?

    A. Scope control

    B. Procurement management

    C. Contract closure

    D. No additional process is needed because the project has been canceled.

20. Management has determined that your project must be completed by December 30. This date is an input to your planning process group and is considered what?

    A. A constraint

    B. An enterprise environmental factor

    C. An organizational process asset

    D. An assumption

Questions and Answers

1. Yolanda is the project manager of the Data Migration Project for her organization. As the project manager Yolanda should identify which project management processes are most appropriate for this type of project. What is a project process?

    A. The creation of a product

    B. The progressive elaboration resulting in a product

    C. A series of actions that bring about a product, result, or service

    D. A series of actions that allow the project to move from concept to deliverable

    C. A process, the focus of this chapter, is a set of interrelated activities that brings about a product, result, or service. A is incorrect because it does not fully describe a process, but describes more of a project. B is incorrect because progressive elaboration is not a description of a process, but rather a description of incremental refinements of a definition of a product, service, or result. D is also incorrect because this statement describes project phases.

2. There are five project management process groups that allow projects to move from start to completion. Which one of the following is NOT one of the project management process groups?

A. Initiating

B. Planning

C. Communicating

D. Closing

C. Communicating is a process, but it is not a process group. A, B, and D are all incorrect choices because they are project management process groups.

3. Of the following, which is the logical order of the project management processes?

A. Initiating, planning, monitoring and controlling, executing, closing

B. Initiating, planning, executing, monitoring and controlling, closing

C. Planning, initiating, monitoring and controlling, executing, closing

D. Planning, initiating, executing, closing, monitoring and closing

B. Projects logically move through initiating, planning, executing, monitoring and controlling, and closing. A, C, and D are all incorrect because they are not in the logical order of the project management process groups.

4. You are the project manager of the GRT Construction Project. Your project team announces how they are happy to be done with project planning. You inform the team, however, that you and they will likely be returning to project planning throughout the project. This ongoing process of project planning is also known as _____.

A. Constant integration planning

B. Rolling wave planning

C. Continuous planning

D. Phase gates

B. Rolling wave planning is the progressive detailing of the project management plan. A is not a valid project management term. C is not an appropriate answer. D, phase gates, describes the end of a project phase.

5. You are the project manager for the AQA Project. You would like to include several of the customers in the project planning sessions. Your project leader would like to know why the stakeholders should be involved since your project team will be determining the best method to reach the project objectives. You should include the stakeholders because _____.

A. It generates goodwill between the project team and the stakeholders.

B. It allows the stakeholders to see the project manager as the authority of the project.

C. It allows the project team to meet the stakeholders and express their concerns regarding project constraints.

D. It allows the project team to leverage the skills and knowledge of the stakeholders to develop the project plan.

D. Stakeholders should be involved in the planning processes because they have specific skills and knowledge that the project team can use to develop the project plan. A may be true, but it is not the best answer for this question. B is not valid because it is not the reason for involving the stakeholders. In addition, the project manager may not be seen as the project authority in every project (consider public projects and functional organizations). C is incorrect because this is not the purpose of involving the stakeholders.

6. You are the project manager of a new mobile application project for a client. You have requested that several of the stakeholders participate in the initiation of the project. Why is this important?

A. It improves the probability of shared ownership.

B. It allows for scope constraints.

C. It prevents scope creep.

D. It allows for effective communications.

A. Stakeholders should participate in project initiation because it improves shared ownership of the project, deliverable acceptance, and stakeholder satisfaction. B, C, and D are all false statements about the involvement of stakeholders in the initiation processes.

7. You are coaching several new project managers in your organization about the project management life cycle and the purpose of each group. There is some confusion, however, about the actual purpose of the project management planning process group. What is the primary purpose of the planning process group?

A. To initiate the project work

B. To determine the project cost

C. To determine the Iron Triangle of Project Management

D. To develop the project management plan

D. The purpose of planning is to develop the project management plan. A is incorrect. This is the purpose of the initiating process group. B and C are incorrect because these may occur during planning, but these are not the primary purpose of the planning process group.

8. Beth is the project customer for a home construction project. The project is likely to be awarded to your company's design firm, but there are still some questions regarding the proposal your company has offered to Beth. Robert, your manager, wants you to be the project manager on this project even though it technically hasn't been awarded to your company. When is a project manager typically selected?

A. Planning phase

B. Executing phase

C. Initiation phase

D. When the project charter is approved

> **C.** The project manager is selected during the initiation process group. A, B, and D are all false because these answers do not define when the project manager is selected.

9. Gary is teaching a group of project managers about the PMP and the *PMBOK Guide*. Gary wants to clearly communicate what project management is according to the *PMBOK Guide*. Which one of the following statements best describes what project management is?

   A. Project management is the application of knowledge, skills, tools, and techniques to project team members to meet project requirements.

   B. Project management is the application of knowledge, skills, tools, and techniques to project activities to meet project requirements.

   C. Project management is the collection of the project management processes used on every project.

   D. Project management is the application of the project management processes that are used on every project.

> **B.** Project management is the application of knowledge, skills, tools, and techniques to project activities to meet project requirements. A, C, and D are not valid definitions of what project management is. A is incorrect because the tools and techniques are not applied to the project team members. C is incorrect because not every project management process is used on every project. And D, while similar to C, is incorrect because not every process is applied on every project.

10. In order for a project to be successful, there must be four conditions. Which one of the following is not a condition required for project success?

    A. The project team must select the appropriate processes to meet the project objectives.

    B. The project team must select applicable knowledge areas in order to meet the project objectives.

    C. The project team must comply with requirements to meet stakeholder needs, wants, and expectations.

    D. The project team must balance the competing demands of scope, time, cost, quality, resources, and risk to create a quality product.

> **B.** The project team does not select which knowledge areas are needed for the project to be successful, so this statement is false. Thus, it is not a condition

required for project success. Chapters 4 through 12 in this book and the *PMBOK* describe the ten knowledge areas that are applicable for every project. A, C, and D are correct statements for a successful project. The fourth condition of a successful project is that a defined approach to adapt the product specifications and plans to meet the project requirements is used within the project.

11. When a project manager and a project team choose the processes that they deem applicable to their project, this is called what?

    A. Tailoring

    B. Faulty project management

    C. Functional project management

    D. Rolling wave planning

    A. The project team tailors the project processes to their individual project. B is incorrect because this is good project management, not faulty project management. C describes an organizational structure, not tailoring. D is incorrect because rolling wave planning defines the iterations of project planning.

12. Ron is the project manager of a new project and he's eager to meet the project team to get the project planned and the work moving. However, he's confused as to when he will actually acquire the team. In which process group will the project team be acquired?

    A. Initiating

    B. Planning

    C. Executing

    D. Monitoring and controlling

    C. The project team is acquired in the executing process group. A, B, and D are all incorrect because the team is not acquired during these groups. This is a tricky question for some people. Remember, the project management life cycle isn't a series of phases or step-by-step directions. You'll move from one process group to another as needed in the project.

13. You are the project manager of a new project. You have worked with management to identify several initial assumptions and constraints for your project. Where will these items be documented?

    A. Project management plan

    B. Project scope statement

    C. Project charter

    D. Risk management plan

C. The initial constraints and assumptions are documented in the project charter. A, B, and D are all incorrect because the initial constraints and assumptions are documented in the project charter, not in the project management plan, the project scope statement, or the risk management plan.

14. Ben is the project manager for his company. A customer has requested a new website and asked that Ben serve as the project manager since he's done great work in the past for her company. Based on this information, when does a project become officially authorized?

    A. When the project charter is written

    B. When the project is funded

    C. When the project team is assembled

    D. When the project charter is approved

    D. The project is not authorized until the charter is approved. A is incorrect because a charter can be written by the project management team and still not be approved. B is incorrect because a project is chartered, typically and technically, before being funded. Recall that the contract, or agreement, is needed as one of the possible inputs to the project charter. C is incorrect because team acquisition happens during the execution process group—well after project initiation, which is where the charter comes from.

15. You are the project manager of a new project to construct a children's playground in your community. The project is being funded by a private donor, but they expect you to manage the project with the fullest attention. When does the vast majority of a project's budget get expended?

    A. During the planning process group activities

    B. During the execution process group activities

    C. During the initiation process group activities

    D. During the procurement process group activities

    B. When the project team completes the project work, the project's budget is expended. A, C, and D are all incorrect because the vast majority of the project's budget is not consumed during these process groups.

16. You have identified a negative risk within your project and would like to implement a work-around to the risk. A work-around is an example of what?

    A. A corrective action

    B. A defect repair

    C. Preventive action

    D. Poor project management

    A. A work-around is an example of a corrective action. A, corrective action, is an action to bring future project performance in alignment with the project plan. B, defect repair, is the repair of flawed work. C is incorrect because a preventive action attempts to reduce the probability of a risk from coming into play. D is not a valid answer.

17. You are working on a new high-profile project. Management has asked that you pause the project at the end of each project phase to communicate with them about the work and the project progress, and provide cost and schedule forecasts. Which process group can provide feedback between project phases?

   A. Planning

   B. Executing

   C. Monitoring and controlling

   D. Closing

   C. The monitoring and controlling process group provides feedback between project phases. A, B, and D are all incorrect because these process groups do not provide feedback between project phases.

18. You are the project manager of an IT upgrade project for a health care client. The client demands perfection in the project's product because of the lives your project's product will affect. Which process aims to eliminate causes of unsatisfactory performance?

   A. Scope definition

   B. Scope validation

   C. Quality control

   D. Cost control

   C. Quality control aims to eliminate causes of unsatisfactory performance. This process is part of the monitoring and controlling process group. A, scope definition, is the process of defining what the scope and its requirements for acceptance are. B, scope validation, is the inspection-drive process the project manager and the project customer (or a third party) will do together to inspect the project deliverables for acceptability. D, cost control, is concerned with controlling project costs.

19. Mick is the project manager of the CHA Design Project. The project has been performing poorly on both costs and schedule. The customer has become very aggravated with the project problems and has decided to cancel the project. Which process must happen next?

   A. Scope control

   B. Procurement management

   C. Contract closure

   D. No additional process is needed because the project has been canceled.

> **C.** When a project is canceled, the closing processes must still happen. In this example, the only closing process mentioned was contract closure. A, B, and D are all invalid because these processes do not happen if a project is closed or canceled.

20. Management has determined that your project must be completed by December 30. This date is an input to your planning process group and is considered what?

    A. A constraint

    B. An enterprise environmental factor

    C. An organizational process asset

    D. An assumption

> **A.** A preset project deadline is an example of a project constraint. B is incorrect because enterprise environmental factors are not constraints. C, organizational process assets, are not constraints but resources for the project management team. D is incorrect because assumptions are things believed to be true but not proven to be true.

PART II

Project Management Professional Testing Areas

Project Integration Management

In this chapter, you will
- Learn what project integration management does for the project manager
- Develop the project charter
- Create the project management plan
- Manage the project work
- Monitor and control the project work
- Understand how integrated change control works
- Close a project or phase

What the heck is *project integration management*? This is the heart of project management and is made up of the day-to-day processes the project manager relies upon to ensure that all parts of the project work together. Project integration management is about the project manager making the best decisions for work, resources, project issues, and all the logistics of the project so it is completed as planned. What you do in one area of the project directly affects all the other areas of the project.

Project integration management is also about making trade-offs between competing objectives and alternatives. I'm certain you, as a project manager, have worked with stakeholders who want something that would cancel out a characteristic another stakeholder wants: Bob says he wants the house painted green, and Nancy wants it painted red. Or your client wants your organization to design a reliable, fast network operating system for thousands of users as long as it doesn't cost more than a few thousand dollars. Competing objectives require negotiations, balance, and lots and lots of aspirin.

VIDEO For a more detailed explanation, watch the *Working with Project Integration Management* video now.

In the first part of this book, I discussed the project management life cycle and the 47 project management processes. These processes are not isolated elements, but they overlap, interact, and complement one another. Project integration management is the coordination and support of these project management plans. It also considers the interrelationship of the ten knowledge areas and how actions in one knowledge area affect all the others.

Developing the Project Charter

All projects officially start with a project charter—a formal document that authorizes the project to exist in the organization and gives the project manager authority over the project resources. So what's so great about the charter? It's the document that gives you, the project manager, the authority to use resources to do the project work—and authority over resources like equipment and facilities. It's a powerful document and needs to be signed by someone with power in the organization. The project manager is assigned to the project as early as possible, and ideally while the charter is still being developed. The project manager needs to be assigned, without a doubt, before the project moves into the project planning process group.

In many organizations, the project manager is the person writing the charter, and that's fine—really!—but the charter cannot be signed by the project manager. While the project may be backed by the project customer, the project champion, or even the organization's project management office, the charter is officially backed by a project initiator, typically called the *project sponsor*, at a level within the organization where this person can allocate funding and resources for the project. In other words, the project manager can't sign the charter because he's not "powerful" enough within the organization to assign resources and funds to his own project.

 EXAM TIP The project charter authorizes the project, names the project manager, and also defines the project manager's level of authority.

Charters are created by an enterprise, a government agency, a program manager, or a project steering committee (sometimes called the portfolio organization). Charters are written so that a project can answer or satisfy one of the following:

- Market demand
- Business need
- Customer request
- Technological advance
- Legal requirement
- Ecological impacts
- Social need

Your organization might call these opportunities, problems, or business requirements. Once you're a project manager, you'll just call 'em your favorite project. (Your favorite project is always the one you're managing right now.) Why some projects within an organization get selected and others do not can be due to finances, the project owner, sponsor influence, legal requirements, or any number of reasons. The message to take away is that regardless of why a project gets selected, you, the project manager, must have a charter for the project to be officially authorized. Charters should always include the following project information:

- Requirements for satisfaction of project stakeholder needs, wants, and expectations
- Business needs, a description of the project's product, or a mile-high view of the project's purpose
- The reason why the project was chartered
- The project manager and his or her level of autonomy
- Summary milestone schedule
- Stakeholder influences
- Functional organizations and how they'll be involved with the project
- Project constraints and assumptions (environment, external, and organizational)
- Business case for the project and the project return on investment
- Summary project budget
- High-level risks
- Project approval requirements
- Name and authority level of the project sponsor

Believe it or not, the project charter may be updated. For example, the summary project budget may be based on a simple, rough order-of-magnitude estimate. As the project moves deeper into planning, the estimates become clearer and more precise. The more accurate estimate may cause the budget to change, requiring the project charter to be modified to reflect the new information.

Preparing to Create the Project Charter

The project charter is often written by the project manager and then signed by the project sponsor, so you'll need to know what goes into it, how it gets created, and then what you can do with your charter—especially for the Certified Associate in Project Management (CAPM) or Project Management Professional (PMP) examination. When preparing to create the project charter, you'll need five things, described in the following sections.

Contract

Okay, I confess—you won't always need a contract, or an agreement, in order to create a project charter, but it's an input in the Project Management Body of Knowledge (PMBOK), so work with me a moment. If you're working in an organization that performs projects for other entities, such as a consulting firm, architectural firm, or even an event planning company, you'll need a contract to make the project official. Chapter 12 explores contracting, but for now know that you may need a contract if it's appropriate for your project.

Project Statement of Work (SOW)

This document defines all the products and services that the project will provide. For a project completed internally, the SOW comes from the project sponsor and defines the business need, products, and services the project will create. If the project is to be completed for another organization, the customer should provide the performing organization with the SOW as part of their procurement package. For example, if your company were to receive a Request for Proposal (RFP) to create a new warehouse, the customer would include the SOW with the RFP so you could know what the proposal is to address. Every SOW should include:

- **Business need** Why the project needs to exist.

- **Product scope description** This document describes the product or service the project will create. Consider the RFP to create the new warehouse: The customer's RFP would detail the square footage, requirements of the warehouse, and other details that would allow your company to respond intelligently to their request. As you may have experienced, especially in the world of information technology, the product description is usually broad, vague, and dreamy in the early stages of a project. As the project moves through the planning phases, the details of the product scope become clearer.

- **Strategic plan** The strategic plan defines how the project will mesh with the organization's goals. This is a key input when an organization decides whether to do a project. You won't find a car manufacturer hosting projects to create chandeliers—it's just not within their strategic plan to undertake such a project.

Business Case

The business case defines why the project is worthy of the organization's monies to be invested into the project. It explains why the project is needed and what type of return the organization can expect for its investment. A cost-benefit analysis is usually included in the business case to support the project's purpose in the organization. The business case may be written by the project manager, business analyst, or even by a customer if the project is sponsored by someone external to your organization.

Business cases can evolve from feasibility studies because some of the information may overlap. The business case will define the market demand for the project's creation, the organizational need, ecological impacts, legal requirements, a social need, or the technological advance that the project will bring the organization. In some instances, the business case could be based on a customer's request for additional services or on products that are opportunities for the organization to grow.

Enterprise Environmental Factors

The project charter also considers the organization where the project will take place and its culture, standards, regulations, and environment. You'll see enterprise environmental factors throughout the remainder of this book. Just so you've got these fun things once and for all, here are the enterprise environmental factors you'll need to be familiar with:

- Organization's culture and structure
- Industry standards and regulations
- Organization's facilities and equipment (the general infrastructure of the company)
- Human resources and their talents, skills, and availability
- Human resources administration
- Work authorization system
- Marketplace conditions
- Stakeholders' tolerance for risk (also known as the utility function)
- Commercial databases for the organization's industry (Think of cost-estimating databases for a builder or manufacturer.)
- Project management information system (PMIS). Think of—yes, I'll say it—Microsoft Project. Don't worry, you won't have to know any software vendors or their goods for the PMI exam. All of your favorite, or least favorite, project management software is just lumped into the generic term "project management information system."

Organizational Process Assets

Anything that your organization has in its possession that can help your current project succeed is part of the organizational process assets. This also means that the policies, procedures, plans, and documentation of past projects are part of the organizational process assets. The Project Management Institute (PMI) breaks down the organizational process assets into two big categories. Let's explore them in detail.

- Processes and procedures for project work:
  - Standard processes and procedures for getting project work done. Consider purchase requests, team member acquisitions, the quality programs your projects subscribe to, checklists, and generally the way your company requires your projects to operate.
  - Guidelines on how your project team is to complete their work, proposal evaluations, and how you measure your project for performance.
  - Templates for project management.

- How the project manager is allowed to tailor the project management processes to fit any given project.
- Communication, archival, and security requirements, and allowed modalities for communication:
  - How a project manager is to close a project
  - Financial controls and procedures
  - Issue and product defect management
  - Change control procedures
  - Risk management procedures
  - Work authorization system processes
  - Processes and procedures for contributing to and accessing a corporate knowledge base
  - Process measurements
  - Project files
  - Historical information and lessons learned documentation
  - Issue and defect records of past projects and products
  - Configuration management for versioning, baselines, company standards, procedures, and prior project documents (for example, the versions of software, blueprints, and manuals)
  - Financial databases

Choosing a Project to Charter

Once the organization and the project manager are armed with these inputs, they're ready to go about creating the project charter. Preparing to create the charter is often trickier than actually writing it. However, before the project management team can actually create a charter, there needs to be a project. This means the organization, the project steering committee, or the project portfolio management team needs to choose a project to initiate.

Unless you work for an incredible organization and/or are extremely lucky, you've probably discovered that not every good project ends up being authorized through a charter. After all, most companies only have a limited amount of funds to invest in new projects. There are two approaches an organization takes to choose new projects—and no, "heads or tails" is not one of them.

The first method is by using a mathematical model to determine the likelihood of success. These models include:

- Linear programming
- Nonlinear programming
- Dynamic programming

- Integer programming
- Multiobjective programming

Sounds like fun, doesn't it? Don't worry. You do not need to know how to perform any of the preceding math tricks for your CAPM or PMP examination. Just be topically aware of these, and know that they are examples of geeky mathematical models.

 EXAM TIP Mathematical models are also known as "constrained optimization."

The second method, however, you will want to be a bit more familiar with. This project selection uses a benefits-comparison model to determine project success. Let's look at these in more detail in the following sections.

Murder Boards

Murder boards are committees full of folks that ask every conceivable negative question about the proposed project. Their goals are to expose strengths and weakness of the project—and to kill the project if it's deemed unworthy for the organization to commit to. Not a pleasant decision-making process. You might also know murder boards by a slightly friendlier name: project steering committees or project selection committees.

Scoring Models

Scoring models (sometimes called weighted scoring models) are models that use a common set of values for all of the projects up for selection. For example, values can be profitability, complexity, customer demand, and so on. Each of these values has an assigned weight. Values of high importance have a high weight, while values of lower importance have a lower weight. The projects are measured against these values and assigned scores by how well they match the predefined values. The projects with higher scores take priority over projects with lower scores. Figure 4-1 demonstrates the scoring model.

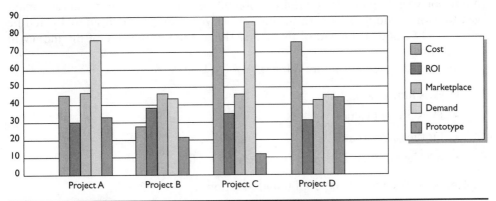

Figure 4-1 A scoring model bases project selection on predefined values.

Benefit/Cost Ratios

Just like they sound, benefit/cost ratio (BCR) models examine the benefit-to-cost ratio. A typical measure is the cost to complete the project and the cost of ongoing operations of the project product compared against the expected benefits of the project. For example, consider a project that will cost $575,000 to create a new product, market the product, and provide ongoing support for the product for one year. The expected gross return on the product, however, is $980,000 in year one. The benefit of completing the project is greater than the cost to create the product.

 EXAM TIP BCR statements can be written as ratios. For example, a BCR of 3:2 has three benefits to two costs—a good choice. A BCR of 1:3, however, is not a good choice. Pay special attention to which side of the ratio represents the cost. It should not exceed the benefit if you want it to be selected.

Payback Period

How long does it take the project to "pay back" the associated costs? For example, the AXZ Project will cost the organization $500,000 to create over five years. The expected cash inflow (income) on the project deliverable, however, is $40,000 per quarter. From here, it's simple math: 500,000 divided by $40,000 is 12.5 quarters, or a little over three years to recoup the expenses.

This selection method, while one of the simplest, is also the weakest. Why? The cash inflows are not discounted against the time to begin creating the cash. This is the time value of money. The $40,000 per quarter five years from now is worth less than $40,000 in your pocket today. Remember when sodas were a nickel? It's the same idea—the soda hasn't gotten better; the nickel is just worth less today than it was way back then.

Considering the Discounted Cash Flow

Discounted cash-flow accounts for the time value of money. If you were to borrow $100,000 for five years from your uncle, you'd be paying interest on the money, yes? (If not, you've got a great uncle.) If the $100,000 were invested for five years and managed to earn a whopping 6 percent interest per year, compounded annually, it'd be worth $133,822.60 at the end of five years. This is the future value of the money in today's terms.

The magic formula for future value is $FV = PV(1 + I)^n$, where:

- FV is future value
- PV is present value
- I is the interest rate
- n is the number of periods (years, quarters, etc.)

Here's the formula with the $100,000 in action:

1. $FV = 100,000(1 + .06)^5$

2. FV = 100,000(1.338226)

3. FV = 133,822.60

The future value of the $100,000 five years from now is worth $133,822.60. So how does that help? Now we've got to calculate the discounted cash-flow across all of the projects up for selection. The discounted cash-flow is really just the inverse of the preceding formula. We're looking for the present value of future cash flows: $PV = FV \div (1 + I)^n$.

In other words, if a project says it'll be earning the organization $160,000 in five years, that's great, but what's $160,000 five years from now really worth today? This puts the amount of the cash flow in perspective with what the projections are in today's money. Let's plug it into the formula and find out (assuming the interest rate is still 6 percent):

1. $PV = FV \div (1 + I)^n$

2. PV = 160,000 ÷ (1.338226)

3. PV = $119,561

So... $160,000 in five years is really only worth $119,561 today. If we had four different projects of varying time to completion, cost, and project cash inflows at completion, we'd calculate the present value and choose the project with the best present value because it'll likely be the best investment for the organization.

EXAM TIP You should be able to look at the present value of two proposed projects and make a decision as to which one should be green-lighted. The project with the highest present value is the best choice if that's the only factor you're presented with.

Calculating the Net Present Value

The net present value (NPV) is a somewhat complicated formula, but it allows you to predict a project's value more precisely than the lump-sum approach found with the PV formula. NPV evaluates the monies returned on a project for each period the project lasts. In other words, a project may last five years, but there may be a return on investment (ROI) in each of the five years the project is in existence, not just at the end of the project.

For example, a retail company may be upgrading the facilities at each of their stores to make shopping and purchasing easier for their customers. The company has 1,000 stores. As each store makes the conversion to the new facility design, the project deliverables will begin, hopefully, generating cash flow. (Uh, we specifically want cash inflow from the new stores, not cash outflow. That's some nerdy accounting humor.) The project can begin earning money when the first store is completed with the conversion to the new facilities. The faster the project can be completed, the sooner the organization will see a complete ROI.

Here's how the NPV formula works:

1. Calculate the project's cash flow for time unit (typically quarters or years).
2. Calculate each time unit total into the present value.
3. Sum the present value of each time unit.
4. Subtract the investment for the project.
5. Take two aspirins.
6. Examine the NPV value. An NPV greater than zero is good, and the project should be approved. An NPV less than zero is bad, and the project should be rejected.

When comparing two projects, the one with the greater NPV is typically better, although projects with high returns (PVs) early in the project are better than those with low returns early in the project. Table 4-1 provides an example of an NPV calculation.

 EXAM TIP   You likely will not have to calculate NPV for your CAPM or PMP exam. I've included the whole scenario here to provide an understanding of the formula. Basically, better than zero is good; less than zero means your project is losing money.

Considering the Internal Rate of Return

The last benefit measurement method is the internal rate of return (IRR). The IRR is a complex formula to calculate when the present value of the cash inflow equals the original investment. Don't get too lost in this formula—it's a tricky business, and you won't need to know how to calculate the IRR for the exam. You will need to know, however, that when comparing IRRs of multiple projects, projects with high IRRs are better choices than projects with low IRRs. This makes sense. Would you like an investment with a high rate of return or a lower rate of return?

Organizations use the IRR to determine if the organization should invest capital into the project. IRR is, technically, the yield on the funds invested into the project. You really know that you have a good, efficient investment when the IRR beats other rates

Table 4-1 Net Present Value Calculation	Period	Cash Flow	Present Value
	1	15,000.00	14,150.94
	2	25,000.00	22,249.91
	3	17,000.00	14,273.53
	4	25,000.00	19,802.34
	5	18,000.00	13,450.65
	Totals	$100,000.00	83,927.37
	Investment		78,000.00
	NPV		$ 5,927.37

of return for investing the capital in bonds, other projects, or even letting the cash stay in the bank. Organizations usually have a minimum acceptable rate of return (MARR) that the project needs to beat before it's even worth their time and cash to invest in the project. You might also know MARR as the hurdle rate—you've got to clear the hurdle before it's worth the risk of taking capital out of sure-thing investments and putting it into the chancy world of projects.

> **EXAM TIP** The formulas on the time value of money are important for project selection and for the exam. You'll need to be familiar with the present value, future value, and net present value formulas, what they do, and why organizations use them to select projects. You should be topically familiar with the internal rate of return concepts, but I doubt you'll have to calculate any IRR.

Knowing the Project Management Methodology

Before the project management team can dive in and create the project charter, they also need to understand how their organization approaches project management in general. When I teach my project management seminars, I find that some companies have a formal, highly structured, rigid project management approach. Other companies are, well, loosey-goosey. Their approach can vary from project manager to project manager, and they don't mind.

Whatever methodology an organization has adopted, the project management team must understand how this affects the level of detail they'll need to provide in their project charter. The great thing about this point, in light of your exam, is that every company in the world can use a different project management methodology, so it's tough to ask questions about what's proper or not.

Creating the Charter—Finally

Now that the project management team is armed with all the inputs, has considered the project selection methodology, and understands the project management methodology in place in their organization, they're ready to create the project. There are just two tools the project management team can use to create the charter:

- **Expert judgment** Experts within the organization or external experts such as consultants, agencies, firms, or subject matter experts (SMEs) can help the project management team create all the needed elements for the charter.

- **Facilitation techniques** You'll use facilitation techniques often in your role as the project manager. These are approaches like brainstorming, problem solving with stakeholders, conflict resolution, and group dynamics to reach a consensus for the project charter.

The project charter, as a final reminder for your exam, is endorsed by an entity outside of the project boundaries. This person or entity has the power to authorize the project and grant the project manager the power to assign resources to the project work.

The project charter should define the business needs and what the project aims to create in order to solve those business needs. The project charter typically defines:

- Metrics for the key project objectives (like time, cost, and quality)
- High-level requirements for the project
- The high-level description of the project's purpose
- The high-level risk within the project
- The summary milestone schedule
- The summary budget
- Key stakeholders the project will include
- Stakeholders needed for approvals and sign-off on the project acceptance
- The project manager's name and level of authority
- The project sponsor or entity authorizing the project

Many organizations create a standardized project charter as part of their organizational process assets and then adapt the project charter to each project. Whatever approach you take in your project, from scratch or from template, the most important thing is that the person who signs the project charter has the authority to back up the project manager for conflict resolution and issues in case there's a challenge to the project or the resources needed.

Developing the Project Management Plan

You wouldn't go about building a house, creating a new piece of software, or launching any project without a project plan, right? The project management plan, however, is more than how the *work* will be done, it's how the *project* will be done. That's right, the project management plan defines how the project is executed, monitored and controlled, and then closed. It's a plan on how to manage, coordinate, and integrate all the different knowledge areas and processes within a project. It's multifaceted. Figure 4-2 shows the process necessary before the project management plan can be developed. Think of all the things a project manager and the project team will decide within the project plan that need to be documented:

- Which project management processes and their level of implementation are appropriate for the project
- What tools and techniques will be used with which processes
- How the selected processes will be used to manage the project, including how the processes will interact as the project moves through its phases
- How the project work will be completed
- How change control will happen

- How configuration management will be performed
- The integrity of the project's baselines and how the measurements will be used to better manage the project
- Communication demand and techniques with the project stakeholders
- How the project phases will commence and proceed
- How stakeholder inclusion and management will occur
- When and how management will review the project performance

Creating the Project Management Plan

As the project completes project planning activities, the outputs will be assimilated into a collection of subsidiary project plans. The collection of these subsidiary project plans will address all of the previous points and help the project manager and the project team know where the project is going and how they will get there. Let's take a moment and look at each of the minimum project management subsidiary plans the project management plan will include:

- **Scope management plan**   This defines how the project scope will be planned, managed, and controlled. This plan is covered in detail in Chapter 5.
- **Requirements management plan**   This plan defines how the project requirements will be defined, gathered, documented, and managed. This plan is covered in detail in Chapter 5.
- **Schedule management plan**   This defines how the project schedule will be created and managed. The schedule management plan and its creation are covered in Chapter 6.

Figure 4-2
It's a logical approach to get to the project management planning phase.

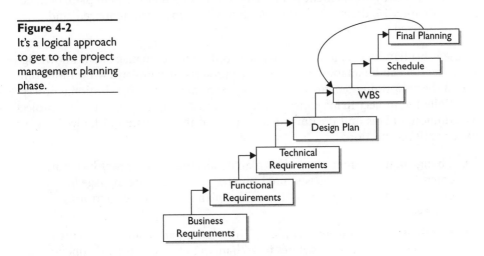

- **Cost management plan**   This plan details how the project costs will be planned for, estimated, budgeted, and then monitored and controlled. Cost management is described in Chapter 7.

- **Quality management plan**   Quality is expected on every project. This plan defines what quality means for the project, how the project will achieve quality, and how the project will map to organizational procedures pertaining to quality. Chapter 8 covers quality management in more detail.

- **Process improvement plan**   Who wants an extra helping of waste in their project? This plan aims to eliminate non-value-added activity, eliminate waste, and determine how the project work, execution, and management can be made better. This plan is covered in Chapter 8.

- **Human resource plan**   This plan defines how project team members will be brought onto the project team, managed, and released from the project team. It also defines team training, safety issues, roles and responsibilities, and how the project's reward and recognition system will operate. Chapter 9 defines the human resource plan in detail.

- **Communications management plan**   This plan defines who will get what information, how they will receive it, and in what modality the communication will take place. Chapter 10 explains communication in more detail.

- **Risk management plan**   Risk is an uncertain event or condition that may affect the project's outcome. The risk management plan defines how the project will manage risk. Chapter 11 includes a conversation on this plan.

- **Procurement management plan**   The procurement management plan, defined in Chapter 12, controls how the project will be allowed to contract goods and services.

- **Stakeholder management plan**   The stakeholder management plan, defined in Chapter 13, defines how stakeholders will be included, managed, and prioritized for the project.

These subsidiary plans are directly related to the project management knowledge areas. Each plan can be adapted from previous projects or templates within the company that the performing organization has created as part of its organizational process assets. While the project management is, for the most part, a compilation of project plans, additional plans and documents are included that you should know for your CAPM or PMP certification:

- **Change management plan**   This plan details the project procedures for entertaining change requests, and how change requests are managed, documented, approved, or declined. This plan is part of the control scope process.

- **Configuration management plan**   This plan is part of an input to the control scope process. It defines how changes to the features and functions of the project deliverable, the product scope, may enter the project.

- **Staffing management plan** This is a subsidiary plan of the human resource management plan. It specifically addresses how the human resource requirements will be met in the project. It can address internal staffing, procurement of resources, or negotiations with other projects for shared resources.

- **Risk response plan** This subsidiary plan defines the risk responses that are to be used in the project for both positive and negative risks.

- **Milestone list** This list details the project milestones and their attributes. It is used for several areas of project planning, but also helps determine how quickly the project may be achieving its objectives.

- **Resource calendar** Resources are people and things like equipment, rooms, and other facilities. This calendar defines when the resources are available to contribute to the project.

- **Schedule baseline** This is the planned start and finish of the project. The comparison of what was planned and what was experienced is the schedule variance.

- **Cost baseline** This is the aggregated costs of all of the work packages within the work breakdown structure (WBS).

- **Quality baseline** This documents the quality objectives for the project, including the metrics for stakeholder acceptance of the project deliverable.

- **Scope baseline** The scope baseline is a combination of three project documents: the project scope statement, the work breakdown structure, and the WBS dictionary. The creation of the project's deliverable will be measured against the scope baseline to show any variances from what was expected and what the project team has created.

- **Risk register** The risk register is a centralized database consisting of the outcome of all the other risk management processes. Consider the outcome of risk identification, qualitative analysis, and quantitative analysis.

- **Issue log** Issues are points of contention where some question of the project's direction needs to be resolved. All identified issues are documented in the issue log, along with an issue owner and a deadline to resolve the issue. The outcome of the issue is also recorded.

- **Assumption log** An assumption is something that is believed to be true or false, but it has not yet been proven to be true or false. Assumptions that prove wrong can become risks for the project. All identified project assumptions are recorded in the assumption log for testing and analysis, and the outcomes are recorded.

- **Change log** All changes that enter into a project are recorded in the change log. The characteristics of the change, such as the time, cost, risk, and scope details, are also recorded.

EXAM TIP You'll be seeing these documents throughout the remainder of this book. Basically, every knowledge area has one project management subsidiary plan, except for quality, which has two: the quality management plan and the process improvement plan.

Executing the Project Plan

So you've got a project plan—great! Now the work of executing the project plan begins. The PMBOK process for this chunk of the project is to direct and manage the project work. This is where the project manager manages the project and the project team does the work. The project manager and the project team will go about completing the promises made in the plan to deliver, document, measure, and complete the project work. The project plan will communicate to the project team, the stakeholders, management, and even to the vendors what work happens next, how it begins, and how it will be measured for quality and performance.

NOTE You'll likely be using a project management information system, like Microsoft Project, Basecamp, or some other software to help you manage your project. For your exam you won't be tested on these products, but you'll need to know that a project management information system helps the project manager make decisions and track project progress.

The product of the project is created during these execution processes. The largest percentage of the project budget will be spent now. The project manager and the project team must work together to orchestrate the timing and integration of all the project's moving parts. A flaw in one area of the execution can have ramifications in cost and additional risk, and can cause additional flaws in other areas of the project.

As the project work is implemented, the project manager refers to the project plan to ensure that the work is meeting the documented expectations, requirements, quality demands, target dates, and more. The completion of the work is measured and then compared against the cost, schedule, and scope baselines as documented in the project plan. Should there be—gasp!—discrepancies between the project work and the baselines, prompt and accurate reactions are needed to adjust the slipping components of the project. The execution of the project includes many activities:

- Doing the work to reach the project objectives
- Spending the project budget to reach the objectives
- Building, training, and developing the project team
- Getting quotes, bids, and proposals for project vendors
- Selecting the project sellers
- Purchasing, managing, and using the resources, materials, equipment, and facilities the project needs to reach its objectives

- Implementing the organization's mandated methods and standards for the project
- Managing and verifying the project deliverables
- Completing risk assessment, monitoring, and response
- Managing those pesky sellers
- Dovetailing the approved changes into the project
- Communicating with and managing the project stakeholders
- Gathering project data on cost, schedule, quality, and status to forecast where the project will be in the future
- Collecting and creating the lessons learned documentation

Directing and managing the project work also requires the project management team to respond to conditions within the project. Consider a new immediate risk that demands a response. A new condition warrants that the project management team plan and then directly confront the problem. Four activities coincide with executing the project plan:

- Apply corrective actions to bring future project performance back into alignment with the project plan.
- Apply preventive actions to avoid negative risks within the project.
- Apply defect repairs to fix flaws and problems identified through quality control.
- Update the project management plan and execution as a result of change requests within the project.

Monitoring and Controlling the Project Work

As soon as a project begins, the project management monitoring and controlling processes also begin. These processes monitor all the other processes within the project to ensure they are being done according to plan, according to the performing organization's practices, and to ensure that a limited number of defects enters the project. The monitoring and controlling process group has several key activities:

- Collecting project statistics
- Measuring project performance
- Distributing project information
- Analyzing project trends and measurements to improve the project
- Looking for new risks and managing known risks

Monitoring the Project

Monitoring and controlling the project is not a one-time or random event. It's important for the project management team to continue to monitor the project and not to assume that all's well simply because the project work is being completed. A constant monitoring of the project confirms that the project work is being done properly and that if the work is flawed, a response can be prepared. Monitoring and controlling is also concerned with its results. For example, a defect repair review follows a defect repair to ensure that the repair is accurate and that the project work may continue.

Monitoring and controlling the project work has eight activities:

- Comparing actual performance to what was promised in the project management plan

- Determining if corrective and preventive actions should be applied to the project

- Performing ongoing risk assessment, risk tracking, and analyzing the risk responses and their effectiveness on the identified risks

- Maintaining a project information base on the project's product throughout the project life cycle

- Providing information for status updates, progress measurement, and project forecasting

- Forecasting cost and schedule information

- Monitoring the approved change requests as they are implemented into the project and tracking the rejected change requests and their associated documentation

- Reporting on the project to the program manager if the project is part of the program

NOTE Forecasting the project's performance on its cost and schedule is part of monitoring and controlling. In Chapter 7, we'll dive headfirst into earned value management and how it helps the project manager control the project and respond to cost and schedule variances and make forecasts about the likelihood of the project's success.

Managing Integrated Change Control

Project managers must protect the project scope from changes. Management, team members, customers, and other stakeholders are going to want changes to the project deliverables. Changes to the product often stem from the customer. Changes may also stem from suggestions of the stakeholders—such as small, innocent changes that bloom into additional time and costs. Finally, changes may come from the project team. When it comes to integrated change control, the project manager must provide for:

- Identifying a change that is proposed or that has already occurred
- Influencing the stakeholders so that only approved changes are incorporated into the project work
- Reviewing and, when needed and applicable, approving change requests
- Managing changes by regulating the flow of change requests
- Reflecting the approved changes in the project baselines: time, cost, scope, and quality
- Reviewing and approving corrective and preventive actions
- Considering the impact of a change request on the rest of the project, as well as considering all of the knowledge areas and the impact of a change on each one
- Documenting the change request and the impact it may have on the project
- Communicating the change to the appropriate stakeholders
- Completing defect repair validation
- Continuing quality control

EXAM TIP   Think of integrated change control as the domino effect. Any proposed changes to the project can have serious impacts on other areas of the project. Because of this, all of the project management knowledge areas have to be evaluated with each project change.

When you're doing integrated change control, you might be working with the change control board. This is a committee of executives, project stakeholders, and other experts who'll examine and evaluate the change and make a determination on how the change should be managed. This management of the change includes approving, rejecting, or postponing the change. Not all projects utilize a change control board, but all projects should document the change control process and communicate how it'll work in the project.

Reacting to Change

Every project needs a change control system to review, consider, track, and, if needed, approve the change requests. Rejected change requests should also be tracked and documented. Most often, projects rely on a change control board (CCB) to evaluate the worthiness of a proposed change before it is approved. Whatever approach a project management team elects or is required to take when dealing with changes, the approach should be documented. The key stakeholders must all agree to abide by the rules of the change control system before the project work begins. The project's change management plan provides the governance for all changes in the project, the role of the project manager and change requests, and how (and often when) the change control board will review proposed changes.

When changes are approved, the project manager must then update the project baselines, as changes will likely affect a combination of scope, cost, and time. The updated baselines allow the project to continue with the new changes fleshed in and provide for an accurate measurement of the project performance.

This is an important concept: *update the project baselines*. Consider a project to which work has been added but for which the schedule baseline has not been updated. The project end date will be sooner than is possible to meet, because the project baseline does not reflect the additional work that should extend that date. In addition, a failure to revise the project baseline could skew reporting, variances, future project decisions—and even future projects.

 EXAM TIP Undocumented change requests should not be implemented into the project.

Consider a project manager who does not update the project baseline after a change. The completion of the project goes into the archives and can serve as historical information for future projects. The historical information is skewed because it does not accurately account for the added work and the projected end date or budget. Note that change requests do include any corrective or preventive actions, but these actions do not justify changes to the project baselines. Basically, if you have an error in the project and need corrective actions, you should also have a change request for that corrective action, but the error doesn't justify a change to the cost and schedule baseline. Only changes that are additions or reductions to the existing project scope can justify a change to the performance baselines. In some cases, like with a really flawed time estimate, the change control board may allow a rebaselining of the schedule, but usually an error counts as a variance against the project performance.

Using the Project Management Information System

You already know that the PMIS is a software tool that helps the project management team plan, execute, monitor and control, and then close the project. The PMIS, contrary to what some managers want to believe, does not replace the project manager. Within the PMIS are two important systems that you will need to know for your CAPM or PMP exam and for the remainder of this book. Let's get these down now and be happy for the next nine chapters.

The Configuration Management System

We all know that changes are likely to happen to the project scope. How these change requests are submitted, reviewed, have their status tracked, and are approved are part of the configuration management system. This system, established early in the project, defines how stakeholders are allowed to submit change requests, the conditions for approving a change request, and how approved change requests are validated in the project scope. Configuration management also is in charge of several activities:

- Documenting the functional and physical characteristics of a product or component

- Controlling changes to any of a product's physical characteristics

- Recording changes to the product's physical characteristics and the conditions surrounding the changes

- Contributing and supporting the audit of a product or component for quality

The Change Control System

You'll be hearing an awful lot about change control throughout the remainder of this book. It's essential for a project to have an established change control system, or the project will be riddled with change requests. The change control system (CCS) communicates the process for controlling changes to the project deliverables. This system works with the configuration management system and seeks to control and document proposals to the project's product. Figure 4-3 demonstrates an example of a change control system.

NOTE I won't bash Microsoft Project—it's an excellent, excellent tool. However, some managers believe that if you have Microsoft Project installed on your PC, you should be able to manage a project without any flaws, questions, or issues. Ha! That's like saying that just because you have Microsoft Word installed, you should be able to write a novel. Project management is more than a piece of software.

Figure 4-3
All change requests must be documented and must pass through a change control system.

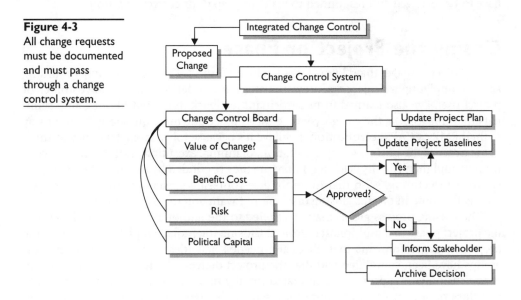

Configuration Identification

The configuration of the project's product or service must be accurately and completely defined. This includes the labeling of the components, how changes are made to the product, and the accountability of the changes. Specifically, accountability refers to the ownership of the change, the cost of the change, the schedule impacts, and the influence the product change has over the remainder of the product features and components. For example, a change to add a basement to a new home construction project would affect the project baselines, the configuration of the product, and, depending on the project status when the change was approved, possibly other components of the house.

Configuration Status Accounting

Configuration management also includes the documentation of the product information so that the project management team can quickly and effectively manage the product. This process means organization of the product materials, details, and prior documentation. For example, a new home construction project would have blueprints, permits, field drawings, vendor and customer specifications, and more information that needs to be cataloged, managed, and quickly accessed throughout the project.

Configuration Verification and Auditing

Configuration management is concerned with the performance and functional attributes of the product. In the new home construction project, the role of configuration management is to ensure that the new home is built according to the configuration documentation. Variances between what was completed and what was planned would have to be reviewed and responded to via defect repair or corrective actions.

Closing the Project or Phase

Every project manager that I know loves to close a project. There's something rewarding about completing a project and then transferring the deliverable to the customer or project user. I've also learned from participant feedback in my PMP Boot Camp seminars that this topic is the category where they missed the most questions on their way to their PMP or CAPM certification. I believe it's because folks have a tendency to study in the order of the process groups: initiation, planning, executing, monitoring and controlling, and then (finally) closing. I imagine they're winded by the time their studying efforts get to closing. With that in mind, give yourself a stretch, another sip of coffee, and really home in on this closing discussion. I want you to pass your exam!

The closing process group may be applied to the end of a project or to the end of the project phase in a multiphased project. Closing the project or phase means that the project manager confirms that all of the needed activities within the other process groups have been completed and that the project deliverables have been handed over to the customer. If a project is terminated for any reason, the project manager should still close out the project to account for the work that has been performed on the project and to learn why the project may have failed.

NOTE   Projects can be moving along swimmingly and still get terminated. Consider an organization's cash flow, the project's priority, or that the project deliverable may not be needed any longer. Just because a project was canceled doesn't always mean the project was a failure.

Completing Closure

This is the guts of the closing process group. First, the project manager documents everyone who is involved in the project closure: team members, vendors, management, the sponsor, and often the project customer. Part of this documentation defines each person's role and related responsibility to close out the project. Consider a large construction project. Lots of people are involved in the formal closing proceedings, so documentation explaining who'll be needed, what they'll be doing, and when they'll be doing it makes great sense for the project manager.

The second part of closure collects all of the project records, the lessons learned, and communications for the project archives. Yes, archives. All project information should be archived—this becomes part of the organizational process assets. Project and phase closure includes the examination and analysis of the project records and determines the success or failure of the project, as well as why the project succeeded or failed. This information helps future project managers, or if it's a phase that's being closed, allows the project manager to make corrective actions for the remainder of the project.

Part of project closure is to analyze the success of the project. One of the most common approaches is regression analysis. It's a mathematical model to examine the relationship among project variables, like cost, time, labor, and other project metrics. Regression analysis can use a scatter diagram to help visualize the correlation between the dependent variable, like the project's budget, against the independent variables, like errors in the project, changes to the project, and any delays stakeholders may have caused to the project. This helps to identify trends, especially in phases, and helps prepare for future projects and other phases yet to begin within the project.

The goal of project closure is to get formal acceptance of the project deliverables. *Formal acceptance* means that the project customer or sponsor agrees that the deliverable provided is in alignment with the project scope and that it is acceptable. A formal documentation of project acceptance, such as a project certificate of closure or a project closure sign-off, is needed to confirm that the project deliverable has been transferred from the project manager to the recipient of the project.

Completing Contract Closure

Vendors like to get paid, but the project manager must confirm that everything the vendor promised has been delivered according to the contract between the vendor and the project manager's organization. Contract closure documents the completed contract and its outputs. This information is also stored as part of the project archives.

PART II

Above any other conversation, e-mail, or promises, the details of the project contract are paramount. The project manager consults the contract not only to confirm that the vendor has lived up to its obligations, but also to confirm that the project manager's organization has held up its part of the bargain. Sometimes, and they are not fun times, the vendor didn't live up to the agreement and the contract was canceled. Contracts can be canceled for any number of reasons: poor performance, schedule and/or cost overruns, quality issues, and more. Whatever the reason, the documentation surrounding the cancellation of the contract is included as part of the contract closure, and this information is also included in the project archives for future reference.

Chapter Summary

Project integration management is an ongoing process the project manager completes to ensure that the project moves from initiation to closure. It is the gears, guts, and grind of project management—the day-in, day-out business of completing the project work. Project integration management coordinates the activities, project resources, constraints, and assumptions of the project plans and massages them into a working model. Once the model exists, it's up to the project management team to monitor and control the project from initiation to closure, and to ensure that everything goes according to plan. And if it doesn't, to fix it.

Of course, project integration management isn't an automatic process. It requires you, the project manager, to negotiate, finesse, and adapt to project circumstances. It relies on general business skills (such as leadership), organizational skills, and communication to get all the parts of the project working together. Project integration management has six events:

- **Developing the project charter** The project charter authorizes the project. It names the project manager and allows the project to commence. Projects are chartered for varying reasons: market demand, customer requests, to solve a problem, or even to address a social need. While the charter authorizes the project, it also defines the requirements for stakeholder satisfaction, the project purpose, and the project assumptions and constraints.

- **Developing the project management plan** Project management plan development is an iterative process that requires input from the project manager, the project team, the project customers, and other key stakeholders. It details how the project work will accomplish the project goals. The project comprises 11 subsidiary plans and several other documents.

- **Directing and managing the project work** Once the project management plan has been created, the project manager and the project team can implement the plan. Directing and managing the project work creates the project deliverables for the project or phase. Corrective actions, preventive actions, and defect repair all happen through directing and managing the project work

- **Monitoring and controlling the project work**   This process starts with the project's conception and finishes with the project completion. Its goal is to make certain that the project stays on track and finishes according to the project plan. Measurements for project performance, time, cost, and quality are implemented. If there are variances, responses to these will happen through preventive, corrective, or defect repair actions.

- **Performing integrated change control**   Changes can kill a project. Change requests must be documented and sent through a formal change control system to determine their worthiness for implementation. Integrated change control manages changes across the entire project. Change requests are evaluated and considered for impacts on risk, costs, schedule, and scope. Not all change requests are approved—but all change requests must be documented and reviewed.

- **Closing the project or phase**   Projects and phases are closed. Administrative closure confirms that all of the needed processes for each process group have been completed. Administrative closure also gathers all project records for archival purposes, including documentation of the project's success or failure. Contracts, when used, must also be closed after inspection of the contract deliverables. Contracts are always closed according to the agreed-upon terms.

Key Terms

Assumption log   An assumption is something that is believed to be true or false, but it has not yet been proven to be true or false. Assumptions that prove wrong can become risks for the project. All identified project assumptions are recorded in the assumption log for testing and analysis, and the outcomes are recorded.

Benefit/cost ratio (BCR) models   This is an example of a benefits comparison model. It examines the benefit-to-cost ratio.

Change control board (CCB)   A committee that evaluates the worthiness of a proposed change and either approves or rejects the proposed change.

Change control system (CCS)   The change control system communicates the process for controlling changes to the project deliverables. This system works with the configuration management system and seeks to control and document proposals to change the project's product.

Change log   All changes that enter into a project are recorded in the change log. The characteristics of the change, such as the time, cost, risk, and scope details, are also recorded.

Change management plan   This plan details the project procedures for entertaining change requests: how change requests are managed, documented, approved, or declined.

PART II

Closure processes   This final process group of the project management life cycle is responsible for closing the project phase or project. This is where project documentation is archived and project contracts are also closed.

Communications management plan   This plan defines who will get what information, how they will receive it, and in what modality the communication will take place.

Configuration identification   This includes the labeling of the components, how changes are made to the product, and the accountability of the changes.

Configuration management plan   This plan is an input to the control scope process. It defines how changes to the features and functions of the project deliverable, the product scope, may enter the project.

Configuration management system   This system defines how stakeholders are allowed to submit change requests, the conditions for approving a change request, and how approved change requests are validated in the project scope. Configuration management also documents the characteristics and functions of the project's products and any changes to a product's characteristics.

Configuration status accounting   The organization of the product materials, details, and prior product documentation.

Configuration verification and auditing   The scope verification and completeness auditing of project or phase deliverables to ensure that they are in alignment with the project plan.

Contract closure   The formal verification of the contract completeness by the vendor and the performing organization.

Cost baseline   This is the aggregated costs of all of the work packages within the work breakdown structure (WBS).

Cost management plan   This plan details how the project costs will be planned for, estimated, budgeted, and then monitored and controlled.

Enterprise environmental factors   The culture, structure, standards, regulations, organizational logistics, and other organizational characteristics that influence how a project operates.

Future value   A benefit comparison model to determine a future value of money. The formula to calculate future value is $FV = PV(1 + I)^n$, where PV is present value, I is the given interest rate, and n is the number of periods.

Human resource plan   This plan defines how project team members will be brought onto the project team, managed, and released from the project team. It also defines team training, safety issues, roles and responsibilities, and how the project's reward and recognition system will operate. Chapter 9 defines the human resource plan in detail.

Integrated change control A process to consider and control the impact of a proposed change on the project's knowledge areas.

Issue log Issues are points of contention where some question of the project's direction needs to be resolved. All identified issues are documented in the issue log, along with an issue owner and a deadline to resolve the issue. The outcome of the issue is also recorded.

Mathematical model A project selection method to determine the likelihood of success. These models include linear programming, nonlinear programming, dynamic programming, integer programming, and multiobjective programming.

Milestone Milestones are significant points or events in the project's progress that represent accomplishment in the project. Projects usually create milestones as the result of completing phases within the project.

Milestone list This list details the project milestones and their attributes. It is used for several areas of project planning, but also helps determine how quickly the project may be achieving its objectives.

Murder boards These are committees that ask every conceivable negative question about the proposed project. Their goals are to expose the project's strengths and weaknesses, and to kill the project if it's deemed unworthy for the organization to commit to. Also known as project steering committees or project selection committees.

Net present value Evaluates the monies returned on a project for each period the project lasts.

Organizational process assets Anything that an organization has to help a current project succeed. Policies, procedures, documentation of past projects, and plans are part of the organizational process assets.

Payback period An estimate to predict how long it will take a project to pay back an organization for the project's investment of capital.

Present value A benefit comparison model to determine the present value of a future amount of money. The formula to calculate present value is $PV = FV \div (1 + I)^n$, where FV is future value, I is the given interest rate, and n is the number of periods.

Process improvement plan This plan aims to eliminate non-value-added activity, eliminate waste, and determine how the project work, execution, and management can be made better.

Procurement management plan The procurement management plan controls how the project will acquire goods and services.

Project charter This document authorizes the project. It defines the initial requirements of the project stakeholders. The project charter is endorsed by an entity outside of the project boundaries.

PART II

Project management plan   The documented approach of how a project will be planned, executed, monitored and controlled, and then closed. This document is a collection of subsidiary management plans and related documents.

Project scope management plan   Defines how the project scope will be planned, managed, and controlled.

Project statement of work (SOW)   This document defines all the products and services the project will provide.

Quality baseline   Documents the quality objectives for the project, including the metrics for stakeholder acceptance of the project deliverable.

Quality management plan   This plan defines what quality means for the project, how the project will achieve quality, and how the project will map to organizational procedures pertaining to quality.

Regression analysis   A mathematical model to examine the relationship among project variables, like cost, time, labor, and other project metrics.

Risk management plan   Risk is an uncertain event or condition that may affect the project outcome. The risk management plan defines how the project will manage risk.

Risk register   The risk register is a centralized database consisting of the outcome of all the other risk management processes, such as the outcome of risk identification, qualitative analysis, and quantitative analysis.

Risk response plan   This subsidiary plan defines the risk responses that are to be used in the project for both positive and negative risks.

Schedule baseline   This is the planned start and finish of the project. The comparison of what was planned and what was experienced is the schedule variance.

Schedule management plan   Defines how the project schedule will be created and managed.

Scope baseline   The scope baseline is a combination of three project documents: the project scope statement, the work breakdown structure, and the WBS dictionary. The creation of the project deliverable will be measured against the scope baseline to show any variances from what was expected and what the project team has created.

Scoring models   These models use a common set of values for all of the projects up for selection. For example, values can be profitability, complexity, customer demand, and so on.

Staffing management plan   This is a component of the human resource management plan. It specifically addresses how the human resource requirements will be met in the project. It can address internal staffing, procurement of resources, or negotiations with other projects for shared resources.

Questions

1. You are the project manager for a pharmaceutical company. You are currently working on a project for a new drug your company is creating. A recent change in a law governing drug testing will impact your project and change your project scope. The first thing you should do as project manager is:

   A. Create a documented change request.

   B. Proceed as planned since the project will be grandfathered beyond the new change in the law.

   C. Consult with the project stakeholders.

   D. Stop all project work until the issue is resolved.

2. You are the project manager for the HALO Project. You and your project team are preparing the project plan. Of the following, which one is a project plan development constraint you and your team must consider?

   A. The budget as assigned by management

   B. Project plans from similar projects

   C. Project plans from similar projects that have failed

   D. Interviews with SMEs who have experience with the project work in your project plan

3. You are the project manager of a new project to develop a new software product. Management has not required a formal project management plan in the past, but they'd like you to develop a project management plan to serve as a model or template for all other projects in the organization. The primary purpose of your project management plan is:

   A. To define the work to be completed to reach the project end date.

   B. To define the work needed in each phase of the project life cycle.

   C. To prevent any changes to the scope.

   D. To provide accurate communication for the project team, project sponsor, and stakeholders regarding how the project will be executed, controlled, and closed.

4. In your project management plan development, you'll need several inputs. Of the following, which one is an input to project plan development?

   A. Assumptions

   B. Outputs from other project management processes

   C. Earned value management

   D. Business needs

5. Robert is the project manager of the HBQ Project. This project requires all of the telephones in the organization to be removed and replaced with an Internet phone. He's learned that the removal of some of the phones has

damaged the walls in the office building and they will need to be repaired. This project has a deadline and little time for repairing errors that weren't anticipated. Based on this information, which one of the following is the best example of defect repair review?

A. Adding labor to a project to reduce errors during the installation of hardware

B. Retraining the project team on how to install a new material so that all future work with the new materials is done correctly

C. Repairing an incorrectly installed door in a new home construction project

D. Inspecting work that has been corrected because it was done incorrectly the first time

6. You are the project manager of the NHG Project. You have had to terminate a contract with a vendor. What is this an example of?

A. A special case of contract closure

B. Mitigation

C. A contract claim

D. Scope closure

7. The project plan provides a baseline for several things. Which one of the following does the project plan NOT provide a baseline for?

A. Scope

B. Cost

C. Schedule

D. Control

8. You are the project manager for your organization. When it comes to integrated change control, you must ensure that which one of the following is present?

A. Supporting detail for the change

B. Approval of the change from the project team

C. Approval of the change from a subject matter expert

D. Risk assessment for each proposed change

9. Keisha is the project manager for her organization and she's working with her project team to develop the project management plan for a new project. The project team is confused about the change management plan and how it governs changes within the project. The project plan provides what in regard to project changes?

A. A methodology to approve or decline changes

B. A guide to all future project risk management decisions

PART II

C. A vision of the project deliverables

D. A fluid document that may be updated as needed based on the CCB

10. You are assisting the project manager for the DGF Project. This project is to design and implement a new application that will connect to a database server. Management has requested that you create a method to document technical direction on the project and any changes or enhancements to the technical attributes of the project deliverable. Which one of the following would satisfy management's request?

A. The configuration management system

B. Integrated change control

C. Scope control

D. The change management plan

11. You are a project manager of a project that is part of a program. There has been some conflict among the project team about who assigns activities and directs the project execution. In this scenario, who directs the performance of the planned project activities?

A. The project manager and the project management team

B. The project team

C. The project sponsor

D. The program manager

12. You have just informed your project team that each team member will be contributing to the lessons learned documentation. Your team does not understand this approach and wants to know what the documentation will be used for. Which one of the following best describes the purpose of the lessons learned documentation?

A. Offers proof of concept for management

B. Offers historical information for future projects

C. Offers evidence of project progression as reported by the project team

D. Offers input to team member evaluations at the project's conclusion

13. Fred is the project manager of a bridge construction project. His organization and the city inspectors both have an interest in the success and overall performance of the project and have asked Fred to identify the approach he'll use to measure and report project performance. Which one of the following measures project performance?

A. WBS

B. The project plan

C. The earned value technique

D. The work authorization system

14. Configuration management is a process for applying technical and administrative direction and surveillance of the project implementation. Which activity is not included in configuration management?

A. Controlling changes to the project deliverables

B. A method to communicate changes to stakeholders

C. Automatic change request approvals

D. Identification of the functional and physical attributes of the project deliverables

15. The project manager can help write the project charter, but is not the person signing the project charter. Regardless of who actually writes the charter, there are several elements that should be included in the document. All of the following are addressed in the project charter, except for which one?

A. Requirements to satisfy the project customer, project sponsor, and other stakeholders

B. Assigned project management and level of authority

C. Summary budget

D. Risk responses

16. Terri's organization is moving through the process of selecting one of several projects. Her organization utilizes mathematical models to determine the projects that should be initiated. Which one of the following is an example of a mathematical model used to select projects for selection?

A. Future value

B. Linear programming

C. Present value

D. Benefits/cost ratio

17. You and the project management team are creating a project statement of work. As part of this activity, which one of the following should be referenced in the project statement of work document?

A. Risk responses

B. Organizational process assets

C. The initial work breakdown structure

D. A reference to the strategic plan

18. The project management plan has several purposes and all projects should have a plan. What is the purpose of the project management plan?

A. It defines the project manager and their level of authority on the project.

B. It authorizes the project manager to assign resources to the project work.

C. It defines how the project will be planned and executed.

    D. It defines how the project will be executed, monitored and controlled, and then closed.

19. The project steering committee is considering which project they should invest capital in. Mary's project promises to be worth $175,000 in four years. The project steering committee is interested in Mary's project, but they would like to know the present value of the return if the interest rate is 6 percent. What is the present value of Mary's project?

    A. $175,000

    B. $139,000

    C. $220,000

    D. $43,750

20. You are the project manager for your organization. A change has recently been approved by your organization's change control board. You need to update the scope baseline and what other document?

    A. The cost baseline

    B. The quality baseline

    C. The risk management plan

    D. The change log

Questions and Answers

1. You are the project manager for a pharmaceutical company. You are currently working on a project for a new drug your company is creating. A recent change in a law governing drug testing will impact your project and change your project scope. The first thing you should do as project manager is:

    A. Create a documented change request.

    B. Proceed as planned since the project will be grandfathered beyond the new change in the law.

    C. Consult with the project stakeholders.

    D. Stop all project work until the issue is resolved.

    A. Change requests should first be documented in the project's change control system. B is incorrect because the new law will require changes to the project. C is incorrect because it may be inappropriate to consult with the project stakeholders, especially on a large project. D is incorrect because we do not know the impact of the change, and it may not justify halting the project work.

2. You are the project manager for the HALO Project. You and your project team are preparing the project plan. Of the following, which one is a project plan development constraint you and your team must consider?

    A. The budget as assigned by management

B. Project plans from similar projects

C. Project plans from similar projects that have failed

D. Interviews with SMEs who have experience with the project work in your project plan

A. A predetermined budget set by management is an example of a project constraint. B and C are examples of organizational process assets that the project manager will use as inputs to project management planning. D, interviews with subject matter experts, is an example of expert judgment, and is a tool and technique used in project management plan development.

3. You are the project manager of a new project to develop a new software product. Management has not required a formal project management plan in the past, but they'd like you to develop a project management plan to serve as a model or template for all other projects in the organization. The primary purpose of your project management plan is:

A. To define the work to be completed to reach the project end date.

B. To define the work needed in each phase of the project life cycle.

C. To prevent any changes to the scope.

D. To provide accurate communication for the project team, project sponsor, and stakeholders regarding how the project will be executed, controlled, and closed.

D. The primary purpose of the project management plan is to define how the project will proceed. A and B are incorrect because these address only the project work. C is incorrect because this answer only addresses the project's change control system.

4. Of the following, which one is an input to project plan development?

A. Assumptions

B. Outputs from other project management processes

C. Earned value management

D. Business needs

B. The outputs from other project management processes need to be identified as part of the planning process. The project management processes are the 47 processes described in Chapter 3 and throughout the remainder of this book. Because the development of the project management plan is an iterative activity, the outputs of the project management processes can affect your project management planning. A, C, and D are incorrect because these are not inputs to the project plan development processes. There are four inputs to developing your project management plan: the project charter, outputs from other processes, enterprise environmental factors, and organizational process assets.

5. Robert is the project manager of the HBQ Project. This project requires all of the telephones in the organization to be removed and replaced with an Internet phone. He's learned that the removal of some of the phones has damaged the walls in the office building and they will need to be repaired. This project has a deadline and little time for repairing errors that weren't anticipated. Based on this information, which one of the following is the best example of defect repair review?

   A. Adding labor to a project to reduce errors during the installation of hardware

   B. Retraining the project team on how to install a new material so that all future work with the new materials is done correctly

   C. Repairing an incorrectly installed door in a new home construction project

   D. Inspecting work that has been corrected because it was done incorrectly the first time

   D. Defect repair review is a review of the defect repair. Even though the project may be on a deadline, Robert's project team will still need to repair the walls and confirm the repair is acceptable. A is an example of a preventive action. B is an example of a corrective action. C is an example of defect repair.

6. You are the project manager of the NHG Project. You have had to terminate a contract with a vendor. What is this an example of?

   A. A special case of contract closure

   B. Mitigation

   C. A contract claim

   D. Scope closure

   A. Terminating a contract with a vendor is a special case of contract closure. B, C, and D are not appropriate answers for this question because mitigation is a risk response, a contract claim is a disagreement between the buyer and seller, and scope closure describes the completion of the project scope activities.

7. The project plan provides a baseline for several things. Which one of the following does the project plan NOT provide a baseline for?

   A. Scope

   B. Cost

   C. Schedule

   D. Control

   D. The project management plan provides baselines for the schedule, cost, and scope. Control is a project activity and part of the monitoring and controlling process group. A, B, and C are all incorrect because scope, cost, and schedule do have associated baselines. Recall that a baseline is what's predicted and the actuals are the experiences of the project. The difference between the baseline and what actually happened reveals the variances of the project.

8. You are the project manager for your organization. When it comes to integrated change control, you must ensure that which one of the following is present?

   A. Supporting detail for the change

   B. Approval of the change from the project team

   C. Approval of the change from a subject matter expert

   D. Risk assessment for each proposed change

   A. Integrated change control requires detail for implementing the change. Without evidence of the need for the change, there is no reason to implement it. B is incorrect because the project team does not approve change requests. C is incorrect because a subject matter expert is not always needed for a requested change. D is incorrect because risk assessment for a proposed change is not always needed. The change could be rejected or approved for other reasons besides the potential of risk events.

9. Keisha is the project manager for her organization and she's working with her project team to develop the project management plan for a new project. The project team is confused about the change management plan and how it governs changes within the project. The project plan provides what in regard to project changes?

   A. A methodology to approve or decline changes

   B. A guide to all future project risk management decisions

   C. A vision of the project deliverables

   D. A fluid document that may be updated as needed based on the CCB

   A. The project management plan defines how changes will be monitored and controlled. B describes the risk management plan. C defines the project charter and project scope. D is an incorrect statement.

10. You are assisting the project manager for the DGF Project. This project is to design and implement a new application that will connect to a database server. Management has requested that you create a method to document technical direction on the project and any changes or enhancements to the technical attributes of the project deliverable. Which one of the following would satisfy management's request?

    A. The configuration management system

    B. Integrated change control

    C. Scope control

    D. The change management plan

A. The configuration management system documents all functional physical characteristics of the project's product. It also controls changes to the project's product. B, C, and D are not correct answers.

11. You are a project manager of a project that is part of a program. There has been some conflict among the project team about who assigns activities and directs the project execution. In this scenario, who directs the performance of the planned project activities?

    A. The project manager and the project management team

    B. The project team

    C. The project sponsor

    D. The program manager

    A. The project manager and the project management team direct the performance of the project activities. In a program, the program manager assigns the project manager authority over the project resources and authorizes the project manager to direct the project work. B, C, and D, the project team, sponsor, and the program manager, do not direct performance.

12. You have just informed your project team that each team member will be contributing to the lessons learned documentation. Your team does not understand this approach and wants to know what the documentation will be used for. Which one of the following best describes the purpose of the lessons learned documentation?

    A. Offers proof of concept for management

    B. Offers historical information for future projects

    C. Offers evidence of project progression as reported by the project team

    D. Offers input to team member evaluations at the project's conclusion

    B. Lessons learned documentation serves as part of organizational process assets for future projects. A, the proof of concept, is not a PMI theme. C, project progress, is reported through status reports and performance measurements. D is incorrect because team member evaluations are based on performance, not lessons learned.

13. Fred is the project manager of a bridge construction project. His organization and the city inspectors both have an interest in the success and overall performance of the project and have asked Fred to identify the approach he'll use to measure and report project performance. Which one of the following measures project performance?

    A. WBS

    B. The project plan

    C. The earned value technique

    D. The work authorization system

C. The earned value technique, commonly called earned value management (EVM), measures project performance on several factors, including cost and schedule. A, the WBS, is a breakdown of the project scope. B, the project plan, defines how the project will be controlled, executed, and closed. D, the work authorization, allows work to progress within a project.

14. Configuration management is a process for applying technical and administrative direction and surveillance of the project implementation. Which activity is not included in configuration management?

    A. Controlling changes to the project deliverables

    B. A method to communicate changes to stakeholders

    C. Automatic change request approvals

    D. Identification of the functional and physical attributes of the project deliverables

    C. Change requests should not be automatically approved. All documented change requests should flow through the change control system, be evaluated, and then a decision should be made. A, B, and D are all part of configuration management.

15. The project manager can help write the project charter, but is not the person signing the project charter. Regardless of who actually writes the charter there are several elements that should be included in the document. All of the following are addressed in the project charter, except for which one?

    A. Requirements to satisfy the project customer, project sponsor, and other stakeholders

    B. Assigned project management and level of authority

    C. Summary budget

    D. Risk responses

    D. Risk responses are not addressed in the project charter. High-level risks may be identified, but the responses to those risks are not included in the project charter. These responses will be documented in the project's risk response plan. B, the project manager, C, the summary budget, and A, the requirements to satisfy the project customer, are defined in the charter.

16. Terri's organization is moving through the process of selecting one of several projects. Her organization utilizes mathematical models to determine the projects that should be initiated. Which one of the following is an example of a mathematical model used to select projects for selection?

    A. Future value

    B. Linear programming

    C. Present value

    D. Benefits/cost ratio

B. Linear programming is an example of a mathematical model that can be used for project selection. Recall that mathematical models are also known as constrained optimization. A, future value, C, present value, and D, the benefit/cost ratio, are all examples of the benefits comparison model.

17. You and the project management team are creating a project statement of work. As part of this activity, which one of the following should be referenced in the project statement of work document?

    A. Risk responses

    B. Organizational process assets

    C. The initial work breakdown structure

    D. A reference to the strategic plan

    D. The project statement of work should reference or include the business that justified the project, the product scope description that defines the product the project will create, and the strategic plan for the organization. A, risk responses, is not a valid answer because risk responses are not needed in the project statement of work. Organizational process assets are not included in the project statement of work, so B is incorrect, too. C, the initial work breakdown structure, is also not part of the project scope statement.

18. The project management plan has several purposes and all projects should have a plan. What is the purpose of the project management plan?

    A. It defines the project manager and their level of authority on the project.

    B. It authorizes the project manager to assign resources to the project work.

    C. It defines how the project will be planned and executed.

    D. It defines how the project will be executed, monitored and controlled, and then closed.

    D. The project management plan communicates how the project will be executed, monitored and controlled, and then closed. A and B both describe components of the project charter. C does not answer the question as completely as D.

19. The project steering committee is considering which project they should invest capital in. Mary's project promises to be worth $175,000 in four years. The project steering committee is interested in Mary's project, but they would like to know the present value of the return if the interest rate is 6 percent. What is the present value of Mary's project?

    A. $175,000

    B. $139,000

    C. $220,000

    D. $43,750

B. $139,000 is the present value of Mary's project. This is found through the following formula: $PV = FV \div (1 + I)^n$, which is future value divided by one plus the interest rate to the power of the periods the project will last. This question would read ($175,000)/(1.26) because the interest rate provided was 6 percent. A, C, and D are all incorrect calculations.

20. You are the project manager for your organization. A change has recently been approved by your organization's change control board. You need to update the scope baseline and what other document?

    A. The cost baseline

    B. The quality baseline

    C. The risk management plan

    D. The change log

D. When a change enters the project, the change log must be updated to reflect the change. The question did not indicate that new costs or risks will be entering the project, so these choices, A and C, are incorrect. The quality baseline, B, is not a valid answer because quality is a reflection of the completion of the project scope.

Managing the Project Scope

In this chapter, you will

- Plan project scope management
- Collect project requirements
- Create the project scope statement
- Create the work breakdown structure
- Validate the project scope
- Control the project scope

You're the project manager of a large, complex project. Everyone agrees that the project must be completed within one year, the budget is tight, and there's little room for error. One of your project team members, Tony, has taken it upon himself to incorporate "extras" into the project deliverable to make it snappier, better, and easier for the product customer to use. While his project additions are clever, they aren't in the project scope.

Tony argues that his creative additions don't cost the project anything extra and the customer will love what he's come up with. The trouble for you, the customer, and Tony, is that the time he's spent changing the scope should have been spent doing the things that are in the scope. In addition, the extras weren't managed and reviewed as change requests, and will likely be a surprise to the project customer. Not to mention the added risks, potential for defect, and the contempt shown for an established change control system.

 VIDEO For a more detailed explanation, watch the *Managing the Project Scope* video now.

Managing the project scope, according to the *PMBOK Guide,* is the project manager's job and ensures that all of the required work—and only the required work—is done to complete the project successfully. Project scope management doesn't permit Tony's, or anyone else's, additions. Scope management is agreeing on what's in the scope and then defending that agreement.

Plan the Project Scope Management

One of the first things you'll have to achieve in your role as the project manager of a new project is to define the project's scope management plan. Now, your organization may rely on organizational process assets in the form of a template for all projects, but it's possible that you'll be creating this scope management plan from scratch. In this section, you'll learn both approaches that you can apply to your projects and your PMI exam.

This process is all about creating the scope management plan and the requirements management plan. These are two subsidiary plans for the overall project management plan that you'll assemble and never touch again. Kidding! Because these are planning processes, chances are you'll be editing these plans as you move through planning over and over. The point is that these two plans shape your approach to how you'll define and control both the project's scope and the project's requirements.

In order to begin this process, you'll need the information already gathered and included in the project charter. That's right—the project charter. You'll use the charter because it's the launching point of the project and already maps out the high-level requirements and vision for the project. The project charter sets the direction for the project, while the scope management plan and the requirements management plan define how the project will achieve those objectives.

Creating the Project Scope Management Plan

Once the project moves from the initiating processes into planning, one of the first plans to be created is the project scope management plan. This plan defines the following:

- How the project scope will be defined
- How the detailed project scope statement will be created
- How the work breakdown structure will be created
- How scope validation will be performed at the end of each phase and at the end of the project
- How the project scope will be controlled

The project scope management plan is based first on the details of the project charter. Recall that the project charter authorizes the project within an organization and defines the general project boundaries and goals. When the project management team is ready to begin creating the project scope management plan, they'll actually rely on four things as inputs to this project management process:

- Enterprise environmental factors
- Organizational process assets
- The project charter
- The project management plan

The project management team can use expert judgment to help them analyze these four inputs to create the best project scope management plan. Don't get too hyped over expert judgment. You'll see this term throughout the *PMBOK* and this book. Expert judgment is just an approach that uses people such as experts and consultants (assuming they're truly experts—wink, wink) who have exceptional knowledge about the product the project will be creating. For example, in the skyscraper project, expert judgment could be world-renowned architects, city planners, union representatives, and more.

The project management team can also use templates, forms, and standards as part of the process to create the project scope management plan. If an organization is completing the same type of project over and over, there's no real benefit to starting from scratch each time. Instead, they'll logically use previous projects' plans, forms, work breakdown structures (WBSs), and more as part of the current planning. These are collectively referred to as organizational process assets.

You now know that the project scope management plan will be used to define, validate, manage, and control the project scope. There are four more juicy facts you need to know about this hefty plan:

- The project scope management plan defines how the official project scope statement will be defined based on the project charter.

- The project scope management plan defines how the work breakdown structure will be created, controlled, and approved. We'll talk about the WBS in more detail later in this chapter.

- The plan documents the process for scope validation. To clarify, scope validation is the inspection of the project deliverables by the project customer. The goal of scope validation is to validate that the deliverables are in alignment with the project goals and then are formally accepted.

- The project scope management plan documents and defines how changes to the project scope will be managed and controlled. This is linked to our conversation in Chapter 4 on integrated change control. As a refresher, integrated change control acknowledges that a change in one knowledge area can affect any of the other knowledge areas.

The project scope management plan is a subsidiary of the project management plan. This plan sets the tone for the remainder of the project. As you may have already guessed, the larger the project, the more important this plan is. As a general rule, larger projects require more detail.

The scope management plan can rely heavily on organizational process assets and enterprise environmental factors. From organizational process assets, you can call on the policies and procedures that you must follow as a project manager in your organization. From the enterprise environmental factors, you'll allow the organization's culture, organizational structure, project team administration rules, and the overall marketplace conditions to influence your planning and development. The marketplace conditions are especially important if you're a vendor completing a project for someone else. When you're a vendor, the relationship is different than if you're a project manager completing a project right inside your organization.

The primary tool and technique for creating the scope management plan is planning—and this means meetings. Every project manager loves meetings and you'll have lots of these in order to shape this plan. You'll call on the project sponsor, in some cases the project team (assuming they've been selected), key stakeholders that can help with the processes, and any other experts. "Any other experts" means that you might be calling on the program manager if this project takes place within a program, other project managers who can help with the drafting of the plan, and even consultants.

Creating the Requirements Management Plan

The second plan that comes out of this process is the requirements management plan. While similar in nature, this plan explains how the project will collect, analyze, record, and manage the requirements throughout the project. Like the scope management plan, this plan doesn't list the actual requirements, but sets the rules for how the project manager, team, and stakeholders will interact with the project's requirements. This plan is also a subsidiary plan for the overall project management plan.

This plan can be based on a template, just like the scope management plan can be, but you can tailor it to your project as needed. The elements of this plan include:

- The process for planning, tracking, and recording all of the project requirements
- Configuration management activities for the product (changing the product, specs for the product scope, and who can approve any changes to the product)
- The process for analyzing and prioritizing requirements
- Metrics for measuring the acceptability of the requirements
- How the requirements will be tracked through the project (usually through a requirements tracing matrix)

Collecting the Project Requirements

It's great to have a project, but it's even greater to understand what the stakeholders want the project to create. The collect requirements process aims to identify and document what the stakeholders need from the project. The requirements you'll identify from the project sponsor, customer, and other stakeholders need to be quantifiable, measurable, and documented in order to confirm that the results of the project satisfy the needs of the stakeholder. You don't want requirements that use subjective terms to describe the project deliverables. What's "good" to you may not be "good" to someone else.

You'll rely on the project charter as one of the inputs to this process. Recall that the project charter identifies the project and defines the business need of the project. This should give you some direction for collecting the project requirements. The project

PART II

charter will also contain high-level requirements that can be refined for details regarding the project stakeholder's expectations.

The other input for this process is the stakeholder register. The stakeholder register is a directory of all the stakeholders, their contact information, and details about their relationship with the project. You'll need this document to contact the stakeholders so you can begin the process of collecting project requirements. When you're dealing with large groups of stakeholders—for example, all of the users of a particular software your project centers on—a smaller part of the group can represent the larger group in the project.

EXAM COACH What are your requirements for your upcoming Project Management Institute (PMI) examination? Have you made your own list of requirements that you'll need to satisfy to achieve your Certified Associate in Project Management (CAPM) or Project Management Professional (PMP) status? You need to know what you must create in order to create it.

Working with Project Stakeholders

You'll have to work with the project stakeholders in order to identify the requirements your project needs. This is where the *stakeholder register* comes in handy because you'll need to contact the stakeholders to schedule times to elicit their project requirements. One favorable approach is to categorize the types of users and stakeholders to streamline your requirements collection process. By grouping stakeholders together, you can save time and effort and keep the project moving along. There are many tools you can use to collect requirements from the stakeholders, such as the following.

Interviews

Perhaps the most common requirements elicitation technique is the interview. The interviewer must prepare questions to guide the interviewee to discussing the needs that the project will satisfy. Usually interviews are performed one-on-one, though it's not unusual for the project manager to interview several stakeholders at once. Open-ended questions are best for essay-type answers, while closed-ended questions can nail down the specifics of the requirements.

Focus Groups and Facilitated Workshops

A focus group is a collection of stakeholders that interacts with a trained moderator. The moderator leads the group through a conversation, engages all of the participants, and remains neutral about the topic at hand. Focus groups can build trust, create new relationships, and help the group of stakeholders reach consensus on the project requirements. A scribe or recorder documents the conversation for analysis after the focus group is concluded.

A facilitated workshop is a meeting with all of the key stakeholders to define the project requirements quickly and as a group. Facilitated workshops are interactive, often have stakeholders from different functional areas of the project, and can expose conflicting objectives and disagreements. A good facilitator keeps the group focused on the project requirements and can help resolve conflicts and disagreements in requirements.

 NOTE You might know a focus group through a facilitated workshop called the Joint Application Design (JAD) session. These software development workshops allow the designers and the users to interact and discuss the software requirements.

Group Creativity Techniques

A group creativity technique is an approach to identify requirements quickly in hopes of reaching a consensus. You're probably already familiar with brainstorming and mind mapping, but this technique also includes several other approaches:

- **Nominal group technique** As with brainstorming, participants are encouraged to generate as many ideas as possible, but the suggested ideas are ranked by a voting process.

- **Affinity diagrams** When stakeholders create a large number of ideas, you can use an affinity diagram to cluster similar ideas together for further analysis.

- **Delphi Technique** This approach uses rounds of anonymous surveys to build consensus. Because the surveys are anonymous, participants are more likely to be honest with their requirements, opinions, and statements. The project manager organizes these comments and inputs, and then sends them back to the participants for another round of anonymous input.

- **Brainstorming** This approach encourages participants to generate as many ideas as possible about the project requirements. No idea is judged or dismissed during the brainstorming session.

- **Mind mapping** This approach maps ideas to show the relationship among the requirements and the differences between them. The map can be reviewed to identify new solutions or to rank the identified requirements.

Making a Group Decision

Group decisions can help the project manager prioritize, classify, and even generate requirements. The participants in the group determine the appropriate method for reaching a group decision, and there are four approaches:

- **Unanimity** Everyone must be in agreement.

- **Majority** More than 50 percent of the group must be in agreement.

- **Plurality** The largest block of voters makes the decision, even if they don't represent more than 50 percent of the group. (Consider three or four factions of stakeholders for three or more different choices, none of which receives more than 50 percent of the vote.)

- **Dictatorship** Only one individual makes the decision for the group.

Questionnaires and Surveys

When you have hundreds, even thousands, of stakeholders to identify requirements from, a survey is an ideal tool and technique to rely on. The project manager can leverage web tools to quickly disseminate the survey, track responses, and organize the participants' responses.

Observations

One of the best requirements gathering techniques is observation. The project manager goes into the field and observes the work being done to determine what requirements are appropriate for the project work. You might know this approach as shadowing. *Passive* observation, sometimes called invisible observation, requires the project manager to observe the work without asking questions or interrupting the workflow. *Active* observation allows the project manager to talk and interact with the participant to fully understand the work. In some instances, the project manager might actually work alongside the participant to understand the work that the project requirements may affect.

Prototypes

A prototype is a model of the finished deliverable that allows the stakeholder to see how the final project deliverable may operate. In software development, a *vertical* prototype approach details the interface, the functionality, and sometimes both. A *horizontal* prototype shows a very broad view of the deliverable, with very little operability at this point. Either prototype can be considered a throwaway prototype, or the model can be developed in more detail by the project team.

Context Diagrams

Imagine a project to design a computer network. You'd have servers, workstations, wireless access points, even the physical network. A context diagram would show how data moves around on the network, how people would interact with the network, what the network would provide, and how people will contribute information to and from the devices on your network. A context diagram shows all of these components, called actors, and how they will interact with the thing.

Document Analysis

Most projects have lots of documents that contribute to the project scope and requirements: plans, brochures, blueprints, organizational process assets, proposals, and more. Document analysis requires the project manager and the project team study these documents for anything that should be included in the requirements and referenced from the document. You'll keep all of the documentation that you reference as part of the project's supporting detail. At the end of the project, these documents are included in the project archives and become part of organizational process assets.

Examining the Outputs of Requirement Collection

So once you've gathered all of the project requirements, you'll need to do something with them. The first place to start is the requirements documentation—a listing of all of the project requirements and the supporting detail for the identified requirements. Requirements need to be measurable and consistent and then presented to the key stakeholders for their confirmation of what you've captured and what the stakeholders were expecting to receive from you. Examples of requirement types are:

- Business requirements
- Stakeholder requirements
- Project objectives
- Solution requirements
- Quality requirements
- Operational transfer requirements
- Training and support of the requirements for production

Because requirements can be a long, long list, it's better to record them in a table called a requirements traceability matrix. This table documents and numbers each requirement, their status in the project, and shows how each requirement is linked to a specific deliverable that the project will create or has created. You'll also, usually, give a little narrative about the requirement in the matrix as a point of reference. For more detail, you'll reference the actual requirements documentation. This matrix helps the project manager and the project customer see the product of the project and compare it against the requirements to confirm that all of the requirements have been met and are in existence in the final deliverable for the customer.

Defining the Project Scope

Building a skyscraper has to be one of the largest projects a project manager could manage. Think of all the different facets of the project: the art and design of the building, the structural requirements, the building codes, and the concern and interest of all the stakeholders within the project. The skyscraper would require months, if not years, of serious planning, tight change control, and incredible organization to complete. The scope of the skyscraper would be massive, and any change within the scope could have ramifications further down the blueprinted line.

Now imagine a project to build a barn. There would still be considerable planning, and the stakeholders of the barn might be concerned with its planning and construction, but probably not to the same depth as with the skyscraper project. The priority and impact of each project is important to the key stakeholders of each, but no doubt the skyscraper has a much broader impact than a barn. My point? Larger projects require more detail when it comes to scope creation and planning. Lots more.

Let's define scope, er, scopes, before moving forward.

Project scope and product scope are different entities. *Project* scope deals with the required work to create the project deliverables. For instance, our projects to create a new barn and the new skyscraper would focus only on the work required to complete the projects, with the specific attributes, features, and characteristics called for by the project plan. The scope of the project is specific to the work required to complete the project objectives. The project scope focuses on what must be done to create the deliverable.

Product scope, on the other hand, refers to the attributes and characteristics of the deliverables the project is creating. As in the preceding barn and skyscraper projects, the product scope would define the features and attributes of the barn and skyscraper. In this instance, the project to create a barn would not include creating a flower garden, a wading pool, and the installation of a fence, just as the skyscraper project likely wouldn't include a neighboring park. There would be specific requirements regarding the features and characteristics of each project: the materials to be used, the dimensions of the space, the function of each building, and all the related details that make a skyscraper a skyscraper and a barn a barn. The product scope is what the customer of the project envisions.

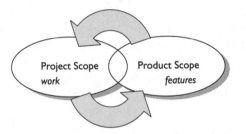

The project scope and the product scope are bound to each other. The product scope constitutes the characteristics and features of the product that the project creates. The end result of the project is measured against the requirements for that product. The project scope is the work required to deliver the product. Throughout the project execution, the work is measured against the project plan to validate that the project is on track to fulfill the product scope. The product scope is measured against requirements, while the project scope is measured against the project plan.

NOTE When it comes to *project* scope management, as is covered in the bulk of this chapter, focus on the work required to complete the project according to the project plan. The *product* scope, meanwhile, is specific to the deliverable of the project. Just remember, the exam will focus on project scope management. If you're stumped on any exam questions about project management processes, consider a huge project scope, like the skyscraper project.

Defining the Project Scope

A project manager and the project team can't plan how to complete the project until they know what it is and exactly what they are trying to complete. That's where the project scope statement is needed. Before the project management team can get to the good stuff of deciding how the project work will be done, they first must create the project scope statement.

When a project is first initiated, the focus is on what the project will deliver: the product scope. It's all dreamy and blue sky. Now that the project has moved into planning, things are tightened through the project scope statement. The project scope statement is built on the foundations defined in the project's initiation: major deliverables, constraints, and assumptions. In planning, more information about the exactness of the project deliverables comes to light through planning, research, stakeholder analysis, and product analysis. The wants and needs of the stakeholders are considered, and eventually they evolve into the project requirements.

The project manager, the project team, and the key stakeholders need to work together to examine the project for additional constraints and assumptions so that the project can be planned completely. The key stakeholders are needed because their insight into the project's deliverables can help the project manager and the project team define all that the project is to deliver. The key stakeholders help create the scope and agree on what's out of the project scope. For example, a project to build a web site may include the layout, design, and database functionality—all within scope—but the photography needed for the web site may be out of scope. The photography activity may be in an entirely different project, so it's not relevant to the current scope definition.

Creating the project scope involves four inputs:

- The scope management plan
- The project charter
- Requirements documentation
- Organizational process assets

These four inputs help the project management team work together to define all of the contents of the project scope. This isn't a quick or necessarily easy process, but it's vital to prepare an accurate and complete project scope statement, otherwise the project will be haunted by errors and omissions. You'll especially rely on the outputs of the collect requirements process as a foundation for what goes into the project scope.

 EXAM TIP Projects fail in the beginning, not the end. Poor planning early in the project will lead to poor execution later in the project. A rushed scope definition will likely cause problems later on in the project. This is the stakeholders' opportunity to define all that they want in the scope. Changes to the scope are easy early in the project, but are much more difficult later in the project because of the work, time, and monies already invested.

Using Product Analysis

If you were the project manager for a company that wanted to create a new camera, you might choose several of your competitors' cameras to study, experiment with, and improve upon. You'd compare the features and functions of the other cameras in light of the requirements and goals of your current project. Product analysis is the study of how a thing was made and how it works.

This approach to creating the project scope statement is product analysis. Product analysis, however, is more than just analyzing a product. It focuses on how it works, the function of the product, and what's the most profitable approach to creating the product. There are six flavors of product analysis. Don't be consumed with memorizing these approaches for your CAPM or PMP examination, just be topically aware of these product analysis methods.

Product Breakdown

This approach breaks down a product much as the project management team breaks down the project scope into a WBS. For example, a computer could be broken down into the physical components, such as the hard drive, processor, memory, network card, and so on. A product breakdown structure illustrates the hierarchical structure of the product.

Systems Analysis

This approach studies and analyzes a system, its components, and the relationship of the components within the system. For example, a manufacturing company's system for placing an order from a customer through delivery may have several steps, from sale to completion and interaction between departments on that journey. Systems analysis would study the relationship between each component and how the process could be improved or the time reduced, or how practically any variable within the system could be documented for additional study.

System Engineering

This project scope statement creation process studies how a system should work, designs and creates a system model, and then enacts the working system based on the project goals and the customer's expectations. Systems engineering aims to balance the time and cost of the project in relation to the project scope. A successfully designed system can be profitable, productive, and create quality that is acceptable to the project sponsor and the project customer.

Value Engineering

This approach to project scope statement creation attempts to find the correct level of quality in relation to a reasonable budget for the project deliverable while still achieving an acceptable level of performance of the product. Basically, this approach wants the biggest bang for the project's buck—as long as the bang and the buck create a deliverable that performs as expected. Consider a home remodeling project: the homeowners could choose silk drapes and gold doorknobs or wool drapes and brass doorknobs and get the same function. Their demand for a quality, grade, and function is in relation to how much capital they'd like to invest in their home project.

Value Analysis

Like value engineering, this approach examines the functions of the project's product in relation to the cost of the features and functions. This is where, to some extent, the grade of the product is in relationship to the cost of the product. Consider Microsoft Word's features and cost in relation to the features and cost of your computer's Notepad application. While the price range is broadly different, the functions associated with Word are far more powerful than those of Notepad.

Functional Analysis

This is the study of the functions within a system, project, or—what's more likely in the project scope statement—the product the project will be creating. Functional analysis studies the goals of the product, how the product will be used, and the expectations the customer has of the product once it leaves the project and moves into operations. Functional analysis may also consider the cost of the product in operations, which is known as life-cycle costing.

Using Alternatives Generation

Your customer wants you to install an e-mail system for their organization. They don't care which solution you and your project team come up with, as long as it's reliable, easy to manage, and provides a central calendaring system. If you're from the IT world, I imagine you immediately thought of several different approaches to solving this project for your customer. That's alternative identification at its root.

Alternatives generation is more than just differing products that can solve the customer's problem. It also means examining what solution makes the most economical sense for the project and for the customer's ongoing support of the product once it's been created. In the e-mail system, the project manager, project team, and experts would need to examine how the customer will use all of the different aspects of the e-mail system, their long-term goals for the system, and what their budget for the project and any ongoing maintenance of the system would be.

To do alternatives generation, the project management team will do research, brainstorming, and lateral thinking. Their focus is to identify all of the feasible alternatives to the project's deliverable or even to components within the project. Alternatives generation also broaches a quality topic: grade. *Grade* is the ranking of materials or services, such as first class versus coach, or plywood versus oak. We'll see this again in Chapter 8.

Using Stakeholder Analysis

Stakeholder analysis is almost always involved when it comes to creating the project scope statement. It's all about the customer's demands, wishes, and goals for the project. The project management team interviews the stakeholders and categorizes, prioritizes, and documents what the customer wants and needs. This is fundamental to project management: You and the key stakeholders must be in agreement on what the project will create, or the project scope statement cannot be created and approved. Without an agreement on what the requirements for acceptance are, the project is moving toward inevitable failure.

Here's another gotcha with stakeholder analysis: If you can't quantify it, if you can't measure it, you can't create it. For example, a "fast" office network isn't quantified. "Customer satisfaction" isn't quantified. And "happy," "warm-fuzzy," and "good" aren't quantified. The project scope statement needs to define in exact terms the acceptable ranges for all of the project deliverables. All project requirements must be quantifiable. Here's a general rule: If you can measure it, you can quantify it.

 EXAM TIP Failure to quantify the project objectives raises risks that the project won't achieve the customer's expectations. After all, what's fast and good to you may mean something entirely different to the project customer.

Examining the Project Scope Statement

The project scope statement identifies all of the project deliverables and defines the work required to create the deliverables. This document creates a common lexicon and understanding of what the project will deliver for all of the project stakeholders. The project scope statement clearly states the project objectives and communicates the goals of the project so that all of the project team members, the project sponsor, and the key stakeholders are in agreement as to what the project will accomplish.

The project scope statement also guides the remainder of the project planning processes. Should changes be proposed to the project, the project scope statement helps determine if the proposed changes are within or outside the project's boundaries. A well-written scope can ward off change requests, while a loose, poorly written scope is often an invitation for change requests and additional work by the project team.

So what goes into a project scope statement? Glad you asked! There are a bunch of things, which the following sections explain.

Product Scope Description

This is a narrative of what the project is creating as deliverables for the project customer. Early in the project, the product scope may be somewhat vague, but as the project scope is progressively elaborated, the product scope description may be updated to reflect its evolution and clarifications.

 EXAM TIP *Progressive elaboration* is a PMI term to describe an incremental process of redefining and clarifying any facet of a project. For example, a house project may start broad, as a three-bedroom, two-car garage home, and then, through progressive elaboration, all of the details down to the kitchen sink and doorknobs are defined.

Product Acceptance Criteria

The project scope statement components work with the project requirements, but focus specifically on the product and on what the conditions and processes are for formal acceptance of the product.

Project Deliverables

These are all the things that the project will create. Consider that the project deliverables are more than just the product, but also ancillary deliverables, such as project reports, communications, and lessons learned that the organization may use for future projects. The documentation and experience within the current project become part of the organizational process assets for future projects.

Project Exclusions

A project exclusion clearly states what is included with the project and what's excluded from it. This helps to eliminate assumptions between the project management team and the project customer. For example, a software programmer may create a new application for a customer as part of the project, but the distribution of the software to the customer's 10,000 computer workstations is defined as out of scope.

Project Constraints

A constraint is anything that limits the project team's options. Common constraints include the cost, schedule, technical, and quality demands. The project objectives can have qualifiers, such as "U.S. dollars," "less than $4 million," or "within 10 percent of the stated budget." If your project is operating under a contract, the contractual obligations are constraints.

Project Assumptions

A project assumption is anything that is held to be true but not proven to be true. Within the scope, the assumptions are defined, as is their impact on the project if an assumption proves to be false. For example, in construction, there are assumptions that the warmer seasons will be cooperative for outdoor work. No one can necessarily prove this, but it's believed to be true based on history. However, should the weather not cooperate, it could have huge impacts on the project.

Creating the Work Breakdown Structure

The WBS is all about the project deliverables. It's a breakdown of the project scope into hierarchical deliverables. The WBS takes the project scope and breaks it down into smaller, manageable chunks of deliverables. Each layer of the WBS breaks down the layer above it into smaller deliverables, until it arrives at the smallest item in the WBS, the work package.

NOTE The work in the WBS refers to the deliverables the project will create, not the effort your project team will have to put forth to create the deliverables.

Figure 5-1 is an example of a simple WBS. The house project has five major categories of deliverables: project management, paperwork, construction, interior design, and landscaping. Each of these first-tier deliverables can be broken down again. In Figure 5-1, the construction deliverable has been broken down to a second level consisting of the basement, first floor, and second floor. Each of these deliverables could be broken down again to another level, and so on. The smallest item in the WBS is called a *work package*, which can be an effective unit to estimate cost and time, and can be monitored and controlled within the project.

So how far must the project scope be broken down? There's no right answer, other than to the level of detail that's appropriate for the project priority, scope, and objectives.

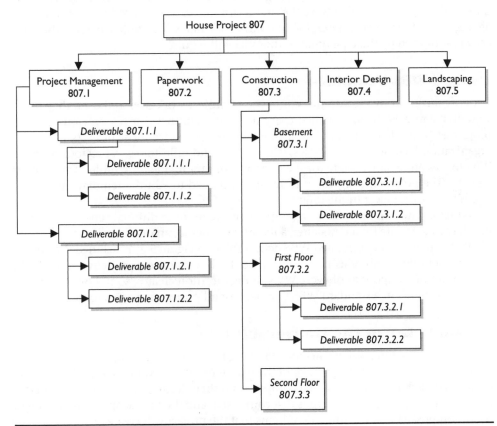

Figure 5-1   A WBS is the breakdown of a project scope.

A guideline for WBS breakdown is the *8/80 Rule*. This rule recommends that the labor to create a work package equate to no more than 80 hours and no fewer than 8 hours of labor for the associated activities. Of course, that's just a guideline, not a regulation. Some projects may call for work packages, such as a quality control result, that may take far less than eight hours. For your CAPM or PMP exam, know that the smallest element in the WBS is a work package and that it can be scheduled, estimated for costs, and then monitored and controlled.

 EXAM TIP The WBS is primarily about things, not activities. The work package is just a label for the smallest deliverable within the WBS. The PMI has lightened their stance on allowing appropriate activities, such as testing, into the WBS. A work package can be scheduled, have its cost estimated, and be controlled.

Usually, the WBS is a visual mapping of the subdivision of the project deliverables, though this approach isn't always the best technique to use. The WBS can also be created by using the project phases, by subcontractors that will complete parts of the project work, or even by the type of labor the WBS will require.

Using a WBS Template

If an organization were to do the same type of project work over and over, they likely wouldn't start a WBS from scratch every time. Instead, they'd use a previous, similar project as a template for the current one. This is ideal since most projects within an organization have similar life cycles, deliverables, and milestones. A previous project's WBS makes an ideal template for the current project, provided the projects are similar enough. The project management team may still need to edit the template, but using one is a huge timesaver in the long run.

Other organizations may use a template in the more traditional sense. Just as you may have a template for a newsletter, a report, or a memo, an organization could create a WBS template of prepopulated WBS deliverables. In Figure 5-1, I included the project management deliverables as part of the WBS. Project management deliverables could be a common component of every WBS an organization creates, so it'd be ideal to include these items in a standard WBS template for all project managers to use.

Breaking Down the Deliverables

Horrible joke warning: What's Beethoven doing now? Decomposing.

All right, so it's not the best joke in the world, but it's relevant. Like Beethoven, the project management team will first compose and then decompose. In project management, the project scope statement is first composed, and then the scope is broken down (or decomposed) into the individual items that the project will create.

Some items in the WBS may not be available for decomposition because they're far off in the future. In these instances, the project management team will break down those items as more information regarding the deliverables becomes available. This is an example of *rolling wave planning*. Some projects may elect to create their WBS based on the phases within the project, rather than on the total deliverables of the project. Either approach is fine, but the following activities are required to break down the project scope into a WBS:

- Identify the project deliverables and related work.
- Form the WBS structure.
- Decompose the upper-tier deliverables into lower-tier deliverables.
- Create and assign WBS identification codes to the WBS packages. (This is called the code of accounts and is a numbering system to identify each element within the WBS.)
- Confirm that the decomposition is appropriate for the type of project.

Creating the WBS Dictionary

Along with the WBS, a WBS dictionary defines all of the characteristics of each element within the WBS. The primary documentation of the WBS dictionary is on the work package, the smallest item in the WBS, but upper-tier deliverables can also be documented. Each work package in the WBS is cross-referenced in this companion document and includes the following details where appropriate:

- Code of account identifier and charge number
- Work package description
- Statement of work
- Work package owner or responsible role
- Schedule milestones
- Contract information
- Quality requirements
- Technical references
- Associated activities and work packages
- Schedule
- Resources
- Cost

 EXAM TIP   You'll see the scope baseline often in your PMP or CAPM endeavor. The *scope baseline* is the combination of the project scope, the work breakdown structure, and the WBS dictionary.

Validating the Project Scope

Imagine a project to create a full-color, slick catalog for an electronics manufacturer. The project manager has completed the initiation processes, moved through planning, and is now executing the project work. The only trouble is that the project manager and the experts on the project team aren't sharing the work progress with the customer. The work they are completing is not in alignment with the product description or the customer requirements.

The project team has created a trendy 1950s-style catalog with funky green and orange colors, lots of beehive hairdo models, horn-rimmed glasses, and tongue-in-cheek jokes about "the future" of electronics. The manufacturer wants to demonstrate a professional, accessible, current look for its publications. What do you think will happen if the project manager presents the catalog with his spin rather than following the request of the customer?

Scope validation is the process of the project customer accepting the project deliverables. It happens either at the end of each project phase or as major deliverables are created. Scope validation ensures that the deliverables the project creates are in alignment with the project scope. It is concerned with the acceptance of the work. A related activity, *quality control* (*QC*), is concerned with the correctness of the work. Scope validation and QC can happen in tandem because the quality of the work contributes to scope validation. Poor quality will typically result in scope validation failure.

Preparing for Project Inspection

You could just rush into scope validation, but that'd be a waste of time and not a very organized approach to confirming that the project deliverables are accurate. It's better to collect some inputs to help you prepare for the project inspection. You'll need the following:

- **Project management plan**   The project management plan contains the scope management plan, which you'll need because it defines how the scope can be validated and by which stakeholders in the project.

- **Requirements documentation**   This documentation of what the stakeholders expected from the project defines all of the technical requirements that must be present for the work to be accepted by the stakeholders.

- **Requirements traceability matrix**   This is a table that maps the requirements throughout the project all the way to their completion.

- **Verified deliverables**   These are deliverables that your project team has completed that have passed your project's quality control process.

- **Work performance data**   This information defines how well the deliverables are in compliance and records those requirements that are not in compliance with the project scope.

These five things will help you and the project stakeholders inspect the project work to confirm that what you've created is what was promised to the customer.

Inspecting the Project Work

To complete scope validation, the deliverables must be inspected. Inspection may require measuring, examining, and testing the product to prove that it meets the customer's requirements. Inspection usually requires the project manager and the customer to inspect the project deliverables for verification, which, in turn, results in acceptance. Depending on the industry, inspections may also be known as:

- Reviews
- Product reviews
- Audits
- Walkthroughs
- Group decision-making techniques

Assuming the scope has been validated, the customer accepts the deliverable. This is a formal process that requires signed documentation of the acceptance by the sponsor or customer. Scope validation can also happen at the end of each project phase or when major deliverables within the project are achieved. In these instances, scope validation may be conditional, based on the work results. When the scope is not validated, the project may undergo one of several actions. It may be canceled and deemed a failure, sent through corrective actions, or put on hold while a decision is made based on the project or phase results.

Should a project get canceled before it has completed the scope, scope validation is measured against the deliverables to the point of the project cancellation. In other words, scope validation measures the completeness of the work up to the cancellation, not the work that was to be completed after project termination.

EXAM TIP If a project scope has been completed, the project is complete. Resist the urge to do additional work once the project scope has been fulfilled. Also, be cautious of instances where the scope is fulfilled and the product description is exact, but the customer is not happy with the product. Technically, for the exam, the project is complete even if the customer is not happy.

Controlling the Project Scope

Scope control is about protecting the project scope from change and, when change does happen, managing those changes. Ideally, all requested changes follow the scope change control system, which means that change requests must be documented. Those changes that sneak into the project scope are lumped into that project poison category of scope creep. Scope creep is, of course, bad, bad news.

Corrective actions—those steps taken to move the project back into alignment with the project scope—do require formal change requests, because the project manager isn't changing the scope, but rather the work that's outside of the project scope. Corrective actions are a part of scope control because you're nudging, and sometimes shoving, work back into alignment with the project scope. The trouble with scope creep and corrective actions is that the project team is doing or fixing work that should never have entered the scope in the first place—and that means wasted time and dollars. That's one sure way for a project to be late and over budget.

 NOTE Corrective actions will require a formal change request especially if they involve additional time or cost to complete.

Controlling the project scope is also concerned with "influencing the factors that create project scope changes." That's the PMBOK way of saying that the project manager must control the project team and the project stakeholders from doing anything, absolutely anything, that's outside of the project scope. It also means that the project management team should capture the customer's vision in planning before much of the project work begins. For example, it's always easier to make changes on a blueprint than in construction. Gathering all requirements and creating an accurate project scope statement can ward off changes during execution.

You'll need five things as inputs to the control scope process:

- **Project management plan**   Within the project management plan, you'll reference the scope baseline, scope management plan, change management, configuration management plan, and the requirements management plan for scope control.

- **Work performance data**   This is the status of the deliverables—the work that's been started, finished, or has yet to begin.

- **Requirements documentation**   You'll still need to identify the requirements as approved by the stakeholders.

- **Requirements traceability matrix**   This table identifies and tracks requirements through the project and is needed to help identify which requirements have been completed and how changes may affect any identified requirement.

- **Organizational process assets**   Your organization may have scope management policies, guidelines, and reporting methods that you must use as part of scope control.

Using a Change Control System

While it's dreamy and ideal for requirements to be completely gathered before the work begins, change requests to the project work are still likely. Every project demands a change control system that defines and controls how changes to the project and to the product can be approved. The scope management plan defines the change control system, its procedure, and how the change decisions can be made—often with a fee just to entertain the change request. The change control system should be reviewed during the project kickoff meeting so that all of the stakeholders are aware of the process. Change control is part of the project management information system to help control changes to the project scope. This helps automate the procedure, but doesn't necessarily make approving or denying change requests any easier. The change control system also considers integrated change control. Integrated change control examines the proposed change and how it affects all of the project's knowledge areas. For example:

- How does this change affect the project scope?
- What is the cost of the change?
- How does this change affect the project schedule?
- How does this change affect quality?
- What resources are needed or affected by the change?
- How does this change affect communications?
- What risks does this change present?
- Will procurement be affected by this change?

The change control system should do several things for the project management team:

- Document all change requests.
- Track each change request.
- Document approval levels required for a scope change.
- Provide the status of each change request.

NOTE Technically, there are four change control systems. While this chapter includes information on the most common changes, in the project scope there are also change control systems for cost, schedule, and contract. All four change control systems invoke integrated change control when a change is proposed.

Planning for Project Scope Changes

When a change is presented, part of considering the change involves additional planning. The project manager and the project team must reconvene to examine the change and how it may affect the project work and the knowledge areas discussed earlier. Changes are sometimes rejected, such as when a project team member takes the initiative for a change and does not follow the change control procedures. In these instances, the project management team must consider the change and examine the variance to determine the response.

Consider a team member who moves the light fixtures in a kitchen construction project by 2 feet. The team member believes the kitchen would be better lit with the lights moved to their new position, but he didn't follow the change control process to make the change. Now there is a variance in the scope—a difference between what the specification documents called for and what the team member did. The project management team has to consider how to manage the variance. Should they redo the work or accept the change the team member has made? If they redo the work, they may lose time and money, but they'll be in scope. If they leave the change as is, then they're out of scope.

Another consideration for all changes is the configuration management system. Configuration management documents all of the features and functions of the project's product. When a change is requested, the impact on the features and functions of the product is documented with the change request before the change is allowed to move through the integrated change control process. For example, a change to add French doors to a home construction project would need all of the features and functions of those French doors so that the true impact on the project's knowledge areas could be examined fully. Failure to accurately document the change can lead to assumptions proving false, new risks, schedule slippage, and financial costs within the project.

 EXAM TIP Undocumented change requests should not be considered at all. Change requests must be documented according to the project scope management plan. When there is a difference between what was planned and what was created, variance analysis is needed to determine what corrective actions should be implemented.

Approving a Change

It's a safe bet that changes to the project scope will happen during a project. Why do change requests happen? And which ones are most likely to be approved? Most change requests are a result of:

- **Value-added changes**   These are changes that will reduce costs. (This is often due to technological advances made since the time the project scope was created.)

- **External events**   These could be such things as new laws or industry requirements.

- **Errors or omissions**   Ever hear this one: "Oops! We forgot to include this feature in the product description and WBS!" Errors and omissions can happen to both the project scope, which is the work to complete the project, and the product scope, which is the features and functions of the deliverable, and they typically constitute an overlooked feature or requirement.

- **Risk response**   A risk has been identified, and changes to scope are needed to mitigate the risk.

When change requests are approved, the effects of that change should be documented throughout the project. The Iron Triangle of Project Management is a good example: If the project scope increases, then the project schedule and the project costs will likely need to be changed to reflect these changes. Here are all of the project components that will most likely need to be updated to reflect any approved changes to the project:

- Requirements documentation
- Requirements traceability matrix (RTM)
- Project scope statement
- Work breakdown structure (WBS)
- WBS dictionary
- Scope baseline
- Additional requested changes
- Organizational process assets
- Risk register
- Project management plan

Change requests must always follow the change control system, or they are considered out of scope. As the project manager and the project team discover and report changes that are out of scope, the project management team must deal with the changes to remove them through corrective actions or incorporate them through the change control process. Those changes that are incorporated into the project must still be documented and then reflected in the preceding project components. No changes sneak by!

Chapter Summary

Project scope management is the ability to complete all of the project's required work—and only the required work. This means no extras, no favors, and no cutting corners. The project scope is the focus of the project—the necessary work to complete the project. Project scope management is a tool the project manager uses to determine what work is in the project and what work is extraneous.

The project scope management plan will help the project management team determine how the project scope will be defined, how the WBS will be created, how the scope will be controlled throughout the remainder of the project, and how the scope will be verified by the project customer, both at the end of the project and at the end of each project phase. The project scope management plan makes the project team consider all of the knowledge areas and how they may be affected by changes to the project scope.

To determine what the project scope actually is, plenty of scope planning is needed. The project manager and the project team must have a clear vision of the project, the business need for the project, the requirements, and the stakeholder expectations for the project. The end result of the scope planning processes is the project scope statement. The scope statement says, in no uncertain terms, what is within the project and what is not. This is a more detailed project scope statement than what's created during project initiation.

For your CAPM or PMP exam, focus on protecting the project scope. This includes finding the real purpose of the project so that the scope is in alignment with the identified need. Once the scope has been created, the project team, stakeholders, the project sponsor, and even the project manager should not change it, unless there is overwhelming evidence of why the scope needs to be changed. All changes should be documented and must follow the change control system as defined in the project scope management plan.

Key Terms

8/80 Rule   A planning heuristic for creating the WBS. This rule states that the work package in a WBS must take no more than 80 hours of labor to create and no fewer than 8 hours of labor to create.

Active observation   The observer interacts with the worker to ask questions and understand each step of the work being completed. In some instances, the observer could serve as an assistant in doing the work.

Affinity diagrams   When stakeholders create a large number of ideas, you can use an affinity diagram to cluster similar ideas together for further analysis.

Alternatives generation   A scope definition process of finding alternative solutions for the project customer while considering the customer's satisfaction, the cost of the solution, and how the customer may use the product in operations.

Brainstorming   This approach encourages participants to generate as many ideas as possible about the project requirements. No idea is judged or dismissed during the brainstorming session.

Change control system (CCS)   Documented in the scope management plan, this system defines how changes to the project scope are managed and controlled.

Change management plan   This subsidiary plan defines how changes will be allowed and managed within the project.

Code of accounts   A numbering system for each item in the WBS. The *PMBOK* is a good example of a code of accounts, as each chapter and its subheadings follow a logical numbering scheme. For example, *PMBOK* 5.3.3.2 identifies an exact paragraph in the *PMBOK*.

Configuration management plan   This subsidiary plan defines how changes to the features and functions of the project deliverables will be monitored and controlled within the project.

Context diagram   These diagrams show the relationship between elements of an environment. For example, a context diagram would illustrate the networks, servers, workstations, and people that interact with the elements of the environment.

Delphi Technique   This approach uses rounds of anonymous surveys to build consensus. Because the surveys are anonymous, participants are more likely to be honest with their requirements, opinions, and statements. The project manager organizes these comments and inputs and then sends them back to the participant for another round of anonymous input.

Dictatorship   A decision method where only one individual makes the decision for the group.

Focus groups   A moderator-led requirements collection method to elicit requirements from stakeholders.

Functional analysis   This is the study of the functions within a system, project, or, what's more likely in the project scope statement, the product the project will be creating. Functional analysis studies the goals of the product, how the product will be used, and the expectations the customer has of the product once it leaves the project and moves into operations. Functional analysis may also consider the cost of the product in operations, which is known as life-cycle costing.

Funding limit   Most projects have a determined budget in relation to the project scope. There may be a qualifier on this budget, such as plus or minus 10 percent based on the type of cost estimate created.

Initial project organization   The project scope statement identifies the project team and the key stakeholders. In some organizations, especially on larger projects, the team organization and structure are also documented.

Interviews   A requirements collection method used to elicit requirements from stakeholders in a one-on-one conversation.

Majority   A group decision method where more than 50 percent of the group must be in agreement.

Mind mapping   This approach maps ideas to show the relationship among requirements and the differences between requirements. The map can be reviewed to identify new solutions or to rank the identified requirements.

Nominal group technique   As with brainstorming, participants are encouraged to generate as many ideas as possible, but the suggested ideas are ranked by a voting process.

Passive observation   The observer records information about the work being completed without interrupting the process; sometimes called the invisible observer.

Plurality   A group-decision method where the largest part of the group makes the decision when it's less than 50 percent of the total. (Consider three or four factions within the stakeholders.)

Product acceptance criteria   This project scope statement component works with the project requirements, but focuses specifically on the product and what the conditions and processes are for formal acceptance of the product.

Product breakdown   A scope definition technique that breaks down a product into a hierarchical structure, much like a WBS breaks down a project scope.

Product scope description   This is a narrative description of what the project is creating as a deliverable for the project customer.

Product scope   Defines the product or service that will come about as a result of completing the project. It defines the features and functions that characterize the product.

Project assumptions   A project assumption is a factor in the planning process that is held to be true but not proven to be true.

Project boundaries   A project boundary clearly states what is included with the project and what's excluded from the project. This helps to eliminate assumptions between the project management team and the project customer.

Project constraints   A constraint is anything that limits the project manager's options. Consider a predetermined budget, deadline, resources, or materials the project manager must use within the project—these are all examples of project constraints.

Project objectives   These are the measurable goals that determine a project's acceptability to the project customer and the overall success of the project. Objectives often include the cost, schedule, technical requirements, and quality demands.

Project requirements   These are the demands set by the customer, regulations, or the performing organization that must exist for the project deliverables to be acceptable. Requirements are often prioritized in a number of ways, from "must have" to "should have" to "would like to have."

Project scope   This defines all of the work, and only the required work, to complete the project objectives.

Project scope management plan   This project management subsidiary plan controls how the scope will be defined, how the project scope statement will be created, how the WBS will be created, how scope validation will proceed, and how the project scope will be controlled throughout the project.

Prototype   A model of the finished deliverable that allows the stakeholder to see how the final project deliverable may operate.

Requirements documentation   This documentation of what the stakeholders expected in the project defines all of the requirements that must be present for the work to be accepted by the stakeholders.

Requirements management plan   This subsidiary plan defines how changes to the project requirements will be permitted, how requirements will be tracked, and how changes to the requirements will be approved.

Requirements traceability matrix (RTM)   This is a table that maps the requirements throughout the project all the way to their completion.

Schedule milestones   The project customer may have specific dates when phases of the project should be completed. These milestones are often treated as project constraints.

Scope creep   Undocumented, unapproved changes to the project scope.

Scope validation   The formal inspection of the project deliverables, which leads to project acceptance.

Stakeholder analysis   A scope definition process where the project management team interviews the stakeholders and categorizes, prioritizes, and documents what the project customer wants and needs. The analysis is to determine, quantify, and prioritize the interests of the stakeholders. Stakeholder analysis demands quantification of stakeholder objectives; goals such as "good," "satisfaction," and "speedy" aren't quantifiable.

Systems analysis   A scope definition approach that studies and analyzes a system, its components, and the relationship of the components within the system.

Systems engineering   This project scope statement creation process studies how a system should work, designs and creates a system model, and then enacts the working system based on the project's goals and the customer's expectations. Systems engineering aims to balance the time and cost of the project in relation to the scope of the project.

Unanimity   A group decision method where everyone must be in agreement.

Value analysis   As with value engineering, this approach examines the functions of the project's product in relation to the cost of the features and functions. This is where, to some extent, the grade of the product is in relationship to the cost of the product.

Value engineering   This approach to project scope statement creation attempts to find the correct level of quality in relation to a reasonable budget for the project deliverable while still achieving an acceptable level of performance of the product.

WBS dictionary   A WBS companion document that defines all of the characteristics of each element within the WBS.

WBS template   A prepopulated WBS for repetitive projects. Previous projects' WBSs are often used as templates for current similar projects.

Work breakdown structure (WBS)   A deliverables-oriented breakdown of the project scope.

Work package   The smallest item in the WBS.

Work performance information   Status of the deliverables: the work that's been started, finished, or has yet to begin.

Questions

1. Henry is the project manager for his organization, and management has asked him to create a project management plan to define the scope statement. Which project management plan guides the creation of the detailed project scope statement?

   A. The charter

   B. The project management plan

   C. The project scope plan

   D. The project scope management plan

2. You are the project manager of the GYH Project. This project will create a walking bridge across the Tennessee River. You've been asked to start the process of creating the project scope statement and you need to gather the elements for this process. Which one of the following is not needed to define the project scope?

   A. A project charter

   B. Organizational process assets

   C. A risk management plan

   D. Requirements documentation

3. You are the project manager of the BHY Project. Your project customer has demanded that the project be completed by December 1. December 1 is an example of which one of the following?

   A. A constraint

   B. An assumption

   C. A project boundary

   D. Product acceptance criteria

4. Marty is the project manager of the Highway 41 Bridge Project and he's working with his project team members to create the WBS. Marty shows the team how to break down the project scope into the WBS components, but the team doesn't understand how far down the breakdown should occur. Marty should call the lowest-level item in a WBS what?

   A. A deliverable

   B. A work package

   C. An activity

   D. A leaf object

5. You are working with the project team to create the WBS. There are some elements in the WBS that can't be broken down yet. You and the team elect to break down these items later in the project as more details become available. This approach to creating the WBS is also known as what?

A. Decomposition

B. The 8/80 Rule

C. Parkinson's Law

D. Rolling wave planning

6. You are the project manager for your organization and you're creating the WBS for a new project. In your WBS, you're numbering each level of the components following a project sequenced numbering order. Your WBS is numbered in a hierarchical fashion for easy identification and reference. This numbering scheme is called what?

A. Code of accounts

B. Chart of accounts

C. WBS template

D. WBS dictionary

7. You'll use the scope management plan to define the project scope statement. You'll also use this plan to build the scope baseline. Which two items are parts of the scope baseline for the project?

A. The project scope management plan and project charter

B. The project scope management plan and the WBS

C. The WBS and WBS dictionary

D. Time and cost baselines

8. Throughout the project, you have milestones scheduled at the end of each phase. Tied to these milestones you have a project management requirement of scope validation. Scope validation leads to what?

A. Defect repair

B. Formal acceptance of the complete project scope

C. Rework

D. Inspection

9. You've just reached the end of your project and management has asked you and several key stakeholders to begin the scope validation process. What is a tool and technique used during scope validation?

A. Inspection

B. Quality control

C. Stakeholder analysis

D. Defect repair review

10. David, one of your project team members, has been making changes to his work, which, as a result, changes the project scope. David's changes are also known as what?

    A. Gold plating

    B. Scope control defect

    C. Scope creep

    D. Improvised scope composition

11. As the project manager, you are averse to change once the scope statement has been approved. You do not want changes to enter the project because these changes can have a wide impact on the project as a whole. Which system defines how the project scope and the product scope can be changed?

    A. The project scope change control system

    B. The project integrated management system

    C. The project management information system

    D. Change control

12. A scope change has been approved in Marcy's project. All of the following must be updated to reflect the change except for which one?

    A. The project scope statement

    B. The WBS

    C. The WBS dictionary

    D. Defect repair review

13. A project team member has, on his own initiative, added extra vents to an attic to increase air circulation. The project plan did not call for these extra vents, but the team member decided they were needed based on the geographical location of the house. The project team's experts concur with this decision. This is an example of:

    A. Cost control

    B. Ineffective change control

    C. Self-led teams

    D. Value-added change

14. It's important for you, the project manager, to understand what each of the project management processes create. One of the key processes you'll do is scope control throughout your project. Which of the following is an output of scope control?

    A. Work-around

    B. Change request for a corrective action

    C. Transference

    D. Risk assessment

15. You are the project manager for the JHG Project. Your project is to create a new product for your industry. You have recently learned that your

competitor is also working on a similar project, but their offering will include a computer-aided program and web-based tools, which your project does not offer. You have implemented a change request to update your project accordingly. This is an example of which of the following?

A. A change due to an error and omission in the initiation phase

B. A change due to an external event

C. A change due to an error or omission in the planning phase

D. A change due to a legal issue

16. You are the project manager of a large project. Your project sponsor and management have approved you to outsource portions of the project plan. What must be considered if a change request affects the procured work?

A. The project sponsor

B. The contractual agreement

C. Vendor(s)

D. The cause of the change request

17. A project team member has asked you what a scope statement is. Which of the following is a characteristic of a project scope statement?

A. Defines the scope baseline for the project

B. Defines the requirements for each project within the organization

C. Defines the roles and responsibilities of each project team member

D. Defines the project deliverables and the work needed to create those deliverables

18. One of the stakeholders of the project you are managing asks why you consider the project scope statement so important in your project management methodology. You answer her question with which of the following?

A. It is mandatory to consult the plan before authorizing any change.

B. Project managers must document any changes before approving or declining them.

C. The project scope helps the project manager determine if a change is within or outside of scope.

D. The project plan and earned value management (EVM) work together to assess the risk involved with proposed changes.

19. You are the project manager for a large construction project. The architect has provided your project team with blueprints detailing the exact layout of the building your team will be creating. He insists that the team follow the blueprints as he's designed them. The blueprints are an example of which one of the following?

A. Project specifications

B. Approval requirements

C. Project constraints

D. Initially defined risks

20. Complete this sentence: Project scope management is primarily concerned with defining and controlling _____.

A. What is and is not included in the project

B. What is and is not included in the product

C. Changes to the project scope

D. Changes to the configuration management system

Questions and Answers

1. Henry is the project manager for his organization, and management has asked him to create a project management plan to define the scope statement. Which project management plan guides the creation of the detailed project scope statement?

A. The charter

B. The project management plan

C. The project scope plan

D. The project scope management plan

D. The project scope management plan defines the creation of the detailed project scope statement. A, the charter, does include the preliminary project scope statement, but not the detailed one the project scope management plan defines. B, the project management plan, is a parent of the project scope management plan. C is not a valid plan, so this answer is incorrect.

2. You are the project manager of the GYH Project. This project will create a walking bridge across the Tennessee River. You've been asked to start the process of creating the project scope statement and you need to gather the elements for this process. Which one of the following is not needed to define the project scope?

A. A project charter

B. Organizational process assets

C. A risk management plan

D. Requirements documentation

C. At this point, you won't need, or likely have, the risk management plan to define the project scope. A, B, and D are incorrect statements because you'll need the project charter, organizational process assets, and the requirements documentation to define the project scope.

3. You are the project manager of the BHY Project. Your project customer has demanded that the project be completed by December 1. December 1 is an example of which one of the following?

A. A constraint

B. An assumption

C. A project boundary

D. Product acceptance criteria

A. This is an example of a project constraint. B is incorrect because this is a requirement, not an assumption. C is incorrect because project boundaries define things that are within and outside of the project scope. D is incorrect because product acceptance criteria are an example of functions and features the product must have to be acceptable to the customer.

4. Marty is the project manager of the Highway 41 Bridge Project and he's working with his project team members to create the WBS. Marty shows the team how to break down the project scope into the WBS components, but the team doesn't understand how far down the breakdown should occur. Marty should call the lowest-level item in a WBS what?

A. A deliverable

B. A work package

C. An activity

D. A leaf object

B. The smallest item in the WBS is called the work package. A, deliverables, may be true to a degree, but B is a more precise answer. C is incorrect because activities are found in the activity list. D is an invalid WBS term.

5. You are working with the project team to create the WBS. There are some elements in the WBS that can't be broken down yet. You and the team elect to break down these items later in the project as more details become available. This approach to creating the WBS is also known as what?

A. Decomposition

B. The 8/80 Rule

C. Parkinson's Law

D. Rolling wave planning

D. This is a clear example of rolling wave planning. A is incorrect because decomposition describes the breakdown process of the project scope. B is incorrect because the 8/80 Rule defines the guideline for the amount of labor that should be related to each work package in the WBS. C, Parkinson's Law, is not relevant to this question. Parkinson's Law states that work will expand to fulfill the amount of time allotted to it.

6. You are the project manager for your organization and you're creating the WBS for a new project. In your WBS, you're numbering each level of the components following a project sequenced numbering order. Your WBS is numbered in a hierarchical fashion for easy identification and reference. This numbering scheme is called what?

   A. Code of accounts

   B. Chart of accounts

   C. WBS template

   D. WBS dictionary

   A. The WBS numbering scheme is called the code of accounts. B, chart of accounts, is a project management accounting system. C, a WBS template, can be a prepopulated WBS or a WBS from a previous project used to define the current project's WBS. D is incorrect because the WBS dictionary defines the attributes of each WBS element.

7. You'll use the scope management plan to define the project scope statement. You'll also use this plan to build the scope baseline. Which two items are parts of the scope baseline for the project?

   A. The project scope management plan and project charter

   B. The project scope management plan and the WBS

   C. The WBS and WBS dictionary

   D. Time and cost baselines

   C. The WBS and WBS dictionary are two of the three components of the scope baseline. The approved detailed project scope statement is the third portion of the scope baseline. A, B, and D are all incorrect because they do not accurately define the scope baseline.

8. Throughout the project, you have milestones scheduled at the end of each phase. Tied to these milestones you have a project management requirement of scope validation. Scope validation leads to what?

   A. Defect repair

   B. Formal acceptance of the complete project scope

   C. Rework

   D. Inspection

   B. Scope validation leads to one thing: formal acceptance of the complete project scope. A, C, and D are incorrect because defect repair, rework, and inspection are not outputs of scope validation.

9. You've just reached the end of your project and management has asked you and several key stakeholders to begin the scope validation process. What is a tool and technique used during scope validation?

   A. Inspection

   B. Quality control

   C. Stakeholder analysis

   D. Defect repair review

   A. Inspection is a tool and technique used during scope validation. You might also use group-decision making techniques as part of the validate scope process. B, quality control, is tempting, but this is not a correct choice for scope validation. C and D are incorrect as well because these two choices are not used during the scope validation process.

10. David, one of your project team members, has been making changes to his work, which, as a result, changes the project scope. David's changes are also known as what?

    A. Gold plating

    B. Scope control defect

    C. Scope creep

    D. Improvised scope composition

    C. Undocumented changes are examples of scope creep. A, gold plating, is when the project team adds changes to consume the project budget. B and D, scope control defect and improvised scope composition, are not valid change management terms.

11. As the project manager, you are averse to change once the scope statement has been approved. You do not want changes to enter the project because these changes can have a wide impact on the project as a whole. Which system defines how the project scope and the product scope can be changed?

    A. The project scope change control system

    B. The project integrated management system

    C. The project management information system

    D. Change control

    A. The only system that defines how project and product scope can be changed is the project scope change control system. B, the project integrated management system, is not a valid term. C, the project management information system, is the parent system of the project scope change control system. D, change control, is a process, not a system.

12. A scope change has been approved in Marcy's project. All of the following must be updated to reflect the change except for which one?

A. The project scope statement

B. The WBS

C. The WBS dictionary

D. Defect repair review

D. Defect repair and its review do not require a change request, so this choice is correct. A, B, and C, the project scope statement, the WBS, and the WBS dictionary, do require updates when change requests are approved.

13. A project team member has, on his own initiative, added extra vents to an attic to increase air circulation. The project plan did not call for these extra vents, but the team member decided they were needed based on the geographical location of the house. The project team's experts concur with this decision. This is an example of:

A. Cost control

B. Ineffective change control

C. Self-led teams

D. Value-added change

B. Even though the change is agreed upon, this is an example of ineffective change control. The team member should follow the change control process as defined in the project scope management plan. A, C, and D are incorrect choices.

14. It's important for you, the project manager, to understand what each of the project management processes create. One of the key processes you'll do is scope control throughout your project. Which of the following is an output of scope control?

A. Work-around

B. Change request for a corrective action

C. Transference

D. Risk assessment

B. Change requests for corrective actions are an output of scope control. This is because the project team may be doing work outside of the project scope. Corrective action would stop the extraneous work and bring the project team member's actions back into the work within the project scope. A, C, and D are not outputs of scope control.

15. You are the project manager for the JHG Project. Your project is to create a new product for your industry. You have recently learned that your competitor is also working on a similar project, but their offering will include a computer-aided program and web-based tools, which your project does

not offer. You have implemented a change request to update your project accordingly. This is an example of which of the following?

A. A change due to an error and omission in the initiation phase

B. A change due to an external event

C. A change due to an error or omission in the planning phase

D. A change due to a legal issue

B. This is a change due to an external event—the event being the product your competitor has in their project. This is not an example of an error or omission in the initiation phase, so A is incorrect. C is incorrect because this is not an error or omission in the planning phase, but a response to a competitor. D is incorrect because this is not a legal issue.

16. You are the project manager of a large project. Your project sponsor and management have approved you to outsource portions of the project plan. What must be considered if a change request affects the procured work?

A. The project sponsor

B. The contractual agreement

C. Vendor(s)

D. The cause of the change request

B. If a change to the project scope affects the procured work, the project manager must consider the contract. This is because the change may affect the existing contract the project manager and the vendor have entered into. While A, the project sponsor, and C, the vendor, are likely to be involved with the change, the contractual agreements override all other internal systems. D, the cause of the change request, is not as relevant as the contract.

17. A project team member has asked you what a scope statement is. Which of the following is a characteristic of a project scope statement?

A. Defines the scope baseline for the project

B. Defines the requirements for each project within the organization

C. Defines the roles and responsibilities of each project team member

D. Defines the project deliverables and the work needed to create those deliverables

D. The project scope statement defines the project deliverables and the associated work to create those deliverables. A is incorrect because the project scope statement, the WBS, and the WBS dictionary are considered to be the project scope baseline. B is incorrect. The project scope statement does define the requirements for every project, but it is project-specific. C is incorrect because the project scope statement does not define the roles and responsibilities of the project.

18. One of the stakeholders of the project you are managing asks why you consider the project scope statement so important in your project management methodology. You answer her question with which of the following?

    A. It is mandatory to consult the plan before authorizing any change.

    B. Project managers must document any changes before approving or declining them.

    C. The project scope helps the project manager determine if a change is within or outside of scope.

    D. The project plan and earned value management (EVM) work together to assess the risk involved with proposed changes.

    C. The project scope statement can help the project management team determine if a proposed change is within or outside of the project boundaries. A, B, and D are correct statements, but they do not answer the question in regard to the importance of the project scope statement.

19. You are the project manager for a large construction project. The architect has provided your project team with blueprints detailing the exact layout of the building your team will be creating. He insists that the team follow the blueprints as he's designed them. The blueprints are an example of which one of the following?

    A. Project specifications

    B. Approval requirements

    C. Project constraints

    D. Initially defined risks

    A. Blueprints are an example of the project specifications. B is incorrect because this is not an example of approval requirements. C is incorrect because this is not an example of a constraint. D is also incorrect because the blueprints are not examples of initially defined risks.

20. Complete this sentence: Project scope management is primarily concerned with defining and controlling _____.

    A. What is and is not included in the project

    B. What is and is not included in the product

    C. Changes to the project scope

    D. Changes to the configuration management system

    A. Project scope management is primarily concerned with defining and controlling what is and is not included in the project. B, C, and D are all incorrect statements.

Managing Project Time

In this chapter, you will

- Plan schedule management
- Define the project activities
- Sequence the project activities
- Estimate the resources for the defined activities
- Estimate how long the activities will take to complete
- Develop the project schedule
- Control the project schedule

Time has a funny way of sneaking up on you—and then easing on by. As a project manager, you've got stakeholders, project team members, and management all worried about your project deliverables, how the project is moving forward, and when, oh when, the project will be done. You've also got vacations, sick days, demands from other project managers, and delays from vendors to deal with.

Management frets over how much a project will cost. Project customers fret over the deliverables the project will create. Everyone, as it turns out, frets over how long the project will take. Of course I'm talking about the Triple Constraints of Project Management: cost, scope, and time. If any one of these constraints is out of balance with the other two, the project is unlikely to succeed. Time, as it happens, is often the toughest of the three constraints to manage, because interruptions come from all sides of the project.

Your Project Management Institute (PMI) exam and this chapter will focus on seven key project management processes in project time management. The processes within project time management, like much of project management, are interdependent on one another and on other processes in the project management life cycle.

Let's get into project time management right now!

Planning Schedule Management

The project management planning processes are iterative, as you know, and will happen over and over throughout the project. You and the project team—and even some key stakeholders—will work together to define the project's schedule management plan. This will happen early in the project's planning processes, but chances are good you'll need to return to schedule management planning to adjust, replan, or focus on the schedule you've created for the project.

Planning schedule management is not the creation of the actual project schedule. That'd be too easy. Instead, the schedule management plan defines how the project's policies and procedures for managing the project schedule will take place. You'll define the procedures for doing the other six processes within the knowledge area of time management:

- Define the project activities
- Sequence the project activities
- Estimate activity resources
- Estimate activity durations
- Develop the project schedule
- Control the schedule

In order to do this planning process, you'll gather your project team, your key stakeholders, and subject matter experts like people from management and consultants to help you plan what it is you're about to schedule. You'll need the project management plan, the project charter, enterprise environmental factors, and organizational process assets. I like to highlight organizational process assets in my PMP Boot Camp because this is like a PMI code word for templates from past projects.

Creating the Schedule Management Plan

The actual process of creating the schedule management plan involves you, the project team, and other experts meeting to discuss and agree upon the policies and procedures the schedule management processes should have. You'll rely on organizational process assets for much of the discussion: historical information, past project information, and existing organizational processes.

This event of creating the schedule management plan may also include the identification and approval of the tools and techniques for scheduling and controlling the project work. For example, an organization may not allow more than a certain number of hours per employee on the project. Or the organization could prevent certain activities from being done in tandem because of the associated risks. Every organization and their approach will be different, so you'll need to know if your company has any restrictions, scheduling rules, or policies on overtime, labor utilization, or coordination of resources. These will all affect the actual schedule of the project and should be documented in the project's schedule management plan.

During the creation of the schedule management plan, you'll also identify any software you'll utilize for scheduling the project work, tracking project performance, task completion, workflow management, and reporting. This is the project management information system that will assist you in the project management duties.

Examining the Schedule Management Plan

The schedule management plan could be adapted from a previous project or, if you need to, you could design the plan from scratch. For your CAPM and the PMP examination, you should be familiar with the information documented in the plan:

- **Project schedule model development**   This is the approved scheduling methodology and project management information system that will help you develop the project schedule.

- **Project schedule model maintenance**   This component of the plan is what you'll use when you update the project progress.

- **Level of accuracy**   Define the confidence need in the project duration estimating (such as +/–48 hours or 10 percent), any rounding of hours (for example, you could say the smallest task assignment is one work day), and how confident you are to meet the project's deadline if one exists.

- **Units of measure**   Your schedule management plan can define the schedule in hours, days, weeks, or even percentage of employee schedule.

- **Organizational procedure links**   The schedule management plan is part of the overall project management plan and is a project deliverable that will become part of historical information. The schedule management plan should be linked to the approved organizational policies and preferences.

- **Control thresholds**   Depending on the confidence in the activity duration estimates, a level of tolerance for the project schedule should be identified, such as +/–10 percent. This is considered the threshold or tolerance for error. Any value outside of the 10 percent will be a cause for a corrective action in the project.

- **Rules of performance measurement**   The schedule management plan should define how the project will be measured for performance. The most common approach is a suite of formulas called earned value management. (I'll discuss these in detail in Chapter 7 on cost management.)

- **Reporting formats**   Based on project performance, the project manager will need to report the schedule status to management, key stakeholders, and project customers.

- **Process descriptions**   The schedule management plan will define the schedule management activities and the associated activities the project manager and project team are expected to complete.

Defining the Project Activities

When a project is first initiated, project managers often focus immediately on the labor and activities that will be required to complete the project work. But that focus ignores the scope. In Chapter 5, I discussed the project scope and the work breakdown structure (WBS) as prerequisites to defining the project activities. For your PMI examination, here's the sequence of events that the project manager should have in place before getting to the work the project team will complete:

- Project scope statement
- Work breakdown structure (WBS)
- WBS dictionary
- Work packages
- Schedule activities

The work package, the smallest item in the WBS, is broken down into *schedule activities*, which include the labor to create the things defined in the WBS. The WBS, of course, reflects the project scope statement. While the preceding list is the logical sequence of how the project management team will work together to create the activity list, there are actually just four inputs to activity definition:

- Enterprise environmental factors
- Organizational process assets
- Scope baseline
- Schedule management plan

These inputs and the order of precedence mentioned earlier will help the project manager define the activities to actually create the components of the project scope. We're still in the planning process group, so this process is iterative. Any changes to the project scope will likely cause the project manager to revisit these processes throughout the project.

Making the Activity List

You and your project team are armed with the inputs I've listed previously and are ready to start defining the activities in order to create the project schedule.

Sounds like fun, huh? This process and its complexity will be in proportion to the size of the project scope. In other words, larger projects require more detail and more planning time, while smaller projects, like changing all the keyboards in your company, won't be all that complicated or too time-consuming to plan. My advice to you—the Certified Associate in Project Management (CAPM) or Project Management Professional (PMP) candidate—on your exam is to think of the largest project you can imagine, such as creating a skyscraper, and then you'll see the reason to use all or most of these project processes.

Let's take a look at the methods used to define the project activities, which the following sections explain in detail.

Decomposing the Work Packages

Yep, more decomposition. You know that the project scope is decomposed into deliverables, and then those deliverables continue to be decomposed into work packages. Work packages, of course, are the smallest item in the WBS. Now that you and your project team are focused on defining the project activities, you'll be breaking down the work packages into the labor needed to create each work package.

Some project managers follow a sequential pattern for this process. First, they decompose the project scope into first-tier deliverables, then they decompose those project deliverables into second-tier deliverables, and so on, until they've created the work packages. Armed with the work packages, they'll decompose those into the schedule activities we're discussing here. Other project managers will decompose the project scope, then the work packages, and then create the schedule activities in one swoop.

Either approach, in fact, is just fine—even with our pals at the PMI. Complete decomposition of the project scope down to the schedule activities is needed—how you get there doesn't matter. It only matters that all of the work packages are decomposed and that the project management team follows the internal policies and procedures (if they exist) to create the schedule activities.

EXAM TIP Use a logical approach to defining the activities: project scope statement, WBS, work packages, and then schedule activities.

Relying on Templates

Who wants to start a project from scratch when you've got an older, similar project just waiting to be manipulated? That older, similar project is a template. Sometimes in the project management world, we think of a template as an empty shell with pre-populated fields and deliverables—and that's fine. A *template* can also be an older, similar project that can be used and updated for the current project.

A project manager can use a standard activity list if the project work is similar to past projects. There's no real advantage to starting from scratch. Templates can include not only the activity list, but also the resource skills, estimated hours of effort, risks, deliverables, and any relevant project work information.

EXAM TIP Think of templates as past project files that can be manipulated and used for the current project.

Using Rolling Wave Planning

Have you ever done "the wave" at a football game? You can see the wave moving toward you from across the stadium, then you're in it, and then it surges past. "Rolling wave" in project management planning is iterations of planning the work and then doing the project work. Progressive elaboration, which you use to create the WBS and the WBS dictionary, is an example of rolling wave planning.

Rolling wave planning considers the big picture of what the project scope will create, but focuses on the short-term activities to move the project along. Figure 6-1 shows how a project to create a piece of software considers all of the project requirements for the deliverable, but focuses on the immediate activities necessary to complete a portion of the deliverable. Once that work is done, the project management team convenes and plans how to create the next portion of the project. The team plans, does the work, and then reconvenes for more planning.

 EXAM TIP Rolling wave planning focuses on the immediate while considering the big picture of the project. (Which is easier to plan and accomplish: what you must do this week or what you must do during a week a year from now?)

Using Expert Judgment

Let's face facts. As a project manager, you aren't always the person who knows the most about the work that the project centers on. Using expert judgment is working smart, not hard. The project manager relies on the project team, subject matter experts, and consultants to help determine the work that needs to be completed to create the project scope. You'll see expert judgment throughout this book and the Project Management

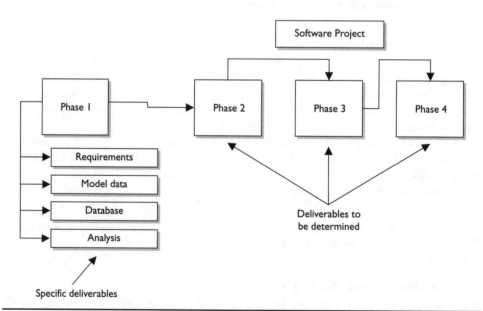

Figure 6-1 Rolling wave planning details the imminent work and keeps future work at the high level.

Body of Knowledge (PMBOK). It's simply leveraging other people's brainpower so that the project manager can make the best decisions with regard to the project.

Creating Planning Components

A third element of the scope baseline is the work breakdown structure. The WBS uses a component that has hooks into project time performance: a control account. A *control account* is a marker within the WBS that tracks the performance of the work packages associated with the control account. For example, a home construction project could create a control account for the basement, first floor, and second floor. The work packages associated with each floor of the house are tracked by the corresponding control account. Now you can see an overall performance of the project, or just see how each control account is performing.

Of course, there's no predetermined rule about how you use control accounts, except that a work package can be associated only with one control account at a time. In the home construction project, you could create control accounts for framing, electrical, plumbing, even landscaping, and track the performance by these categories. The performance information you'll most likely use is earned value management—something we'll get into in detail later in Chapter 7. For now, know that control accounts allow you to track performance for separate chunks of the WBS by using earned value management to track performance in time and cost.

Sometimes enough information just isn't available in the WBS to determine what activities are needed in the activity list. Let's go back to the new home construction project. Your customer in this instance knows the dimensions of the kitchen, but doesn't know what type of appliances, cabinets, or even tile they want to put into their deluxe kitchen. This isn't a problem at the beginning of the project because your construction team can get to work building the home, but eventually the homeowners must make a decision on the materials and components they'll want in their schmancy kitchen.

The kitchen may have a budget, but how the budget will be consumed isn't yet known, because the homeowners haven't decided where in the kitchen they'll spend their monies. The effort to create the deliverables in the kitchen may also fluctuate based on the type of materials and deliverables the homeowners elect to include in their kitchen.

What you can use in these instances is a planning package. A *planning package* is a signal that decisions need to be made by a given date or instance. In our home construction project example, a control account could capture the kitchen, while a planning package could represent the decision for the cabinets. Another planning package could capture the appliances, and the third could capture the decision for the kitchen flooring. We know these three things are needed in the kitchen (cabinets, appliances, and floor), but we don't know exactly what schedule activities are needed, because not enough information is yet known.

Examining the Activity List

The primary output of decomposing the work is the activity list, which is a collection of all the work elements required to complete the project. The activity list is actually an extension of the WBS and will serve as a fundamental tool in creating the project schedule. The activity list is needed to ensure that all the deliverables of the WBS are accounted for and that the necessary work is mapped to each work package.

The activity list also ensures that there is no extra work included in the project. Extra work costs time and money—and defeats the project scope. The WBS comprises all of the components the project will create, while the activity list is made up of all the work required to create the components within the WBS. In addition, the work on the activity list includes attributes of each identified activity. This ensures three things:

- That the team members are in agreement on what each activity accomplishes
- That the work supports and creates the WBS deliverables
- That the work is within the project scope

Documenting the Activity Attributes

Every activity in the activity list has attributes that must be documented. The documentation of the activities' characteristics will help with additional planning, risk identification, resource needs, and more. Of course the activities and depth of the attributes will vary by project discipline. For your PMI exam, here are some attributes you should consider:

- Activity identifier
- Activity codes
- Activity description
- Predecessor and successor activities
- Logical relationships
- Leads and lags
- Resource requirements
- Imposed dates
- Constraints and assumptions
- Responsibility of the project team member(s) completing the work
- Location of the work
- Type and amount of effort needed to complete the work

These activity attributes are especially useful for generating reports. With this information, you could quickly filter the activities to identify the work where a particular vendor is involved. Or you could filter the events based on location, risk, and project team member. You could use the activity attributes in nearly endless ways to help you communicate information to management to stakeholders, and to your project team.

EXAM TIP   Level of effort (LOE) and apportioned effort (AE) can be part of the activity description. LOE activities are the project maintenance type activities that have to be done over and over: budgeting, reporting, communicating. These activities almost always go to the project manager. AE activities are activities that can't be easily broken down into individual, traceable events. For example, quality assurance is part of every project activity, but isn't just one activity in the project.

Updating the Work Breakdown Structure

When creating the activity list, the project team and the project manager may discover discrepancies or inadequacies in the existing WBS. Updates to the WBS allow the project manager to ensure that all the needed project deliverables are included in the WBS and then to map the discovered deliverables to the identified work in the activity list.

In addition, the elements within the WBS may not be defined fully or correctly. During the decomposition of the work, elements of the WBS may need to be updated to reflect the proper description of the WBS elements. The descriptions should be complete and full and leave no room for ambiguity or misinterpretation. Finally, updates to the WBS may also include cost estimates to the discovered deliverables.

 EXAM TIP   Updates to the WBS are called refinements. As the project moves toward completion, refinements ensure that all of the deliverables are accounted for within the WBS. They may also call for, indirectly, updates to the activity list.

Sequencing the Project Activities

Now that the activity list has been created, the activities must be arranged in a logical sequence. This process calls on the project manager and the project team to identify the logical relationships between activities, as well as the preferred relationship between those activities. This can be accomplished in a few different ways:

- **Computer-driven**   Many different scheduling and project management software packages are available. These programs can help the project manager and the project team determine which actions need to happen in what order and with what level of discretion.

- **Manual process**   In smaller projects, and on larger projects in the early phases, manual sequencing may be preferred. An advantage of manual sequencing is that it's easier to move around dependencies and activities than it is in some programs.

- **Blended approach**   A combination of manual and computer-driven scheduling methods is fine. It's important to determine the correctness of the activity sequence, however. Sometimes a blended approach can be more complex than relying on just one or the other.

Considering the Inputs to Activity Sequencing

Figure 6-2 shows the complete process of activity sequencing. There are many approaches to completing activity sequencing. Perhaps the best approach, however, is activity sequencing that involves the entire project team and is not just a solo activity.

The project manager must rely on the project team and the inputs to activity sequencing:

- **Schedule management plan**   This plan is needed because it will direct how the activity sequence is to occur.

- **Activity list**   As just mentioned, this is the list of actions needed to complete the project deliverables.

- **Activity attributes**   Each scheduled activity has attributes that need to be documented. For example, the successor and predecessor of each activity, the lead and lag information, and the person responsible for completing the activity should all be documented. This information is important when it comes to schedule development and project control.

- **Project scope statement**   The scope statement is needed, since it may influence the sequence of events. For example, in construction, technology, or community planning (among other project types), the scope statement may include requirements, constraints, and assumptions that will logically affect the planning of activity sequencing.

- **Milestone list**   Milestones must be considered and evaluated when sequencing events to ensure that all of the work needed to reach the milestones is included.

- **Organizational process assets**   If you've done this type of work in the past, you can rely on historical information to help you sequence the current work.

Figure 6-2
Activity sequencing relies on several inputs to create the schedule.

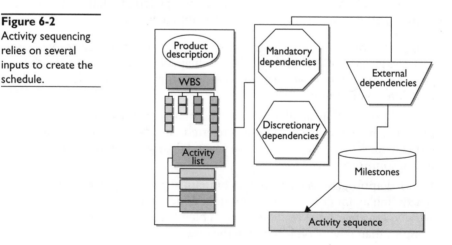

- **Enterprise environmental factors** Any rules or regulations that you must follow in your project's activity sequencing must be documented and upheld.

Creating Network Diagrams

Network diagrams visualize the project work. A network diagram shows the relationship of the work activities and how they will progress from start to completion. Network diagrams can be extremely complex or easy to create and configure. Most network diagrams in today's project management environment use an approach called "activity-on-node" to illustrate the activities and the relationships among those activities.

 EXAM TIP Older network diagramming methods used "activity-on-arrows" to represent the activities and their relationships. Don't be tempted to choose activity-on-arrows, because this diagramming method is long gone from the PMBOK.

Using the Precedence Diagramming Method

The precedence diagramming method (PDM) is the most common method of arranging the project work visually. The PDM puts the activities in boxes or circles, called *nodes*, and connects the boxes with arrows. The arrows represent the relationships and the dependencies of the work packages. The following illustration shows a simple network diagram using PDM:

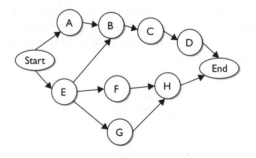

 EXAM TIP PDM is the most common approach to network diagramming since it's used by most project management information systems. It can also be done manually, however.

Relationships between activities in a PDM constitute one of four different types (as shown in Figure 6-3):

- **Finish-to-start (FS)** This relationship means that Task A must be completed before Task B can begin. This is the most common relationship. For example, the foundation must be set before the framing can begin.

Figure 6-3
Task relationships can vary, but finish-to-start is the most common.

Finish-to-Start

Task A must finish before Task B can start.

Start-to-Start

Task A must start before Task B can start.

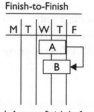

Finish-to-Finish

Task A must finish before Task B can finish.

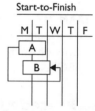

Start-to-Finish

Task A must start before Task B can finish.

- **Start-to-start (SS)** This relationship means that Task A must start before Task B can start. This relationship allows both activities to happen in tandem. For example, a crew of painters is painting a house. Task A is to scrape the flecking paint off the house, and Task B is to prime the house. The workers scraping the house must start before the other workers can begin priming the house. All of the scraping doesn't have to be completed before the priming can start, just some of it.

- **Finish-to-finish (FF)** This relationship means that Task A must be completed before Task B is completed. Ideally, the two tasks should finish at exactly the same time, but this is not always the case. For example, two teams of electricians may be working together to install new telephone cables throughout a building by Monday morning. Team A is pulling the cable to each office. Team B, meanwhile, is connecting the cables to wall jacks and connecting the telephones. Team A must pull the cable to the office so that Team B can complete their activity. The activities need to be completed at nearly the same time, by Monday morning, so that the new phones are functional.

- **Start-to-finish (SF)** This relationship is unusual and is rarely used. It requires that Task A start so that Task B may finish. Such relationships may be encountered in construction and manufacturing. It is also known as just-in-time (JIT) scheduling. An example is a construction of a shoe store. The end of the construction is soon, but an exact date is not known. The owner of the shoe store doesn't want to order the shoe inventory until the construction is nearly complete. The start of the construction tasks dictates when the inventory of the shoes is ordered.

> **EXAM TIP**   I like to use the just-in-time scheduling as a practical way to describe a start-to-finish relationship. In my examples, it's really some *soft logic* by the scheduler, as lead time for the ordering of the shoes could account for the construction of the project. Having said that, I still like to use something physical that most people can visualize and relate to. Now I'll get geeky—well, geekier. A true example of a start-to-finish relationship involves chemical reactions, where a chemical reaction cannot finish before another reaction starts. In this chemical environment, it is *hard logic*—the reaction must happen in a particular order to get the desired effect.

Utilizing Network Templates

Just as a project manager can rely on WBS templates, network templates may be available to streamline the planning process or to conform to a predetermined standard. Network templates can represent an entire project, if appropriate, although portions of a network template, such as the required project management activities, are common.

The portions of a network template are also known as *subnets* or fragnets. Subnets are often associated with repetitive actions within a network diagram. For example, each floor in a high-rise apartment building may undergo the same or similar actions during construction. Rather than complete the network diagram for each floor, a subnet can be implemented.

Determining the Activity Dependencies

The progression of the project is built on the sequence of activities. In other words, predecessor activities must be complete before successor activities can begin. The following are the dependencies you should know for your CAPM or PMP exam:

- **Mandatory dependencies**   These dependencies are the natural order of activities. For example, you can't begin building your house until your foundation is in place. These relationships are called *hard logic*.

- **Discretionary dependencies**   These dependencies are the preferred order of activities. Project managers should use these relationships at their discretion, and document the logic behind the decision. Discretionary dependencies allow activities to happen in a preferred order because of best practices, conditions unique to the project work, or because of external events. For example, a painting project typically allows the primer and the paint to be applied within hours of each other. Due to the expected high humidity during the project, however, all of the building will be completely primed before the paint can be applied. These relationships are also known as *soft logic*, preferred logic, or preferential logic.

- **External dependencies**   As the name implies, these are dependencies outside of the project's control. Examples include the delivery of equipment from a vendor, the deliverable of another project, or the decision of a committee, lawsuit, or expected new law.

- **Internal dependencies**   Some relationships are internal to the project or the organization. For example, the project team must create the software as part of the project's deliverable before the software can be tested for quality control.

 EXAM COACH   You have dependencies for passing your PMI exam. It's mandatory that you apply for the exam. You've an external dependency with the PMI approving your application—it's somewhat out of your hands. You also have some discretionary dependencies, such as when you study, your mental attitude, and the order of the chapters you study. Take charge and keep pressing yourself toward passing the exam. You can do this!

Considering Leads and Lags

Leads and lags are values added to activities to slightly alter the relationship between two or more activities. For example, a finish-to-start relationship may exist between applying primer to a warehouse and applying the paint. The project manager in this scenario has decided to add one day of lead time to the activity of painting the warehouse. Now the painting can begin one day before the priming is scheduled to end. Lead time is considered a negative value, because time is subtracted from the downstream activity to bring it closer to the start of the project.

Lag time is waiting time. Imagine a project to install wood floors in an office building. Currently, there is a finish-to-start relationship between staining the floors and adding a layer of shellac to seal them. The project manager has elected, because of the humidity in the building, to add two days of lag time to the downstream activity of sealing the floors. Now the shellac cannot be applied immediately after the stain, but must wait two additional days. Lag time is considered a positive value, since time is added to the project schedule.

The following illustration shows the difference between lead and lag times. Leads and lags must be considered in the project schedule, since an abundance of lag time can increase the project's duration. An abundance of lead time, while decreasing duration, may increase risks.

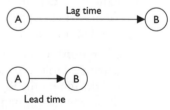

 EXAM TIP   Lead time is always "accelerated time" and is negative time because the work is moving closer to the project start date. *Lag* time is always waiting time and is considered positive time because the project manager is adding time to the project schedule.

Estimating the Project Resources

Resources include materials, equipment, and people. After the project manager and the project team have worked together to determine the sequence of the activities, they now have to determine which resources are needed for each activity, as well as how much of each resource. As you can guess, resource estimating goes hand in hand with cost estimating (which we'll discuss in Chapter 7). After all, if you need a metric ton of pea gravel, that's a resource estimate, but someone's got to pay for that metric ton of pea gravel.

To estimate the demand for the project resources, you'll need several inputs:

- Schedule management plan
- Activity list
- The attributes of each activity
- The availability of the resources you'll need, in the form of two calendars:
  - *Resource* calendars let you know when individual resources are available. This calendar tells you when Bob has scheduled a vacation, when a piece of equipment that your project needs is already scheduled for use, and even when facilities like meeting rooms are available.
  - *Project* calendars communicate when the project work may take place. For example, your project may allow work to happen between 6 A.M. and 6 P.M., Monday through Friday. Your project calendar will also identify any holidays when the project work won't happen.
- Risk register
- Activity cost estimates
- Enterprise environmental factors
- Organizational process assets

Using Expert Judgment

The project manager and the project team have worked together to create the WBS, the activity list, and the sequence of activities, so it makes sense that they'll continue to work together to create the resource estimates. And they do. According to the PMBOK, the project management team may work with experts to help make the best decisions. This is using the old standby, "expert judgment," when the project manager relies on someone more knowledgeable to help make the best decision.

Identifying Alternatives

As the project management team determines what resources are needed, there will be plenty of opportunities to determine which solution is the best solution for the project. Whenever more than one solution is presented, this is called *Alternative analysis*. Alternative analysis comes in many different flavors:

- **Resources**   For example, employees or consultants, junior or senior engineers
- **Tools and equipment**   Such as power tools or hand-held tools, newer versus older machinery
- **Types of materials**   For example, oak versus plywood
- **Make-or-buy decisions**   For instance, build your own software or buy a solution from a vendor

 EXAM TIP   *Alternative analysis* is used throughout the PMBOK, so you'll likely see this term on the PMP exam. Whenever you have two feasible choices for a component in your project, you're working with alternative analysis.

Relying on Published Estimating Data

If you are a project manager in construction, the cost of the labor you use, the materials you routinely work with, and seasonal factors you consider for each project typically vary, depending on what part of the country, or even the world, your project is operating within. Many companies provide estimating data on the resources your project can purchase based on the geographical locales the project takes place in, supply and demand, and the season of your purchases. Published estimating data helps the project management team determine an exact cost of the resources the project will utilize.

Using Bottom-Up Estimating

Every time I mention bottom-up estimating in one of my seminars, someone snickers and pantomimes drinking a shot of booze. Ha-ha.

Bottom-up estimating is the most accurate time-and-cost estimating approach a project manager can use. This estimating approach starts at "the bottom" of the project and considers every activity, its predecessor and successor activities, and the exact amount of resources needed to complete each activity. Bottom-up estimating accounts for all of the resources needed to complete all of the project work. While it is the most accurate estimating approach, it is also the most time-consuming.

 EXAM TIP   You'll see bottom-up estimating again in Chapter 7, which examines cost estimating. To complete bottom-up estimating, especially for costs, a WBS must be present. Bottom-up estimating for costs is also known as creating the definitive estimate.

Examining the Activity Resource Estimates

So what do you get when the project manager, the project team, and all your experts complete the activity resource process? You get the requirements for all the project resources. Not a trick question! The process allows the project manager, the project team, management, and your key stakeholders to see the needed resources to complete each work package in the WBS. Specifically, at the end of this process you'll have:

- **Resource requirements for each activity** You'll know what resources are needed, the assumption your project management team used to create the requirements, and the basis for each estimate.

- **Updates to the project documents** You may have errors and omissions, change requests, and discoveries about and around the activities that you're estimating. If the activities or their attributes change, you'll have to update your original activity list to reflect these changes. Updates to the calendar are based on the creation of the activity resource requirements. If change requests enter the project, the resource availability and demand may shift, which could affect the resource calendar.

- **Resource breakdown structure** This is a hierarchical breakdown of the project resources by category and resource type. For example, you could have a category of equipment, a category of human resources, and a category of materials. Within each category, you could identify the types of equipment your project will use, the types of human resources, and the types of materials.

Estimating Activity Durations

How many times have you heard management ask, "Now how long will all of this take?" Countless times, right? And maybe right after that: "How much will all of this cost?" We'll talk about cost estimates in Chapter 7. For now, let's talk about time.

The answer to the question "How long will it take?" depends on the accuracy of the estimates, the consistency of the work, and other variables within the project. The best a project manager can do is to create honest estimates based on the information provided. Until the schedule is finalized, no one will know the duration of the project.

First, you identify the activities, sequence the activities, define the resources, and then estimate durations. These processes are needed to complete the project schedule and the project duration estimate. These four processes are iterated as more information becomes available. If the proposed schedule is acceptable, the project can move forward. If the proposed schedule takes too long, the scheduler can use a few strategies to compress the project. We'll discuss the art of scheduling in a few moments.

Activity duration estimates, like the activity list and the WBS, don't come from the project manager—they come from the people completing the work. The estimates may also undergo progressive elaboration. In this section, we'll examine the approach to completing activity duration estimates, the basis of these estimates, and allow for activity list updates.

Considering the Activity Duration Estimate Inputs

The importance of accurate estimates is paramount. The activity duration estimates will be used to create the project schedule and to predict when the project should end. Inaccurate estimates could cost the performing organization thousands of dollars in fines, missed opportunities, lost customers, or worse. To create accurate estimates, the project manager and the project team will rely on several inputs:

- **Schedule management plan** You'll need this as an input because it guides the process of estimating the activity durations.

- **Activity lists** You know this, right? Activity lists are the work elements necessary to create the deliverables.

- **Activity attributes** Effort is the amount of labor applied to a task. Duration, on the other hand, is how long the task is expected to take with the given amount of labor. For example, a task to unload a freight truck may take eight hours with two people assigned to the task. If the effort is increased by adding more labor to the task (in this instance, more people), then the duration of the task is decreased. Some activities, however, have a fixed duration and are not affected by the amount of labor assigned to the task. For example, installing a piece of software on a computer will take the same amount of time if one computer administrator is completing the work or if two computer administrators are doing it.

- **Activity resource requirements** Activity resource requirements define the resources (human or otherwise) needed to complete a particular activity. For example, a project to build a home will require lots of different resources: plumbers, electricians, architects, framers, and landscapers. The project manager would not, however, assign all of the different resources to every task, but only to the tasks that the resource was qualified to complete. Remember that resources also include equipment and materials, so those are identified as part of the activity resource requirements as well.

- **Resource calendars** The project manager will need to know when resources are, or are not, available for utilization on the project.

- **The project scope statement** Identification of the project constraints and assumptions is needed, since they may influence the estimates. The project scope statement provides this information.

- **Risk register** The risk register can help the project manager and the project team identify key activities and their associated risks. This information may influence the constraints and task relationships in the project. Should risks come true, there may also be consideration of the timing of risk responses. (I'll talk more about risk management in Chapter 11.)

- **Resource breakdown structure** The resource breakdown structure visualizes the categories of resources and their characteristics. Remember that resources may not be just people, but could also represent facilities, equipment, and materials.

- **Organizational process assets** Okay, the big one here is historical information. Historical information is always an excellent source of data on activity duration estimates. It can come from several sources, such as the following:

- Historical information can come from project files on other projects within the organization.

- Commercial duration-estimating databases can offer information on how long industry-specific activities should take. These databases should take into consideration the materials, the experience of the resources, and define the assumptions the predicted work duration is based upon.

- Project team members may recollect information regarding the expected duration of activities. While these inputs are valuable, they are generally less valuable than documented sources, such as other project files or the commercial databases.

- **Enterprise environmental factors**   Your organization may require the project manager to use duration-estimating datasets, productivity metrics based on your industry, or other commercially available information.

You'll need to consider the resource capabilities of your project team. Consider a task in an architectural firm. Reason says that a senior architect assigned to the task will complete it faster than a junior architect will. Material resources can also influence activity time. Consider predrilled cabinets versus cabinets that require the carpenter to drill each cabinet as it's installed. The predrilled cabinets allow the job to be completed faster.

The project manager should also reference the project management plan. Specifically, the project manager and the project team must evaluate the risk register. We'll discuss risk in detail in Chapter 11. Risks, good or bad, can influence the estimated duration of activities. The risks of each activity should be identified, analyzed, and then predicted as to their probability and impact. If risk mitigation tasks are added to the schedule, the mitigation activities will need their duration estimated and then sequenced into the schedule in the proper order.

Using Analogous Estimating

Analogous estimating relies on historical information to predict current activity durations. Analogous estimating is also known as top-down estimating and is a form of expert judgment. To use analogous estimating, activities from the historical project that are similar in nature are used to predict similar activities in the current project.

A project manager must consider if the work has been done before and, if so, what help the historical information provides. The project manager must consider the resources, project team members, and equipment that completed the activities in the previous project compared with the resources available for the current project. Ideally, the activities should be more than similar; they should be identical. And the resources that completed the work in the past should be the same resources used in completing the current work. When the only source of activity duration estimates is the project team members, instead of expert judgment and historical information, your estimates will be uncertain and inherently risky.

EXAM TIP Analogous estimating uses historical information and is more reliable than predictions from the project team members.

Applying Parametric Estimates

Quantitatively based durations use mathematical formulas to predict how long an activity will take based on the "quantities" of work to be completed. For example, a commercial printer needs to print 100,000 brochures. The workers include two press operators and two bindery experts to fold and package the brochures. Notice how the duration is how long the activity will take to complete, while the effort is the total number of hours (labor) invested because of the resources involved. The decomposed work, with quantitative factors, is shown in Table 6-1.

EXAM TIP Duration is how long an activity takes, while *effort* is the billable time for the labor to complete the activity. Consider an activity that is scheduled to last 40 hours. The project manager must consider the cost of the time of the person assigned to complete the project work. For example, a senior engineer may be able to complete the activity in 40 consecutive work hours, but the cost of this employee's time may be more than the value of the activity. A part-time employee may be able to complete the task in two segments of 20 hours, at a substantially lower rate.

Creating a Three-Point Estimate

How confident can a project manager be when it comes to estimating? If the project work has been done before in past projects, then the level of confidence in the duration estimate is probably high. But if the work has never been done before, there are lots of unknowns—and with them comes risk. To mitigate the risk, the project manager can use a three-point estimate. A three-point estimate requires that each activity have three estimates: optimistic, most likely, and pessimistic estimates. This is also known as simple averaging. Based on these three estimates, an average can be created to predict how long the activity should take (see Figure 6-4).

Workers	Units per Hour	Duration for 100,000	Effort
Press operators (two)	5000	20 hours	40 hours
Bindery experts (two)	4000	25 hours	50 hours
Totals		45 hours	90 hours

Table 6-1 Decomposed Work with Quantitative Factors

Figure 6-4
Three-point estimates use the formula (optimistic + most likely + pessimistic)/3 to predict an activity's duration.

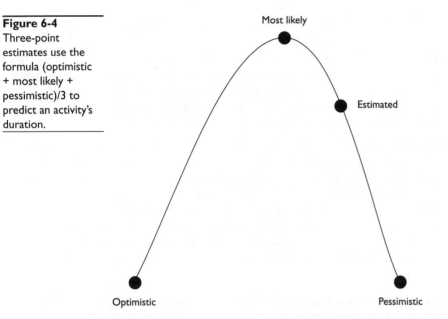

Most likely

Estimated

Optimistic

Pessimistic

EXAM TIP   If this sounds familiar to the Program Evaluation and Review Technique (PERT), you're correct. The formula for PERT is similar to the three-point estimate. PERT is (Optimistic + (4 × Most Likely) + Pessimistic)/6. The denominator is six in PERT because you're using six factors. This is also known as weighted averaging.

Factoring in Reserve Time

Parkinson's Law states: "Work expands so as to fill the time available for its completion." This little nugget of wisdom is oh-so-true. Consider a project team member who knows an activity should last 24 hours. The team member decides, in his own wisdom, to say that the activity will last 32 hours. These extra 8 hours, he figures, will allow plenty of time for the work to be completed should any unforeseen incidents pop up. The trouble is, however, that the task will magically expand to require the complete 32 hours. Why does this happen? Consider the following:

- **Hidden time**   Hidden time, the time factored in by the project team member, is secret. No one, especially the project manager, knows why the extra time has been factored into the activity. The team member can then "enjoy" the extra time to complete the task at his leisure.

- **Procrastination**   Most people put off starting a task until the last possible minute. The trouble with bloated, hidden time is that people may wait through the additional time they've secretly factored into the activity.

Unfortunately, if something does go awry in completing the activity, the work result is later than predicted.

- **Demands**   Project team members may be assigned to multiple projects with multiple demands. The requirement to move from project to project can shift focus, result in a loss of concentration, and require additional ramp-up time as workers shift from activity to activity. The demand for multitasking allows project team members to take advantage of hidden time.

- **On schedule**   Activities are typically completed on schedule or later, but rarely early. Workers who have bloated the activity duration estimates may finish their task ahead of when they promised, but they have a tendency to hold onto those results until the activity's due date. This is because workers aren't usually rewarded for completing work early. In addition, workers don't want to reveal the inaccuracies in their time estimates. Workers may believe future estimates may be based on actual work durations rather than estimates, so they'll "sandbag" the results to protect themselves—and finish "on schedule."

So what's a project manager to do? First off, the project manager should strive to incorporate historical information and expert judgment on which to predicate accurate estimates. Second, the project manager should stress a genuine need for accurate duration estimates. Finally, the project manager can incorporate a reserve time.

A *reserve time* is a percentage of the project duration or a preset number of work periods, and is usually added to the end of the project schedule or just in front of reaching project milestones. Reserve time may also be added to individual activity durations based on risk or uncertainty in the activity duration. When activities are completed late, the additional time for the activity is subtracted from the reserve time. As the project moves forward, the reserve time can be reduced or eliminated as the project manager sees fit. Reserve time decisions should be documented.

Evaluating the Estimates

Estimating activities provides two outputs:

- **Activity duration estimates**   Activity duration estimates reflect how long each activity will take to complete. Duration estimates should include an acknowledgment of the range of variance. For example, an activity whose duration is expected to be one week may have a range of variance of one week plus or minus three days. This means that the work can take up to eight days or as few as two days, assuming a five-day week.

- **Project documents updates**   Any assumptions made during the activity estimating process should be identified. In addition, any historical information, subject matter experts, or commercial estimating databases that were used should also be documented for future reference. During the estimating process, there may be discoveries of missing activities within the

PART II

activity list. The project manager should confirm that the new activities are reflected in the activity list for the project

Developing the Project Schedule

The project manager, the project team, and possibly even the key stakeholders, will examine the inputs previously described and apply the techniques discussed in this section to create a feasible schedule for the project. The point of the project schedule is to complete the project scope in the shortest possible time without incurring exceptional costs, risks, or a loss of quality.

Creating the project schedule is part of the planning process group. It is calendar-based and relies on both the project network diagram and the accuracy of time estimates. When the project manager creates the project schedule, she'll also reference the risk register. The identified risks and their associated responses can affect the sequence of the project work and when the project work can take place. In addition, if a risk comes to fruition, the risk event may affect the scheduling of the resources and the project completion date.

Applying Mathematical Analysis

Mathematical analysis is the process of factoring theoretical early and late start dates and theoretical early and late finish dates for each activity within the project network diagram (PND). The early and late dates are not the expected schedule, but rather a potential schedule based on the project constraints, the likelihood of success, the availability of resources, and other constraints.

The most common approach to calculating when a project may finish is by using the critical path method. It uses a "forward" and "backward" pass to reveal which activities are considered critical. Activities on the critical path may not be delayed; otherwise, the project end date will be delayed. The *critical path* is the path with the longest duration to completion. Activities not on the critical path have some float (also called slack) that allows some amount of delay without delaying the project end date.

EXAM TIP The critical path is used to determine which activities have no float. You can also use the critical path to determine the earliest date for when the project may be completed. There can be more than one critical path in a project, and it's possible for the critical path to change.

Calculating Float in a PND

Float, or slack, is the amount of time an activity can be delayed without postponing the project's completion. Technically, there are three different types of float:

- **Free float** This is the total time a single activity can be delayed without affecting the early start of any successor activities.

- **Total float**   This is the total time an activity can be delayed without affecting project completion.

- **Project float**   This is the total time the project can be delayed without passing the customer-expected completion date.

EXAM COACH   There are a couple of different approaches to calculating float. I'm sharing the approach that I learned and that I think is the best approach. You may have learned a different method that you prefer. You won't hurt my feelings if you use your method to get the same result as my method. What's most important is that you understand the concepts of forward and backward passes, and that you can find the critical path and float in a simple network diagram.

Most project management software will automatically calculate float. On the CAPM or PMP exam, however, candidates will be expected to calculate float manually. Don't worry—it's not too tough. The following describes the process.

Examine the PND and find the critical path. The critical path is typically the path with the longest duration and will always have zero float. The critical path is technically found once you complete the forward and backward passes. Start with the forward pass. After the backward pass, you can identify the critical and near-critical paths, as well as the float.

VIDEO   For a more detailed explanation, watch the *How to Calculate Float* video now.

1. The early start (ES) and early finish (EF) dates are calculated first by completing the forward pass. The ES of the first task is one. The EF for the first task is its ES, plus the task duration, minus one. Don't let the "minus one value" throw you. If Task A is scheduled to last three days, it would only take three days to complete the work, right? The ES is one, the duration is three, and the EF is three, because the activity would finish within three days, not four days. The following illustration shows the start of the forward pass:

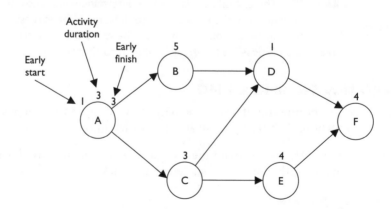

2. The ES of the next task(s) will be the EF for the previous activity, plus one. In other words, if Task A finishes on day 3, Task B and Task C can begin on day 4.

3. The EF for the next task(s) equals its ES plus the task duration, minus one. Sound familiar?

4. Now each task moves forward with the forward pass. Use caution when there are multiple predecessor activities; the EF with the largest value is carried forward. The following illustration shows the completed forward pass:

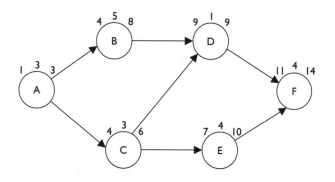

5. After the forward pass is completed, the backward pass starts at the end of the PND. The backward pass is concerned with the late finish (LF) and the late start (LS) of each activity. The LF for the last activity in the PND equals its EF value. The LS is calculated by subtracting the duration of the activity from its LF and then adding one. The one is added to accommodate the full day's work; it's just the opposite of subtracting the one day in the forward pass. Here's a tip: The last activity is on the critical path, so its LS will equal its ES.

6. The next predecessor activity's LF equals the LS of the successor activity, minus one. In other words, if Task F has an LS of 11, Task D and Task E will have an LF of 10. The following illustration shows the process of the backward pass:

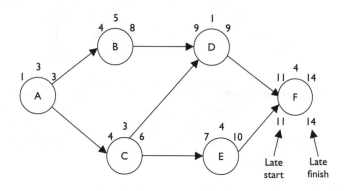

7. The LS is again calculated by subtracting the task's duration from the task's LF and then adding one. The following shows the completed backward pass:

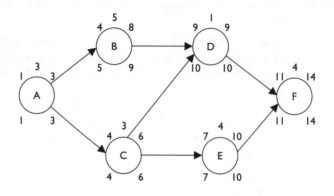

8. To officially calculate float, the ES is subtracted from the LS, or the EF is subtracted from the LF. Recall the total float is the amount of time a task can be delayed without affecting the project completion date. The next illustration shows the completed PND with the float exposed.

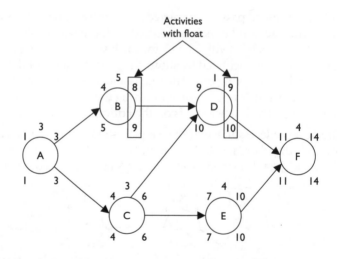

DIGITAL CONTENT I bet you're wishing you could try this one out for yourself, right? The Adobe PDF document titled "Chapter Six Float Exercise" includes a project network diagram that you can print and use to test your float-ability. You can also just create your own diagrams and practice finding float.

VIDEO For a more detailed explanation, watch the *Float Exercise Explained* video now.

Encountering Scheduling on the CAPM or PMP Exam

Out here in the real world, where you and I work every day, we likely aren't calculating float manually. On your PMI exam, however, you'll need to be able to calculate float. Why? You're proving that you understand the theory and application of managing project time. On your regular gig, you'll use your project management software to do this magic for you. You'll encounter float, scheduling, and critical path activities on the exam. You should count these questions as "gimmes" if you remember a few important rules:

- Always draw out the network diagram presented on your scratch paper. It may be used in several questions.

- Know how to calculate float. (The complete process was shown earlier in the "Calculating Float in a PND" section.)

- You may encounter questions that ask on what day of the week a project will end if no weekends or holidays are worked. No problem. Add up the critical path, divide by 5 (Monday through Friday), and then figure out which day of the week the activity will end on.

- You may see something like Figure 6-5 when it comes to scheduling. When three numbers are presented, think three-point estimate. Optimistic is the smallest number and pessimistic is the largest, so most likely, it's somewhere between the two. When a number is positioned directly over the tasks, it is the task duration. When a number is positioned to the upper-right of a task, this represents the EF date.

Applying Schedule Compression

Schedule compression is also a mathematical approach to scheduling. The trick with schedule compression, as its name implies, is calculating ways the project can get done sooner than expected. Consider a construction project. The project may be slated to last

Figure 6-5
Scheduling follows
many rules to
arrive at a project
completion date.

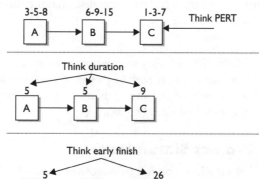

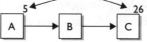

eight months, but due to the expected cold and nasty weather typical of month 7, the project manager needs to rearrange activities, where possible, to end the project as soon as possible.

In some instances, the relationship between activities cannot be changed due to hard logic or external dependencies. The relationships are fixed and must remain as scheduled. Now consider the same construction company that is promised a bonus if they can complete the work by the end of month 7. Now there's incentive to complete the work, but there's also the fixed relationship between activities.

To apply duration compression, the performing organization can rely on two different methods. These methods can be used independently or together, and are applied to activities or to the entire project based on need, risk, and cost. The methods are as follows:

- **Crashing** This approach adds more resources to activities on the critical path to complete the project earlier. In the crashing process, costs grow as the labor is added. Crashing doesn't always work. Consider activities that have a fixed duration and won't finish faster with additional resources. The project manager must also consider the expenses in relation to the gains of completing on time. For example, a construction company may have been promised a bonus to complete the work by a preset date, but the cost incurred to hit the targeted date may be more than the bonus.

- **Fast tracking** This method changes the relationship of activities. With fast tracking, activities that would normally be done in sequence are allowed to be done in parallel or with some overlap. Fast tracking can be accomplished by changing the relation of activities from FS (finish-to-start) to SS (start-to-start) or by adding lead time to downstream activities. For example, a construction company could change the relationship between painting the rooms and installing the carpet by adding lead time to the carpet installation task. Before the change, all of the rooms had to be painted before the carpet installers could begin. With the added lead time, the carpet can be installed hours after a room is painted. However, fast tracking can increase risk and may cause rework in the project. Can't you just imagine those workers getting fresh paint on the new carpet?

 EXAM TIP It's easy to remember the difference between these two actions. Crashing and cost both begin with C—we're adding resources, and too many people will "crash" into each other. Fast tracking is about speeding things up. However, haste can be risky.

Using a Project Simulation

Project simulations allow a project manager to examine the feasibility of the project schedule under different conditions, variables, and events. For example, the project manager can see what would happen to a project if activities were delayed, vendors missed shipment dates, or external events affected the project.

Simulations are often completed by use of the Monte Carlo analysis. The Monte Carlo analysis, named after the world-famous gambling district of Monaco, predicts how scenarios may work out, given any number of variables. The process doesn't actually churn out a specific answer, but a range of possible answers. When Monte Carlo is applied to a schedule, it can examine, for example, the optimistic completion date, the pessimistic completion date, and the most likely completion date for each activity in the project.

As you can imagine in a typical network diagram, there are likely thousands, if not millions, of combinations of tasks that complete early, late, or as expected. Monte Carlo analysis shuffles these combinations, usually through computer software, and offers a range of possible end dates coupled with an expected probability for achieving each end date.

In other words, Monte Carlo analysis is an odds-maker. The project manager chooses, or is at least influenced by, the end date with the highest odds of completion in ratio to the demands for completion by an expected time. The project manager can then predict with some certainty that the project has an 85 percent chance of completion by a specific date.

 EXAM TIP Monte Carlo analysis can be applied to more than just scheduling. It can also be applied to cost, project variables, and, most often, to risk analysis.

Simulations also provide time to factor in "what-if" questions, worst-case scenarios, and potential disasters. The end result of simulations is to create responses to the feasible situations. Then, should the situations come into play, the project team is ready with a planned response.

Using Resource-Leveling Heuristics

First off, a *heuristic* is a fancy way of saying "rule of thumb." A resource-leveling heuristic is a method to flatten the schedule when resources are overallocated. Resource leveling can be applied using different methods to accomplish different goals. One of the most common methods is to ensure that workers are not overextended on activities.

Resource leveling usually limits the total amount of labor a resource can contribute in a given period. For example, you may have a constraint that says your project team members can only work 25 hours per week on your project. If you've created a schedule that requires your project team members to work 40 hours per week on your project, then each team member is now overallocated on your project by 15 hours. So now you have to lop off 15 hours per week per resource, which increases the total duration of your project. There won't be more hours of labor, but it'll take longer on the calendar to do the same amount of work.

Another method for resource leveling is to take resources off of noncritical path activities and apply them to critical path activities to ensure that the project end date is met. This method takes advantage of available slack and balances the expected duration of the noncritical path with the expected duration of the critical path. When you're doing resource leveling on noncritical path activities, it's also known as resource smoothing.

Finally, some resources may be scarce to the project. Consider a highly skilled technician or consultant who is only available on a particular date to contribute to the project. These resources are scheduled from the project end date, rather than from the start date. This is known as reverse resource-allocation scheduling.

Using the Critical Chain Method

The critical chain method (CCM) aims to eliminate Parkinson's Law by eliminating bottlenecks that hold up project progression. In the critical chain method, deadlines associated with individual tasks are removed, and the only date that matters is the promised due date of the project deliverable. CCM works to modify the project schedule based on the availability of project resources rather than the pure sequence of events, as in the critical path method.

CCM first requires the discovery of the critical path, but then applies available resources to determine the true resource-limited schedule. Based on the availability of resources to complete the project work, the critical path is often different than what it would have been using the pure critical path method.

CCM scheduling evaluates each activity's latest possible start and finish dates. This allows project managers to manage the buffer activity duration—that is, the activities that are not on the critical path, but whose completion contributes to the start of critical path activities. In other words, the focus is on completing each activity in order to complete the entire project by the promised end date.

The path in the network diagram that is resource-constrained is considered the critical chain. To accommodate the resource constraints, you can add buffers of time, called *feeder buffers*, between noncritical chain activities before they connect to the critical chain. In other words, you can pause work that's not on the critical chain so things don't get crunched for the resources on the critical chain. You can also add a buffer of time at the end of the project just as you would in using management reserve time.

Using Project Management Software

When it comes to project management software, take your pick: The market is full of it. Project management applications are tools, not replacements, for the project management processes. Many of the software tools today automate the processes of scheduling, activity sequencing, work authorization, and other activities. The performing organization must weigh the cost of the PMIS (project management information system) against the benefits the project managers will actually see.

Relying on a Project Coding Structure

The coding structure identifies the work packages within the WBS and is then applied to the PND. This allows the project manager, the project team, experts, and even key stakeholders, to extract areas of the project to examine and evaluate. For example, a project to create a catalog for a parts distributor may follow multiple paths to completion. Each path to completion has its own "family" of numbers that relate to each activity on the path, as outlined in Table 6-2.

Considering the Outputs of Schedule Development

After all the challenges of examining, sequencing, and calculating the project activities, a working schedule is created. Schedule development, like most project management planning processes, moves through progressive elaboration. As the project moves forward, discoveries, risk events, or other conditions may require the project schedule to be adjusted. In this section, we'll discuss the project schedule and how it is managed.

Examining the Project Schedule

The project schedule includes, at a minimum, a date when the project begins and a date when the project is expected to end. The project schedule is considered "proposed" until the resources needed to complete the project work are ascertained. In addition to

Table 6-2 Possible Paths in Creating a Catalog	**Path**	**Coding for Path**	**Typical Activities**
	Artwork	4.2	Concept (4.2.1) Logos (4.2.2) Font design (4.2.3)
	Photography	4.3	Product models (4.3.1) Airbrushing (4.3.2) Selection (4.3.3)
	Content	4.4	Message (4.4.1) Copywriting (4.4.2) Editing (4.4.3) Rewrites (4.4.4)
	Print	4.5	Signatures (4.5.1) Plates (4.5.2) Four-color printing (4.5.3)
	Bind	4.6	Assembly (4.6.1) Bindery (4.6.2) Trimming (4.6.3) Shrink-wrap (4.6.4)
	Distribution	4.7	Packaging (4.7.1) Labeling (4.7.2) Shipping (4.7.3)

the schedule, the project manager should include all of the supporting details. Project schedules can be presented in many different formats, such as:

- **Project network diagram (PND)** This illustrates the flow of work, the relationships among activities, the critical path, and the expected project end date. PNDs, when used as the project schedule, should have dates associated with each project activity to show when the activity is expected to start and end.

- **Bar charts** These show the start and end dates for the project and the activity duration against a calendar. They are easy to read. Scheduling bar charts are also called Gantt charts.

- **Milestone charts** These plot the high-level deliverables and external interfaces, such as a customer walkthrough, against a calendar. Milestone charts are similar to a Gantt chart, but with less detail regarding individual activities. The following is an example of a milestone chart:

Milestone	July	Aug	Sep	Oct	Nov	Dec
Customer sign-off	△ ▼					
Architect signature		△	▼			
Foundation			△			
Framing					△ ▼	
Roofing						△

Legend
△ Planned
▼ Actual

Utilizing the Schedule Management Plan

The schedule management plan is a subsidiary plan of the overall project plan. It is used to control changes to the schedule. A formal schedule management plan has procedures that control how changes to the project plan can be proposed, accounted for, and then implemented. An informal schedule management plan may consider changes on an instance-by-instance basis.

Updating the Resource Requirements

Due to resource leveling, additional resources may need to be added to the project. For example, a proposed leveling may extend the project beyond an acceptable completion date. To reach the project end date, the project manager elects to add additional resources to the critical path activities. The resources the project manager adds should be documented, the associated costs accounted for, and everything approved.

Controlling the Project Schedule

Schedule control is part of integrated change management, as discussed in Chapter 4. Throughout a typical project, events may require updates to the project schedule. Schedule control is concerned with three processes:

- The project manager works with the factors that can cause changes in the schedule in an effort to confirm that the changes are agreed upon. Factors can include project team members, stakeholders, management, customers, and project conditions.

- The project manager examines the work results and conditions to determine whether the schedule has changed.

- The project manager manages the actual change in the schedule.

Managing the Inputs to Schedule Control

Schedule control, the process of managing changes to the project schedule, is based on several inputs:

- Project management plan
- Project schedule
- Work performance data
- Project calendars
- Schedule data
- Organizational process assets

Applying a Schedule Control System

A schedule control system is a formal approach to managing changes to the project schedule. It considers the conditions, reasons, requests, costs, and risks of making changes. It includes methods of tracking changes, approval levels based on thresholds, and the documentation of approved or declined changes. The schedule control system process is part of integrated change management.

Measuring Project Performance

Poor performance may result in schedule changes. Consider a project team that is completing its work on time, but all of the work results are unacceptable. The project team may be rushing through their assignments to meet their deadline. To compensate for this, the project may be changed to allow for additional quality inspections and more time for activity completion. Project performance is often based on earned value management, which we'll discuss in Chapter 7.

Examining the Schedule Variance

The project manager must actively monitor the variances between when activities are scheduled to end and when they actually end. An accumulation of differences between scheduled and actual dates may result in a schedule variance.

The project manager must also pay attention to the completion of activities on paths with float, not just the critical path. Consider a project that has eight different paths to completion. The project manager should first identify the critical path, but should also identify the float on each path. The paths should be arranged and monitored in a hierarchy from the path with smallest float to the path with the largest float. As activities are completed, the float of each path should be monitored to identify any paths that may be slipping from the scheduled end dates.

Updating the Project Schedule

So what happens when a schedule change occurs? The project manager must ensure that the project schedule is updated to reflect the change, document the change, and follow the guidelines within the schedule management plan. Any formal processes, such as notifying stakeholders or management, should be followed.

Revisions are a special type of project schedule change that cause the project start date and, more likely, the project end date to be changed. They typically stem from project scope changes. Because of the additional work the new scope requires, additional time is needed to complete the project.

Schedule delays, for whatever reason, may be so drastic that the entire project has to be *rebaselined*—that is, all of the historical information up to the point of the rebaseline is eliminated. Rebaselining is a worst-case scenario and should only be used when adjusting for drastic, long delays. Schedule revision is the preferred, and most common, approach to changing the project end date.

EXAM TIP You only want to rebaseline in extreme, drastic scenarios.

Applying Corrective Action

Corrective action is any method applied to bring the project schedule back into alignment with the original dates and goals for the project end date. Corrective actions are efforts to ensure that future performance meets the expected performance levels. It includes the following:

- Ensuring that the work packages are complete as scheduled. Completing a work package early isn't always a good thing.

- Extraordinary measures to ensure that work packages complete with as little delay as possible.

- Root-cause analysis of schedule variances.

- Implementing measures to recover from schedule delays.

Chapter Summary

All projects take time—time to plan the project, do the work, control the work, and confirm that the work has been done according to plan. Of course, there are all those other things that eat into a project's schedule: change request reviews, corrective and preventive actions, defect repair, defect repair review, and scope verification. When a project manager first looks at planning the project work, she and her project team will consider all of the activities that will need to be completed based on the project WBS.

Once all the project work has been identified and the activity list has been generated, it's time to put the activities into the order necessary to reach the project completion. This means the activity attributes are considered. Those activities that must happen in a particular order are using hard logic, while those activities that don't have to happen sequentially can use soft logic. The sequencing of the project activities happens with the project management team.

Putting the activities in the order in which they'll happen leads to the creation of a project network diagram. It's pretty. The PND most likely will be using the precedence diagramming method—that's where you can clearly identify the predecessors and successors within the project. The relationships between the activities signal the conditions that must be true to allow the work to progress.

Once the work has been organized and visualized, it's time to staff it. This is project resource estimating, which also contributes to the cost of the project. Resource utilization considers not only the people that your project will need, but also the materials and equipment. This activity considers the quantity of resources the project demands and when the resources are available. This is a tricky business in large projects, so rolling wave planning may be incorporated into the project.

Of course, management and the project stakeholders will want to know how long the project work will take to complete. Now that the network diagram has been created and the resources have been identified, the project management team can more accurately estimate the project duration. The project manager can use the identified labor, which is commonly done, or the project manager can rely on analogous estimating, which isn't as accurate as bottom-up estimating. In some instances, the project manager can also use parametric estimating to predict the project duration.

As the project manager examines the network diagram, he'll want to find opportunities to shift resources and determine where delays will affect the project end date. Of course, I'm talking about the critical path—the path with no float and whose activities cannot, better not, be delayed, or the project end date will go beyond what's been scheduled. Activities not on the critical path have float and can often be delayed if needed. You'll have a few questions on float, and I encourage you to watch the videos to nail down the float process.

A project manager must control the project schedule. Sometimes this means compressing the project schedule. Recall that crashing adds resources to the project work, but crashing adds cost. The project manager can only crash the project work if the activities are effort-driven. Activities that are of fixed duration, such as printing a million booklets on a particular printing press, won't get done faster just because the project manager adds labor to the activities. The printing press can only print so many booklets per hour. Other activities can benefit from fast tracking; this approach allows phases to overlap, but increases the project risk.

Key Terms

Activity list The primary output of breaking down the WBS work packages.

Alternative analysis The identification of more than one solution. Consider roles, materials, tools, and approaches to the project work.

Analogous estimating A somewhat unreliable estimating approach that relies on historical information to predict what current activity durations should be. Analogous estimating is more reliable, however, than team member recollections. Analogous estimating is also known as top-down estimating and is a form of expert judgment.

Bottom-up estimating The most accurate time-and-cost estimating approach a project manager can use. This estimating approach starts at "the bottom" of the project and considers every activity, its predecessor and successor activities, and the exact amount of resources needed to complete each activity.

Control account A WBS entry that considers the time, cost, and scope measurements for that deliverable within the WBS. The estimated performance is compared against the actual performance to measure overall performance for the deliverables within that control account. The specifics of a control account are documented in a control account plan.

Control threshold A predetermined range of acceptable variances, such as +/–10 percent off schedule. Should the variance exceed the threshold, then project control processes and corrected actions will be enacted.

Crashing A schedule compression approach that adds more resources to activities on the critical path to complete the project earlier. When crashing a project, costs are added because the associated labor and sometimes resources (such as faster equipment) cause costs to increase.

Critical chain method A network analysis approach where the deadlines associated with individual tasks are removed and the only date that matters is the promised due date of the project deliverable. CCM works to modify the project schedule based on the availability of project resources rather than on the pure sequence of events, as in the critical path method.

Critical path The path in the project network diagram that cannot be delayed, otherwise the project completion date will be late. There can be more than one critical path. Activities in the critical path have no float.

Discretionary dependencies These dependencies are the preferred order of activities. Project managers should use these relationships at their discretion and should document the logic behind the decision. Discretionary dependencies allow activities to happen in a preferred order because of best practices, conditions unique to the project work, or external events. Also known as preferential or soft logic.

Early finish The earliest a project activity can finish. Used in the forward pass procedure to discover the critical path and the project float.

Early start The earliest a project activity can begin. Used in the forward pass procedure to discover the critical path and the project float.

External dependencies As the name implies, these are dependencies outside of the project's control. Examples include the delivery of equipment from a vendor, the deliverable of another project, or the decision of a committee, lawsuit, or expected new law.

Fast tracking A schedule compression method that changes the relationship of activities. With fast tracking, activities that would normally be done in sequence are allowed to be done in parallel or with some overlap. Fast tracking can be accomplished by changing the relation of activities from FS to SS or even FF or by adding lead time to downstream activities. However, fast tracking does add risk to the project.

Finish-to-finish An activity relationship type that requires the current activity to be finished before its successor can finish.

Finish-to-start An activity relationship type that requires the current activity to be finished before its successor can start.

Fragnet A representation of a project network diagram that is often used for outsourced portions of a project, repetitive work within a project, or a subproject. Also called a subnet.

Free float   This is the total time a single activity can be delayed without affecting the early start of its immediately following successor activities.

Hard logic   Logic that describes activities that must happen in a particular order. For example, the dirt must be excavated before the foundation can be built. The foundation must be in place before the framing can begin. Also known as a mandatory dependency.

Internal dependencies   Internal relationships to the project or the organization. For example, the project team must create the software as part of the project's deliverable before the software can be tested for quality control.

Lag time   Positive time that moves two or more activities further apart.

Late finish   The latest a project activity can finish. Used in the backward pass procedure to discover the critical path and the project float.

Late start   The latest a project activity can begin. Used in the backward pass procedure to discover the critical path and the project float.

Lead time   Negative time that allows two or more activities to overlap where ordinarily these activities would be sequential.

Management reserve   A percentage of the project duration to combat Parkinson's Law. When project activities become late, their lateness is subtracted from the management reserve.

Mandatory dependencies   These dependencies are the natural order of activities. For example, you can't begin building your house until your foundation is in place. These relationships are called hard logic.

Monte Carlo analysis   A project simulation approach named after the world-famous gambling district in Monaco. This predicts how scenarios may work out, given any number of variables. The process doesn't actually churn out a specific answer, but a range of possible answers. When Monte Carlo analysis is applied to a schedule, it can examine, for example, the optimistic completion date, the pessimistic completion date, and the most likely completion date for each activity in the project and then predict a mean for the project schedule.

Parametric estimate   A quantitatively based duration estimate that uses mathematical formulas to predict how long an activity will take based on the quantities of work to be completed.

Parkinson's Law   A theory that states: "Work expands so as to fill the time available for its completion." It is considered with time estimating, because bloated or padded activity estimates will fill the amount of time allotted to the activity.

Planning package   A WBS entry located below a control account and above the work packages. A planning package signifies that there is more planning that needs to be completed for this specific deliverable.

Precedence diagramming method A network diagram that shows activities in nodes and the relationship between each activity. Predecessors come before the current activity, and successors come after the current activity.

Project calendars Calendars that identify when the project work will occur.

Project float This is the total time the project can be delayed without passing the customer-expected completion date.

Project network diagram A diagram that visualizes the flow of the project activities and their relationships to other project activities.

Refinement An update to the work breakdown structure.

Resource breakdown structure (RBS) This is a hierarchical breakdown of the project resources by category and resource type. For example, you could have a category of equipment, a category of human resources, and a category of materials. Within each category, you could identify the types of equipment your project will use, the types of human resources, and the types of materials.

Resource calendars Calendars that identify when project resources are available for the project work.

Resource-leveling heuristic A method to flatten the schedule when resources are overallocated. Resource leveling can be applied using different methods to accomplish different goals. One of the most common methods is to ensure that workers are not overextended on activities.

Rolling wave planning The imminent work is planned in detail, while the work in the future is planned at a high level. This is a form of progressive elaboration.

Schedule management plan A subsidiary plan in the project management plan. It defines how the project schedule will be created, estimated, controlled, and managed.

Soft logic The activities don't necessarily have to happen in a specific order. For example, you could install the light fixtures first, then the carpet, and then paint the room. The project manager could use soft logic to change the order of the activities if so desired.

Start-to-finish An activity relationship that requires an activity to start so that its successor can finish. This is the most unusual of all the activity relationship types.

Start-to-start An activity relationship type that requires the current activity to start before its successor can start.

Subnet A representation of a project network diagram that is often used for outsourced portions of projects, repetitive work within a project, or a subproject. Also called a fragnet.

Template A previous project that can be adapted for the current project and forms that are pre-populated with organizational-specific information.

Three-point estimate   An estimating technique for each activity that requires optimistic, most likely, and pessimistic estimates to be created. Based on these three estimates, an average can be created to predict how long the activity should take.

Total float   This is the total time an activity can be delayed without delaying project completion.

Work package   The smallest item in the work breakdown structure.

Questions

1. You are the project manager of the HGF Project. You would like to use a portion of the activity list from the HGB Project, which is similar to your current project. The portion of the activity list from the HGB Project is best described as which one of the following?

   A. Rolling wave planning

   B. Analogous estimating

   C. A template

   D. Expert judgment

2. You are the project manager of a large project for your organization. Much of the project will center on new software which you'll be installing on 4500 laptops in stages. Because of the likelihood of change, you've recommended a rolling wave planning approach. Which one of the following is the best example of rolling wave planning?

   A. Using expert judgment for the current project

   B. Using a portion of the activity list from a previous project

   C. Breaking down the project scope

   D. Planning the immediate portions of the project in detail and the future project portions at a higher level

3. You are working with your project team to break down the project work into activities. Which component in the WBS must be broken down to get to the schedule activities?

   A. Project scope

   B. Work packages

   C. Planning packages

   D. Product scope

4. You and the project team have created the work breakdown structure based on the project scope and requirements. Your next step is to create the project's activity list. Which one of the following will NOT be included in the activity list created with the project management team?

   A. Activities that are not part of the project scope

   B. Quality control activities

   C. Activities to create the work packages

   D. Physical terms, such as linear feet of pipe to be installed

5. Mary has created an activity list with her project team. She has included activity attributes for each of the activities in her project activity list. Of the following, which one is not an example of an activity attribute that Mary likely included?

   A. Scope verification processes

   B. Predecessor activities

   C. Leads and lags

   D. Geographic area where the work must take place

6. Your project team agrees that the server operating system must first be installed before the application can be installed. This best describes which one of the following?

   A. Hard logic

   B. Soft logic

   C. Start-to-start relationship

   D. Finish-to-finish relationship

7. You are working with your project team to schedule activities for your construction project. You have scheduled the painting activity to be completed before the carpet installation activity may begin. The relationship between the painting activity and carpet installation activity can best be described as which one of the following?

   A. Lag

   B. Lead

   C. Finish-to-start

   D. Start-to-finish

8. You are the project manager for your organization, and the following illustration represents your project. Based on the following illustration. How long will the project last?

   A. 15 days

   B. 12 days

   C. 14 days

   D. 41 days

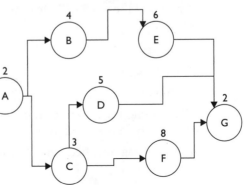

9. Beth is the project manager of her company and she's asked you to help her with project schedule network analysis. Examine the illustration to the right. If Activity B is delayed by two days, how late will the project be?

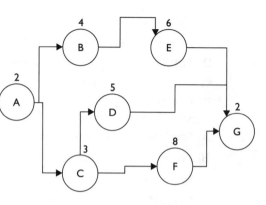

A. The project will not be late because Activity B may use float.

B. The project will be late by one day.

C. The project will be late by two days.

D. The project will be late by four days.

10. Ronald is the project manager for his company. He has created a project network diagram for the activities in the activity list and he's trying now to begin the process of float determination. He's asked for your help. Examine the following illustration. Which path is the critical path?

A. ABFGJL

B. ACFGJL

C. ADEHJL

D. ADIKL

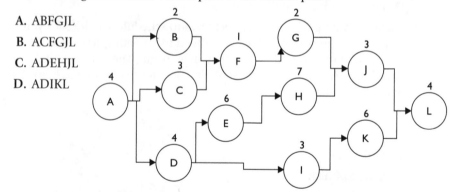

11. Consider a project that is to begin work on a Monday and a project team that will not work any weekends. The critical path of the project is 17 days. On what day of the week will the project be completed?

A. Monday

B. Tuesday

C. Wednesday

D. Thursday

12. Mike, a project manager in your company, is falling behind on the project schedule. He has elected to crash the project. What is crashing?

A. Adding lag time between all project activities

    B. Adding lead time between all project activities

    C. Adding additional project resources to the project work

    D. Removing all unneeded project deliverables

13. You are the project manager of the PJG Project for your company. This project is similar to a project you completed a few months ago and you'd like to reference the older project for information. Which estimating technique uses a similar project to predict how long the current project will take to complete?

    A. Analogous estimating

    B. Parametric estimating

    C. Organizational process assets

    D. Bottom-up estimating

14. You are using a three-point estimate for your project. Howard reports that his optimistic estimate is 16 hours, his most likely estimate is 24 hours, and the pessimistic estimate is 65 hours. What is the estimated duration for Howard's activity?

    A. You won't know until Howard actually does the work.

    B. 105 hours.

    C. 24 hours.

    D. 35 hours.

15. The framing activity cannot begin until the concrete has cured for 36 hours. The time between the concrete activity and the framing activity is best described as which one of the following?

    A. Hard logic

    B. Lag time

    C. Lead time

    D. Finish-to-start relationship

16. You are the project manager of the Data Warehouse Project. You've just recently created the project network diagram and you now want to identify the critical path. Which one of the following best describes the critical path?

    A. It is always one path with no float.

    B. It determines the earliest the project can finish.

    C. It has the most activities.

    D. It has the most important project activities.

17. Management has asked that you create the schedule management plan to identify the different processes and procedures your project will require. During the creation of the plan, you need to identify schedule control and its components. Schedule control is part of which project management process?

    A. Change control

    B. Cost control

    C. WBS refinements

    D. Integrated change control

18. Terry is the project manager of the network update project and the project stakeholders have requested that four new servers be added to the project. This addition will cause changes in the project costs and schedule. Which system can manage changes to the project schedule?

    A. Change control system

    B. Schedule change control system

    C. Integrated change control

    D. Change control board

19. Which schedule development tool does not consider the availability of the project resources, only when the work may take place in the project?

    A. The critical path method

    B. The critical chain method

    C. Schedule compression

    D. Arrow on the node method

20. You are working with your project team to respond to some delays in the project schedule. You have elected to crash the project schedule and management wants to know what effect this will have on the project as a whole. What happens when a project manager elects to crash a project?

    A. The project will end early.

    B. The project will end on time.

    C. The project costs will increase.

    D. The project team morale will decrease.

Questions and Answers

1. You are the project manager of the HGF Project. You would like to use a portion of the activity list from the HGB Project, which is similar to your current project. The portion of the activity list from the HGB Project is best described as which one of the following?

    A. Rolling wave planning

    B. Analogous estimating

    C. A template

    D. Expert judgment

C. This is an example of using the previous project as a template. A, rolling wave planning, is incorrect because rolling wave planning describes the detailed planning of the imminent project work, and the high-level planning of work is further away in the project schedule. B is incorrect. Analogous estimating describes the method of using a similar project to create the current project's time and/or cost estimate. D is incorrect because expert judgment is using an expert to provide needed information for the current project.

2. You are the project manager of a large project for your organization. Much of the project will center on new software which you'll be installing on 4500 laptops in stages. Because of the likelihood of change, you've recommended a rolling wave planning approach. Which one of the following is the best example of rolling wave planning?

A. Using expert judgment for the current project

B. Using a portion of the activity list from a previous project

C. Breaking down the project scope

D. Planning the immediate portions of the project in detail and the future project portions at a higher level

D. Rolling wave planning is the planning of the immediate portions of the project in detail and the future work at a higher level. A is incorrect because expert judgment is using an expert to help the project manager make informed decisions within the project. B describes using a template for the current project. C is the process of creating the WBS by breaking down the project scope.

3. You are working with your project team to break down the project work into activities. Which component in the WBS must be broken down to get to the schedule activities?

A. Project scope

B. Work packages

C. Planning packages

D. Product scope

B. The work packages are broken down into schedule activities. A, the project scope, is incorrect because this is the root of the WBS. C, planning packages, is incorrect because the planning packages represent portions of the WBS where known work content does not have schedule activities. D is incorrect because the product scope describes the thing or service the project will create.

4. You and the project team have created the work breakdown structure based on the project scope and requirements. Your next step is to create the project's activity list. Which one of the following will NOT be included in the activity list created with the project management team?

A. Activities that are not part of the project scope

B. Quality control activities

C. Activities to create the work packages

D. Physical terms, such as linear feet of pipe to be installed

A. The activity list must not include any activities that are not part of the project scope. B, C, and D are all incorrect because these activities and terms are included in the activity list.

5. Mary has created an activity list with her project team. She has included activity attributes for each of the activities in her project activity list. Of the following, which one is not an example of an activity attribute that Mary likely included?

A. Scope verification processes

B. Predecessor activities

C. Leads and lags

D. Geographic area where the work must take place

A. Scope verification leads to acceptance decisions with the project customer, but it is not part of the activity attributes. B, C, and D are all part of the activity attributes that Mary may include.

6. Your project team agrees that the server operating system must first be installed before the application can be installed. This best describes which one of the following?

A. Hard logic

B. Soft logic

C. Start-to-start relationship

D. Finish-to-finish relationship

A. The operating system must be installed before the application, so this is an example of hard logic. B is incorrect because soft logic describes a scenario in which the activities can happen in any order. C and D are incorrect because these activities cannot start at the same time nor may they finish at the same time.

7. You are working with your project team to schedule activities for your construction project. You have scheduled the painting activity to be completed before the carpet installation activity may begin. The relationship between the painting activity and carpet installation activity can best be described as which one of the following?

A. Lag

B. Lead

C. Finish-to-start

D. Start-to-finish

C. The painting activity must finish first, and then the carpet installation activity can begin. A, lag, is incorrect because this describes the waiting time between project activities. B, lead, is also incorrect because this describes a schedule compression technique to move project activities closer together. D, start-to-finish, is a relationship between activities, typically used in just-in-time scheduling, but that is not what is described in this example.

8. You are the project manager for your organization, and the following illustration represents your project. Based on the following illustration. How long will the project last?

A. 15 days

B. 12 days

C. 14 days

D. 41 days

A. The project will last 15 days. The path ACFG is the critical path that will take 15 days to complete. B and C are both representative of paths that are less than the critical path, so these answers are incorrect. D, 41 days, is the sum of the number of days of labor if you added the duration of each project activity in the project. The total of 41 days, however, is not an accurate calculation of the total number of days to complete the project based on the critical path.

9. Beth is the project manager of her company and she's asked you to help her with project schedule network analysis. Examine the illustration to the right. If Activity B is delayed by two days, how late will the project be?

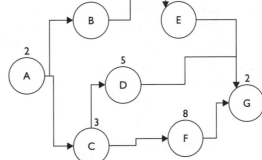

A. The project will not be late because Activity B may use float.

B. The project will be late by one day.

C. The project will be late by two days.

D. The project will be late by four days.

B. If activity B is delayed by two days, the total duration of the project changes to 16 total days—one more day than the critical path will allow. A, C, and D are all incorrect calculations for this project. For more information, see the PMBOK, Section 6.5.2.2.

10. Ronald is the project manager for his company. He has created a project network diagram for the activities in the activity list and he's trying now to begin the process of float determination. He's asked for your help. Examine the following illustration. Which path is the critical path?

A. ABFGJL

B. ACFGJL

C. ADEHJL

D. ADIKL

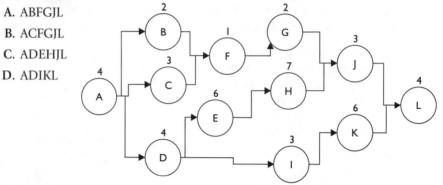

C. ADEHJL is the critical path because this one takes the longest to complete. A, B, and D are examples of paths that have float, so they are not on the critical path.

11. Consider a project that is to begin work on a Monday and a project team that will not work any weekends. The critical path of the project is 17 days. On what day of the week will the project be completed?

A. Monday

B. Tuesday

C. Wednesday

D. Thursday

B. The project will complete on a Tuesday. This can be quickly determined by counting each set of Monday through Friday as five days. Three weeks allows the project to end on day 17, a Tuesday. A, C, and D are incorrect.

12. Mike, a project manager in your company, is falling behind on the project schedule. He has elected to crash the project. What is crashing?

A. Adding lag time between all project activities

B. Adding lead time between all project activities

C. Adding additional project resources to the project work

D. Removing all unneeded project deliverables

C. Crashing is when a project manager elects to add resources to the project work in an attempt to compress the project schedule. Crashing adds costs to the project. A would cause the project duration to increase. B, adding lead time, is an example of fast tracking. D is not a valid choice.

13. You are the project manager of the PJG Project for your company. This project is similar to a project you completed a few months ago and you'd like to reference the older project for information. Which estimating technique uses a similar project to predict how long the current project will take to complete?

    A. Analogous estimating

    B. Parametric estimating

    C. Organizational process assets

    D. Bottom-up estimating

    A. Analogous estimating uses an analogy between similar projects to determine the current project's duration. B, parametric estimating, uses a parameter—such as 10 hours per unit installed—to predict the project duration. C is not a valid answer. D, bottom-up estimating, accounts for every work package in the WBS and the total amount of time for each deliverable. It is the most reliable time-estimating technique, but also takes the longest to create.

14. You are using a three-point estimate for your project. Howard reports that his optimistic estimate is 16 hours, his most likely estimate is 24 hours, and the pessimistic estimate is 65 hours. What is the estimated duration for Howard's activity?

    A. You won't know until Howard actually does the work.

    B. 105 hours.

    C. 24 hours.

    D. 35 hours.

    D. A three-point estimate takes the sum of the optimistic, pessimistic, and most likely estimates and divides it by three. A is not a reflection of the estimated duration. B and C do not reflect the result of a three-point estimate.

15. The framing activity cannot begin until the concrete has cured for 36 hours. The time between the concrete activity and the framing activity is best described as which one of the following?

    A. Hard logic

    B. Lag time

    C. Lead time

    D. Finish-to-start relationship

    B. The framing activity cannot begin immediately after the concrete activity; there is waiting time, which is commonly known as lag time. A, hard logic, describes the order in which activities must happen; it does not describe the time between activities. C, lead time, would actually allow activities to overlap. D, finish-to-start, does describe the relationship between the concrete and the framing activities, but it does not answer the question.

16. You are the project manager of the Data Warehouse Project. You've just recently created the project network diagram and you now want to identify the critical path. Which one of the following best describes the critical path?

   A. It is always one path with no float.

   B. It determines the earliest the project can finish.

   C. It has the most activities.

   D. It has the most important project activities.

   B. The critical path reveals the earliest that a project may finish. A is incorrect because the project may have more than one critical path. C is incorrect because the critical path may have fewer activities than other paths in the project, but may still take longer to complete. D is also incorrect because the critical path does not reflect the importance of the path's activities, just their duration.

17. Management has asked that you create the schedule management plan to identify the different processes and procedures your project will require. During the creation of the plan, you need to identify schedule control and its components. Schedule control is part of which project management process?

   A. Change control

   B. Cost control

   C. WBS refinements

   D. Integrated change control

   D. Schedule control is part of the integrated change control process. A, B, and C are incorrect because neither completely answers the question.

18. Terry is the project manager of the network update project and the project stakeholders have requested that four new servers be added to the project. This addition will cause changes in the project costs and schedule. Which system can manage changes to the project schedule?

   A. Change control system

   B. Schedule change control system

   C. Integrated change control

   D. Change control board

   B. The only system that deals directly with schedule is B, the schedule change control system. A is not a valid choice. C, integrated change control, actually describes a project process. D is a group that determines scope changes and their effect on the project constraints.

19. Which schedule development tool does not consider the availability of the project resources, only when the work may take place in the project?

A. The critical path method

B. The critical chain method

C. Schedule compression

D. Arrow on the node method

A. The critical path method only considers when the work may take place and not the availability of the resources. B, the critical chain method, does consider when the resources are available. C and D are not valid choices for this question.

20. You are working with your project team to respond to some delays in the project schedule. You have elected to crash the project schedule and management wants to know what effect this will have on the project as a whole. What happens when a project manager elects to crash a project?

A. The project will end early.

B. The project will end on time.

C. The project costs will increase.

D. The project team morale will decrease.

C. Crashing adds cost to the project because it adds labor, and labor costs money. A and B are incorrect because crashing a project does not necessarily ensure that the project will end early or on time. D is also incorrect because there's no evidence that the team morale will decrease if the project manager elects to crash the project.

Managing Project Costs

7

In this chapter, you will

- Plan for project cost management
- Estimate the project costs
- Administer the project budget
- Manage project cost control
- Work with earned value management

Money. Cash. Greenbacks. Dead presidents. It's all the same thing when you get down to it: Projects require finances to get from start to completion, and it's often the project manager's job to estimate, control, and account for the finances a project demands. Projects consume the project budget during execution, when all of those project management plans we've discussed are put into action, and the project budget is monitored and controlled during, well, the monitoring and controlling processes.

What's that you say? You don't have any control over the monies your project requires? Management gives you a predetermined budget, and it's up to you to make it all work out? Yikes! While this book centers on your Certified Associate in Project Management (CAPM) and Project Management Professional (PMP) examinations, that's always one of the scariest things I hear. Or is it? If management's decision is based on previous projects, business analysts' research, or should-cost estimates from experts, then it's not so scary. I'll give you this much: A predetermined project budget is always a constraint, and it's rarely fun for the project manager.

And what about those projects that don't have any monies assigned to the project work? You know… the projects where the project scope is completed just by the project team's work, and there really aren't any materials or items to purchase. That's okay—there are still costs associated with the project, because someone, somewhere, is paying for the project team's time. Salaries can also be considered a project cost. After all, time is money.

 VIDEO For a more detailed explanation, watch the *Using Earned Value Management* video now.

Finally—and here's the big whammy—it doesn't really matter where your project monies come from, whether you actually control them, and the processes your organization uses to spend them. Your Project Management Institute (PMI) exam makes you understand all of the appropriate processes and procedures of how projects are estimated, budgeted, and then financially controlled. And that's what we'll discuss in this chapter.

You know by now, I'm assuming, that there are 47 project management processes. Guess how many of them center on cost? Four: planning cost management, cost estimating, cost budgeting, and cost controlling. Isn't that reassuring? Your PMI exam will, no doubt, have questions on costs, but so much of the content of this chapter refers to your enterprise environmental factors. (Remember that term? It's how your company does business.) Your cost management plan defines and outlines your organization's and project's procedures for cost management and control. I'll not pass the buck anymore. Let's go through this chapter like a wad of cash at an all-night flea market.

Planning for Project Cost Management

You need a plan just for project costs. You need a plan that will help you define what policies you and the project team have to adhere to in regard to costs, a plan that documents how you get to spend project money, and a plan for how cost management will happen throughout your entire project. Well, you're in luck! This plan, a subsidiary plan of the project management plan, is the project cost management plan.

Like most of these subsidiary plans, you can use a template from past projects, your project management office, or your program manager to build the plan that's specific to your project. Or, if you really have to, you can create a project cost management plan from scratch. It's not much fun, but I'll show you how to do it. You'll also need to know the business of preparing this cost management plan for your PMI examination—you'll certainly have some questions about what's included in the plan and how you and the project team work together to build the plan and execute it throughout the project.

Preparing the Project Cost Management Plan

In order to prepare to complete the process of cost management planning, you'll need four inputs:

- Project management plan
- Project charter
- Enterprise environmental factors
- Organizational process assets

Now don't let the idea of the project management plan scare you. Remember that planning is an iterative activity. You'll have some elements of the project management plan already completed when you start this cost management planning—and some parts of the project management plan won't be completed yet. As more and more information becomes available, you can return to this cost management plan and adjust it as necessary. For example, you may not know the specific rules about how your company can purchase materials. You might need to go speak with your project sponsor, the purchasing department, or your program manager to confirm these rules and then you could return to the cost management plan and update the information accordingly.

You'll also need the project management plan and its scope baseline to help the cost management planning. Recall that the scope baseline is the WBS, the WBS dictionary, and the project scope statement. The WBS will help you determine what resources you need to purchase, how estimating the expenses relate to the project's deliverables, and the time accountability for nonexempt project team members such as contractors.

NOTE   You'll reference the project charter for just one reason: the summary budget. Remember, the project charter includes a summary budget for the project so you'll use that amount as a foundation for project cost management.

The actual creation of the cost management plan relies heavily on meetings. Nothing like some meetings about the project budget, right? You'll need meetings specifically with your key stakeholders and subject matter experts. These people can help guide and direct you about the organization's environment, tell you about similar projects they've worked on or sponsored, and help with the enterprise environmental factors and organizational processes you'll have to adhere to in cost management.

These meetings will likely include some analytical techniques to analyze the anticipated cost of the project, the return on investment, and how the project should be funded. Self-funding means the organization pays for the project expenses from their cash flow. Funding with equity means the organization balances the project expenses with equity they have in their assets. Funding with debt means the company pays for the project through a line of credit or bank loan. There are pros and cons to each approach, and an analysis of the true cost of the project, the cost of the funding, and the risk associated with the project is examined as part of the decision.

NOTE   The time value of money was covered in Chapter 4. Present value, future value, net present value, and the internal rate of return are all applicable here, too.

Examining the Project Cost Management Plan

Once you've created the cost management plan, you have a clear direction on how you'll estimate, budget, and manage the project costs. This plan defines, much like the schedule management plan, the level of accuracy defined for the project and the units of measurement. For example, you might round financial figures to the nearest $100 or keep track of costs to the exact penny. Your unit of measurement isn't just dollars, yen, or euros, but also things like a workday, hours, or even weeks for labor. Keep in mind, some organizations do not include the cost of labor in the project, while other companies do.

If you're using control accounts in your WBS, you'll reference those control accounts in your cost management plan. Recall that a control account is like a "mini-budget" for a chunk of the WBS. For example, a house project may have a control account for the basement, the first floor, the second floor. Or you could get more specific and have a control account for the kitchen in the house project. Whatever approach you're using, you'd reference that information in the cost management plan—the *PMBOK Guide* calls this an organizational procedure link.

Just as you defined control thresholds for your schedule, you'll do the same for your project costs. Control thresholds, as a reminder, are the limits of variance before a corrective action is needed in the project. For example, a project may have a control threshold of 10 percent off budget before a predefined action is taken. Or the control threshold could be any cost variance greater than $5,000 requires project management action. The action could be a corrective action, but also may include an exceptions report or variance report to management.

Determining the Project Costs

One of the first questions a project manager is likely to be asked when a project is launched is, "How much will this cost to finish?" That question can only be answered through progressive elaboration. To answer the question, the project manager, or the project estimator as the case may be, first needs to examine the costs of the resources needed to complete each activity in the project. Resources, of course, are people, but also things: equipment, material, training, even pizza if the project demands it.

On top of the cost of the resources, there's also all the variances that must be considered: project risks, fluctuations in the cost of materials, the appropriate human resources for each activity, and oddball elements like shipping, insurance, inflation, and monies for testing and evaluations.

Estimates, as Figure 7-1 depicts, usually come in one of three flavors through a series of refinements. As more details are acquired as the project progresses, the estimates are refined. Industry guidelines and organizational policies may define how the estimates are refined.

- **Rough order of magnitude (ROM)** This estimate is rough and is used during the initiating processes and in top-down estimates. The range of variance for the estimate can be from –25 percent to +75 percent.

- **Budget estimate** This estimate is also somewhat broad and is used early in the planning processes and also in top-down estimates. The range of variance for the estimate can be from –10 percent to +25 percent.

Figure 7-1
There are three generally accepted types of cost estimates.

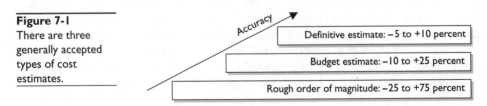

Accuracy

Definitive estimate: –5 to +10 percent

Budget estimate: –10 to +25 percent

Rough order of magnitude: –25 to +75 percent

- **Definitive estimate** This estimate type is one of the most accurate. It's used late in the planning processes and is associated with bottom-up estimating. You need the work breakdown structure (WBS) in order to create the definitive estimate. The range of variance for the estimate can be from –5 percent to +10 percent.

EXAM TIP The range of variance percentages are pretty typical of these estimate types, but there's no steadfast rule that the estimates must follow these ranges. Your organization may use entirely different ranges of variance for each estimate type.

While project managers typically think of project estimates as some unit of measure such as dollars, euros, or yen, it's possible and often feasible to estimate project costs based on labor. Consider the number of hours the project team must work on creating a new piece of software. You could even estimate based on the number of full-time employees assigned to the project for a given duration.

EXAM TIP If your organization doesn't use a cost estimator, the project manager and the project team work together to estimate the project costs.

Estimating the Project Costs

Assuming that the project manager and the project team are working together to create the cost estimates, there are many inputs to the cost-estimating process. For your PMI exam, it would behoove you to be familiar with these inputs because these are often the supporting details for the cost estimate the project management team creates. Let's have a look, shall we?

Referencing the Cost Management Plan

You've created the cost management plan, so might as well use it. The plan is used as an input for cost estimating because it defines the level of detail needed in the cost estimates you're creating. You'll follow the cost management plan's requirements for cost estimating, rounding, and adherence to enterprise environmental factors.

Including the Human Resource Plan

If your organization includes an accounting of the cost of labor, you'll obviously need this project management subsidiary plan. The human resource plan, which is covered in Chapter 9, defines the cost of labor, contracted labor rates, and the budget allotted for rewards and recognition for the project. You'll need this information to predict what the costs of the project will be.

Using the Project Scope Baseline

You'll need the project scope baseline often enough. First, the project scope statement is an input to the cost-estimating process. What a surprise! The project scope statement is needed because it defines the business case for the project, the project justifications, and the project requirements—all things that'll cost cash to achieve. The project scope statement can help the project manager and the stakeholders negotiate the funding for the project based on what's already been agreed upon. In other words, the size of the budget has to be in proportion to the demands of the project scope statement.

While the project scope statement defines constraints, it also defines assumptions. In Chapter 11, which discusses risk management, we'll discuss how assumptions can become risks. Basically, if the assumptions in the project scope statement prove false, the project manager needs to assess what the financial impact may be.

Consider all of the elements in the project scope statement that can contribute to the project cost estimate:

- Contractual agreements
- Insurance
- Safety and health issues
- Environment expenses
- Security concerns
- Cost of intellectual rights
- Licenses and permits

Last, and perhaps one of the more important elements in the project scope statement, is the requirements for acceptance. The cost estimate must reflect the monies needed to attain the project customer's expectations. If the monies are not available to create all of the elements within the project scope, then either the project scope must be trimmed to match the monies that are available, or more cash needs to be dumped into the project.

Next, you'll need the second part of the scope baseline: the work breakdown structure (WBS). The WBS is needed to create a cost estimate, especially the definitive estimate, because it clearly defines all of the deliverables the project will create. Each of the work packages in the WBS will cost something in the way of materials, time, or often both. You'll see the WBS as a common theme in this chapter, because the monies you spend on a project are for the things you've promised in the WBS.

Finally, you'll need the WBS's pal, the WBS dictionary, because it includes all of the details and the associated work for each deliverable in the WBS. As a general rule, whenever you have the WBS involved, the WBS dictionary tags along.

Examining the Project Schedule

The availability of resources, when the resources are to do the work, when capital expenses are to happen, and so on are needed for cost estimating. The schedule management plan can also consider contracts with collective bargaining agreements (unions) and their timelines, the seasonal cost of labor and materials, and any other timings that may affect the overall cost estimate. The project schedule can help you determine not only when resources are needed, but when you'll have to pay for those resources.

Referencing the Risk Register

A risk is an uncertain event that may cost the project time, money, or both. The risk register is a central repository of the project risks and the associated status of each risk event. Some risks the project team can buy their way out of, while other risks will cost the project if they come true. We'll discuss risks in detail in Chapter 11, but for now, know that the risk register is needed because the cost of the risk exposure helps the project management team create an accurate cost estimate.

 EXAM TIP Risks may not always cost monies directly, but could affect the project schedule. Keep in mind, however, that this could in turn cause a rise in project costs because of vendor commitment, penalties for lateness, and added expenses for extra labor.

Relying on Enterprise Environmental Factors

Every time I have to say or write "enterprise environmental factors," I cringe. It's just a fancypants way of saying how your organization runs its shop. Within any organization, "factors" affect the cost-estimating process. Surprise, surprise, there are two for your exam:

- **Marketplace conditions** When you have to buy materials and other resources, the marketplace dictates the price, what's available, and from whom you will purchase them. We'll talk all about procurement in Chapter 12, but for now, there are three conditions that can affect the price of anything your project needs to purchase:

    - Sole source When there's only one vendor that can provide what your project needs to purchase. Examples include a specific consultant, a specialized service, or a unique type of material.

    - Single source When there are many vendors that can provide what your project needs to purchase, but you prefer to work with a specific vendor. They are your favorite.

    - Oligopoly This is a market condition in which the market is so tight that the actions of one vendor affect the actions of all the others. Can you think of any? How about the airline industry, the oil industry, or even training centers and consultants?

- **Commercial databases** One of my first consulting gigs was for a large commercial printer. We used a database—based on the type of materials the job was to be printed on, the number of inks and varnish we wanted to use, and the printing press we'd use—to predict how much the job would cost. That's a commercial database. Another accessible example is any price list your vendors may provide so that you can estimate the costs accurately.

EXAM TIP Here's a goofy way to remember all the market conditions for your PMI exam. For a sole source, think of James Brown, the Godfather of Soul. There's only one James Brown, just as there's only one vendor. For a single source, think of all the single people in the world and how you only want to date your sweetie instead of all the others. With a single source, you consider all the different available vendors, but you have your favorite. And for oligopoly? It sounds like "oil" which we know is a classic example of an oligopoly market. Hey, I warned you these were goofy!

Using Organizational Process Assets

Here's another term that makes my teeth hurt: organizational process assets. These are just things your organization has learned, created, or purchased that can help the project management team manage a project better. When it comes to cost estimating, an organization can use many assets:

- **Cost-estimating policies** An organization can, and often will, create a policy on how the project manager or the cost estimator is to create the project cost estimate. It's just their rule. Got any of those where you work?

- **Cost-estimating templates** In case you've not picked up on this yet, the PMI and the Project Management Body of Knowledge (PMBOK) love templates. Templates in project management don't usually mean a shell in the way that Microsoft Word thinks of templates. We're talking about using past similar projects to serve as a template for the current project.

- **Historical information** Beyond the specific costs of previous projects, historical information is just about anything that came before this project that can help the project manager and the project team create an accurate cost estimate.

- **Project files** Project archives and files from past projects can help with the cost-estimating process. Specifically, the project manager is after the performance of past similar projects in areas of cost control, the cost of risks, and quality issues that could affect costs.

- **Project team knowledge** Your project team usually consists of the experts closest to the project work and can be a valuable input to the project cost-estimating process. Be forewarned—for the real world and your PMI exam, project team recollections are great, but aren't the most reliable input. In other words, Marty's war stories about how Project XYZ was $14 billion over budget don't compare with historical information that says Project XYZ was $14 over budget.

- **Lessons learned** It's always good to rely on lessons learned as an input during planning. After all, it's better to learn from someone else's mistakes.

EXAM TIP   Sometimes an organization has two projects, or opportunities, and they can only choose one of the projects to complete. For example, Project A is worth $75,000, and Project B is worth $250,000. The organization will likely choose Project B because it is worth more, and let Project A go because it is worth considerably less. *Opportunity cost* is a term to describe the total amount of the project that was let go in lieu of the project that was selected. In this instance, the opportunity cost is $75,000: the worth of Project A.

Creating the Cost Estimate

All of the cost inputs are needed so that the project cost estimator, likely the project management team, can create a reliable cost estimate. The estimates you'll want to know for the CAPM and PMP exam, and for your career, reflect the accuracy of the information the estimate is based upon. The more accurate the information, the better the cost estimate will be. Basically, all cost estimates move through progressive elaboration: as more details become available, the more accurate the cost estimate is likely to be. Let's examine the most common approaches to determining how much a project is likely to cost.

Using Analogous Estimating

Analogous estimating relies on historical information to predict the cost of the current project. It is also known as top-down estimating and is the least reliable of all the cost-estimating approaches. The process of analogous estimating uses the actual cost of a historical project as a basis for the current project. The cost of the historical project is applied to the cost of the current project, taking into account the scope and size of the current project, as well as other known variables.

Analogous estimating is considered a form of expert judgment. This estimating approach takes less time to complete than other estimating models, but is also less accurate. This top-down approach is good for fast estimates to get a general idea of what the project may cost. The trouble, or risk, with using an analogous estimate, however, is that the historical information that estimate is based upon must be accurate. For example, if I were to create a cost estimate for Project NBG based on a similar project Nancy did two years ago, I'd be assuming that Nancy kept accurate records and that her historical information is accurate. If it isn't, then my project costs are not going to be accurate, and I'm going to be really mad at Nancy.

Determining the Cost of Resources

One of the project management plans needed for cost estimating is the human resource management plan, which defines all of the attributes of the project staff, including the personnel rates. Armed with this plan and a determination of what resources are needed to complete the project, the project manager can extrapolate what the cost of the human resource element of the project will likely be.

Resources include more than just the people doing the project work. The cost estimate must also reflect all of the equipment and materials that will be utilized to complete the work. In addition, the project manager must identify the quantity of the needed resources and when the resources are needed for the project. The identification of the resources, the needed quantity, and the schedule of the resources are directly linked to the expected cost of the project work.

There are four variations on project expenses to consider:

- **Direct costs**   These costs are attributed directly to the project work and cannot be shared among projects (airfare, hotels, long-distance phone charges, and so on).

- **Indirect costs**   These costs are representative of more than one project (utilities for the performing organization, access to a training room, project management software license, and so on).

- **Variable costs**   These costs vary depending on the conditions applied in the project (the number of meeting participants, the supply and demand of materials, and so on).

- **Fixed costs**   These costs remain constant throughout the life cycle of the project (the cost of a piece of rented equipment for the project, the cost of a consultant brought onto the project, and so on).

And yes, you can mix and match these terms. For example, you could have a variable cost based on shipping expenses that is also a direct cost for your project. Don't get too hung up on these cost types—just be topically familiar with them for your PMI exam.

Using Bottom-Up Estimating

Bottom-up estimating starts from zero, accounts for each component of the WBS, and arrives at a sum for the project. It is completed with the project team and can be one of the most time-consuming methods used to predict project costs. While this method is more expensive because of the time invested to create the estimate, it is also one of the most accurate. A fringe benefit of completing a bottom-up estimate is that the project team may buy into the project work since they see the value of each cost within the project.

Using Parametric Estimating

"That'll be $465 per metric ton."

"You can buy our software for $765 per license."

"How about $125 per network drop?"

These are all examples of parameters that can be integrated into a parametric estimate. *Parametric estimating* uses a mathematical model based on known parameters to predict the cost of a project. The parameters in the model can vary based on the type of work being completed and can be measured by cost per cubic yard, cost per unit, and so on. A complex parameter can be cost per unit, with adjustment factors based on the conditions of the project. The adjustment factors may have several modifying factors, depending on additional conditions.

There are two types of parametric estimating:

- **Regression analysis** This is a statistical approach that predicts future values based on historical values. Regression analysis creates quantitative predictions based on variables within one value to predict variables in another. This form of estimating relies solely on pure statistical math to reveal relationships between variables and to predict future values.

- **Learning curve** This approach is simple: The cost per unit decreases the more units workers complete, because workers learn as they complete the required work (see Figure 7-2). The more an individual completes an activity, the easier it is to complete. The estimate is considered parametric, since the formula is based on repetitive activities, such as wiring telephone jacks, painting hotel rooms, or other activities that are completed over and over within a project.

EXAM TIP Don't worry too much about regression analysis for the exam. The learning curve is the topic you're more likely to have questions on.

Using Good Old Project Management Software

Who's creating estimates with their abacus? Most organizations rely on software to help the project management team create an accurate cost estimate. While the CAPM and PMP examinations are vendor neutral, a general knowledge of how computer software

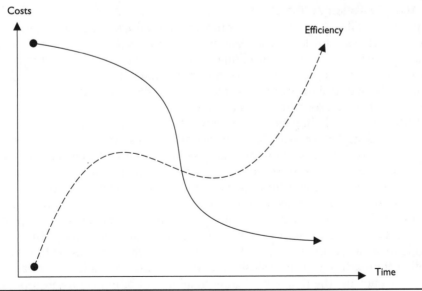

Figure 7-2 The learning curve affects the cost of efficiency.

can assist the project manager is needed. Several different computer programs are available that can streamline project work estimates and increase their accuracy. These tools can include project management software, spreadsheet programs, and simulations.

Examining the Vendor Bids

Sometimes it's just more cost-effective (and easier) to hire someone else to do the work. Other times, the project manager has no choice, because the needed skill set doesn't exist within the organization. In either condition, the vendors' bids need to be analyzed to determine which vendor should be selected based on their ability to satisfy the project scope, the expected quality, and the cost of their services. We'll talk all about procurement in Chapter 12.

Implementing Three-Point Estimating

A three-point estimate uses three factors to predict a cost: pessimistic, optimistic, and most likely. A three-point estimate can use a simple average of the three factors or it can use a weighted factor for the most likely factor. For example, a project manager predicts the pessimistic cost to be $5,600, the most likely cost to be $4,800, and the optimistic cost to be $3,500. With the simple average, you'd just add up the three amounts and divide by three for a value of $4,633.

With the weighted average, you'll consider all of the same costs, but the most likely amount is multiplied by four, and then you'll divide the sum of the three values by six. Here's what this looks like with the same costs ($5,600 + (4 × 4,800) + 3,500)/6 = $4,716. So in this instance the weight average leans more toward the most likely amount than does the simple average.

Creating a Reserve Analysis

Do you think it'll snow next December in Michigan? I do, too. But do we know on what exact date? That's a quick and easy example of a *known unknown*. You know that something is likely to occur, but you just don't know when or to what degree. Projects are full of known unknowns, and the most common unknown deals with costs. Based on experience, the nature of the work, or fear, you suspect that some activities in your project will cost more than expected—that's a known unknown.

Rather than combating known unknowns by padding costs with extra monies, the PMBOK suggests that we create "contingency allowances" to account for these overruns in costs. The contingency allowances are used at the project manager's discretion to counteract cost overruns for scheduled activities. In Chapter 6, we discussed the concept of management reserve for time overruns. This is a related concept when it comes to the cost reserve for projects. This reserve is sometimes called a *contingency reserve* and is traditionally set aside for cost overruns due to risks that have affected the project cost baseline. Contingency reserves can be managed in a number of ways. The most common is to set aside an allotment of funds for the identified risks within the project. Another approach is to create a slush fund for the entire project for identified risks and known unknowns. The final approach is an allotment of funds for categories of components based on the WBS and the project schedule.

Considering the Cost of Quality

The *cost of quality*, which we'll discuss in Chapter 8, defines the monies the project must spend to reach the expected level of quality within a project. For example, if your project will use a new material that no one on the project team has ever worked with, the project team will likely need training so they can use it. The training, as you can guess, costs something. That's an example of the cost of quality.

On the other side of the coin (cost pun intended, thank you), there's the cost of poor quality, sometimes called the *cost of nonconformance to quality*. These are the costs your project will pay if you don't adhere to quality the first time. In our example with the project team and the new materials, a failure to train the team on the new materials will mean that the team will likely not install the materials properly, take longer to use the materials, and may even waste materials. All of these negative conditions cost the project in time, money, team frustration, and even loss of sales.

Examining the Cost Estimate

Once all of the inputs have been evaluated and the estimate creation process is completed, you get the cost estimate. The estimate is the likely cost of the project—it's not a guarantee, so there is usually a modifier—sometimes called an acceptable range of variance. That's the plus/minus qualifier on the estimate—for example, $450,000 + $25,000 to −$13,000, based on whatever conditions are attached to the estimate. The cost estimate should, at the minimum, include the likely costs for all of the following:

- Labor
- Materials
- Equipment
- Services
- Facilities
- Information technology
- Special categories, such as inflation and contingency reserve

It's possible for a project to have other cost categories, such as consultants, outsourced solutions, and so on, but the preceding list is the most common. Consider this list when studying to pass your exam.

Along with the cost estimate, the project management team includes the basis of the estimate. These are all the supporting details of how the estimate was created and why the confidence in the estimate exists at the level it does. Supporting details typically include all of the following:

- Description of the work to be completed in consideration of the cost estimate
- Explanation of how the estimate was created
- What assumptions were used during the estimate creation

- The constraints that the project management team had to consider when creating the cost estimate

A project's cost estimate may lead to some unpleasant news in the shape of change requests. I say "unpleasant," because changes are rarely enjoyable. Changes can affect the scope in two primary ways when it comes to cost:

We don't have enough funds to match the cost estimate, so we'll need to trim the scope.

We have more than enough funds to match the cost estimate, so let's add some stuff into the scope.

All change requests must be documented and fed through the integrated change control system, as discussed in Chapter 4. What the project manager wants to be leery of is gold plating. *Gold plating* is when the project manager, the project sponsor, or even a stakeholder adds in project extras to consume the entire project budget. It's essentially adding unneeded features to the product in order to use up all the funds allocated to the project. While this often happens in the final stages of a project, it can begin right here during the project cost estimating. Gold plating delivers more than what's needed and can create new risks and work, and can contribute to a decline in team morale.

If changes are approved, then integrated change control is enacted, the project scope is updated, the WBS and WBS dictionary are updated, and so on, through all of the project management plans as needed. The cost management plan needs to be updated as well to reflect the costs of the changes and their impact on the project cost estimate.

Budgeting the Project

Now that the project estimate has been created, it's time to create the official cost budget. Cost budgeting is really cost aggregation, which means the project manager will be assigning specific dollar amounts for each of the scheduled activities or, more likely, for each of the work packages in the WBS. The aggregation of the work package cost equates to the summary budget for the entire project. This process creates the cost baseline, as Figure 7-3 shows.

Cost budgeting and cost estimates may go hand in hand, but estimating is completed before a budget is created—or assigned. Cost budgeting applies the cost estimates over time. This results in a time-phased estimate for cost, which allows an organization to predict cash flow, to project return on investment, and to perform forecasting. The difference between cost estimates and cost budgeting is that cost *estimates* show costs by category, whereas a cost *budget* shows costs across time.

Creating the Project Budget

Good news! Many of the tools and techniques used to create the project cost estimates are also used to create the project budget. The following is a quick listing of the tools you can expect to see on the CAPM and PMP exams:

- **Cost aggregation**   Costs are parallel to each WBS work package. The costs of each work package are aggregated to their corresponding control accounts. Each control account is then aggregated to the sum of the project costs.

- **Reserve analysis**   Cost reserves are for unknown unknowns within a project. The contingency reserve is not part of the project cost baseline, but is included as part of the project budget.

- **Historical relationships**   This is kind of a weird term. Historical relationships in cost estimating describe the history of costs in a given industry. For example, construction uses a cost per square foot, while software development can charge a fee per hour depending on the type of resource being used. This approach uses a parametric model to extrapolate what costs will be for a project (for example, cost per hour and cost per unit). It can include variables and the additional percentage of fee points based on conditions.

- **Funding limit reconciliation**   Organizations only have so much cash to allot to projects—and no, you can't have all the monies right now. Funding limit reconciliation is an organization's approach to managing cash flow against the project deliverables based on a schedule, milestone accomplishment, or data constraints. This helps an organization plan when monies will be devoted to a project rather than using all of the funds available at the start of a project. In other words, the monies for a project budget will become available based on dates and/or deliverables. If the project doesn't hit predetermined dates and products that were set as milestones, the likelihood of additional funding becomes questionable.

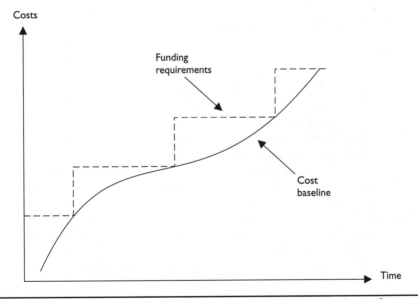

Figure 7-3   The cost baseline is how much the project will cost demonstrated on an S-curve.

Examining the Project Budget

As with most parts of the PMBOK, you don't get just one output after completing a process, you get several. Creating the project budget is no different because there are three outputs to know for the PMI examination: cost baseline, project funding requirements, and project documents. The following sections look at these in detail.

Working with the Cost Baseline

The *cost baseline*, shown in Figure 7-3, is actually a time-lapse exposure of when the project monies are to be spent in relation to cumulative values of the work completed in the project. Most baselines are shown as an S-curve, where the project begins in the left and works its way to the upper-right corner. When the project begins, it's not worth much and usually not much has been spent. As the project moves toward completion, the monies for labor, materials, and other resources are consumed in relation to the work. In other words, the monies spent on the project over time will equate to the work the project is completing.

Some projects, especially projects that are of high priority or are large, may have multiple cost baselines to track cost of labor, cost of materials, even the cost of internal resources compared with external resources. This is all fine and dandy, as long as the values in each of the baselines are maintained and consistent. It wouldn't do a project manager much good if the cost baseline for materials was updated regularly and the cost baseline for labor was politely ignored.

 EXAM TIP Monies that have already been spent on a project are considered sunk into the project. These funds are called *sunk costs*—they're gone.

Determining the Project Funding Requirements

Projects demand a budget, but when the monies in the project are made available depends on the organization, the size of the project, and just plain old common sense. For example, if you were building a skyscraper that costs $850 million, you wouldn't need all of the funds on the first day of the project, but you would forecast when those monies would be needed. That's cash-flow forecasting.

The funding of the project, based on the cost baseline and the expected project schedule, may happen incrementally or may be based on conditions within the project. Typically, the funding requirements have been incorporated into the cost baseline. The release of funds is treated like a step function, which is what it is. Each step of the project funding allows the project to move on to the next milestone, deliverable, or whatever step of the project the project manager and the stakeholders have agreed to.

The project funding requirements also account for the management contingency reserve amounts. This is a pool of funds for cost overruns. Typically, the management contingency reserve is allotted to the project in each step, though some organizations may elect to only disburse contingency funds on an as-needed basis—that's just part of organizational process assets.

To be crystal clear, the *cost baseline* is what the project should cost in an ideal, perfect world. The *management contingency reserve* is the "filler" between the cost baseline and the maximum funding. In most cases, the management contingency reserve bridges the gap between the project cost baseline and the maximum funding to complete the project. Figure 7-4 demonstrates the management contingency reserve at project completion.

The Usual Suspects

There are three more outputs of the cost-budgeting process. The outputs are:

- **Cost baseline**   The cost baseline is the budget of the project—usually in ratio to when the funds are needed and how far along the project has progressed. In other words, in larger projects you don't get all of the project budgeting at the start, but rather the monies are spent throughout the project. This is where you might see an S-curve of how much the project is predicted to spend in relation to the progress the project is to make. Ideally, you'll run out of money right when the project reaches its conclusion.

- **Project funding requirements**   Part of the project's budget is a prediction of when you'll need the money: capital expenses, monthly labor burn rates, contractual obligations, and project liabilities. You will need to consider the total budget requirements as part of the funding requirements. This includes the cost baseline and any management reserves for risk events.

- **Project document updates**   You may need to update the risk register, cost estimates, and delete project schedule.

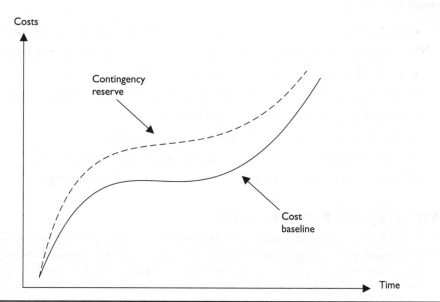

Figure 7-4   Contingency reserve provides funding for cost overruns.

Controlling Project Costs

Once a project has been funded, it's up to the project manager and the project team to work effectively and efficiently to control costs. This means doing the work right the first time. It also means, and this is tricky, avoiding scope creep and undocumented changes, as well as getting rid of any non-value-added activities. Basically, if the project team is adding components or features that aren't called for in the project, they're wasting time and money.

Cost control focuses on controlling the ability of costs to change and on how the project management team may allow or prevent cost changes from happening. When a change does occur, the project manager must document the change and the reason why it occurred and, if necessary, create a variance report. Cost control is concerned with understanding why the cost variances, both good and bad, have occurred. The "why" behind the variances allows the project manager to make appropriate decisions on future project actions.

 **EXAM TIP** Variance reports are sometimes called exception reports.

Ignoring the project cost variances may cause the project to suffer from budget shortages, additional risks, or scheduling problems. When cost variances happen, they must be examined, recorded, and investigated. Cost control allows the project manager to confront the problem, find a solution, and then act accordingly. Specifically, cost control focuses on:

- Controlling causes of change to ensure that the changes are actually needed
- Controlling and documenting changes to the cost baseline as they happen
- Controlling changes in the project and their influence on cost
- Performing cost monitoring to recognize and understand cost variances
- Recording appropriate cost changes in the cost baseline
- Preventing unauthorized changes to the cost baseline
- Communicating the cost changes to the proper stakeholders
- Working to bring and maintain costs within an acceptable range

Managing the Project Costs

Controlling the project costs is more than a philosophy—it's the project manager working with the project team, the stakeholders, and often management to ensure that costs don't creep into the project, and then managing the cost increases as they happen. To implement cost control, the project manager must rely on several documents and processes:

- **Cost baseline** You know this one already. The cost baseline is the expected cost the project will incur and when those expenses will happen. This time-phased budget reflects the amount that will be spent throughout the project. Recall that the cost baseline is a tool used to measure project performance.

- **Project funding requirements** The funds for a project are not allotted all at once, but stair-stepped in alignment with project deliverables. Thus, as the project moves toward completion, additional funding is allotted. This allows for cash-flow forecasting. In other words, an organization doesn't have to have the project's entire budget allotted at the start of the project. It can predict, based on expected income and predicted expenses, that the budget will be available in incremental steps.

- **Performance reports** These reports focus on project cost performance, project scope, and planned performance versus actual performance. The reports may vary according to stakeholder needs. We'll discuss performance reporting in detail in Chapter 10 and everyone's favorite, earned value management, in just one moment.

- **Change requests** When a change to the project scope is requested, an analysis of the associated costs to complete the proposed change is required. In some instances, such as when removing a portion of the project deliverable, a change request may reduce the project cost. (I know, that's wishful thinking. But in the PMI's world, it's possible.)

- **Cost management plan** The cost management plan dictates how cost variances will be managed. A *variance* is a difference between what was expected and what was experienced. In some instances, the management contingency reserve allowance can "cover" the cost overruns. In other instances, depending on the reason why the overrun occurred, the funding may have to come from the project customer. Consider a customer who wanted the walls painted green, and after the work was completed, changed his mind and wanted the walls orange. This cost overrun is due only to a change request and not to a defect.

Creating a Cost Change Control System

Way, way back in Chapter 5, I discussed the scope change control system. Whenever some joker wants to add something to the project scope, or even take something out of our project scope, the scope change control system is engaged. Similarly, the cost change control system examines any changes associated with scope changes, the costs of materials, and the cost of any other resources you can imagine.

When a cost change enters the system, there is appropriate paperwork, a tracking system, and procedures the project manager must follow to obtain approval on the proposed change. Figure 7-5 demonstrates a typical work flow for cost change approval. If a change gets approved, the cost baseline is updated to reflect the approved changes. If a request gets denied, the denial must be documented for future potential reference. You don't want a stakeholder wondering at the end of the project why his or her change wasn't incorporated into the project scope without having some documentation as to why.

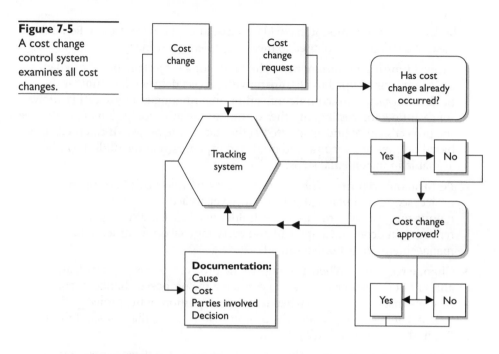

Figure 7-5
A cost change
control system
examines all cost
changes.

 EXAM TIP   There are four specific change control systems in project management: the scope change control system, the schedule change control system, the cost change control system, and the contract change control system.

Using Earned Value Management

When I teach a PMP Boot Camp, attendees snap to attention when it comes to earned value management and their exam. This topic is foreign to many folks, and they understandably want an in-depth explanation of this suite of mysterious formulas. Maybe you find yourself in that same position, so here's some good news: It's not that big a deal. Relax—you can memorize these formulas, answer the exam questions correctly, and worry about tougher exam topics. I'll show you how.

First, earned value management (EVM) is the process of measuring the performance of project work against what was planned to identify variances, opportunities to improve the project, or just to check the project's health. EVM can help predict future variances and the final costs at completion. It is a system of mathematical formulas that compares work performed against work planned, and measures the actual cost of the work your project has performed. EVM is an important part of cost control since it allows a project manager to predict future variances from the expenses to date within the project.

Learning the Fundamentals

EVM, in regard to cost management, is concerned with the relationships among three formulas that reflect project performance. Figure 7-6 demonstrates the connection between the following EVM values:

- **Planned value (PV)**   Planned value is the work scheduled and the budget authorized to accomplish that work. For example, if a project has a budget of $500,000 and month 6 represents 50 percent of the project work, the PV for that month is $250,000.

- **Earned value (EV)**   Earned value is the physical work completed to date and the authorized budget for that work. For example, if your project has a budget of $500,000 and the work completed to date represents 45 percent of the entire project work, its earned value is $225,000. You can find EV by multiplying the percent complete times the project budget at completion (BAC).

- **Actual cost (AC)**   Actual cost is the actual amount of monies the project has required to date. In your project, your BAC, for example, is $500,000, and your earned value is $225,000. As it turns out, your project team had some waste, and you spent $232,000 in actual monies to reach the 45-percent-complete milestone. Your actual cost is $232,000.

That's the fundamentals of earned value management. All of our remaining formulas center on these simple formulas. Just remember that earned value is always the percent of work complete times the given budget at completion. On your PMI exam, you'll always be provided with the actual costs, which are the monies that have already been spent on the project. You'll have to do some math to find the planned value, which is the value your project should have by a given time. The formula for planned value is the percentage of project completion based on how complete the project should

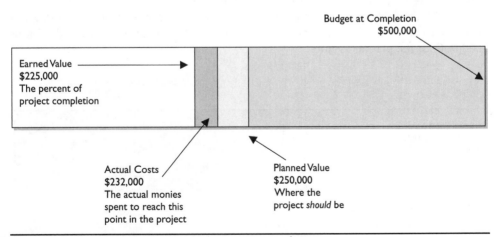

Figure 7-6   Earned value management shows project performance.

be at a given time. For example, let's say you're supposed to be 80 percent complete by December 15. If your budget is $100,000, in this instance your planned value is $80,000.

Finding the Project Variances

Out in the real world, I'm sure your projects are never late and never over budget (ha-ha—pretty funny, right?). For your exam you'll need to be able to find the cost and schedule variances for your project. I'll stay with the same $500,000 budget I've been working with in the previous examples and as demonstrated in Figure 7-7. Finding the variances helps the project manager and management determine a project's health, set goals for project improvement, and benchmark projects against each other based on the identified variances.

Finding the Cost Variance

Let's say your project has a BAC of $500,000 and you're 40 percent complete. You have spent, however, $234,000 in real monies. To find the cost variance, we'll find the earned value, which is 40 percent of the $500,000 budget. As Figure 7-7 shows, this is $200,000. In this example, you spent $234,000 in actual costs. The formula for finding the cost variance is earned value minus actual costs. In this instance, the cost variance is –$34,000.

This means you've spent $34,000 dollars *more* than what the work you've done is worth. Of course, the $34,000 is in relation to the size of the project. On this project, that's a sizeable flaw, but on a billion-dollar project, $34,000 may not mean too much. On either project, a $34,000 cost variance would likely spur a cost variance report (sometimes called an exceptions report).

Finding the Schedule Variance

Can you guess how the schedule variance works? It's basically the same as cost variance, only this time, we're concerned with planned value instead of actual costs. Let's say your project with the $500,000 budget is supposed to be 45 percent complete by today, but we know that you're only 40 percent complete. We've already found the earned value as $200,000 for the planned value.

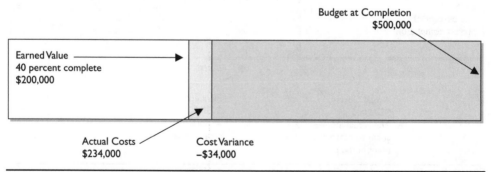

Budget at Completion
$500,000

Earned Value
40 percent complete
$200,000

Actual Costs
$234,000

Cost Variance
–$34,000

Figure 7-7   Cost variance is the difference between earned value and actual costs.

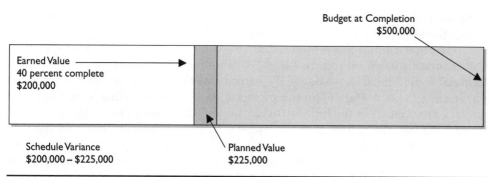

Figure 7-8   Schedule variance is the difference of earned value and planned value.

Recall that planned value, where you're supposed to be and what you're supposed to be worth, is planned completion times the BAC. In this example, it's 45 percent of the $500,000 BAC, which is $225,000. Uh-oh! You're behind schedule. The schedule variance formula, as Figure 7-8 demonstrates, is earned value minus the planned value. In this example, the schedule variance is $25,000.

Finding the Indexes

In mathematical terms, an index is an expression showing a ratio—and that's what we're doing with these indexes. Basically, an index in earned value management shows the health of the project's time and cost. The index, or ratio, is measured against one: the closer to one the index is, the better the project is performing. As a rule, you definitely don't want to be less than one because that's a poorly performing project. And, believe it or not, you don't want to be too far from one in your index, as this shows estimates that were bloated or way, way too pessimistic. Really.

Finding the Cost Performance Index

The cost performance index (CPI) measures the project based on its financial performance. It's an easy formula: earned value divided by actual costs, as Figure 7-9 demonstrates. Your project, in this example, has a budget of $500,000 and you're 40 percent

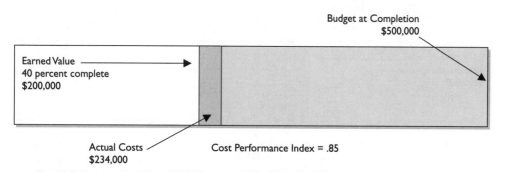

Figure 7-9   The CPI is found by dividing earned value by the actual costs.

complete with the project work. This is an earned value of how much? Yep. It's 40 percent of the $500,000, for an earned value of $200,000.

Your actual costs for this project to date (the cumulative costs) total $234,000. Your PMI exam will always tell you your actual costs for each exam question. Let's finish the formula. To find the CPI, we divide the earned value by the actual costs, or $200,000 divided by $234,000. The CPI for this project is .85, which means that we're 85 percent on track financially, not too healthy for any project, regardless of its budget.

Another fun way to look at the .85 value is that you're actually losing 15 cents on every dollar you spend on the project. Yikes! That means for every dollar you spend for labor, you actually only get 85 cents worth. Not a good deal for the project manager. As stated earlier, the closer to 1 the number is, the better the project is performing.

Finding the Schedule Performance Index

The schedule performance index (SPI) measures the project schedule's overall health. The formula, as Figure 7-10 demonstrates, is earned value divided by planned value. In other words, you're trying to determine how closely your project work is being completed in relation to the project schedule you created. Let's try this formula.

Your project with the $500,000 budget is 40 percent complete, for an earned value of $200,000, but you're supposed to be 45 percent complete by today. That's a planned value of $225,000. The SPI for this project at this time is determined by dividing the earned value of $200,000 by the planned value of $225,000, for an SPI of .88. This tells me that this project is 88 percent on schedule, or, if you're a pessimist, the project is 12 percent off track.

Predicting the Project's Future

Notice in the preceding paragraph I said, "at this time." That's because the project will, hopefully, continue to make progress, and the planned value and earned value numbers will change. Naturally, as the project moves toward completion, the earned value amounts will increase, and so will the planned value numbers. Typically, these indexes, both schedule and costs, are measured at milestones, and they allow the project management team to do some prognosticating as to where the project will likely end up by its completion. That's right—we can do some forecasting.

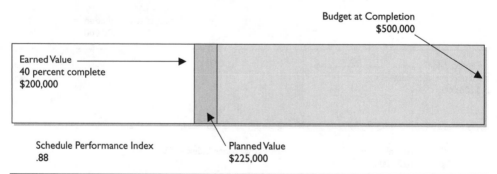

Figure 7-10 The SPI is found by dividing the earned value by the planned value.

EXAM TIP The forecasting formulas are swift and easy to calculate, but they're not really all that accurate. After all, you never really know how much a project will cost until you've completed all of the project work.

Finding the Estimate to Complete

So your project is in a pickle, and management wants to know how much more this project is going to cost. They're after the estimate to complete (ETC) equation. There are three flavors of this formula, based on conditions within your project.

ETC Based on a New Estimate Sometimes you just have to accept the fact that all of the estimates up to this point are flawed, and you need a new estimate. Imagine a project where the project manager and the project team estimate that the work will cost $150,000 in labor, but once they get into the project, they realize it'll actually cost $275,000 in labor because the work is much harder than they anticipated. That's a reason for the ETC on a new estimate.

ETC Based on Atypical Variances This formula, shown in Figure 7-11, is used when the project has experienced some wacky fluctuation in costs, and the project manager doesn't believe the anomalies will continue within the project. For example, the cost of wood was estimated at $18 per sheet. Due to a hurricane in another part of the country, however, the cost of wood has changed to $25 per sheet. This fluctuation in the cost of materials has changed, but the project manager doesn't believe the cost change will affect the cost to deliver the other work packages in the WBS. Here's the formula for atypical variances: ETC = BAC – EV.

Let's say that this project has a BAC of $500,000 and is 40 percent complete. The earned value is $200,000, so our ETC formula would be ETC = $500,000 – $200,000, for an ETC of $300,000. Obviously, this formula is shallow and won't be the best forecasting formula for every scenario. If the cost of the materials has changed drastically, a whole new estimate would be more appropriate.

ETC Based on Typical Variances Sometimes in a project, a variance appears and the project management team realizes that this is going to continue through the rest of the project. Figure 7-12 demonstrates the formula: ETC = (BAC – EV)/CPI. For

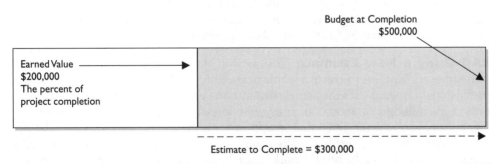

Budget at Completion
$500,000

Earned Value
$200,000
The percent of
project completion

Estimate to Complete = $300,000

Figure 7-11 The estimate to complete can consider atypical variances.

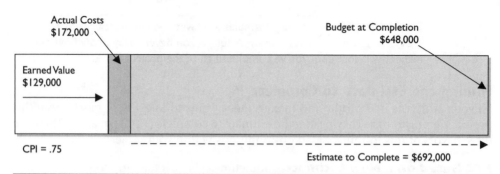

Figure 7-12 ETC may consider expected variances within a project.

example, consider a project to install 10,000 light fixtures throughout a university campus. You and the project team have estimated it'll take 12,000 hours of labor to install all of the lights, and your cost estimate is $54 per hour, which equates to $648,000 to complete all of the installations.

As the project team begins work on the install, however, the time to install the light fixtures actually takes slightly longer than anticipated for each fixture. You realize that your duration estimate is flawed and the project team will likely take 16,000 hours of labor to install all of the lights.

The ETC in this formula requires that the project manager know the earned value and the cost performance index. Let's say that this project is 20 percent complete, so the EV is roughly $129,000. As the work is taking longer to complete, the actual cost to reach the 20 percent mark turns out to be $172,000. The CPI is found by dividing the earned value, $129,000, by the actual costs of $172,000. The CPI for this project is .75.

Now let's try the ETC formula: (BAC – EV)/CPI, or ($648,000 – $129,000)/.75, which equates to $692,000. That's $692,000 more that this project will need in its budget to complete the remainder of the project work. Yikes!

Finding the Estimate at Completion

One of the most fundamental forecasting formulas is the estimate at completion (EAC). This formula accounts for all those pennies you're losing on every dollar if your CPI is less than one. It's an opportunity for the project manager to say, "Hey! Based on our current project's health, this is where we're likely to end up at the end of the project. I'd better work on my resume." Let's take a look at these formulas.

EAC Using a New Estimate   Just as with the estimate to complete formulas, sometimes it's best just to create a whole new estimate. This approach with the EAC is pretty straightforward—it's the actual costs plus the estimate to complete. Let's say your project has a budget of $500,000, and you've already spent $187,000 of it. For whatever reason, you've determined that your estimate is no longer valid, and your ETC for the remainder of the project is actually going to be $420,000—that's how much you're going to need to finish the project work. The EAC, in this instance, is the actual costs of $187,000 plus your ETC of $420,000, or $607,000.

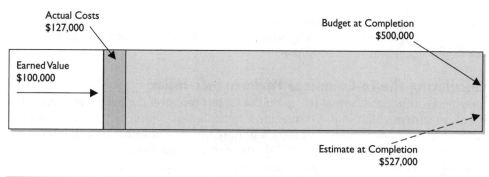

Figure 7-13   The EAC can also account for anomalies in project expenses.

EAC with Atypical Variances   Sometimes anomalies within a project can skew the project estimate at completion. The formula for this scenario, as Figure 7-13 demonstrates, is the actual costs plus the budget at completion minus the earned value. Let's try it. Your project has a BAC of $500,000, and the earned value is $100,000. However, you've spent $127,000 in actual costs. The EAC would be $127,000 + $500,000 – $100,000, or $527,000. That's your new estimate at completion for this project.

EAC Using the CPI   If a project has a CPI of .97, you could say the project is losing three pennies on every dollar. Those three pennies are going to add up over time. This approach is most often used when the project manager realizes that the cost variances are likely going to continue through the remainder of the project. This formula, as Figure 7-14 demonstrates, is EAC = AC + ((BAC – EV)/CPI). Don't you just love nested formulas? Let's try this one out.

Your project has a BAC of $500,000, and your earned value is $150,000. Your actual costs for this project are $162,000. Your CPI is calculated as .93. The EAC would be $162,000 + (($500,000 – $150,000)/.93), or $538,344. Wasn't that fun?

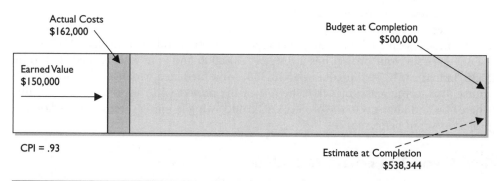

Figure 7-14   The EAC can also use the CPI as a modifier.

EXAM TIP There won't be as many questions on these EVM formulas as you might hope, but knowing these formulas can help you nail down the few questions you'll likely have.

Calculating the To-Complete Performance Index

Imagine a formula that would tell you if the project can meet the budget at completion based on current conditions. Or imagine a formula that can predict if the project can even achieve your new estimate at completion. Forget your imagination and just use the To-Complete Performance Index (TCPI). This formula can forecast the likelihood of a project to achieve its goals based on what's happening in the project right now. There are two different flavors for the TCPI, depending on what you want to accomplish:

- If you want to see if your project can meet the budget at completion, you'll use this formula: TCPI = (BAC – EV)/(BAC – AC).

- If you want to see if your project can meet the newly created estimate at completion, you'll use this version of the formula: TCPI = (BAC – EV)/ (EAC – AC).

Anything greater than 1 in either formula means that you'll have to be more efficient than you planned in order to achieve the BAC or the EAC, depending on which formula you've used. Basically, the greater the number is than 1, the less likely it is that you'll be able to meet your BAC or the EAC, depending on which formula you've used. The lower the number is than 1, the more likely you are to reach your BAC or EAC (again, depending on which formula you've used).

Finding Big Variances

Two variances relate to the entire project, and they're both easy to learn. The first variance you don't really know until the project is 100 percent complete. This is the project variance, and it's simply BAC – AC. If your project had a budget of $500,000 and you spent $734,000 to get it all done, then the project variance is $500,000 – $734,000, which equates, of course, to –$234,000.

The second variance is part of our forecasting model, and it predicts the likely project variance. It's called the variance at completion (VAC), and the formula is VAC = BAC – EAC. Let's say your project has a BAC of $500,000 and your EAC is predicted to be $538,344. The VAC is $500,000 – $538,344, for a predicted variance of –$38,344. Of course, this formula assumes that the rest of the project will run smoothly. In reality, where you and I hang out, the project VAC could swing in either direction based on the project's overall performance.

The Five EVM Formula Rules

For EVM formulas, the following five rules should be remembered:

1. Always start with EV.
2. Variance means subtraction.

3. Index means division.

4. Less than 1 is bad in an index, and greater than 1 is good. Except for TCPI, which is the reverse.

5. Negative is bad in a variance.

The formulas for earned value analysis can be completed manually or through project management software. For the exam, you'll want to memorize these formulas. Table 7-1 shows a summary of all the formulas, as well as a sample, albeit goofy, mnemonic device.

DIGITAL CONTENT   These aren't much fun to memorize, I know, but you should. While you won't have an overwhelming number of EVM questions on your exam, these are free points if you know the formulas and can do the math. I have a present for you—it's an Excel spreadsheet called "EV Worksheet." It shows all of these formulas in action. I recommend you make up some numbers to test your ability to complete these formulas and then plug in your values to Excel to confirm your math. Enjoy!

Name	Formula	Sample Mnemonic Device
Planned Value	PV = percent complete of where the project should be	Please
Earned Value	EV = percent complete × BAC	Eat
Cost Variance	CV = EV – AC	Carl's
Schedule Variance	SV = EV – PV	Sugar
Cost Performance Index	CPI = EV/AC	Candy
Schedule Performance Index	SPI = EV/PV	S (This and the following two spell "SEE")
Estimate at Completion (typical variance)	EAC = BAC/CPI	E
Estimate at Completion (atypical variance)	EAC = BAC + AC – EV	E
Estimate at Completion	EAC = AC + ETC	Everyone
Estimate to Complete	ETC = EAC – AC	Eat
To-Complete Performance Index (BAC)	(BAC – EV)/(BAC – AC)	The
To-Complete Performance Index (EAC)	(BAC – EV)/(EAC – AC)	Taffy
Variance at Completion	VAC = BAC – EAC	Violin

Table 7-1   A Summary of EVM Formulas

Chapter Summary

Projects require resources and time, both of which cost money. Projects are estimated, or predicted, according to how much the project work will likely cost to complete. There are multiple flavors and approaches to project estimating. Project managers can use analogous estimating, parametric estimating, or, the most reliable, bottom-up estimating. Whatever estimating approach the project manager elects to use, the basis of the estimate should be documented in case the estimate should ever be called into question.

When a project manager creates the project estimate, he should also factor in a contingency reserve for project risks and cost overruns. Based on the enterprise environmental factors of an organization, and often the project priority, the process to create and receive the contingency reserve may fluctuate. The contingency reserve is not an allowance to be spent at the project manager's discretion but more of a safety net should the project go awry. Variances covered by the contingency reserve can't be swept under the rug, but must be accounted for and hopefully learned from.

Cost budgeting is the aggregation of the costs to create the work packages in the WBS. Sometimes, cost budgeting refers to the cost aggregation as the "roll-up" of the costs associated with each work package. Cost budgeting effectively applies the cost estimates over time. Most project managers don't receive the entire project funding in one swoop, but rather in step functions over the life of the project.

Once the project moves from planning into execution, it also moves into monitoring and control. The project manager and the project team work together to control the project costs and monitor the performance of the project work. The most accessible method to monitor the project cost is through earned value management. Earned value management demonstrates the performance of the project and allows the project manager to forecast where the project is likely to end up financially.

Key Terms

Actual cost (AC)   The actual amount of monies the project has spent to date.

Analogous estimating   An approach that relies on historical information to predict the cost of the current project. It is also known as top-down estimating and is the least reliable of all the cost-estimating approaches.

Bottom-up estimating   An estimating approach that starts from zero, accounts for each component of the WBS, and arrives at a sum for the project. It is completed with the project team and can be one of the most time-consuming and most reliable methods to predict project costs.

Budget estimate   This estimate is also somewhat broad and is used early in the planning processes and also in top-down estimates. The range of variance for the estimate can be from –10 percent to +25 percent.

Commercial database   A cost-estimating approach that uses a database, typically software-driven, to create the cost estimate for a project.

Contingency reserve   A contingency allowance to account for overruns in costs. Contingency allowances are used at the project manager's discretion and with management's approval to counteract cost overruns for scheduled activities and risk events.

Cost aggregation   Costs are parallel to each WBS work package. The costs of each work package are aggregated to their corresponding control accounts. Each control account then is aggregated to the sum of the project costs.

Cost baseline   A time-lapse exposure of when the project monies are to be spent in relation to cumulative values of the work completed in the project.

Cost budgeting   The cost aggregation achieved by assigning specific dollar amounts for each of the scheduled activities or, more likely, for each of the work packages in the WBS. Cost budgeting applies the cost estimates over time.

Cost change control system   A system that examines any changes associated with scope changes, the cost of materials, and the cost of any other resources, and the associated impact on the overall project cost.

Cost management plan   The cost management plan dictates how cost variances will be managed.

Cost of poor quality   The monies spent to recover from not adhering to the expected level of quality. Examples may include rework, defect repair, loss of life or limb because safety precautions were not taken, loss of sales, and loss of customers. This is also known as the cost of nonconformance to quality.

Cost of quality   The monies spent to attain the expected level of quality within a project. Examples include training, testing, and safety precautions.

Cost performance index (CPI)   Measures the project based on its financial performance. The formula is CPI = EV/AC.

Cost variance (CV)   The difference of the earned value amount and the cumulative actual costs of the project. The formula is CV = EV − AC.

Definitive estimate   This estimate type is one of the most accurate. It's used late in the planning processes and is associated with bottom-up estimating. You need the WBS in order to create the definitive estimate. The range of variance for the estimate can be from −5 percent to +10 percent.

Direct costs   Costs are attributed directly to the project work and cannot be shared among projects (for example, airfare, hotels, long-distance phone charges, and so on).

Earned value (EV)   Earned value is the physical work completed to date and the authorized budget for that work. It is the percentage of the BAC that represents the actual work completed in the project.

Estimate at completion (EAC)   These forecasting formulas predict the likely completed costs of the project based on current scenarios within the project.

Estimate to complete (ETC)   An earned value management formula that predicts how much funding the project will require to be completed. Three variations of this formula are based on conditions the project may be experiencing.

Fixed costs   Costs that remain constant throughout the life of the project (the cost of a piece of rented equipment for the project, the cost of a consultant brought on to the project, and so on).

Funding limit reconciliation   An organization's approach to managing cash flow against the project deliverables based on a schedule, milestone accomplishment, or data constraints.

Indirect costs   Costs that are representative of more than one project (for example, utilities for the performing organization, access to a training room, project management software license, and so on).

Known unknown   An event that will likely happen within the project, but when it will happen and to what degree is unknown. These events, such as delays, are usually risk-related.

Learning curve   An approach that assumes the cost per unit decreases the more units workers complete, because workers learn as they complete the required work.

Oligopoly   A market condition where the market is so tight that the actions of one vendor affect the actions of all the others.

Opportunity cost   The total cost of the opportunity that is refused to realize an opposing opportunity.

Parametric estimating   An approach using a parametric model to extrapolate what costs will be needed for a project (for example, cost per hour and cost per unit). It can include variables and points based on conditions.

Planned value (PV)   Planned value is the work scheduled and the budget authorized to accomplish that work. It is the percentage of the BAC that reflects where the project should be at this point in time.

Project variance   The final variance, which is discovered only at the project's completion. The formula is VAR = BAC – AC.

Regression analysis   This is a statistical approach to predicting what future values may be, based on historical values. Regression analysis creates quantitative predictions based on variables within one value to predict variables in another. This form of estimating relies solely on pure statistical math to reveal relationships between variables and to predict future values.

Reserve analysis   Cost reserves are for unknown unknowns within a project. The management reserve is not part of the project cost baseline, but is included as part of the project budget.

Rough order of magnitude   This rough estimate is used during the initiating processes and in top-down estimates. The range of variance for the estimate can be from −25 percent to +75 percent.

Schedule performance index (SPI)   Measures the project based on its schedule performance. The formula is SPI = EV/PV.

Schedule variance (SV)   The difference between the earned value and the planned value. The formulas is SV = EV − PV.

Single source   Many vendors can provide what your project needs to purchase, but you prefer to work with a specific vendor.

Sole source   Only one vendor can provide what your project needs to purchase. Examples include a specific consultant, specialized service, or unique type of material.

Sunk costs   Monies that have already been invested in a project.

To-Complete Performance Index   A formula to forecast the likelihood of a project to achieve its goals based on what's happening in the project right now. There are two different flavors for the TCPI, depending on what you want to accomplish. If you want to see if your project can meet the budget at completion, you'll use this formula: TCPI = (BAC − EV)/(BAC − AC). If you want to see if your project can meet the newly created estimate at completion, you'll use this version of the formula: TCPI = (BAC − EV)/(EAC − AC).

Variable costs   Costs that change based on the conditions applied in the project (the number of meeting participants, the supply of and demand for materials, and so on).

Variance   The difference between what was expected and what was experienced.

Variance at completion (VAC)   A forecasting formula that predicts how much of a variance the project will likely have based on current conditions within the project. The formula is VAC = BAC − EAC.

Questions

1. You are using a previous similar project to predict the costs of the current project. Which of the following best describes analogous estimating?

   A. Regression analysis

   B. Bottom-up estimating

   C. Organizational process assets

   D. Enterprise environmental factors

2. You are the project manager for a new technology implementation project. Management has requested that your estimates be as exact as possible. Which one of the following methods of estimating will provide the most accurate estimate?

    A. Top-down estimating

    B. Top-down budgeting

    C. Bottom-up estimating

    D. Parametric estimating

3. Amy is the project manager for her company and she's working with the project team to determine the effect of a proposed change on the project's budget. When Amy looks at the change, she tells the team that the change will pass through project's cost change control system. What does the cost change control system do?

    A. It defines the methods to change the cost baseline.

    B. It defines the methods to create the cost baseline.

    C. It evaluates changes to the project costs based on changes to the project scope.

    D. This is not a valid change control system.

4. You have just started a project for a manufacturer. Project team members report they are 30 percent complete with the project. You have spent $25,000 of the project's $250,000 budget. What is the earned value for this project?

    A. 10 percent

    B. $75,000

    C. $25,000

    D. Not enough information to know

5. You and your project team are about to enter a meeting to determine project costs. You have elected to use bottom-up estimating and will base your estimate on the WBS. Which one of the following is not an attribute of bottom-up estimating?

    A. People doing the work create the estimates.

    B. It creates a more accurate estimate.

    C. It's more expensive to do than other methods.

    D. It's less expensive to do than other methods.

6. You are the project manager for a consulting company. Your company has two possible projects to manage, but they can only choose one. Project WQQ is worth $217,000, while Project LB is worth $229,000. Management elects to choose Project LB. The opportunity cost of this choice is which one of the following?

    A. $12,000

    B. $217,000

    C. $229,000

  D. Zero, because project LB is worth more than Project WQQ

7. You are the project manager for the CSR Training Project, and 21,000
   customer service reps are invited to attend the training session. Attendance
   is optional. You have calculated the costs of the training facility, but the
   workbook expense depends on how many students register for the class. For
   every 5,000 workbooks created, the cost is reduced by a percentage of the
   original printing cost. The workbook expense is an example of which one of
   the following?

   A. Fixed costs

   B. Parametric costs

   C. Variable costs

   D. Indirect costs

8. You are the project manager of a construction project scheduled to last 24
   months. You have elected to rent a piece of equipment for the project's
   duration, even though you will need the equipment only periodically
   throughout the project. The costs of the equipment rental per month are
   $890. This is an example of which of the following?

   A. Fixed costs

   B. Parametric costs

   C. Variable costs

   D. Indirect costs

9. You are the project manager of the BHG Project. Your BAC is $600,000. You
   have spent $270,000 of your budget. You are now 40 percent done with the
   project, though your plan called for you to be 45 percent done with the work
   by this time. What is your CPI?

   A. 100

   B. 89

   C. .89

   D. .79

10. Management has requested that you complete a definitive cost estimate
    for your current project. Which one of the following must exist in order to
    complete this estimate?

    A. Project scope statement

    B. Work breakdown structure (WBS)

    C. Project team

    D. Expert judgment

11. You need to procure a highly specialized chemical for a research project. There is only one vendor available that provides the materials you need. This scenario is an example of what market condition?

    A. Constraint

    B. Single source

    C. Sole source

    D. Oligopoly

12. You are the project manager of the Network Upgrade Project for your company. Management has asked that you create a cost estimate of the project so they can determine the project funding. You gather the inputs for the cost estimate and begin the process of cost estimating. Of the following cost-estimating inputs, which one is the least reliable?

    A. Team member recollections

    B. Historical information

    C. Project files

    D. Cost-estimating templates

13. You can purchase pea gravel for your project at $437 per metric ton. You need four tons of the pea gravel, so you predict your costs will be $1,748. This is an example of which cost-estimating approach?

    A. Parametric

    B. Analogous

    C. Bottom-up

    D. Top-down

14. Which one of the following is an example of resource cost rates that a project manager could use to predict the cost of the project?

    A. Analogous estimating

    B. Bottom-up estimating

    C. Commercial database

    D. Procurement bid analysis

15. You have created a cost estimate for a new project that you'll be managing in your organization. All of the following should be included in your cost estimate except for which one?

    A. Description of the schedule activity's project scope of work

    B. Assumptions made

    C. Constraints

    D. Team members the project will utilize

16. Linda is the project manager of a construction project. The budget for her project is $275,000. The project team made a mistake early in the project that cost $34,000 in added materials. Linda does not believe the mistakes will likely happen again because the team is 30 percent complete with the project and things are once again going smoothly. Her sponsor wants to know how much more funding Linda will likely need on the project. What should Linda tell the sponsor?

   A. $192,500

   B. $241,000

   C. $309,000

   D. $275,000

17. A project had a budget of $750,000 and was completed on time. The project expenses, however, were 15 percent more than what the project called for. What is the earned value of this project?

   A. Impossible to know—not enough information

   B. $112,500

   C. $637,500

   D. $750,000

18. A project had a budget of $750,000 and was completed on time. The project expenses, however, were 15 percent more than what the project called for. What is the variance at the completion for this project?

   A. Impossible to know—not enough information

   B. $112,500

   C. $637,500

   D. $750,000

19. Marty is the project manager of a software development project. He has reviewed the project's costs and progress and he realizes that he has a cost variance of $44,000. He needs to complete what type of report?

   A. Status report

   B. Exceptions report

   C. Forecast report

   D. Lessons learned

20. You are a construction manager for a construction project. The project will be using a new material that the project team has never worked with before. You allot $10,000 to train the project team on the new materials so that the project will operate smoothly. The $10,000 for training is known as what?

   A. Cost of quality

    B. Cost of poor quality

    C. Sunk costs

    D. Contingency allowance

Questions and Answers

1. You are using a previous similar project to predict the costs of the current project. Which of the following best describes analogous estimating?

    A. Regression analysis

    B. Bottom-up estimating

    C. Organizational process assets

    D. Enterprise environmental factors

    C. Analogous estimating is based on historical information, which is part of organizational process assets. A, regression analysis, is incorrect because this choice describes the study of a project moving backward so that it may ultimately move forward. B is incorrect because this is the most reliable cost-estimating technique and is based on the current project's WBS. D, enterprise environmental factors, is a term that describes the internal policies and procedures a project manager must follow within the project.

2. You are the project manager for a new technology implementation project. Management has requested that your estimates be as exact as possible. Which one of the following methods of estimating will provide the most accurate estimate?

    A. Top-down estimating

    B. Top-down budgeting

    C. Bottom-up estimating

    D. Parametric estimating

    C. Bottom-up estimating takes the longest to complete of all the estimating approaches, but it is also the most reliable approach. A, top-down estimating, is also known as analogous estimating, and it is not reliable. B, top-down budgeting, is not a valid term for this question. D, parametric estimating, is an approach that predicts the project costs based on a parameter, such as cost per hour, cost per unit, or cost per usage.

3. Amy is the project manager for her company and she's working with the project team to determine the effect of a proposed change on the project's budget. When Amy looks at the change, she tells the team that the change will pass through project's cost change control system. What does the cost change control system do?

    A. It defines the methods to change the cost baseline.

B. It defines the methods to create the cost baseline.

C. It evaluates changes to the project costs based on changes to the project scope.

D. This is not a valid change control system.

A. The cost change control system defines how changes to the cost baseline may be approved. B, C, and D are all invalid choices.

4. You have just started a project for a manufacturer. Project team members report they are 30 percent complete with the project. You have spent $25,000 of the project's $250,000 budget. What is the earned value for this project?

A. 10 percent

B. $75,000

C. $25,000

D. Not enough information to know

B. Earned value is found by multiplying the percentage of the project that is completed by the project's budget at completion. In this instance, it's $75,000. A, C, and D are all incorrect.

5. You and your project team are about to enter a meeting to determine project costs. You have elected to use bottom-up estimating and will base your estimate on the WBS. Which one of the following is not an attribute of bottom-up estimating?

A. People doing the work create the estimates.

B. It creates a more accurate estimate.

C. It's more expensive to do than other methods.

D. It's less expensive to do than other methods.

D. Bottom-up estimating is typically more expensive to do than other estimating approaches, because of the time required to create this type of estimate. A, B, and C are all accurate attributes of a bottom-up estimate.

6. You are the project manager for a consulting company. Your company has two possible projects to manage, but they can only choose one. Project WQQ is worth $217,000, while Project LB is worth $229,000. Management elects to choose Project LB. The opportunity cost of this choice is which one of the following?

A. $12,000

B. $217,000

C. $229,000

D. Zero, because project LB is worth more than Project WQQ

B. The opportunity cost is the amount of the project that the organization cannot do. A is incorrect because the $12,000 represents the difference between the two projects. C, $229,000, is incorrect because this is the amount of the LB project. D is incorrect because this is not an accurate statement.

7. You are the project manager for the CSR Training Project, and 21,000 customer service reps are invited to attend the training session. Attendance is optional. You have calculated the costs of the training facility, but the workbook expense depends on how many students register for the class. For every 5,000 workbooks created, the cost is reduced by a percentage of the original printing cost. The workbook expense is an example of which one of the following?

A. Fixed costs

B. Parametric costs

C. Variable costs

D. Indirect costs

C. This is an example of a variable cost, since the cost of the training will fluctuate based on the number of participants that choose to come to the project session. A is incorrect because fixed costs do not vary. B is incorrect because parametric costs can be identified as cost per unit. D is incorrect because indirect costs are a way to describe costs that may be shared between projects.

8. You are the project manager of a construction project scheduled to last 24 months. You have elected to rent a piece of equipment for the project's duration, even though you will need the equipment only periodically throughout the project. The costs of the equipment rental per month are $890. This is an example of which of the following?

A. Fixed costs

B. Parametric costs

C. Variable costs

D. Indirect costs

A. This is an example of a fixed cost. The cost of the equipment will remain uniform, or fixed, throughout the duration of the project. B is incorrect because parametric costs can be identified as cost per unit. C is incorrect because the cost of the equipment does not fluctuate. D is incorrect because indirect costs are a way to describe costs that may be shared between projects.

9. You are the project manager of the BHG Project. Your BAC is $600,000. You have spent $270,000 of your budget. You are now 40 percent done with the project, though your plan called for you to be 45 percent done with the work by this time. What is your CPI?

A. 100

B. 89

C. .89

D. .79

C. The CPI is found by dividing the earned value by the actual costs. A is incorrect because the project is not performing at 100 percent. B is incorrect because "89" is not the same value as C. D is an incorrect calculation of the CPI.

10. Management has requested that you complete a definitive cost estimate for your current project. Which one of the following must exist in order to complete this estimate?

A. Project scope statement

B. Work breakdown structure

C. Project team

D. Expert judgment

B. The WBS is needed in order to create a definitive cost estimate. This is the most accurate estimate type, but it also takes the longest to complete. A, C, and D are all incorrect because these items are not required to complete a definitive estimate.

11. You need to procure a highly specialized chemical for a research project. There is only one vendor available that provides the materials you need. This scenario is an example of what market condition?

A. Constraint

B. Single source

C. Sole source

D. Oligopoly

C. Sole source is the best choice because it describes the marketplace condition in which only one vendor can provide the goods or services your project requires. A, constraint, is not a valid market condition. B, single source, describes the marketplace condition in which there are multiple vendors that can provide the goods or services your project demands, but you prefer to work with just one in particular. D, an oligopoly, is a market condition in which the actions of one vendor affect the actions of the other vendors.

12. You are the project manager of the Network Upgrade Project for your company. Management has asked that you create a cost estimate of the project so they can determine the project funding. You gather the inputs for the cost

estimate and begin the process of cost estimating. Of the following cost-estimating inputs, which one is the least reliable?

A. Team member recollections

B. Historical information

C. Project files

D. Cost-estimating templates

A. Team member recollections are the least reliable input to cost estimating. B, C, and D are all valid inputs to the cost-estimating process.

13. You can purchase pea gravel for your project at $437 per metric ton. You need four tons of the pea gravel, so you predict your costs will be $1,748. This is an example of which cost-estimating approach?

A. Parametric

B. Analogous

C. Bottom-up

D. Top-down

A. The cost of the pea gravel is a parametric estimate. B, analogous, is incorrect because no other project cost estimate is being referenced. C, bottom-up, is not described in this instance because the WBS and each work package is not being estimated for cost. D, top-down estimating, is another name for A, analogous estimating, so this choice is invalid.

14. Which one of the following is an example of resource cost rates that a project manager could use to predict the cost of the project?

A. Analogous estimating

B. Bottom-up estimating

C. Commercial database

D. Procurement bid analysis

C. Commercial databases often provide resource cost rates for project estimating, so this is the correct answer for this question. A, B, and D do not include resource cost rates, so these are all incorrect.

15. You have created a cost estimate for a new project that you'll be managing in your organization. All of the following should be included in your cost estimate except for which one?

A. Description of the schedule activity's project scope of work

B. Assumptions made

C. Constraints

D. Team members the project will utilize

D. The team members that the project manager will utilize are not included in the cost estimate. The project manager will include the project scope of work, the assumptions made, and the constraints considered when creating a cost estimate, so A, B, and C are incorrect.

16. Linda is the project manager of a construction project. The budget for her project is $275,000. The project team made a mistake early in the project that cost $34,000 in added materials. Linda does not believe the mistakes will likely happen again because the team is 30 percent complete with the project and things are once again going smoothly. Her sponsor wants to know how much more funding Linda will likely need on the project. What should Linda tell the sponsor?

    A. $192,500

    B. $241,000

    C. $309,000

    D. $275,000

    A. The formula for this instance, because the conditions experienced were atypical, is ETC = BAC − EV. The formula for Linda's project would be ETC = $275,000 − $82,500. B, C, and D are all incorrect calculations of the estimate-to-complete formula.

17. A project had a budget of $750,000 and was completed on time. The project expenses, however, were 15 percent more than what the project called for. What is the earned value of this project?

    A. Impossible to know—not enough information

    B. $112,500

    C. $637,500

    D. $750,000

    D. The earned value is simply the percent complete times the BAC. In this instance, the project's budget was $750,000, and since the project is 100 percent complete, the answer is D. A, B, and C are all incorrect.

18. A project had a budget of $750,000 and was completed on time. The project expenses, however, were 15 percent more than what the project called for. What is the variance at the completion for this project?

    A. Impossible to know—not enough information

    B. $112,500

    C. $637,500

    D. $750,000

    B. The formula for this problem is variance at completion minus the actual costs for the project. A, C, and D are all incorrect.

19. Marty is the project manager of a software development project. He has reviewed the project's costs and progress and he realizes that he has a cost variance of $44,000. He needs to complete what type of report?

   A. Status report

   B. Exceptions report

   C. Forecast report

   D. Lessons learned

   B. Because Marty has a variance, he needs to complete a variance report. A variance report is also known as an exceptions report, so B is the best answer. A, a status report, is used to communicate the status of the project, not the variances. C is not a valid report type. D, lessons learned, is an ongoing project document, not a report type.

20. You are a construction manager for a construction project. The project will be using a new material that the project team has never worked with before. You allot $10,000 to train the project team on the new materials so that the project will operate smoothly. The $10,000 for training is known as what?

   A. Cost of quality

   B. Cost of poor quality

   C. Sunk costs

   D. Contingency allowance

   A. Training for the project team is known as the cost of quality. B, the cost of poor quality, is incorrect because this would be the costs the project would incur if it did not attain the expected level of quality. Sunk costs describe the monies that have been spent on a project already, so C is incorrect. D, contingency allowance, is an amount of funds allotted to cover cost overruns in a project.

Managing Project Quality

8

In this chapter, you will
- Plan for quality
- Work with quality assurance programs
- Perform quality control
- Recognize the quality control charts

What good does it do if a project launches, the project execution consumes the monies and time, but the project deliverable is of unacceptable quality? Imagine a project to build a new house, and at the project completion, the house is tilting to one side, the windows all have cracks and holes in them, and the roof has obvious gaps for the rain and birds. This is not, I'm sure, what the homeowners had in mind.

Fortunately, in project management—in good project management—mechanisms are in place to plan and implement quality throughout the project, and not just as an afterthought. Project quality management is all about the project manager, the project team, and the performing organization working together to ensure that the project performs as the project plan calls for, so that the project deliverable aligns with the project scope statement. Quality in a project is really all about getting the project done and creating a deliverable that satisfies the project requirements and that can actually be used by the project customer.

According to the American Society for Quality (ASQ), "Quality is the degree to which a set of inherent characteristics fulfill requirements." Well, isn't that interesting? Let's go back in time. A project is launched and a project charter is issued to the project manager. Then the project manager and the project team create what document? The project scope statement. The project scope statement defines all of the requirements for the project, including what's in and what's out of scope. Quality is, therefore, satisfying everything that the project scope statement requires.

In the project scope statement, we define what the project will create, its requirements for acceptance, and the metrics to measure project success. In project quality management, we plan quality into the project, inspect the project and deliverables for the existence of quality, and then move toward the scope validation process, which confirms that we've created what our customer expected. Quality is about delivering on promises.

No discussion on quality is complete without a nod to our pal W. Edwards Deming. You likely won't need to know much about Deming for the exam, other than his famed plan-do-check-act (PDCA) cycle. (I highly recommend Mary B. Walton's book *The Deming Management Method* [Perigee Books, 1988] for the complete story of Deming— maybe after you pass your PMI examination.) For your PMP and CAPM exams, know that Deming's philosophy on quality management considers of paramount importance customer satisfaction, prevention over inspection, a call for management responsibility, and a desire to do the work correctly the first time.

 VIDEO For a more detailed explanation, watch the *Examining Quality Control* video now.

This chapter is core to the PMI's idea of project integration management. If quality suffers, then all of the knowledge areas are affected by the absence of quality. You can also see the effect on integration management if any of the other knowledge areas suffers in performance. Quality is directly affected by all of the other areas of project management, and they likewise are affected if quality is missing. It's a busy, two-way street.

Planning for Quality

Quality planning is the process of first determining which quality standards are relevant to your project and then finding the best methods of adhering to those quality standards. This is a great example of project integration management, which was referred to earlier. Quality planning is core to the planning process group because each knowledge area has relevant standards that affect quality, and quality planning is integrated into each planning process.

In other words, if a project manager rushes through planning for each of the knowledge areas, then quality is likely to suffer. When change requests are proposed, the impact of each change request on each of the knowledge areas is considered. You already know that a change request could have a financial impact, a schedule impact, and more. Quality management asks: What impact does quality have on this proposed change, and what impact does this change have on the overall quality of the project?

Throughout the project planning, the focus is on completing the project by satisfying the project requirements. Quality is fleshed into all of the project planning. The foundation of quality planning states that quality is planned into the project, not inspected in. In other words, planning how to achieve the expected level of quality and then executing the project plan is easier, more cost-effective, and less stressful for everyone involved than catching and fixing mistakes as the project moves toward completion. Like my dad used to say, "Do it right the first time."

There are six inputs to planning for quality in a project:

- **Project management plan** The project management plan needs the scope, cost, and schedule baselines as part of the quality management planning. The project scope baseline defines all of the project requirements and the expectations of the project customer. By satisfying the requirements in the scope baseline, nothing less and nothing more, quality can be achieved. The goal of project quality management is to satisfy the acceptance criteria for the project as defined in the project scope baseline. The cost baseline is needed to help balance the expected quality with the monies you spend. Finally, the schedule baseline is needed to determine how the schedule may affect the quality processes. Time can directly affect quality. If the project schedule starts to slip, the project team may feel rushed, and rushed people often make more mistakes. More mistakes will increase the project cost and further delay the project. As Ben Franklin said, "Haste makes waste."

- **Stakeholder register**   You'll need to know which stakeholders have a specific interest in the quality objectives of the project and how to contact them. Some stakeholders may have concerns about specific deliverables, so you'll want to communicate with those folks when quality issues arise.

- **Risk register**   The risk register contains all of the identified risks and information on how potential risks may affect the overall quality of the project.

- **Requirements documentation**   The requirements of the project are needed because these reflect the expectations of the project stakeholders. The project's work is to create all of the requirements and fulfill the product scope.

- **Enterprise environmental factors**   You know that enterprise environmental factors are the policies and procedures your organization must adhere to. In particular, the enterprise environmental factors I'm discussing here are those mandates that affect the application area your project is dealing with. In other words, a construction project has different codes and regulations to follow than a project to bake a million cookies does.

- **Organizational process assets**   These are the methods of operation your organization follows and the guidelines that are specific to your organization. Historical information, lessons learned, and guidelines within your organization are there for the project managers to rely on. Within the organization, a quality policy may have been issued by senior management for all projects to adhere to—this is part of organizational process assets. And what if a quality policy doesn't exist? It's up to the project management team to create one for their project.

Using Quality Planning Tools

The project manager and the project team can use several tools to plan for quality in the project. The goal of all these tools is to plan quality into the project rather than attempt to inspect quality into the project. (To repeat, do the work right the first time.) Let's take a look at these tools and how the project manager and the project team can use them to their benefit.

Using a Cost-Benefit Analysis

Ever go shopping and compare prices? For example, you might consider the cost of two cars in relation to features both cars provide. Or you might consider hiring a more experienced worker because he or she has some competencies that make the extra dollars worth the costs. Part of planning for quality is moving through this process of cost-benefit analysis.

Using a cost-benefit analysis is more than just considering how much to spend for features and materials used in the project deliverable, although that is part of the process. Cost-benefit analysis also considers the cost of completing the project work and the best approach to achieving quality in the project in relation to the monies to complete the work. For example, you could always use senior engineers to complete even the most menial tasks, but that wouldn't be a good use of their time or of the monies to pay for the senior engineers' time. Figure 8-1 is an example of using a cost-benefit analysis.

Cost-benefit analysis is simply the study of the quality received in proportion to the cost to reach those quality expectations. The project management team must understand how much money is appropriate to spend to satisfy the project customer. If the project spends too much to reach a level of quality that is far beyond what the customer expects or wants, then that's waste. The same is true if the project team produces less than the level of quality the customer expects and rework is needed.

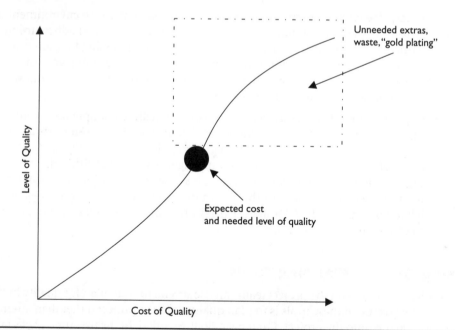

Figure 8-1   Quality should meet, not exceed, the customer's expectations.

EXAM COACH Quality is achieved by satisfying exactly what the scope calls for. What's the scope for your exam? It's a pass or fail exam, so your scope is probably to pass, right? Don't aim for a 100 percent—aim for a passing grade. Put your efforts into the biggest exam objectives to get the biggest bang for your exam buck.

Benchmarking Performance

Benchmarking is simply comparing two similar things to measure which one performs best. For example, you could benchmark the same activities on two different computers, test-drive several different cars, or even benchmark an organization before and after a project. Benchmarking, in regard to quality planning, examines project practices against other projects to measure performance, and then selects the best practices for performance in the current project.

Using Design of Experiments

The design-of-experiments approach relies on statistical what-if scenarios to determine what variables within a project will result in the best outcome. This type of approach is most often used on the product of the project rather than on the project itself. For example, a project team creating a new bicycle may experiment with the width of the tires, the weight of the frame, and the position of the handlebars in relation to the bike seat to determine the most comfortable ride at an acceptable cost to the consumer.

Although design of experiments is most often associated with product design, it can be applied to project management activities. For example, a project manager may evaluate the activities within a project and determine the time and cost of activities, depending on which employees are assigned to complete the work. A more experienced worker may cost the project more money on an hourly basis, but this individual is expected to complete the work in a third of the time that a less experienced worker would. This is design of experiments: experimenting with different variables to find the best solution at the best cost.

Design of experiments is also used as a method to identify which variables within a project or product are causing failures or unacceptable results. The goal of design of experiments is to isolate the root cause of an effect and to adjust that cause to eliminate the unacceptable results.

Considering the Cost of Quality

The cost of quality (COQ) considers how much must be spent to achieve the expected level of quality within the project. There are two types of costs directly tied to quality:

- **Cost of conformance to quality**   This is the cost associated with the monies spent to attain the expected level of quality. For example, training, safety issues, and purchasing the right equipment and materials all contribute to the expected levels of quality. This is sometimes called the cost of conformance to quality.

- **Cost of nonconformance to quality**   This is the cost associated with not satisfying the quality expectations. For example, if the project manager does not train the project team, or if the correct materials are not used in the project implementation, quality will suffer, and additional costs will be incurred to do the work over. Cost of poor quality can also result in rejected deliverables, loss of sales and customers, and, if safety concerns are not met, loss of life or limb. The cost of nonconformance to quality is also known as the cost of poor quality or the cost of failure.

 EXAM TIP There are actually eight tools and techniques you can use to plan quality: cost-benefit analysis, cost of quality, seven basic quality tools, benchmarking, design of experiments, statistical sampling, additional quality tools, and meetings. You'll use some of these same tools over and over, and I'm going to cover all of the tools in this chapter. In particular, the seven basic quality tools are used in planning and in quality control.

Using Other Quality Planning Tools

The project manager can use lots of other tools and approaches to plan for quality within the project. I recommend that you be aware of these tools, but don't invest too much time learning their ins and outs:

- Brainstorming
- Affinity diagrams
- Force field analysis
- Nominal group techniques
- Matrix diagrams
- Flowcharts
- Prioritization matrices

Creating the Quality Management Plan

The end result of the quality planning phase is to find a method to implement the quality policy. Because planning is iterative, the quality planning sessions often require several revisits to the quality planning processes. Longer projects may have scheduled quality planning sessions to compare the performance of the project in relation to the quality that was planned.

One of the major outputs of quality planning is the quality management plan. This document describes how the project manager and the project team will fulfill the quality policy. In an ISO 9000 environment, the quality management plan is referred to as the "project quality system." The quality management plan addresses the following three things about the project and the project work:

- **Quality control** Work results are monitored to see if they meet relevant quality standards. If the results do not meet the quality standards, the project manager applies root cause analysis to determine the cause of the poor performance and then eliminates the cause. Quality control is inspection-oriented.

- **Quality assurance** The overall performance is evaluated to ensure that the project meets the relevant quality standards. Quality assurance maps to an organization's quality policy and is typically a managerial process. Quality assurance is generally considered the work of applying the quality plan.

- **Quality improvement** The project performance is measured and evaluated, and corrective actions are applied to improve the product and the project. The improvements can be large or small, depending on the condition and the quality philosophy of the performing organization.

Establishing Quality Metrics

You need some quality metrics. If you don't measure, then your project cannot improve. Specifically, I'm talking about the quantifiable terms and values to measure a process, activity, or work result. An example of quality metrics is an expected value for the required torque to tighten a bolt on a piece of equipment. By testing and measuring the torque, the operational definition would prove or disprove the quality of the product. Other examples can include hours of labor to complete a work package, required safety measures, cost per unit, and so on.

Operational definitions are clear, concise measurements. Designating that 95 percent of all customer service calls should be answered by a live person within 30 seconds is a metric. A statement that all calls should be answered in a timely manner is not.

Applying Checklists

Checklists are simple approaches to ensure that work is completed according to the quality policy. It's usually a list of activities that workers will check off as each task is completed. Checklists can be quick instructions of what needs to be done to clean a piece of equipment or questions that remind the employee to complete a task: "Did you turn off the printer before opening the cover?"

Creating the Process Improvement Plan

One of the goals of quality project management is continuous process improvement. The process improvement plan looks to improve the project, not just the end result of the project. Its aim is to identify and eliminate waste and non-value-added activity. Specifically, this plan aims to accomplish the following:

- Increase customer value by eliminating waste within the project.
- Establish process boundaries.
- Determine process configuration through a flowchart for evaluation and analysis in order to improve the project as a whole.

- Process metrics within the project.
- Establish targets for performance improvement.

Updating the Baseline and the Project Management Plan

Just as there is a baseline for costs, schedule, and scope, there is also a baseline for quality. The quality baseline records and compares the quality objectives for the project. It's the measurement of the project performance and the quality of the project objectives. The variances show the project management team where the project should be improving.

The project management plan includes two plans that are outputs of quality planning: the quality management plan and the process improvement plan. Based on the outputs of quality management planning, the project plan can be updated to reflect how the expected level of quality will be achieved. As usual, changes to the project scope that change the project plan will also need to be examined for their impact on quality or on the processes of the project. In addition, the project team's work to complete the changes may affect the quality of the deliverable.

Performing Quality Assurance

Quality assurance (QA) is the sum of the creation and implementation of the plans by the project manager, the project team, and management to ensure that the project meets the demands of quality. QA is not something that is done only at the end of the project, but is done before and during the project as well. Quality management is prevention-driven; you want to do the work correctly the first time.

In some organizations, the quality assurance department or another entity will complete the QA activities. QA is interested in preventing defects and assuring that quality control fixes any product problems.

There are many different approaches to QA, depending on the quality system the organization or project team has adapted. QA is, to some extent, a parent for continuous process improvement. Continuous process improvement aims to remove waste and non-value-added activities, so it works hand in hand with quality assurance.

Preparing for Quality Assurance

The project manager and the project team will need several inputs to prepare for QA:

- **The quality management plan** This plan defines how the project team will implement and fulfill the quality policy of the performing organization. You'll also reference the process improvement plan.

- **Process improvement plan** The activities you and your project team will perform in quality assurance should mesh and align with the goals of the process improvement plan.

- **Quality metrics** Quality control tests will provide these measurements. The values must be quantifiable so that results can be measured, compared, and analyzed. In other words, "pretty close to on track" is not adequate; "95 percent pass rate" is more acceptable.

- **Results of quality control**   The measurements taken by the project manager and the project team to inspect the project deliverables' quality are fed back into the QA process.

- **Project documents**   The project documentation may influence the quality assurance approaches for the project and should be reviewed to see what requirements the project should adhere to.

Applying Quality Assurance

The QA department, management, or, in some instances, even the project manager can complete the requirements for QA. QA can be accomplished using the following tools (many of the same tools used during quality planning):

- **Affinity diagram**   This diagram takes the breakdown of ideas, solutions, and project components and groups them together with likeminded ideas. For example, an IT solution might group all of the thoughts about hardware, then software, then the network, and so on.

- **Process decision program chart (PDPC)**   This chart helps the project team define all of the steps to get from the current state to a desired goal. It facilitates a conversation about what must be completed to reach the goal.

- **Interrelationship diagraphs**   These are used for complex solutions where the causes and effects of problems and benefits are intertwined with one another. For example, in a construction project the plumbing, framing, and foundation are all related and decisions and benefits in one area can cause decisions and benefits (or problems) in another area of the project.

- **Tree diagram**   Tree diagrams show hierarchies and the decomposition of a solution, an organization, or a project team. The WBS and an org chart are examples of tree diagrams.

- **Prioritization matrices**   This is a table to rank and score project decisions and alternatives to determine the best solution for the project.

- **Activity network diagrams**   These are diagrams, such as the project network diagram, to show the flow of the project work.

- **Matrix diagrams**   A data analysis table that shows the strength between variables and relationships in the matrix.

Completing a Quality Audit

Quality audits are about learning. The idea of a quality audit is to identify the lessons learned on the current project to determine how to make things better for this project—as well as for other projects within the organization. The idea is that Susan the project manager can learn from the implementations of Bob the project manager and vice versa.

Quality audits are formal reviews of what's been completed within a project, what worked, and what didn't work. The end result of the audit is improved performance for the current project, other projects, or the entire organization.

Quality audits can be scheduled at key intervals within a project or—surprise!—they can come without warning. The audit process can vary, depending on who is completing the audit: internal auditors or hired, third-party experts.

Analyzing the Project Processes

Process *improvement* is executed to examine the project-specific processes to see if they are improving. Process *analysis* is the examination of the project processes to see what's working, what isn't working, and to make recommendations of what should be improved. This is an opportunity for the project manager to streamline processes, remove non-value-added activities, and purge waste from the project.

If the process analysis leads to changes in the approach in the project, the change should be documented and communicated. You'll also want to measure the performance after the change has been implemented to see how the change has affected the project.

Improving the Project

The goal of QA is project improvement. It's not only the quality of the project's deliverables, but also the quality of the process to complete the project work. This is *process analysis*, and it follows the guidelines of the process improvement plan. Process analysis is completed through any or all of the following measures:

- An examination of problems or constraints
- An analysis of the project for non-value-added activities
- Root cause analysis
- The creation of preventive actions for identified problems

Quality improvement requires action to improve the project's effectiveness. The actions to improve the effectiveness may have to be routed through the change control system, which means change requests, analysis of the costs and risks, and involvement from the change control board (CCB). There are four outputs of quality assurance in a project:

- Change requests
- Project management plan updates
- Project document updates
- Organizational process assets updates

Performing Quality Control

This is the section of the project where the project manager and the project team have control and influence. Quality assurance (QA), for the most part, is specific to your organization, and the project manager doesn't have much control over the QA processes—he just has to do them. Quality control (QC), on the other hand, is specific to the project manager, so the project manager has lots of activities.

 EXAM TIP Pay close attention to the quality control mechanisms—there are things the project manager has control over in every project.

Quality control requires the project manager, or another qualified party, to monitor and measure project results to determine whether they are up to the quality standards. If the results are unsatisfactory, root cause analysis follows the quality control processes. Root cause analysis lets the project manager determine the cause and apply corrective actions. On the whole, QC occurs throughout the life of a project, not just at its end.

QC is not only concerned with the product the project is creating, but also with the project management processes. QC measures performance, scheduling, and cost variances. The experience of the project should be of quality—not just the product the project creates. Consider a project manager who demands that the project team work extreme hours to meet an unrealistic deadline. Team morale suffers, and likely so does the project work the team is completing.

The project team should do the following to ensure competency in quality control:

- Conduct statistical quality control measures, such as sampling and probability.
- Inspect the product to avoid errors.
- Perform attribute sampling to measure conformance to quality on a per-unit basis.
- Conduct variable sampling to measure the degree of conformance.
- Study special causes to determine anomalies.
- Research random causes to determine expected variances of quality.
- Check the tolerance range to determine if the results are within or outside an acceptable level of quality.
- Observe control limits to determine if the results are in or out of quality control.

Preparing for Quality Control

Quality control relies on several inputs, such as the following:

- **The project management plan** The project management plan contains the quality management plan as a subsidiary plan. This defines how QC will be applied to the project, the expectations of QC, and the organization's approach for performing quality control.

- **Quality metrics**   The operational definitions that define the metrics for the project are needed so that QC can measure and react to the results of project performance.

- **Quality checklists**   If the project is using checklists to ensure that project work is completed, copies of the checklists will be needed as part of quality control. The checklists can then serve as indicators of completed work, as well as of expected results.

- **Work performance data**   The results of the project work are needed to compare with the quality standards. The expected results of the product and the project can be measured from the project plan. In other words, the project must meet the expected quality metrics, or corrective action needs to be done.

- **Approved change requests**   Approved change requests affect how the project work is scheduled and performed, which may affect the project's overall quality. Quality control verifies that approved change requests are implemented properly.

- **Deliverables**   You need something to inspect. Deliverables are the results of the project work, and these are things that will be inspected to confirm that they're great and full of quality as the customer (and you, the project manager) expect.

- **Project documents**   Project documents will help you determine what the specific levels of quality are to be as you measure the project deliverables. You may reference things like any contractual agreements, corrective actions results, and outputs of previous quality control measurements.

- **Organizational process assets**   This shouldn't be a surprise, because I'd bet dollars to donuts your organization has quality standards that you must adhere to.

Relying on the Seven Basic Quality Tools

There are seven basic quality tools as referenced by the *PMBOK Guide*, 5th edition, that you should be familiar with for your PMI examination. You can use these tools in quality planning, quality assurance, and, most likely, here in quality control. Here they are:

- **Cause-and-effect diagrams**   These are also known as fishbone diagrams and Ishikawa diagrams and they help determine causal factors for an effect you'd like to solve.

- **Flowcharts**   A flowchart shows the sequence of events with possible branching and loopbacks to reach an end result of a process or a series of processes.

- **Checksheets** These are used to tally up problems, effects, conditions, or other aspects about a project's product during quality control inspection. The results of checksheets help project managers quickly ascertain problems within the project.

- **Pareto diagrams** These charts show the categorization of problems from largest to smallest.

- **Histograms** A histogram is a bar chart and can be used for frequency of problems, ranking of services, or any other distribution of data.

- **Control charts** These show trends over time and help a project manager determine the stability of a process, improvement, or other analysis of the project work. These are ideal for repeatable processes as in manufacturing.

- **Scatter diagrams** These charts measure the relationship between a dependent project variable and an independent project variable. The closer the variables trend, the more likely there is a connection.

Inspecting Results

Although quality is planned, not inspected, into a project, inspections are needed to prove conformance to the requirements. An inspection can be done on the project as a whole, on a portion of the project work, on the project deliverable, or even on an individual activity. Inspections are also known as:

- Reviews

- Product reviews

- Audits

- Walkthroughs

Creating a Flowchart

Technically, a flowchart is any diagram illustrating how components within a system are related. An organizational flowchart shows the bottom crew of operations up to the "little squirt" on top. A heating, ventilation, and air conditioning (HVAC) blueprint shows how the air flows through a building from the furnace to each room. Flowcharts show the relation between components, as well as help the project team determine where quality issues may be present and plan accordingly.

You'll need to be concerned with two types of flowcharts for these exams:

- **Cause-and-effect diagrams** These diagrams show the relation between the variables within a process and how those relations may contribute to inadequate quality. They can help organize both the process and team opinions, as well as generate discussion on finding a solution to ensure quality. Figure 8-2 is an example of a cause-and-effect diagram. (As stated in

PART II

Figure 8-2
Cause-and-effect diagrams show the relation of variables to a problem.

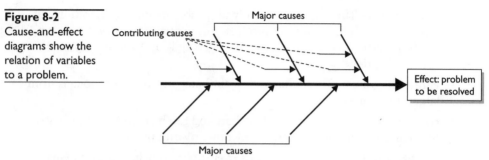

the previous section, these diagrams are also known as Ishikawa diagrams and fishbone diagrams.)

 EXAM TIP A cause-and-effect diagram is also called an Ishikawa diagram—same thing, just a fancier name.

- **System or process flowcharts** These flowcharts illustrate the flow of a process through a system, such as a project change request through the change control system or work authorization through a quality control process. A process flowchart does not have to be limited to the project management activities. It could instead demonstrate how a manufacturer creates, packages, and ships the product to the customer (as seen in Figure 8-3).

Creating a Control Chart

Ever feel like your project is out of control? A control chart can prove it.

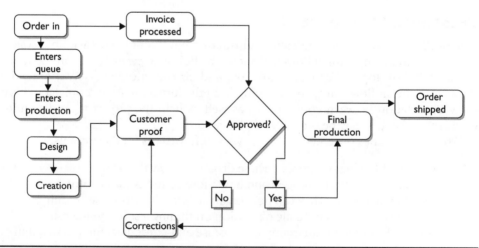

Figure 8-3 Flowcharts demonstrate how processes within a system are related.

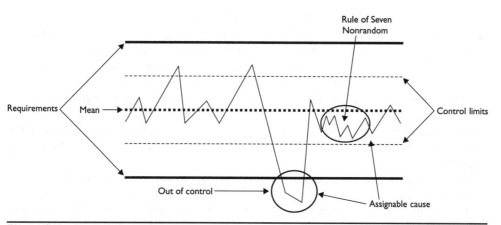

Figure 8-4 Control charts demonstrate the results of inspections.

Control charts illustrate the performance of a project over time. They map the results of inspections against a chart, as seen in Figure 8-4. Control charts are typically used in projects or operations where there are repetitive activities—such as manufacturing, a series of tests, or help desks.

The outer limits of a control chart are set by the customer requirements. Within the customer requirements are the upper control limits (UCLs) and the lower control limits (LCLs). The UCL is typically set at +3 or +6 sigma, while the LCL is set at –3 or –6 sigma. Sigma results show the degree of correctness. Table 8-1 outlines the four sigma values representing normal distribution. You'll need to know these for the PMP exam.

So what happened to sigma four and five? Nothing. They're still there. It's just that the difference between three sigma at 99.73 and six sigma at 99.99 is so small that statisticians just jump to six sigma. The *mean* in a control chart represents the expected result, while the *sigma* values represent the expected spread of results based on the inspection. A true six sigma allows only two defects per million opportunities, and the percentage to represent that value is 99.99985 percent. For the exam, you can go with the 99.99 percent.

For example, if a manufacturer creates 1,000 units per hour and expects 50 units each hour to be defective, the mean would be 950 units. If the control limits were set at +/– three sigma, the results of testing would actually expect as many as 953 correct units and as few as 947 correct units.

Table 8-1 The Four Sigma Values Representing Normal Distribution	Value	Percent Correct
	+/– 1 sigma	68.26 percent
	+/– 2 sigma	95.46 percent
	+/– 3 sigma	99.73 percent
	+/– 6 sigma	99.99 percent

Over time, the results of testing are plotted in the control chart. Whenever a result of testing is plotted beyond the upper or lower control values, it is considered to be "out of control." When a value is out of control, there is a reason why—it's called an *assignable cause*. Something caused the results to change for better or for worse, and the result must be investigated to understand the why behind the occurrence.

Another assignable cause is the Rule of Seven. The Rule of Seven states that whenever seven consecutive results are all on one side of the mean, this is an assignable cause. Thus, there's been some change that caused the results to shift to one side of the expected mean. Again, the cause must be investigated to determine why the change happened.

While control charts are easily associated with recurring activities, like manufacturing, they can also be applied to project management. Consider the number of expected change requests, delays within a project, and other recurring activities. A control chart can plot out these activities to measure performance, show positive and negative results, and track corrective actions.

Creating Pareto Diagrams

A Pareto diagram is somewhat related to Pareto's Law: 80 percent of the problems come from 20 percent of the issues. This is also known as the *80/20 Rule*. A Pareto diagram illustrates the problems by assigned cause, from largest to smallest, as Figure 8-5 shows. The project team should first work on the larger problems and then move on to the smaller problems.

Creating a Histogram

A histogram is a bar chart showing the frequency of variables within a project. For example, a histogram could show which states have the most customers. Within project management, a common histogram is a resource histogram that shows the frequency of resources used on project work.

Figure 8-5
A Pareto diagram is a histogram that ranks the issues from largest to smallest.

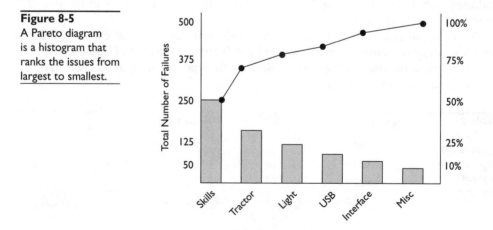

Creating a Run Chart

A run chart, as Figure 8-6 shows, is a line graph that shows the results of inspection in the order in which they've occurred. The goals of a run chart are first to demonstrate the results of a process over time and then to use trend analysis to predict when certain trends may reemerge. Based on this information, an organization can work to prevent the negative trend or work to capitalize on an identified opportunity.

Creating a Scatter Diagram

A scatter diagram tracks the relationship between two variables. The two variables are considered related the closer they track against a diagonal line. For example, a project manager could track the performance of two team members, the time and cost, or even changes between functional managers and the project's schedule.

Completing a Statistical Sampling

Statistical sampling is the process of choosing a percentage of results at random. For example, a project creating a medical device may have 20 percent of all units randomly selected to check quality. This process must be completed on a consistent basis throughout the project, rather than on a sporadic schedule.

Statistical sampling can reduce the costs of quality control, but mixed results can follow if an adequate testing plan and schedule are not followed. The science of statistical sampling (and its requirements to be effective) is an involved process. There are many books, seminars, and professionals devoted to the process. For the CAPM and PMP exams, know that statistical sampling uses a percentage of the results to test for quality. This process can reduce quality control cost.

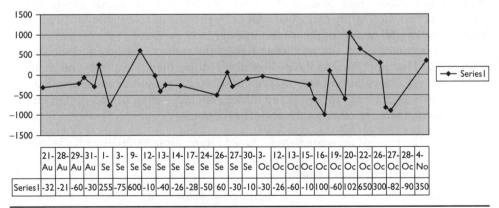

Figure 8-6 Run charts track the results of inspections over time.

Revisiting Flowcharting

Flowcharting uses charts to illustrate how the different parts of a system operate. This is valuable in QC, because the process can be evaluated and tested to determine where in the process quality begins to break down. Corrective actions can then be applied to the system to ensure that quality continues as planned—and as expected.

Applying Trend Analysis

Trend analysis is the science of taking past results to predict future performance. Sports announcers use trend analysis all the time: "The Cubs have never won in St. Louis on a Tuesday night in the month of July when the temperature at the top of the third inning was above 80 degrees."

The results of trend analysis allow the project manager to apply corrective action to intervene and prevent unacceptable outcomes. Trend analysis on a project requires adequate records to predict results and set current expectations. It can monitor the following:

- **Technical performance** Trend analysis can ask, "How many errors have been experienced up to this point in the project schedule, and how many additional errors were encountered?"

- **Cost and schedule performance** Trend analysis can ask, "How many activities were completed incorrectly, came in late, or had significant cost variances?"

Examining Quality Control Results

Quality control should, first and foremost, result in quality improvement. The project manager and project team, based on the results of the tools and techniques to implement quality control, apply corrective actions to prevent unacceptable quality and to improve the overall quality of the project management processes.

The corrective actions and the defect repairs the project manager and the project team want to incorporate into the project may require change requests and management approval. The value and importance of the change should be evident so that the improvement to quality is approved and folded into the project. In addition to quality improvement, there are other results of quality control:

- **Quality control measurements** Based on the project's quality management plan, quality control measurements need to be documented and kept as part of the project's documentation.

- **Validated changes** If you've identified an error in the project work, then the project team has to take corrective action and fix the error. Then someone has to come back and validate that the defect has been fixed to an acceptable level. If not, then it's more rework.

- **Validated deliverables** The goal of quality control is to keep mistakes out of customers' hands. If you've inspected the deliverables and they're acceptable by the quality metrics, then they should be acceptable for the project customer. Validated deliverables are an output of quality control and an input to scope validation.

- **Work performance information** The information created by the project's controlling processes is one of the outputs of quality control. This includes schedule control, scope control, cost control, and quality control. The integrated relationship of the project causes the control of other knowledge areas to affect the quality of the project's deliverables.

- **Change requests** Should the quality in the project be less than what was planned for, there may be change requests for corrective actions, preventive actions, or defect repair.

- **Project management plan updates** Based on the experiences of quality control, the project management plan could be updated. You should primarily be concerned with the possibility that the quality management plan and process improvement plan will require an update in the project.

- **Project document updates** Updates to the quality standards, contracts, training plans, and other process documentation could be an output of quality control.

- **Organizational process assets updates** If the project is using checklists to confirm the completion of work, then the completed checklists should become part of the project records. Some project managers require the project team member completing the checklists to initial them as whole and complete. Lessons learned documentation is also updated as a result of the quality control process.

Chapter Summary

What good is a project deliverable if it doesn't work, is unacceptable, or is faulty? Project quality management ensures that the deliverables that project teams create meet the expectations of the stakeholders. For your CAPM or PMP examination, quality means delivering the project at the exact level of the design specifications and the project scope—no more, no less.

Grade and quality are two different things. Grade is the ranking assigned to different components that have the same functional purpose. For example, sheet metal may come in different grades based on what it is needed for. Another example is the grade of paper based on its thickness, ability to retain ink, and so on. Low quality is always a problem; low grade may not be.

Quality planning happens before project work begins, but also as work is completed. Quality planning can confirm the preexistence of quality or the need for quality improvements. Quality is planned into a project, not inspected in. However, quality control uses inspections to prove the existence of quality within a project deliverable.

The cost of quality is concerned with the monies invested in the project to attain the expected level of quality. Examples of these costs include training, safety measures, and quality management activities. The cost of nonconformance centers on the monies lost by not completing the project work correctly the first time. In addition, this cost includes the loss of sales, loss of customers, and downtime within the project.

Quality assurance is prevention-driven and is a management process. Quality control is inspection-driven and is a project process. On your PMI exam, keep those two thoughts separate and you'll be ahead of the game.

Key Terms

Activity network diagram   These diagrams, such as the project network diagram, show the flow of the project work.

Affinity diagram   This diagram breaks down ideas, solutions, causes, and project components and groups them together with other similar ideas and components.

Benchmarking   Comparing any two similar entities to measure their performance.

Cause-and-effect diagrams   Diagrams that show the relationship between variables within a process and how those relationships may contribute to inadequate quality. The diagrams can help organize both the process and team opinions, as well as generate discussion on finding a solution to ensure quality.

Checklist   A simple approach to ensure that work is completed according to the quality policy.

Control chart   A quality control chart that maps the performance of project work over time.

Cost of conformance   This is the cost associated with the monies spent to attain the expected level of quality. It is also known as the cost of quality.

Cost of nonconformance to quality   The cost associated with not satisfying quality expectations. This is also known as the cost of poor quality.

Cost-benefit analysis   A process to study the trade-offs between costs and the benefits realized from those costs.

Design of experiments   An approach that relies on statistical scenarios to determine what variables within a project will result in the best outcome.

External QA   Assurance provided to the external customers of the project.

Flowchart   A diagram illustrating how components within a system are related. Flowcharts show the relation between components, as well as help the project team determine where quality issues may be present and, once done, plan accordingly.

Internal QA   Assurance provided to management and the project team.

Interrelationship diagraphs Used for complex solutions where the causes and effects of problems and benefits are intertwined with one another.

ISO The abbreviation for the International Organization for Standardization. ISO is Greek for "equal," while "International Organization for Standardization" in a different language would be abbreviated differently. The organization elected to use "ISO" for all languages.

Matrix diagram A data analysis table that shows the strength between variables and relationships in the matrix.

Pareto diagram A histogram that illustrates and ranks categories of failure within a project.

Prioritization matrices A table to rank and score project decisions and alternatives to determine the best solution for the project.

Process decision program chart (PDPC) Helps the project team define all of the steps to get from the current state to a desired goal. It facilitates a conversation about what must be completed to reach the goal.

Process improvement plan A project management subsidiary plan that aims to improve the project, not just the end result of the project. It strives to identify and eliminate waste and non-value-added activities.

Quality According to ASQ, the degree to which a set of inherent characteristics fulfills requirements.

Quality assurance A management process that defines the quality system or quality policy that a project must adhere to. QA aims to plan quality into the project rather than to inspect quality into a deliverable.

Quality control An inspection-driven process that measures work results to confirm that the project is meeting the relevant quality standards.

Quality management plan This plan defines how the project team will implement and fulfill the quality policy of the performing organization.

Quality metrics The operational definitions that specify the measurements within a project and the expected targets for quality and performance.

Quality planning The process of first determining which quality standards are relevant to your project and then finding out the best methods of adhering to those quality standards.

Rule of Seven A component of a control chart that illustrates the results of seven measurements on one side of the mean, which is considered "out of control" in the project.

Run chart A quality control tool that shows the results of inspection in the order in which they've occurred. The goal of a run chart is first to demonstrate the results of a process over time and then to use trend analysis to predict when certain trends may reemerge.

Scatter diagram   A quality control tool that tracks the relationship between two variables over time. The two variables are considered related the closer they track against a diagonal line.

Seven basic quality tools   These seven tools are used in quality planning and in quality control: cause-and-effect diagrams, flowcharts, checksheets, Pareto diagrams, histograms, control charts, and scatter diagrams.

Statistical sampling   A process of choosing a percentage of results at random. For example, a project creating a medical device may have 20 percent of all units randomly selected to check for quality.

System or process flowcharts   Flowcharts that illustrate the flow of a process through a system, such as a project change request through the change control system, or work authorization through a quality control process.

Tree diagram   Tree diagrams show the hierarchies and decomposition of a solution, an organization, or a project team. The WBS and an org chart are examples of tree diagrams.

Trend analysis   The science of using past results to predict future performance.

Work performance information   The results of the project work as needed. This includes technical performance measures, project status, information on what the project has created to date, corrective actions, and performance reports.

Questions

1. You are the project manager for the BBB Project. Stacy, a project team member, is confused about what QA is. Which of the following best describes QA?

   A. QA is quality assurance for the overall project performance.

   B. QA is quality acceptance according to scope verification.

   C. QA is quality assurance for the project deliverable.

   D. QA is quality assurance for the project stakeholders.

2. You are the project manager for the Photo Scanning Project. This project is similar to another project you have completed. Your project is to electronically store thousands of photos for your city's historical society. Quality is paramount on this project. Management approaches you and asks why you have devoted so much of the project time to planning. Your response is which of the following?

   A. This is a first-time, first-use project, so more time is needed for planning.

   B. Planning for a project of this size, with this amount of quality, is mandatory.

   C. Quality is planned into a project, not inspected in.

D. Quality audits are part of the planning time.

3. You are the project manager for the recently initiated Floor Installation Project. Today you plan to meet with your project team to ensure that the project is completed with no deviations from the project requirements. This process is which of the following?

    A. Quality planning

    B. Quality management

    C. Quality control

    D. Quality assurance

4. You are the project manager for the ASE Project, which must map to industry standards in order to be accepted by the customer. You and your team have studied the requirements and have created a plan to implement the deliverables with the appropriate level of quality. What is this process called?

    A. Quality planning

    B. Quality management

    C. Quality control

    D. Quality assurance

5. Juan is the project manager for his organization and he's asked Beth, a project team member, to help him create a fishbone diagram. Beth doesn't know what this is and asks for your help. A fishbone diagram is the same as a(n) _____ diagram.

    A. Ishikawa

    B. Pareto

    C. Flow

    D. Control

6. Management has asked you to define the correlation between quality and the project scope. Which of the following is the best answer?

    A. The project scope includes metrics for quality.

    B. Quality metrics are applied to the project scope.

    C. Quality is the process of completing the scope to meet stated or implied needs.

    D. Quality is the process of evaluating the project scope to ensure that quality exists.

7. You are the project manager of the Condo IV Construction project and you're working with your project team and the project sponsor to identify the quality metrics and develop the quality management plan for the project. In light of this planning event, which of the following is most true about quality?

    A. It will cost more money to build quality into the project.

    B. It will cost less money to build quality into the project process.

    C. Quality is inspection-driven.

    D. Quality is prevention-driven.

8. You are the project manager for the KOY Project, which requires quality that maps to federal guidelines. To ensure that you can meet these standards, you have elected to put the project team through training specific to the federal guidelines your project must adhere to. The costs of these classes can be assigned to which of the following?

    A. The cost of doing business

    B. Cost of quality

    C. Cost of adherence

    D. Cost of nonconformance

9. You are the project manager for the KOY Project, which requires quality that maps to federal guidelines. During a quality audit, you discover that a portion of the project work is faulty and must be done again. The requirement to do the work is an example of which of the following?

    A. Cost of quality

    B. Cost of adherence

    C. Cost of nonconformance

    D. The cost of doing business

10. You are the project manager of the JKL Project, which currently has some production flaws. Which analysis tool will allow you to determine the cause and effect of the production faults?

    A. A flowchart

    B. A Pareto diagram

    C. An Ishikawa diagram

    D. A control chart

11. Linda is the project manager of a manufacturing project. She and her project team are using design of experiments to look for ways to improve quality. Which of the following best describes design of experiments?

    A. It allows the project manager to move the relationship of activities to complete the project work with the best resources available.

    B. It allows the project manager to experiment with the project design to determine what variables are causing the flaws.

    C. It allows the project manager to experiment with variables to attempt to improve quality.

D. It allows the project manager to experiment with the project design document to become more productive and to provide higher quality.

12. You are the project manager of the Global Upgrade Project. Your project team consists of 75 project team members around the world. Each team member will be upgrading a piece of equipment in many different facilities. Which of the following could you implement to ensure that project team members are completing all of the steps in the install procedure with quality?

   A. Checklists

   B. Work breakdown structure (WBS)

   C. Project network diagram (PND)

   D. The WBS dictionary

13. Mark is the project manager of the PMH Project. Quality inspection of the deliverables show several problems. Management has asked Mark to create a chart showing the distribution of problems and their frequencies. Given this, management wants which of the following?

   A. A control chart

   B. An Ishikawa diagram

   C. A Pareto diagram

   D. A flowchart

14. In the illustration to the right, what does the circled area represent?

   A. Out-of-control data points

   B. In-control data points

   C. The Rule of Seven

   D. Standard deviation

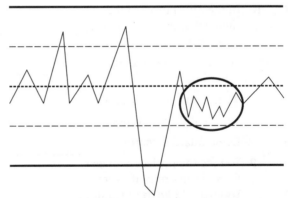

15. You are an IT project manager and are working with the project team to determine the best computer system for the project. You and the project team decide to measure the performance of both systems to determine which one performs best. This is an example of which one of the following?

   A. Cost-benefit analysis

   B. Benchmarking

   C. Design of experiments

   D. Determining the cost of quality

16. A project manager has elected not to enforce safety measures on his construction project. One of the project team members has been injured because of this oversight, and the job site is closed until an investigation into the lack of safety measures is completed. The project will now likely be late, be fined for the error, and lose credibility with the customer. This is an example of which one of the following?

    A. Risk

    B. Trigger

    C. Cost of poor quality

    D. Cost of quality

17. Your organization uses total quality management as part of its quality assurance program. Maria, a leader in your organization's quality assurance program, informs you that she will be reviewing your project to determine if your project management activities comply with the total quality management program. This is an example of which one of the following?

    A. Process analysis

    B. A quality control mechanism

    C. Enterprise environmental factors

    D. A quality audit

18. In the illustration to the right, what does the circled area represent?

    A. Out-of-control data points

    B. In-control data points

    C. The Rule of Seven

    D. Standard deviation

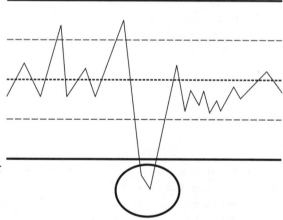

19. You are the project manager for a plastics manufacturer. You would like to illustrate the categories of quality failure within your project so that you and your project team can attack the largest areas of failure first. This type of chart is known as which one of the following?

    A. A control chart

    B. An Ishikawa diagram

    C. A Pareto diagram

    D. A flowchart

20. What is the type of chart to the right called?

A. A Pareto diagram

B. A control chart

C. A fishbone diagram

D. An Ishikawa diagram

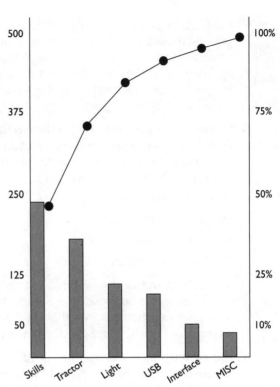

Questions and Answers

1. You are the project manager for the BBB Project. Stacy, a project team member, is confused about what QA is. Which of the following best describes QA?

A. QA is quality assurance for the overall project performance.

B. QA is quality acceptance according to scope verification.

C. QA is quality assurance for the project deliverable.

D. QA is quality assurance for the project stakeholders.

A. QA is concerned with overall project quality performance. B, C, and D are incorrect because they do not correctly explain quality assurance.

2. You are the project manager for the Photo Scanning Project. This project is similar to another project you have completed. Your project is to electronically store thousands of photos for your city's historical society. Quality is paramount on this project. Management approaches you and asks why you have devoted so much of the project time to planning. Your response is which of the following?

A. This is a first-time, first-use project, so more time is needed for planning.

B. Planning for a project of this size, with this amount of quality, is mandatory.

C. Quality is planned into a project, not inspected in.

D. Quality audits are part of the planning time.

C. Of all the choices presented, this is the best answer. Quality is planned into the project, and the planning requires time. A is incorrect because a project of this nature has been completed before. B is incorrect because there isn't enough information provided to determine what the quality demands of the project are. D is incorrect because quality audits are not part of the planning processes.

3. You are the project manager for the recently initiated Floor Installation Project. Today you plan to meet with your project team to ensure that the project is completed with no deviations from the project requirements. This process is which of the following?

A. Quality planning

B. Quality management

C. Quality control

D. Quality assurance

A. Quality planning should be completed prior to the work beginning—and should thereafter be revisited as needed. B is incorrect because quality management is not an applicable answer to the scenario. C and D are incorrect because QC and QA are part of quality management.

4. You are the project manager for the ASE Project, which must map to industry standards in order to be accepted by the customer. You and your team have studied the requirements and have created a plan to implement the deliverables with the appropriate level of quality. What is this process called?

A. Quality planning

B. Quality management

C. Quality control

D. Quality assurance

A. Quality planning is the process of creating a plan to meet the requirements of quality. B, C, and D are incorrect because they do not explain the process in the question's scenario.

5. Juan is the project manager for his organization and he's asked Beth, a project team member, to help him create a fishbone diagram. Beth doesn't know what this is and asks for your help. A fishbone diagram is the same as a(n) _____ diagram.

A. Ishikawa

B. Pareto

C. Flow

D. Control

> A. A fishbone diagram is the same as an Ishikawa diagram. B, C, and D are incorrect. These charts and diagrams accomplish goals other than the cause-and-effect outcome of the Ishikawa.

6. Management has asked you to define the correlation between quality and the project scope. Which of the following is the best answer?

   A. The project scope includes metrics for quality.

   B. Quality metrics are applied to the project scope.

   C. Quality is the process of completing the scope to meet stated or implied needs.

   D. Quality is the process of evaluating the project scope to ensure that quality exists.

   > C. Quality, in regard to the project scope, is about completing the work as promised. A is incorrect because though the project scope will have requirements for acceptance, it may not have metrics for quality defined. B and D are also incorrect statements.

7. You are the project manager of the Condo IV Construction project and you're working with your project team and the project sponsor to identify the quality metrics and develop the quality management plan for the project. In light of this planning event, which of the following is most true about quality?

   A. It will cost more money to build quality into the project.

   B. It will cost less money to build quality into the project process.

   C. Quality is inspection-driven.

   D. Quality is prevention-driven.

   > D. Quality is prevention-driven. Quality wants to complete the work correctly the first time to prevent poor results, a loss of time, and a loss of funds. A and B are incorrect. There is no guarantee that a project will cost more or less depending on the amount of expected quality. Incidentally, lack of quality will likely cost more than quality planning because of the cost of nonconformance. C is incorrect because quality is planned into a project, not inspected in.

8. You are the project manager for the KOY Project, which requires quality that maps to federal guidelines. To ensure that you can meet these standards, you have elected to put the project team through training specific to the federal guidelines your project must adhere to. The costs of these classes can be assigned to which of the following?

   A. The cost of doing business

   B. Cost of quality

   C. Cost of adherence

D. Cost of nonconformance

B. Training to meet the quality expectations is attributed to the cost of quality. A, C, and D are incorrect because these choices do not describe training as a cost of quality.

9. You are the project manager for the KOY Project, which requires quality that maps to federal guidelines. During a quality audit, you discover that a portion of the project work is faulty and must be done again. The requirement to do the work is an example of which of the following?

 A. Cost of quality

 B. Cost of adherence

 C. Cost of nonconformance

 D. The cost of doing business

C. When project work results are faulty and must be done over, it is attributed to the cost of nonconformance to quality. A, B, and D are all incorrect. These values do not describe faulty work or the cost of nonconformance.

10. You are the project manager of the JKL Project, which currently has some production flaws. Which analysis tool will allow you to determine the cause and effect of the production faults?

 A. A flowchart

 B. A Pareto diagram

 C. An Ishikawa diagram

 D. A control chart

C. The key words "cause and effect" equate to the Ishikawa diagram. A is incorrect because a flowchart will show how a process moves through the system, not the cause and effect of the problems involved. B is incorrect as well. A Pareto diagram maps out the causes and frequency of problems. D is incorrect because a control chart plots the results of sampling, but it doesn't show the cause and effect of problems.

11. Linda is the project manager of a manufacturing project. She and her project team are using design of experiments to look for ways to improve quality. Which of the following best describes design of experiments?

 A. It allows the project manager to move the relationship of activities to complete the project work with the best resources available.

 B. It allows the project manager to experiment with the project design to determine what variables are causing the flaws.

 C. It allows the project manager to experiment with variables to attempt to improve quality.

D. It allows the project manager to experiment with the project design document to become more productive and to provide higher quality.

C. Design of experiments uses experiments and "what-if" scenarios to determine what variables are affecting quality. A is incorrect because design of experiments, in regard to quality, is not interested in changing the relationship of activities to complete project work. B and D are also incorrect because design of experiments will not be changing project design to determine where flaws exist or to become more productive.

12. You are the project manager of the Global Upgrade Project. Your project team consists of 75 project team members around the world. Each team member will be upgrading a piece of equipment in many different facilities. Which of the following could you implement to ensure that project team members are completing all of the steps in the install procedure with quality?

A. Checklists

B. Work breakdown structure (WBS)

C. Project network diagram (PND)

D. The WBS dictionary

A. Checklists are simple but effective quality management tools that the project manager can use to ensure that the project team is completing the required work. B, C, and D are all incorrect. The WBS, PND, and WBS dictionary are not tools the project team can necessarily use to prove they've completed required work. Checklists are the best approach for this scenario.

13. Mark is the project manager of the PMH Project. Quality inspections of the deliverables show several problems. Management has asked Mark to create a chart showing the distribution of problems and their frequencies. Given this, management wants which of the following?

A. A control chart

B. An Ishikawa diagram

C. A Pareto diagram

D. A flowchart

C. Management wants Mark to create a Pareto diagram. Recall that a Pareto diagram maps out the causes of defects and illustrates their frequency. A is incorrect because a control chart does not identify the problems, only the relation of the results to the expected mean. B is incorrect because a cause-and-effect diagram does not map out the frequency of problems. D is also incorrect. Flowcharts show how a process moves through a system and how the components are related.

14. In the illustration to the right, what does the circled area represent?

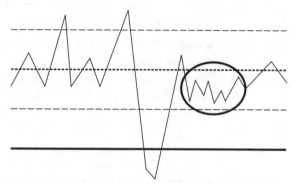

A. Out-of-control data points

B. In-control data points

C. The Rule of Seven

D. Standard deviation

C. The circled area shows seven consecutive sampling results, all on one side of the mean. This is known as the Rule of Seven and is an assignable cause. A is incorrect because these values are in control. B is correct, but it does not fully answer the question as C does. D is incorrect because standard deviation is a predicted measure of the variance from the expected mean of a sampling.

15. You are an IT project manager and are working with the project team to determine the best computer system for the project. You and the project team decide to measure the performance of both systems to determine which one performs best. This is an example of which one of the following?

A. Cost-benefit analysis

B. Benchmarking

C. Design of experiments

D. Determining the cost of quality

B. This is an example of benchmarking because the project team is comparing one system to another. A is incorrect because the cost-benefit analysis would compare the costs and associated benefits of each system, rather than just how the two systems compare with each other. C is incorrect because the design of experiments is a method that determines which factors influence the variables of the project's deliverable. D is not a valid answer because the cost of quality is the dollar amount the project must invest to achieve the expected level of quality.

16. A project manager has elected not to enforce safety measures on his construction project. One of the project team members has been injured because of this oversight, and the job site is closed until an investigation into the lack of safety measures is completed. The project will now likely be late, be fined for the error, and lose credibility with the customer. This is an example of which one of the following?

A. Risk

B. Trigger

C. Cost of poor quality

D. Cost of quality

> **C.** This is an example of the cost of poor quality. The project manager should have followed the safety measures for the job site, and costs associated with the safety measures are considered part of D, the cost of quality. A is incorrect because risk is inherent to application work, while the ramifications of not enforcing the safety measures is an example of the cost of poor quality. B is incorrect because trigger is a risk management term that references a condition or warning sign that a risk is coming into the project.

17. Your organization uses total quality management as part of its quality assurance program. Maria, a leader in your organization's quality assurance program, informs you that she will be reviewing your project to determine if your project management activities comply with the total quality management program. This is an example of which one of the following?

A. Process analysis

B. Quality control mechanism

C. Enterprise environmental factors

D. Quality audit

> **D.** This is an example of a quality audit to confirm that your project is adhering to the quality assurance program established within your organization. A and B are incorrect choices for this question. C is incorrect because although enterprise environmental factors may be a valid characteristic of the total quality management program, it is not the best answer for the question, which centers on the audit process rather than on how the audit will be performed.

18. In the illustration to the right, what does the circled area represent?

A. Out-of-control data points

B. In-control data points

C. The Rule of Seven

D. Standard deviation

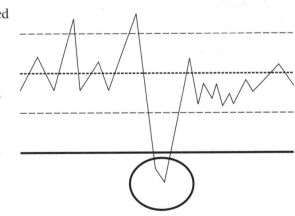

A. The circled area shows out-of-control data points. B is incorrect because "in-control data points" does not best answer the question. C is incorrect because the Rule of Seven refers to seven consecutive measurements, all on one side of the mean. D is incorrect because standard deviation is a predicted measure of the variance from the expected mean of a sampling.

19. You are the project manager for a plastics manufacturer. You would like to illustrate the categories of quality failure within your project so that you and your project team can attack the largest areas of failure first. This type of chart is known as which one of the following?

    A. A control chart

    B. An Ishikawa diagram

    C. A Pareto diagram

    D. A flowchart

    C. You want to create a Pareto diagram. A is incorrect because a control chart does not identify the problems, only the relation of the results to the expected mean. B is incorrect because a cause-and-effect diagram does not map out the frequency of problems. D is also incorrect. Flowcharts show how a process moves through a system and how the components are related.

20. What is the type of chart to the right called?

    A. A Pareto diagram

    B. A Control chart

    C. A Fishbone

    D. An Ishikawa

    A. This is a Pareto diagram. B is incorrect because a control chart shows the results of measurements over time. C and D are both incorrect because a fishbone diagram and an Ishikawa diagram are essentially the same type of chart.

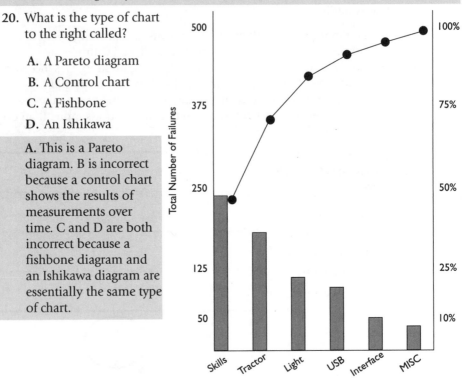

9

Managing Project Human Resources

In this chapter, you will
- Plan for human resources
- Acquire the project team
- Develop the project team
- Manage the project team

Your project relies on people to get the work done. Those people, your project team, look to you, the project manager, to provide leadership, direction, motivation, and your general management skills to help them know what their project assignments are, get their work done, and resolve issues and dilemmas within the project.

It's a blast! Okay, that's a bit of sarcasm. In reality, and on your PMI exam, the resources involved with the project know what is expected of them by the project manager, management, and the stakeholders, and then they complete those expectations. And if they don't? Then it's up to the project manager, the functional managers, and even the other project team members to enforce the project's ground rules so that all team members work toward the requirements in the project scope statement.

VIDEO For a more detailed explanation, watch the *Exploring Human Resource Theories* video now.

The type of organizational structure, from functional to projectized, will also influence how the project manager may discipline, motivate, and manage the project team. In a functional environment, the project manager won't have much autonomy to discipline or offer rewards beyond what management has deemed appropriate. In a projectized structure, for example, the project manager has much more autonomy to both discipline and reward.

Your project team may be assigned to you or you may have to build the team one person at a time. Chances are that you'll have a core project team at the beginning of the project and then more and more team members will join as the project scope is defined and the activities are identified. Adding people to the project team can influence how you do the work and introduce new risks and opportunities—based on their interest in the project, experience levels, and, frankly, their competency about the project work. An analysis of the project team can help you plan your team development approach.

A subset of the project team is the project management team—you've seen this term already in this book. The *project management team* is the core group of project team members that help with the project management decisions. Sometimes this bunch of folks may also be called the core, executive, or leadership team. Your pal, the project sponsor, works directly with you, the project manager, and the project management team to help the team make the best decisions and to keep the project moving forward.

As the project manager, you'll need to manage and lead the project—yes, there is a difference between management and leadership. Management is about getting things done. Leadership is about aligning, motivating, and directing people. I believe that people will work harder, smarter, and better for someone they want to work for than they will for someone they are required to work for. As part of your leadership and management, you want to maintain a professional and ethical behavior. Avoid playing favorites, balance the tasks among the project team, and get involved in the work when the team needs your help.

For your PMI examination, you'll need to know some vital facts about managing the project team. We'll cover these vital facts in this chapter.

Planning for Human Resources

Here we go again. Have you noticed that every knowledge area for your PMI examination starts with a planning process? Hmmm, I hope so. Planning is an iterative process that begins early in the project and continues through the project management life cycle. Planning for project human resources is vital to a successful project. After all, you've got to plan how the project work will be completed and which resources will complete that work.

When it comes to planning human resources, the project manager is aiming to plan for several facets of the project. Specifically, this planning process answers the following questions:

- What project roles are needed on the project?
- What is the responsibility of each role on the project?
- To whom does each role report?
- Will resources on the project be from inside or outside of the organization?
- How will project team members be acquired?
- How will project team members be released from the project?
- What training needs to be completed for the project team?
- What are the rewards and recognition systems the project may utilize?
- What are the compliance and safety issues that must be addressed?

- How will the usage of the team resources affect the operations of the
  organization?

Phew! That's a bunch of questions the project management team must answer during this portion of planning. The good news is that some of these questions can be answered when doing other project management planning exercises, such as time and cost estimating. All of the answers to these questions are documented in the staffing management plan. The human resource plan, of which the staffing management plan is a component, is the primary output of the human resources planning process.

Relying on Enterprise Environmental Factors

You've seen enterprise environmental factors over and over throughout this book. When it comes to relying on the good ol' enterprise environmental factors for human resource planning, the reliance is on how the organization identifies and utilizes roles and responsibilities and on the interaction of the organization with the project management team. The project management team must consider five interfaces in its planning. These are project interfaces that the project team will likely have to interact with throughout the project:

- **Organizational** The project management team needs to identify which departments are going to be involved in the project. The team considers how the project will interact with these different departments and organizations, as well as what relationships exist between the departments, the project team, and management.

- **Technical** The project team identifies the disciplines and specialties that the project will require to complete the project scope statement. The technical interfaces are the resources that will be doing the project work. In that light, the project manager needs to examine what work needs to be completed, how the project moves from phase to phase, and even the nature of the work and how different disciplines may need to work together to allow the project to move forward. The project manager must also consider the technical interfaces required for the project deliverables to interact with the ongoing operations of the organization.

- **Interpersonal** This organization interface considers the formal and informal reporting relationships that may exist among the project team members. The interpersonal interface also considers the job descriptions of the project team members, existing reporting structures between supervisors and subordinates, and what, if any, existing relationships may affect the project work. This interface also considers any cultural or language differences among the project team members that may need to be addressed.

- **Logistical** Have you ever worked with project team members who are located around the world? What about project team members who are within footsteps of each other? The logistical interface considers just that—the logistics of the project team and the stakeholders in relation to managing the project. The project manager must consider the geographical locales, the time zones, countries, and any other logistics that may affect the project.

- **Political** Uh-oh, here come the politics. This interface considers the hidden goals, personal agendas, and alliances among the project team and the stakeholders. Yep, politics is considered in project management and on the PMI examination.

While the interfaces mentioned previously should be considered during the human resource planning phase for every project, constraints also could be introduced through these interfaces or as independent constraints. Recall that a constraint is anything that limits the project team's options. Here are three common constraints that may affect your human resources planning:

- **Organizational structure** The structure of the organization has a direct correlation to the amount of power a project manager has. Figure 9-1 provides a refresher on the organizational structures. For a more in-depth refresher, see Chapter 2.

- **Collective bargaining agreements** Contracts and agreements with unions or other employee groups may serve as constraints for the project.

- **Economic conditions** Your organization may experience a hiring freeze, slash the training budget, or even cut out most travel expenses. These cuts are all examples of economic conditions that can serve as constraints on your project.

 EXAM TIP Contracts and grievances with unions are constraints. But the unions, themselves, are stakeholders.

Figure 9-1
The organizational structure affects the project manager's power.

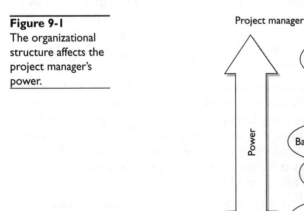

Project manager

Projectized

Strong matrix

Balanced matrix

Weak matrix

Power

Functional

Functional manager

Using the Organizational Process Assets

Many projects within any organization are similar to past projects. For example, an architecture firm designs buildings, an IT consultancy may design software or networks, and a manufacturer manufactures things. Within each of these disciplines, and countless others, some projects are similar to projects that have gone before. The past project records, lessons learned, and even past staffing management plans can be adapted for the current project. Organizational process assets provide four elements for human resources planning that you should know for your PMI exam:

- **Organization standards** You need to understand the human resources policies, procedures, expectations, role descriptions, and rules that you, the project manager, will need to adhere to.

- **Templates** Using past project records, including older staffing management plans as a base for the current project, is a great example of using past projects as templates for the current project. Historical information can serve as a type of template.

- **Escalation procedures** Are you in charge of the project team when it comes to issue resolution? Or do you have to escalate the issue along to management when there are problems? You need to know the process for escalation and your level of authority over the project team.

- **Checklists** When it comes to planning for human resources, checklists, which are part of organizational process assets, attempt to identify common elements within similar projects. Ideal things that a checklist can help the project management team identify include:
  - Roles and responsibilities
  - Competencies for the project work
  - Training programs
  - Team ground rules
  - Safety issues
  - Compliancy
  - Rewards and recognition considerations

Referencing the Project Management Plan

The project management plan has many things to consider when it comes to staffing the project. Let's take a quick peek at each subsidiary plan, elements within the project management plan, and how they may affect what resources the project manager will require on the project team. Here are the elements of the project management plan:

- **Project scope management plan** Defines how the project scope will be planned, managed, and controlled. This plan is considered, because the project team will be doing the work to create the things the scope promises.

- **Schedule management plan**   Defines how the project schedule will be created and managed. The availability of, and the demand for, the project team are influenced by the schedule management plan.

- **Cost management plan**   This plan details how the project costs will be planned for, estimated, budgeted, and then monitored and controlled. In most projects, the project manager will need to account for the cost of the project team and their contributions to the project work. In some instances, the cost is more related to the time the team member is utilized, rather than the actual salary of the project team member.

- **Change management plan**   Changes are likely to happen on the project, so you'll need to communicate the change management process to the project team. You want to explain how all changes will be captured, analyzed, and then, if approved, implemented into the project. Changes can affect what the project will do and you don't want this to be a surprise to the project team.

- **Configuration management plan**   Documentation, control, and confirmation of the features and functions of the project's product are needed. Tied to scope management, the configuration management plan communicates how changes to the product may be permitted.

- **Quality management plan**   Quality is expected on every project. This plan defines what quality means for the project, how the project will achieve quality, and how the project will map to organizational procedures pertaining to quality. The project team members will need to adhere to quality expectations, which may include training, team development, peer reviews, and inspections.

- **Process improvement plan**   Who wants an extra helping of waste in their project? This plan aims to eliminate non-value-added activities, eliminate waste, and determine how the project work, execution, and management can be better executed and managed. The project manager wants the project team to get rid of non-value-added activities.

- **Human resource plan**   This plan defines project roles, responsibilities, and the reporting structure, and includes the staffing management plan. The staffing management plan defines how your project will get and manage the needed resources on your project.

- **Communications management plan**   This plan defines who will get what information, how they will receive it, and in what modality the communication will take place. The project team will need to communicate with the project manager, the sponsor, stakeholders, vendors, and each other.

- **Risk management plan**   Risk is an uncertain event or condition that may affect the project's outcome. Project team members will need to know what risks are within the project, which risk owners will be identified, and how risk responses will be planned and communicated.

- **Procurement management plan**   The project may need to procure goods and services. The project team may need to interact with vendors, consultants, and even internal stakeholders, such as a procurement office or purchasing department. This plan may also address how procured consultants will serve as project team members.

- **Milestone list**   This list details the project milestones and their attributes. The milestone list is used for several areas of project planning, but also helps track how quickly the project may be achieving its objectives.

- **Resource calendar**   Resources are people and things like equipment, rooms, and other facilities. This calendar defines when resources are available to contribute to the project.

- **Schedule baseline**   This is the planned start and finish of the project. The comparison of what was planned and what was experienced is the schedule variance.

- **Cost baseline**   This is the aggregated costs of all of the work packages within the work breakdown structure (WBS).

- **Quality baseline**   This documents the quality objectives for the project, including the metrics for stakeholder acceptance of the project deliverable.

- **Risk register**   The risk register is a centralized database consisting of the outcome of all the other risk management processes. Consider the outcome of risk identification, qualitative analysis, and quantitative analysis.

Charting the Human Resources

Lots of charts can help the project manager and the project management team determine what resources are needed, what responsibilities are within the project, reporting relationships, accountability concerns, and lots more. Your PMI examination will quiz you on these schmancy charts and how they're used. Don't worry—they're not difficult. Let's have a look.

Using a Hierarchical Chart

A hierarchical chart shows the relationship between superior and subordinate employees, groups, disciplines, even departments. You've already seen one hierarchical chart: the WBS. When it comes to human resource planning, there are five types of charts to consider:

- **Organization chart**   This traditional chart shows how the organization is broken down by departments and disciplines. It is sometimes called the organizational breakdown structure (OBS) and is arranged by departments, units, or teams. With regard to project management, an OBS can be used to show which project responsibilities are linked with which departments.

- **Resource breakdown structure (RBS)**   This hierarchical chart can decompose the project by the types of resources it contains. For example, your project might be using mechanical engineers in several different deliverables throughout the project. The RBS would organize all of the usage of the mechanical engineers, as well as other resources, by their disciplines rather than by where the disciplines are being utilized. A RBS is an excellent tool for tracking resource utilization and resource costs.

- **Responsibility assignment matrix (RAM)**   A RAM chart shows the correlation between project team members and the work they've been assigned to complete. A RAM chart doesn't necessarily have to be specific to individual team members; it can also be decomposed to project groups or units. Most often, however, RAM charts depict activities and individual workers.

- **RACI chart**   A RACI chart is another matrix chart that only uses the activities of responsible, accountable, consult, and inform (hence, the acronym RACI). Technically, a RACI chart is a form of the responsibility assignment matrix, but I want to include it here as a separate entry. This chart, depicted in Figure 9-2, has gained some popularity in recent years, so I'd wager you'll see it on your PMI examination. Notice how the different roles have only one of four responsibilities: responsible, accountable, consult, and inform for each assignment.

- **Text-oriented chart**   A text-oriented chart is really more of a shopping list of what a team member is responsible for within the project. These listings define project responsibilities, reporting relationships, project authority, competencies, and qualifications. You might also know these as position descriptions or role-responsibility-authority forms.

	Project Team Member				
Activity	Steve	Martha	Sam	Liza	Mike
Foundation	A	R	A	I	C
Framing	R	A	A	I	C
Wiring	A	C	C	R	C
Testing	R	I	A	C	A

Figure 9-2   RACI charts show the relation between activities and project team members.

Networking Human Resources

My buddy, Rick, and I do an exaggerated used-car salesman thumbs-up whenever one of us mentions networking. We know networking works—it's a great way to meet new people, find new business, and make friends. Networking events, such as your PMI chapter meetings, luncheons, and just working a room, are all ways to help your project move forward by furthering better understanding of how your organization moves through political and interpersonal relationships.

Basically, networking supports the old adage that people like to do business with people they like. If people don't know you, they won't get a chance to like you. Networking functions, especially those internal to your organization, are great methods to meet and greet and share news about your projects. Attending networking events on an ongoing basis is effective. Some project managers fall into the trap of networking only at the launch of a project. However, it's the steady networking that builds relationships.

Identifying the Roles and Responsibilities

Human resource planning accomplishes wonderful things. It communicates what resources the project will need, the roles and responsibilities the project team will play on the project, the structure of the project team, and more. One of the fundamental things that human resource planning does for the project is to identify the attributes of the project team. You'll need to know these four terms for your PMI examination:

- **Role** This denotes what a person is specifically responsible for in a project. Roles are usually tied to job titles, such as network engineer, mechanical engineer, and electrician. It's what a person does.

- **Responsibility** A responsibility is the work that a role performs. More precisely, it's the work that a project team member is responsible for within the project.

- **Authority** Project team members may have authority over other project team members, have the ability to make decisions, and even sign approvals for project work and purchases. The authority level defines which project team member has what level of authority within the project.

- **Competency** This attribute defines what talents, skills, and capacities are needed to complete the project work. If there is a skill gap, then training, development, hiring, and even schedule and scope changes should be enacted.

Creating a Project Organization Chart

Another output of the human resource planning process for your project is a project organization chart. This chart, as its name implies, illustrates the organization of the project, the project team members, and all the associated reporting relationships. The level of detail of the project organization chart is relative to the size of the project team and the priority of the project. In other words, a massive international project with 3,000 project team members around the globe will likely have more detail than a 20-person project team to create a new piece of software.

Examining the Staffing Management Plan

Here's the meat of planning for project human resources: you and the project management team create the human resource plan. The human resource plan includes the more project manager–specific plan: the staffing management plan. The staffing management plan details all of the following concerns:

- **Staff acquisition** This portion of the project plan defines how the project team will be assembled. In some organizations, the project team is assigned to the project manager. In others, the project manager petitions for the project team members that he'd like on the project. This portion of the plan also defines how the organization's human resources department will interact with the project management team and if the project team will be all internal, all external, or a blend of resources. Staff acquisition also deals with the geographical location of the project team members and the costs associated with acquiring team members with the appropriate expertise.

- **Timetable** In most projects, not all team members will be utilized on the project all of the time. A timetable can identify when project team members are needed on the project and when related activities, such as team acquisitions, can be scheduled. In some projects, a resource histogram, as Figure 9-3 shows, demonstrates when resources will be utilized across the project. Typically, each bar in the histogram represents a project team member, although some resource histograms can be created to show when a

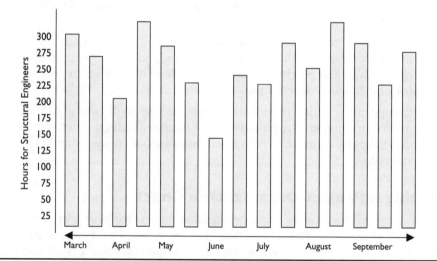

Figure 9-3 Resource histograms depict when project team resources are utilized.

project unit or department is involved in the project. Timetables are linked to the resource calendar to see the days when a particular resource is available for project work. This is especially important in a matrix structure when the project team member may be assigned to work on multiple projects.

 EXAM TIP   When an individual bar in a resource histogram extends beyond the maximum allowed hours, resource leveling is needed. Resource leveling lops off the exceeded labor amount and often causes the project duration to increase.

- **Staff release plan**   The staffing management plan defines the conditions and circumstances regarding when a project staff member may be released from the project team. Technically, you'll create a staff release plan. This plan defines how the project manager, functional managers, and other project managers in the organization will use the identified resources in future projects and operations. Once the staff has been released from the project, the project expenses can go down, assuming that project is paying directly for the labor of the staff.

- **Training needs**   If the project team doesn't know how to complete the work within the project, the project manager must hire a contracted resource or train the project team. This section of the staffing management plan defines the need for training, the benefits of certification, and how the training can help the project—and often the organization—reach its goals.

- **Rewards and recognition**   This is a key PMI point. A clearly defined system for rewards and recognition will reinforce the behavior the project manager wants from her project team. Rewards and recognition, however, must be based on conditions within a person's control. For example, if Bob is to be rewarded for managing costs within the project, but Bob has no authority over the decisions that affect costs, he'll feel pretty insecure in his ability to realize the reward your project promises.

 EXAM TIP   You want to avoid zero-sum awards. These are awards where only one person can win the award, such as team member of the month. (More on this shortly in "Rewarding the Project Team.")

- **Compliance issues**   The staffing management plan also details how the project will adhere to government regulations, union contracts, and human resource practices your organization abides by.

- **Safety**   Many projects must consider the safety of the project team. While safety for the project team is part of the cost of quality, as I discussed in Chapter 8, it's revisited here to reinforce the need for attention to safety issues. We'll see this issue again in Chapter 11 when we discuss risks and the project team.

Acquiring the Project Team

You need people to complete your project. But have you ever managed a project where the resources you wanted on the project were not available? Or have you managed a project where the resources you were assigned weren't the best resources to complete the project work? Staff acquisition is the process of getting the needed resources on the project team to complete the project work. It focuses on working within the policies and procedures of the performing organization to obtain the needed resources to complete the project work. Negotiation, communication, and political savvy are the keys to getting the desired resources on the project team.

Examining the Staffing Pool

Sometimes the project manager doesn't have any say over the project team members who are assigned to the project team. In other instances, the project manager can influence the decision makers to get the best team members. Your project team might also include contractors that you'll have to manage. These are all part of enterprise environmental factors—how an organization operates. The project manager should always ask about the following things:

- **Experience** What is the experience of the project team member? Has he done similar work in the past? Has he done it well?

- **Interest level** Are the project team members interested in working on this project?

- **Characteristics** How will each individual team member work with other project team members?

- **Availability** Will the project team members desired for the project be available? Project managers should confer with functional managers on the availability of potential team members.

- **Knowledge** What is the competency and proficiency of the available project team members?

Negotiating for Resources

Most projects require the project manager to negotiate for resources. The project manager will likely have to negotiate with functional managers to obtain the needed resources to complete the project work. The functional managers and the project manager may struggle over an employee's time due to demands from ongoing operations, other projects, and desires to effectively use resources. In other instances, functional managers may want to assign under-utilized resources on projects in order to consume their otherwise idle employees' time.

Project managers may also have to negotiate with other project managers to share needed resources among projects. Scheduling the needed resources between the project teams will need to be coordinated so that both projects may complete successfully.

Working with Preassigned Staff

Project team members are often preassigned to a project for a number of reasons:

- Availability of the individual

- Promised as part of a competitive contract

- Required as part of the project charter for an internal project

- Opportunity for the staff member to complete on-the-job training

Whatever the reasoning behind the assignment of the staff to the project, the project manager should evaluate the project team for skill gaps, availability to complete the project work, and expectations of the project team members. The project manager must address any discrepancies between the requirements of the project work and the project team's ability to complete the work.

Procuring Staff

In some instances, the project manager may have no alternative but to procure the project team or individuals to complete the project work. I'll talk all about procurement in Chapter 12. With regard to project team procurement, reasons why the project manager can use this alternative include, but are not limited to, the following:

- The performing organization lacks the internal resources with the needed skills to complete the project work.

- The work is more cost-effective to procure.

- The project team members are present within the organization, but they are not available to the current project because of the organizational structure, such as a functional or projectized structure.

- The project team members are present within the organization, but they cannot complete the needed work due to other project assignments.

Managing a Virtual Team

Placing all of the project team members in one geographical location is ideal for many project managers. In theory, having all of the project team members together allows the team members to quickly communicate, work with each other, and generally work better as a team. In reality, that's not always possible: Team members are spread around the globe, space isn't necessarily available in one locale, and other logistics could prevent bringing all of the project team together in a project war room. (And yes, there's no fighting in the war room.)

Virtual teams, however, are more likely in today's world. Collaboration software, Internet tools, phone calls, and e-mails can help increase communications and the sense of a co-located team without the expense and improbability of a co-located team. Virtual teams allow the organization to:

- Create a project team that comprises experts from around the globe
- Permit people to work from home offices
- Permit people to work different shifts and hours
- Include people on the project team who may have mobility limitations
- Save monies by not incurring travel expenses

 EXAM TIP The negative side to virtual teams is that communication can be more difficult, and costs can be incurred from coordinating and managing the needed communication among the virtual team.

Utilizing a Multicriteria Decision Analysis Process

A multicriteria decision analysis process sounds real formal, scientific, and scary, but it's mainly a method to rank a potential project team member on several factors to see if the person should be on the project team. To use this approach, you'd identify several factors, assign scores to the different factors, and then measure each team member by those factors. Here's a quick example I made up with scoring:

- **Skills, 5 points** What skills does the person have that the project needs?
- **Knowledge, 3 points** Does this person have specialized knowledge about the processes, the customer, or the project life cycle?
- **Costs, 6 points** How much is this person going to cost the project?
- **Availability, 3 points** Will this person be available for the duration of the project?
- **Experience, 4 points** Does this person have experience with the technology the project will be implementing?

Using these simple factors, you could measure and compare each potential team member and make a determination of their scored value to the project. You can add as many factors as needed and perhaps create a minimum threshold of points that the person must have to be invited onto your project team.

Assembling the Project Team

With the project team assembled, the project manager can continue planning, assigning activities, and managing the project progression. Project team members can be assigned to the project on a full- or part-time basis, depending on the project conditions. Once the project team is built, a project team directory should be assembled. The project team directory should include the project team members':

- Names
- Phone numbers
- E-mail addresses
- Mailing addresses, if the team is geographically dispersed

As well as:

- Contact information for key stakeholders
- Additional relevant contact information for team members, such as photos, web addresses, and so on

Developing the Project Team

The project team is developed by enhancing the competencies of the individual project team members and promoting the interaction of all the project team members. Throughout the project, the project manager will have to work to develop the project team. The project manager may have to develop an individual team member's skills so that she can complete her assignments. The project manager will also have to work to develop the project team as a whole so that the team can work together to complete the project.

In matrix organizations, the project team members are accountable to the project manager and to their functional managers. Developing the project team can prove challenging, since the project team members may feel pulled between multiple bosses. The project manager must strive to involve and develop the project team members as individuals completing project work—and as team members completing the project objectives together.

Preparing for Team Development

Team development is a natural process, but it's also a process that the project manager can usher along. If you're the project manager and you want your team to work together, get along, and focus on completing the project rather than on who's really in charge of the project, you'll need these inputs:

- **Staff assignments**   The assignments of the project team members define their skills, their needs for development, and their abilities to complete the project work as individuals and as part of the team.

- **Human resource plan**   Recall that the human resource plan details how project team members will be brought onto the project, managed, and released from the project team.

- **Resource availability**   You'll need to know when your project team members are available and when they're vacationing in the desert. This component also considers when project team members are on multiple projects within your organization and allows you to plan for when you'll utilize the project team members best.

Leading Project Team Development

Due to the temporary nature of projects, it can be tough for a group of strangers to form relationships and immediately create a successful project. Team development is the guidance, direction, and leadership the project manager offers to influence a project team. The project manager needs interpersonal skills, sometimes called "soft" skills, to help alleviate the project team's fears, concerns, and anxiety about the project. The project manager should use empathy, leadership, and group facilitation to move team development along.

Training the project team is one of the best team development exercises. The staffing management plan defines the need for training, and team development is the execution of that plan. In other words, if team members don't know how to do the project work, train them!

Another facet of team development is a focus on getting the project work completed. The project managers are the power on the project team. While there may be some resistance from the project team to cooperate with the project manager, complete assigned duties, or participate as requested, the project team should realize that the project manager is the project authority. There are five types of powers that the project manager wields:

- **Expert** The project manager's authority comes from both experience with the technology the project focuses on and from expertise in managing projects.
- **Reward** The project manager has the authority to reward the project team.
- **Formal** The project manager has been assigned the role of project manager by senior management and is in charge of the project. This is also known as *positional* power.
- **Coercive** The project manager has the authority to discipline the project team members. This is also known as *penalty* power. When the team is afraid of the project manager, the project manager has *coercive* power.
- **Referent** The project team personally knows the project manager. *Referent* can also mean that the project manager refers to the person who assigned him or her the position—for example, "The CEO assigned me to this position, so we'll do it this way." This power can also mean the project team wants to work on the project or with the project manager due to the high priority and impact of the project.

Creating Team-Building Activities

Team-building activities are approaches to developing the team through facilitated events. The goal of team-building exercises is to allow the project team to learn about each other, rely on each other, and form cohesiveness among the project team members. Events can include:

- Involving the team during planning processes
- Defining rules for handling team disagreements

- Holding off-site activities
- Facilitating quick team-involvement activities
- Facilitating activities to improve interpersonal skills and form relationships

There's a general belief that project teams actually go through their own natural development processes. These processes can shift, linger, and even stall based on the dynamics of the project team. This theory of team development was created by Dr. Bruce Tuckman in 1965. Here are the five phases of team development that project managers may face:

- **Forming** The project team meets and learns about their roles and responsibilities on the project. Little interaction among the project team happens in this stage, as the team is learning about the project and project manager. The project manager guides the project team through this stage of team development by introducing members and helping them learn about one another.

- **Storming** The project team struggles for project positions, leadership, and project direction. The project team can become hostile toward the project leader, challenge ideas, and try to establish and claim positions about the project work. The amount of debate and fury can vary depending on whether the project team is willing to work together, the nature of the project, and the control of the project manager. The project manager's role in this stage is to mediate disagreement and squelch unproductive behavior.

- **Norming** Project team members go about getting the project work, begin to rely on one another, and generally complete their project assignments. In this stage of team development, the project manager allows the project team to manage themselves.

- **Performing** If a project team can reach the performing stage of team development, they trust one another, work well together, and issues and problems get resolved quickly and effectively. The project manager stays out of the project team's way, but is available to help the project team get their work done.

- **Adjourning** Once the project is done, either the team moves onto other assignments as a unit, or the project team is disbanded and individual team members go on to other work. The project manager uses the staffing management plan as a guide for how project team members are released from the project team.

NOTE Tuckman originally used just the first four stages of team development, but added adjourning to the model in the 1970s.

Establishing Project Ground Rules

Creating ground rules for the project team is part of team development. Ground rules establish the project expectations for the project team and define what is and is not acceptable behavior by all of the project team members, including the project manager. When all of the project team members agree to abide by the defined ground rules, misunderstandings diminish while productivity increases. Once ground rules are defined, it's the responsibility of all the project team members to enforce them.

 EXAM TIP Ground rules are enforced by the project team, not just the project manager.

Relying on Interpersonal Management Skills

As a project manager, you need interpersonal skills to lead the project team. You might know these as soft skills or emotional intelligence, but they're really about understanding what motivates a person, how you can lead the person, and how to really listen to a person on your project team. While project management is about getting things done, you're dealing with people that have issues, concerns, stress, anxiety, and a life beyond your project. You need to listen to the project team, empathize with them as needed, and help them manage their project work and assignment. This is a great example where a more experienced project manager can shift from the project manager role and see the project from the perspective of the team member.

A chunk of project management relies on interpersonal skills. Specifically, the project manager relies on:

- **Leading** Good project managers master the art of establishing direction, aligning people, and motivating the project team to complete the project work.
- **Communicating** Good project managers are good communicators. Remember, half of communicating is listening.
- **Negotiating** Project managers will likely negotiate for scope, cost, terms, assignment, and resources.
- **Problem solving** Project managers must have the ability to confront and solve problems.
- **Influencing** Project managers use their influence to get things done.

Rewarding the Project Team

When discussing human resource planning, I mentioned that you, the project manager, should create the rewards and recognition system. This system is part of team development and encourages the behavior you want from your project team—that is, the behavior that promotes the project to completion and meets the project scope statement. Performance appraisals tell the project manager, and sometimes functional management, which team members should be rewarded based on the confines of the reward system.

Obviously, positive behavior should be rewarded. If a project team member willingly agrees to work overtime to ensure that the project will hit its schedule objective, that should be rewarded or recognized by the project manager. However, if a project team member has to work overtime because he has wasted time or resources, a reward is not in order.

Win-lose awards, sometimes called zero-sum awards, should be avoided because they can hurt the project team's cohesiveness. Any award where only some of the project team members can qualify shouldn't be given. For instance, I once worked on a project where the project manager awarded the software developer who created the most code a bonus every month. Well, since I wasn't a software developer, I could never qualify for that bonus. (Thanks a lot, Ron! Ron was my boss then, and oh what sweet printed vengeance this is. Just kidding... He dropped the bonus program when he saw the trouble with his plan.)

> **EXAM TIP** Your reward and recognition system should also consider cultural differences. Creating team rewards in a culture that encourages individualism can be difficult. In other words, the reward system must mesh with the culture within which the project manager is operating.

Assessing the Project Team

You want your project team to be the best unit of people possible. You want them to rely on one another, help each other, and communicate without fear of retribution. You also want the project team to be competent in the project work and execution of the project management plan. Personnel assessment tools, such as exams and surveys, can help you gain some insight into the project team and where each person's strengths and weaknesses lie. This can help you determine how to better manage the project team, improve performance, and gain insight into what motivates team members.

The assessments of the project team can measure all sorts of factors, but there are some common measurements as a result of the assessment program:

- Technical success of the project execution
- Project schedule adherence
- Cost baseline management
- Improvement in competencies
- Reduction in staff turnover
- Team functionality in communications and problem solving

Project team members' performance is reviewed and tied to their overall performance on the project team. Performance appraisals can be in the form of a 360-degree appraisal, where a project team member is reviewed in all directions by the project team, the project manager, stakeholders, and even vendors, where appropriate.

Managing the Project Team

Now that the project manager has planned for the human resources and developed the project team, he can focus on managing the project team. This process involves tracking each team member's performance, offering feedback, taking care of project issues, and managing those pesky change requests that can affect the project team and its work. The staffing management plan may be updated based on lessons learned and changes within the team management process.

In a matrix environment, where the project team members are accountable to both the project manager and a functional manager, team management is a tricky business. The project manager and the functional managers need to work together to communicate the utilization of the project team member in both operations and on the project. The project team's demand for dual reporting to the project manager and the functional manager also has to be considered—and is often the responsibility of the project manager rather than the functional manager or project team member.

Preparing for Team Management

Managing the project team is based on many conditions and scenarios within the project. Management of the project team is really about one thing: getting the project work done as promised in the project scope statement. There are many inputs to project team management:

- **Human resource plan** You know this plan, right? Just in case you forgot, it defines when project team members will complete their project work, the training needs for the project, certification requirements, and any labor compliance issues. It's an output of human resources planning.

- **Project staff assignments** The project manager and the project management team both need a listing of the project staff assignments in order to monitor and evaluate each project team member's project performance.

- **Team performance assessments** You'll know if your project team is doing a good job or not, but you'll want to quantify their performance so that you can make recommendations where needed. Assessments include information on the project team's skills, competencies, turnover rate, and team cohesion.

- **Issue log** Any issues that have been found in the project should be documented in this log. A project team member is assigned to the resolution of the issue by a given date, so this log is considered an input to managing the project team.

- **Work performance reports** The project management team observes and records the work a project team member performs. This doesn't necessarily mean the project management team peers over the shoulder of the project team member, but rather observes the team member's participation in team activities, their delivery on action items, and thoroughness in communication.

- **Organizational process assets**   Consider the organization's approach to rewarding employees for their work in a project. Organizational process assets in team management rely on dinners, certificates of appreciation, newsletters, and other methods to recognize a project team's hard work on a project.

All of these inputs feed directly into the actual process of managing the project team. The project manager and the project management team will use the evidence of these things to better manage the team in order to move the project toward completion.

Dealing with Team Disagreements

In most projects, there will be instances when the project team, management, and other stakeholders disagree on the progress, decisions, and proposed solutions within the project. It's essential for the project manager to keep calm, lead, and direct the parties to a sensible solution that's best for the project. Here are seven reasons for conflict, listed from most common to least common:

- Schedules
- Priorities
- Resources
- Technical beliefs
- Administrative policies and procedures
- Project costs
- Personalities

 EXAM TIP   You can expect questions on these areas of conflict on the exam. Don't be duped into thinking personality conflicts are the biggest problem with conflict resolution. They are the least important.

So what's a project manager to do with all the potential for strife in a project? There are five different approaches to conflict resolution:

- **Collaborate/Problem Solve**   This approach utilizes multiple viewpoints and perspectives to find a resolution. To utilize this method, the participants need a collaborative attitude to confront the problem rather than each other.

- **Force/Direct**   The person with the power makes the decision. The decision made may not be the best decision for the project, but it's fast. As expected, this autocratic approach does little for team development and is a win-lose solution. It should be used when the stakes are high and time is of the essence, or if relationships are not important.

- **Compromise/Reconcile**   This approach requires that both parties give up something. The decision made is a blend of both sides of the argument. Because neither party really wins, it is considered a lose-lose solution. The project manager can use this approach when the relationships are equal and no one can truly "win." This approach can also be used to avoid a fight.

- **Smoothing/Accommodating**   This approach smoothes out the conflict by minimizing the perceived size of the problem. It is a temporary solution, but can calm team relations and boisterous discussions. Smoothing may be acceptable when time is of the essence or when any of the proposed solutions will not currently settle the problem. This can be considered a lose-lose situation as well, since no one really wins in the long run. The project manager can use smoothing to emphasize areas of agreement between disagreeing stakeholders and thus minimize areas of conflict.

- **Withdrawal/Avoidance**   This conflict resolution has one side of the argument walking away from the problem, usually in disgust. The conflict is not resolved, and it is considered a yield-lose solution. The approach can be used, however, as a cooling-off period or when the issue is not critical.

Creating an Issue Log

It's okay to have issues within a project as long as the issues are recorded in the issue log. An *issue*, technically, is something that may be preventing the project team from reaching the project objectives. Typically, issues are identified and recorded in the issue log. Each issue is assigned to an owner who needs to find a method that will resolve the issue by a given date. Each issue should also be identified as to its status and possible resolution. Common issues are:

- Differences of opinion
- Situations to be investigated
- Unanticipated responsibilities that need to be assigned to someone on the project team

Examining the Outputs of Team Management

Team management begins as soon as the project team comes together, and ends as soon as the project is closed. Throughout the project, different conditions and scenarios will affect how the project manager and the project management team will manage the project and the resources within it. There are five outputs of managing the project team:

- **Requested changes**   Seems like just about everything can result in a change request, doesn't it? Changes to the project team can have ripple effects on the project scheduling, project cost, and even the project scope statement, so a change request is needed when these conditions are true. Corrective actions can include moving people to different assignments, outsourcing some of the project work, and replacing project team members who may have left the organization or project. Preventive actions can include cross-training, role clarification, and even additional labor through hiring or procurement to ensure that all of the project work is completed as planned.

- **Project management plan updates**   Just like any other area of project management, if the project management plan needs to be updated, it should be. Project management plan updates could include approved change requests, corrective actions, new project team member roles, and training decisions.

- **Project document updates**   Updates to the issue log, role description, and staff assignments should be reflected in the project documents as needed. You may need to update the roles and responsibility charts, such as your RACI chart, to reflect the changes within the project and/or project team.

- **Enterprise environmental factor updates**   It is possible that your management approach could affect the enterprise environmental factors within your organization. You may need to update the process for performance appraisals and any information about project team members' new skills as a result of the project training.

- **Organizational process assets updates**   You'll need to update the organizational process assets for your project as a result of managing the project team. This will likely include any templates you've created, historical information, and lessons learned documentation. What the project management team learns in the project becomes part of organizational process assets for future projects. For example, lessons learned in human resources include:

  - Staffing management plan
  - Organizational charts
  - Position descriptions
  - Ground rules
  - Conflict management techniques
  - Successful rewards and recognition approaches
  - Procedures for virtual team management
  - Negotiating techniques
  - Training programs

- Successful team-building exercises
- Issues and solutions documented in the project log

Relating to Organizational Theories

You can expect to see some of these topics on your exam, so let's have a look at these theories in more detail.

Maslow's Hierarchy of Needs

According to Abraham Maslow, people work to take care of a hierarchy of needs. The pinnacle of their needs is self-actualization. People want to contribute, prove their worth, and use their skills and abilities. Figure 9-4 shows the pyramid of needs that all people try to ascend by fulfilling each layer, one at a time.

Maslow's five layers of needs, from lowest to highest, are:

- **Physiological**   People require these necessities to live: air, water, food, clothing, and shelter.
- **Safety**   People need safety and security. This can include stability in life, work, and culture.
- **Social**   People are social creatures and need love, approval, and friends.
- **Esteem**   People strive for the respect, appreciation, and approval of others.
- **Self-actualization**   At the pinnacle of needs, people seek personal growth, knowledge, and fulfillment.

Figure 9-4
Maslow's theory states that people ultimately work for self-actualization.

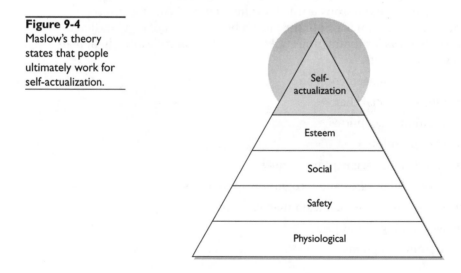

Herzberg's Theory of Motivation

According to Frederick Herzberg, a psychologist and authority on the motivation of work, there are two catalysts for success with people:

- **Hygiene agents** These elements are the expectations all workers have. They include job security, a paycheck, clean and safe working conditions, a sense of belonging, civil working relationships, and other basic attributes associated with employment.

- **Motivating agents** These are the elements that motivate people to excel. They include responsibility, appreciation of work, public recognition for a job well done, the chance to excel, education, and other opportunities associated with work aside from financial rewards.

This theory says that the presence of hygiene factors will not motivate people to perform because these are expected attributes. However, the absence of these elements will demotivate performance. For people to excel, the presence of motivating factors must exist. Figure 9-5 illustrates Herzberg's Theory of Motivation.

EXAM COACH Use Herzberg's Theory for your exam. Find some things that will motivate you to excel so you can pass your exam: a career advancement, a day off work, new clothes, or some other reward. Create an incentive that means something to you. After all, part of Herzberg's Theory is that the motivating agents have to interest the person that's being motivated.

McGregor's Theory of X and Y

Douglas McGregor's theory states that, from their perspective, management believes there are two types of workers, good and bad, as seen in Figure 9-6. Theory X sees workers as lazy, uninterested in doing the project work, and that they must be micromanaged

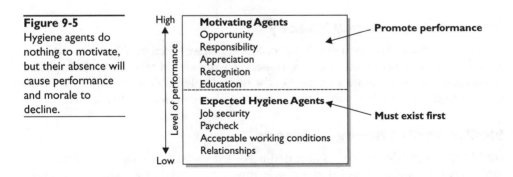

Figure 9-5
Hygiene agents do nothing to motivate, but their absence will cause performance and morale to decline.

Figure 9-6
Management believes that "X" people are bad and "Y" people are good.

and coerced to do the work. Theory Y sees workers as good, self-directed, and able to do the work that's assigned to them.

- *X is bad.* These people need to be watched all the time, micromanaged, and cannot be trusted. X people avoid work, shun responsibility, and lack the aptitude to achieve.

- *Y is good.* These people are self-led, motivated, and can accomplish new tasks proactively.

Ouchi's Theory Z

William Ouchi's theory is based on the participative management style of the Japanese. This theory states that workers are motivated by a sense of commitment, opportunity, and advancement. Workers in an organization subscribing to Theory Z learn the business by moving up through the ranks of the company.

Ouchi's theory also credits the idea of *lifetime employment.* Workers will stay with one company until they retire because they are dedicated to the company, which is in turn dedicated to them.

EXAM TIP If you need a way to keep McGregor's X and Y and Ouchi's Z theories separate in your mind, think of this: X is bad; Y is good; Z is the best.

Vroom's Expectancy Theory

Vroom's Expectancy Theory states that people will behave based on what they expect as a result of their behavior. In other words, people will work in relation to the expected reward of the work. If the attractiveness of the reward is desirable to the worker, she will work to receive it. In other words, people expect to be rewarded for their effort.

McClelland's Theory of Needs

David McClelland developed his acquired-needs theory based on his belief that a person's needs are acquired and develop over time. These needs are shaped by circumstance, conditions, and life experiences for each individual. McClelland's Theory of Needs is also known as the Three Needs Theory because there are just three needs for each individual. Depending on the person's experiences, the order and magnitude of each need shifts:

- **Need for Achievement**   These people need to achieve, so they avoid both low-risk and high-risk situations. Achievers like to work alone or with other high achievers, and they need regular feedback to gauge their achievement and progress.

- **Need for Affiliation**   People who have a driving need for affiliation look for harmonious relationships, want to feel accepted by people, and conform to the norms of the project team.

- **Need for Power**   People who have a need for power are usually seeking either personal or institutional power. Personal power generally is the ability to control and direct other people. Institutional power is the ability to direct the efforts of others for the betterment of the organization.

McClelland developed the Thematic Apperception Test to determine what needs are driving individuals. The test is a series of pictures that the test taker must create a story about. Through the storytelling, the test taker will reveal which need is driving his or her life at that time.

Chapter Summary

The project manager has to plan for the needed human resources to complete the project work. In addition, the project manager plans for how the human resources will be managed, trained, motivated, and led throughout the duration of the project. The project management team works to identify the roles within the project and their responsibilities, which are the activities needed to complete the project work. The key output of planning for human resources is the staffing management plan, which defines how the project team will be acquired, managed, trained, rewarded for the work, and then released from the project team. The staffing management plan also defines how the project management team will comply with government regulations and will manage team safety concerns.

The project team is acquired just as the staffing management plan specifies. The team, however, isn't always selected—it's often preassigned to the project. Sometimes, the project manager gets to negotiate with the functional managers and other project managers to get the best resources possible on the project. When the resources aren't available inside the organization, the project manager often has to deal with contracted help, which means procurement.

Some teams all work together in one locale and might huddle in the project's war room. This idea of a co-located team supports ad-hoc conversations, team cohesiveness, and project performance. However, in many cases, the project team is not co-located, and a virtual team is created. Virtual teams allow people with mobility handicaps or travel issues, as well as home office workers, to be actively involved in the project.

Whatever conditions surround the project team, the project manager must work to develop the team. Team development centers on building team cohesiveness through team-building exercises, training, and team involvement. One team development tool and technique is the creation of ground rules. Ground rules are created and agreed upon by the project team to promote performance within the project. Once ground rules are created, it's up to the project team to enforce them.

Through conversations, observations, performance appraisals, conflict management, and the issue log, the project manager will manage the project team. The goal of team management is getting the project done—meaning, it's all about results.

Human resource theories, such as Maslow's Hierarchy of Needs, McGregor's Theory of X and Y, Ouchi's Theory Z, and Vroom's Expectancy Theory, all seek to determine what motivates an employee to complete her project tasks. Project managers can use these theories to determine the best approach to motivate or inspire a project team member to elicit the behavior the project manager expects.

Key Terms

Adjourning   Once the project is done, either the team moves onto other assignments as a unit, or the project team is disbanded and individual team members go on to other work.

Authority power   Project management team members may have authority over other project team members, may have the ability to make decisions, and perhaps even sign approvals for project work and purchases.

Coercive power   The project manager has the authority to discipline the project team members. This is also known as penalty power.

Collaborate/Problem solving   This approach confronts the problem head-on and is the preferred method of conflict resolution. Multiple viewpoints and perspectives contribute to the solution.

Collective bargaining agreement constraints   Contracts and agreements with unions or other employee groups may serve as constraints on the project.

Competency   This attribute defines what talents, skills, and capabilities are needed to complete the project work.

Compromising   This approach requires that both parties give up something.

Vroom's Expectancy Theory   This theory states that people will behave based on what they expect as a result of their behavior. In other words, people will work in relation to the expected reward.

Expert power   The project manager's authority comes both from experience with the technology the project focuses on and from expertise in managing projects.

Forcing power   The person with the power makes the decision.

Formal power The project manager has been assigned the role of project manager by senior management and is in charge of the project.

Forming The project team meets and learns about their roles and responsibilities on the project. Little interaction among the project team happens in this stage as the team is learning about the project and project manager.

Herzberg's Theory of Motivation Frederick Herzberg's theory of the motivating agents and hygiene agents that affect a person's willingness to excel in his career.

Hierarchical organizational chart A chart showing the relationship between superior and subordinate employees, groups, disciplines, and even departments.

Human resource plan This plan defines staff acquisition, the timetable for staff acquisition, the staff release plan, training needs for the project team, any organizational compliance issues, rewards and recognitions, and safety concerns for the project team doing the project work.

Interpersonal interfaces This organizational interface considers the formal and informal reporting relationships that may exist among the project team members. The interpersonal interface also considers the job descriptions of the project team members, existing reporting structures between supervisors and subordinates, and existing relationships, if any, that may affect the project work. This interface also considers any cultural or language differences among the project team that may need to be addressed.

Issue log A logbook of the issues the project team has identified and dates as to when the issues must be resolved by. The issue log may also include team members or stakeholders who are responsible for finding a solution to the identified issues.

Logistical interfaces The logistics of the team locale, time zones, geographical boundaries, and travel requirements within a project.

Maslow's Hierarchy of Needs Abraham Maslow's theory of the five needs all humans have and work toward.

McClelland's Theory of Needs David McClelland developed this theory, which states our needs are acquired and developed by our experiences over time. All people are, according to this theory, driven by one of three needs: achievement, affiliation, or power.

McGregor's Theory of X and Y Douglas McGregor's theory that states management views workers in the Y category as competent and self-led and workers in the X category as incompetent and needing to be micromanaged.

Multicriteria Decision Analysis A method to rate potential project team members based on criteria such as education, experience, skills, knowledge, and more.

Norming Project team members go about getting the project work, begin to rely on one another, and generally complete their project assignments.

Organization chart Traditional chart that depicts how the organization is broken down by department and disciplines. This chart is sometimes called the organizational breakdown structure (OBS) and is arranged by departments, units, or teams.

Organizational interfaces The project management team needs to identify which departments are going to be involved in the project.

Organizational structure constraint The structure of the organization has a direct correlation to the amount of power a project manager has within a project.

Ouchi's Theory Z William Ouchi's theory is based on the participative management style of the Japanese. This theory states that workers are motivated by a sense of commitment, opportunity, and advancement.

Performing If a project team can reach the performing stage of team development, they trust one another, work well together, and issues and problems get resolved quickly and effectively.

Political interfaces The hidden goals, personal agendas, and alliances among the project team members and the stakeholders.

RACI chart A RACI chart is a matrix chart that only uses the activities of responsible, accountable, consult, and inform.

Referent power The project team personally knows the project manager. Referent can also mean that the project manager refers to the person who assigned him the position.

Resource breakdown structure (RBS) This hierarchical chart can decompose the project by the type of resources used throughout it.

Responsibility assignment matrix (RAM) A RAM chart shows the correlation between project team members and the work they've been assigned to complete.

Responsibility A responsibility is the work that a role performs.

Reward The project manager has the authority to reward the project team.

Role This denotes what a person is specifically responsible for in a project. Roles are usually tied to job titles, such as network engineer, mechanical engineer, and electrician.

Smoothing This approach smooths out the conflict by minimizing the perceived size of the problem. It is a temporary solution, but can calm team relations and boisterous discussions.

Staffing management plan A subsidiary plan of the project management plan that defines staff acquisition, timetables, release criteria, training needs, reward and recognition systems, compliance issues, and safety concerns for the project.

Storming The project team struggles for project positions, leadership, and project direction. The project team can become hostile toward the project leader, challenge ideas, and try to establish and claim positions about the project work. The amount of debate and fury can vary depending on if the project team is willing to work together, the nature of the project, and the control of the project manager.

Technical interfaces   The project team identifies the disciplines and specialties that the project will require to complete the project scope statement. The technical interfaces are the resources that will be doing the project work.

Withdrawal   This conflict resolution method sees one side of the argument walking away from the problem, usually in disgust.

Questions

1. You are the project manager for the JHG Project. This project requires coordination with the director of manufacturing, HR, the IT department, and the CIO. This is an example of what type of input to organizational planning?

   A. Organizational interfaces

   B. Technical interfaces

   C. Interpersonal interfaces

   D. Human resource coordination

2. You are the project manager of the Newton Construction Project. This project will use internal and external employees on your project team. Your project requires an electrician at month 8. This is an example of which of the following?

   A. Organizational interfaces

   B. Staffing requirements

   C. Contractor requirements

   D. Resource constraints

3. You are the project manager of the PUY Project. This project requires a chemical engineer for seven months of the project, although there are no available chemical engineers within your department. This is an example of which of the following?

   A. Organizational interfaces

   B. Staffing requirements

   C. Contractor requirements

   D. Resource constraints

4. You are the project manager in an organization with a weak matrix. Your project team will come from three different lines of business within the organization and they are also working on at least two other projects. Who will have the authority in your project?

   A. The project manager

    B. The customer

    C. Functional management

    D. The team leader

5. You are the project manager for the LMG Project. Your project will have several human resource issues that must be coordinated and approved by the union. Which of the following statements is correct about this scenario?

    A. The union is considered a resource constraint.

    B. The union is considered a management constraint.

    C. The union is considered a project stakeholder.

    D. The union is considered a project team member.

6. You are the project manager of the PLY Project. This project is similar to the ACT Project you have completed. What method can you use to expedite the process of organizational planning?

    A. Use the project plan of the ACT Project on the PLY Project.

    B. Use the roles and responsibilities defined in the ACT Project on the PLY Project.

    C. Use the project team structure of the ACT Project on the PLY Project.

    D. Use the project team of the ACT Project on the PLY Project.

7. You are the project manager in your organization. Your project is part of a larger program led by Nancy Whitting. Nancy is a believer of McGregor's Theory of X and Y. Which of the following is an example of Theory X?

    A. Self-led project teams

    B. Micromanagement

    C. Team members able to work on their own accord

    D. Earned value management

8. You are the project manager of the PLN Project. The team members are somewhat afraid of you as project manager because they see you as management. They know that a negative review from you about their project work will impact their yearly bonus. This is an example of which of the following?

    A. Formal power

    B. Coercive power

    C. Expert power

    D. Referent power

9. You are the project manager of the MMB Project. The president of the company has spoken to the project team and told them of the confidence

and respect he has in you to lead the project to a successful completion. The project manager has what type of power on this project?

A. Formal power

B. Coercive power

C. Expert power

D. Halo power

10. Management has approached Tyler, one of your project team members. Tyler is a database administrator and developer whose work is always on time, accurate, and of quality. He also has a reputation of being a "good guy" and is well liked. Because of this, management has decided to move Tyler into the role of a project manager for a new database administration project. This is an example of which of the following?

A. Management by exception

B. The halo effect

C. Management by objectives

D. McGregor's Theory of X and Y

11. You are the project manager of the Holson Implementation Project for your company. It's come to your attention that three of your project team members are in a disagreement about the direction the project work should take. This disagreement is stalling the project schedule and causing the other project team members to become uncomfortable. You need to resolve this situation quickly and professionally. Which problem-solving technique is the best for most project management situations?

A. Collaborating/Problem Solving

B. Compromising

C. Forcing

D. Avoiding

12. Harold is an outspoken project team member. All of the project team members respect Harold for his experience with the technology, but often things have to go in Harold's favor, otherwise the team's in for a bumpy ride. During a discussion on a solution, a project team member waves her arms and says, "Fine, Harold, do it your way." This is an example of which of the following?

A. A win-win solution

B. A leave-lose solution

C. A lose-lose solution

D. A yield-lose solution

13. You are the project manager for the GBK Project. This project affects a line of business, and the customer is anxious about the success of the project. Which of the following is likely not a top concern for the customer?

    A. Project priorities

    B. Schedule

    C. Cost

    D. Personality conflicts

14. There are several management theories that you should understand for your PMI exam and for your role as a project manager. Which theory believes that workers need to be involved with the management process?

    A. McGregor's Theory of X and Y

    B. Ouchi's Theory Z

    C. Herzberg's Theory of Motivation

    D. Vroom's Expectancy Theory

15. You need a method to keep workers motivated and inspired on your project. This project has many conditions that the project team sees as unfavorable, but they do like you as a project manager. _____ states that as long as workers are rewarded, they will remain productive.

    A. McGregor's Theory of X and Y

    B. Ouchi's Theory Z

    C. Herzberg's Theory of Motivation

    D. Vroom's Expectancy Theory

16. You are the project manager for Industrial Lights Project. You have been hired by your organization specifically because of your vast experience with the technology and with projects of this nature. The project team is aware of your experience. You likely have what type of power on this project?

    A. Formal power

    B. Coercive power

    C. Expert power

    D. Referent power

17. You are the project manager for GHB Project. You have served as a project manager for your organization for the past ten years. Practically all of your projects come in on time and on budget. The project team has worked with you in the past, and they consider you to be an expert project manager. They also like working with you. Given all of this, you likely have what type of power on this project?

    A. Formal power

B. Coercive power

C. Expert power

D. Referent power

18. You are the project manager for your organization and it's come to your attention that some of the project team members are in disagreement with the senior network engineer about the installation of some equipment. You need to resolve this situation quickly before the project stalls any longer. Which of the following is an example of coercive power?

   A. A project manager who has lunch with the project team every Thursday

   B. A project manager who will openly punish any team member who is late with an activity

   C. A project manager who has worked with the technology on the project for several years

   D. A project manager who is friends with all of the project team members

19. Mike is the project manager for a project with a very tight schedule. The project is running late, and Mike feels that he does not have time to consider all the possible solutions that two team members are in disagreement over. He quickly decides to go with the team member with the largest amount of seniority. This is an example of which of the following?

   A. Problem solving

   B. Compromising

   C. Forcing

   D. Withdrawal

20. You are a project manager in a projectized organization. Your job as a project manager can be described best by which of the following?

   A. Full-time

   B. Part-time

   C. Expeditor

   D. Coordinator

Questions and Answers

1. You are the project manager for the JHG Project. This project requires coordination with the director of manufacturing, HR, the IT department, and the CIO. This is an example of what type of input to organizational planning?

   A. Organizational interfaces

   B. Technical interfaces

   C. Interpersonal interfaces

D. Human resource coordination

> A. The reporting interfaces for this project—the director of manufacturing, HR, the IT department, and the CIO—are examples of the organizational interfaces. B is incorrect because technical interfaces are the technical gurus for the project, such as the engineers and designers. C, the interpersonal interfaces, is not the best choice because this relationship describes the different individuals working on the project. D, human resource coordination, is also incorrect.

2. You are the project manager of the Newton Construction Project. This project will use internal and external employees on your project team. Your project requires an electrician at month 8. This is an example of which of the following?

    A. Organizational interfaces

    B. Staffing requirements

    C. Contractor requirements

    D. Resource constraints

> B. Because the project requires the electrician, a project role, this is a staffing requirement. A is incorrect because it does not accurately describe the situation. C is incorrect because contractor requirements would specify the procurement issues, the minimum qualifications for the electrician, and so on. D is incorrect because a resource constraint, while a tempting choice, deals more with the availability of the resource or the requirement to use the resource.

3. You are the project manager of the PUY Project. This project requires a chemical engineer for seven months of the project, although there are no available chemical engineers within your department. This is an example of which of the following?

    A. Organizational interfaces

    B. Staffing requirements

    C. Contractor requirements

    D. Resource constraints

> B. The project needs the resource of the chemical engineer to be successful. When the project needs a resource, it is a staffing requirement. A, C, and D are all incorrect. This is not a situation describing an organizational interface or contractor requirements. Resource constraints might include a requirement to use a particular resource or that a resource must be available when certain project activities are happening.

4. You are the project manager in an organization with a weak matrix. Your project team will come from three different lines of business within the

organization and they are also working on at least two other projects. Who will have the authority in your project?

A. The project manager

B. The customer

C. Functional management

D. The team leader

C. In a weak matrix structure, functional management will have more authority than the project manager. A, B, and D are all incorrect because these choices do not have as much authority on a project in a weak matrix environment as functional management will have.

5. You are the project manager for the LMG Project. Your project will have several human resource issues that must be coordinated and approved by the union. Which of the following statements is correct about this scenario?

A. The union is considered a resource constraint.

B. The union is considered a management constraint.

C. The union is considered a project stakeholder.

D. The union is considered a project team member.

C. In this instance, the union is considered a project stakeholder because it has a vested interest in the project's outcome. A is incorrect because the union is not a resource constraint; they are interested in the project management methodology and the project human resource management. B is incorrect because the union is the counterweight to the management of the organization, not to the project itself. D is also incorrect because the union is not a project team member.

6. You are the project manager of the PLY Project. This project is similar to the ACT Project you have completed. What method can you use to expedite the process of organizational planning?

A. Use the project plan of the ACT Project on the PLY Project.

B. Use the roles and responsibilities defined in the ACT Project on the PLY Project.

C. Use the project team structure of the ACT Project on the PLY Project.

D. Use the project team of the ACT Project on the PLY Project.

B. When projects are similar in nature, the project manager can use the roles and responsibilities defined in the historical project to guide the current project. A is incorrect because the entire project plan of the ACT Project is not needed. Even the roles and responsibilities matrix of the historical project may not be an exact fit for the current project. C is incorrect because copying the project team structure is not the best choice of all the answers presented. D is also incorrect because using the same project team may not be feasible at all.

7. You are the project manager in your organization. Your project is part of a larger program led by Nancy Whitting. Nancy is a believer of McGregor's Theory of X and Y. Which of the following is an example of Theory X?

A. Self-led project teams

B. Micromanagement

C. Team members able to work on their own accord

D. Earned value management

B. Theory X states that workers have an inherent dislike of work and will avoid it if possible. With regard to this theory, micromanagement is a method used to make certain workers complete their work. A and C are actually examples of McGregor's Theory Y. D is incorrect because EVM is not directly related to McGregor's Theory of X and Y.

8. You are the project manager of the PLN Project. The team members are somewhat afraid of you as project manager because they see you as management. They know that a negative review from you about their project work will impact their yearly bonus. This is an example of which of the following?

A. Formal power

B. Coercive power

C. Expert power

D. Referent power

B. When the project team is afraid of the power the project manager yields, this is called coercive power. A, C, and D are incorrect because they describe assigned, technical, and referential power over the project, respectively.

9. You are the project manager of the MMB Project. The president of the company has spoken to the project team and told them of the confidence and respect he has in you to lead the project to a successful completion. The project manager has what type of power on this project?

A. Formal power

B. Coercive power

C. Expert power

D. Halo power

A. The company president has assigned you to the position of the project manager, so you have formal power. B is incorrect because coercive power is the fear associated with the project manager. C is incorrect because expert power is derived from the project manager's experience with the technology being implemented. D is also incorrect because halo power is not a viable answer to the question.

10. Management has approached Tyler, one of your project team members. Tyler is a database administrator and developer whose work is always on time, accurate, and of quality. He also has a reputation of being a "good guy" and is well liked. Because of this, management has decided to move Tyler into the role of a project manager for a new database administration project. This is an example of which of the following?

    A. Management by exception

    B. The halo effect

    C. Management by objectives

    D. McGregor's Theory of X and Y

    B. The halo effect is the assumption that because the person is good at a technology, he would also be good at managing a project dealing with that said technology. A, C, and D are all incorrect because these do not describe the halo effect.

11. You are the project manager of the Holson Implementation Project for your company. It's come to your attention that three of your project team members are in a disagreement about the direction the project work should take. This disagreement is stalling the project schedule and causing the other project team members to become uncomfortable. You need to resolve this situation quickly and professionally. Which problem-solving technique is the best for most project management situations?

    A. Collaborating/Problem Solving

    B. Compromising

    C. Forcing

    D. Avoiding

    A. Collaborating/Problem Solving is the best problem-solving technique because it meets the problem directly. B is incorrect because compromising requires both sides on an argument to give up something. C is incorrect because forcing requires the project manager to force a decision based on external inputs, such as seniority, experience, and so on. D is also incorrect because avoiding ignores the problem and does not solve it.

12. Harold is an outspoken project team member. All of the project team members respect Harold for his experience with the technology, but often things have to go in Harold's favor, otherwise the team's in for a bumpy ride. During a discussion on a solution, a project team member waves her arms and says, "Fine, Harold, do it your way." This is an example of which of the following?

    A. A win-win solution

    B. A leave-lose solution

    C. A lose-lose solution

    D. A yield-lose solution

D. When Harold always has to win an argument and team members begin to give in to Harold's demands simply to avoid the argument rather than finding an accurate solution, this is a yield-lose situation. A is incorrect because both parties do not win. B is incorrect because the project team member did not leave the conversation, but instead ended it. C is incorrect because a lose-lose is a compromise where both parties give up something.

13. You are the project manager for the GBK Project. This project affects a line of business, and the customer is anxious about the success of the project. Which of the following is likely not a top concern for the customer?

    A. Project priorities

    B. Schedule

    C. Cost

    D. Personality conflicts

D. Personality conflicts are likely a concern for the customer, but are not as important as project priorities, schedule, and cost. The customer hired your company to solve the technical issues. A, B, and C are all incorrect because these are most likely the top issues for a company in a project of this magnitude.

14. There are several management theories that you should understand for your PMI exam and for your role as a project manager. Which theory believes that workers need to be involved with the management process?

    A. McGregor's Theory of X and Y

    B. Ouchi's Theory Z

    C. Herzberg's Theory of Motivation

    D. Expectancy Theory

B. Ouchi's Theory Z states that workers need to be involved with the management process. A is incorrect because McGregor's Theory of X and Y believes that X workers don't want to work and need constant supervision, while Z workers will work if the work is challenging, satisfying, and rewarding. C is incorrect because Herzberg's Theory of Motivation describes the type of people and what excites them to work. D, the expectancy theory, describes how people will work based on what they expect in return.

15. You need a method to keep workers motivated and inspired on your project. This project has many conditions that the project team sees as unfavorable, but they do like you as a project manager. _____ states that as long as workers are rewarded, they will remain productive.

A. McGregor's Theory of X and Y

B. Ouchi's Theory Z

C. Herzberg's Theory of Motivation

D. Vroom's Expectancy Theory

D. Vroom's Expectancy Theory describes how people will work based on what they expect in return. If people are rewarded because of the work they complete, and they like the reward (payment), they will continue to work. A, B, and C are all incorrect because these theories do not accurately describe the scenario presented.

16. You are the project manager for Industrial Lights Project. You have been hired by your organization specifically because of your vast experience with the technology and with projects of this nature. The project team is aware of your experience. You likely have what type of power on this project?

A. Formal power

B. Coercive power

C. Expert power

D. Referent power

C. You, the project manager, have expert power on this project because of your experience with the technology and with projects that are similar in nature. A, B, and D are all incorrect. These project management powers do not accurately describe the scenario. Formal power is appointed power. Coercive power describes fear of the project manager. Referent power describes power by association and personal knowledge.

17. You are the project manager for GHB Project. You have served as a project manager for your organization for the past ten years. Practically all of your projects come in on time and on budget. The project team has worked with you in the past, and they consider you to be an expert project manager. They also like working with you. Given all of this, you likely have what type of power on this project?

A. Formal power

B. Coercive power

C. Expert power

D. Referent power

D. This is referent power because the project team knows the project manager personally. A and B are incorrect choices because these do not describe the scenario. C is incorrect because expert power does not deal with the ability to lead and complete a project, but instead focuses on being an expert in the technology that the project deals with.

18. You are the project manager for your organization and it's come to your attention that some of the project team members are in disagreement with the senior network engineer about the installation of some equipment. You need to resolve this situation quickly before the project stalls any longer. Which of the following is an example of coercive power?

    A. A project manager who has lunch with the project team every Thursday

    B. A project manager who will openly punish any team member who is late with an activity

    C. A project manager who has worked with the technology on the project for several years

    D. A project manager who is friends with all of the project team members

    B. Coercive power is the formal authority a project manager wields over the project team. A is incorrect because only referent power may come through lunch meetings. C is incorrect because experience is expert power. D is incorrect because interpersonal relationships are examples of referent power.

19. Mike is the project manager for a project with a very tight schedule. The project is running late, and Mike feels that he does not have time to consider all the possible solutions that two team members are in disagreement over. He quickly decides to go with the team member with the largest amount of seniority. This is an example of which of the following?

    A. Problem solving

    B. Compromising

    C. Forcing

    D. Withdrawal

    C. Forcing happens when the project manager makes a decision based on factors that are not relevant to the problem. Just because a team member has more seniority does not mean this individual is correct. A, B, and D are incorrect choices. A, problem solving, is not described in the scenario. B, compromising, happens when both parties agree to give up something. D, withdrawal, happens when a party leaves the argument.

20. You are a project manager in a projectized organization. Your job as a project manager can be described best by which of the following?

    A. Full-time

    B. Part-time

    C. Expeditor

    D. Coordinator

    A. Project managers are typically assigned to a project on a full-time basis in a projectized organization. B, C, and D do not accurately describe the work schedule of a project manager in a projectized environment.

CHAPTER 10

Managing Project Communications

In this chapter, you will
- Plan for project communications
- Manage project communications
- Control project communications

In the movie *Cool Hand Luke*, the prison captain says, "What we got here is a failure to communicate." It's a famous line that has been repeated by musicians and politicians, and even muttered by project managers. Hopefully, when you, the project manager, quote this line, you aren't viewed as the prison captain by your project team.

The point is, many projects experience a breakdown in communications. It's been said that 90 percent of a project manager's time is spent communicating. If you think about it, this certainly makes sense. Your project plans all communicate what you're going to do. Your project reports and forms communicate what you are doing or have done. And all of your status meetings, ad-hoc meetings, and presentations are examples of communicating.

 VIDEO For a more detailed explanation, watch the *Learning the Communications Formula* video now.

Managing project communications is all about the creation, collection, distribution, storage, and handy retrieval of project information. It's what the project manager does day in and day out. The project manager is at the hub of communications and works with the project team, the project stakeholders, the sponsor, the vendors, and often the public to send and receive communications about the project. It can be exhausting because somebody always needs to tell you something, or you need to tell somebody else something. The key, of course, is to plan how to communicate, and then to share that plan and those expectations at the launch of the project.

This chapter discusses the three processes that project communication centers on. Of course, you'll also need to know these processes to pass your Project Management Institute (PMI) exam.

Examining the Communications Foundation

Communications are central to project management and, as part of communications management, work with and through all of the other knowledge areas. A poor job of communicating ensures that the other knowledge areas will likely suffer. Integration management, which I discussed in Chapter 4, revisits us in this chapter since communication is the monitor of the other knowledge areas and serves as the vehicle for reporting information on these other facets of project management.

Communication Factors

In the Project Management Body of Knowledge's (PMBOK) introduction to Chapter 10, some interesting tips and terms sneak into the chapter that you'll likely see on your PMI examination. The first foundation you've got to know in regard to project communications is some of the skills a project manager uses to communicate. Consider the following:

- **Sender–receiver models** These are feedback loops and barriers to communications. Your project status meeting is a great example of a feedback loop because all of your project team members hear what the other team members say, offer feedback to the speaker, hear the speaker respond, and so on. Basically, a feedback loop is a conversation between one or more speakers centering on one specific topic. A barrier to communication is anything that prevents communication from occurring at optimum levels. For example, if you and I are on the same project team but we're mad at each other, we're not going to communicate effectively—if at all.

- **Choice of media** The best modality to use when communicating is the one that is relevant to the information that's being communicated. Some communications demand a formal report, whereas others only warrant a phone call, a face-to-face meeting, or a few sentences on a sticky note. The right medium is dictated by what needs to be communicated.

- **Writing style** You don't have to be E.B. White to write effectively (look at me!). You should, however, be conscious of the message you want to communicate, and choose the appropriate writing style.

- **Presentation techniques** Some people cannot stand to be in front of an audience, but as a project manager, they often find themselves having to present project news and status. The presentation techniques, such as confidence, body language, and visual aids, promote or distract from the message the presenter is offering to the audience.

- **Meeting management techniques**   Ever attend a WOT meeting? That's a "waste of time" meeting. Meetings should have an agenda and order, and someone needs to keep the meeting minutes for the project.

Understanding the Communication Model

The second foundation that is tucked into the introduction of Chapter 10 of the PM-BOK is the communication model. As you can see in Figure 10-1, the model demonstrates how communication moves from one person to another. I like to think of each portion of the model as a fax machine to visualize all the components. Take a look:

- **Sender**   This is the person who wants to send the message. Let's say I want to fax you a contract.
- **Encoder**   This is the device that encodes the message to be sent. My fax machine is the encoder.
- **Medium**   This is the device or technology that transports the message. The telephone line is the medium between our fax machines.
- **Decoder**   This is the device that decodes the message as it is being received. Your fax machine is the decoder.
- **Receiver**   This is the person who receives the message. You receive my fax, jot a note to me, and then send it back through your fax machine to mine. When you send the message back to me, the communication model is reversed.
- **Noise**   Anything that interferes with or disrupts the message. It's possible that static on the phone line may distort the fax message between the two fax machines.

You'll likely see some of this business on your PMI exam. However, throughout this chapter, this model affects how communication happens between people.

Figure 10-1
The communications model demonstrates the flow of communication.

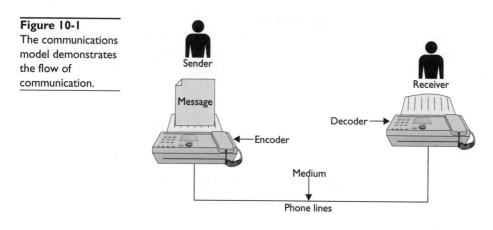

Planning for Communications

As expected, effective communications begin with effective planning. The point of planning for communications is to determine and answer five fundamental project management questions:

- Who needs what information?
- When do they need the information?
- In what modality is the information needed?
- Who will provide the information?
- Who should have access to the information?

Communication planning, although it comes late in this book and in the *PMBOK Guide*, is actually done very early in the project planning processes. It's essential to answer the previous questions as early as possible because their outcomes can affect the remainder of the project planning. Throughout the project, updates to communications planning are expected. Even the responses to the five project management communication questions can change as stakeholders, project team members, vendors, and other project interfaces change.

Preparing for Communications

The outputs of the communications planning process are the communications management plan and project document updates. The communications management plan answers in detail the five questions previously mentioned and provides information on communication requirements, expectations, and timings. When the project management team begins to plan for communications in their project and answer those five essential questions, they've got four inputs they'll rely on, which the following sections describe.

Using Enterprise Environmental Factors

Many of the communications management processes are linked to the enterprise environmental factors. Enterprise environmental factors that affect project communications planning are:

- Organizational culture and structure
- Standards and regulations the project must comply with
- The logistics and organizational infrastructure
- The human resources the project will rely on and interact with
- The policies and procedures for personnel administration
- The project's work authorization system
- The marketplace conditions

- Stakeholder risk tolerances
- Commercial databases that the project may use for estimating
- Project management information system

Using Organizational Process Assets

The organizational process assets affect how the project manager, the project team, and the stakeholders will communicate within a project. The primary organizational process assets that affect communication are:

- Standards and policies unique to the organization
- Organizational guidelines, work instructions, and performance measurement criteria
- Organizational communication requirements for all projects, considering required and approved technology, security issues, archiving, and allowed communication media
- Project closure requirements
- Financial controls and procedures
- Issue and defect management procedures for all projects
- Change control procedures
- Risk control procedures
- Work authorization systems
- Process measurement databases
- Project file structure, organization, and retention
- Historical information and lessons learned requirements
- Issue and defect management databases
- Configuration management databases
- Project financial databases detailing labor hours, costs, budget issues, and cost overruns

Relying on the Stakeholder Register

The stakeholder register defines whom you'll communicate with. Based on the stakeholder register and the stakeholder analysis you've completed, you'll know which stakeholders are most interested in your project and how much influence they have over your project. For each stakeholder, you should know:

- The interest in the project
- The influence over the project
- Strategies for gaining stakeholder support

- Strategies for removing obstacles

This information can be sensitive, so it's important for the project manager to guard this information and share it only with the people who need to know this information. In other words, you don't want to document how much of a pain the IT director is and then post it on your blog. While it's important to create a definitive strategy for managing stakeholders' fears, threats, concerns, and objections, it's just as important to guard the strategy from reaching the wrong people in your organization.

EXAM COACH Most project managers are good communicators to begin with. You're probably going to do fine on this exam topic if you do fine in your role as project manager, but don't let your guard down. Pay attention to the terms and communications management plan in this chapter. These may be things you don't use in your day-to-day role as a project manager, but you'll find them on your exam. Keep positive communications with yourself. You can pass this exam!

Identifying Communication Requirements

The project manager and the project team work together to identify who needs what information. In other words, the project management team needs to know what the requirements for successful communications are in order to plan how to achieve those requirements.

Stakeholders will need different types of information, depending on their interest in the project and the priority of the project. The project manager will need to complete an analysis of the identified stakeholders to determine what information they actually need, as well as how often the information is needed.

There is no value in expending resources on generating information, reports, and analyses for stakeholders who have no interest in the information. An accurate assessment of stakeholders' needs for information is required early in the project planning processes. As a rule of thumb, provide information when its presence contributes to success or when a lack of information can contribute to failure.

The project manager and the project team can identify the demand for communications using the following:

- Organization charts
- The project structure within the performing organization
- Stakeholder responsibility relationships
- Departments and disciplines involved with the project work
- The number of individuals involved in the project and their locales
- Internal and external information needs
- Stakeholder information

On the Certified Associate in Project Management (CAPM) and Project Management Professional (PMP) exams, and in the real world, the project manager will need to identify the number of communication channels within a project. Here's a magic formula to calculate the number of communication channels: $N(N - 1)/2$, where N represents the number of identified stakeholders. For example, if a project has ten stakeholders, the formula would read $10(10 - 1)/2$, for a total of 45 communication channels. Figure 10-2 illustrates the formula.

EXAM TIP Know this formula: $N(N - 1)/2$, where N represents the number of stakeholders. It's easy, and you'll probably encounter it on the PMP exam.

Exploring Communication Technologies

Let's face it: A project manager and a project team can use many different avenues to communicate. Project teams can effectively communicate through hallway meetings or formal project status meetings. Information can be transferred from stakeholder to stakeholder through anything from written notes to complex online databases and tracking systems.

As part of the communications planning, the project manager should identify all of the required and approved methods of communicating. Some projects may be highly sensitive and contain classified information that not all stakeholders are privy to, while other projects may contain information that's open for anyone to explore. Whatever the case, the project manager should identify what requirements exist, if any, for the communication modalities.

Communication modalities can also include meetings, reports, memos, e-mails, and so on. The project manager should identify the preferred methods of communicating based on the conditions of the message to be communicated. Consider the following, which may have an effect on the communications plan:

- **Urgency of the information** *When* the information is communicated can often be as important as *what's* being communicated. For some projects, information should be readily available, while other projects are less demanding.

Figure 10-2
Communication channels can be calculated using a simple formula.

Step 1
Know the formula.
$$\frac{N(N-1)}{2}$$

Step 2
Enter the values.
$$\frac{10(9)}{2}$$

Step 3
Get your answer.
$$\frac{90}{2} = 45$$

- **Technology**   Because of the demands of the project, technology changes may be needed to fulfill the project request. For example, the project may require an internal web site that details project progress. If such a web site does not exist, time and monies will need to be invested into this communication requirement. Also consider that some technologies you're currently using on the project may be replaced by newer, better communication technologies. That's right, the length of the project can influence the project technology.

- **Ease of use**   The communication tool(s) that's selected for the project should be easy to use, have training available if necessary, and be widely available for all of the project team to utilize. You can imagine the frustration if the project team is required to use a particular tool and that tool is difficult to use by the project team.

- **Project environment**   How a team communicates often depends on its structure. Consider a co-located team versus a virtual team. Each type can be effective, but there will be differing communication demands for each type of team.

- **Protecting the information**   Some of the information that's available in the project will likely be sensitive and confidential. Pay grades, contracts, team member discipline, and even stakeholder management will be confidential and not all stakeholders should see this information. You'll need to take steps to protect this information during and after the project. You'll also need to determine the most appropriate method to communicate this sensitive information.

There are loads of ways that communication can happen: e-mail, faxes, text messaging, web technologies—and new ways of communicating are being created all the time. Just think of all the new technologies that can help your project team communicate that didn't exist just a few years ago. While all these new methods of communicating have been created, they're still part of the basic communication model. And when you consider all of the different ways to communicate, you'll still find all communication falls into one of three categories:

- **Interactive communication**   This is the most common and most effective approach to communication. It's where two or more people exchange information. Consider status meetings, ad-hoc meetings, phone calls, and videoconferences.

- **Push communication**   This approach pushes the information from the sender to the receiver without any real acknowledgment that the information was really received or understood. Consider letters, faxes, voicemail messages, e-mails, and other communication modalities in which the sender packages and sends information to the receivers through some intermediary network.

- **Pull communication**   This approach pulls the information from a central repository, like a database of information. Pull communications are good for large groups of stakeholders who want to access project information at their discretion. Consider a project web site where stakeholders can periodically drop by for a quick update on the project status.

Creating the Communications Management Plan

Based on stakeholder analysis, the project manager and the project team can determine what communications are needed. There's no advantage to supplying stakeholders with information that isn't needed or desired, and the time spent creating and delivering such information is a waste of resources.

A communications management plan can organize and document the process, types, and expectations of communications. It provides the following:

- The stakeholder communications requirements in order to communicate the appropriate information as demanded by the stakeholders.

- Information on what is to be communicated. This plan includes the expected format, content, and detail—think project reports versus quick e-mail updates.

- Details on how needed information flows through the project to the correct individuals. The communication structure documents where the information will originate, to whom the information will be sent, and in what modality the information is acceptable.

- Appropriate methods for communicating include e-mails, memos, reports, and even press releases.

- Schedules of when the various types of communication should occur. Some communications, such as status meetings, should happen on a regular schedule, while other communications may be prompted by conditions within the project.

- Escalation processes and time frames for moving issues upward in the organization when they can't be solved at lower levels.

- Instructions on how the communications management plan can be updated as the project progresses.

- A project glossary.

- Identification of the stakeholder who will communicate specific project information.

- Identification of the stakeholder responsible for managing, controlling, and releasing confidential project information.

- Schedule, budget, and resource allocation for communication activities.

- Communication constraints such as technology, regulations, policies, and other enterprise environmental factors.

The communications management plan may also include information and guidelines for project status meetings, team meetings, e-meetings (that's electronic meetings, not meetings about the letter *e*), and even e-mail. Setting expectations for communications and meetings early in the project establishes guidelines for the project team and stakeholders.

Managing Project Communications

Now that the project's communications management plan has been created, it's time to execute it. Managing project communications is the process of ensuring that the proper stakeholders get the appropriate information when and how they need it. Essentially, it's the implementation of the communications management plan. This plan details how the information is to be created and dispersed, and also how the dispersed information is archived.

Examining Communication Skills

Here's a newsflash: Communication skills are used to send and receive information. Sounds easy, right? If communication is so easy, then why do so many problems on projects stem from misunderstandings, miscommunications, failures to communicate, and similar communication failings? Communication skills are part of the project manager's arsenal of general management skills—basically, it's delivering on the promise that the right stakeholders will get the right information at the right time. General management skills, in regard to project communications, are also about managing stakeholder requirements.

In the communication model that your PMI exam will quiz you on, it's the sender's responsibility to make the message clear, complete, and concise so that the recipient can receive it. The sender must also confirm that the recipient truly understands the information. Have you ever been in a project team meeting where a team member implied he understood the message that was being sent, but later proved that he really didn't understand what was being sent?

 EXAM TIP Face-to-face meetings, like those in ad-hoc meetings, are ideal for project communications.

Communication happens when information is transferred from one party to another. Transmission of a message is just like a radio signal—it's transmitting, but there's no evidence that anyone is actually picking up the signal. Along these same lines, the acknowledgment of a message means that the receiver has indeed received the message, but she may not necessarily agree with the message that has been sent.

Examining Communication Factors and Technologies

The most common type of communication between a sender and a receiver is verbal communication. When verbal communications are involved, the project manager should remember that half of communication is listening. This means that the project manager must confirm that the receiver understands the message being sent. The confirmation of the sent message can be seen in the recipient's body language, feedback, and verbal confirmation of the sent message. Five terms are used to describe the process of communicating:

- **Paralingual** The pitch, tone, and inflections in the sender's voice affect the message being sent.

- **Feedback** The sender confirms that the receiver understands the message by directly asking for a response, questions for clarification, or other confirmation of the sent message.

- **Active listening** The receiver confirms that the message is being received through feedback, questions, prompts for clarity, and other signs of confirmation.

- **Effective listening** The receiver is involved in the listening experience by paying attention to visual cues from the speaker and paralingual characteristics and also by asking relevant questions.

- **Nonverbal** It's been said that approximately 55 percent of communication is nonverbal. Facial expressions, hand gestures, and body language contribute to the message.

As pictured in Figure 10-3, the words in an oral message actually only account for 7 percent of the message. The tonality of the message accounts for 38 percent of the message. The remaining 55 percent is body language. A classic example involves a person talking to a dog. If the person has a friendly voice and posture, the dog will likely be receptive. However, if the person has a mean voice and guarded posture, the dog may feel threatened and on guard. When project managers talk with stakeholders, they must be aware of their body language and posture—not just the words they are communicating.

Figure 10-3
The words used in communication are only a small portion of a message.

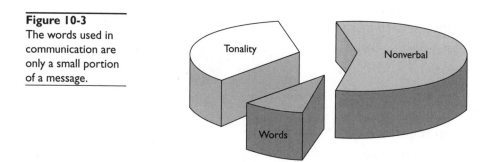

The medium in communication can help or hinder the message. For example, when a project manager talks to a stakeholder in person, the stakeholder has the advantage not only of hearing the message and tone, but also of seeing the body language. Remove body language from a conversation, and the message is interpreted by just the words and tonality. Always be aware of the downsides of various non-direct communication modalities: e-mail, reports, memos, and letters.

Creating Information Management Systems

What good is information if no one can find it? An information management system allows for fast and accurate access to project information. It can be a simple manual filing system, an advanced database of information storage, or a robust project management software suite. Whatever the approach, the information must be accessible, organized, and secure.

Project information can be hard-copy, printed information—like letters, reports, and brochures from vendors. You will also have electronic information such as e-mails, voicemails, videos, web resources, and even text messages. Your project may also rely on project management tools that are software-based for project organization, communication among the project team, and interfaces with stakeholders. All of this information and how it's sorted, stored, and retrieved is part of the information management system.

The project team, the project manager, the customer, and other stakeholders may need access to design specs, blueprints, plans, and other project information. A good information retrieval system is reliable, easy to navigate, and updated as new information becomes available.

Distributing Information

Throughout the project, the project manager, project sponsor, project team, and other stakeholders are going to need to supply information to one another. The methods for distributing information can vary, but the best modality is the one that's most appropriate to the information being conveyed. In other words, an e-mail may not be the correct format in which to share variance information regarding project costs.

Information can be distributed through some of the following methods, given project demands and available technology:

- Project meetings
- Hardcopy documentation
- Databases
- Faxes
- E-mail
- Telephone calls
- Videoconferences
- A project web site

Creating Lessons Learned

Do you ever wish you could travel back in time? With lessons learned, you almost can. The whole point of lessons learned is to improve future projects by sharing what was learned during the current project.

A lessons learned session is completed with the project manager, the project team, and key stakeholders to identify lessons they've learned in the technical, managerial, and project processes. Think of it: You're helping other project managers in the future by documenting what works and what doesn't in your project.

Lessons learned should happen throughout the project, not just at the project's conclusion. As a project moves through each phase, project managers can use a lessons learned session as a good team-building exercise. This means documenting and learning from what worked and what didn't within the project.

Examining the Results of Communications Management

Communications management results in the following:

- **Lessons learned**   When lessons learned sessions are completed, they're available to be used and applied. They are now part of the organizational process assets.

- **Project records**   All project communications are also part of the organizational process assets. This includes e-mails, memos, letters, and faxes. In some instances, the project team can also contribute by keeping their records in a project notebook.

- **Project reports**   Reports are formal communications on project activities, their status, and conditions. Management, customers, and policies within the performing organization may have differing requirements for when reports are required.

- **Project presentations**   Presentations are useful in providing information to customers, management, the project team, and other stakeholders. The delivery and degree of formality of the presentation should be appropriate for the conditions and information being delivered within the project.

- **Feedback from stakeholders**   Stakeholders are usually happy to offer their feedback on the project performance. Project managers should document this feedback and apply it to improve the project's performance.

- **Stakeholder notifications**   As the project rolls along, there undoubtedly will be notifications to the stakeholders about resolved issues, approved changes, and the overall health of the project. This information should be kept for future reference.

Controlling Communications

Throughout the project, customers and other stakeholders are going to need updates on the project performance, work status, and project information. The work performance information—the status of what's been completed and what's left to do—is always at the heart of performance reporting. Stakeholders want to be kept abreast of how the project is performing, but also what issues, risks, and conditions in the project have evolved.

Controlling communication is the process of following the communications management plan, distributing information, and sharing how the project is performing. Performance reporting is the process of collecting, organizing, and disseminating information on how project resources are being used to complete the project objectives. In other words, the people footing the bill and who are affected by the outcome of the project need some confirmation that things are going the way the project manager has promised.

Based on changing conditions within the project, the project manager and team may need to go back to communications planning, update the communications management plan, and then manage communications accordingly. At the heart of controlling communications is performance reporting. Performance reporting covers more than just cost and schedule, although these are the most common concerns. Another huge issue is the influence of risks on the project's success. The project manager and the project team must continue to monitor and evaluate risks, including pending risks and their impact on the project's success.

Another major concern with reporting is the level of quality. No one will praise the project manager and the project team for completing the project on time and on budget if the quality of the work is unacceptable. In fact, the project could be declared a failure and canceled as a result of poor quality, or the project team may be forced to redo the work, business could be lost, or individuals could even be harmed as a result of the poor quality of the project work.

Examining the Tools for Controlling Communications

Stakeholders expect you to keep them abreast of the project's performance, issues, conditions, changes, risk, and other concerns about the project. You'll utilize three tools to control communications, but understand that you, the project manager, being involved and available is the strongest asset for communications. The three tools you'll use are:

- **Reporting systems** You'll need some tool, probably part of your project management information system, to collect, assemble, and generate information about the project. You could use a simple spreadsheet, but the collection of project information is going to be more cumbersome, while a large, complex PMIS requires the knowledge and skill of both the project manager and the project team to use it effectively.

- **Expert judgment** One of the best tools and techniques you can use is to rely on the expertise of others. Experts, such as the project team, stakeholders, and consultants, can help you identify shortcomings or problems in your communications. These experts can help you ensure that your message is timely, appropriate, and on-target with the correct stakeholders.

- **Meetings**   Meetings allow the project manager, the project team, stakeholders, and experts to have conversations about the project. Communication meetings can help you and the stakeholder determine if the current communication approach is working or if there should be refinements to how you and the stakeholders communicate.

Reviewing Project Performance

The project manager will host performance review meetings to ascertain the progress and level of success the project team is having with the project work. Performance review meetings focus on the work that has been completed and how the work results are living up to the time and cost estimates. In addition, the project manager and the project team will evaluate the project scope to protect it from change and creep. The project manager and the project team will also examine quality and its effect on the project as a whole. Finally, the project manager must lead a discussion on pending or past risks, and then determine any new risks, as well as the overall risk likelihood and its potential impact on the project's success.

Analyzing Project Variances

Performance review meetings are not the only tools the project manager uses to assess project performance. Prior to the performance reviews, or spurred by a performance review, the project manager needs to examine the time, scope, quality, and cost variances within the project. The project manager will examine the estimates supplied for the time and cost of activities and compare it with the time and cost actually experienced.

The goals of analyzing project variances include the following:

- Prevent future variances.
- Determine the root cause of variances.
- Determine if the variances are an anomaly or if the estimates were flawed.
- Determine if the variances are within a predetermined acceptable range, such as −10 percent or +5 percent.
- Determine if the variances can be expected on future project work.

In addition to examining the time and cost variances, which are the most common, the project manager must examine any scope, resource, and quality variances. A change in the scope can skew time and cost predictions. A variance in resources, such as the expected performance by a given resource, can alter the project schedule and even the predicted costs of a project. Quality variances may result in rework, lost time, lost monies, and even the rejection of the project product.

EXAM TIP Performance reporting is often based on the results of earned value management (EVM). See Chapter 7 for detailed information on how to calculate EVM.

Examining the Results of Controlling Communications

The goal of controlling communications is to share information regarding the project's performance with the appropriate stakeholders and to improve upon the established communication process. Of course, performance reporting is not something done only at the end of the project or after a project phase. Instead, it is done according to a regular schedule, as detailed in the communications plan or as project conditions warrant. There are five outputs of controlling communications:

- **Performance reports** These are the results and summation of the project performance analysis. The communications management plan will detail the type of report needed, based on the conditions within the project, the timing of the communication, and the demands of the project stakeholder.

- **Change requests** Performance results may prompt change requests to some areas of the project. The change requests should flow into the change control system (CCS) for consideration and then be approved or denied.

- **Project document updates** Will the project end on schedule? Will the project be on budget? How much longer will it take to complete the project? And how much more money will this project need to finish? Earned value management can answer many of these questions for the project management team. You'll update the appropriate project documents based on the conditions within the project.

- **Project management plan updates** You may have to edit the project management plan based on the outcome of this process. Stakeholder communication preferences may change, interests on different project areas can change, and reactions to how the information is sent may also prompt updates to the project management plan.

- **Organizational process assets updates** Controlling communications may create lessons learned, templates, reporting formats, and other assets that could be used in other projects.

Chapter Summary

Communication is a project manager's most important skill. Project managers have to communicate with management, customers, the project team members, and the rest of the stakeholders involved with the project. The project manager's foundation is communication. Without effective communication, how will work get completed, progress reported, and information dispersed?

Communications planning centers on asking, "Who needs what information and when do they need it?" Consider all of the different channels for communication on any project. There are many different possibilities for information to be lost, messages to be skewed, and progress to be hindered. The formula for calculating the communication channels is $N(N-1)/2$, where N represents the number of stakeholders. As a general rule, larger projects require more detail—and detail means more planning for communications.

The communications management plan organizes and documents the communication processes, acceptable modalities for types of communication, and the stakeholder expectations for communication. The plan should detail how information is gathered, organized, accessed, and dispersed. The plan should also provide a schedule of expected communication based on a calendar schedule, such as project status meetings. Some communications are prompted by conditions within the project, such as cost variances, schedule variances, or other performance-related issues.

Key Terms

Acknowledgment   The receiver signals that the message has been received. An acknowledgment shows receipt of the message, but not necessarily agreement with the message.

Active listening   The receiver confirms that the message is being received through feedback, questions, prompts for clarity, and other signs of confirmation.

Choice of media   The best modality to use when communicating that is relevant to the information being communicated.

Communication assumptions   Anything that the project management team believes to be true but hasn't proven to be true. For example, the project management team may assume that all of the project team can be reached via cell phone, but parts of the world, as of this writing, don't have a cell signal.

Communication barrier   Anything that prohibits communication from occurring.

Communication channels formula $N(N-1)/2$, where N represents the number of identified stakeholders. This formula reveals the total number of communication channels within a project.

Communication constraints   Anything that limits the project management team's options. When it comes to communication constraints, geographical locales, incompatible communications software, and even limited communications technology can constrain the project team.

Communications management plan   A project management subsidiary plan that defines the stakeholders who need specific information, the person who will supply the information, the schedule for the information to be supplied, and the approved modality to provide the information.

Cost reporting system   A system to record the actual costs of the project activities.

Decoder   The device that decodes a message as it is being received.

Effective listening   The receiver is involved in the listening experience by paying attention to visual cues from the speaker and paralingual characteristics, and by asking relevant questions.

Encoder   The device that encodes the message being sent.

Feedback   The sender confirms that the receiver understands the message by directly asking for a response, questions for clarification, or other confirmation.

Influence/impact grid   Stakeholders are mapped on a grid based on their influence over the project in relation to their influence over the project execution.

Information presentation tools   A software package that allows the project management team to present the project's health through graphics, spreadsheets, and text. (Think of Microsoft Project.)

Information retrieval system   A system to quickly and effectively store, archive, and access project information.

Interactive communication   This is the most common and most effective approach to communication. It's where two or more people exchange information. Consider status meetings, ad-hoc meetings, phone calls, and videoconferences.

Lessons learned   This is documentation of what did and did not work in the project implementation. Lessons learned documentation is created throughout the project by the entire project team. When lessons learned sessions are completed, they're available to be used and applied by the entire organization. They are now part of the organizational process assets.

Medium   The device or technology that transports a message.

Noise   Anything that interferes with or disrupts a message.

Nonverbal   Facial expressions, hand gestures, and body language are nonverbal cues that contribute to a message. Approximately 55 percent of communication is nonverbal.

Paralingual   The pitch, tone, and inflections in the sender's voice affecting the message being sent.

Performance report   A report that depicts how well a project is performing. Often, the performance report is based on earned value management and may include cost or schedule variance reports.

Project presentations   Presentations are useful in providing information to customers, management, the project team, and other stakeholders.

Project records   All the business of the project communications is also part of the organizational process assets. This includes e-mails, memos, letters, and faxes.

Project reports   Reports are formal communications on project activities, their status, and conditions.

Pull communication This approach pulls the information from a central repository, like a database of information. Pull communications are good for large groups of stakeholders who want to access project information at their discretion. Consider a project web site where stakeholders can periodically drop by for a quick update on the project status.

Push communication This approach pushes the information from the sender to the receiver without any real acknowledgment that the information was really received or understood. Consider letters, faxes, voicemail messages, e-mails, and other communications modalities that the sender packages and sends to receivers through some intermediary network.

Receiver The person who receives the message.

Sender The person who is sending the message.

Sender–receiver models Feedback loops and barriers to communications.

Stakeholder notifications Notices to the stakeholders about resolved issues, approved changes, and the overall health of the project.

Status review meeting A regularly scheduled meeting to discuss the status of the project and its progress toward completing the project scope statement.

Time reporting system A system to record the actual time to complete project activities.

Questions

1. You are the project manager of the BlueSky Network Upgrade Project. You have 15 project team members and you're speaking with them about the importance of communication. You show them the communication model and give examples of each of the components of the model. One of the project team members asks for an example of noise. Of the following, which one is an example of noise?

   A. Fax machine

   B. Ad-hoc conversations

   C. Contractual agreements

   D. Distance

2. You are the project manager for the JHG Project. Management has requested that you create a document detailing what information will be expected from stakeholders and to whom that information will be disseminated. Management is asking for which one of the following?

   A. The roles and responsibilities matrix

   B. The scope management plan

   C. The communications management plan

   D. The communications worksheet

3. Which of the following will help you, the project manager, complete the needed communications management plan by identifying the stakeholders' communication needs?

A. Identification of all communication channels

B. Formal documentation of all communication channels

C. Formal documentation of all stakeholders

D. Lessons learned from previous similar projects

4. You are the project manager for the JGI Project. You have 32 stakeholders on this project. How many communication channels do you have?

A. Depends on the number of project team members

B. 496

C. 32

D. 1

5. You are the project manager for the KLN Project. You had 19 stakeholders on this project and have added three team members to the project. How many more communication channels do you have now compared with before?

A. 171

B. 231

C. 60

D. 1

6. A memo has been sent to you, the project manager, the project team members, and the project customers from the project sponsor. In this instance, who is the sender?

A. The project sponsor

B. The project manager

C. The project team members

D. The project customers

7. Beth is a project manager for her organization and she is working with the stakeholders to develop a communications management plan. She wants to acknowledge the assumptions and constraints in the project. Which one of the following is an example of a project communication constraint?

A. Ad-hoc conversations

B. Demands for formal reports

C. Stakeholder management

D. Team members in different geographical locales

8. Project managers can present project information in many different ways. Which one of the following is not a method a project manager can use to present project performance?

   A. Histograms

   B. S-curves

   C. Bar charts

   D. RACI charts

9. There are many terms that you'll need to know for your PMI examination that deal with project communications. Of the following, which term describes the pitch and tone of an individual's voice?

   A. Paralingual

   B. Feedback

   C. Effective listening

   D. Active listening

10. You are the project manager of the KMH Project. This project is slated to last eight years. You have just calculated EVM and have a cost variance (CV) of –$3,500, which is outside of the acceptable thresholds for your project. What type of report is needed for management?

    A. Progress report

    B. Forecast report

    C. Exception report

    D. Trends report

11. You are presenting your project performance to your key stakeholders. Several of the stakeholders are receiving phone calls during your presentation, and this is distracting people from your message. This is an example of what?

    A. Noise

    B. Negative feedback

    C. Outside communications

    D. Message distracter

12. You are the project manager for the OOK Project. You will be hosting project meetings every week. Of the following, which one is not a valid rule for project meetings?

    A. Schedule recurring meetings as soon as possible.

    B. Allow project meetings to last as long as needed.

    C. Distribute meeting agendas prior to the meeting start.

    D. Allow the project team to have input to the agenda.

13. What percentage of a message is sent through nonverbal communications, such as facial expressions, hand gestures, and body language?

    A. Greater than 50 percent

    B. 30 to 40 percent

    C. 20 to 30 percent

    D. 10 to 20 percent

14. Gary is the project manager of the HBA Update Project and his company has hired you as a project management consultant. Gary is confused about the timing of some of the project management processes. In particular, Gary doesn't understand the concept, purpose, and timing of the lessons learned documentation. He asks for your help. When does lessons learned identification take place?

    A. At the end of the project

    B. At the end of each project phase

    C. Throughout the project life cycle

    D. Whenever a lesson has been learned

15. Gary is the project manager of the HBA Update Project and his company has hired you as a project management consultant. Gary is confused about the timing of some of the project management processes. He now has a good understanding of the lessons learned purpose, but he's still confused about why you've recommended that the project team participate in the lessons learned documentation, too. Why should a project team complete lessons learned documentation?

    A. To ensure project closure

    B. To show management what they've accomplished on the project

    C. To show the project stakeholders what they've accomplished on the project

    D. To help future project teams complete their projects more accurately

16. You are the project manager for the PMU Project. Your project has 13 members. You have been informed that next week your project will receive the seven additional members you requested. How many channels of communication will you have next week?

    A. 1

    B. 78

    C. 190

    D. 201

17. Performance reporting should generally provide information on all of the following except for which one?

    A. Scope

    B. Schedule

    C. Labor issues

    D. Quality

18. You are the project manager of a project that will last 18 months and includes three different countries. As part of your communications management plan you've scheduled face-to-face meetings with the project team and you're utilizing web conferencing software for the virtual team. Based on this information, the process of sending information from the project manager to the project team is called what?

    A. Functioning

    B. Matrixing

    C. Blended communications

    D. Transmitting

19. George is the project manager of the 7YH Project. In this project, George considers the relationship between himself and the customer to be of utmost importance. Which one of the following is a valid reason for George's belief in the importance of this relationship?

    A. The customer will complete George's performance evaluation. A poor communication model between George and the customer will affect his project bonus.

    B. The customer is not familiar with project management. George must educate the customer about the process.

    C. The customer is always right.

    D. The communication between the customer and George can convey the project objectives more clearly than can the language in the project contract.

20. You are the project manager for your company and you're working with the project team to develop the project's communication management plan. The project team is confused about some of the communication terms. Basically, they want to know how communication actually happens and how you can prove the communication was effective. Which one of the following means that communications occur?

    A. The transfer of knowledge

    B. The outputting of knowledge

    C. The presence of knowledge

    D. The transmission of knowledge

Questions and Answers

1. You are the project manager of the BlueSky Network Upgrade Project. You have 15 project team members and you're speaking with them about the importance of communication. You show them the communication model and give examples of each of the components of the model. One of the project team members asks for an example of noise. Of the following, which one is an example of noise?

   A. Fax machine

   B. Ad-hoc conversations

   C. Contractual agreements

   D. Distance

   D. Noise is anything that interferes with the transmission and understanding of the message. Distance is an example of noise. A, a fax machine, is an example of a decoder. B is incorrect because ad-hoc conversations are informal conversations. C, contractual agreements, are a type of formal communication.

2. You are the project manager for the JHG Project. Management has requested that you create a document detailing what information will be expected from stakeholders and to whom that information will be disseminated. Management is asking for which one of the following?

   A. The roles and responsibilities matrix

   B. The scope management plan

   C. The communications management plan

   D. The communications worksheet

   C. Management is requesting a communications management plan, which details the requirements and expectations for communicating information among the project stakeholders. A is incorrect because a roles and responsibilities matrix depicts who does what and who makes which decisions. B, the scope management plan, is also incorrect because this plan explains how changes to the scope may be allowed, depending on the circumstances. D is not a valid choice for the question.

3. Which of the following will help you, the project manager, complete the needed communications management plan by identifying the stakeholders' communication needs?

   A. Identification of all communication channels

   B. Formal documentation of all communication channels

   C. Formal documentation of all stakeholders

   D. Lessons learned from previous similar projects

PART II

D. Lessons learned and historical information from a previous project are ideal inputs to communications planning. A, B, and C are incorrect because these choices do not fully answer the question. Lessons learned from previous, similar projects are the best tool to identify stakeholders' requirements for communication.

4. You are the project manager for the JGI Project. You have 32 stakeholders on this project. How many communication channels do you have?

   A. Depends on the number of project team members

   B. 496

   C. 32

   D. 1

   B. Using the formula N(N − 1)/2, where N represents the number of stakeholders, gives us 496 communication channels. A, C, and D are incorrect. These values do not reflect the number of communication channels on the project.

5. You are the project manager for the KLN Project. You had 19 stakeholders on this project and have added three team members to the project. How many more communication channels do you have now compared with before?

   A. 171

   B. 231

   C. 60

   D. 1

   C. This is a tough question, but typical of the CAPM and PMP exams. The question asks how many more communication channels exist. You'll have to calculate the new value, which is 231, and then subtract the original value, which is 171, for a total of 60 new channels. A is incorrect because 171 is the original number of communication channels. B is incorrect because this value reflects the new number of communication channels. D is not a valid choice.

6. A memo has been sent to you, the project manager, the project team members, and the project customers from the project sponsor. In this instance, who is the sender?

   A. The project sponsor

   B. The project manager

   C. The project team members

   D. The project customers

   A. The project sponsor is the source of the memo, since this is the sender of the message. B, C, and D are all recipients of the memo, not the sender, so they cannot be the source of the message.

7. Beth is a project manager for her organization and she is working with the stakeholders to develop a communications management plan. She wants to acknowledge the assumptions and constraints in the project. Which one of the following is an example of a project communication constraint?

   A. Ad-hoc conversations

   B. Demands for formal reports

   C. Stakeholder management

   D. Team members in different geographical locales

   D. Team members who are not located physically close together can be a communications constraint, since it can be tougher to communicate when distance between team members exists. A, B, and C are all incorrect because these are not project communications constraints.

8. Project managers can present project information in many different ways. Which one of the following is not a method a project manager can use to present project performance?

   A. Histograms

   B. S-curves

   C. Bar charts

   D. RACI charts

   D. RACI charts do not show project performance, but instead accountability of the resources involved in the project. A, B, and C are incorrect because these choices do present project performance.

9. There are many terms that you'll need to know for your PMI examination that deal with project communications. Of the following, which term describes the pitch and tone of an individual's voice?

   A. Paralingual

   B. Feedback

   C. Effective listening

   D. Active listening

   A. *Paralingual* is a term used to describe the pitch and tone of a voice. B, feedback, is a request to confirm the information sent in the conversation. C, effective listening, is the ability to understand the message through what is said, through facial expressions, gestures, tone, pitch, and so on. D, active listening, is the process of confirming what is understood and asking for clarification when needed.

10. You are the project manager of the KMH Project. This project is slated to last eight years. You have just calculated EVM and have a cost variance (CV) of

–$3,500, which is outside of the acceptable thresholds for your project. What type of report is needed for management?

A. Progress report

B. Forecast report

C. Exception report

D. Trends report

C. An exception report is typically completed when variances exceed a given limit. A is incorrect. Progress reports describe the progress of the project or phase. B is incorrect because this is not a valid answer. D, a trends report, is an analysis of project trends over time.

11. You are presenting your project performance to your key stakeholders. Several of the stakeholders are receiving phone calls during your presentation, and this is distracting people from your message. This is an example of what?

A. Noise

B. Negative feedback

C. Outside communications

D. Message distracter

A. Noise is the correct answer, since their phone calls are distracting from your message. B, C, and D are incorrect because they do not answer the question. Negative feedback can mean the recipient didn't respond well to the message you've sent. Outside communications isn't a valid term. And a message distracter can be the pitch, inflection, and body language that sends a conflicting message to what you're saying to your audience.

12. You are the project manager for the OOK Project. You will be hosting project meetings every week. Of the following, which one is not a valid rule for project meetings?

A. Schedule recurring meetings as soon as possible.

B. Allow project meetings to last as long as needed.

C. Distribute meeting agendas prior to the meeting start.

D. Allow the project team to have input to the agenda.

B. Project meetings should have a set time limit. A, C, and D are incorrect answers, even though these are good attributes of project team meetings.

13. What percentage of a message is sent through nonverbal communications, such as facial expressions, hand gestures, and body language?

A. Greater than 50 percent

B. 30 to 40 percent

C. 20 to 30 percent

D. 10 to 20 percent

A. Greater than 50 percent of a message is sent through nonverbal communications. B, C, and D are incorrect.

14. Gary is the project manager of the HBA Update Project and his company has hired you as a project management consultant. Gary is confused about the timing of some of the project management processes. In particular, Gary doesn't understand the concept, purpose, and timing of the lessons learned documentation. He asks for your help. When does lessons learned identification take place?

   A. At the end of the project

   B. At the end of each project phase

   C. Throughout the project life cycle

   D. Whenever a lesson has been learned

   C. Lessons learned takes place throughout the project life cycle, not just at the end of the project or its phases. A, B, and D are incorrect choices.

15. Gary is the project manager of the HBA Update Project and his company has hired you as a project management consultant. Gary is confused about the timing of some of the project management processes. He now has a good understanding of the lessons learned purpose, but he's still confused about why you've recommended that the project team participate in the lessons learned documentation, too. Why should a project team complete lessons learned documentation?

   A. To ensure project closure

   B. To show management what they've accomplished on the project

   C. To show the project stakeholders what they've accomplished on the project

   D. To help future project teams complete their projects more accurately

   D. Lessons learned documentation helps future project teams complete their projects with more efficiency and effectiveness. A, B, and C are incorrect because each statement does not reflect the intent of lessons learned documentation: to help future project teams.

16. You are the project manager for the PMU Project. Your project has 13 members. You have been informed that next week your project will receive the seven additional members you requested. How many channels of communication will you have next week?

   A. 1

   B. 78

   C. 190

   D. 201

C. The project currently has 13 team members, and next week, seven additional team members will come aboard, thus making a total of 20 team members. Using the formula $N(N - 1)/2$, where N is the number of identified stakeholders, the communication channels equal 190. A, B, and D are all incorrect.

17. Performance reporting should generally provide information on all of the following except for which one?

    A. Scope

    B. Schedule

    C. Labor issues

    D. Quality

    C. Labor issues are not part of performance reporting. A, B, and D are all part of performance reporting.

18. You are the project manager of a project that will last 18 months and includes three different countries. As part of your communications management plan you've scheduled face-to-face meetings with the project team and you're utilizing web conferencing software for the virtual team. Based on this information, the process of sending information from the project manager to the project team is called what?

    A. Functioning

    B. Matrixing

    C. Blended communications

    D. Transmitting

    D. When information is sent, it is considered to be transmitted regardless of the technology involved. A, B, and C are all incorrect.

19. George is the project manager of the 7YH Project. In this project, George considers the relationship between himself and the customer to be of utmost importance. Which one of the following is a valid reason for George's belief in the importance of this relationship?

    A. The customer will complete George's performance evaluation. A poor communication model between George and the customer will affect his project bonus.

    B. The customer is not familiar with project management. George must educate the customer about the process.

    C. The customer is always right.

    D. The communication between the customer and George can convey the project objectives more clearly than can the language in the project contract.

D. George and the customer's relationship can allow clearer communication on the project objectives than what may be expressed in the project contract. The contract should take precedence on any issues, but direct contact is often the best way to achieve clear and concise communication. A is an incorrect choice because the focus is on personal gain rather than the good of the project. B is incorrect because the customer does not necessarily need to be educated about the project management process. C is incorrect because the customer is not always right—the contract will take precedence in any disagreements.

20. You are the project manager for your company and you're working with the project team to develop the project's communication management plan. The project team is confused about some of the communication terms. Basically, they want to know how communication actually happens and how you can prove the communication was effective. Which one of the following means that communications occur?

   A. The transfer of knowledge

   B. The outputting of knowledge

   C. The presence of knowledge

   D. The transmission of knowledge

   A. The transfer of knowledge is evidence that communication has occurred. B and C do not necessarily mean the knowledge has originated from the source and been transferred to the recipient. D is also incorrect because messages are transmitted, but knowledge is transferred.

Managing Project Risks

In this chapter, you will
- Plan for risk management
- Identify project risks
- Complete qualitative risk analysis
- Complete quantitative risk analysis
- Plan the risk responses
- Monitor and control project risks

A *project risk* is an uncertain event or condition that can have a positive or negative impact on the project. That's correct—it's possible for a risk to have a positive impact. Risks that have a positive impact are also known as opportunities. Technically, risk isn't a bad thing. It's the impact that can be painful, costly, or delay the project work. Most project managers look at risk the same way they'd look at leftover shrimp cocktail. Yuck. Some risks, though, are good for the project, and the project manager wants to accept them; other risks aren't so welcome.

Let's look at this from another point of view. Imagine a golfer teeing up. To the right of the tee box, there's a water hazard, but just beyond the water is the green. The golfer can either avoid the water and take longer to get to the green, or try to shoot over the water and get on the green in fewer strokes. Driving up the fairway is the safer play, but cutting over the water will improve the golfer's score. The risk with the water hazard is that if he can't make the shot, then he's down a penalty stroke.

VIDEO For a more detailed explanation, watch the *Creating a Risk Matrix* video now.

Risk, as in the golfing scenario, must be in proportion to the reward the risk taker can realize as a result of taking the chance. The willingness to accept the risk is called the *utility function*. Some call the utility function your risk tolerance—the amount of risk you'll take on in relation to the impact the risk event may bring. Your risk appetite (think yummy!) is how much risk you'll accept in relation to the reward the risk may bring. An experienced golfer may have a high risk appetite, so he's willing to accept the water hazard. A golf hack like me would likely have a low risk tolerance and drive up the fairway away from the water. Someone with a high tolerance for risk is called a risk seeker, while someone with a low tolerance for risk is called risk-averse.

It's true in project management, too. With some projects, you and your organization are willing to accept risks to realize rewards such as cost savings, time savings, or on-the-job training. On other projects—typically, those projects with high-impact and high-profile characteristics—you're not so willing to accept the risks. In this chapter, we'll look at the six processes that dictate project risk management, and you'll have plenty of risk management questions on your Project Management Institute (PMI) exam.

Let me be very clear: The risks you can readily identify are the known risks. The risks that are more ambiguous, like the weather or vendor delays, are called known unknowns. You can anticipate and plan for the known unknowns, but the planning is about the probability of the event and the impact the risk might have on the project objectives. Project risk describes the likelihood of the overall project being successful for the organization. Individual project risks are the risks within the project. When a risk event actually happens, it can shift from being just a risk to being an issue in the project.

The project management processes described here are presented in the most logical order. They are actually iterative processes throughout the project life cycle. Pay special attention to monitoring and controlling project risks because new risks can creep into the project or be discovered as the project moves toward closure.

Planning for Risk Management

Risk management planning is not the identification of risks or even the response to known risks within a project. Risk management planning is how the project management team will complete the risk management activities within the project. These activities really set up the project to effectively manage the five other risk management activities. Risk management planning creates the risk management plan.

By deciding the approach to each of the risk management activities before moving into them, the project management team can more effectively identify risks, complete risk analysis, and then plan risk responses. In addition, planning for risk management also allows the project management team to create a strategy for the ongoing identification and monitoring of existing risks within the project.

Preparing for Risk Management Planning

There are five inputs to risk management planning, although some are more important than others. It's essential for the project management team to understand the priority of the project, which shouldn't be too tough to do. Important projects, high-profile projects, or projects with hefty budgets are generally risk-averse. Smaller projects are generally more willing to accept risks. You'll need the following to prepare for risk management:

- **Project management plan**   Risk management planning considers all of the project's subsidiary plans, baselines, project documentation, and supporting detail. The project manager will pay special attention to the project scope, project communications, cost, and schedule because these knowledge areas can be most widely affected by risk.

- **Project charter**   The project charter is needed because it defines the high-level objectives for the project and also identifies the initial known risks.

- **Stakeholder register**   The stakeholder register is referenced for stakeholder concerns, threats, perceived threats, contact information, and roles involved in the project.

- **Enterprise environmental factors**   An organization's attitude toward risk may vary (as I mentioned) based on the type, size, and profile of the project.

- **Organizational process assets**   An organization may have a predefined approach to risk management. If that's the case, the project management team uses the organization's approach and follows its established procedures. For example, an organization could define risk tolerance levels, risk categories, templates, roles and responsibilities, and more. A project team may also use other similar projects to guide the current risk management planning activities.

Completing Risk Management Planning

Planning for risk happens in—surprise, surprise!—planning meetings, where the project team develops the risk management plan and analyzes the inputs previously mentioned to make the best decisions for the current project. While the project team is the primary participant at the risk management planning meeting, the attendees may actually include the project manager, stakeholders, and other subject matter experts within an organization who influence the risk management processes.

The purpose of these risk management planning meetings is to create the risk management plan and to define the cost and schedule for risk management activities. Let's face facts: It'll take time and monies for most projects to identify, test, and challenge the risks that may exist within the project. These initial meetings allow monies and time to be incorporated within the project. Risk responsibilities are also assigned in these meetings, as are the risk terminologies the project will use. Risk management planning also defines and tailors the following for the project:

- Risk templates the project should use
- Definitions and terms for risk levels
- Probability according to risk type
- Impact of the risks
- Guidelines for the probability and impact matrix to be used during risk analysis

Creating the Risk Management Plan

The whole point of risk management meetings and analysis is to create the risk management plan. This plan does not detail the planned responses to individual risks within the project—this is the purpose of the risk response plan. The risk management plan is responsible for determining how:

- The project will utilize the selected risk management methodology
- Risks will be identified
- Quantitative analysis will be completed
- Qualitative analysis will be completed
- Risk response planning will happen
- Risks will be monitored and tracked
- Ongoing risk management activities will happen throughout the project's life cycle

Defining the Risk Management Methodology

The methodology is concerned with how the risk management processes will take place. It asks the following:

- What tools are available to use for risk management?
- What approaches are acceptable within the performing organization?
- What data sources can be accessed and used for risk management?
- What approach is best for the project type and the phase of the project?
- Which approach is most appropriate given the conditions of the project?
- How much flexibility is available for the project given the conditions, time frame, and the project budget?

Identifying Risk Roles and Responsibilities

The roles and responsibilities identify the groups and individuals who will participate in the leadership and support of each of the risk management activities within the project plan. In some instances, risk management teams outside of the project team may have a more realistic, unbiased approach to the risk identification, impact, and overall risk management needs than the actual project team does.

Creating a Risk Management Budget

Based on the size, impact, and priority of the project, a budget may need to be established for the project's risk management activities. This section of the risk management plan defines a cost estimate for the resources needed to complete risk management. These costs are rolled into the project's cost baseline. A project with high priority and no budget allotment for risk management activities may face uncertain times ahead.

Identifying the Risk Management Schedule

The risk management process needs a schedule to determine how often, and when, risk management activities should happen throughout the project. If risk management happens too late in the project, the project could be delayed because of the time needed to identify, assess, and respond to the risks. A realistic schedule should be developed early in the project to accommodate risks, risk analysis, and risk reaction.

Defining a Project's Risk Categories

Based on the nature of the work, there should be identified categories of risks within the project. Figure 11-1 depicts one approach to identifying risk categories by using a risk breakdown structure (RBS). Throughout the project, the risk categories should be revisited to update and reflect the current status of the project. If a similar risk management plan is available from a previous project, the project team may elect to use this plan as a template and tailor the risk categories accordingly. There are four general categories of risks:

- **Technical, quality, or performance risks** Technical risks are associated with new, unproven, or complex technologies being used on the project. Changes to the technology during the project implementation can also be a risk. Quality risks are the levels set for expectations of impractical quality and performance. Changes to industry standards during the project can also be lumped into this category of risks.

- **Project management risks** These risks deal with faults in the management of the project: the unsuccessful allocation of time, resources, and scheduling; unacceptable work results (low-quality work); and poor project management as a whole.

- **Organizational risks** The performing organization can contribute to the project's risks through unreasonable cost, time, and scope expectations; poor

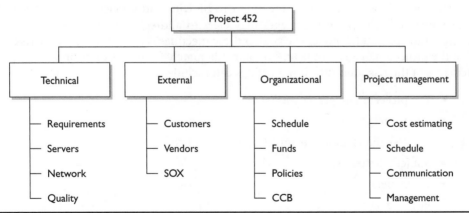

Figure 11-1 A risk breakdown structure (RBS) can organize risks by categories.

project prioritization; inadequate funding or the disruption of funding; and competition with other projects for internal resources.

- **External risks** These risks are outside of the project, but directly affect it—for example, legal issues, labor issues, a shift in project priorities, or weather. "Force majeure" risks can be scary, and usually call for disaster recovery rather than project management. These are risks caused by earthquakes, tornadoes, floods, civil unrest, and other disasters.

The discipline that you work in may allow you to identify and categorize risk beyond these generic categories I've listed here. The idea is to create risk themes so you can group associated risks by topic. This allows you to identify trends in the risk and look for root causes to attack many risks at once. An RBS is an ideal way to visualize where project risks are lurking in each phase or within the project as a whole.

Identifying the Project Risks

Risk identification is the systematic process of combing through the project, the project plan, the work breakdown structure (WBS), and all supporting documentation to identify as many of the risks that may affect the project as possible. Remember, a risk is an uncertain event or condition that may affect the project outcome. Risks can be positive or negative. In the big picture of risk identification, there are two categories of risks:

- **Pure risks** These risks have only a negative outcome. Examples include loss of life or limb, fire, theft, natural disasters, and the like. These risks are often referred to as insurable risks.

- **Business risks** These risks may have a negative or a positive outcome. Examples include using a less experienced worker to complete a task, allowing phases or activities to overlap, or forgoing the expense of formal training for on-the-job education. These risks are also known as speculative risks.

The initial risk identification meeting can be wild and unwieldy if the approach isn't structured. The project manager may elect to address risks by category, project phase, or the project life cycle. The goal of these meetings is to capture all of the risks so that the project management team can plan adequately for the risk responses. The participants of the risk identification meetings can include:

- The project manager
- The project team
- The risk management team (if one exists, of course)
- Subject matter experts
- Customers
- End users
- Other project managers

- Stakeholders

- Risk management experts

Risk identification is not a one-time event. The project manager should encourage the project team and these participants to continually be on the lookout for risk events as the project moves toward closure. The risk management plan also includes timings for iterations of risk identification and management. Risk identification is an iterative process, because new risks can creep into the project, or existing risks may be identified later as more detail becomes available. You'll need several inputs to complete risk identification:

- **Risk management plan** This lone output of risk management planning is needed during risk identification because the plan will identify the organization's and the project's proper approach for identifying risks within the project.

- **Cost management plan** You'll likely need funds for risk identification and for risk responses. Your cost management plan should address the organization's approach to requesting funds for contingency reserves and risk responses.

- **Schedule management plan** How the project is structured can actually create risks or avoid risks. Generally, the faster the pace of the project, the more risks the project will experience.

- **Quality management plan** The quality management plan and the organization's approach to quality management may create risks or, more likely, help the project avoid risks.

- **Human resource plan** This plan helps the project manager anticipate how the project will be staffed and the roles that can contribute to risk identification and management. The staffing management plan can also help the project manager anticipate any risks associated with the resources leaving the project team.

- **Project scope baseline** The project scope statement includes the assumptions that the project is based on. These assumptions are often sources of risk within the project. You'll use the work breakdown structure (WBS) and the WBS dictionary to examine the work packages and deliverables for risk events.

- **Activity cost estimates** The project's activity cost estimates are needed to determine the likelihood of achieving the cost estimates based on the identified risks in the project. If risks come into fruition in the project, the cost of the activities will increase. An examination of the cost of the estimates, the cost of the risks, and the cost of risk responses is often needed as part of risk management planning and risk identification.

- **Activity duration estimates** Just as risks can affect the cost of the activities, so too can risks affect the duration of an activity. In addition, you may need to adjust activity duration to slow the work down to avoid risks, add labor, or consider risk responses and how these may affect the duration of activities.

- **Stakeholder register**   Customers and other stakeholders need to participate in the risk identification process. You'll need their expert judgment, experience, and knowledge to help identify risks in the project.

- **Project documents**   The project manager will need several project documents to identify project risks. Consider the following:

  - An assumptions log

  - Work performance reports

  - Project network diagrams

  - Earned value findings

  - Time, cost, and scope baselines

- **Procurement documents**   There is always risk associated with hiring a third party to complete a portion of the project work. An analysis of the agreements is needed to identify the risks associated with the vendor completion of the project work, the reliability of the vendor, and the ramifications of vendor-based work on the project schedule, costs, quality, and scope.

- **Enterprise environmental factors**   When it comes to risk identification, having commercial databases, academic studies, benchmarking results, white papers, and other statistics and information related to your discipline is ideal.

- **Organizational process assets**   If an organization has completed projects similar to the current project, using the historical information can help with the risk identification.

Finding Project Risks

Now the fun part of risk identification: Anything goes as long as it can be perceived as a risk. All of the risk identification participants should identify as many risks as possible, regardless of their perceived initial threat. I'm not really talking about sunspots and asteroid crashes here, but relevant risks should be recorded, regardless of their size and impact on the project. What begins as a small risk can bloom into something much larger as the project progresses.

Reviewing the Project Documentation

One of the first steps the risk identification participants can take is to review the project documentation. The project plan, scope, and other project files should be reviewed. Constraints and assumptions should be reviewed, considered, and analyzed for risks. This structure review takes a broad look at the project plan, the scope, and the activities defined within the project.

Relying on Risk Identification Methods

There are five methods you can use when it comes to gathering project information regarding risks. You'll likely see these on your exam:

- **Brainstorming**   Good, old-fashioned brainstorming is the most common approach to risk identification. It's usually completed by a project team with subject matter experts to identify the risks within the project. The risks are identified in broad terms and posted, and then the risks' characteristics are detailed. Your pal, the risk breakdown structure (RBS), can help facilitate the brainstorming process. The identified risks are categorized and will pass through the qualitative and quantitative risk analyses later. I'll discuss those in just a few pages—no peeking!

- **The Delphi Technique**   The Delphi Technique, shown in Figure 11-2, is an anonymous method used to query experts about foreseeable risks within a project, phase, or component of a project. The results of the survey are analyzed by a third party, organized, and then circulated to the experts. There can be several rounds of anonymous discussion with the Delphi Technique without fear of backlash or offending other participants in the process. The Delphi Technique is completely anonymous, and the goal is to gain consensus on project risks within the project. The anonymous nature of the process ensures that no single expert's advice overtly influences the opinion of another participant.

    I'm often asked why this approach is called the Delphi Technique. It was developed during the Cold War as a forecasting and consensus-building device, and was named after the "Oracle at Delphi." Delphi is a Greek

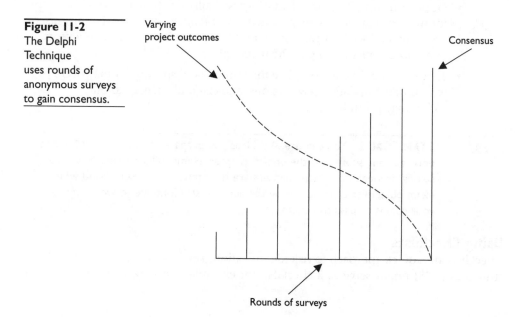

Figure 11-2
The Delphi Technique uses rounds of anonymous surveys to gain consensus.

Varying project outcomes

Consensus

Rounds of surveys

archeological site that, according to legend, is the center of the universe. However, as fascinating as Greek mythology is, there won't be any legends on your PMI examination. Sorry.

- **Hosting interview sessions**   Interviewing subject matter experts and project stakeholders is an excellent approach to identifying risks on the current project based on the interviewees' experiences. The people responsible for risk identification share the overall purpose of the project, the project's work breakdown structure (WBS), and, likely, the same assumptions as the interviewee. The interviewee, through questions and discussion, shares his insight on what risks he perceives within the project. The goal of the process is to learn from the expert what risks may be hidden within the project, what risks this person has encountered in similar work, and what insight the person has into the project work.

- **Root cause identification**   Project managers and the project team often see the impact of a risk, but not always its cause. Root cause identification aims to find out why a risk event may be occurring, the causal factors creating the risk events, and then, eventually, how the events can be mitigated or eliminated.

- **Implementing SWOT analysis**   *SWOT* stands for strengths, weaknesses, opportunities, and threats. SWOT analysis is the process of examining the project from the perspective of each characteristic. For example, a technology project may identify SWOT as:

  - **Strengths**   The technology to be installed in the project has been installed by other large companies in our industry.

  - **Weaknesses**   We have never installed this technology before.

  - **Opportunities**   The new technology will allow us to reduce our cycle time for time-to-market on new products. *Opportunities* are things, conditions, or events that allow an organization to differentiate itself from competitors and improve its standing in the marketplace.

  - **Threats**   The time to complete the training and simulation may overlap with product updates, new versions, and external changes to our technology portfolio.

EXAM COACH   You can use SWOT as you prepare to pass your PMI exam. Look at your scores for the end-of-chapter exams. Which chapters are you strong or weak in? Which chapters are threatening your exam? And which exam objectives can you ace on the actual test? Continue to work smart— your goal is to pass the exam.

Using Checklists

Checklists are a quick approach to risk identification. The lowest of the risk breakdown structures (RBS) might serve as a checklist, for example. More likely, similar projects that have been completed in the past have risk registers that the current risk identification process can benefit from. While checklists can be created quickly and easily, it's impossible to build an exhaustive risk checklist.

 EXAM TIP The danger in using or relying on risk identification checklists is that the risk identification participants don't consider risks that aren't on the checklists. Even for projects that have been completed over and over, based on the nature of the work, the project team must actively seek to identify risks that are outside of the organizational process assets checklists.

Examining the Assumptions

All projects have assumptions. Assumption analysis is the process of examining the assumptions to see what risks may stem from false assumptions. Examining assumptions is about gauging the validity of the assumptions. For example, consider a project to install a new piece of software on every computer within an organization. The project team has made the assumption that all of the computers within the organization meet the minimum requirements to install the software. If this assumption were wrong, cost increases and schedule delays would occur.

Examining the assumptions also requires a review of assumptions across the whole project for consistency. For example, consider a project with an assumption that a senior employee will be needed throughout the entire project work; the cost estimate, however, has been billed at the rate of a junior employee.

Utilizing Diagramming Techniques

Several diagramming techniques can be utilized by the project team to identify risks:

- **Ishikawa** These cause-and-effect diagrams are also called fishbone diagrams, as seen in Figure 11-3. They are great for analyzing the root causes of risk factors within the project. The goal is to identify and treat the root of the problem, not the symptom.

- **Flowchart** System or process flowcharts show the relationships between components and how the overall process works. These are useful for identifying risks between system components.

- **Influence** An influence diagram charts out a decision problem. It identifies all of the elements, variables, decisions, and objectives, and also how each factor may influence another.

Creating a Risk Register

The only output of risk identification is the project's risk register. The risk register is a component of the project management plan that contains all of the information related to the risk management activities. It's updated as risk management activities are

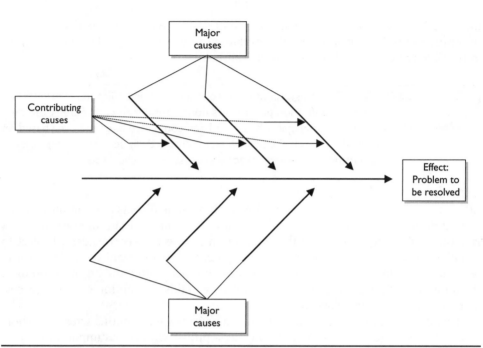

Figure 11-3 Ishikawa diagrams are also known as fishbone diagrams.

conducted to reflect the status, progress, and nature of the project risks. The risk register includes the following:

- **Risks** Of course, the most obvious output of risk identification is the risk that has been successfully identified. Recall that a risk is an uncertain event or condition that could potentially have a positive or negative effect on project success.

- **Potential responses** The initial risk identification process may yield solutions and responses to identified risks. This is fine, as long as the responses are documented here. Along with the risk responses, the identification of risk triggers may also occur. *Triggers* are warning signs or symptoms that a risk has occurred or is about to occur. For example, should a vendor fail to complete her portion of the project as scheduled, the project completion may be delayed.

- **The root causes of risk** Risk identification can identify why risk conditions exist. Project managers can also use *if-then* statements based on the *cause* of the risk event to predict the *effect* of the risk event.

- **Updated risk categories** Risk identification may prompt the project team to identify new categories of risks. These new categories should be documented in the risk register, and if a risk breakdown structure (RBS) is utilized, it will need to be updated as well.

Using Qualitative Risk Analysis

The first, and somewhat shallow, risk analysis is qualitative analysis. Qualitative risk analysis "qualifies" the risks that have been identified in the project. Specifically, qualitative risk analysis examines and prioritizes the risks based on their probability of occurring and the impact on the project if the risks do occur. Qualitative risk analysis is a broad approach to ranking risks by priority, which then guides the risk reaction process. The end result of qualitative risk analysis (once risks have been identified and prioritized) can either lead to more in-depth quantitative risk analysis or move directly into risk response planning.

The status of the project will also affect the process of qualitative risk analysis. Early in the project, there may be several risks that have not yet surfaced. Later in the project, new risks may become evident and need to pass through qualitative analysis. The status of the project is linked to the available time needed to analyze and study the risks. There may be more time early in the project, while a looming deadline near the project's end may create a sense of urgency to find a solution for the newly identified risks.

EXAM TIP When you think of "qualitative," think of qualifying. You are qualifying, or justifying, the seriousness of the risk for further analysis. Some Certified Associate in Project Management (CAPM) and Project Management Professional (PMP) candidates like to remember that qualitative is a list. The "L" in *qualitative* and *list* ties the two together.

Preparing for Qualitative Analysis

As with most of the project planning processes, the project management team is included in the rapid analysis of the project risks. There are five inputs to qualitative analysis:

- **Risk management plan** The risk management plan is the key input to qualitative risk analysis. The plan will dictate the process, the methodologies to be used, and the scoring model for identified risks. In addition to the risk management plan, the identified risks from the risk register will obviously be needed to perform an analysis. These are the risks that will be scored and ranked based on their probability and impact.

- **Project scope baseline** Consider an organization that does the same type of projects over and over, such as installing networks or constructing bridges. These repetitive projects have known risks and known risk responses. An organization that is attempting project work that it has never done before has more unknowns, which can represent risks in a project. The project scope baseline can help identify a project's uniqueness. The project scope statement's assumptions and constraints can also be examined for risks.

- **Risk register** This project-centric database of identified risks and their status is referenced to qualify risks.

- **Enterprise environmental factors**   Risk databases, industry studies, internal risk management policies, and program governance can all be considered as part of the risk analysis.

- **Organizational process assets**   Past projects and lessons learned—the organization's historical information—are ideal resources for the qualitative risk analysis process. No need to reinvent the wheel.

 EXAM TIP   You'll always update the risk register when any new information about a risk is discovered.

Completing Qualitative Analysis

During the risk identification process, all possible risks are identified. Of course, not all risks are worth responding to, while others demand attention. Qualitative analysis is a subjective approach to organizing and prioritizing risks. Through a methodical and logical approach, the identified risks are rated according to probability and potential impact.

The outcome of the ranking determines four things:

- It identifies the risks that require additional analysis through quantitative risk analysis.

- It identifies the risks that may proceed directly to risk response planning.

- It identifies risks that are not critical, project-stopping risks, but that still must be documented.

- It prioritizes risks.

Applying Probability and Impact

The project risks are rated according to their probability and impact. Risk *probability* is the likelihood that a risk event may happen, while risk *impact* is the consequence that the result of the event will have on the project objectives. Two approaches exist to ranking risks:

- Cardinal scales identify the probability and impact on a numerical value, from .01 (very low) to 1.0 (certain).

- Ordinal scales identify and rank the risks from very high to very unlikely.

Creating a Probability-Impact Matrix

Each identified risk is fed into a probability-impact matrix, as seen in Figure 11-4. The matrix maps out the risk, its probability, and its possible impact. The risks with higher probability and impact are a more serious threat to the project objectives than risks with lower impact and consequences. The risks that are threats to the project require

Figure 11-4

A probability-impact matrix measures the identified risks within the project.

Odds and impact

Risk	Probability	Impact	Risk Score
Data loss	Low	High	Moderate
Network speed	Moderate	Moderate	Moderate
Server downtime	High	Low	Moderate
E-mail service down	Low	Low	Low

Each identified risk

Subjective score

quantitative analysis to determine the root causes, the methods to control the risks, and effective risk management. We'll discuss quantitative risk management later in this chapter.

The project is best served when the probability scale and the impact scale are pre-defined prior to qualitative analysis. For example, the probability scale rates the likelihood of an individual risk happening and can be on a linear scale (.1, .3, .5, .7, .9), or on an ordinal scale. The scale, however, should be defined and agreed upon in the risk management plan. The impact scale, which measures the severity of the risk on the project's objectives, can also be ordinal or cardinal.

By identifying and assigning the scales to use prior to the process of qualitative analysis, all risks can be ranked by the system, including future identified risks. A shift in risk-rating methodologies midproject can cause disagreements with regard to how the project risks should be handled.

A probability-impact matrix multiplies the value for the risk probability by the risk impact, giving a total risk score, as seen in Figure 11-5. The risk's scores can be cardinal, and then preset values can qualify the risk for a risk response. For example, an identified risk in a project is the possibility that the vendor may be late in delivering the

Figure 11-5

The results of a probability-impact matrix create the risk score.

Risk Scores					
Probability					
0.9	0.05	0.09	0.18	0.36	0.72
0.7	0.04	0.07	0.14	0.28	0.56
0.5	0.03	0.05	0.10	0.20	0.40
0.3	0.02	0.03	0.06	0.12	0.24
0.1	0.01	0.01	0.02	0.04	0.08
	0.05	0.10	0.20	0.40	0.80
	Impact				

Legend	☐ Low
	☐ Moderate
	☐ High

hardware. The probability is rated at .9, but the impact of the risk on the project is rated at .1. The risk score is calculated by multiplying the probability times the impact—in this case, resulting in a score of .09.

The scores within the probability-impact matrix can be referenced against the performing organization's policies for risk reaction. Based on the risk score, the performing organization can place the risk in differing categories to guide risk reaction. There are three common categories, based on an RAG (Red, Amber, Green) rating risk score:

- **Red condition**   High risk. These risk scores are high in impact and probability.
- **Amber condition (also called yellow condition)**   These risks are somewhat high in impact and probability.
- **Green condition**   Risks with a green label are generally fairly low in impact, probability, or both.

Relying on Data Precision

Here's the truth about qualitative risk analysis: It's easy, fast, cheap, and not very reliable. One of the toughest parts of qualitative risk analysis is the biased, subjective nature of the process. A project manager and the project team must question the reliability and reality of the data that leads to the ranking of the risks. For example, Susan may have great confidence in herself when it comes to working with new, unproven technologies. Based on this opinion, she determines the probability of the work to be a very low score. However, because she has no experience with the technology due to its newness, the probability of the risk of failure is actually very high. The biased opinion that Susan can complete the work with zero defects and problems is slightly skewed because she has never worked with the technology before. Obviously, a low-ranked score on a risk that should be ranked high can have detrimental effects on the project's success.

Data precision ranking takes into consideration the biased nature of the ranking, the accuracy of the data submitted, and the reliability of the nature submitted to examine the risk scores. Data precision ranking is concerned with the following:

- The level of understanding of the project risk
- The available data and information about the identified risk
- The quality of the data and information about the identified risk
- The reliability of the data about the identified risk

Assessing the Risk Score

Once the qualitative risk assessment has been completed, you can step back, heave a sigh of relief, and then acknowledge that this process will need to be repeated throughout the project as new risks come into play. Risk assessment is an ongoing, iterative process that lasts throughout the project. Want some more sad news? The risk ratings in the qualitative risk matrix can change based on conditions in the project or as more information about the risks becomes available.

One nice thing about the qualitative risk analysis process is the ability to categorize risks. Remember the RBS? The qualitative risk analysis process may give you an opportunity to create new risk categories that you've identified or to reorganize the RBS. The goal of updating the RBS is to group risks by common categories to create better risk responses later on in the risk management processes.

Finally, assessing the risk score gives the project manager an opportunity to address near-term risks. Imminent risks are usually considered of higher urgency than future risks. Consider the risk ranking, the time needed for the risk response, and the conditions that indicate the risk is coming to fruition.

Updating the Risk Register

At the beginning of the qualitative risk analysis process, the risk register was fairly simple. The list of identified risks, some potential responses, and supporting detail for the risks are all that you'd likely find in that database. Now that more information has become available, the project manager and the project team can update the risk register accordingly.

As qualitative risk analysis happens throughout the project, new risks will be identified. The project manager should route the risks through the qualitative risk analysis process. The end results of qualitative risk analysis are all updated in the risk register:

- **Overall risk ranking of the project** This allows the project manager, management, customers, and other interested stakeholders to comprehend the risk, the nature of the risks, and the condition between the risk score and the likelihood of success for a project. The risk score can be compared with other projects to determine project selection, the placement of talent in a project, prioritization, the creation of a benefit/cost ratio, or even the cancellation of a project because it is deemed too risky.

- **Risk categories** Within the risk register, categories of risks should be created. The idea is that not only will related risks be lumped together, but also there may be some trend identification and root cause analysis of identified risks. As risks are categorized, it should be easier to create risk responses as well.

- **Near-term risks** Qualitative analysis should also help the project team identify which risks require immediate or near-term risk responses. However, risks that are likely to happen later in the project can be acknowledged, allowing imminent risks to be managed first.

- **Risks requiring additional analysis** The risks categorized as high will likely need additional analysis, such as quantitative analysis. Some risks may demand immediate risk management based on the nature of the risks and the status of the project.

- **Low-priority risk watch list**   Let's face it: Not all risks need additional analysis. However, these low-priority risks should be identified and assigned to a watch list for periodic monitoring.

- **Trends in qualitative analysis**   As the project progresses and risk analysis is repeated, trends in the ranking and analysis of the risks may become apparent. These trends can allow the project manager and other risk experts to respond to the root cause and predicted trends to either eliminate or respond to the risks within the project.

Preparing for Quantitative Risk Analysis

Quantitative risk analysis attempts to numerically assess the probability and impact of the identified risks. It also creates an overall risk score for the project. This method is more in-depth than qualitative risk analysis and relies on several different tools to accomplish its goal.

Qualitative risk analysis typically precedes quantitative risk analysis. I like to say that qualitative analysis qualifies risks, while quantitative analysis quantifies risks. All or a portion of the identified risks in qualitative risk analysis can be examined in the quantitative analysis. The performing organization may have policies on the risk scores in qualitative analysis that require the risks to advance to the quantitative analysis. The availability of time and budget may also be a factor in determining which risks should pass through quantitative analysis. Quantitative analysis is a more time-consuming process, and is, therefore, also more expensive. The goals of quantitative risk analysis are to:

- Quantify the cost and impact of the risk exposure
- Ascertain the likelihood of reaching project success
- Ascertain the likelihood of reaching a particular project objective
- Determine the risk exposure for the project
- Determine the likely amount of the contingency reserve needed for the project
- Determine the risks with the largest impact on the project
- Determine realistic time, cost, and scope targets

Interviewing Stakeholders and Experts

Interviews with stakeholders and subject matter experts can be one of the first tools to quantify the identified risks. These interviews can focus on worst-case, best-case, and most-likely scenarios if the goal of the quantitative analysis is to create a triangular distribution. Most quantitative analysis, however, uses continuous probability distributions. Figure 11-6 shows five sample distributions: normal, lognormal, beta, triangular, and uniform.

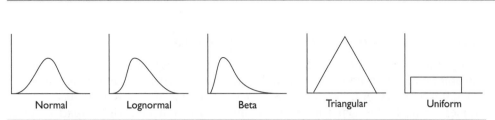

Figure 11-6 Risk distributions illustrate the likelihood and impact of an event within a project.

Continuous probability distribution examines the probability of all possibilities within a given range. For each variable, the probability of a risk event and the corresponding consequence of the event may vary. In other words, dependent on whether the risk event occurs and how it happens, a reaction to the event may also occur. The distribution of the probabilities and impact includes:

- Normal
- Lognormal
- Beta
- Triangular
- Uniform

 EXAM TIP   It's doubtful you'll be tested on these risk distributions for the exam. The PMBOK mentions them only briefly, so you just need to be topically aware of them. Don't invest hours memorizing the subject.

Applying Sensitivity Analysis

Sensitivity analysis examines each risk to determine which one has the largest impact on the project's success. All other risks in the project are set at a baseline value and then compared against all of the other risks individually. The individual risk is then examined to see how it may affect the success of the project. The goal of sensitivity analysis is to determine which individual risks have the greatest impact on the project's success and then to escalate the risk management processes based on these risk events.

The tornado diagram is best used when completing sensitivity analysis. The tornado diagram maps out all the variables in a situation from largest to smallest impact on the project or situation. If you've ever seen a tornado, you know it's really big on top and small at the bottom—that's what the tornado diagram looks like, too. The closer the bar is to the top of the diagram, the more impact it has on the situation, project, or investment. The closer the bar is to the bottom of the chart, the less impact it has on the situation. Tornado diagrams are also sometimes called tornado plots or tornado charts.

Finding the Expected Monetary Value

The expected monetary value (EMV) of a project or event is based on the probability of outcomes that are uncertain. For example, one risk may cost the project an additional $10,000 if it occurs, but there's only a 20 percent chance of the event occurring. In its simplest form, the expected monetary value of this individual risk impact is, thus, $2,000. Project managers can also find the expected monetary value of a decision by creating a decision tree.

Table 11-1 is an example of a simple risk matrix that determines the expected monetary value for some sample risks. Note that the sum of the EMV reveals what the contingency reserve for these risks should be.

Using a Decision Tree

A decision tree is a method used to determine which of two or more decisions is the best one. For example, it can be used to determine buy-versus-build scenarios, lease-or-purchase equations, or whether to use in-house resources rather than outsourcing project work. The decision tree model examines the cost and benefits of each decision's outcome and weighs the probability of success for each of the decisions.

The purpose of the decision tree is to make a decision, calculate the value of that decision, or determine which decision costs the least. Follow Figure 11-7 through the various steps of the decision tree process.

Completing a Decision Tree

As the project manager of the new GFB Project, you have to decide whether to create a new web application in-house or send the project out to a developer. The developer you would use (if you were to outsource the work) quotes the project cost at $175,000. Based on previous work with this company, you are 85 percent certain they will finish the work on time.

Your in-house development team quotes the cost of the work as $165,000. Again, based on previous experience with your in-house developers, you feel 75 percent certain they can complete the work on time. Now let's apply what we know to a decision tree:

- Buy or Build is simply the decision name.

Risk	Probability	Impact	EMV
Data loss	.40	−$12,000	−$4,800
New regulation	.80	−$34,000	−$27,200
Vendor discount	.30	+$10,000	+$3,000
Hardware issue	.45	−$65,000	−$29,250
		Contingency reserve =	$58,250

Table 11-1   Creating the Contingency Reserve

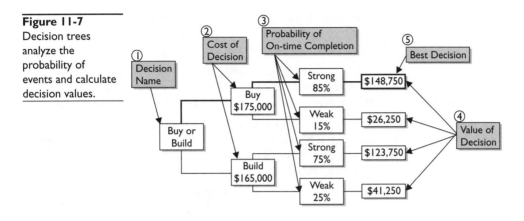

Figure 11-7
Decision trees analyze the probability of events and calculate decision values.

*   The cost of the decision if you "buy" the work outside of your company is $175,000. If you build the software in-house, the cost is $165,000.

*   Based on your probability of completion by a given date, you apply the 85 percent certainty to the "strong" finish for the Buy branch of the tree. Because you're 85 percent certain, you're also 15 percent uncertain; this value is assigned to the "weak" value on the Buy branch. You complete the same process for the Build branch of the tree.

*   The value of the decision is the percentage of strong and weak applied to each branch of the tree.

*   The best decision is based solely on the largest value of all possible decisions.

Using a Project Simulation

Project simulations allow the project team to play "what-if" games without affecting any areas of production. The Monte Carlo analysis (sometimes called the Monte Carlo technique) is the most common simulation. This technique got its name from Monte Carlo, Monaco (world-renowned for its slot machines, roulette wheels, and other games of pure chance). The Monte Carlo technique, typically completed using a computer software program, completely simulates a project by using values for all possible variables to predict the most likely model.

Examining the Results of Quantitative Risk Analysis

Quantitative risk analysis is completed throughout the project as risks are identified and passed through qualitative analysis, as project conditions change, or on a preset schedule. The end result of quantitative risk analysis should be reflected in the risk register and includes the following:

*   **Probabilistic analysis**   The risks within the project allow the project manager or other experts to predict the likelihood of project success. The project may

be altered by the response to certain risks. This response can increase cost and push back the project completion date.

- **Probability of costs and schedule objectives** Based on the identified risks, their impact, and the probability of occurrence, forecasts for the project schedule and the project costs are created. The more negative the risks that occur within a project, the greater the chance of delays and increased costs.

- **A prioritized list of risks** This list of quantified risks demonstrates those with the highest potential for endangering project success. This list includes the risks that have the greatest opportunity to affect the project. Each risk is identified with its probability and impact.

- **Trends** As the project moves toward completion, quantitative risk analysis may be repeated over and over. In each round of analysis, trends in the identified risks may become visible. These trends can help the project team eliminate the root cause of the risks, reduce their probability, or control their impact.

Updating the Risk Register

You guessed it. After completing a round of quantitative risk analysis, the risk register needs to be updated to reflect all the new information the project manager has learned about the project and its risks. Here's what gets updated in the risk register:

- Probability of the project succeeding
- Probability of achieving the project's cost and time objectives
- Prioritized list of quantified risks
- Trends the project management team has discovered

The risk register and the risk information will be updated throughout the project. This is a PMI-ism—the risk register is part of the project management plan and has to be updated throughout the project.

Planning for Risk Responses

Risk response planning is all about options and actions. It focuses on how to decrease the possibility of risks adversely affecting the project's objectives and also on how to increase the likelihood of positive risks that can aid the project. Risk response planning assigns responsibilities to people and groups close to the risk event. Risks will increase or decrease based on the effectiveness of risk response planning.

The responses to identified risks must be in balance with the risks themselves. The cost and time invested in a risk must be met with the gains from reducing the risk's impact and probability. In other words, a million-dollar solution for a hundred-dollar problem is unacceptable. The individuals who are assigned to the risk must have the authority to react to the project risk as planned. In most cases, several risk responses may be viable for the risk—the best choice for the identified risk must be documented, agreed upon, and then followed through should the risk come to fruition.

Preparing for Risk Responses

To successfully prepare for risk response, the project manager, project team, and appropriate stakeholders rely on several inputs—many of which stem from qualitative and quantitative risk analyses. The risk management plan is needed during the risk response planning, but the risk register is also needed to provide the following:

- A list of prioritized risks
- A risk ranking
- A prioritized list of quantified risks
- A probabilistic analysis of the project
- The probability of the project meeting the cost and schedule goals
- The list of potential responses decided upon when risks were first identified
- Any risk owners who have been identified
- A list of risks with common causal factors
- Trends from qualitative and quantitative analyses

Creating Risk Responses

The project team can employ several tools and techniques to respond to risks. Each risk should be evaluated to determine which category of risk response is most appropriate. When a category has been selected, the response must then be developed, refined, documented, and readied for use if needed. In addition, secondary responses may be selected for each risk. The purpose of risk response planning is to bring the overall risk of the project down to an acceptable level. In addition, risk response planning must address any risks that have unacceptably high scores.

Avoiding Negative Risks

Avoidance is simply avoiding the risk. This can be accomplished in many different ways and generally happens early in the project, when any change will result in fewer consequences than later in the project plan. Examples of avoidance include the following:

- Changing the project plan to eliminate the risk
- Clarifying project requirements to avoid discrepancies
- Reducing the project scope to avoid the risk
- Using a proven methodology rather than a new approach

EXAM TIP One avoidance risk strategy is to shut down the entire project to avoid the risk entirely.

Transferring Negative Risks

Transference is the process of transferring the risk (and the ownership of the risk) to a third party. The risk doesn't disappear—it just becomes someone else's problem. Transference of a risk usually costs a premium for the third party to own and manage. Common examples of risk transference include:

- Insurance
- Performance bonds
- Warranties
- Guarantees
- Fixed-priced contracts

Mitigating Negative Risks

Mitigating risks is an effort to reduce the probability and/or impact of an identified risk in the project. Mitigation is done based on the logic before the risk happens. The cost and time to reduce or eliminate the risks is more cost-effective than repairing the damage caused by the risk. The risk event may still happen, but hopefully the cost and impact of the risk will both be very low.

Mitigation plans can be created so that they are implemented should an identified risk cross a given threshold. For example, a manufacturing project may have a mitigation plan to reduce the number of units created per hour should the equipment's temperature cross a given threshold. The reduction is the number of units per hour that it may cost the project in time. In addition, the cost of extra labor to run the equipment longer because the machine is now operating at a slower pace may be attributed to the project. However, should the equipment fail, the project would have to replace the equipment and be delayed for weeks while awaiting repairs.

Examples of mitigation include:

- Adding activities to the project to reduce the risk probability or impact
- Simplifying the processes within the project
- Completing more tests on the project work before implementation
- Developing prototypes, simulations, and limited releases

Managing the Positive Risk and Opportunities

While most risks have a negative connotation, not all risks are bad. There are instances when a risk may create an opportunity that can help the project, other projects, or the organization as a whole. The type of risk and the organization's willingness to accept the risks will dictate the appropriate response.

Exploiting Positive Risks or Opportunities

When an organization would like to take advantage of a positive risk that will likely happen, it can exploit the risk. Positive risk exploitation can be realized by adding resources to finish faster than was originally planned, increasing quality to recognize sales and customer satisfaction, utilizing a better way of completing the project work, or any other method that creates the positive outcomes of the identified risk.

Sharing Positive Risks

The idea of sharing a positive risk really means sharing a mutually beneficial opportunity between two organizations or projects, or creating a risk-sharing partnership. When a project team can share the positive risk, ownership of the risk is given to the organization that can best capture its benefits.

Enhancing Positive Risks

This risk response seeks to modify the size of the identified opportunity. The goal is to strengthen the cause of the opportunity to ensure that the risk event does happen. Enhancing a project risk looks for solutions, triggers, or other drivers to ensure that the risk does come to fruition so that the rewards of the risk can be realized by the performing organization.

Accepting the Risks

Risk acceptance is the process of simply accepting the risks because no other action is feasible, or because the risks are deemed to be of small probability, impact, or both, and a formal response is not warranted. *Passive* acceptance requires no action; the project team deals with the risks as they happen. *Active* acceptance entails developing a contingency plan should the risk occur. Acceptance may be used for both positive and negative risks.

A *contingency plan* is a predefined set of actions the project team will take should certain events occur. Events that trigger the contingency plan should be tracked. A *fallback plan* is a reaction to a risk that has occurred when the primary response proves to be inadequate.

Updating the Risk Register

Are you noticing a theme here? Every time new information about the project's risks is learned, the risk register has to be updated. Since I'm dealing with risk responses in this section, the updates to the risk register are:

- Identified risks and how each one can threaten the project
- Risk owners and their responsibilities for the risk events
- Risk response strategies and the responses to risk events
- Symptoms and warning signs of risk
- Budget and schedule impact of the risk response activities

- Contingency reserves for time and costs
- Contingency plans and triggers to implement the plan
- Fallback plans
- Residual risks (risks that are expected to remain after a risk response)
- Secondary risks (new risks created as a result of a risk response)

Creating Contracts for Risk Response

When multiple entities are involved in a project, contractual agreements may be necessary to identify the responsible parties for identified risks. The contract may be needed for insurance purposes, customer acceptance, or the acknowledgment of responsibilities between the entities completing the project. Transference is an example of contractual agreements for the responsibility of risks within a project.

Justifying Risk Reduction

To reduce risk, additional time or monies are typically needed. The process and logic behind the strategies to reduce the risk should be evaluated to determine if the solution is worth the trade-offs. For example, a risk may be eliminated by adding $7,500 to a project's budget. However, the likelihood of the risk occurring is relatively low. Should the risk happen, it would cost, at a minimum, $8,000 to correct, and the project would be delayed by at least two weeks.

The cost of preventing the risk versus the cost of responding to it must be weighed and justified. If the project manager gambles that the risk won't happen and doesn't spend the $7,500 cost for the risk response, and the project moves forward as planned without the risk happening, it has theoretically saved $15,500 because the risk did not happen and the response to the risk did not need to happen.

However, if the risk does happen without the $7,500 preventive risk response, the project will lose at least $8,000 and be delayed at least two weeks. The cost inherent in the project delay may be more expensive than the solution to the risk. The judgment of solving the risk to reduce the likelihood of delaying the project may be wiser than ignoring the risk.

Updating the Project Plan

The risk reactions, contingency plans, and fallback plans should all be documented and incorporated into the project plan—for example, updating the schedule, budget, and WBS to accommodate additional time, money, and activities for risk responses. The responses to the risks may change the original implementation of the project and should be updated to reflect the project plan and intent of the project team, management, and other stakeholders. A failure to update the project plan and the risk register may cause risk reactions to be missed—and skew performance measurements.

There's a chance you'll also need to update the scope, cost, and schedule baselines to reflect the changes to these components of the project. For example, you may edit the project scope as part of risk response. This change in the project scope may in fact affect the costs and schedule of the project so you'd need to reflect these baselines, too. This is a great example of the integrated nature of project management. Any decision you make here in risk management, in particular risk responses, can affect the entire project and will cause a need to update the project management plan accordingly.

You'll also need to update the assumption log if you've identified risks that change the project assumptions. It's also possible that during the management of the risk, you had to generate new assumptions about how the project would behave if you were to enact certain risk responses. The technical documentation that supports the project management plan may also need to be updated if you've added risk responses that affect the project deliverables.

Monitoring and Controlling Project Risks

Risks must be actively monitored, and new risks must be responded to as they are discovered. Risk monitoring and control is the process of monitoring identified risks for signs that they may be occurring, controlling identified risks with the agreed-upon responses, and looking for new risks that may creep into the project. Risk monitoring and control also is concerned with the documentation of the success or failure of risk response plans and keeping records of metrics that signal risks are occurring or disappearing from the project.

Risk monitoring and control is an active process that requires participation from the project manager, the project team, key stakeholders, and, in particular, risk owners within the project. As the project progresses, risk conditions may change and require new responses, additional planning, or the implementation of a contingency plan.

There are several goals to risk monitoring and control:

- Confirm that risk responses are implemented as planned
- Determine if risk responses are effective or if new responses are needed
- Determine the validity of the project assumptions
- Determine if risk exposure has changed, evolved, or declined due to trends in the project progression
- Monitor risk triggers
- Confirm that policies and procedures happen as planned
- Monitor the project for new risks

Preparing for Risk Monitoring and Control

A project manager's work is never done—at least, not until the project is closed. Risk monitoring and controlling is an active process. There are several inputs the project team and the project manager must rely on to effectively monitor and control risks:

- **The project management plan**   Specifically, it's the risk management plan that you're after. This plan defines the organization's approach to risk management. It is not the strategy for specific risks within a project, but the overall strategy for risk analysis and planning.

- **The risk register** The risk register is the central repository for all project risk information. It includes the identified risks, the potential responses, the root causes of risks, and any identified categories of risk.

- **Work performance information** The results of project work can inform the project manager and the project team of new and impending risks. In addition, project team members may create reports to monitor or document risks. These reports are known as issue logs, action items, jeopardy warnings, and escalation notices.

- **Work performance data** The project performance focuses on the balance of the project schedule, costs, and deliverables that have been created. Should any of these factors suffer, new risks are likely to enter the project.

Monitoring and Controlling Risks

Risk monitoring and control happens throughout the project. These are not solitary activities that are completed once and never revisited. The project manager and the project team must actively monitor risks, respond with the agreed-upon actions, and scan the horizon for risks that have not been addressed. Risk monitoring and control is a recurring activity that requires input from all project participants.

Project risk should be on the agenda at every project team meeting. The periodic risk review is a regularly scheduled discussion throughout the project to ascertain the level of foreseeable risks, the success of risk responses in the project to date, and a review of pending risks. Based on circumstances within the project, risk rankings and prioritization may fluctuate. Changes to the project scope, team, or conditions may require qualitative and quantitative analyses.

Completing Risk Response Audits

You don't just assume your risk responses work—you have to test them. A risk response audit examines the planned risk responses, how well the planned actions work, and the effectiveness of the risk owners in implementing the risk responses. The audits happen throughout the project to measure the effectiveness of mitigating, transferring, and avoiding risks. The risk response audit should measure the effectiveness of the decision and its impact on time and cost. Of course, you'll update the risk register once the audit has been completed.

Analyzing Project Variances

A variance is the difference between what was planned and what was experienced. No one likes to hear that variances are in the project, but ignoring variances can only lead to more risks, more troubles, and more headaches. Cost variances can eat into the project budget, which in turn creates new risks, such as running out of cash, having to choose a lower grade of materials, or even removing deliverables from the scope. Cost variances can also force the project manager to have to ask for more funds, which is not a pleasant experience.

Schedule variances are just as deadly. Delays in the project work, vendor deliveries, and time estimates that were too optimistic can eat into the management reserve and consume the project's float. These risks can create new risks. Consider the risks inherent to the schedule variance responses:

- Crashing the project
- Fast-tracking the project
- Overworking the project team
- Rushing the project work
- Rushing through quality control and quality audits to regain time

Remember earned value analysis? Earned value analysis measures project performance. When project performance is waning, the project is likely missing targeted costs and schedule goals. The results of earned value analysis can signal that risks are happening within the project or that new risks may be developing.

For example, a schedule performance index (SPI) of .93 means the project is off schedule by 7 percent. A risk based on this value could mean that the project team is having difficulty completing the project work as planned. Additional work will continue to be late, the project will finish late, and quality may suffer as the team attempts to rush to complete assigned tasks.

Measuring Technical Performance

Throughout the project, the project team's technical competence with the technology being used in the project should increase. The level of technical achievement should be in proportion to the expected level of technical performance within the project. If the project team is not performing at a level of expected technical expertise, the project may suffer additional risks due to the discrepancy. Technical performance can be measured by the successful completion of activities throughout the project or project phases.

Monitoring Contingency Reserve

As risk events happen, you'll need to keep an eye on the risk reserves and how this budget for risk events is being depleted. Let's say you have a risk reserve of $250,000 based on your quantitative analysis. When a risk begins, you'll use some of the reserve to offset the impact of the event or to pay for the risk response. The cost of the actual risk event is subtracted from the $250,000—let's pretend in this instance it's $90,000. Now the reserve only has $160,000 to cover the remaining risk events in the project. To monitor the contingency reserve, you'll need to see what events are still left in the project, what their probability and impact are, and compare the remaining risk exposure to what's left in the reserve.

Examining the Results of Risk Monitoring and Control

Risk monitoring and control helps the project become more successful. Risk monitoring and control measures the planned responses to risks and creates reactions to unplanned risks. The outputs of risk monitoring and control also aim to help the project reach its objectives. Consider these outputs:

- **Risk register updates** As the project moves along and the project manager and the project team complete the risk assessments, audits, and risk reviews, they'll need to record their findings in the risk register. This update may include the reevaluation of the risk's impact, probability, and expected monetary value. For those risks that have passed in the project, the risk register should record what actually happened with the risk event and its impact on the project.

- **Change requests** Your favorite, I'm sure. As workarounds and contingency plans are used, they require changes to the project plan. Changes that occur as a result of the risks are completed through integrated change control. The changes are documented, approved, and incorporated into the project plan.

- **Recommended corrective actions** As risks come to fruition, corrective actions are needed to bypass them. The two types of corrective action are work-arounds and contingency plans. Corrective actions are actions taken to bring the project back into compliance with the project plan.

- **Recommended preventive actions** Preventive actions are steps taken to bring the project back into alignment with the project management plan.

- **Risk response plan updates** As risks occur, the responses to them should be documented and updated in the risk response plan. Should risk rankings change during the project, the change in ranking, the logic behind the change, and the results of the risk rank change should be documented in the risk response plan. For the risks that do not occur, the risks should be documented and considered closed in the risk response plan.

- **Organizational process asset updates** The risks from the current project can help other project managers in the future. Therefore, the project manager must work to ensure that the current risks, their anticipated impact, and their actual impact are recorded. The current risk probability and impact matrix, for example, can become a risk template for other projects in the future. This is true for just about any risk document—from the risk register to the risk breakdown structure, lessons learned, and checklists.

- **Project management plan updates** Some change requests and risk responses may require updates to the project management plan.

Chapter Summary

All projects have some level of risks—just how much the project stakeholders are willing to accept varies by project and organization. The quantification of the stakeholders' tolerance for risk is called the utility function: the higher the project's importance, the lower the utility function. Low-priority projects are generally more likely to accept risks than those projects that have a big impact on your organization. Some organizations may define their utility function as a risk-reward ratio, where a project with a large amount of risk must equate to a large amount of reward for doing the project.

Recall that at the launch of the risk planning process, there's the creation of the risk management plan. This plan addresses how the project's risk management approach will be directed. This plan is not specific to the risks within the project, but creates the boundaries, expectations, and general rules for the risk management process. Once this plan is in place and everyone is in agreement to abide by it, the project-specific risk management activities can commence.

The first stop is all about risk identification. This isn't a private meeting—the project team, project manager, project sponsor, vendors, stakeholders, end users, and even customers can participate if it's necessary. Any project-relevant risks are documented. It's good to have a variety of participants, as their point of view can help identify risks that may have been overlooked otherwise.

As risks are identified, the project manager can use the Delphi Technique to build a consensus on which risks have the highest impact on the project. This anonymous approach allows participants to speak freely about the risks, unhindered by the opinions of other stakeholders. The comments on the identified risks are distributed to all of the participants, allowing participants to comment, concur, or dismiss opinions on the identified risks. Through rounds of discussion, a consensus on the risks is reached.

Quick, subjective, qualitative risk analysis almost always happens before quantitative analysis. Qualitative analysis qualifies the risk for more analysis or identifies the risk as a low-level risk event and adds it to the low-level risk watch list. More serious risk events and the prioritized risk events of qualitative analysis go onto quantitative analysis. Quantitative analysis provides an in-depth look at the risk events and aims to quantify the risks.

Specifically, the risk exposure for the project is tied to a dollar amount. The risk exposure is offset by a contingency reserve. Should risk events happen, monies from the contingency reserve are used to counteract the risk events. Ongoing monitoring and controlling of the risk events and their impact is essential to effective risk management.

Involved with all of these processes is the risk register. It's the project's journal and database of risks, their status, their impact, and any supporting detail about the risk events. As more information is gathered about the risks, the project management team updates the risk register. As the project moves past risk events, their status and outcomes are updated in the risk register. The risk register is part of the project management plan and becomes, once the project closes, part of organizational process assets for future projects.

Key Terms

Acceptance   A risk response appropriate for both positive and negative risks, but often used for smaller risks within a project.

Avoidance   A risk response to avoid the risk.

Brainstorming   The most common approach to risk identification; usually completed by a project team with subject matter experts to identify the risks within the project.

Business risks   These risks may have negative or positive outcomes. Examples include using a less experienced worker to complete a task, allowing phases or activities to over-lap, or forgoing the expense of formal training for on-the-job education.

Cardinal scales   A ranking approach to identify the probability and impact by using a numerical value, from .01 (very low) to 1.0 (certain).

Checklists   A quick and cost-effective risk identification approach.

Data precision   The consideration of the risk ranking scores that takes into account any bias, the accuracy of the data submitted, and the reliability of the nature of the data submitted.

Decision tree   A method to determine which of two or more decisions is the best one. The model examines the costs and benefits of each decision's outcome and weighs the probability of success for each of the decisions.

Delphi Technique   An anonymous method of querying experts about foreseeable risks within a project, phase, or component of a project. The results of the survey are analyzed by a third party, organized, and then circulated to the experts. There can be several rounds of anonymous discussion with the Delphi Technique, without fear of backlash or offending other participants in the process. The goal is to gain consensus on project risks within the project.

Enhancing   A risk response that attempts to enhance the conditions to ensure that a positive risk event will likely happen.

Expected monetary value (EMV)   The monetary value of a risk exposure based on the risk's probability and impact in the risk matrix. This approach is typically used in quantitative risk analysis because it quantifies the risk exposure.

Exploit   A risk response that takes advantage of the positive risks within a project.

External risks   These risks are outside of the project, but directly affect it—for example, legal issues, labor issues, a shift in project priorities, or weather. "Force majeure" risks call for disaster recovery rather than project management. These are risks caused by earthquakes, tornadoes, floods, civil unrest, and other disasters.

Flowcharts   System or process flowcharts show the relationship between components and how the overall process works. These are useful for identifying risks between system components.

Influence diagrams   An influence diagram charts out a decision problem. It identifies all of the elements, variables, decisions, and objectives and also how each factor may influence another.

Ishikawa diagrams   These cause-and-effect diagrams are also called fishbone diagrams and are used to find the root cause of factors that are causing risks within the project.

Low-priority risk watch list   Low-priority risks are identified and assigned to a watch list for periodic monitoring.

Mitigation   A risk response effort to reduce the probability and/or impact of an identified risk in the project.

Monte Carlo technique   A simulation technique that got its name from the casinos of Monte Carlo, Monaco. The simulation is completed using a computer software program that can simulate a project, using values for all possible variables, to predict the most likely model.

Ordinal scales   A ranking approach that identifies and ranks the risks from very high to very unlikely or to some other value.

Organizational risks   The performing organization can contribute to the project's risks through unreasonable cost, time, and scope expectations; poor project prioritization; inadequate funding or the disruption of funding; and competition with other projects for internal resources.

Probability and impact matrix   A matrix that ranks the probability of a risk event occurring and its impact on the project if the event does happen; used in qualitative and quantitative risk analyses.

Project management risks   These risks deal with faults in the management of the project: the unsuccessful allocation of time, resources, and scheduling; unacceptable work results; and poor project management.

Pure risks   These risks have only a negative outcome. Examples include loss of life or limb, fire, theft, natural disasters, and the like.

Qualitative risk analysis   This approach "qualifies" the risks that have been identified in the project. Specifically, qualitative risk analysis examines and prioritizes risks based on their probability of occurring and their impact on the project should they occur.

Quantitative risk analysis   This approach attempts to numerically assess the probability and impact of the identified risks. It also creates an overall risk score for the project. This method is more in-depth than qualitative risk analysis and relies on several different tools to accomplish its goal.

RAG rating   An ordinal scale that uses red, amber, and green (RAG) to capture the probability, impact, and risk score.

Residual risks   Risks that are expected to remain after a risk response.

Risk   A project risk is an uncertain event or condition that can have a positive or negative impact on the project.

Risk identification   The systematic process of combing through the project, the project plan, the work breakdown structure, and all supporting documentation to identify as many risks that may affect the project as possible.

Risk management plan   A project management subsidiary plan that defines how risks will be identified, analyzed, responded to, and monitored within the project. The plan also defines the iterative risk management process that the project is expected to adhere to.

Risk management planning   The agreed-upon approach to the management of the project risk processes.

Risk owners   The individuals or entities that are responsible for monitoring and responding to an identified risk within the project.

Risk register   The risk register is a project plan component that contains all of the information related to the risk management activities. It's updated as risk management activities are conducted to reflect the status, progress, and nature of the project risks.

Risk response audit   An audit to test the validity of the established risk responses.

Risk responsibilities   The level of ownership an individual or entity has over a project risk.

Risk score   The calculated score based on each risk's probability and impact. The approach can be used in both qualitative and quantitative risk analysis.

Root cause identification   Root cause identification aims to find out why a risk event may be occurring, the causal factors for the risk events, and then, eventually, how the events can be mitigated or eliminated.

Secondary risks   New risks that are created as a result of a risk response.

Sensitivity analysis   A quantitative risk analysis tool that examines each risk to determine which one has the largest impact on the project's success.

Sharing   A risk response that shares the advantages of a positive risk within a project.

SWOT analysis   SWOT analysis is the process of examining the project from the perspective of each characteristic: strengths, weaknesses, opportunities, and threats.

Technical, quality, or performance risks   Technical risks are associated with new, unproven, or complex technologies being used on the project. Changes to the technology during the project implementation can also be a risk. Quality risks are the levels set for expectations of impractical quality and performance.

Transference   A risk response that transfers the ownership of the risk to another party. Insurance, licensed contractors, or other project teams are good examples of transference. A fee and contractual relationships are typically involved with the transference of a risk.

Questions

1. Mary and Thomas are project managers for their organization and they're discussing risk management and risk responses. Thomas insists that an organization should never accept a project risk and Mary says that sometimes it's okay. They've called on you, a project management expert, to help with this decision. When is it appropriate to accept a project risk?

   A. It is never appropriate to accept a project risk.

   B. All risks must be mitigated or transferred.

   C. It is appropriate to accept a risk if the project team has never completed this type of project work before.

   D. It is appropriate if the risk is in balance with the reward.

2. Frances is the project manager of the LKJ Project. Which of the following techniques will she use to create the risk management plan?

   A. Risk tolerance

   B. Status meetings

   C. Planning meetings

   D. Variance meetings

3. You are the project manager of the GHK Project. You and the manufacturer have agreed to substitute the type of plastic used in the product to a slightly thicker grade should there be more than 7 percent error in production. The thicker plastic will cost more and require the production to slow down, but the errors should diminish. This is an example of which of the following?

   A. Threshold

   B. Tracking

   C. Budgeting

   D. JIT manufacturing

4. You are a project manager consultant for the Allen T1 Company and you're helping them create a risk management plan for their project management office. You're explaining the concept of risk tolerance and how it affects the risk management policies. An organization's risk tolerance is also known as what?

   A. The utility function

   B. Herzberg's Theory of Motivation

   C. Risk acceptance

   D. The risk-reward ratio

5. The customers of the project have requested additions to the project scope. The project manager notifies you that additional risk planning will need to be added to the project schedule. Why?

    A. The risk planning should always be the same amount of time as the activities required by the scope change.

    B. Risk planning should always occur whenever the scope is adjusted.

    C. Risk planning should only occur at the project manager's discretion.

    D. The project manager is incorrect. Risk planning does not need to happen at every change in the project.

6. Jason is the project manager for his organization and he's working with his project team to identify and analyze project risks. Jason begins to create a risk register as part of this process, but his team doesn't understand what a risk register is or its purpose. Which one of the following best describes the risk register?

    A. It documents all of the outcomes of the other risk management processes.

    B. It's a document that contains the initial risk identification entries.

    C. It's a system that tracks all negative risks within a project.

    D. It's part of the project's project management information system (PMIS) for integrated change control.

7. You are a project management consultant for the Steinberg Organization and you're helping them categorize risks they may encounter in their projects. For starters, you identify some basic risk categories but your client wants to see some examples of these categories. You tell them, for example, that _____ include(s) fire, theft, or injury, and offer(s) no chance for gain.

    A. Business risks

    B. Pure risks

    C. Risk acceptance

    D. Life risks

8. Complete this sentence: A project risk is a(n) _____ occurrence that can affect the project for good or bad.

    A. Known

    B. Potential

    C. Uncertain

    D. Known unknown

9. Bradley is the project manager for his organization and he's working with his project team to identify risks. Some of the project team members are confused as to when risk identification should happen in the project. When should risk identification happen?

    A. As early as possible in the initiation process

    B. As early as possible in the planning process

C. Throughout the product management life cycle

D. Throughout the project life cycle

10. You are the project manager of the KLJH Project. This project will last two years and has 30 stakeholders. How often should risk identification take place?

A. Once at the beginning of the project

B. Throughout the execution processes

C. Throughout the project

D. Once per project phase

11. Ruth is a project management expert and consultant for businesses creating project management offices. Ruth's current client wants help to better identify risks. Which one of the following is an acceptable tool for risk identification?

A. Decision tree analysis

B. Decomposition of the project scope

C. The Delphi Technique

D. Pareto charting

12. You are the project manager for a project that will create a new and improved web site for your company. Currently, your company has over 8 million users around the globe. You would like to poll experts within your organization with a simple, anonymous form asking about any foreseeable risks in the design, structure, and intent of the web site. With the collected information, subsequent anonymous polls are submitted to the group of experts. This is an example of _____.

A. Risk identification

B. A trigger

C. An anonymous trigger

D. The Delphi Technique

13. Alice is a project manager for her organization and she's working with the project team to identify project risks and rank them by impact and probability. Which risk analysis technique provides the project manager with a risk ranking?

A. Quantifiable

B. Qualitative

C. The utility function

D. SWOT analysis

14. A table of risks, their probability, impact, and a number representing the overall risk score is called a _____.

A. Risk table

B. Probability-impact matrix

C. Quantitative matrix

D. Qualitative matrix

15. You are presented with the following table:

Risk Event	Probability	Impact Cost/Benefit	EMV
1	.20	−4,000	
2	.50	5,000	
3	.45	−300	
4	.22	500	
5	.35	−4,500	

What is the EMV for Risk Event 3?

A. $135

B. −$300

C. $45

D. −$135

16. You are presented with the following table:

Risk Event	Probability	Impact Cost/Benefit	Ex$V
1	.35	−4,000	
2	.40	50,000	
3	.45	−300,000	
4	.30	50,000	
5	.35	−45,000	

Based on the preceding numbers, what is the amount needed for the contingency fund?

A. Unknown with this information

B. 249,000

C. 117,150

D. 15,750

17. The water sanitation project manager has determined that the risks associated with handling certain chemicals are too high. He has decided to allow someone else to complete this portion of the project, and so has outsourced the handling and installation of the chemicals and filter equipment to an experienced contractor. This is an example of which of the following?

A. Avoidance

    B. Acceptance

    C. Mitigation

    D. Transference

18. A project manager and the project team are actively monitoring the pressure gauge on a piece of equipment. Sarah, the engineer, recommends a series of steps to be implemented should the pressure rise above 80 percent. The 80 percent mark represents what?

    A. An upper control limit

    B. The threshold

    C. Mitigation

    D. A work-around

19. You are presented with the following table:

Risk Event	Probability	Impact Cost/Benefit	Ex$V
1	.20	−4,000	
2	.50	5,000	
3	.45	−300	
4	.22	500	
5	.35	−4,500	
6			

What would Risk Event 6 be, based on the following information: Marty is 60 percent certain that he can get the facility needed for $45,000, which is $7,000 less than what was planned for.

    A. .60, 45,000, 27,000

    B. .60, 52,000, 31,200

    C. .60, 7,000, 4,200

    D. .60, −7,000, −4,200

20. You are the project manager for your organization and you're working with the project team to identify the project risks, rank the risks on probability and impact, and then create a risk contingency reserve. As part of these processes, you want to explore multiple scenarios of risk events in the project so you're utilizing different tools to analyze the project risks. Based on this information, which of the following can determine multiple scenarios, given various risks and the probability of their impact?

    A. A decision tree

    B. The Monte Carlo technique

    C. A Pareto chart

    D. A Gantt chart

Questions and Answers

1. Mary and Thomas are project managers for their organization and they're discussing risk management and risk responses. Thomas insists that an organization should never accept a project risk and Mary says that sometimes it's okay. They've called on you, a project management expert, to help with this decision. When is it appropriate to accept a project risk?

   A. It is never appropriate to accept a project risk.

   B. All risks must be mitigated or transferred.

   C. It is appropriate to accept a risk if the project team has never completed this type of project work before.

   D. It is appropriate if the risk is in balance with the reward.

   D. Risks that are in balance with the reward are appropriate for acceptance. Risk acceptance as a response planning technique to an identified risk is appropriate when the cost of a mitigation strategy is equal to or greater than the cost of the risk event to the project should the risk event occur. A, B, and C are all incorrect because these solutions are all false responses to risk management.

2. Frances is the project manager of the LKJ Project. Which of the following techniques will she use to create the risk management plan?

   A. Risk tolerance

   B. Status meetings

   C. Planning meetings

   D. Variance meetings

   C. Planning meetings are used to create the risk management plan. The project manager, project team leaders, key stakeholders, and other individuals with the power to make decisions regarding risk management attend the meetings. A, B, and D are incorrect because these choices do not fully answer the question.

3. You are the project manager of the GHK Project. You and the manufacturer have agreed to substitute the type of plastic used in the product to a slightly thicker grade should there be more than 7 percent error in production. The thicker plastic will cost more and require the production to slow down, but the errors should diminish. This is an example of which of the following?

   A. Threshold

   B. Tracking

   C. Budgeting

   D. JIT manufacturing

A. An error value of 7 percent represents the threshold the project is allowed to operate under. Should the number of errors increase beyond 7 percent, the current plastic will be substituted. B is incorrect because tracking is the documentation of a process through a system or workflow, or the documentation of events through the process. C, budgeting, is also incorrect. D is incorrect because JIT manufacturing is a scheduling approach to ordering the materials only when they are needed in order to keep inventory costs down.

4. You are a project manager consultant for the Allen T1 Company and you're helping them create a risk management plan for their project management office. You're explaining the concept of risk tolerance and how it affects the risk management policies. An organization's risk tolerance is also known as what?

A. The utility function

B. Herzberg's theory of motivation

C. Risk acceptance

D. The risk-reward ratio

A. The utility function describes an organization's willingness to tolerate risk. B is incorrect. Herzberg's Theory of Motivation is a human resource theory that describes motivating agents for workers. C is also incorrect. Risk acceptance describes the action of allowing a risk to exist because it is deemed low in impact, low in probability, or both. D, the risk-reward ratio, is incorrect. This describes the potential reward for taking on a risk in the project.

5. The customers of the project have requested additions to the project scope. The project manager notifies you that additional risk planning will need to be added to the project schedule. Why?

A. The risk planning should always be the same amount of time as the activities required by the scope change.

B. Risk planning should always occur whenever the scope is adjusted.

C. Risk planning should only occur at the project manager's discretion.

D. The project manager is incorrect. Risk planning does not need to happen at every change in the project.

B. When the scope has been changed, the project manager should require risk planning to analyze the changes for risks to the project's success. A is incorrect. The scope changes may not require the same amount of time as the activities needed to complete the risk planning. C is incorrect because risk planning should not occur at the project manager's discretion. Instead, it should be based on evidence within the project and the policies adopted in the risk management plan. D is also incorrect. When changes are added to the project scope, risk planning should occur.

6. Jason is the project manager for his organization and he's working with his project team to identify and analyze project risks. Jason begins to create a risk register as part of this process, but his team doesn't understand what a risk register is or its purpose. Which one of the following best describes the risk register?

   A. It documents all of the outcomes of the other risk management processes.

   B. It's a document that contains the initial risk identification entries.

   C. It's a system that tracks all negative risks within a project.

   D. It's part of the project's project management information system (PMIS) for integrated change control.

   A. The risk register documents all of the outcomes of the other risk management processes. B, C, and D are all incorrect definitions of the risk register.

7. You are a project management consultant for the Steinberg Organization and you're helping them categorize risks they may encounter in their projects. For starters, you identify some basic risk categories but your client wants to see some examples of these categories. You tell them, for example, that _____ include(s) fire, theft, or injury, and offer(s) no chance for gain.

   A. Business risks

   B. Pure risks

   C. Risk acceptance

   D. Life risks

   B. Pure risks are the risks that could threaten the safety of the individuals on the project. A is incorrect because business risks affect the financial gains or losses of a project. C and D are incorrect because these terms are not relevant.

8. Complete this sentence: A project risk is a(n) _____ occurrence that can affect the project for good or bad.

   A. Known

   B. Potential

   C. Uncertain

   D. Known unknown

   C. Risks are not planned; they are left to chance. The accommodation and the reaction to a risk can be planned, but the event itself is not planned. If risks could be planned, Las Vegas would be out of business. A, B, and D are all incorrect because these terms do not accurately complete the sentence.

9. Bradley is the project manager for his organization and he's working with his project team to identify risks. Some of the project team members are confused

as to when risk identification should happen in the project. When should risk identification happen?

A. As early as possible in the initiation process

B. As early as possible in the planning process

C. Throughout the product management life cycle

D. Throughout the project life cycle

D. Risk identification is an iterative process that happens throughout the project's life cycle. A and B are both incorrect because risk identification is not limited to any one process group. C is incorrect because risk identification happens, technically, throughout the project management life cycle, which is unique to each project, and not through the product management life cycle.

10. You are the project manager of the KLJH Project. This project will last two years and has 30 stakeholders. How often should risk identification take place?

A. Once at the beginning of the project

B. Throughout the execution processes

C. Throughout the project

D. Once per project phase

C. Risk identification happens throughout the project. Recall that planning is iterative: as the project moves toward completion, new risks may surface that call for identification and planned responses. A is incorrect. Risk identification should happen throughout the project, not just at the beginning. B is incorrect because risk identification is part of planning. D is incorrect because the nature of the project phase may require and reveal more than one opportunity for risk identification.

11. Ruth is a project management expert and consultant for businesses creating project management offices. Ruth's current client wants help to better identify risks. Which one of the following is an acceptable tool for risk identification?

A. Decision tree analysis

B. Decomposition of the project scope

C. The Delphi Technique

D. Pareto charting

C. The Delphi Technique, an anonymous risk identification method, is the correct answer. A is incorrect. Decision tree analysis is appropriate for calculating the expected monetary value of a decision, but not risk identification. B is incorrect because the decomposition of the project scope will result in the WBS. D is incorrect. Creating a Pareto chart is part of quality control, not risk identification.

12. You are the project manager for a project that will create a new and improved web site for your company. Currently, your company has over 8 million users around the globe. You would like to poll experts within your organization with a simple, anonymous form asking about any foreseeable risks in the design, structure, and intent of the web site. With the collected information, subsequent anonymous polls are submitted to the group of experts. This is an example of _____.

    A. Risk identification

    B. A trigger

    C. An anonymous trigger

    D. The Delphi Technique

    D. An anonymous poll that allows experts to freely submit their opinion without fear of backlash is an example of the Delphi Technique. A, B, and C are incorrect. These choices do not accurately answer the question.

13. Alice is a project manager for her organization and she's working with the project team to identify project risks and rank them by impact and probability. Which risk analysis technique provides the project manager with a risk ranking?

    A. Quantifiable

    B. Qualitative

    C. The utility function

    D. SWOT analysis

    B. The risk ranking is based on the very high, high, medium, low, and very low attributes of the identified risks. A is incorrect because it is not relevant to the question. This answer is quantifiable, not quantitative. C is incorrect. "Utility function" describes an organization's tolerance for risk. D, SWOT analysis, is part of risk identification.

14. A table of risks, their probability, impact, and a number representing the overall risk score is called a _____.

    A. Risk table

    B. Probability-impact matrix

    C. Quantitative matrix

    D. Qualitative matrix

    B. A table of risks, their probability, and impact equate to a risk score, and is a risk probability-impact matrix. A is incorrect because it does not fully answer the question. C and D are incorrect because a risk matrix can be used in both quantitative and qualitative risk analyses.

15. You are presented with the following table:

Risk Event	Probability	Impact Cost/Benefit	EMV
1	.20	−4,000	
2	.50	5,000	
3	.45	−300	
4	.22	500	
5	.35	−4,500	

What is the EMV for Risk Event 3?

A. $135

B. −$300

C. $45

D. −$135

D. Risk Event 3 has a probability of 45 percent and an impact cost of −$300, which equates to −$135. A, B, and C are incorrect because their values are wrong answers for the formula.

16. You are presented with the following table:

Risk Event	Probability	Impact Cost/Benefit	Ex$V
1	.35	−4,000	
2	.40	50,000	
3	.45	−300,000	
4	.30	50,000	
5	.35	−45,000	

Based on the preceding numbers, what is the amount needed for the contingency fund?

A. Unknown with this information

B. 249,000

C. 117,150

D. 15,750

C. The calculated amount for each of the risk events is shown in the following table:

Risk Event	Probability	Impact Cost/Benefit	Ex$V
1	.35	−4,000	−1,400
2	.40	50,000	20,000
3	.45	−300,000	−135,000
4	.30	50,000	15,000
5	.35	−45,000	−15,750
			−117,150

A, B, and D are incorrect answers because they do not reflect the contingency amount needed for the project based on the preceding table.

17. The water sanitation project manager has determined that the risks associated with handling certain chemicals are too high. He has decided to allow someone else to complete this portion of the project, and so has outsourced the handling and installation of the chemicals and filter equipment to an experienced contractor. This is an example of which of the following?

A. Avoidance

B. Acceptance

C. Mitigation

D. Transference

D. Because the risk is not eliminated but transferred to someone else or another entity, it is considered transference. A is incorrect because the risk still exists—it is just being handled by another entity. B is incorrect because the project manager has not accepted the risk, deciding instead to allow another entity to deal with it. C is incorrect. The risk has not been mitigated in the project.

18. A project manager and the project team are actively monitoring the pressure gauge on a piece of equipment. Sarah, the engineer, recommends a series of steps to be implemented should the pressure rise above 80 percent. The 80 percent mark represents what?

A. An upper control limit

B. The threshold

C. Mitigation

D. A work-around

B. The 80 percent mark is a threshold. A is incorrect. An upper control limit is a boundary for quality in a control chart. C is incorrect. Mitigation is a planned response should a risk event happen. D is also incorrect. A work-around is an action to bypass the risk event.

19. You are presented with the following table:

Risk Event	Probability	Impact Cost/Benefit	Ex$V
1	.20	−4,000	
2	.50	5,000	
3	.45	−300	
4	.22	500	
5	.35	−4,500	
6			

What would Risk Event 6 be, based on the following information: Marty is 60 percent certain that he can get the facility needed for $45,000, which is $7,000 less than what was planned for.

A. .60, 45,000, 27,000

B. .60, 52,000, 31,200

C. .60, 7,000, 4,200

D. .60, −7,000, −4,200

> C. Marty is 60 percent certain that he can save the project $7,000. The $4,200 represents the 60 percent certainty of the savings. A, B, and D are all incorrect since these values do not reflect the potential savings of the project.

20. You are the project manager for your organization and you're working with the project team to identify the project risks, rank the risks on probability and impact, and then create a risk contingency reserve. As part of these processes you want to explore multiple scenarios of risk events in the project so you're utilizing different tools to analyze the project risk. Based on this information, which of the following can determine multiple scenarios, given various risks and the probability of their impact?

A. A decision tree

B. The Monte Carlo technique

C. A Pareto chart

D. A Gantt chart

> B. The Monte Carlo technique can reveal multiple scenarios and examine the risks and probability of impact. A, a decision tree, helps guide the decision-making process. C, a Pareto chart, helps identify the leading problems in a situation. D, a Gantt chart, compares the lengths of activities against a calendar in a bar chart format.

Managing Project Procurement

In this chapter, you will

- Plan for project procurement
- Select the project vendors
- Create contracts for the project work
- Control and administer the contractual relationships
- Close out the contract with the project vendors

Projects routinely require procurements. Projects need materials, equipment, consultants, training, books, software, hardware, and lots of other stuff in order for the project to be successful. Project procurement management is the process of purchasing the products necessary to meet the needs of the project scope. It's also the control and delivery of the promises made between the buyer and the seller.

Procurement management also involves planning, requesting seller information, choosing a source, administering the contract, and closing out the contract. Procurement management, as far as your Certified Associate in Project Management (CAPM) and Project Management Professional (PMP) exams are concerned, focuses on the practices from the buyer's point of view, not the seller's. Usually. Sometimes, you may be presented as the vendor that is completing a project for your customer, the buyer. You should also recognize that the seller can be seen as a contractor, subcontractor, vendor, or supplier. In whatever situation you're put into on your exam, always do what's "fair" for both parties and what's in the best interest of the project scope.

When buying anything from a vendor, the buyer needs a contract. A contract becomes a key input to many of the processes within the project. The contract, above anything else, specifies the rules and agreements for the project.

 VIDEO For a more detailed explanation, watch the *Build versus Buy* video now.

Here's a neat twist: When the seller is completing his or her obligations to supply a product, the Project Management Institute (PMI) treats those obligations as a project. In other words, if ABC Electricians was wiring a building for your company, ABC Electricians would be the performing organization completing its own project. Your company becomes the customer of their project—and is, of course, a stakeholder in their project.

In the scenarios described in this chapter, the seller will be outside of the performing organization. The buyer will be managing a project and procuring resources from a vendor. However, all of the details in this chapter can be applied to internal work orders, formal agreements, and contracts between organizational units within a single entity.

Planning for Procurement

Procurement planning is the process of identifying which part of the project should be procured from resources outside of the organization. Generally, procurement decisions are made early on in the planning processes. Procurement planning centers on four elements:

- Whether procurement is needed
- What to procure
- How much to procure
- When to procure

The project schedule is also taken into consideration when procurement decisions are made. Consider the lead time from when the purchase decision is made to when the purchase actually happens. And then consider the time from when the purchase happens to the time when the vendor actually delivers the goods or services. In light of the schedule, it's often more practical to just hire an expert to complete the work than to do the work in-house because of limited resources, the expertise of the internal resources, and the promised (or demanded) project completion date.

There are nine inputs to the plan purchases and acquisitions processes:

- **Project management plan**   The project management plan is needed because the decisions made in the project may affect the procurement processes, and the procurement process can alter previous plans and decisions in the project. From the project management plan, you'll pay special attention to the scope baseline as part of your procurement planning. Because the project scope statement defines the project work—and only the required work—to complete the project, it also defines the limitations of the project. The work breakdown structure (WBS) is needed during procurement decisions because it exposes all of the project deliverables and what needs to be purchased to create all of the promised deliverables. And if you're going to use the WBS, you might as well rely on the WBS dictionary, too. The WBS dictionary provides the full description of the WBS deliverables. This can, of course, help the project manager and the project team determine exactly what should be procured and what should not.

- **Requirements documentation**   You need to know exactly what the project is required to deliver so that the customer will accept what the project creates. The requirements documentation will define the requirements for project acceptance.

These documents may also contain information about the contractual and legal obligations the project must adhere to. Consider safety, licenses and permits, insurance, environmental, and industry-specific requirements.

- **Risk register**   In Chapter 11, I discussed the risk register: the centralized database of all project risks and their impact. The risk exposure, risk owners, and risk responses may all need to be considered for possible procurement decisions.

- **Activity resource requirements**   Resources are people and things. A project manager may need to hire a consultant, a contractor, or a new employee to complete the project work. Resource requirements may also include tools, equipment, and materials. All of this costs—cha-ching!—money.

- **Project schedule**   The project schedule helps with cash-flow forecasting, the consideration of purchase decisions, and the timing for procurement processes.

- **Activity cost estimates**   Remember these from Chapter 7? You'll need your cost estimates to complete cost budgeting and to track your expenses for activities.

- **Stakeholder register**   The project manager and team will need the contact information for the stakeholders interested in the procurement decisions. Some decisions in procurement may affect the interests of stakeholders— consider costs, materials, schedules, and contractual obligations.

- **Enterprise environmental factors**   These are the conditions of the marketplace; the available products, services, and results; the availability of the things you'd like to purchase; and the terms and conditions of the purchase agreement. If your organization doesn't have a formal purchasing department, the project team has to step up and complete the project procurement activities.

- **Organizational process assets**   When it comes to purchases, you likely have rules and procedures unique to your organization on how you can buy anything for your project. The internal rules in your organization police how the project manager may purchase, negotiate, agree to contractual obligations, and pay the vendor. (If you don't have these rules and policies in your organization, allow me to offer my services directly to you. Sign on the dotted line.)

Determining the Contract Type

There are multiple types of contracts when it comes to procurement. The project work, the market, and the nature of the purchase determine the contract type. Here are some general rules that CAPM and PMP exam candidates, and project managers, should know:

- A *contract* is a formal agreement between the buyer and the seller. Contracts can be oral or written—although written is preferred.

- The United States backs all contracts through the court system.

- Contracts should clearly state all requirements for product acceptance.

- Any changes to the contract must be formally approved, controlled, and documented.

- A contract is not fulfilled until all of its requirements are met.

- Contracts can be used as a risk mitigation tool, as in transferring the risk. All contracts have some level of risk; depending on the contract type, the risk can be transferred to the seller. If a risk response strategy is to transfer, risks associated with procurement are considered secondary risks and must go through the risk management process.

- There are legal requirements governing contracts. For a contract to be valid, it must:

  - Contain an offer

  - Have been accepted

  - Provide for a consideration (payment)

  - Be for a legal purpose

  - Be executed by someone with the capacity and authority

- The terms and conditions of the contract should define breaches, copyrights, intellectual rights, and force majeure.

 EXAM TIP *Force majeure* is a powerful and unexpected event, such as a hurricane or other natural disaster.

Fixed-Price Contracts

These contracts must clearly define the requirements the vendor is to provide. These contracts may also provide incentives for meeting or exceeding contract requirements—such as meeting deadlines—and require the seller to assume the risk of cost overruns, as Figure 12-1 demonstrates.

Cost-Reimbursable Contracts

These contract types pay the seller for the product. The payment to the seller includes a profit margin—the difference between the actual costs of the product and the sales amount. The actual costs of the product fall into two categories:

- **Direct costs**   Costs incurred by the project in order for the project to exist. Examples include the equipment needed to complete the project work, the salaries of the project team, and other expenses tied directly to the project's existence.

- **Indirect costs**   Costs attributed to the cost of doing business. Examples include utilities, office space, and other overhead costs.

Figure 12-1
Fixed-price contracts transfer risk to the seller.

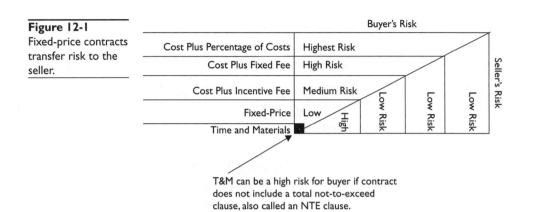

T&M can be a high risk for buyer if contract does not include a total not-to-exceed clause, also called an NTE clause.

- Cost-reimbursable contracts require the buyer to assume the risk of cost overruns. There are three types of cost-reimbursable contracts:
  - Cost plus fixed fee
  - Cost plus percentage of costs
  - Cost plus incentive fee

 EXAM TIP Cost plus percentage of costs is not used often—and isn't allowed in many organizations. Don't plan on seeing this contract type on your exam.

Time and Materials Contracts

Time and materials (T&M) contracts are sometimes called unit price contracts. They are ideal when an organization contracts out a small project or when smaller amounts of work within a larger project are to be completed by a vendor. T&M contracts, however, can grow dangerously out of control as more work is assigned to the seller. While time and materials is an easy to create and administer contract type, it can pose a threat to the buyer if a "not-to-exceed" clause is not included in the contract. A not-to-exceed clause states the maximum amount of monies the vendor can bill for the contracted work. Figure 12-2 is an example of how T&M contracts can pose a risk for the buyer.

Figure 12-2
Time and materials must have a not-to-exceed clause to protect the buyer.

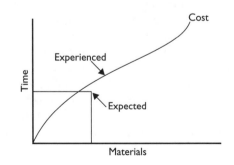

Understanding Contract Types

On the CAPM and PMP examinations, you can anticipate a few questions on contract types. Familiarize yourself with Table 12-1.

 EXAM TIP The contractual relationship between the buyer and the seller is often considered confidential. The terms, conditions, and private nature of a contractual relationship are known as *privity*.

Using the Procurement Planning Tools

Procurement planning should be done early in the planning processes, with certain exceptions. As needs arise, as project conditions change, or as other circumstances demand, procurement planning may be required throughout the project. Whenever procurement planning happens early in the project, as preferred, or later in the project, as needed, a logical approach to securing the proper resources is necessitated.

Determining to Make or Buy

The decision to make or buy a product is a fundamental aspect of project management. In some conditions, it is more cost-effective to buy; in others, it makes more sense to create an in-house solution. The make-or-buy analysis should be made in the initial scope definition to determine if the entire project should be completed in-house or procured. As the project evolves, additional make-or-buy decisions are often needed.

The initial costs of the solution for the in-house or procured product must be considered, but so, too, must the ongoing expenses of the solutions. For example, a company may elect to lease a piece of equipment. The ongoing expense of leasing the piece of equipment should be weighed against the expected ongoing expense of purchasing the equipment and the monthly costs to maintain, insure, and manage the equipment.

For example, Figure 12-3 shows the mathematical approach to determining whether it is better to create a software program in-house or to buy one from a software company. The in-house solution will cost your company $25,000 to create your own software package and, based on historical information, another $2,500 per month to maintain it.

The development company has a solution that will cost your company $17,000 to purchase, but the development company requires a maintenance plan for each software program installed, which will cost your company $2,700 per month. The difference between making the software and buying it is $8,000. The difference between supporting the software the organization has made and allowing the external company to support their software is only $200 per month.

The $200 per month is divided into the difference between creating the software internally and buying it—which is $8,000 divided by $200, or 40 months. If the software is to be replaced within 40 months, the company should buy the software. If the software will not be replaced within 40 months, it should build the software.

Contract Type	Acronym	Attribute	Risk Issues
Cost plus fixed fee	CPFF	Actual costs plus profit margin for seller.	Cost overruns represent risk to the buyer.
Cost plus percentage of cost	CPPC	Actual costs plus profit margin for seller.	Cost overruns represent risk to the buyer. This is the most dangerous contract type for the buyer.
Cost plus incentive fee	CPIF	Actual costs plus profit margin for seller.	Cost overruns represent risk to the buyer.
Cost plus award fee	CPAF	Actual costs plus a buyer-determined award for completing the project.	Award is at the discretion of the buyer, and the seller may be disappointed in the award fee.
Fixed-price	FP	Agreed price for contracted product. Can include incentives for the seller.	Seller assumes risk.
Lump-sum	LS	Agreed price for contracted product. Can include incentives for the seller.	Seller assumes risk.
Firm fixed-price	FFP	Agreed price for contracted product.	Seller assumes risk.
Fixed-price incentive fee	FPIF	Agreed price for contracted product. Can include incentives for the seller.	Seller assumes risk.
Fixed-price with economic price adjustments	FP-EPA	Mostly used for long-term contracts. This fixed-price contract has provisions for economic adjustments, like inflation, cost increases, or regulatory cost increases. These typically refer to a financial index as a guide for approved cost increases.	Changes in agreed-upon provisions, such as the cost of materials or inflation, can drive the overall costs of the project up. There is uncertainty in this longer-term contractual agreement, and uncertainty brings risk.
Time and materials	T&M	Price assigned for the time and materials provided by the seller.	Contracts without "not-to-exceed" clauses can lead to cost overruns.
Unit price	UP	Price assigned for a measurable unit of product or time. (For example, $130 for engineer's time on the project.)	Risk varies with the product. Time represents the biggest risk if the amount needed is not specified in the contract.

Table 12-1   Common Contract Types

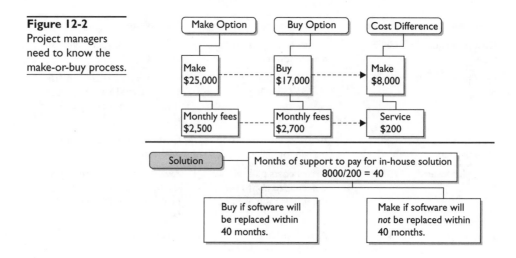

Figure 12-2
Project managers
need to know the
make-or-buy process.

There are multiple reasons why an organization may choose to make or buy. Table 12-2 provides some common reasons for making and buying.

EXAM TIP You may be presented with one or two questions on make-or-buy analysis. In the preceding example, and on the exam, you won't be confronted with the tax benefits of make-or-buy—although in your job as a project manager, you may be. For the exam, focus on determining which is the most cost-effective, fair solution.

Using Expert Judgment
Procurement planning can rely on expert judgment. It may be beneficial to rely on the wisdom of others—whether those in the performing organization or subject matter

Reasons to Make	Reasons to Buy
Less costly	Less costly
Can use in-house skills	In-house skills are not available or don't exist
Can control the work	Small volume of work
Can control intellectual property	More efficient
Learn new skills	Transfer risks
Available staff	Available vendor
Can focus on core project work	Project team can focus on other work items

Table 12-2 Common Reasons to Make or Buy Software

experts—to determine the need for procurement. Expert judgment for procurement management planning can come from the following:

- Units or individuals within the performing organization

- Consultants and subject matter experts

- Professional, trade, or technical associations

- Industry groups

Examining the Results of Procurement Planning

Procurement planning is a process that should happen early in the planning processes. The outputs of procurement planning allow the project manager and the project team to proceed with confidence in the procuring of products and services needed to successfully complete the project. If it is determined early in the project that there's no need for procurements, then, obviously, the remaining procurement processes are unnecessary for the project.

The Procurement Management Plan

This subsidiary project plan documents the decisions made in the procurement planning processes and specifies how the remaining procurement activities will be managed. The plan details the following:

- How vendors will be selected

- The type of contracts to be used

- The risk management approach for contracted work

- The process of independent estimating

- The relationship between the project team and the procurement office within the performing organization (if one exists)

- The management of lead time for procurement and vendor delivery

- Requirements for performance bonds and vendor insurance

- Identification of an approved vendors list (if appropriate according to organizational requirements)

- The procurement forms, such as contracts, the project team is required to use

- How multiple vendors will be managed to supply their contracted product

- The coordination between sellers and the project team and among project activities, project reporting, scheduling, business operations, and other project concerns

Using the Procurement Statement of Work

In the procurement statement of work (often just called the SOW), the seller fully describes the work to be completed and/or the product to be supplied. The SOW becomes part of the contract between the buyer and the seller. It is typically created as part of the procurement planning process, and it allows the seller to determine if he or she can meet the written requirements of the SOW.

Particular industries have different assumptions about what constitutes an SOW. What one industry calls an SOW may be a statement of objectives (SOO) in another. An SOO is a document describing a problem to be solved by the seller.

 EXAM TIP The SOW can be updated as the project moves through negotiations with the vendor or as more details about the purchase become available.

Creating the Procurement Documents

The primary outputs of the plan-contracting process are the procurement documents. These documents guide the relationship between the buyer and the seller. Communication between the buyer and the seller should always be specific as to the requirements and expectations of the seller. In initial communications, especially when requesting a price or proposal, the buyer should include the contract statement of work, relevant specifications, and, if necessary, any nondisclosure agreements (NDAs). Requests from buyers to sellers should be specific enough to give the seller a clear idea of what the buyer is requesting, but general enough to allow the seller to provide viable alternatives.

Here are some specific documents the project manager—and the PMP and CAPM candidate—should be familiar with:

- **Invitation for Bid (IFB)** From buyer to seller. Requests the seller to provide a price for the procured product or service.

- **Request for Quote (RFQ)** From buyer to seller. Requests the seller to provide a price for the procured product or service.

- **Request for Proposal (RFP)** From buyer to seller. Requests the seller to provide a proposal to complete the procured work or to provide the procured product.

- **Purchase order (PO)** A purchase order is a form of a unilateral contract that the buyer provides to the vendor and shows the purchase has been approved by the buyer's organization.

- **Request for Information (RFI)** From buyer to seller. Requests the seller to provide more information about the seller's products and/or services.

- **Bid** From seller to buyer. Price is the determining factor in the decision-making process.

- **Quotation** From seller to buyer. Price is the determining factor in the decision-making process.

- **Proposal** From seller to buyer. Other factors, such as skill sets, reputation, or ideas for the project solution may be used in the decision-making process.

EXAM COACH Obviously, there's a financial commitment from you to pass the PMP, but have you made a contract with yourself? Have you set the terms of your study efforts, your positive outlook for passing the exam, and the reward you'll receive for a passing score? Make a deal with yourself for passing your PMI exam—you deserve it!

Creating Source Selection Criteria

Another output of the plan-contracting process is the evaluation criteria. This is used to rate and score proposals from the sellers. In some instances, such as with a bid or quote, the evaluation criteria are focused just on the price the seller offers. In other instances, such as a proposal, the evaluation criteria can be multiple values: experience, references, certifications, and more. The project management team can use any combination of the following questions to help determine which vendor should be selected to supply the project's procurement needs:

- Does the vendor understand the project needs?
- What's the overall cost of the project?
- What's the life-cycle cost of the deliverable?
- Does the seller have the technical capability to complete the deliverable?
- What's the vendor's technical approach to the project's needs?
- What's the vendor's management approach to creating the deliverable?
- Does the seller have the financial backing to deliver as promised?
- Will the vendor have sustained capacity and interest in the project's deliverable for future assignments?
- What is the vendor's business model? Is it a small business, woman-owned, or disadvantaged business that may qualify for the contract as defined in some governmental agencies?
- Can the vendor provide references?
- Who retains the intellectual and proprietary property rights?

These questions—and others—can help the project management team make the best decision when it comes to choosing which vendor should support the project. For your PMP or CAPM exam, always choose the vendor that offers the best solution for the project.

Conducting Procurements

Once the plan-contracting process has been completed, the actual process of asking the sellers to participate can begin. Fortunately, the sellers, not the buyers, perform most of the activity in this process—usually at no additional cost to the project. The sellers are busy trying to win the business. There are eight inputs to the conduct procurement process:

- **Procurement management plan** This plan is needed because it directs the procurement processes. Go figure.

- **Procurement documents** These are created in plan-contracting processes. These are the Invitation for Bid (IFB), Request for Proposal (RFP), and Request for Quote (RFQ) documents.

- **Source selection criteria** The project management team and the organization identify what attributes the vendor must have to qualify for the contract.

- **Seller proposals** Vendors will provide the project manager a response to a RFP, IFB, or RFQ. Proposals will undergo an evaluation to determine how well the proposals satisfy the procurement need of the organization.

- **Project documents** You'll need to reference the risk register and risk-related contractual agreements if the project is to use the risk response of transference.

- **Make-or-buy decisions** The results of the project's make-or-buy decisions are needed because these direct the project manager to purchase resources for the project.

- **Procurement statement of work** The statement of work defines what your project wants to procure from the vendors. It lists the specifics of what you want to buy and what you want the vendors to provide. It's this document that the vendors will utilize to create their responses.

- **Organizational process assets** Yes, you've seen organizational process assets throughout the project, but the specific asset you're considering is a history of qualified sellers. A list of qualified sellers (also preferred sellers or approved sellers) generally has contact information, history of past experience with the seller, and other pertinent information. In addition to the internal qualified seller list, there are other resources that can help determine which sellers may qualify for the proposed work: Internet resources, industry directories, trade associations, and so on.

Hosting a Bidder Conference

Buy some donuts and make the coffee—all your bidders are coming over! A bidder conference, also called a contractor conference or vendor conference, is a meeting with prospective sellers to ensure that all sellers have a clear understanding of the product or service to be procured and are all on equal footing. Bidder conferences allow sellers to query the buyer on the details of the project statement of work to help ensure that their proposals are adequate and appropriate for the proposed agreement. At this point in the process, all sellers are considered equal.

Advertising for Sellers

Have you ever opened your Sunday newspaper and checked out the classifieds? Chances are, you've seen classified ads announcing opportunities for organizations to bid on upcoming projects. That's the idea behind this tool and technique. These advertisements usually run in newspapers or trade journals specific to the industry of the organization. Some government agencies require advertisements inviting sellers to solicit the project work, attend a bidder conference, or present a proposal for the described work.

Creating a Qualified Sellers List

One of the inputs to this process is to rely on your organizational process assets' qualified sellers list. If the organization doesn't have such a list, the project management team can start creating one. The qualified sellers list can be created through trade magazines, interviews, the Internet, interviews with past customers, and even site visits. It's a bunch of fun!

Selecting a Seller

Once the sellers have presented their proposals, bids, or quotes (depending on what the buyer requested), their documents are examined so that the project manager can select which sellers are the best choice for the project work. In many instances, price may be the predominant factor for choosing a particular seller—but not always. Other factors besides price may also be taken into consideration:

- The cost of an item may not reflect the true cost to the performing organization if the item cannot be delivered in a timely manner. If a seller promises to have a product on site by a specific date and fails to do so, the project can be delayed, costing the organization thousands—or more—in losses.

- Proposals can be separated into two categories: technical and commercial. The technical category describes the approach and methodology to complete the project work. The commercial category delves into the price to complete the project work. An evaluation takes into consideration both categories in order to determine the best choice for the project.

- Critical, high-priority projects may rely on multiple sellers to complete the project work. This redundancy can balance risk, cost, and opportunity among multiple vendors.

Examining Vendor Responses

The *procurement document package* is a collection of documents prepared by the buyer and sent to each of the vendors that may participate in the procurement process. The procurement document package defines the requirements of the purchase, specifies the needs, and describes how the vendor should respond.

The end result of requesting a seller response is, as expected, a collection of proposals, bids, or quotations, depending on what the buyer asked for. These documents indicate the sellers' ability and preparedness to complete the project work. The proposals should be in alignment with the stated expectations of the buyer, and they may be presented orally, electronically, or in hardcopy format. Of course, the relationship between the buyer and seller—and the type of information being shared—will determine which modality is the best choice of communication.

Choosing the Seller

For the performing organization to finalize the process of selecting a vendor, there must first be eligible sellers. Assuming more than one seller can satisfy the demands of the project, there are seven tools and techniques the project manager can rely on:

- **Weighting system**   A weighting system takes out the personal preferences of the decision maker in the organization to ensure that the best seller is awarded the contract. A weighting system creates a matrix, as seen in Figure 12-4. Weights are assigned to the values of the proposals, and each proposal is scored. Because the weights are determined before reviewing the proposals, the process is guaranteed to be free of personal preferences and bias. The seller with the highest score is awarded the contract.

- **Independent estimates**   These estimates are often referred to as "should/cost" estimates. These estimates are created either by the performing organization or outside experts to predict what the cost of the procured product should be. If there is a significant difference between what the organization has predicted and what the sellers have proposed, either the statement of work was inadequate, or the sellers have misunderstood the requirements.

Possible Score	20	20	15	10	10	5	20	100
Value	Experience	Certifications	Level IV Engineers	Security Clearance	Start Date	Waste Removal	Price	Total Score
ABC Constructions	15	20	7	10	10	5	12	79
Allen Builders	12	20	12	10	10	0	10	74
FRJ Construction	18	20	11	0	10	5	18	82
Howe & Who Construction	18	15	5	0	5	5	15	73
Martin & Martin	9	20	13	10	5	0	18	65
Ralph Engineers	15	8	8	0	10	5	17	73

Figure 12-4   A weighting system scores values to the seller's ability to deliver goods or services.

- **Screening system** A screening system is a tool that filters or screens out vendors that don't qualify for the contract. For example, the project manager could say that only vendors that have built eight bridges in Utah can qualify for the contract. Sellers that don't meet the requirements are removed from the selection process, and their proposals are not considered.

- **Contract negotiation** The performing organization creates an offer, and the seller considers the offer. The contract negotiation process is an activity to create a fair price for the work the seller is to complete. The performing organization and the seller must be in agreement on the expectations, requirements, authorities, terms, technical and business management approaches, price—and any other pertinent factors covered within and by the contract—prior to signing the contract.

- **Seller rating systems** Seller rating systems are used by organizations to rate prior experience with each vendor that it has worked with in the past. The seller rating system can track performance, quality ratings, delivery, and even contract compliance. The project manager of the current project can reference this internal seller rating system to determine the expectations of working with a vendor based on the vendor's past performance.

- **Expert judgment** Sometimes, the project manager isn't the best person to make a decision as to which vendor should be selected. Consider very large projects, like building a new skyscraper. The project manager likely wouldn't be the only person involved in making the procurement decision, but rather a team comprising different experts would contribute to the decision.

- **Proposal evaluation techniques** This big bucket of tools and techniques can include objective and subjective considerations from experts within the organization, weighting systems, multiple reviewers, scoring systems, screening systems—just about any source-selection technique that the project management team feels like using. The point is that there are many different approaches to compare and contrast proposals, so the project management team should use all of the appropriate techniques available to make the best decision for the good of the project.

- **Internet search** No doubt the Internet has changed the way companies buy and sell goods and services. Many commercially available goods can be located online at a guaranteed fixed-price for organizations. However, complex goods and services often can't use the Internet for cost estimating, budgeting, and exact pricing. The Internet can be used as a tool for procurement, but it's often just the start of the buyer–seller communication process.

Examining the Results of Seller Selection

The primary output, other than the selected seller, of the selecting seller process is a contract between the buyer and the seller. A contract is a legally binding agreement between the buyer and seller in which the seller provides the described product and the buyer pays for the product. Contracts are known by many names:

- Agreement
- Subcontract
- Purchase order
- Memorandum of understanding

 EXAM TIP A *letter of intent* is not a contract, but a letter stating that the buyer is intending to create a contractual relationship with the seller. A *letter contract* is a contract that may be used when the work needs to start immediately. A letter contract is often considered a "stopgap" solution in procurement.

Contracts have to be signed by a person with the power to authorize the requirements and payment specified in the contract. This role is called the delegation of procurement authority. Whether this person is the project manager depends on the procurement policies of the performing organization.

In some organizations, all contracts flow through centralized contracting. Centralized contracting requires all contracts for all projects to be approved through a central unit within the performing organization. Other organizations use a decentralized contracting approach, which assigns a contract administrator or contract officer to the project.

There are five other outputs of the conduct procurement process that PMP and CAPM candidates should be familiar with:

- **Project management plan updates** When dealing with large, unwieldy contracts, a new subsidiary management plan may need to be created. This subsidiary plan, the contract management plan, defines how the contract will be administered through the duration of the project. The contract may cause integration management to kick in. Changes to the procurement process, or changes to the procured item itself, may cause ripples in the procurement management plan, which also means updates to the project management plan.

- **Project document updates** The procurement process can create a need for the project documents to be updated. You may need to update the requirements documentation and the associated requirement traceability matrix. Based on the details of the contract type selected, there may be new risks introduced into the project, so the risk register and risk response plans may also need to be updated.

- **Resource calendars** The demand and availability of resources related to the contracted decision should be documented. This documentation includes when resources are active in the project and when they're not needed and can be utilized elsewhere.

- **Contract award**   The vendor that is selected for the project work is awarded the project contract. The contract includes the statement of work, schedule, performance requirements of the vendor, seller requirements, pricing, payment obligations, warranty of the work, and any terms for penalties. Some contracts define termination and alternative dispute resolution should there be claims or should the need diminish for the goods and services the contract provides.

- **Change requests**   We all know that change requests are likely to happen, and when dealing with procurement management, it's no different. Change requests are fed into the change control system, considered through integration change control, and, if approved, are then reflected in the time, cost, and scope baselines. Nothing new or surprising here.

Controlling Project Procurements

Controlling procurements is the process of ensuring that both the buyer and the seller live up to the agreements in the contract. The project manager and the contract administrator must work together to make certain the seller meets its obligations, just as the vendor will ensure that the buyer lives up to its agreements as well. If either party does not fulfill its contractual requirements, legal remedies may ultimately be pursued.

EXAM TIP   Because of the legalities associated with the contract, contract administration is often handled as an operation of the organization rather than as part of project management.

Another aspect of contract administration, especially on larger projects with multiple sellers providing various products, is the coordination between the contractors. The project manager or contract officer schedules and confirms the performance of the sellers so that the deliverables, schedule, and performance of a contractor do not infringe or adversely affect the performance of another contractor.

Within the contract must be the terms for payment. Typically, the performance and progress of the contractor is directly linked to payments it receives. The project manager must track performance and quality to approve or decline payment as needed. The contract should define the metrics for acceptance to avoid disagreements on performance.

This process is integrated into the project's control as a whole. You will likely perform procurement control along with other project management control processes to ensure that what happens in procurement doesn't adversely affect the remainder of the project. You'll direct and manage the procurement work and do quality control on what the vendor provides. You'll also need to perform integrated change control on any of the changes the procurement may bring about—or that get introduced to the project that could affect the contracted work. Finally, you will always be looking to control the risks associated with the procured work.

Completing the Procurement Control Process

The actual process of completing procurement control relies heavily on communication between the project manager, the contract officer, and the seller. The communications plan may have considerations for how and when the communication between the buyer and seller should take place and what the purpose of the communication should be. There are several tools and techniques to assist the project management team with the contract administration process:

- **Contract change control system** The contract change control system defines the procedures for how the contract may be changed. The process for changing the contract includes the forms, documented communications, dispute resolution procedures, tracking methods, the procedures for getting the changes approved within the performing organization, and the conditions within the project, business, or marketplace that justify the need for the change. The system is part of integrated change control.

- **Procurement performance reviews** The buyer has to confirm that the seller is living up to the terms of the contract. Specifically, the buyer reviews the quality of what the vendor has created, the cost of what's been created, and if the vendor is on schedule and in alignment with the agreement and the project scope. All of these items are documented in the terms of the contract—no fudging from the vendors is allowed.

- **Inspections and audits** If you hired an architect to build your dream home, would you wait until the house is completely built before inspecting the work? Of course not. You'd have to, and likely want to, perform periodic inspections, audits, and walkthroughs of the home as it's under construction. The same is true in project management: the buyer completes inspections and audits to confirm that the seller is abiding by the contracted requirements for the project.

- **Performance reporting** Performance reporting is the communication between the project manager and management on how the seller is performing under the guidelines in the contract. This is part of communications and should be documented within the communications management plan. The buyer has to confirm that the vendor is living up to the terms of the contract.

- **Payment systems** Sellers like to be paid when they have completed their obligations. How the sellers are paid is controlled by the payment system, which includes the interaction of the project manager and the accounts payable department. The performing organization may have strict guidelines for how payment requests are submitted and approved and how payments are completed. On larger projects, the project management team may have specific procedures for submitting the payment requests.

- **Claims administration** Uh-oh! Claims are disagreements between the buyer and the seller, usually centering on a change, who did the change, and even whether a change has occurred. Claims are also called disputes and appeals, and are monitored and controlled through the project in accordance with the contract terms. The contract can, and usually does, determine the path to resolution, which may include arbitration or litigation to resolve the claims between the buyer and seller. No fun. Alternative dispute resolution is an agreed-upon approach to work out the claim without, usually, involving the expense of lawyers and court cases.

- **Records management system** Guess what this system does. Yep. It records and organizes all of the documentation of the contract, the related communications, the work results, and the performance of the vendor. The records management system is part of the project management information system.

EXAM TIP Who's administering a contract manually? Information technology (IT) can help the project manager, the project management team, and the vendor efficiently abide by the terms of the contract and keep the project moving forward.

Reviewing the Results of Procurement Control

Procurement control calls for communication between the seller and buyer, the project manager and the vendor, and the stakeholders. There must be significant documentation of the agreement that both the buyer and the seller agree to before the procured work begins. Once the procured work, service, or product has been delivered from the seller to the buyer, there must be agreement that the delivery is in alignment with the original agreement. There are five outputs of the procurement control process:

- **Work performance information** Performance reporting is the communication between the project manager and management on how the seller is performing under the guidelines in the contract. This is part of communications and should be documented within the communications management plan. The buyer has to confirm that the vendor is living up to the terms of the contract. Specifically, the buyer reviews the quality of what the vendor has created, the cost of what's been created, and if the vendor is on schedule. All of these items are documented in the terms of the contract—no fudging from the vendors is allowed. Performance reviews can be an input to future procurement decisions.

- **Change requests** Changes to the project's scope, costs, or schedule can directly influence the contracted work between the buyer and the seller. Changes that affect the project contracts must flow through the contract change control system. Recall that the contract change control system defines the procedures for how the contract may be changed. The process for changing the contract includes the forms, documented communications, tracking methods, dispute resolution procedures, the procedures for getting the changes approved within the performing organization, and the conditions within the project, business, or marketplace that justify the need for the change. The system is part of integrated change control. The vendor may not be obligated to accept the changes to the contract and this can create claims and disputes between the vendor and the buyer.

- **Project management plan updates**   You may need to update the project management plan based on the outcomes of controlling procurement. For example, the project's procurement management plan could be updated based on procurement decisions. You may also need to update the schedule baseline based on the abilities of vendors to deliver the goods and services requested.

- **Project document updates**   Any procurement documentation should be included as part of the project's supporting detail and will become part of organizational process assets. Change requests related to the procured goods and services, technical specifications from the vendor, performance reports, and other communications are all included as part of project documentation.

- **Organizational process assets updates**   All procurement communications, outcomes of performance reporting, outcomes of inspections and audits, vendor invoices, and any documentation created and submitted by the vendor will become part of the project's archive and is technically an update to the organizational process assets.

Performing Contract Closure

Contract closure is analogous to administrative closure. Its purpose is to confirm that the obligations of the contract were met as expected. The project manager, the customer, key stakeholders, and, in some instances, the seller, may finalize product verification together to confirm that the contract has been completed.

Contract closure can also be linked to administrative closure, because it is the process of confirming that the work was finished. In instances where the contract was terminated, contract closure is reviewed, and the contract is considered closed because of the termination. The project records should be updated to reflect the contract closure and the acceptance of the work or product.

Auditing the Procurement Process

The successes and failures within the procurement process of the project are reviewed from the procurement planning stage through to contract closure. The intent of the audit is to learn what worked and what didn't during the procurement processes. This knowledge can then be applied to other areas within the current project and to other projects within the performing organization.

Negotiating Settlements

Before the contract can be officially closed, all issues, disputes, claims, and disagreements must be settled between the buyer and the seller. The terms of the contract override all other agreements, so this is one of the first things the two parties must agree upon (again!). The goal is to settle the disagreement in a fair manner, usually through alternative dispute resolution—which can include mediation and arbitration. If the buyer and seller can agree upon a settlement to an issue, then the claim is escalated to litigation and the court system. Almost all contracts define the court where the claim and associated lawsuit will be filed.

Completing Contract Closure

Once the deliverables have been accepted and the contract has been closed, it's essential to collect all of the contract information and to record it in the contract file. A *contract file* is a complete indexed set of records of the procurement process and is incorporated into the administrative closure process. These records include financial information as well as information on the performance and acceptance of the procured work.

Assuming the procured work is acceptable and meets the requirements of the contract, the contract can be closed. The formal closure of a project comes in a written notice from the contract officer to the seller. The notice informs the seller that the work is acceptable and that the contract is considered closed. The formal closure process may vary according to the size of the project. The requirements for contract closure should be documented within the contract.

Chapter Summary

Projects can buy or build as much as they need in order to be successful. Part of the procurement process is deciding what needs to be procured. The WBS and the project scope can help the project management team determine what things or services need to be procured in order for the project to be completed. Once the decision of what needs to be procured is made, the project manager can, often with the help of expert judgment, query the vendors for bids, quotes, or proposals based on the details of the project manager's SOW.

Vendors may need to attend a bidder conference in order to get clarification on the SOW—plus, it helps to chat with the project manager to get a clear understanding of what the project calls for. Vendors will then provide their quotes, bids, or proposals, according to what the project manager has requested. And then they'll hope they win the gig.

Once the project manager's organization has made the decision as to what vendor will be providing the service, the contract is issued. Now both parties have to live up to the terms and conditions of the contract. Of course, if there are issues that escalate during contract administration, there can be—gulp!—claims between the buyer and seller.

The project manager and the vendor should work together for the best interest of the project. During contract closure, the buyer inspects the project work and confirms that the vendor delivered and performed according to the contract terms. And then everyone lives happily ever after.

Key Terms

Alternative dispute resolution   When there is an issue or claim that must be settled before the contract can be closed, the parties involved in the issue or claim will try to reach a settlement through mediation or arbitration.

Bid   From seller to buyer. Price is the determining factor in the decision-making process.

Bidder conference   A meeting of all the project's potential vendors to clarify the contract statement of work and the details of the contracted work.

Claims   These are disagreements between the buyer and the seller, usually centering on a change, who did the change, and even whether a change has occurred. Claims are also called disputes and appeals, and are monitored and controlled through the project in accordance with the contract terms.

Contract   A contract is a formal agreement between the buyer and the seller. Contracts can be oral or written—though written is preferred.

Contract change control system   This defines the procedures for how the contract may be changed. The process for changing the contract includes the forms; documented communications; tracking; conditions within the project, business, or marketplace that justify the needed change; dispute resolution procedures; and the procedures for getting the changes approved within the performing organization.

Contract statement of work (SOW also CSOW)   This document requires that the seller fully describe the work to be completed and/or the product to be supplied. The SOW becomes part of the contract between the buyer and the seller.

Cost plus award fee contract   A contract that pays the vendor all costs for the project, but also includes a buyer-determined award fee for the project work.

Cost plus fixed fee contract   A contract that requires the buyer to pay for the cost of the goods and services procured plus a fixed fee for the contracted work. The buyer assumes the risk of a cost overrun.

Cost plus incentive fee   A contract type that requires the buyer to pay a cost for the procured work, plus an incentive fee, or a bonus, for the work if terms and conditions are met.

Cost plus percentage of costs   A contract that requires the buyer to pay for the costs of the goods and services procured plus a percentage of the costs. The buyer assumes all of the risks for cost overruns.

Direct costs   These are costs incurred by the project in order for the project to exist. Examples include the equipment needed to complete the project work, salaries of the project team, and other expenses tied directly to the project's existence.

Fixed-price contracts   Also known as firm fixed-price and lump-sum contracts, these are agreements that define a total price for the product the seller is to provide.

Fixed-price incentive fee   A fixed-price contract with opportunities for bonuses for meeting goals on costs, schedule, and other objectives. These contracts usually have a price ceiling for costs and associated bonuses.

Fixed-price with economic price adjustments   A fixed-price contract with a special allowance for price increases based on economic reasons such as inflation or the cost of raw materials.

Force majeure   An "act of God" that may have a negative impact on the project. Examples include fire, hurricanes, tornadoes, and earthquakes.

Independent estimates   These estimates are often referred to as "should cost" estimates. They are created by the performing organization or outside experts to predict what the cost of the procured product should be.

Indirect costs   These are costs attributed to the cost of doing business. Examples include utilities, office space, and other overhead costs.

Invitation for Bid (IFB)   From buyer to seller. Requests the seller to provide a price for the procured product or service.

Letter contract   A letter contract allows the vendor to begin working on the project immediately. It is often used as a stopgap solution.

Letter of intent   A letter of intent is not a contract, but a letter stating that the buyer is intending to create a contractual relationship with the seller.

Make-or-buy decision   A process in which the project management team determines the cost-effectiveness, benefits, and feasibility of making a product or buying it from a vendor.

Privity   The contractual relationship between the buyer and the seller is often considered confidential and secret.

Procurement management plan   A project management subsidiary plan that documents the decisions made in the procurement planning processes.

Procurement planning   A process to identify which parts of the project warrant procurement from a vendor by the buyer.

Proposal   A document the seller provides to the buyer. The proposal includes more than just a fee for the proposed work. It also includes information on the vendor's skills, the vendor's reputation, and ideas on how the vendor can complete the contracted work for the buyer.

Purchase order (PO)   A purchase order is a form of unilateral contract that the buyer provides to the vendor showing that the purchase has been approved by the buyer's organization.

Quotation   From seller to buyer. Price is the determining factor in the decision-making process.

Request for Proposal (RFP)   From buyer to seller. Requests the seller to provide a proposal to complete the procured work or to provide the procured product.

Request for Quote (RFQ)   From buyer to seller. Requests the seller to provide a price for the procured product or service.

Risk-related contractual agreements   When the project management team decides to use transference to respond to a risk, a risk-related contractual agreement is created between the buyer and the seller.

Screening system   A tool that filters or screens out vendors that don't qualify for the contract.

Seller rating systems   These are used by organizations to rate prior experience with each vendor that they have worked with in the past. The seller rating system can track performance, quality ratings, delivery, and even contract compliance.

Time and materials contract   A contract type in which the buyer pays for the time and materials for the procured work. This is a simple contract, usually for smaller procurement conditions. These contract types require a not-to-exceed clause, or the buyer assumes the risk for cost overruns.

Weighting system   This takes out the personal preferences of the decision maker in the organization to ensure that the best seller is awarded the contract. Weights are assigned to the values of the proposals, and each proposal is scored.

Case Study

Litke Greenhouse and Nursery: Procurement Processes

Litke Greenhouse and Nursery is Knoxville, Tennessee's agricultural supplier. They specialize in commercial and home-based plants, ranging from orchids and roses to dogwood and jasmine trees. Ros Litke, owner, sponsored a project to create a year-round garden and showcase that would serve multiple purposes:

- A greenhouse that could hold plants
- An educational facility for classes and seminars
- A marketing piece that could gain national attention
- A tourist destination for gardeners, photographers, and local residents

The project scope called for the design and installation of a large greenhouse like no other facility in the Southeast. The greenhouse simulates a lush Smoky Mountain cove with adult trees, younger saplings, indigenous plants, a water feature with rainbow trout, and a limited number of birds. The project was dubbed "Snapshot of East Tennessee" because it reflected the ideal East Tennessee environment.

Planning for Procurement

Ros Litke, the project sponsor, named Jen Stein as the project manager and Ty Koenig as the project manager assistant. When Jen, Ty, and the project team planned this project, they identified which deliverables in the WBS they would be able to feasibly create in-house and which items needed to be procured. The internal team was qualified to complete the placement of the plants, the design of the garden environment, and the installation of the water feature. The deliverables in the WBS that required procurement included:

- The architectural design and construction of the greenhouse
- The fish and wildlife for the greenhouse
- The marketing process to inform the public of the final product

The project team, Jen, and Ty determined that Litke Greenhouse and Nursery would need to procure these resources because the internal talent did not have the skill sets to complete the required work. In addition, the fish and birds required for the project would need to come from a supplier. While Litke Greenhouse and Nursery does have a full-time marketing manager, it was determined that this individual, Jeff Honeycutt, did not have the time to dedicate to the complete campaign. In addition, Jeff did not have the skill set to create the desired web site to promote the new space. Jeff Honeycutt was, however, involved with selecting the vendor for the marketing campaign.

As there were multiple items to procure, different procurement documents were created.

Procuring the Architectural Design

The vision of the finished project was discussed in detail with Ros Litke, Jen Stein, and Ty Koenig. The details of the facility were documented and mapped to a statement of work (SOW). The statement of work defined the design of the architectural plans according to the specifications of Litke Greenhouse and Nursery.

With the SOW created, Jen created a request for proposal that she submitted to five selected architectural and construction organizations.

Procuring the Wildlife

Based on the planned space of the facility, it was determined that eight birds and 144 rainbow trout would need to be procured. Jen created a Request for Quote (RFQ) for this procurement, because price was the only determining factor in the selection. The RFQ was sent to five suppliers of the birds and fish.

Procuring the Marketing

Jeff Honeycutt, the full-time marketing pro at Litke Greenhouse and Nursery, worked with Jen and Ty to define the SOW for the marketing. Because of the nature of the work to be procured, a Request for Proposal (RFP) was created. Jeff wanted a marketing company to see the whole vision of the project and then share that vision with the public.

Hosting a Bidder Conference

Jen and Ty agreed to meet with each of the proposed bidders to discuss the RFP, the project, and to answer any questions the bidders might have. The conferences were held on a preset date, as detailed in the RFP, and each bidder had the opportunity to schedule a 40-minute session with Jen and Ty. This allowed the vendor to clarify any issues and to gather as much detail as possible to create the proposal that he or she believed would be most valuable to the buyer.

A bidder conference was allowed for both the architectural and the marketing procurement processes. During the marketing bidder conferences, Jen and Ty relied on Jeff's marketing experience to help lead the conversation and to answer vendor questions.

A bidder conference was not needed for the procurement of the fish and birds. Jen and Ty did allow the bidders to call them to clarify any questions on the procured items. Only one bidder for the wildlife called with a question: "How many female rainbow trout would the project require?"

Selecting a Vendor

Jen and Ty read each of the proposals and bids supplied by the sellers. The bid for the wildlife was the easiest decision to make because it was driven solely by price. While all of the bids supplied for the wildlife were close, Jen and Ty selected the vendor with the lowest price. All of the vendors guaranteed their fish and fowl to be healthy and disease-free.

The architectural selection process was not as clear because of the proposals involved. Ty assisted Jen in creating evaluation criteria to compare and contrast each proposal. Proposals were ranked according to the following specifications:

- Qualifications and experience of each firm
- Ability to address all issues in the provided statement of work
- Ability to fulfill the design and construction based on the determined timeline
- New ideas presented within the proposal
- Price

Based on this ranking of information, Jen selected an architectural firm to design and build the facility. Jen and Ty followed a similar approach in selecting the marketing vendor, but also involved Jeff Honeycutt to make the best decision.

Negotiating the Contract

After selecting the vendors for each of the items that needed procurement, Jen worked with the vendors to negotiate the contract. Each contract was relative to the type of work or item to be procured. For example, the architectural firm initially wanted a cost plus percentage of costs contract. This would have caused the final price for the project to fluctuate based on the costs of the materials throughout the project.

Jen negotiated with the seller to use a fixed-price and incentive fee contract for the project. This contract ensured that the vendor would receive a guaranteed fee for the project work, but also created an opportunity to gain a bonus if the contracted work was completed ahead of schedule.

The contracted work for the marketing was assigned to a time and materials contract. This contract type allowed the selected marketing firm to bill for time invested in the project's marketing creation, the web site, and on marketing literature. The contract did, however, include a not-to-exceed fee for the entire project work. Jen and the seller agreed that reports on the expense of the work would be provided every two weeks. This would allow Jen to track the marketing expenses against the deliverables the seller was creating.

Questions

1. You are the project manager of the Adams Construction Project. Some of the work in the project contains pure risk that you're not willing to accept. You decided to mitigate the pure risks in this project. Which of the following may be used as a risk mitigation tool?

   A. The vendor proposal

   B. The contract

   C. The quotation

   D. Project requirements

2. You are the project manager for the 89A Project. You have created a contract for your customer. The contract must have what two things?

   A. An offer and consideration

   B. Signatures and the stamp of a notary public

   C. Value and worth of the procured item

   D. Start date and acceptance of start date

3. Britney is the project manager of the FTG Software Project. She's relying on the project scope to help her analyze the procurement needs of the project. The project scope statement can help a project manager create procurement details. Which one of the following best describes this process?

   A. The project scope statement defines the contracted work.

   B. The project scope statement defines the requirements for the contract work.

   C. The project scope statement defines the contracted work, which must support the requirements of the project customer.

   D. Both parties must have and retain their own copy of the product description.

4. Yolanda has outsourced a portion of a project to a vendor. The vendor has discovered some issues that will influence the cost and schedule of its portion of the project. How must the agreement be updated?

   A. As a new contract signed by Yolanda and the vendor.

   B. As directed by the contract change control system.

   C. As a memo and SOW signed by Yolanda and the vendor.

   D. Project management contracts have clauses that allow vendors to adjust their work according to unknowns.

5. You are creating a new contract for some procured work in the project. Your manager wants you to define how issues and claims will be resolved including the possibility of any lawsuits related to the procured work. The United States backs all contracts through which of the following?

   A. Federal law

   B. State law

   C. The court system

   D. Lawyers

6. Terry is the project manager of the MVB Project. She needs to purchase a piece of equipment for her project. The accounting department has informed Terry that she needs a unilateral form of contract. Accounting is referring to which of the following?

   A. The statement of work (SOW)

   B. A legally binding contract

   C. A purchase order

   D. An invoice from the vendor

7. You are a project management consultant for the Hopson Company and you're working with them to determine the best vendor and contract choice for a portion of their project. The purpose of a contract is to distribute between the buyer and seller a reasonable amount of what?

   A. Responsibility

   B. Risk

   C. Reward

   D. Accountability

8. You are the project manager of the Communications Projects for your organization. Management has stressed that you use privity throughout this project. Privity is what?

   A. The relationship between the project manager and a known vendor

   B. The relationship between the project manager and an unknown vendor

C. The contractual, confidential information between customer and vendor

D. The professional information regarding the sale between customer and vendor

9. Sammy is the project manager of the DSA Project. He is considering proposals and contracts presented by vendors for a portion of the project work. Of the following, which contract is least risky to the DSA Project from Sammy's perspective?

A. Cost plus fixed fee

B. Cost plus percentage of cost

C. Cost plus incentive fee

D. Fixed-price

10. Bradley is the project manager of the Warehouse Remodeling Project for his company. He is in the process of determining which contracts to use in this project. His company is risk-averse, so the correct choice of contract is important to Bradley. Of the following contract types, which one requires the seller to assume the risk of cost overruns?

A. Cost plus fixed fee

B. Cost plus incentive fee

C. Lump-sum

D. Time and materials

11. Benji is the project manager of the PLP Project. He has hired an independent contractor for a portion of the project work. The contractor is billing the project $120 per hour plus materials. This is an example of what?

A. Cost plus fixed fee

B. Time and materials

C. Unit price

D. Lump-sum

12. Mary is the project manager of the JHG Project. She has created a procurement statement of work (SOW) for a vendor. What project component is the procurement statement of work based on?

A. The project scope statement

B. The work breakdown structure (WBS)

C. The scope baseline

D. The WBS dictionary

13. You are the project manager for a software development project for an accounting system that will operate over the Internet. Based on your research, you have discovered that it will cost you $25,000 to write your own code.

Once the code is written, you estimate you'll spend $3,000 per month updating the software with client information, government regulations, and maintenance. A vendor has proposed to write the code for your company and charge a fee based on the number of clients using the program every month. The vendor will charge you $5 per month per user of the web-based accounting system. You will have roughly 1,200 clients using the system per month. However, you'll need an in-house accountant to manage the time and billing of the system, so this will cost you an extra $1,200 per month. How many months will you have to use the system before it is better to write your own code than to hire the vendor?

A. 3 months

B. 4 months

C. 6 months

D. 15 months

14. Henry has been negotiating with the ABN Contracting Company for two weeks regarding some procured work on the project. Henry has sent the ABN Contracting Company a letter of intent. This means what?

A. Henry intends to sue the ABN Contracting Company.

B. Henry intends to buy from the ABN Contracting Company.

C. Henry intends to bid on a job from the ABN Contracting Company.

D. Henry intends to fire the ABN Contracting Company.

15. Martha is the project manager of the MNB Project. She wants a vendor to offer her one price to do all of the detailed work. Martha will issue which type of document?

A. A Request for Proposal (RFP)

B. A Request for Information (RFI)

C. A proposal

D. An Invitation for Bid (IFB)

16. You are the project manager for your company and you have six vendors on your project. You've worked with the vendors collectively to organize and schedule their overlapping work, scope control, and changes within their contract requirements. You have created many procurement documents in this project. Which one of the following is true about procurement documents?

A. They offer no room for bidders to suggest changes.

B. They ensure receipt of complete proposals.

C. They inform the performing organization why the bid is being created.

D. The project manager creates and selects the bid.

17. You are the project manager of the SRQ City Network Project for your company. You will be managing the selection of several vendors to participate in this process and your project team wants to know when seller selection actually happens. In what process group does the select seller event happen?

    A. Initiating

    B. Planning

    C. Executing

    D. Closing

18. You have an emergency on your project. You have hired a vendor who is to start work immediately. What contract is needed now?

    A. T&M

    B. Fixed-price

    C. Letter contract

    D. Incentive contract

19. You are the project manager for a seller and are managing another company's project. Things have gone well on the project, and the work is nearly complete. There is still a significant amount of funds in the project budget. The buyer's representative approaches you and asks that you complete some optional requirements to use up the remaining budget. You should do what?

    A. Negotiate a change in the contract to take on the additional work.

    B. Complete a contract change for the additional work.

    C. Gain the approval of the project stakeholder for the requested work.

    D. Deny the change because it was not in the original contract.

20. There are some risks that you can do little about. In your most recent project, for example, a tornado has wrecked your construction project. The tornado is known as what?

    A. A force majeure

    B. A risk transference

    C. Direct costs

    D. An unknown unknown

Questions and Answers

1. You are the project manager of the Adams Construction Project. Some of the work in the project contains pure risk that you're not willing to accept. You decided to mitigate the pure risks in this project. Which of the following may be used as a risk mitigation tool?

    A. The vendor proposal

B. The contract

C. The quotation

D. Project requirements

> **B.** Contracts can be used as a risk mitigation tool. Procurement of risky activities is known as transference; the risk does not disappear, but the responsibility for the risk is transferred to the vendor. A, C, and D are all incorrect. A vendor proposal, a quotation, and project requirements do nothing to serve as a risk mitigation tool.

2. You are the project manager for the 89A Project. You have created a contract for your customer. The contract must have what two things?

A. An offer and consideration

B. Signatures and the stamp of a notary public

C. Value and worth of the procured item

D. Start date and acceptance of start date

> **A.** Of all the choices presented, A is the best choice. Contracts have an offer and a consideration. B is incorrect because not all contracts demand -signatures and notary public involvement. C is incorrect because a contract may not explicitly determine what the value and worth of the procured product or service is. D is also incorrect because a contract may specify a start date, but the acceptance of the start date is vague and not needed for all contracts.

3. Britney is the project manager of the FTG Software Project. She's relying on the project scope to help her analyze the procurement needs of the project. The project scope statement can help a project manager create procurement details. Which one of the following best describes this process?

A. The project scope statement defines the contracted work.

B. The project scope statement defines the requirements for the contract work.

C. The project scope statement defines the contracted work, which must support the requirements of the project customer.

D. Both parties must have and retain their own copy of the product description.

> **C.** The project scope statement defines the details and requirements for acceptance of the project, serves as a valuable input to the process of determining what needs to be procured, and defines what the end result will be. When dealing with vendors to procure a portion of the project, the procured work must support the requirements of the project's customer. A is incorrect because the project scope statement defines the project as a whole, not just the contracted work, which may be just a portion of the project. B is

incorrect because the project scope statement does not define the requirements for the contract work. D is also incorrect because the vendor likely will not have a copy of the product description.

4. Yolanda has outsourced a portion of a project to a vendor. The vendor has discovered some issues that will influence the cost and schedule of its portion of the project. How must the agreement be updated?

   A. As a new contract signed by Yolanda and the vendor.

   B. As directed by the contract change control system.

   C. As a memo and SOW signed by Yolanda and the vendor.

   D. Project management contracts have clauses that allow vendors to adjust their work according to unknowns.

   B. This is the best answer of all the choices presented. The contract change control system will determine the best route to incorporate the change. A, while feasible, is not the best answer to the question. A new contract does not update the original agreement and may cause delays because the contract may have to be resubmitted, reapproved, and so on. C and D are not viable answers.

5. You are creating a new contract for some procured work in the project. Your manager wants you to define how issues and claims will be resolved including the possibility of any lawsuits related to the procured work. The United States backs all contracts through which of the following?

   A. Federal law

   B. State law

   C. The court system

   D. Lawyers

   C. All contracts in the United States are backed by the U.S. court systems. A, B, and D are all incorrect answers.

6. Terry is the project manager of the MVB Project. She needs to purchase a piece of equipment for her project. The accounting department has informed Terry that she needs a unilateral form of contract. Accounting is referring to which of the following?

   A. The statement of work (SOW)

   B. A legally binding contract

   C. A purchase order

   D. An invoice from the vendor

   C. A purchase order is an example of a unilateral contract. A, B, and D are all incorrect answers. An SOW is a statement of work, and a legally binding contract does not fully answer the question. D, an invoice from the vendor, is not what the purchasing department is requesting.

7. You are a project management consultant for the Hopson Company and you're working with them to determine the best vendor and contract choice for a portion of their project. The purpose of a contract is to distribute between the buyer and seller a reasonable amount of what?

A. Responsibility

B. Risk

C. Reward

D. Accountability

B. A fair contract shares a reasonable amount of risk between the buyer and the seller. A is incorrect because a contract may transfer the majority of the responsibility to the vendor. C is incorrect because the reward is not an appropriate answer to the question. D is also incorrect because the accountability of the services contracted to the vendor is not shared between the buyer and the seller.

8. You are the project manager of the Communications Projects for your organization. Management has stressed that you use privity throughout this project. Privity is what?

A. The relationship between the project manager and a known vendor

B. The relationship between the project manager and an unknown vendor

C. The contractual, confidential information between customer and vendor

D. The professional information regarding the sale between customer and vendor

C. Privity is a confidential agreement between the buyer and seller. A, B, and D are incorrect choices because these do not fully answer the question.

9. Sammy is the project manager of the DSA Project. He is considering proposals and contracts presented by vendors for a portion of the project work. Of the following, which contract is least risky to the DSA Project from Sammy's perspective?

A. Cost plus fixed fee

B. Cost plus percentage of cost

C. Cost plus incentive fee

D. Fixed-price

D. A fixed-price contract contains the least amount of risk for a buyer. The seller assumes all of the risk. A, B, and C are incorrect because these contract types carry the risk of cost overruns being assumed by the buyer.

10. Bradley is the project manager of the Warehouse Remodeling Project for his company. He is in the process of determining which contracts to use in this project. His company is risk-averse so the correct choice of contract is

important to Bradley. Of the following contract types, which one requires the seller to assume the risk of cost overruns?

A. Cost plus fixed fee

B. Cost plus incentive fee

C. Lump-sum

D. Time and materials

C. A lump-sum contract provides a fixed fee to complete the contract; the seller absorbs any cost overruns. A and B are incorrect because these contracts do not require the seller to carry the risk of cost overruns. D is incorrect because a time and materials contract requires the buyer to pay for cost overruns on the materials and the time invested in the project work.

11. Benji is the project manager of the PLP Project. He has hired an independent contractor for a portion of the project work. The contractor is billing the project $120 per hour plus materials. This is an example of what?

A. Cost plus fixed fee

B. Time and materials

C. Unit price

D. Lump-sum

B. The contractor's rate of $120 per hour plus the cost of the materials is an example of a time and materials contract. A is incorrect because a cost plus fixed fee contract charges the cost of the materials, plus a fixed fee, for the installation or work to complete the contract. C is incorrect because a unit price contract has a set price for each unit installed on the project. D is also incorrect because a lump-sum contract does not break down the time and materials.

12. Mary is the project manager of the JHG Project. She has created a procurement statement of work (SOW) for a vendor. What project component is the procurement statement of work based on?

A. The project scope statement

B. The work breakdown structure (WBS)

C. The scope baseline

D. The WBS dictionary

C. The statement of work is developed from the scope baseline. A, B, and D are all incorrect because these are the three components of the scope baseline.

13. You are the project manager for a software development project for an accounting system that will operate over the Internet. Based on your research, you have discovered that it will cost you $25,000 to write your own code. Once the code is written, you estimate you'll spend $3,000 per month

updating the software with client information, government regulations, and maintenance. A vendor has proposed to write the code for your company and charge a fee based on the number of clients using the program every month. The vendor will charge you $5 per month per user of the web-based accounting system. You will have roughly 1,200 clients using the system per month. However, you'll need an in-house accountant to manage the time and billing of the system, so this will cost you an extra $1,200 per month. How many months will you have to use the system before it is better to write your own code than to hire the vendor?

A. 3 months

B. 4 months

C. 6 months

D. 15 months

C. The monies invested in the vendor's solution would have paid for your own code in six months. This is calculated by finding your cash outlay for the two solutions: $25,000 for your own code creation; zero cash outlay for the vendor's solution. The monthly cost to maintain your own code is $3,000. The monthly cost of the vendor's solution is $7,200. Subtract your cost of $3,000 from the vendor's cost of $7,200 and this equals $4,200. Divide this number into the cash outlay of $25,000 to create your own code, and you'll come up with 5.95 months. Of all the choices presented, C, 6 months, is the best answer. A, B, and D are all incorrect because they do not answer the question.

14. Henry has been negotiating with the ABN Contracting Company for two weeks regarding some procured work on the project. Henry has sent the ABN Contracting Company a letter of intent. This means what?

A. Henry intends to sue the ABN Contracting Company.

B. Henry intends to buy from the ABN Contracting Company.

C. Henry intends to bid on a job from the ABN Contracting Company.

D. Henry intends to fire the ABN Contracting Company.

B. Henry intends to buy from the ABN Contracting Company. A, C, and D are all incorrect because these choices do not adequately describe the purpose of the letter of intent.

15. Martha is the project manager of the MNB Project. She wants a vendor to offer her one price to do all of the detailed work. Martha will issue which type of document?

A. A Request for Proposal (RFP)

B. A Request for Information (RFI)

C. A proposal

D. An Invitation for Bid (IFB)

> **D.** An Invitation for Bid (IFB) is a request for a sealed document that lists the seller's firm price to complete the detailed work. A and B, Request for Proposal (RFP) and Request for Information (RFI), are documents from the buyer to the seller requesting information on completing the work. C, a proposal, does not list the price to complete the work, but instead offers solutions to the buyer for completing the project needs.

16. You are the project manager for your company and you have six vendors on your project. You've worked with the vendors collectively to organize and schedule their overlapping work, scope control, and changes within their contract requirements. You have created many procurement documents in this project. Which one of the following is true about procurement documents?

    A. They offer no room for bidders to suggest changes.

    B. They ensure receipt of complete proposals.

    C. They inform the performing organization why the bid is being created.

    D. The project manager creates and selects the bid.

> **B.** Procurement documents detail the requirements for the work to ensure complete proposals from sellers. A is incorrect because procurement documents allow input from the seller to suggest alternative ways to complete the project work. C is incorrect because informing the performing organization as to why the bid is being created is not the purpose of the procurement documents. D is not realistic.

17. You are the project manager of the SRQ City Network Project for your company. You will be managing the selection of several vendors to participate in this process and your project team wants to know when seller selection actually happens. In what process group does the select seller event happen?

    A. Initiating

    B. Planning

    C. Executing

    D. Closing

> **C.** The select seller event happens during the execution process group. The process is the conduct procurement process and is based primarily on the outcomes of the procurement planning process. A, B, and D are all incorrect because these process groups do not include source selection.

18. You have an emergency on your project. You have hired a vendor who is to start work immediately. What contract is needed now?

    A. T&M

    B. Fixed-price

C. Letter contract

D. Incentive contract

> C. For immediate work, a letter contract may suffice. The intent of the letter contract is to allow the vendor to get to work immediately to solve the project problem. A, B, and D are all incorrect because these contracts may require additional time to create and approve. When time is of the essence, a letter contract is acceptable.

19. You are the project manager for a seller and are managing another company's project. Things have gone well on the project, and the work is nearly complete. There is still a significant amount of funds in the project budget. The buyer's representative approaches you and asks that you complete some optional requirements to use up the remaining budget. You should do what?

A. Negotiate a change in the contract to take on the additional work.

B. Complete a contract change for the additional work.

C. Gain the approval of the project stakeholder for the requested work.

D. Deny the change because it was not in the original contract.

> C. Any additional work is a change in the project scope. Changes to the project scope should be approved by the mechanisms in the contract change control system. The stakeholder needs to approve the changes to the project scope. A, B, and D are not realistic expectations of the project. This question borders on the PMP Code of Professional Conduct. Typically, when a project scope has been fulfilled, the project work is done. The difference in this situation is that the additional tasks are optional requirements for the project scope.

20. There are some risks that you can do little about. In your most recent project, for example, a tornado has wrecked your construction project. The tornado is known as what?

A. A force majeure

B. A risk transference

C. Direct costs

D. An unknown unknown

> A. Force majeure, sometimes called "an act of God," is a natural disaster that can wreck a project. B, risk transference, is incorrect because this describes the response to the risk, not the tornado itself. C, direct cost, describes costs that cannot be shared with other organizations but that are attributed directly to your project. D, an unknown unknown, does not fully describe the tornado as A does, so this choice is also incorrect.

Managing Project Stakeholder Management

In this chapter, you will
- Identify the project stakeholders
- Plan for stakeholder management
- Manage stakeholder engagement
- Control stakeholder engagement

I've always said that the hardest part of the project isn't execution, following processes or regulations, or even planning complex work. The hardest part of the project is dealing with people. People can be demanding, unreasonable, rude, shift their priorities, and exhibit many other bad behaviors you've probably already experienced as a project manager. People can also be wonderful, kind, caring, and genuinely interested in the project. They can be reasonable, understand how their demands don't mesh with what they've already asked you for in the project, and can be your biggest allies in getting the project done.

These are the project stakeholders, and they are looking to you to complete the project work, not spend too much money, and beat a deadline. Stakeholders are the people who are affected by your project and those who can affect your project—for better or worse. Stakeholder management, the focus of this chapter, is a new knowledge area in the PMBOK Fifth Edition. In older PMBOK versions, stakeholder management was still considered but was lumped into other knowledge areas rather than pulled out as one big topic. I think the subject is a great addition to the latest PMBOK Guide, and along with project communication, is probably where you'll spend the bulk of your time as a project manager.

 VIDEO For a more detailed explanation, watch the *Mapping the Stakeholders* video now.

Because this is a new knowledge area, I'd reason that you'll see plenty of exam questions on stakeholder management on your CAPM and PMP exams. Spend a little extra time in this chapter and with the chapter key terms to make sure you've got the science, theory, and PMI approach down for stakeholder management. There are just four processes in this new knowledge area: identifying stakeholders, planning stakeholder management, managing stakeholder engagement, and controlling stakeholder engagement. The basic theme of these four processes is that you need to identify, engage, and manage how you interact with the project stakeholders. If you master this knowledge area, you'll be on your way to becoming a fantastic project manager—and a certified one.

Identifying Project Stakeholders

Just to be clear, stakeholders are the people who can affect your project and also be affected *by* your project. Affecting your project means that the stakeholder can positively or negatively influence it. Your project can do the same to stakeholders' lives. For instance, imagine a construction project to replace an existing bridge and all the people that could be involved in that project. You'll work with architects, engineers, construction gurus, and the day-to-day workers on the project. There will be city planners, government inspectors, and other bureaucrats involved in the project. You'll also have all of the people who live near the bridge eagerly awaiting its completion and possibly aggravated by the inconvenience your project causes them.

All of these people are stakeholders who can affect your project, and whose lives you'll be affecting. Now imagine if you didn't take the time to identify the correct stakeholders for the project. What would happen if you forget to identify the government agencies for the bridge project? Or you forget to identify the people who use the bridge every day as part of their commute? Or you miss identifying the architect for the bridge? Stakeholder identification is vital to project success. You and the project team must pause and really think about the stakeholders and how your project affects them, and also how the stakeholders can affect your project.

Stakeholder identification should happen as early as possible in the project. If you wait too long to properly identify the stakeholders, you may end up missing decisions and requirements that will only cause the project to stall, you could possibly create bad relationships with the stakeholders, and perhaps cause turmoil within the project. Stakeholder identification is a project initiating activity and requires the project manager, the project team, and other stakeholders to help identify who should be involved in the project. As you identify stakeholders, you'll classify them according to their power, influence, interests, and other characteristics so as to help you better manage the project and control stakeholder engagement.

Preparing for Stakeholder Identification

Let's go back to that bridge construction project. How do you know who should be included as a stakeholder? You could rely on your experience as a project manager, and those colleagues you know who are part of the project, but what other things would help you really capture all of the stakeholders in the project? There are four definite things you should always have as you begin stakeholder identification:

- **Project charter** The project charter should identify some of the parties involved in the project. The charter can identify the project sponsor, of course, the project manager, and it can identify other parties affected by the project and the people who may also be working with the project manager to plan and complete the project. For example, in the bridge construction project, your project charter may include any vendors that your company has partnered with to complete the work.

- **Procurement documents** When you have a contract between two or more parties you've identified some stakeholders. In the bridge construction project, you'll procure materials and probably hire resources from different companies. These companies are now stakeholders in your project—they can affect your project in a positive way or a negative way depending on how they live up to the terms of the contract. You'll also have internal stakeholders who are identified through procurement documents—consider the employees you work with to complete procurement. Your company may have a central contracting office, an accounts payable office, and a procurement office. These are all stakeholders now as they too can affect your project positively or negatively. In this instance, procurement documents will help you identify project stakeholders.

- **Enterprise environmental factors** You can identify stakeholders through the enterprise environmental factors you're working with in your project. The culture of your company, how your organization is identified, and the departments and offices you're obliged to work with can all reveal project stakeholders. Your industry regulations, government agencies, and industry standards are also part of enterprise environmental factors, and these elements can help you identify stakeholders, too. Depending on where the project is taking place in the world, you may also have local influences that should be considered to be stakeholders.

- **Organizational process assets** Don't forget to look at past projects to identify current stakeholders. If you've done similar work in the past, you'll probably have some of the same or similar stakeholders. Your organizational process assets can also include stakeholder identification approaches, a stakeholder register template, and lessons learned. Use what already exists so you can work smarter and not harder.

These four elements are the inputs to stakeholder identification. You'll want to gather these elements as early as possible in the project to begin identifying the stakeholders. Don't wait too long into the project or you'll find you've not considered all of the stakeholders and their concerns for it.

Identifying the Project Stakeholders

Now that you've gathered the need inputs to stakeholder analysis, it's time to officially launch stakeholder identification. Stakeholder identification aims to identify the stakeholders, document who the stakeholders are, and record their interests, contributions, and expectations for the project. There are just three tools and techniques for stakeholder identification, but they are exhaustive and broad-reaching. You should know these tools not just for your examination, but also for your role as a project manager.

Stakeholder identification is also linked closely with project communications. Recall that you'll plan for project communication and identify who needs what information, when the information is needed, and how the information is to be delivered. Stakeholder identification and communication planning can go hand in hand because you'll need to identify the stakeholders before you can determine what communication demands they may have.

Performing Stakeholder Analysis

Some stakeholders are more important than others. Yeah, I said that. Some stakeholders, like the CEO of your company who's counting on your team to implement a new piece of software, is probably more important than the new receptionist who doesn't like the new software. Too bad for her that she thinks the software looks "icky." She may be a stakeholder, but the CEO of the company has far more power and influence than the receptionist does. Stakeholder analysis is the process of analyzing and classifying the stakeholders and interests in the project. It helps you determine and prioritize the needs and requirements of the stakeholders.

Stakeholder analysis follows three steps:

- Identify and document the stakeholders' contact information, knowledge, expectations of the project, and their level of influence over project decisions.

- Prioritize and classify stakeholders based on their power, influence, expectations, and concerns for the project.

- Plan for managing the stakeholders based on possible negative or positive scenarios in the project that may affect the stakeholders.

 EXAM TIP To identify stakeholders, it's useful to ask known stakeholders who else should be involved in the project.

Classifying Stakeholders

One of the best tools in stakeholder analysis is a classification model. A classification model is a way to group and prioritize stakeholders. There are four models (three of which are very similar) you should know for your PMP or CAPM exam:

- **Power/influence grid** This is a grid, as shown in Figure 13-1, that plots out the amount of power and influence a stakeholder has over the project. You'll position the stakeholder on this grid based on the amount of power and influence they have. Stakeholders with high power and high influence are top priority. Stakeholders with little power and influence are still considered, but they have less priority than other stakeholders in the project.

- **Power/interest grid** This grid also maps out stakeholders' power over the project, but considers their interest in the project as a consideration for prioritization of their project needs, expectations, and contributions.

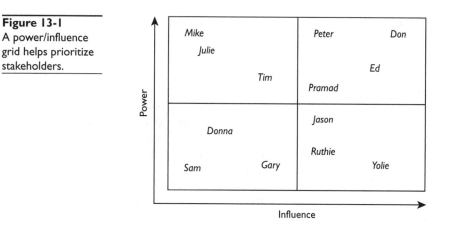

Figure 13-1
A power/influence grid helps prioritize stakeholders.

- **Influence/impact grid**   This classification model considers the influence the stakeholder may have over the project, but also considers the impact the stakeholder can bring to the project. Consider stakeholders who may have little influence, but whose presence or absence from the project could have great impact—such as a key project team member.

- **Salience model**   This model, shown in Figure 13-2, maps out stakeholders' power, urgency, and legitimacy in the project. Power means they can enforce their will on the project's success. Urgency describes the stakeholders' need for attention. Legitimacy describes if their involvement in the project is even warranted.

Finalizing Stakeholder Identification

The final two tools and techniques for stakeholder identification are meetings and expert judgment. First, let's talk about meetings. Stakeholder identification meetings,

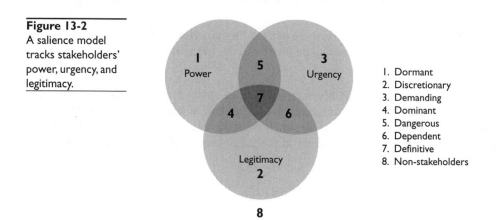

Figure 13-2
A salience model tracks stakeholders' power, urgency, and legitimacy.

1. Dormant
2. Discretionary
3. Demanding
4. Dominant
5. Dangerous
6. Dependent
7. Definitive
8. Non-stakeholders

sometimes called profile analysis meetings, help the project manager and the management team realize the expectations and interests of the key project stakeholders. These meetings are useful to identify and document the different roles in the project, the types of stakeholders you'll work with, and all of the differing objectives, interests, and inputs for the project.

As you meet with your project team and your key stakeholders, you may also rely on expert judgment to help identify and analyze stakeholders. Expert judgment simply means you're working with someone who has more insight on the stakeholders, the type of work being done, or can identify stakeholders you may have overlooked. Experts can be individuals from the project team, business leaders in your company, clients, vendors, consultants, government agencies, focus groups, and more. You're working with these people and groups to ensure that you've identified all of the stakeholders in the project.

Creating the Stakeholder Register

Stakeholder identification is only as good as the documentation that comes out of the process. The stakeholder register is the only output of stakeholder identification. It's a log of all of the stakeholder information you've gathered in the project. It will help you communicate with project stakeholders, ensure you understand the stakeholders' needs, wants, and expectations, and it helps you classify stakeholder objectives and priorities. The stakeholder register is a document that will identify at least three things about your project stakeholders:

- **Identification** You'll need to capture the stakeholder names, project role, company position, contact information, and where they're located should you need to meet with them face to face

- **Assessment information** Stakeholders expectations are documented in the stakeholder register. You'll capture the stakeholders' primary expectations, their expected contributions to the project, influence, and the periods of the project when you anticipate the stakeholder to be most involved and interested in the project.

- **Stakeholder classification** A primary activity of stakeholder identification is to classify the stakeholders by their role, position, attitude toward the project, and other factors.

The creation of the stakeholder register isn't a one-time event. You'll refer to the stakeholder register throughout the project and update it as new information becomes available. For example, stakeholders may leave the project, new stakeholders could be identified in the project, and stakeholder attitudes and influences can change as the project is in motion.

Planning Stakeholder Management

Now that you've identified the stakeholders, how will you manage them? Planning stakeholder management creates the stakeholder management plan and helps you and the project team create a strategy for stakeholder management and engagement. Imagine that you're the project manager of a large project to install new software throughout your company. Some of your stakeholders are excited for the new software—these are positive stakeholders. Other stakeholders hate the idea of changing software and learning something new—these are negative stakeholders. And some of the stakeholders don't care either way—these are neutral stakeholders. Each of these stakeholder types need to be managed by you and the project team.

Planning stakeholder management is the process of determining how stakeholders will be affected and how you'll manage the project in consideration of the stakeholders. This means you'll be working to engage the stakeholders—to get them involved in the project, to maintain their interest, calm their fears and threats the project may be causing—and working with the stakeholder to create relationships among the project team, the customers, vendors, and all stakeholders in the project. You, the project manager, are at the center of stakeholder management, but you also want your project team to work proactively to engage stakeholders support the project objectives.

This planning process, like almost all the planning processes, creates a plan. The stakeholder management plan defines your approach for stakeholder engagement. As the project moves through its life cycle, the stakeholder concerns, interests, support, and interactions may fluctuate. It's because of this fluctuation in stakeholder involvement that you'll likely revisit stakeholder management planning many times throughout the project. Don't worry—this is expected because stakeholder management planning is an iterative activity throughout the entire project.

Preparing to Plan for Stakeholder Management

You won't just rush into stakeholder management planning—surely by this point in the book you know that you'll always arm yourself with some inputs to effectively start off these processes. This planning process is no different. While you may have a good idea what stakeholders expect from the project, you need to consider what stakeholders expect from you as the project manager. This includes the key stakeholders like your project sponsor and the project customer, but you must also consider your most trusted stakeholders: the project team.

To plan for stakeholder management, you'll need four inputs:

- **Project management plan**   Yes, yes, the stakeholder management plan is part of the project management plan, but you're going to need a bunch of other stuff from the project management plan to help you create the stakeholder management plan. You'll need the project management plan because it defines:
  - The life cycle of the project and its phases

- Selected processes for the project

- The plan for project work execution

- Human resource requirements, roles and responsibilities, reporting relationships, and staffing management approaches

- The change management plan

- Communication requirements and strategy

- **Stakeholder register**   Recall that the stakeholder register is an output of stakeholder identification. The stakeholder register will identify the stakeholders, their contact information for communications, and what their expectations of the project are.

- **Enterprise environmental factors**   Recall that organizational structure, the culture of the organization, and even the politics can all affect how you plan for stakeholder management.

- **Organizational process assets**   Of course, you'll rely on organizational process assets to help with the current project's stakeholder management planning. Consider elements like historical files, templates, lessons learned, and other data from past projects as part of your organizational process assets items.

If you're working through project planning, you'll probably already have these inputs readily available. These are similar inputs you'll use in planning the project communications. Stakeholder management and communications work together, but there is a difference. Project communications is about getting the right stakeholder the right information. Stakeholder engagement is about getting stakeholders involved and acting on the communications you give them.

Creating the Stakeholder Management Plan

Now that you've gathered the necessary inputs to planning stakeholder engagement, you'll need to gather the correct experts to help. Stakeholder engagement planning isn't a solo activity—you'll need experts from around your organizations and possibly consultants to help with the planning. Subject matter experts for actually creating the stakeholder engagement plan include senior management, consultants, the project team, leaders within the organization, other project managers with similar project experience, and other needed and identified experts within your organization. The goal is to include as many readily available experts to help you accurately plan an approach to engage your stakeholders.

When you have all of these experts together, either one on one or through a group format, you're going to be hosting meetings. Yes, meetings are one of the tools and techniques for creating the stakeholder engagement plan. These meetings can be traditional conference room events, focus groups, or even panels. The goal isn't to get fancy, just to define the needed engagement level for the stakeholders. Engagement levels define the amount of interest the stakeholder has in the project, but also the amount of support the stakeholder may have, or lose, in the project. There are five engagement levels:

- **Unaware**   The stakeholder doesn't know about the project and the effect the project may have on them.

- **Resistant**   The stakeholder knows about the project and doesn't want the change the project may bring.

- **Neutral**   The stakeholder knows about the project, but neither supports nor resists the project.

- **Supportive**   The stakeholder knows about the project and is supportive of the change the project will bring about.

- **Leading**   The stakeholder knows about the project, is supportive of the change the project may bring about, and is working to make the project successful.

In larger projects with lots of different stakeholders, you may find it beneficial to create a Stakeholder Engagement Assessment Matrix. This is a table that defines all of the stakeholders and their engagement levels in the project. This can help you identify stakeholder trends, commonalities, and group stakeholders together by their level of support in the project. Stakeholders are tagged in the matrix with a C, for current engagement level, and D for their desired engagement level. Not all stakeholders need to be in the leading category, but your strategy may work to get most stakeholders to at least the supportive level for the project.

Examining the Stakeholder Management Plan

There are two results of planning for stakeholder management: the stakeholder management plan and updates to the project documents. The primary output of this process, the stakeholder management plan, aims to engage stakeholders and keep stakeholders engaged throughout the entire project. The stakeholder management plan may contain sensitive information that shouldn't necessarily be shared with everyone. You may need to protect the contents of the stakeholder management plan from the project team and other stakeholders. The stakeholder management plan defines several things:

- Changes the project will bring to stakeholders
- Current and desired levels of stakeholder engagement
- Interrelationships among stakeholders
- Communication requirements throughout the project
- Information to be distributed to stakeholders and why the information is needed by the stakeholders

- Timing of communications
- Conditions and methods for updating the stakeholder management plan

The second output of planning for stakeholder engagement includes the project document updates. The project schedule is a likely candidate for what may be updated as a result of the stakeholder planning process. Consider the timing of communications, meetings, and feedback for the project stakeholders. You might also update the stakeholder register if new stakeholders are identified during planning or if the details of an identified stakeholder changes as a result of planning.

Managing Stakeholder Engagement

As a project manager, you'll constantly work to engage the project stakeholders. This means communication, fostering relationships, facilitating meetings, negotiating, settling disputes, and managing all of the questions, demands, and inputs from the project stakeholders. Managing stakeholder engagement is a constant, ongoing activity—it's what's expected of you as the project manager. You'll have to be available to the project stakeholders, but it also means you must go seek out stakeholders when conditions and situations call for you to get stakeholders more (or less) involved in the project.

Managing stakeholder engagement works right along with the project communications, but it's more than just communicating. Think of all the different types of stakeholders you could have on any of your projects. Surely some of these stakeholders require a bit more attention than others. And some of your stakeholders may offer minimal input, stay out of the way, or dodge the project as much as possible. Other stakeholders may be in your office once, twice, or several times every day with a new fire drill and panic each time. That's stakeholder engagement, giving your time and attention to what's most important in the project while maintaining stakeholder interest, commitment, and buy-in of the project objectives.

Stakeholder influence on the project objectives is usually highest in the early parts of the project. Once you've garnered commitment from the stakeholders, identified the agreed-upon project scope, and set the project to work executing the plans, stakeholder influence should wane. As the project moves forward, some stakeholders may still try to influence the project for their objectives and goals, and you may have to get the project sponsor involved to squelch some of the more overbearing stakeholders. You'll also manage, track, and report on issues that happen in the project that may affect stakeholders. It's an ongoing process.

Preparing to Manage the Stakeholders

The stakeholder management plan will be your primary input to the actual management of stakeholders' engagement. Recall that the stakeholder management plan describes the approach to get the stakeholder involved in the project, how best to communicate with the stakeholders, and the desired level of stakeholder engagement. You'll rely on this plan, along with other parts of the project management plan (such as the communications management plan) to work with the stakeholders to create synergy, promote buy-in, and interact with the stakeholders.

As I mentioned, much of stakeholder engagement is related to the communications management plan. It is the second input for managing stakeholder engagement. This plan will help you review the communication requirements of the project stakeholders. You'll need to know what information is to be communicated and when the stakeholders are expecting the communication. Of course, not all information is to be distributed to all of the stakeholders—some people just don't need (or want) to know everything. The communications management plan defines who needs what information—this is important so you don't send confidential information to the wrong people.

Recall that change is inevitable in most projects. The change log documents the changes that have occurred in the project and the changes that have been proposed in the project. The change log will help you manage stakeholder engagement because you'll need to relay information about change to the appropriate parties. Change can be a sensitive issue in some instances, so always examine the change and think through all of the possible scenarios and reactions the stakeholders may have to the change. Cost and schedule are the two largest concerns most stakeholders have with changes, but you may also need to consider the effect a change has on the project scope. In addition, the project scope may mean changes in other parts of the scope. It's also possible that due to time, costs, risks, or other concerns, you've been forced to remove things from scope. This is another thing that needs to be communicated delicately to stakeholders.

Finally, you'll also rely on organizational process assets to help you prepare in managing stakeholder engagement. Your organization may have forms, templates, and requirements for communications. You may have issue management policies to follow that may alter your approach to stakeholder engagement. Whatever the organizational process assets that can affect your stakeholder engagement, it's a good idea to think through what's being communicated, how you're communicating the information, and what the anticipated reaction is from the stakeholder.

Managing the Stakeholder Engagement

Managing the stakeholder engagement is really about creating and fostering relationships with the people in your project. You want the project to be successful and you need the buy-in and synergy from your project stakeholders. Sure, some low-influence, low-power stakeholders can refuse to buy in to the project, object to the project goals throughout the entire project life cycle, and hate your guts, and you can still be successful. But it's not an enjoyable project when you're fighting a challenging stakeholder the entire time. No one wants to do that.

For your PMI exams, you want stakeholders to be supportive of the project. This means you'll use communication methods and interpersonal skills as your stakeholder engagement tools and techniques. You know communication already—it's how you spend the bulk of your time as a project manager. You have planned the communication, identified who needs what information, documented when the information will be needed, and you know the modality of the information. Good communicators generally make good project managers. Interpersonal skills are the characteristics that make people like you, or at least work with you, as a project manager. Interpersonal skills involve:

- **Trustworthiness**   People need to be able to trust the project manager.

- **Conflict resolution**   Stakeholders will look to the project manager to resolve conflicts.

- **Active listening**   Making sure you understand the message and its underlying meaning.

- **Overcoming resistance to change**   You need to help stakeholders see why the project is important and how it affects their lives.

Of course, project management isn't all about getting people to like you and trust you. Project management is really about getting things done. Management skills are the tools you'll need as part of stakeholder engagement to move the project toward its completion. Management skills are things that involve:

- **Negotiations**   You'll have to lead negotiations regarding give and take on project objectives.

- **Influence**   You'll need to persuade people to buy in and support the project.

- **Facilitation**   Through meetings and messages, you'll build consensus on project goals.

- **Behavior management**   You'll have to modify stakeholder behavior to lead them to accepting the project and its objectives.

Managing stakeholder engagement takes practice and time. The longer you work as a project manager, the better you'll become at engaging stakeholders. Treat people the way they want to be treated, don't make promises you cannot keep, and always do what's in the best interest of the project and you'll be well on your way to not only engaging stakeholders, but also becoming a leader in your project environment.

Reviewing Stakeholder Engagement Results

Because stakeholder engagement is a process—and something you'll do throughout the project—you can expect some outputs of the process. While it may be important to know the results of stakeholder engagement for your PMI exam, it's also important to know what all the actions in this process are creating for your project. Of course, you don't want to just do a process because it's handy and makes sense, you want to do it because you're creating things that can help your project become more successful—and this will make you more successful in your career, too.

Managing stakeholder engagement creates five outputs:

- **Issue log**   An issue log can be created as an output of managing stakeholders. As issues are identified, updated, and resolved, an issue log is updated to reflect the status of the issues.

- **Change requests**   Change requests can come as a result of stakeholder engagement. Changes to the project scope, schedule, corrective actions, and preventive actions are all changes that can stem from stakeholder engagement. Changes can also happen with the communication approach and interaction with the project stakeholders.

- **Project management plan updates**   Based on what you learn in stakeholder engagement, you may need to update the project management plan. Updates are likely going to be in the stakeholder management plan and in the project communications management plan. Stakeholders may change the way they want you to communicate with them, the information they want in the project, or even how they want the information delivered. If there are changes, defects, issues, and even conflict resolution, you may need to update the project management plan to reflect these concerns.

- **Project documents updates**   You may need to update the stakeholder register if new stakeholders are identified in the project, stakeholder information changes, or stakeholders leave the project.

- **Organizational process assets updates**   This involves future historical information, which means you'll be updating organizational process assets with new information that can be leveraged later in the current project or in future projects. Organizational process assets updates can include:

  - **Lessons learned documentation**   What you learn and document in the project can utilized later in the project or in similar projects. Root cause analysis of issues, supporting details of corrective actions, preventive actions, and changes should be included as part of lessons learned documentation. Any other stakeholder management lessons from the project should also be recorded as part of the project's lessons learned documentation.

  - **Stakeholder notifications**   The information you send and receive from stakeholders becomes part of organizational process assets.

  - **Feedback from stakeholders**   Communications from stakeholders become part of the project's organizational process assets.

  - **Project reports**   Reports on the project's performance, issues, risks, and closure are part of organizational process assets.

  - **Project records**   Communications, meeting minutes, reports, and all other types of stakeholder communications are part of organizational process assets.

  - **Project presentations**   Presentations you present to the project stakeholders are part of organizational process assets.

Controlling Stakeholder Engagement

Controlling stakeholder engagement doesn't mean you're controlling what stakeholders do, but rather you're controlling the stakeholder engagement process. Think of it as a check-up for the project management team and key stakeholders to ensure that all of the stakeholder management work is being done properly, effectively, and according to the stakeholder management plan. As the project moves deeper into its project life cycle, you and the project team will work through stakeholder engagement. There can become a lovely rhythm or a dreadful rut in the relationships created in stakeholder engagement. This process ensures that you're following the stakeholder management plan and meeting stakeholder expectations.

Controlling stakeholder engagements also occurs when conditions in the project change. For example, let's revisit a bridge construction project. If the bridge construction project is expected to last six months, that's six months of some unhappy residents that are delayed or detoured because of your bridge project. The residents may be happy for the new bridge, but the pain of the delay and detour is still aggravating. Now imagine there's been rough weather, delays due to poor materials, or other issues that have crept into the project. forcing your timeline to be expanded to ten months. Conditions within the project have changed and you'll need to communicate with the stakeholders about the delay, but you'll also need to continue to engage the stakeholders in the project. You'll have to remind them about the new bridge, how much safer it will be for them, and communicate other upbeat information to keep the stakeholders engaged.

EXAM TIP   Don't engage the stakeholders just when there is good news or bad news. Controlling stakeholder engagement is a continuous process throughout the project.

Preparing to Control Stakeholder Engagement

In order to control the stakeholder engagement, you'll need some inputs to the project. Specifically, you'll need four things to get this process moving:

- **Project management plan**   The project management plan will define the life cycle of the project, the execution of the project work, human resource requirements, roles and responsibilities, staffing management, change management, and communication requirements for stakeholders.

- **Issue log**   You'll use the issue log to document, review, and update issues as part of stakeholder engagement.

- **Work performance data**   You'll need insight into how well the project is performing in order to communicate with and engage the stakeholder appropriately.

- **Project documents** All of the supporting details for the project and the corresponding documentation can contribute to controlling stakeholder engagement. Consider the project schedule, stakeholder register, issue log, change log, and the project communications as the key project documents you'll need for this process.

Controlling Stakeholder Engagement

The actual day-to-day work of controlling stakeholder engagement is reliant on just three tools and techniques. First, you'll need an information management system. An information management system is where you'll document project information like estimated and actual project costs, schedule progress, and overall project performance. It's the system you'll use for project and performance reporting for the project stakeholders. The information management system is the repository of all your project information. This could be inside your favorite project management software, a spreadsheet you've created, or a database. Whatever approach you and your organization decide to use, it's only as good as the last time it was updated.

The second tool and technique is to rely on expert judgment to help control the stakeholder engagement, identify new stakeholders as needed, and do periodic reassessments of the stakeholders' attitudes and concerns toward the project. Expert judgment can come from:

- Project managers
- Senior management
- Other key stakeholders
- Subject matter experts
- Consultants
- Trade associations

Your expert judgment resources can contribute through one-on-one meetings, focus groups, or even surveys. Whatever approach you take, you must document the approach and the outcomes of the event, and then act on what you've learned.

The third and final tool and technique for controlling stakeholder engagement is every project manager's favorite: meetings. Yes, good old meetings help you control stakeholder engagement because they allow you to bring stakeholders together to review status, talk about the project performance, and analyze stakeholder information. Meetings should have an agenda and a set time period, and someone should keep minutes from the meeting.

Reviewing the Outputs of Stakeholder Engagement

So you're working at controlling stakeholder engagement. Guess when this process ends? When execution is done and the project moves into closing, that's when. It's a long, iterative controlling process that you'll do throughout the entire project. As you control stakeholder engagements, you'll be creating five things for your project and organization:

- **Work performance information**   The performance data from across the project is collected and organized into comprehensive work performance information. This is needed for project communications with the stakeholders. You'll share project status, project performance reports, forecasts for costs and schedule, and other information with the stakeholders.

- **Change requests**   Yes, change requests can be a result of controlling stakeholder engagement. Corrective actions and preventive actions are the most likely changes you'll have as a result of controlling stakeholder engagement.

- **Project management plan updates**   You may need to update the project plan as a result of controlling stakeholder engagement. While all areas of the project management plan may need to be updated, the most likely components to be updated are the:
  - Change management plan
  - Communications management plan
  - Cost management plan
  - Human resource management plan
  - Procurement management plan
  - Requirements management plan
  - Risk management plan
  - Schedule management plan
  - Scope management plan
  - Stakeholder management plan

- **Project document updates**   Just as you may need to update the project management plan, you may also need to update the project documents. Specifically, the stakeholder register will likely be updated as a result of controlling the stakeholder engagement, as will the issue log to reflect any issue changes or new issues in the project.

Chapter Summary

Project stakeholder management is an ongoing activity in the project to ensure that the stakeholders are identified, analyzed, and engaged throughout the project life cycle. It's no secret that in many projects people are excited about the new endeavor, but as the project moves into its planning and execution, the excitement and interest can wane.

It's up to the project manager to ensure that stakeholders are communicated with and actively engaged in an ongoing effort during the project.

This new knowledge area in PMBOK Fifth Edition has just four processes. The first process, which is part of project initiation, is to identify the project stakeholders. Recall that this activity should be as early as possible in the project to ensure that the correct stakeholders are identified and classified for proper planning and engagement. If you fail to identify a stakeholder, the stakeholder could, based on their power and influence in the organization, cause your project to be delayed, create additional costs, or even have it canceled. That's why it's imperative to find and classify the project stakeholders.

The second process in this knowledge area is to plan stakeholder management. This process created the stakeholder management plan to ensure that the stakeholders have been identified and that their needs are met during the project. Through the analysis and classification of the stakeholders, you'll identify the level of engagement of the project stakeholders. Recall that there are five levels of stakeholder engagement: unaware, resistant, neutral, supportive, and leading. These classifications can help you set goals in a stakeholders' engagement assessment matrix to move stakeholders to new levels of engagement.

The execution of engaging the project stakeholder really comes down to two key tools: interpersonal skills and management skills. Interpersonal skills are characteristics like being trustworthy, resolving conflict, and overcoming resistance to change. These are more of the soft skills of project management that foster a good working relationship between the project manager and the stakeholders. The second set of skills is lumped into management skills. These are activities like facilitating consensus, influencing people for project support, negotiating agreements, and changing organizational behavior for the betterment of the project.

The final process in project stakeholder management is the controlling of stakeholder engagement. This process ensures that the project manager, the project team, and other stakeholders are all being engaged and contributing to the project as needed. Through information management systems, the project manager can collect performance data and create reports, communications, and track events in the project for the stakeholders. Expert judgment and meetings can also help the project manager ensure that the stakeholders are being engaged and are informed as directed in the stakeholder management plan.

Key Terms

Interactive communications   This type of communication means that information is happening among stakeholders, like in a forum. Examples of interactive communications are meetings, videoconferences, phone calls, and ad-hoc conversations. Interactive communications means that the participants are actively communicating with one another.

Key stakeholder   Stakeholders—such as management, the project manager, program manager, or customers—that have the authority to make decisions in the project.

Leading stakeholder status   Part of stakeholder analysis classification. A leading stakeholder is aware of your project, they want your project to be successful, and the stakeholder is working to make certain the project is a success.

Negative stakeholder   A stakeholder who does not want the project to exist and is opposed to the project.

Neutral stakeholder   A stakeholder who has neither a positive nor negative attitude about the project's existence.

Neutral stakeholder status   Part of stakeholder analysis classification. A neutral stakeholder is aware of your project and is not concerned if the project succeeds or fails.

Positive stakeholder   A stakeholder who sees the benefits of the project and is in favor of the change the project is to bring about.

Profile analysis meeting   This is an analysis meeting to examine and document the roles in the project. The role's interests, concerns, influence, project knowledge, and attitude are documented.

Pull communications   This type of communication pulls information from a central repository. Pull communications allow stakeholders to retrieve information from a central source as needed.

Push communications   This type of communication happens when the sender pushes the same message to multiple people. Good examples of push communications are broadcast text messages, faxes, press releases, and group e-mails.

Reporting system   A reporting system is a software program to store and analyze project data for reporting. A common reporting system will take project data, allow the project manager to pass the data through earned value management, for example, and then create forecasting reports about the project costs and schedule.

Resistant stakeholder status   Part of stakeholder analysis classification. A resistant stakeholder is aware of your project, but they do support the changes your project will create.

Stakeholder   Anyone who is affected by the existence of the project or who can affect the project's existence. Stakeholders can enter and exit the project as conditions change within the project.

Stakeholder analysis   An activity that ranks stakeholders based on their influence, interests, and expectations of the project. Stakeholders are identified and ranked, and then their needs and expectations are documented and addressed.

Stakeholder classification models   These are charts and diagrams that help the project manager determine the influence of stakeholders in relation to their interest in the project. Common classification models include the power/interest grid, the power/influence grid, the influence/impact grid, and the salience model.

Stakeholder engagement   The project manager works to keep the project stakeholders interested, involved, and supportive of the project. Through communication, management skills, and interpersonal skills, the project manager can work to keep the project stakeholders engaged and interested in the project.

Stakeholder identification   A project initiation activity to identify, document, and classify the project stakeholders as early as possible in the project.

Stakeholder management   The project management knowledge area that focuses on the management and engagement of the project stakeholders. There are four processes in this knowledge area: identify stakeholders, plan stakeholder management, manage stakeholder engagement, and control stakeholder engagement.

Stakeholder management plan   The stakeholder management plan documents a strategy for managing the project stakeholders. The stakeholder management plan establishes stakeholder engagement and defines how the project manager can increase and improve stakeholder engagement.

Stakeholder management planning   The project manager works with the project team and subject matter experts to create a strategy to manage the project stakeholders.

Stakeholder register   A documentation of each stakeholder's contact information, position, concerns, interests, and attitude toward the project. The project manager updates the register as new stakeholders are identified and when stakeholders leave the project.

Supportive stakeholder status   This is part of stakeholder analysis classification. A supportive stakeholder is aware of your project and is supportive and hopeful that the project will be successful.

Unaware stakeholder status   Part of stakeholder analysis classification. An unaware status means the stakeholder doesn't know about the project and the effect the project may create on the stakeholder.

Questions

1. You are the project manager of the GUY Project for your organization. This project has recently been chartered and you're starting the process of stakeholder identification. In this process, you're working with your project team, some of the known stakeholders, and your project sponsor. Which one of the following inputs will you NOT need for the stakeholder identification process?

   A. Organizational process assets

   B. Communications management plan

   C. Procurement documents

   D. Project charter

2. Beth is the project manager for a large health care project. She is working with the project sponsor to define the steps she'll use to perform stakeholder analysis. Which of the following correctly defines the steps for stakeholder analysis?

    A. Identify and document the stakeholder information, create a communications management plan, plan for stakeholder management.

    B. Identify and document the stakeholder information, prioritize and classify the stakeholders, create the communications management plan for stakeholder management.

    C. Identify and document the stakeholder information, prioritize and classify the stakeholders, plan for stakeholder management.

    D. Create a focus group for known stakeholders, identify and document the stakeholder information, prioritize and classify the stakeholders, plan for stakeholder management.

3. You are the project manager for your organization. Management has asked you to create a stakeholder classification model to show the amount of authority stakeholders have over project decisions in relation to how much their political capital and position in the company could affect the project. What type of stakeholder classification model should you create?

    A. A power/influence grid

    B. A RAM matrix

    C. An influence/impact grid

    D. A RACI chart

4. Henry has been tasked to create a salience model for his project. This model defines three characteristics for project stakeholders. Which one of the following is NOT one of the three characteristics of the stakeholders mapped in the salience model?

    A. Power

    B. Urgency

    C. Legitimacy

    D. Influence

5. You are the project manager of a large technology project for your company. This project will span the United States and parts of Europe. There are key stakeholders in all countries represented. As part of your stakeholder analysis you'd like to create a document that captures all of the stakeholders' contact information, assessment information, and classification in the project. What type of document are you creating?

    A. Stakeholder directory

    B. Stakeholder management plan

    C. Stakeholder register

    D. Stakeholder communications matrix

6. Terry is the project manager of the ARB project for his company. Terry approaches Scott for his insight about the schedule for releasing the product the project will create. Scott doesn't know anything about the project Terry is working on and is surprised to learn about the product. What type of stakeholder is Scott?

   A. Unaware

   B. Uninformed

   C. Neutral

   D. Sensitive

7. You are a project management consultant for your company and you're meeting the stakeholders for the first time. Mary, a stakeholder, tells you that she hates the project and she hopes that it fails miserably. What type of stakeholder is Mary?

   A. Resistant

   B. Unhappy

   C. Honest

   D. Defiant

8. You are the project manager of the HQL Project for your company. Henry, a stakeholder, is in favor of your project and he's working with you to express the importance of the project. Henry has offered to help with the project, communicate with other stakeholders, and host status meetings. What type of stakeholder is Henry?

   A. Supportive

   B. Cheerleader

   C. Contractual

   D. Leading

9. Sammy is the project manager of the KHG Project. Some of the stakeholders in this project are opposed to the project, some are in favor of the project, and some stakeholders are neutral. Management has asked Sammy to create a chart that shows the current status of engagement for each stakeholder and the desired level of engagement for each stakeholder. What type of chart is management asking for?

   A. Stakeholder engagement mapping

   B. Stakeholder engagement control chart

   C. Stakeholder histogram

   D. Stakeholder engagement assessment matrix

10. You are the project manager of the GUY Project for your company and you're working with your project team on some stakeholder issues. You want to examine the interrelationships among the project stakeholders for better communications. What project management plan will you refer to?

    A. Project communications management plan

    B. Project stakeholder management plan

    C. Project stakeholder register

    D. Project staffing management plan

11. Holly is a new project manager and she's confused about the need for the change log and how it relates to the stakeholder engagement. Why is the change log an input to the management stakeholder engagement process?

    A. Because it documents any changes to the stakeholder contact information

    B. Because it documents any changes to the stakeholder register

    C. Because it communicates changes to the stakeholders

    D. Because it communicates changes about the stakeholders to management

12. Part of stakeholder management is the reliance on interpersonal skills. Which one of the following is an interpersonal skill?

    A. Facilitation

    B. Analysis of product scope

    C. Conflict resolution

    D. Influence

13. Just as you need interpersonal skills, you'll also need management skills to effectively engage the stakeholders in the project. Which one is a management skill?

    A. Trustworthiness

    B. Active listening

    C. Influence

    D. Conflict resolution

14. As a PMP and CAPM candidate, you should be familiar with the inputs, tools and techniques, and outputs of the project management process. The management of stakeholder engagement creates five outputs. Which one of the following is not an output of the process?

    A. An issue log

    B. Change requests

    C. Project management plan updates

    D. Project schedule for stakeholder communications

15. You are coaching several new project managers on effective control of stakeholder engagement. The project managers are confused as to why change requests come from this process. What is the most likely type of change that will come from controlling stakeholder engagements?

    A. Technology change

    B. Errors or omissions in requirements

    C. External changes

    D. Corrective actions

16. Ned is the project manager of the NHQ Project and he's meeting with a few key stakeholders to determine their roles, interests, concerns, influence, and attitude about the project. What type of meeting is Ned hosting?

    A. Kickoff meeting

    B. Stakeholder classification meeting

    C. Profile analysis meeting

    D. Stakeholder status meeting

17. What type of communication is happening in a meeting with several stakeholders exchanging ideas?

    A. Interactive

    B. Push-pull

    C. Conferring

    D. Cooperative

18. You are the project manager of a large construction project. You have created a website that allows the different functional managers to log in to a secured area, run queries, and generate reports on the time, cost, scope, changes, risks, and human resource aspects of your project. What type of communication is this?

    A. Pull

    B. Push

    C. Conferring

    D. Static

19. Which one of the following examples best describes a push communication?

    A. A blog about the project

    B. A secured blog for functional managers

    C. A project newsletter for the stakeholders from the project manager

    D. The project management plan

20. Your project has 45 stakeholders as of today. You've just learned that next week 29 new stakeholders will be joining the project. How many more communication channels will you have next week?

A. 406

B. 990

C. 1711

D. 2701

Questions and Answers

1. You are the project manager of the GUY Project for your organization. This project has recently been chartered and you're starting the process of stakeholder identification. In this process, you're working with your project team, some of the known stakeholders, and your project sponsor. Which one of the following inputs will you NOT need for the stakeholder identification process?

A. Organizational process assets

B. Communications management plan

C. Procurement documents

D. Project charter

B. The communications management plan is not an input to the stakeholder identification process. Choices A, C, and D are incorrect because these answers are inputs to the stakeholder identification process. The four inputs to this process are project charter, procurement documents, enterprise environmental factors, and organizational process assets.

2. Beth is the project manager for a large health care project. She is working with the project sponsor to define the steps she'll use to perform stakeholder analysis. Which of the following correctly defines the steps for stakeholder analysis?

A. Identify and document the stakeholder information, create a communications management plan, plan for stakeholder management.

B. Identify and document the stakeholder information, prioritize and classify the stakeholders, create the communications management plan for stakeholder management.

C. Identify and document the stakeholder information, prioritize and classify the stakeholders, plan for stakeholder management.

D. Create a focus group for known stakeholders, identify and document the stakeholder information, prioritize and classify the stakeholders, plan for stakeholder management.

C. Of all the choices presented, C is the best answer. Stakeholder identification starts with the project manager identifying and documenting the stakeholders' contact information, knowledge, expectations of the project, and their level of influence over project decisions. Then, the project manager must prioritize and classify stakeholders based on their power, influence, expectations, and concerns for the project. Finally, Beth should plan for managing the stakeholders based on possible negative or positive scenarios in the project that may affect the stakeholders. A, B, and D are incorrect because these answers do not reflect the correct ordering of steps for stakeholder analysis.

3. You are the project manager for your organization. Management has asked you to create a stakeholder classification model to show the amount of authority stakeholders have over project decisions in relation to how much their political capital and position in the company could affect the project. What type of stakeholder classification model should you create?

   A. A power/influence grid

   B. A RAM matrix

   C. An influence/impact grid

   D. A RACI chart

   A. Management is asking you to create a power/influence grid. Evaluating the amount of power and influence a stakeholder has over the project will determine where the stakeholder is placed on the grid. Stakeholders with high power and high influence are top priority. Stakeholders with little power and influence are still considered, but they have less priority than other stakeholders in the project. B is incorrect because a RAM is a responsibility assignment matrix. C is incorrect because this classification model focuses on the influence of the stakeholders and the impact, not the power. D is incorrect because RACI is a responsibility matrix that tracks a person's responsibility, accountability, consulted, or informed status for each assignment in the project.

4. Henry has been tasked to create a salience model for his project. This model defines three characteristics for project stakeholders. Which one of the following is NOT one of the three characteristics of the stakeholders mapped in the salience model?

   A. Power

   B. Urgency

   C. Legitimacy

   D. Influence

   D. A salience model plots out a person's power, urgency, and legitimacy in the project. It does not include their influence. A, B, and C are incorrect because these answers are part of the salience model.

5. You are the project manager of a large technology project for your company. This project will span the United States and parts of Europe. There are key stakeholders in all countries represented. As part of your stakeholder analysis you'd like to create a document that captures all of the stakeholders' contact information, assessment information, and classification in the project. What type of document are you creating?

A. Stakeholder directory

B. Stakeholder management plan

C. Stakeholder register

D. Stakeholder communications matrix

C. You are creating a stakeholder register. The stakeholder register is the only output of stakeholder identification. It's a log of all the stakeholder information you've gathered in the project. It will help you communicate with project stakeholders, ensure that you understand the stakeholders needs, wants, and expectations, and helps you classify stakeholder objectives and priorities. A and D are incorrect because there are no project management documents called the stakeholder directory or the stakeholder communications matrix. B is incorrect because the stakeholder management plan defines how the stakeholder will be identified and engaged, and how stakeholder engagement will be controlled.

6. Terry is the project manager of the ARB project for his company. Terry approaches Scott for his insight about the schedule for releasing the product the project will create. Scott doesn't know anything about the project Terry is working on and is surprised to learn about the product. What type of stakeholder is Scott?

A. Unaware

B. Uninformed

C. Neutral

D. Sensitive

A. Scott is an unaware stakeholder. Scott doesn't know about the project and the effect the project may have on him. B and D are incorrect choices because there is no stakeholder classification known as uninformed or sensitive. C is also incorrect because neutral describes a stakeholder who is neither opposed nor in favor of the project.

7. You are a project management consultant for your company and you're meeting the stakeholders for the first time. Mary, a stakeholder, tells you that she hates the project and she hopes that it fails miserably. What type of stakeholder is Mary?

A. Resistant

B. Unhappy

C. Honest

D. Defiant

A. Mary is a resistant stakeholder. Mary, the stakeholder, knows about the project and doesn't want the change the project will bring. While Mary may be unhappy, honest, and defiant, these answers are not stakeholder classification types, so choices B, C, and D are incorrect.

8. You are the project manager of the HQL Project for your company. Henry, a stakeholder, is in favor of your project and he's working with you to express the importance of the project. Henry has offered to help with the project, communicate with other stakeholders, and host status meetings. What type of stakeholder is Henry?

A. Supportive

B. Cheerleader

C. Contractual

D. Leading

D. Henry is considered to be a leading stakeholder. Henry, the stakeholder, knows about the project, is supportive of the change the project may bring about, and is working to make the project successful. A, supportive, isn't the best choice because Henry is doing more than just supporting the project—he's helping the project be successful. B, cheerleader, and C, contractual, are not valid stakeholder classification types.

9. Sammy is the project manager of the KHG Project. Some of the stakeholder in this project are opposed to the project, some are in favor of the project, and some stakeholders are neutral. Management has asked Sammy to create a chart that shows the current status of engagement for each stakeholder and the desired level of engagement for each stakeholder. What type of chart is management asking for?

A. Stakeholder engagement mapping

B. Stakeholder engagement control chart

C. Stakeholder histogram

D. Stakeholder engagement assessment matrix

D. Management is asking Sammy to create a stakeholder engagement assessment matrix to see where stakeholder engagement is now and where it should be in the future. A, B, and C are incorrect because these are not valid charts for stakeholder engagement assessments.

10. You are the project manager of the GUY Project for your company and you're working with your project team on some stakeholder issues. You want to

examine the interrelationships among the project stakeholders for better communications. What project management plan will you refer to?

A. Project communications management plan

B. Project stakeholder management plan

C. Project stakeholder register

D. Project staffing management plan

B. The stakeholder management plan defines several things to the project manager about the stakeholders, including information about the interrelationships among the project stakeholders. A, C, and D are incorrect. The project communications management plan does not define the interrelationships among stakeholders. C, the stakeholder register, defines contact information about each stakeholder. D, the project staffing management plan, addresses human resource needs, not communications and stakeholder management.

11. Holly is a new project manager and she's confused about the need for the change log and how it relates to the stakeholder engagement. Why is the change log an input to the management stakeholder engagement process?

A. Because it documents any changes to the stakeholder contact information

B. Because it documents any changes to the stakeholder register

C. Because it communicates changes to the stakeholders

D. Because it communicates changes about the stakeholders to management

C. The change log will help Holly manage stakeholder engagement because she will need to relay information about changes to the appropriate parties. Change can be a sensitive issue in some instances, so always examine the change and think through all of the possible scenarios and reactions the stakeholders may have to the change. Changes to the stakeholder information are reflected in the stakeholder register, not the change log, so A and B are incorrect. D is also incorrect because the change log isn't needed to update and communicate changes about the stakeholders.

12. Part of stakeholder management is the reliance on interpersonal skills. Which one of the following is an interpersonal skill?

A. Facilitation

B. Analysis of product scope

C. Conflict resolution

D. Influence

C. Conflict resolution is an interpersonal skill a project manager will need to engage and manage stakeholders' interests in the project. A is incorrect because facilitation is a management skill. B is incorrect because analysis of the product scope is not an interpersonal skill. D is also incorrect because influence is part of the managerial skills.

13. Just as you need interpersonal skills, you'll also need management skills to effectively engage the stakeholders in the project. Which one is a management skill?

   A. Trustworthiness

   B. Active listening

   C. Influence

   D. Conflict resolution

   C. Influence is considered a management skill because you'll need to persuade people to buy in and support the project. A, B, and D are all incorrect because these answers are part of the interpersonal skill set for project managers.

14. As a PMP and CAPM candidate, you should be familiar with the inputs, tools and techniques, and outputs of the project management process. The management of stakeholder engagement creates five outputs. Which one of the following is not an output of the process?

   A. An issue log

   B. Change requests

   C. Project management plan updates

   D. Project schedule for stakeholder communications

   D. The schedule for stakeholder communications is more likely a part of the project communications management plan. A, B, and C are incorrect because these answers are outputs of the manage stakeholder engagement process. The process creates five outputs: issue log, change requests, project management plan updates, project document updates, and organizational process assets updates.

15. You are coaching several new project managers on effective control of stakeholder engagement. The project managers are confused as to why the change requests come from this project. What is the most likely type of change that will come from controlling stakeholder engagements?

   A. Technology change

   B. Errors or omissions in requirements

   C. External changes

   D. Corrective actions

   D. Defects are changes that have already happened because the defect is different than what was planned in the project. A defect to be solved requires a change through a corrective action to get the results back in alignment with the project scope. A, B, and C are all examples of common change requests, but the most likely change from controlling stakeholder engagements will be from corrective actions.

16. Ned is the project manager of the NHQ Project and he's meeting with a few key stakeholders to determine their roles, interests, concerns, influence, and attitude about the project. What type of meeting is Ned hosting?

    A. Kickoff meeting

    B. Stakeholder classification meeting

    C. Profile analysis meeting

    D. Stakeholder status meeting

    C. This is an example of a profile analysis meeting. Ned is learning and documenting as much as he can about the stakeholders to better engage them in the project. A is incorrect because the kickoff meeting launches the project. B and D are incorrect because the stakeholder classification meeting and the stakeholder status meeting are not valid meeting types.

17. What type of communication is happening in a meeting with several stakeholders exchanging ideas?

    A. Interactive

    B. Push-pull

    C. Conferring

    D. Cooperative

    A. This is an example of interactive communications. This type of communication means that information is happening among stakeholders, like in a forum or meeting. B, C, and D are incorrect because push-pull, conferring, and cooperative are not valid communication types.

18. You are the project manager of a large construction project. You have created a website that allows the different functional manager to log in to a secured area, run queries, and generate reports on the time, cost, scope, changes, risks, and human resource aspects of your project. What type of communication is this?

    A. Pull

    B. Push

    C. Conferring

    D. Static

    A. This is an example of pull communication because the functional managers are retrieving information from your web server. B is incorrect because push communications require the project manager to push information out to the stakeholders. C and D are incorrect because conferring and static are not valid communication types.

19. Which one of the following examples best describes a push communication?

    A. A blog about the project

    B. A secured blog for functional managers

    C. A project newsletter for the stakeholders from the project manager

    D. The project management plan

    C. Push communication means that one person is sending out the information to other people. Of all the choices, the newsletter from the project manager to the project stakeholders is the best example of a push communication. A and B are incorrect because the blog, secured or not, represents pull communication. D is incorrect because although the project management plan provides information, it's not a definitive communication method.

20. Your project has 45 stakeholders as of today. You've just learned that next week 29 new stakeholders will be joining the project. How many more communication channels will you have next week?

    A. 406

    B. 990

    C. 1711

    D. 2701

    C. To solve this problem, you'll have to use the communications channel formula of $N(N-1)/2$, where N represents the number of stakeholders. You'll first have to find the current number of communication channels, which is 990. Then, you'll find the channels with added stakeholders, which is 2701. Finally, you'll find the difference of 2701 and 990, which is 1711 more communication channels. A is incorrect because 406 represents the communication channels just among the 29 additional stakeholders. B is incorrect because 990 represents the current amount of communication channels. D is incorrect because 2701 is the total amount of communication channels, not the difference in communication channels between this week and next.

Understanding the Code of Ethics and Professional Conduct

In this chapter, you will
- Explore the PMI Code of Ethics and Professional Conduct
- Learn the structure of the Code
- Learn about the Code's stance on fairness and honesty
- Adhere to the Code's mandatory standards

In 1981, back when Jordache jeans and the song "Bette Davis Eyes" were all the rage, some folks at the PMI (Project Management Institute) were more concerned with ethics than parachute pants. The PMI created the Ethics, Standards, and Accreditation Group to generate a code of ethics for the project management profession. Sounds like a bunch of fun, doesn't it? By the end of the '80s, the group's discussions and reports evolved into the "Ethics Standard for the Project Management Professional." In 1998, this document became the early version of a new "Code of Ethics." The Code of Ethics was a code that all PMI members, whether certified as a project manager or not, agreed to abide by in their professional practices. Consequently, in January 1999, the Ethics, Standards, and Accreditation Group approved a process for ethics complaints to be filed, reviewed, and then acted on if the complaint proved valid.

Since the late '90s the global economy has changed. The business world has been rocked by billion-dollar companies going bankrupt, we've all witnessed (or participated in) the dot-com bust, and we've experienced the rise of worldwide competition for jobs. Part of all this chaos is the realization that ethics and moral standards vary among countries, companies, and cultures. The PMI Code of Ethics and Professional Conduct, once just a one-page document, has become outdated.

The PMI also has considered the boom in their membership population. The PMI has grown from just a few hundred U.S.-based members to several hundred thousand members worldwide. From its inception, the goal of the Code of Ethics and Professional Conduct was to create a moral guideline for project managers of all industries to subscribe to a common concept of fairness and honesty, and to be held to a higher level of expectations than project managers who were not members of the PMI. At least that was the theory. I'm sure most of us know project managers who are PMI members but who certainly don't subscribe to the PMI Code of Ethics. Shame, shame, shame on them.

Because the PMI Code of Ethics and Professional Conduct was outdated, the PMI created a new governing body, the Ethics Standard Review Committee, to examine the project management Code of Ethics in regard to this new world that project managers operate within. Part of this committee's work was to include a global approach to the review of the now-defunct Code of Ethics and Professional Conduct, the ethical considerations of the global market, and a desire to create a more exact and detailed description of what the ethics and character of a PMI member should be. The result was the *PMI Code of Ethics and Professional Conduct.*

While the concepts in the PMI Code of Ethics and Professional Conduct are applicable to all project managers, you'll also be tested on these principles. Your PMI examination will include these ethical concepts throughout the exam. You'll be tested on ethics as part of your overall project management, not just on a separate section on the code. After all, ethics are interspersed in your duties as a project manager, thus it is appropriate they be included in your examination as well.

The PMI Code of Ethics and Professional Conduct is arranged by chapters and sections. And, as is the case with most documents from the PMI, you'd think a bunch of attorneys wrote the thing. No offense to my pals at the PMI—it's a great document. Really. However, in this chapter, I'll break down their document into a slightly less formal, and much less official, approach. I hope you like it.

VIDEO   For a more detailed explanation, watch the *Being an Ethical Project Manager—and Passing the PMI Exam* video now.

Learning the Code of Ethics

The first chapter of the PMI Code of Ethics and Professional Conduct paints the big picture of what the code is intended for. The vision of the code is, no doubt, that the project management community will adopt the code in their day-to-day operations and lives as representatives of the PMI. The code is needed because project managers are often in situations where their ethics could be jeopardized. When you consider issues with project labor, unscrupulous vendors, and the temptation of personal gain for project managers, it's a great idea to have a Code of Ethics and Professional Conduct. Let's take a detailed look at this first chapter.

Exploring the Code's Vision and Purpose

The project management community should do what's "right and honorable." I'm sure we all want to reflect those same values in our conduct and see them in the conduct of other project managers. The PMI Code of Ethics and Professional Conduct goes beyond your role as a project manager. The code wants adherence in all areas of our lives: "at

PART II

work, at home, and in service to our profession." Don't most of us live, eat, and sleep project management, anyway?

The real purpose of the code is reputation. From the PMI's point of view, the code and our agreement to adhere to the code will raise the perception of the ethical values project managers agree to—and are expected to abide by—as members and participants in PMI programs. The code is also a motivation to become a better project management practitioner. In theory, establishing a globally accepted code for our ethics and behavior should raise our credibility, reputation, and collective behavior to new standards.

Participating in the Code

In the past, Project Management Professionals (PMPs) were expected to adhere to the PMP Code of Conduct. Certified Associates in Project Management (CAPMs) were expected to adhere to the CAPM Code of Conduct. And members of the PMI who were credentialed as PMPs or CAPMs were also held to a separate ethical standard. It made more sense, of course, to create a blanket code of ethics for all members and certified candidates. So basically, everyone who's a PMI member, a CAPM, a PMP, Program Manager Professional (PgMP), or any other PMI designation must agree to participate in this PMI Code of Ethics and Professional Conduct.

 NOTE   Kudos to the PMI on this decision! A simple solution is usually the best solution. I'm thrilled with this new code, its detailed descriptions, and application to all PMI participants.

Learning the Code Details

The code includes four values that are core to the ethics and standards for project managers:

- Responsibility
- Respect
- Fairness
- Honesty

These four values compose the final four chapters of the Code of Ethics and Professional Conduct. Within each of these values are aspirational standards and mandatory standards. Basically, there are some characteristics of these values that we as project managers should aspire to, and there are other facets of these values that we must adhere to.

The code also contains some comments for examples and clarification. You'll also find a glossary of terms in the code—something our pals at the PMI haven't provided before. I'll list those terms at the end of this chapter. No fair peeking!

Serving Responsibly as a Project Manager

The second chapter of the PMI Code of Ethics and Professional Conduct centers on responsibility. We as project managers already have a level of responsibility based on the organizational structure we operate in (from functional to projectized).

Defining Responsibility

According to the Code of Ethics and Professional Conduct, responsibility is our duty to take ownership for the decisions we make—or fail to make. It's also our duty to take ownership of our actions—or lack of actions. And finally, it's our duty to take ownership of the results of those decisions and actions.

 NOTE That's my favorite section of the entire Code of Ethics and Professional Conduct. I may be on my soapbox here, but I tire of project managers who won't own their decisions or failures. It's an excellent section.

Aspiring to Responsibility Expectations

Project managers need to aspire to responsibility. Here are the details of the responsibility aspirations for this section of the Code of Ethics and Professional Conduct:

- Project managers need to make decisions that don't adversely affect the best interests of society, public safety, and the environment.

- Project managers should only accept assignments that mesh with their background, experience, skills, and qualifications.

- Project managers keep their promises.

- Project managers take ownership of and accountability for their errors and omissions and make quick and accurate corrections. When errors are discovered, project managers are to communicate them to the proper parties and to act to repair those errors immediately.

- Project managers protect proprietary and confidential information. No gossiping or blabbing.

- Project managers uphold the Code of Ethics and Professional Conduct and hold others accountable to it as well.

Remember, these are aspirations of the responsibility portion of the Code of Ethics and Professional Conduct. There will be tough instances, mutually exclusive decisions, and scenarios that will call these aspirations into question.

Adhering to Mandatory Standards

Project managers have to deal with regulations, laws, contracts, and other mandatory requirements in their projects. This section acknowledges those requirements. Let's have a look at what the Code of Ethics and Professional Conduct calls for:

- Project managers have a mandatory responsibility to adhere to regulatory requirements and laws.

- Project managers adhering to this code have a mandatory responsibility to report unethical or illegal conduct to management and those affected by the conduct.

- Project managers are required to bring valid, fact-driven violations of the Code of Ethics and Professional Conduct to the PMI for resolution.

- Disciplinary action should commence for project managers who seek to retaliate against a person raising ethics violations concerns.

Project managers must adhere to these points and agree to participate in them in their roles in the project management community.

Adhering to the Respect Value

Rodney Dangerfield always quipped, "I don't get no respect." And Aretha Franklin sang "R-E-S-P-E-C-T" in *Blues Brothers 2000*. Okay, I may be reaching here when it comes to a topic intro, but how many times in a project management book are you going to see Aretha Franklin *and* Rodney Dangerfield mentioned, and in the same paragraph no less?

My point is that both of these performers were talking about the same thing: the admiration and reverence they believed they deserved from their peers. Respect in the PMI Code of Ethics and Professional Conduct centers not only on the respect we may deserve as project managers, but also on the respect that others are due through their work and contributions to our projects. Respect in project management also is aimed toward our respect for the environment we operate within.

Aspiring to Respect

There are four standards for respect:

- Learn about the norms and customs of others, and avoid behavior that others may find disrespectful.

- Listen to others and seek to understand their points of view and opinions.

- Don't avoid people whom you have conflicts or disagreement with. Approach them in an attempt to resolve your differences.

- Conduct yourself professionally, even when those you deal with don't act professionally.

Respect among individuals and toward the environment promotes trust, confidence, and shared ownership of the project work and deliverables.

Adhering to the Mandatory Values of Respect

As project managers, we demand of ourselves and of fellow project managers four things regarding respect. Here's what the Code of Ethics and Professional Conduct details:

- Project managers negotiate in good faith.
- Project managers don't influence decisions for personal gain at the expense of others.
- Project managers are not abusive toward others.
- Project managers respect the property rights of others.

Project managers are to "take the high road" in their dealings with clients and stakeholders.

Being a Fair Project Manager

Ever hear the phrase, "All's fair in love and war"? Or how about, "Life just isn't fair"? Sure you have. So, what is fairness? Do we need the wisdom of King Solomon to know what's fair? Is fairness different from what's just? These are the types of questions the PMI Code of Ethics and Professional Conduct hopes we will ask ourselves and others.

Fairness is our duty to make decisions and act impartially and objectively. Our behavior, as project managers, is to be void of competing self-interests, prejudice, and favoritism. Sounds wonderfully complex, doesn't it?

Aspiring to Fairness

Project managers are to aspire to four things in the realm of fairness:

- Project managers should demonstrate transparency in decision making.
- Project managers must constantly be impartial and objective and take corrective actions when appropriate.
- Project managers provide equal access to information to those who are authorized to have that information.
- Project managers make opportunities equally available to all qualified candidates.

These are some of the lofty aspirations we must have as project managers. They are also characteristics we should strive toward in our day-to-day lives.

Adhering to the Mandatory Standards on Fairness

There are five values that PMI participants must adhere to regarding fairness. Two of the standards apply to conflict-of-interest scenarios, while the remaining three requirements center on favoritism and discrimination. Project managers are to:

- Fully disclose any real or potential conflict of interest.

- Refrain from participating in any decision where a real or potential conflict of interest exists until we, the project managers, have disclosed the situation, have an approved mitigation plan, and have the consent of the project stakeholders to proceed.

- Refrain from hiring or firing, rewarding or punishing, or awarding or denying contracts based on personal considerations such as favoritism, nepotism, or bribery.

- Refrain from discriminating against others on as the basis of race, gender, age, religion, disability, nationality, or sexual orientation.

- Always apply the rules of the organization (the organization being your employer, the PMI, or other performing organization) without favoritism or prejudice.

I think it's safe to say, in regard to these requirements, that if we follow the rules of our employers, the laws of our country, and the calling voice of our conscience, we'll be all right.

Being an Honest Project Manager

Honesty is being truthful in our conversations and in our actions. This means that we, as project managers, don't over promise, give dates that we know are bad, or sandbag our budgets and deliverables. We do what we say and we say what's truthful. Like the other values in the Code of Ethics and Professional Conduct, honesty has both aspiring and mandatory standards.

Aspiring to Honesty

According to the Code of Ethics and Professional Conduct, project managers should aspire to five traits of honesty:

- Seek the truth.
- Be truthful in communications and conduct.
- Provide accurate and timely information.
- Provide commitments and promises in good faith.
- Strive to create an environment where others feel safe to tell the truth.

These five aspirations are noble. As project managers, we are often rushed by stakeholders to get the work done. These five aspirations cause us to pause and reflect on what's honest and truthful in our communications to project team members, stakeholders, *and ourselves.*

EXAM COACH   To answer project management ethics questions, you should first abide by the laws of the country. Second, follow your company's policies. Third, follow the cultural standards of the location where the project is being managed. Fourth, follow your own ethics. And fifth, as a last resort, if you don't know what to do, imagine what an angel would do and answer the question accordingly.

Living the Honesty Requirements

There are just two mandatory standards for honesty in the Code of Ethics and Professional Conduct:

- We do not engage in or condone behavior that is designed to mislead others. This includes, but isn't limited to:
  - Creating misleading statements
  - Creating false statements
  - Stating half-truths
  - Providing information out of context
  - Withholding information that if known would render our statements as false
- We do not engage in dishonest behavior with the intention of personal gain at the expense of others.

Basically, as project managers, we don't lie. We are required, according to the code, to tell the truth regardless of the impact it may have on us, our project team, or our projects. How many project managers do you know who are living by this requirement already?

Chapter Summary

PMPs and CAPMs agree to abide by the PMI Code of Ethics and Professional Conduct—it's part of the exam application process. While no document can force anyone to behave ethically and professionally, this document encourages all PMI members to adhere to a standard of ethics, morals, and professionalism. While the goal of the PMI Code of Ethics and Professional Conduct is to promote ethics in project management as a profession, you'll also be tested on these concepts on the CAPM and the PMP exams. It will behoove you to read over the actual PMI document from their website and familiarize yourself with the associated concepts, sections, and key terms.

The code includes four values for all PMI members: responsibility, respect, fairness, and honesty. You can apply these four values to all areas of a project, from initiation all the way through closing. As a project manager you'll likely face some ethical choices, but these four values can help guide you through the correct decisions. It's also these four values that make up the major sections of the Code of Ethics and Professional Conduct. In each of these values you'll also find mandatory standards and aspirational standards: things we're required to do and things we should do.

As a project manager you may find yourself working with people from different cultures and countries than your own. You should treat other cultures with respect; just because your culture is different from others doesn't mean your culture is better or worse, only different. When you're working in a different country than your home, you should first educate yourself on how to behave in this new environment. You'll want to understand the politics, the culture, and the work ethic to better operate in the environment. And finally, just because you take the initiative to learn about and respect other cultures doesn't mean they'll do the same for you. Regardless, treat all with respect and you'll win respect in return.

Key Terms

Abusive manner   Treating others with conduct that may result in harm, fear, humiliation, manipulation, or exploitation. For example, berating a project team member because they've taken longer than expected to complete a project assignment may be considered humiliation.

Conflict of interest   A situation where a project manager may have two competing duties of loyalty. For example, purchasing software from a relative may benefit the relative, but it may do harm to the performing organization.

Duty of loyalty   A project manager's responsibility to be loyal to another person, organization, or vendor. For example, a project manager has a duty of loyalty to promote the best interests of an employer rather than the best interests of a vendor.

PMI member   Anyone, whether certified as a project manager or not, who has joined the Project Management Institute.

Practitioner   A person who is serving in the capacity of a project manager or contributing to the management of a project, portfolio of projects, or program. For example, a program manager is considered to be a project practitioner under this definition.

Questions

1. You are the project manager of the JKN Project. The project customer has requested that you inflate your cost estimates by 25 percent. He reports that his management always reduces the cost of the estimates, so this is the only

method to get the monies needed to complete the project. Which of the following is the best response to this situation?

A. Do as the customer asked to ensure that the project requirements can be met by adding the increase as a contingency reserve.

B. Do as the customer asked to ensure that the project requirements can be met by adding the increase across each task.

C. Do as the customer asked by creating an estimate for the customer's management and another for the actual project implementation.

D. Complete an accurate estimate of the project. In addition, create a risk assessment on why the project budget would be inadequate.

2. You are the project manager for the BNH Project. This project takes place in a different country than where you are from. The project leader from this country presents a team of workers that are only from his family. What should you do?

A. Reject the team leader's recommendations, and assemble your own project team.

B. Review the résumés and qualifications of the proposed project team before approving the team.

C. Determine if the country's traditions include hiring from the immediate family before hiring from outside the family.

D. Replace the project leader with an impartial project leader.

3. You are about to begin negotiations on a new project that is to take place in another country. Which of the following should be your guide on what business practices are allowed and discouraged?

A. The project charter

B. The project plan

C. Company policies and procedures

D. The Code of Ethics and Professional Conduct

4. One of your project team members reports that he sold pieces of equipment because he needed to pay for his daughter's school tuition. He says that he has paid back the money by working overtime without reporting the hours worked so that his theft remains private. What should you do?

A. Fire the project team member.

B. Report the team member to his manager.

C. Suggest that the team member report his action to human resources.

D. Tell the team member you're disappointed in what he did, and advise him not to do something like this again.

5. You are the project manager of the SUN Project. Your organization is a functional environment, and you do not get along well with the functional manager leading the project. You disagree with the manager on how the project should proceed, the timings of the activities, the suggested schedule, and the expected quality of the work. The manager has requested that you get to work on several of the activities on the critical path even though you and she have not solved the issues concerning the project. What should you do?

   A. Go to senior management and voice your concerns.

   B. Complete the activities as requested.

   C. Ask to be taken off of the project.

   D. Refuse to begin activities on the project until the issues are resolved.

6. The PMI has contacted you regarding an ethics violation of a PMP candidate. The question is in regard to a friend who said he worked as a project manager under your guidance. You know this is not true, but to save a friendship, you avoid talking with the PMI. This is a violation of what?

   A. The Code of Ethics and Professional Conduct to cooperate on ethics violations investigations

   B. The Code of Ethics and Professional Conduct to report accurate information

   C. The Code of Ethics and Professional Conduct to report any PMP violations

   D. The law concerning ethical practices

7. You are the project manager for the Log Cabin Project. One of your vendors is completing a large portion of the project. You have heard a rumor that the vendor is losing many of its workers due to labor issues. In light of this information, what should you do?

   A. Stop work with the vendor until the labor issues are resolved.

   B. Communicate with the vendor in regard to the rumor.

   C. Look to secure another vendor to replace the current one.

   D. Negotiate with the labor union to secure the workers on your project.

8. You are the project manager for the PMH Project. Three vendors have submitted cost estimates for the project. One of the estimates is significantly higher than similar project work in the past. In this scenario, you should do what?

   A. Ask the other vendors about the higher estimate from the third vendor.

   B. Use the cost estimates from the historical information.

   C. Take the high cost to the vendor to discuss the discrepancy before reviewing the issue with the other vendors.

    D. Ask the vendor that supplied the high estimate for information on how the estimate was prepared.

9. You are the project manager of the LKH Project. This project must be completed within six months. The project is two months into the schedule and is starting to slip. As of now, the project is one week behind schedule. Based on your findings, you believe that you can make some corrective actions and recover the lost time over the next month to get the project back on schedule. Management, however, requires weekly status reports on cost and schedule. What should you do?

    A. Report that the project is one week behind schedule, but will finish on schedule based on cited corrective actions.

    B. Report that the project is on schedule and will finish on schedule.

    C. Report that the project is off schedule by a few days, but will finish on schedule.

    D. Report that the project is running late.

10. As a contracted project manager, you have been assigned a project with a budget of $1.5 million. The project is scheduled to last seven months, but your most recent earned value management (EVM) report shows that the project will finish ahead of schedule by nearly six weeks. If this happens, you will lose $175,000 in billable time. What should you do?

    A. Bill for the entire $1.5 million, since this was the approved budget.

    B. Bill for the $1.5 million by adding additional work at the end of the project.

    C. Report to the customer the project status and completion date.

    D. Report to the customer the project status and completion date, and ask if they'd like to add any additional features to account for the monies not spent.

11. You are the project manager of the PMH Project. You have been contracted to design the placement of several pieces of manufacturing equipment. You have completed the project scope and are ready to pass the work over to the installer. The installer begins to schedule you to help with the installation of the manufacturing equipment. You should do what?

    A. Help the installer place the equipment according to the design documents.

    B. Help the installer place the equipment as the customer sees fit.

    C. Refuse to help the installer, since the project scope has been completed.

    D. Help the installer place the equipment, but insist that the quality control be governed by your design specifications.

12. You are the project manager of the 12BA Project. You have completed the project according to the design documents and have met the project scope.

The customer agrees that the design document requirements have been met; however, the customer is not pleased with the project deliverables and is demanding additional adjustments be made to complete the project. What is the best way to continue?

A. Complete the work as the customer has requested.

B. Complete the work at 1.5 times the billable rate.

C. Do nothing. The project scope is completed.

D. Do nothing. Management from the performing organization and the customer's organization will need to determine why the project failed before adding work.

13. You are the project manager of the AAA Project. Due to the nature of the project, much of the work will require overtime between Christmas and New Year's Day. Many of the project team members, however, have requested vacation during that week. What is the best way to continue?

A. Refuse all vacation requests and require all team members to work.

B. Only allow vacation requests for those team members who are not needed during that week.

C. Divide tasks equally among the team members so each works the same amount of time.

D. Allow team members to volunteer for the overtime work.

14. You are a project manager for your organization. Your project is to install several devices for one of your company's clients. The client has requested that you complete a few small tasks that are not in the project scope. To maintain the relationship with the client, you oblige her request and complete the work without informing your company. This is an example of what?

A. Effective expert judgment

B. Failure to satisfy the scope of professional services

C. Contract change control

D. Integrated change control

15. You are completing a project for a customer in another country. One of the customs in this country is to honor the project manager of a successful project with a gift. Your company, however, does not allow project managers to accept gifts worth more than $50 from any entity. At the completion of the project, the customer presents you with a new car in a public ceremony. What should you do?

A. Accept the car, since it is a custom of the country. To refuse it would be an insult to your hosts.

B. Refuse to accept the car, since it would result in a conflict with your organization's policy on gifts.

   C. Accept the car and then return it, in private, to the customer.

   D. Accept the car and then donate the car to a charity in the customer's name.

16. You have a project team member who is sabotaging your project because he does not agree with it. What should you do?

   A. Fire the project team member.

   B. Present the problem to management.

   C. Present the problem to management with a solution to remove the team member from the project.

   D. Present the problem to management with a demand to fire the project team member.

17. You are the project manager of a project in Asia. You discover that the project leader has hired family members for several lucrative contracts on the project. What should you consider?

   A. Cultural issues

   B. Ethical issues

   C. Organizational issues

   D. Political issues

18. Of the following, which one achieves customer satisfaction?

   A. Completing the project requirements

   B. Maintaining the project cost

   C. Maintaining the project schedule

   D. Completing the project with the defined quality metrics

19. A PMP has been assigned to manage a project in a foreign country. The disorientation the PMP will likely experience as he gets acclimated to the country is known as what?

   A. Sapir-Whorf hypothesis

   B. Time dimension

   C. Ethnocentrism

   D. Culture shock

20. You are the project manager for an information technology project. It has come to your attention that a technical problem has stopped the project work. How should you proceed?

   A. Measure the project performance to date, and account for the cost of the technical problem.

   B. Rebaseline the project performance to account for the technical problem.

C. Work with the project team to develop alternative solutions to the technical problem.

D. Outsource the technical problem to a vendor.

Questions and Answers

1. You are the project manager of the JKN Project. The project customer has requested that you inflate your cost estimates by 25 percent. He reports that his management always reduces the cost of the estimates, so this is the only method to get the monies needed to complete the project. Which of the following is the best response to this situation?

   A. Do as the customer asked to ensure that the project requirements can be met by adding the increase as a contingency reserve.

   B. Do as the customer asked to ensure that the project requirements can be met by adding the increase across each task.

   C. Do as the customer asked by creating an estimate for the customer's management and another for the actual project implementation.

   D. Complete an accurate estimate of the project. In addition, create a risk assessment on why the project budget would be inadequate.

   D. It would be inappropriate to bloat the project costs by 25 percent. A risk assessment describing how the project may fail if the budget is not accurate is most appropriate. A, B, and C are all incorrect, since these choices are ethically wrong. The PMP should always provide honest estimates of the project work.

2. You are the project manager for the BNH Project. This project takes place in a different country than where you are from. The project leader from this country presents a team of workers that are only from his family. What should you do?

   A. Reject the team leader's recommendations, and assemble your own project team.

   B. Review the résumés and qualifications of the proposed project team before approving the team.

   C. Determine if the country's traditions include hiring from the immediate family before hiring from outside the family.

   D. Replace the project leader with an impartial project leader.

   C. You should first confirm what the local practices and customs call for in regard to hiring family members before others. A and D are incorrect, since they do not consider the qualifications of the project team leader and the project team. In addition, they do not take into account local customs. B is incorrect as well. Although it does ponder the qualifications of the project team, it does not consider the local customs.

3. You are about to begin negotiations on a new project that is to take place in another country. Which of the following should be your guide on what business practices are allowed and discouraged?

   A. The project charter

   B. The project plan

   C. Company policies and procedures

   D. The Code of Ethics and Professional Conduct

   C. The company policies and procedures should guide the project manager and the decision he makes in the foreign country. A and B are incorrect because these documents are essential, but usually do not reference allowed business practices. D is incorrect because while the PMI Code of Ethics and Professional Conduct does possess crucial information, the company's policies and procedures are most specific to the project work and requirements.

4. One of your project team members reports that he sold pieces of equipment because he needed to pay for his daughter's school tuition. He says that he has paid back the money by working overtime without reporting the hours worked so that his theft remains private. What should you do?

   A. Fire the project team member.

   B. Report the team member to his manager.

   C. Suggest that the team member report his action to human resources.

   D. Tell the team member you're disappointed in what he did, and advise him not to do something like this again.

   B. This situation calls for the project team member to be reported to his manager for disciplinary action. A is inappropriate because the project manager may not have the authority to fire the project team member. C is inappropriate because the project manager must take action to bring the situation to management's attention. D is also inappropriate because no formal disciplinary actions are taken to address the problem.

5. You are the project manager of the SUN Project. Your organization is a functional environment, and you do not get along well with the functional manager leading the project. You disagree with the manager on how the project should proceed, the timings of the activities, the suggested schedule, and the expected quality of the work. The manager has requested that you get to work on several of the activities on the critical path even though you and she have not solved the issues concerning the project. What should you do?

   A. Go to senior management and voice your concerns.

   B. Complete the activities as requested.

   C. Ask to be taken off of the project.

D. Refuse to begin activities on the project until the issues are resolved.

B. The project manager must respect the delegation of the functional manager. A, C, and D are all inappropriate actions because they do not complete the assigned work the functional manager has delegated to the project manager.

6. The PMI has contacted you regarding an ethics violation of a PMP candidate. The question is in regard to a friend who said he worked as a project manager under your guidance. You know this is not true, but to save a friendship, you avoid talking with the PMI. This is a violation of what?

   A. The Code of Ethics and Professional Conduct to cooperate on ethics violations investigations

   B. The Code of Ethics and Professional Conduct to report accurate information

   C. The Code of Ethics and Professional Conduct to report any PMP violations

   D. The law concerning ethical practices

   A. By avoiding the conversation with PMI in regard to your friend's ethics violation, you are, yourself, violating the Code of Ethics and Professional Conduct to cooperate with the PMI. B, C, and D are incorrect answers because they do not fully answer the question.

7. You are the project manager for the Log Cabin Project. One of your vendors is completing a large portion of the project. You have heard a rumor that the vendor is losing many of its workers due to labor issues. In light of this information, what should you do?

   A. Stop work with the vendor until the labor issues are resolved.

   B. Communicate with the vendor in regard to the rumor.

   C. Look to secure another vendor to replace the current one.

   D. Negotiate with the labor union to secure the workers on your project.

   B. The project manager should confront the problem by talking with the vendor about the rumor. A is incorrect and would delay the project and possibly cause future problems. C is incorrect and may violate the contract between the buyer and seller. D is also incorrect—the agreement is between the performing organization and the vendor, not the labor union.

8. You are the project manager for the PMH Project. Three vendors have submitted cost estimates for the project. One of the estimates is significantly higher than similar project work in the past. In this scenario, you should do what?

   A. Ask the other vendors about the higher estimate from the third vendor.

   B. Use the cost estimates from the historical information.

C. Take the high cost to the vendor to discuss the discrepancy before reviewing the issue with the other vendors.

D. Ask the vendor that supplied the high estimate for information on how the estimate was prepared.

> **D.** Most likely, the vendor did not understand the project work to be procured, so the estimate is skewed. A clear statement of work is needed for the vendors to provide accurate estimates. A and C are inappropriate actions because they discuss another vendor's estimate with the competing vendors. Choice B, historical information, isn't a viable solution because costs may have changed since the historical information was created. In addition, there's no evidence in the question that historical information even exists. This information should be kept confidential between the buyer and seller. In some government projects, the winning bid may be required to be announced.

9. You are the project manager of the LKH Project. This project must be completed within six months. The project is two months into the schedule and is starting to slip. As of now, the project is one week behind schedule. Based on your findings, you believe that you can make some corrective actions and recover the lost time over the next month to get the project back on schedule. Management, however, requires weekly status reports on cost and schedule. What should you do?

A. Report that the project is one week behind schedule, but will finish on schedule based on cited corrective actions.

B. Report that the project is on schedule and will finish on schedule.

C. Report that the project is off schedule by a few days, but will finish on schedule.

D. Report that the project is running late.

> **A.** The project manager should report an honest assessment of the project, with actions on how he plans to correct the problem. B is incorrect because it does not provide an honest answer to management. C is also incorrect because it does not provide an honest answer to management. D is incorrect because it does not provide a solution to the problem.

10. As a contracted project manager, you have been assigned a project with a budget of $1.5 million. The project is scheduled to last seven months, but your most recent earned value management (EVM) report shows that the project will finish ahead of schedule by nearly six weeks. If this happens, you will lose $175,000 in billable time. What should you do?

A. Bill for the entire $1.5 million, since this was the approved budget.

B. Bill for the $1.5 million by adding additional work at the end of the project.

C. Report to the customer the project status and completion date.

D. Report to the customer the project status and completion date, and ask if they'd like to add any additional features to account for the monies not spent.

> **C.** An honest and accurate assessment of the project work is always required. A and B are incorrect because these actions do not reflect an honest assessment of the work. D is incorrect because it offers gold plating and recommends additional changes that were not part of the original project scope. In addition, because this is a contracted relationship, the additional work may not be covered within the original project contract and may result in legal issues.

11. You are the project manager of the PMH Project. You have been contracted to design the placement of several pieces of manufacturing equipment. You have completed the project scope and are ready to pass the work over to the installer. The installer begins to schedule you to help with the installation of the manufacturing equipment. You should do what?

    A. Help the installer place the equipment according to the design documents.

    B. Help the installer place the equipment as the customer sees fit.

    C. Refuse to help the installer, since the project scope has been completed.

    D. Help the installer place the equipment, but insist that the quality control be governed by your design specifications.

> **C.** When the project scope is completed, the contract is fulfilled and the project is done. Any new work items should not be sent through. In this instance, the contract change control system should be invoked, or a new contract should be created. A, B, and D are incorrect because these choices are outside of the scope and have not been covered in the contract.

12. You are the project manager of the 12BA Project. You have completed the project according to the design documents and have met the project scope. The customer agrees that the design document requirements have been met; however, the customer is not pleased with the project deliverables and is demanding additional adjustments be made to complete the project. What is the best way to continue?

    A. Complete the work as the customer has requested.

    B. Complete the work at 1.5 times the billable rate.

    C. Do nothing. The project scope is completed.

    D. Do nothing. Management from the performing organization and the customer's organization will need to determine why the project failed before adding work.

C. When the project scope has been completed, the project is completed. Any additional work, without a contract change or new contract, would be dishonest and would betray the customer or the project manager's company. This is a good example of a question where none of the choices are good, but you must choose the best answer available. Of course, in a real project, you'd have many other choices and options to achieve customer satisfaction. A and B are both incorrect because additional work is not covered in the current contract. D is incorrect because the project did not fail—the deliverables met the requirements of the project scope and the design document.

13. You are the project manager of the AAA Project. Due to the nature of the project, much of the work will require overtime between Christmas and New Year's Day. Many of the project team members, however, have requested vacation during that week. What is the best way to continue?

   A. Refuse all vacation requests and require all team members to work.

   B. Only allow vacation requests for those team members who are not needed during that week.

   C. Divide tasks equally among the team members so each works the same amount of time.

   D. Allow team members to volunteer for the overtime work.

   D. This is the best choice for this scenario, because it allows the project team to be self-led and is sensitive to the needs of the project team. A, B, and C are all autocratic responses to the problem, and while the results may seem fair, D is the best choice.

14. You are a project manager for your organization. Your project is to install several devices for one of your company's clients. The client has requested that you complete a few small tasks that are not in the project scope. To maintain the relationship with the client, you oblige her request and complete the work without informing your company. This is an example of what?

   A. Effective expert judgment

   B. Failure to satisfy the scope of professional services

   C. Contract change control

   D. Integrated change control

   B. When the project manager completes activities outside of the contract and does not inform the performing organization, it is essentially the same as stealing. The PMP must be held accountable for all the time invested in a project. A is incorrect because this is not expert judgment. C is incorrect because the contract has not been changed or attempted to be changed. D is also incorrect because the changes the project manager completed for the customer were not sent through any change control system. Instead, they were completed without documentation or reporting.

15. You are completing a project for a customer in another country. One of the customs in this country is to honor the project manager of a successful project with a gift. Your company, however, does not allow project managers to accept gifts worth more than $50 from any entity. At the completion of the project, the customer presents you with a new car in a public ceremony. What should you do?

  A. Accept the car, since it is a custom of the country. To refuse it would be an insult to your hosts.

  B. Refuse to accept the car, since it would result in a conflict with your organization's policy on gifts.

  C. Accept the car and then return it, in private, to the customer.

  D. Accept the car and then donate the car to a charity in the customer's name.

> **B.** This is the best answer. Although this solution may seem extreme, to accept the car in public would give the impression that the project manager has defied company policy. In addition, accepting the car would appear to be a conflict of interest for the project manager. A, C, and D are all incorrect. Accepting the car, even with the intention of returning it or donating it to charity, would conflict with the company's policies regarding the acceptance of gifts.

16. You have a project team member who is sabotaging your project because he does not agree with it. What should you do?

  A. Fire the project team member.

  B. Present the problem to management.

  C. Present the problem to management with a solution to remove the team member from the project.

  D. Present the problem to management with a demand to fire the project team member.

> **C.** The problem should be presented to management, with a solution to remove the project team member from the project. Remember, whenever the project manager must present a problem to management, she should also present a solution to the problem. A is incorrect because it likely is not the project manager's role to fire the project team member. B is incorrect because it does not address a solution for the problem. D is incorrect because the project manager's focus should be on the success of the project. By recommending that the project team member be removed from the project, the problem is solved from the project manager's point of view. Management, however, may come to the decision on their own accord to dismiss the individual from the company altogether. In addition, a recommendation from the project manager to fire someone may be outside the boundary of human resources' procedure for employee termination.

17. You are the project manager of a project in Asia. You discover that the project leader has hired family members for several lucrative contracts on the project. What should you consider?

A. Cultural issues

B. Ethical issues

C. Organizational issues

D. Political issues

> A. The project manager should first determine what the country's customs and culture call for when hiring relatives. It may be a preferred practice in the country to work with qualified relatives first before hiring other individuals to complete the project work. B, C, and D are not the best choice in this scenario. They may be used to follow up after first examining the cultural issues within the country.

18. Of the following, which one achieves customer satisfaction?

A. Completing the project requirements

B. Maintaining the project cost

C. Maintaining the project schedule

D. Completing the project with the defined quality metrics

> A. The largest factor when it comes to customer satisfaction is the ability to complete the project requirements. B, C, and D are incorrect because achieving these factors, while good, is not as complete as achieving the project requirements, which may include the cost, schedule, and quality expectations.

19. A PMP has been assigned to manage a project in a foreign country. The disorientation the PMP will likely experience as he gets acclimated to the country is known as what?

A. Sapir-Whorf hypothesis

B. Time dimension

C. Ethnocentrism

D. Culture shock

> D. Culture shock is the typical disorientation a person feels when visiting a foreign country. A is incorrect. The Sapir-Whorf hypothesis is a theory that believes an individual can understand a culture by understanding its language. B is incorrect because time dimension is the local culture's general practice for respecting time and punctuality. C is incorrect because ethnocentrism is a person's belief that his or her own culture is the best and that all other cultures should be measured against it.

20. You are the project manager for an information technology project. It has come to your attention that a technical problem has stopped the project work. How should you proceed?

   A. Measure the project performance to date, and account for the cost of the technical problem.

   B. Rebaseline the project performance to account for the technical problem.

   C. Work with the project team to develop alternative solutions to the technical problem.

   D. Outsource the technical problem to a vendor.

   C. When problems arise that stop project tasks, the project manager should work with the team to uncover viable alternative solutions. A and B do nothing to find a solution to the problem, so they are incorrect. D is incorrect because the solution for the problem has not necessarily been addressed. The end result of C, to find an alternative solution, may be D, but outsourcing the problem to a vendor should not be the first choice in this scenario.

PART III

Appendices

Project Management Documents

Projects are full of plans, reports, and other documents. Having a clear understanding of each of the document types and why they may or may not be needed in a project can help you, the Project Management Professional (PMP) or Certified Associate in Project Management (CAPM) candidate, to answer exam questions correctly. The following is a list of project management elements:

Activity attributes   The activity characteristics such as the activity codes, predecessor and successor activities, leads and lags, resource requirements, dates, constraints, and assumptions.

Activity cost estimate supporting detail   This is the collection of documents that detail how the project's cost estimate was created.

- The scope of the work that the estimate is based on
- The basis for the estimate
- Documentation of the assumptions used in the estimate creation
- Documentation of the constraints used in the estimate creation
- The range of possible estimates, such as the +/- percentage or dollar amount

Activity duration estimate   An estimate of the likely time it will take to complete the project, a phase, or individual activities within the project.

Activity list   The collection of schedule activities.

Affinity diagram   A tool that helps the project team sort ideas and data. This simple tool clusters similar ideas; useful to use after a brainstorming session.

Analogous estimate   An estimate based on a previous similar project to predict the current project's time or cost expectations.

Assumption log   All assumptions identified in the project are documented, and the status of each as an assumption is monitored. Assumptions need to be tested to determine risk likelihood.

Backlog   Narratives about the product requirements that need to be completed. These are often prioritized, numbered, and scheduled for creation based on time, budget, and stakeholder demand.

Bar charts   A histogram that typically depicts the project activities and their associated start and end dates. This is also known as a Gantt chart.

Bill of materials (BOM)   Defines the materials and products needed to create the items defined in the corresponding work breakdown structure (WBS). The BOM is arranged in sync with the hierarchy of the deliverables in the WBS.

Business case   A business case is often needed for the project charter to justify the project's existence. Business cases document the financial reasoning for the project and the end result of a feasibility study.

Cause-and-effect diagrams   Also known as Ishikawa diagrams and fishbone diagrams. These illustrate how potential problems within a project may contribute to failure or errors within the project.

Change log   This document records all changes that happen during the project. It's useful for scope verification, quality control, and tracking changes.

Change management plan   A project management plan that defines how the project will manage changes.

Change requests   A documented request to change the project's scope is managed through the project's integrated change control process.

Checksheets   Checklists that are used as part of requirements gathering, task execution, quality control, and other aspects of the project to ensure that a task or process is completed accurately.

Claim   A documented disagreement between the buyer and the seller. Claims are often settled through negotiations, mediation, or in the courts, depending on the terms of the contract.

Communications management plan   This subsidiary plan defines who needs what information, when the information is needed, the frequency of the communication, and the accepted modalities for the communication needs.

Configuration management plan   A project management plan that defines the configurable items and the formal process for how these items are allowed to be changed.

Contingency plan   Part of the monitor and control risk process includes the option of executing a contingency plan to respond to worst-case scenarios with risk impact.

Contract   A legal relationship between the buyer and the seller that describes the work to be completed, the fee for performing the work, a schedule for completing the work, and acceptance criteria to deem the contract complete. If a project is being completed by one organization for another organization, there is typically a contractual relationship between the seller and the customer. Contracts may be inputs for the project charter.

Contract management plan   A plan that is used for significant purchases. This plan directs the acquisition and adherence of both the buyer and the seller to the terms of the contract.

Contract statement of work   This document defines the products and services that are being procured to satisfy portions of the project scope statement.

Control charts   This quality control tool illustrates the stability of a process and allows the project management team to determine if the process may have trends and predictability.

Cost baseline   A time-phased budget that tracks the planned project expenses against the actual project expenses. This document is used to measure, monitor, and control project costs in conjunction with the cost management plan.

Cost management plan   A project management subsidiary plan that defines the structure for estimating, budgeting, and controlling project costs.

Cost plus fee or cost plus percentage of costs   A contract in which the buyer pays the seller a fee for the contract work or deliverable plus an additional fee based on the percentage of the total costs for the goods or services provided.

Cost plus fixed fee   A contract in which the buyer pays the seller the costs of the materials and/or labor to complete the contract work or deliverable, plus a predetermined fee.

Cost plus incentive fee   A contract in which the buyer pays the seller the costs of the materials and labor plus an incentive bonus for reaching objectives set by the buyer. Incentives are typically based on reaching schedule objectives.

Decision tree   A diagram that identifies and evaluates each available outcome of a decision and the decision's implication, consideration of each choice, and the value of each decision.

Defect repair requests   Requests to repair defects within the project deliverables.

Fishbone diagrams   Also known as cause-and-effect diagrams and Ishikawa diagrams. These illustrate how potential problems within a project may contribute to failure or errors within the project.

Fixed-price or lump-sum contract   A contract that defines the total price for the work or product the organization agrees to purchase.

Flowchart   A flowchart is a visual representation of a process through a system.

Force field analysis diagrams   These plot the strengths and weaknesses of the forces (stakeholders) that have influence over project decisions.

Formal acceptance documentation   A document that formally records that the project customer and/or sponsor has accepted the project deliverables.

Gantt chart   A bar chart that shows scheduling information and relationships among tasks. Tasks are represented by nodes. The length of the node combined with the calendar shows the duration of the activity.

Histogram   A bar chart that shows the distribution of values.

Historical information   Past project documentation and lessons learned documents are often used as inputs and references for current projects. Current project documentation and lessons learned documentation become historical information for future projects within an organization.

Human resource plan   This project management plan defines how the project is staffed and how the project team will be defined, managed, and controlled. This plan also includes the staffing management plan.

Independent estimate   Also known as a third-party estimate and a should-cost estimate, this document serves as a means for evaluating estimates provided by potential vendors to complete the work the contract calls for. An independent estimate is often created by a third party for the performing organization for a fee.

Influence diagram   A chart that shows the relationships between and among causal factors, events, situations, and other project conditions.

Invitation for bid   A document inviting a prospective vendor to bid on the contents of the contract statement of work. This is a price-based decision model.

Ishikawa diagrams   Also known as cause-and-effect diagrams and fishbone diagrams. These illustrate how potential problems within a project may contribute to failure or errors within the project.

Lessons learned documentation   The results of quality control and other types of lessons learned are documented and become part of organizational process assets. Lessons learned documentation is created throughout the project's life cycle.

Milestone chart   A chart that depicts the promised milestone completion and the actual milestone completion dates.

Milestone list   The documented collection of the project milestones and their attributes, deadlines, and requirements. The milestone list is part of the overall project management plan.

Nondisclosure agreement (NDA)   A procurement document that requires the vendor to not disclose information about the contract to anyone within or outside of the performing organization.

Organizational breakdown structure   There can be two versions of this document. First, there's the decomposition of the project's hierarchy of organizations, departments, and disciplines related to the work packages in the WBS. This document helps the project management team determine which disciplines or departments are responsible for which work packages as identified in the WBS. Second, this could depict the organization's departments, teams, functional departments, and business units.

Organizational charts   A visual representation of the hierarchy of an organization depicting all of the positions and reporting structures of the organization's members.

Parametric estimate   An estimate based on a parameter, such as a cost per metric ton or number of hours to complete a repetitive activity.

Pareto chart   A histogram that shows the categories of failure within a project. A Pareto chart ranks the failures from largest to smallest, which then allows the project management team to attack the largest problems within the project. Pareto charts are based on Pareto's Law, which states that 80 percent of the problems are related to 20 percent of the causes.

Performance reports   The project's communications management plan defines the expectations and frequency of the project performance reports. Performance reports update the necessary stakeholders on the status and progress information, and may include bar charts, S-curves, histograms, and tables. These reports provide documentation about the project and project team's overall performance during the project execution. Performance can measure work results, time, cost, scope, quality, and other specifics within the project.

PMBOK Guide   A book published by the Project Management Institute (PMI) that serves as a guide to the project management body of knowledge. It is generally accepted in the project management discipline as providing good practices for most projects, most of the time.

Probability and impact matrix   Demonstrates through either a cardinal or an ordinal scale the probability, impact, and risk score of each identified risk event. The process is a result of risk analysis.

Process improvement plan   This project management subsidiary plan instructs the project management team on how to identify and react to any non-value-added activities and waste that may exist or creep into the project.

Procurement management plan   This subsidiary plan of the overall project management plan defines the processes and policies for choosing, selecting, and working with a vendor on the project. The plan defines the contracts that should be used, the standard procurement documents, and the conditions to work with (and sometimes manage) the client–vendor relationship.

Product scope   The features and functions of the product, service, or result that a project may bring about.

Product scope description   This document defines the product, service, or condition that the project promises to create. As the project moves through planning, the product scope description becomes more detailed.

Project calendar   The time when project work is allowed to happen within the project.

Project charter   The document that authorizes the project or project phase. It identifies the business needs and the new product, service, or result the project will bring about in the organization.

Project closure documents   The documentation of the project's completion, closure, and transfer of the project deliverables to other parties within the organization or to the

PART III

project customers. If the project has been canceled, the project closure documents detail why the project has been canceled and what has happened to the project deliverables that may have been created during the limited project execution.

Project management plan   This document defines all of the accepted project management processes for the current project, including how the project will be initiated, planned, executed, monitored, controlled, and closed. The project management plan is comprised of the following subsidiary plans:

- Project scope management plan
- Change management plan
- Configuration management plan
- Requirements management plan
- Schedule management plan
- Cost management plan
- Quality management plan
- Process improvement plan
- Human resource management plan
- Communications management plan
- Risk management plan
- Procurement management plan
- Stakeholder management plan
- Schedule baseline
- Cost performance baseline
- Scope baseline

Project notebook   The project team may elect to keep their individual project records in a project notebook. The project notebooks then become part of the organizational process assets.

Project organization chart   A chart that shows the interrelationship of the project manager, the project sponsor, the project team, and possibly stakeholders.

Project presentations   Formal communication often happens in the form of project presentations. These presentations then become part of the organizational process assets.

Project records   All of the project documentation and communication should be kept and managed by the project management team. These project records become part of the organizational process assets.

Project reports   Project reports vary by organization, but generally include information on the project's status, lessons learned, issue logs, and project closure. Project reports become part of the organizational process assets.

Project schedule network diagram   A visual representation of the sequence of project activities. The most common project schedule network diagram is the precedence diagramming method, which uses predecessors and successors to illustrate the flow of the project work.

Project scope management plan   This is a subsidiary plan of the overall project plan. It defines how the project scope will be defined, documented, verified, managed, and controlled. This plan also defines how the project's WBS will be defined, maintained, and approved. The scope validation process is also documented within the project scope management plan. Finally, this plan defines the scope change control process the project will adhere to.

Project scope statement   This document defines the scope of the project and the work required to deliver the project scope. The project scope statement provides several pieces of project information:

- Project objectives
- Product scope description
- Project requirements
- Project boundaries
- Project deliverables
- Product acceptance criteria
- Project constraints
- Project assumptions
- Initial project organization
- Initial defined risks
- Schedule milestone
- Fund limitations
- Cost estimates
- Project configuration management requirements
- Project specifications
- Approval requirements

Project statement of work   The project statement of work, often just called a SOW, defines the products or processes that the project will provide. This document is an input to the project charter.

Proposal   A response to a Request for Proposal (RFP), which often includes project approaches, ideas, and suggestions to complete the procured work, in addition to a price.

Published estimating data   A collection of production rates, material costs, labor trades, and industry-specific price guidelines.

Qualified seller lists   A list of vendors that are qualified to do business with the performing organization.

Quality baseline   This document defines the quality objectives for the project. Results of project performance measurement are compared against the quality baseline so that improvements may be made. If the work is acceptable, the project may continue.

Quality checklists   A checklist, as the name implies, is a project management tool used to ensure that a series of steps have been performed as planned and required by the project management team.

Quality management plan   This subsidiary project management plan defines how the project management team will adhere to and implement the requirements of the performing organization's quality policy.

RACI chart   A responsibility assignment matrix that documents the project roles and the responsibilities for each within the project. In a RACI chart, the activities of *responsible, accountable, consult,* and *inform* are used (hence, the acronym RACI).

Requirements management plan   This project management plan defines how requirements will be identified, documented, and managed during the project.

Requirements traceability matrix   A table that identifies each requirement at its origin and traces the requirement throughout the project.

Request for Proposal (RFP)   A request from the buyer to potential vendors to provide a price, approaches, and ideas on how to complete the proposed work to be procured.

Request for Quote (RFQ)   A document inviting a prospective vendor to bid on the contents of the contract statement of work. This is a price-based decision model.

Resource breakdown structure (RBS)   A hierarchical decomposition of the resources required to complete the deliverables within the project.

Resource calendar   The calendar that defines when people and equipment are available for the project's use. The resource calendar identifies if a resource is idle, on vacation, or being utilized on the current project or another one within the organization.

Responsibility assignment matrix (RAM)   Illustrates the connection between the project work and the project team members who will complete the project work.

Risk breakdown structure (RBS)   The project risks are depicted in a hierarchy of risk categories.

Risk management plan   This defines how the risk management activities within the project will occur. A risk management plan is a subsidiary plan of the overall project management plan. The risk management plan includes:

- Methodology
- Roles and responsibilities
- Budgeting

- Timing
- Risk categories
- Definitions of risk probability and impact
- Updated risk categories

Risk register   A component of project management planning that documents the outcome of all risk management activities. The risk register includes:

- List of identified risks
- List of potential responses
- Root causes of risk
- Risk prioritization
- Probabilistic analysis
- Risk trends

Risk-related contractual agreements   Should the planned response to a risk event use transference, a contractual agreement is often demanded.

Run charts   Similar to a control chart, these charts show measured trends over time.

Scatter diagram   A quality control diagram that shows the relationship between two variables within a project.

Schedule activities   The work package is decomposed into the tasks needed to create the work package deliverable. The collection of schedule activities may also be called the activity list.

Schedule baseline   A baseline depicting the expected start and completion dates of project activities, dates for the milestones, and finish dates for the entire project or project phase.

Schedule comparison bar charts   A bar chart that depicts the discrepancies between the current activity status and the estimated activity status. This is often referred to as a tracking Gantt chart.

Schedule network templates   An organization that repeats the same type of projects may elect to use a schedule network template. These templates are prepopulated with activities and their preferred sequence. Often, schedule network templates are based on previous similar projects and are adapted for the current project.

Scope baseline   The project's scope baseline comprises the project's scope statement, the WBS, and the WBS dictionary.

Staffing management plan   The project management subsidiary plan that defines when and how staffing needs will be fulfilled in the project's life cycle. The plan defines, at a minimum, the process of staff acquisition, the timetable for resource utilization, release criteria, training needs, the rewards and recognition for the project, human resource compliance, and safety issues for the project team members.

Stakeholder register   A directory of the project stakeholders and their characteristics.

Strategic plan   An organization's strategic plan is considered when a project is being chartered. All projects within an organization should support the organization's strategic plan.

Subnetwork template   When a project includes repetitive work, such as the creation of identical floors within a skyscraper, the network diagram may use a subnetwork template to illustrate the repetition in the project.

Summary budget   Project charters often refer to a summary budget, which may address the predetermined budget allotted for a project or a rough order of magnitude estimate based on the preliminary project scope statement.

Summary milestone schedule   A schedule of when the project management team can expect the milestones within the project to be reached. This schedule is part of the project charter.

Teaming agreement   A contract that defines the limited relationship between two or more organizations in their attempt to seize an opportunity. When the opportunity is done, the contractual relationship defines how the teaming agreement may end.

Text-oriented responsibility formats   When roles and responsibilities need more documentation than a RACI or RAM chart can provide, a text-oriented version is used. These may also be known as position descriptions or role-responsibility-authority forms.

Three-point estimate   An estimate based on the average of the optimistic, most likely, and pessimistic time estimates.

Time and materials contract   A simple contract type in which the buyer pays the seller for the time and materials to deliver the product or service the contract calls for. This contract type should have a not-to-exceed clause to cap the contract's total costs.

Tree diagram   A hierarchical chart that shows the relationship of parent–child objects. Technically, the WBS can be a tree diagram.

WBS dictionary   This is a companion document to the WBS and details each item in it. Every entry in the WBS dictionary includes its related code of account identifier, responsible organization, schedule, quality requirements, and technical references, and may include charge numbers, related activities, and a cost estimate.

WBS template   A WBS from a previous similar project or the organization's methodology that has been adapted and modified to map to the current project's deliverables.

Work breakdown structure (WBS)   A document that visualizes the deliverables that comprise the project scope. The WBS uses a code of accounts to number and identify the elements within the decomposition. The smallest item within the WBS is called the work package.

Work package   The smallest item in the WBS that cannot, or should not, be decomposed any further as a project deliverable.

Work performance information   This is an input to quality control measurement and includes work completion information, status of project deliverables, status of corrective actions, and overall technical performance measurements.

Passing the CAPM and the PMP Exam

Obviously, you want to pass your Project Management Professional (PMP) or Certified Associate in Project Management (CAPM) exam on the first attempt. Why bother sitting for an exam if you know you're not prepared? In this appendix, you'll find the details you must know to pass the exam. These facts won't be everything you need to know to pass the PMP or CAPM exam, but you can bet you won't pass the exam if you don't know the critical information contained in this appendix.

Tips to Pass the Exam

For starters, don't think of this process as preparing to take an exam—think of it as "preparing to pass an exam." Anyone can prepare to take an exam: just show up. Preparing to pass the PMP and the CAPM exam requires project management experience, diligence, and a commitment to study.

Days Before the Exam

In the days leading up to your scheduled exam, here are some basics you should do to prepare yourself for success:

- *Get some moderate exercise.* Find time to go for a jog, lift weights, take a swim, or do whatever workout routine works best for you.

- *Eat smart and healthy.* If you eat healthy food, you'll feel good and feel better about yourself. Be certain to drink plenty of water, and don't overdo the caffeine.

- *Get your sleep.* A well-rested brain is a sharp brain. You don't want to sit for your exam feeling tired, sluggish, and worn out.

- *Time your study sessions.* Don't overdo your study sessions—long, crash-study sessions aren't that profitable. In addition, try to study at the same time every day, at the time your exam is scheduled.

Create Your Own Answer Key

If you could take one page of notes into the exam, what information would you like on this one-page document? Of course, you absolutely cannot take any notes or reference materials into the exam area. However, if you can create and memorize one sheet of notes, you absolutely may re-create this once you're seated in the exam area.

Practice creating a reference sheet so you can immediately, and legally, re-create this document once your exam has begun. You'll be supplied with several sheets of blank paper and a couple of pencils. Once your exam process begins, re-create your reference sheet. The following are key pieces of information you'd be wise to include on your reference sheet (you'll find all of this key information in this appendix):

- Activities within each process group
- Estimating formulas
- Communication formula
- Normal distribution values
- Earned value management formulas
- Project management theories

Testing Tips

The questions on the PMP and CAPM exams aren't always direct and easy; they may offer a few red herrings, and some people have reported that they found taking the exam like reading *War and Peace*. But there are some practical, exam-passing tips. For starters, you may face questions that state, "All of the following are correct options, except for which one?" The question wants you to find the incorrect option or the option that would not be appropriate for the scenario described. You're looking for the answer that doesn't fit with the others listed. Be sure to understand what the question is asking for. It's easy to focus on the scenario presented in a question and then see a suitable option for that scenario in the answer. However, if the question is asking you to identify an option that is not suitable, then you just missed the question. Carefully read the question to understand what is expected for an answer.

Here's a tip that can work with many of the questions: Identify what the question wants for an answer, and then look for an option that doesn't belong with the other possible answers. In other words, find the answer that doesn't fit with the other three options. Find the "odd man out." Here's an example:

EVM is used during the _____.

A. Controlling activities of the project

B. Executing activities of the project

C. Closing activities of the project

D. Entire project

Notice how options A, B, and C are exclusive? If you choose A, the controlling phase, it implies that earned value management (EVM) is not used anywhere else in the project. The odd man out here is D, the entire project; it's considered the "odd" choice because, by itself, it is not an actual process group. Of course, this tip won't work with every question—but it's handy to keep in mind.

For some answer choices, it may seem like two of the four options are both possible correct answers. However, because you may choose only one answer, you must discern which one is the best choice. Within the question, there will usually be some hint describing the progress of the project, the requirements of the stakeholders, or some other clue that can help you determine which answer is the best one for the question.

Answer Every Question—Once

The PMP exam has 200 questions, while the CAPM exam has 150 questions. You need to answer every question. Do not leave any question blank, even if you don't know the answer to the question. A blank answer is a wrong answer. As you move through the exam and you find questions that stump you, use the "mark question" option in the exam software, choose an answer you suspect may be correct, and then move on. When you have answered all of the questions, you are given the option to review your marked answers.

Some questions in the exam may prompt your memory to come up with answers to questions you have marked for review. However, resist the temptation to review those questions you've already answered with confidence and haven't marked. More often than not, your first instinct is the correct choice. When you completed the exams at the end of each chapter, did you change correct answers to wrong answers? If you did it in practice, you'll likely do it on the actual exam.

Use the Process of Elimination

When you're stumped on a question, use the process of elimination. For each question, there'll be four choices. On your scratch paper, write down "ABCD." If you can safely rule out "A," cross it out of the ABCD you've written on your paper. Now focus on which of the other answers won't work. If you determine that "C" won't work, cross it off your list. Now you've got a 50-50 chance of finding the correct choice.

If you cannot determine which answer is best, "B" or "D" in this instance, here's the best approach:

1. Choose an answer in the exam (no blank answers, remember).

2. Mark the question in the exam software for later review.

3. Circle the "ABCD" on your scratch paper, jot any relevant notes, and then write the question number next to the notes.

4. During the review, or from a later question, you may realize which choice is the better of the two answers. Return to the question and confirm that the best answer is selected.

Everything You Must Know

As promised, this section covers all of the information you must know going into the exam. It's highly recommended that you create a method to recall this information. Here goes.

The 47 Project Management Processes

You'll need to know the 47 project management processes and what each process accomplishes in the project. Here's a quick rundown of each process group and their processes:

Initiating the Project

There are just two processes to know for project initiation:

- Develop the project charter
- Identify the project stakeholder

Planning the Project

There are 24 processes to know for project planning:

- Develop project management plan
- Plan scope management
- Collect requirements
- Define scope
- Create WBS
- Plan schedule management
- Define activities
- Sequence activities
- Estimate activity resources
- Estimate activity durations
- Develop schedule
- Plan cost management
- Estimate costs
- Determine budget
- Plan quality management
- Plan HR management
- Plan communications management
- Plan risk management
- Identify risk

- Perform qualitative risk analysis
- Perform a quantitative risk analysis
- Plan risk responses
- Plan procurement management
- Plan stakeholder management

Executing the Project

There are eight executing processes:

- Direct and manage project work
- Perform quality assurance
- Acquire the project team
- Develop the project team
- Manage project team
- Manage communications
- Conduct procurements
- Manage stakeholder engagement

Monitoring and Controlling the Project

There are 11 monitoring and controlling processes:

- Monitor and control the project work
- Perform integrated change control
- Validate scope
- Control scope
- Control schedule
- Control costs
- Control quality
- Control communications
- Control risks
- Control procurements
- Control stakeholder engagement

Closing the Project

There are just two closing processes:

- Close project or phase
- Close procurements

Earned Value Management Formulas

For EVM formulas, the following five rules should be remembered:

1. Always start with *EV*.
2. *Variance* means subtraction.
3. *Index* means division.
4. Less than 1 is bad in an index, greater than 1 is good (with the exception of TCPI).
5. Negative is bad in a variance; positive is good.

The formulas for earned value analysis can be calculated manually or through project management software during your projects. For the exam, you'll want to memorize these formulas. Table A-1 shows a summary of all the formulas, as well as a sample, albeit goofy, mnemonic device.

Quick Project Management Facts

This section has some quick facts you should know at a glance. Hold on—this moves pretty fast.

Name	Formula	Sample Mnemonic Device
Planned Value	PV = percent complete of where the project should be	Please
Earned Value	EV = percent complete × Budget at Completion	Eat
Cost Variance	CV = EV – AC	Carl's
Schedule Variance	SV = EV – PV	Sugar
Cost Performance Index	CPI = EV/AC	Candy
Schedule Performance Index	SPI = EV/PV	S (This and the following two spell "SEE")
Estimate at Completion	EAC = BAC/CPI	E
Estimate to Complete	ETC = EAC – AC	E
To-Complete Performance Index (BAC)	(BAC – EV)/(BAC – AC)	The
To-Complete Performance Index (EAC)	(BAC – EV)/(EAC – AC)	Taffy
Variance at Completion	VAC = BAC – EAC	Violin

Table B-1   A Summary of the Most Common EVM Formulas

Organizational Structures

Organizational structures are relevant to the project manager's authority. A project manager has authority from weakest to highest in the following order:

- Functional
- Weak matrix
- Balanced matrix
- Strong matrix
- Projectized

Work Breakdown Structure (WBS) Facts

The WBS is the big picture of the project deliverables. It is not the activities that will create the project, but the components that the project will create. The WBS helps the project team and the project manager create accurate cost and time estimates. It also helps the project team and the project manager create an accurate activity list. The WBS is an input to five project management activities:

- Define activities
- Estimate costs
- Determine budget
- Identify risks
- Perform qualitative risk analysis

Project Scope Facts

Projects are temporary endeavors to create a unique product or service. They are selected by one of two methods:

- **Benefit measurement methods** These include scoring models, benefit/cost ratios, and economic models.
- **Constrained optimization models** These include mathematical models based on linear, integer, and dynamic programming. (You probably won't see constrained optimization on the CAPM exam.)

The project scope defines all of the required work, and only the required work, to complete the project. Scope management is the process of ensuring that the project work is within scope and protecting the project from scope creep. The scope baseline, which includes the WBS and the WBS dictionary, is the baseline for all future project decisions because it justifies the business need of the project. There are two types of scope:

- **Product scope** Defines the attributes of the product or service the project is creating
- **Project scope** Defines the required work of the project to create the product

Scope validation is the process completed at the end of each phase and of each project to confirm that the project has met the requirements. It leads to formal acceptance of the project deliverable.

Project Time Facts

Time can be a project constraint. Effective time management is the scheduling and sequencing of activities in the best order to ensure that the project completes successfully and in a reasonable amount of time. These are some key terms related to time management:

- **Lag** Waiting between activities.
- **Lead** Activities come closer together and even overlap.
- **Free float** The amount of time an activity can be delayed without delaying the next scheduled activity's early start date.
- **Total float** The amount of time an activity can be delayed without delaying the project's finish date.
- **Float** Sometimes called *slack*—a perfectly acceptable synonym.
- **Duration** May be abbreviated as "du." For example, du=8d means the duration is eight days. Duration is the amount of work periods required to complete an estimated activity.

There are three types of dependencies between activities:

- **Mandatory** This hard logic requires a specific sequence between activities.
- **Discretionary** This soft logic prefers a sequence between activities.
- **External** Due to conditions outside of the project, such as those created by vendors, the sequence must happen in a given order.

There are three types of precedence between activities that you should know for the exam:

- **Finish to start (FS)** The predecessor activity must finish before the successor activity can start.
- **Finish to finish (FF)** The predecessor activity must finish before the successor activity can finish.
- **Start to start (SS)** The predecessor activity must start before the successor activity can start.

Project Cost Facts

There are several methods of providing project estimates:

- **Bottom-up** Project costs start at zero, each component in the WBS is estimated for costs, and then the "grand total" is calculated. This method takes the longest to complete, but provides the most accurate estimate.

- **Analogous** Project costs are based on a similar project. This is a form of expert judgment, but it is also a top-down estimating approach, so it is less accurate than a bottom-up estimate.

- **Parametric modeling** Price is based on cost per unit. Examples include cost per metric ton, cost per yard, and cost per hour.

There are four types of costs attributed to a project:

- **Variable costs** The costs are dependent on other variables. For example, the cost of a food-catered event depends on how many people register to attend the event.

- **Fixed costs** The cost remains constant throughout the project. For example, a rented piece of equipment has the same fee each month even if it is used more in some months than in others.

- **Direct costs** The cost is directly attributed to an individual project and cannot be shared with other projects (for example, airfare to attend project meetings, hotel expenses, and leased equipment that is used only on the current project).

- **Indirect costs** These are the costs of doing business. Examples include rent, phone, and utilities.

Quality Management Facts

The cost of quality is the money spent investing in training, in meeting requirements for safety and other laws and regulations, and in taking steps to ensure quality acceptance. You might see the cost of quality as the cost of conformance. The cost of nonconformance, sometimes called the cost of poor quality, is the cost associated with rework, downtime, lost sales, and waste of materials.

Some common quality management charts and methods include the following:

- **Ishikawa diagrams** (also called fishbone or cause-and-effect diagrams) are used to find causes and effects that contribute to a problem.

- **Flowcharts** show the relationship between components and the flow of a process through a system.

- **Pareto diagrams** identify project problems and their frequencies. These are based on the 80/20 rule: 80 percent of project problems stem from 20 percent of the work.

- **Control charts** plot out the result of samplings to determine if projects are "in control" or "out of control."

- **Just-in-time** ordering reduces the cost of inventory, but requires additional quality because materials would not be readily available if mistakes occurred.

Human Resource Facts

There are several human resource theories that the CAPM and PMP candidate should be familiar with on the exams. They include the following:

- **Maslow's Hierarchy of Needs**   There are five layers of needs for all humans: physiological, safety, social needs (such as love and friendship), esteem, and the crowning jewel, self-actualization.

- **Herzberg's Theory of Motivation**   There are two catalysts for workers: hygiene agents and motivating agents.

    - **Hygiene agents**   These do nothing to motivate, but their absence demotivates workers. Hygiene agents are the expectations all workers have: job security, a paycheck, clean and safe working conditions, a sense of belonging, civil working relationships, and other basic attributes associated with employment.

    - **Motivating agents**   These are the elements that motivate people to excel. They include responsibility, appreciation of work, recognition, opportunity to excel, education, and other opportunities associated with work besides financial rewards.

- **McGregor's Theory of X and Y**   This theory states that "X" people are lazy, don't want to work, and need to be micromanaged. "Y" people are self-led, motivated, and can accomplish things on their own.

- **Ouchi's Theory Z**   This theory holds that workers are motivated by a sense of commitment, opportunity, and advancement. People will work if they are challenged and motivated. Think participative management.

- **McClelland's Theory of Needs**   Also known as the Three Needs Theory, because there are just three needs for each individual: need for achievement, need for affiliation, or the need for power.

- **Vroom's Expectancy Theory**   People will behave based on what they expect as a result of their behavior. In other words, people will work in relation to the expected reward.

Communication Facts

Communicating is the most important skill for the project manager. With that in mind, here are some key facts on communications:

- Communication channels formula: $N(N - 1)/2$. N represents the number of stakeholders. For example, if you have ten stakeholders, the formula would read $10(10 - 1)/2$, or 45 communication channels. Pay special attention to questions wanting to know how many additional communication channels you have based on added stakeholders. For example, if you have 25 stakeholders on your project and have recently added five team members, how many additional communication channels do you now have? You'll have to calculate the original number of communication channels: 25(25 − 1)/2 = 300 and then calculate the new number with the added team members: 30(30 − 1)/2 = 435 and, finally, subtract the difference between the two: 435 − 300 = 135, which is the number of additional communication channels.

- Fifty-five percent of communication is nonverbal; an additional 30 percent is paralingual.

- Effective listening is the ability to watch the speaker's body language, interpret paralingual clues, and decipher facial expressions. Following the message, effective listening has the listener asking questions to achieve clarity and offering feedback.

- Active listening requires receivers of the message to offer cues, such as nodding the head to indicate that they are listening. It also requires receivers to repeat the message, ask questions, and continue the discussion if clarification is needed.

- Communication can be hindered by trendy phrases, jargon, and extremely pessimistic comments. In addition, other communication barriers include noise, hostility, cultural differences, and technical interruptions. Noise is defined as anything that interferes with the transmission and/or the receipt of a communication.

Risk Management Facts

Risks are unplanned events that can have positive or negative effects on the projects. Most risks are seen as threats to the project's success—but not all risks are bad. For example, let's say there is a 20 percent probability that a project will realize a discount in shipping, which will save the project $15,000. If this risk happens, the project will save money; if the risk doesn't happen, the project will have to spend the $15,000. Risks should be identified as early as possible in the planning process. A person's willingness to accept risk is the utility function (also called the utility theory or risk tolerance level). The Delphi Technique can be used to build consensus on project risks.

The only output of the risk planning process is the risk management plan. There are two broad types of risks:

- **Business risk** The loss of time and finances (where a downside and upside exist). Business risk is often referred to as speculative risk.

- **Pure risk** The loss of life, injury, and theft (where only a downside exists). Pure risk is often referred to as insurable risk.

Negative risks can be responded to using one of four methods:

- **Avoidance** Avoid the risk by planning a different technique to remove the risk from the project.

- **Mitigation** Reduce the probability or impact of the risk.

- **Transference** The risk is not eliminated, but the responsibility and ownership of the risk is transferred to another party (for example, through insurance).

- **Acceptance** The risk's probability or impact may be small enough that the risk can be accepted, or the project team is not capable of mitigating the probability of a risk, such as a hurricane.

Positive risks can also be responded to using one of four methods:

- **Exploiting** The organization can take advantage of the benefits a positive risk will create.

- **Sharing** A project or organization can partner with another entity through joint ventures or teaming agreements to share a positive risk event.

- **Enhancing** The project manager tries to make the positive risk event happen in the project by enhancing the conditions for the positive risk event to come true and increasing the positive impact should the risk event come true.

- **Acceptance** The project manager can also accept positive risks.

Risks are ranked and scored to assess their probability and impact on the project:

- **Qualitative analysis** This approach qualifies the risks for further analysis.

- **Quantitative analysis** This method assigns numeric values to probability and impact. This approach calculates a risk factor (or exposure) in dollars or time.

- **Cardinal scale** A numeric ranking.

- **Ordinal scale** A word ranking (high, medium, low).

Procurement Facts

A statement of work (SOW) is provided to the potential sellers so they can create accurate bids, quotes, and proposals for the buyer. A bidder conference may be held so sellers can query the buyer on the product or service to be procured.

A contract is a formal agreement, preferably written, between a buyer and seller. To be valid, a contract must have:

- An offer

- Acceptance

- Consideration

- A legal purpose

- Capacity to enter into a contract

On the CAPM exam, procurement questions are usually from the buyer's point of view. All requirements the seller is to complete should be clearly written in the contract.

Requirements of both parties must be met, or legal proceedings may follow. Contract types include the following:

- **Cost-reimbursable contracts** require the buyer to assume the risk of cost overruns.

- **Fixed-price contracts** require the seller to assume the risk of cost overruns.

- **Time and materials contracts** are good for smaller assignments, but can impose cost overrun risks to the buyer if the contract between the buyer and seller does not include a not-to-exceed clause. This clause, commonly called an NTE clause, puts a cap on the maximum amount for the contract time and materials.

- **A purchase order** is a unilateral form of contract. It is an example of a fixed price contract.

- **A letter of intent** is not a contract, but shows the intent of the buyer to purchase from a specific seller.

Stakeholder Management Facts

Stakeholder management used to be tucked into project communications, but it's so important that it's now its own knowledge area in the PMBOK Guide. Stakeholder management is still closely related to communications management, but it's more than just communicating with stakeholders. You'll complete four processes as part of stakeholder management:

- **Identify stakeholders**   Part of project initiation.
- **Plan stakeholder management**   Part of the planning process group (obviously).
- **Manage stakeholder engagement**   This is an executing process group.
- **Control stakeholder engagement**   Part of the monitoring and controlling process group.

Stakeholder identification is one of the first processes you'll do in a project. You need to identify the stakeholders to ensure you're including all of the right people in the project planning. Once you've identified a stakeholder, you'll record their information in the stakeholder register. There's a three-step approach to stakeholder management:

- Identify stakeholders as early as possible in the project.
- Identify the project impact and support of each stakeholder.
- Plan how to influence the stakeholders.

You'll need to know about the stakeholder classification models for your PMI examination. These are grids to plot out stakeholder power, influence, and interest in the project. Here are four common models:

- **Power/interest grid**   How much power/interest do the stakeholders have?
- **Power/influence grid**   How much power/influence do the stakeholders have?

- **Influence/impact grid**   How much influence (involvement of decisions) and impact on project change do the stakeholders have?

- **Salience model**   Classifies stakeholders based on power, urgency, and legitimacy for the project.

A Letter to You

My goal for you is to pass your exam. As I teach my PMP Boot Camp for different organizations around the globe, I'm struck by one similarity among the most excited course participants: These people want to pass their exam. Sure, project management is not the most exciting topic, but the individuals are excited about passing their exam. I hope you feel the same way. I believe that your odds of passing the PMP or the CAPM are like most things in life; you're going to get out of it only what you put into it. I challenge you to become excited, happy, and eager to pass the exam.

Here are ten final tips for passing your PMP or CAPM examination:

- Prepare to pass the exam, not just take it.

- If you haven't done so already, schedule your exam. Having a deadline makes that exam even more of a reality.

- If you haven't done so already, create a clutter-free area for studying.

- Study in regular intervals right up to the day before your examination.

- Repetition is the mother of learning. If you don't know the formula, repeat it and repeat it. And then repeat it again.

- Create your own flashcards from the terms and glossary in this book.

- Always answer the exam questions according to how the Project Management Institute (PMI) expects something done, not how you'd do it at your organization.

- Practice creating the one page of notes you'll create at the start of your exam.

- Create a significant reward for yourself as an incentive to pass the exam.

- Make a commitment to pass.

If you're stumped on something I've written in this book, or if you'd like to share your PMP or CAPM success story, drop me a line at cs@instructing.com. Finally, I won't wish you good luck on your PMP or CAPM exam—luck is for the ill-prepared. If you follow the strategies I've outlined in this book and apply yourself, I am certain you'll pass the exam.

All my best,
Joseph Phillips, PMP, Project+, CTT+
www.instructing.com

About the CD

The CD-ROM included with this book comes with:

- Total Tester customizable practice exam software with hundreds of practice exam questions for CAPM and PMP
- Process review quiz with 200 questions
- Over an hour of video training from the author
- Worksheets for Time Value of Money and Earned Value
- A Float Exercise
- Process ITTO Quick Review Guide
- CAPM/PMP Cheat Sheets
- An electronic copy of the book in PDF format

System Requirements

The software requires Windows XP or higher and 30MB of hard disk space for full installation. To run, the screen resolution must be set to 1024 × 768 or higher. The electronic copy of the book requires Adobe Acrobat Reader, which is available for installation on the CD-ROM.

Total Tester Premium Practice Exam Software

Total Tester provides you with a simulation of the CAPM and PMP exams. You can create practice exams from selected domains or chapters. You can further customize the number of questions and time allowed.

The exams can be taken in either Practice mode or Exam Simulation mode. Practice mode provides an assistance window with hints, references to the book, an explanation of the answer, and the option to check your answer as you take the test. Both Practice mode and Exam Simulation mode provide an overall grade and a grade broken down by domain.

To take a test, launch the program and select CAPM, PMP, or Combined from the Installed Question Packs list. You can then select either a Practice Exam or an Exam Simulation, or create a Custom Exam.

Process Review Quiz

In addition to the 750 total CAPM and PMP practice exam questions, we have provided you 200 review-style questions to thoroughly test your knowledge of the 47 Project Management Processes. Select Process Review from the Installed Question Packs list and select up to 200 questions. You can further customize your quiz by Domain or Chapter.

Installing and Running Total Tester Premium Practice Exam Software

From the main screen, you may install the Total Tester by clicking the Total Tester Practice Exams button. This will begin the installation process and place an icon on your desktop and in your Start menu. To run Total Tester, navigate to Start | (All) Programs | Total Seminars, or double-click the icon on your desktop.

To uninstall the Total Tester software, go to Start | Settings | Control Panel | Add/Remove Programs (XP) or Programs And Features (Vista/7/8), and then select the Total Tester program. Select Remove—Windows will then completely uninstall the software.

Author Video

Video MP4s provide supplemental instruction that align with the content of the chapter in which they appear. You can access the clips directly from the Author Video menu by clicking the Author Video link on the main launch page.

Additional Resources

The author has provided an exam score spreadsheet, exercises, worksheets, and quick review guides to further aid you in your CAPM and PMP preparation.

Exam Score Spreadsheet

Use this excel spreadsheet to keep track of your performance in the end-of-chapter questions. Enter your score in the Chapter Score tab, then click over to the Chapter Chart tab for a graph of your performance on a chapter-by-chapter level.

Worksheets and Exercises

Excel worksheets for Time Value of Money and Earned Value help you practice and double-check your math when calculating these formulas. The PDF Float Exercise provides additional practice calculating Project Float from Chapter 6 in the book.

Quick Review Guides

The Process ITTO Quick Review PDF offers a handy overview of all 47 Project Management Processes and their corresponding Inputs, Tools and Techniques, and Outputs. The PMP Cheat Sheets PDF help you build your own mental cheat sheets to retain the key PMI-isms that you will see on the CAPM and PMP exams, and they serve as an additional quick review before the exam. You can access these resources directly from the Additional Resources menu by clicking the Additional Resources link on the main launch page.

Electronic Copy of the Book

The entire contents of the book are provided in PDF format on the CD-ROM. This file is viewable on your computer and many portable devices. Adobe's Acrobat Reader is required to view the file on your PC and has been included on the CD-ROM. You may also use Adobe Digital Editions to access your electronic book.

For more information on Adobe Reader and to check for the most recent version of the software, visit Adobe's web site at www.adobe.com and search for the free Adobe Reader or look for Adobe Reader on the product page. Adobe Digital Editions can also be downloaded from the Adobe web site.

To view the electronic book on a portable device, copy the PDF file to your computer from the CD-ROM, and then copy the file to your portable device using a USB or other connection. Adobe does offer a mobile version of Adobe Reader, the Adobe Reader mobile app, which currently supports iOS and Android. For customers using Adobe Digital Editions and the iPad, you may have to download and install a separate reader program on your device. The Adobe web site has a list of recommended applications, and McGraw-Hill Education recommends the Bluefire Reader.

Technical Support

For questions regarding the Total Tester software or operation of the CD-ROM, visit www.totalsem.com or e-mail support@totalsem.com.

For questions regarding the electronic book, videos, or additional resources, e-mail techsolutions@mhedu.com or visit http://mhp.softwareassist.com.

For questions regarding content, please e-mail customer.service@mheducation.com. For customers outside the United States, e-mail international.cs@mheducation.com.

8/80 Rule   A planning heuristic for creating the WBS and the associated activity list. This rule states the work package in a WBS must take no more than 80 hours of labor to create and no fewer than 8 hours of labor to create.

Abusive manner   Treating others with conduct that may result in harm, fear, humiliation, manipulation, or exploitation. For example, berating a project team member because they've taken longer than expected to complete a project assignment may be considered humiliation.

Acceptance   A risk response appropriate for both positive and negative risks, but often used for smaller risks within a project.

Acknowledgment   The receiver signals that the message has been received; an acknowledgment shows receipt of the message, but not necessarily agreement with the message.

Active listening   The receiver confirms that the message is being received through feedback, questions, prompts for clarity, and other signs of confirmation.

Active observation   The observer interacts with the worker to ask questions and understand each step of the work being completed. In some instances, the observer could serve as an assistant in doing the work.

Activity list   The primary output of breaking down the WBS work packages.

Activity network diagrams   These are diagrams, such as the project network diagram, to show the flow of the project work.

Actual cost (AC)   The actual amount of monies the project has spent to date.

Adaptive life cycle   A project life cycle with iterations of planning and executing; project change happens often, but is managed tightly, and the project stakeholders are highly involved in the project. This approach is also known as the agile project management methodology.

Adjourning   Once the project is done, either the team moves on to other assignments as a unit, or the project team is disbanded and individual team members go on to other work.

Affinity diagram   A breakdown of ideas, solutions, causes, and project components that groups them together with other similar ideas.

Alternative dispute resolution   When there is an issue or claim that must be settled before the contract can be closed, the parties involved in the issue or claim will try to reach a settlement through mediation or arbitration.

Alternative identification A scope definition process of finding alternative solutions for the project customer while considering the customer's satisfaction, the cost of the solution, and how the customer may use the product in operations.

Analogous estimating A somewhat unreliable estimating approach that relies on historical information to predict what current activity durations should be. Analogous estimating is more reliable, however, than team member recollections. Analogous estimating is also known as top-down estimating and is a form of expert judgment.

Application areas The areas of expertise, industry, or function where a project is centered. Examples of application areas include architecture, IT, health care, or manufacturing.

Assumption log An assumption is something that is believed to be true or false, but it has not yet been proven to be true or false. Assumptions that prove wrong can become risks for the project. All identified project assumptions are recorded in the assumption log for testing and analysis, and the outcomes are recorded.

Assumption A belief that may or may not be true within a project. Weather is an example of an assumption in construction projects.

Authority power Project management team members may have authority over other project team members, have the ability to make decisions, and even sign approvals for project work and purchases.

Avoidance A risk response to avoid the risk.

Balanced matrix structure An organization where organizational resources are pooled into one project team, but the functional managers and the project managers share the project power.

Benchmarking Comparing any two similar entities to measure their performance.

Benefit/cost ratio (BCR) models This is an example of a benefits comparison model. It examines the benefit-to-cost ratio.

Bid From seller to buyer. Price is the determining factor in the decision-making process.

Bidders conference A meeting of all the project's potential vendors to clarify the contract statement of work and the details of the contracted work.

Bottom-up estimating An estimating approach that starts from zero, accounts for each component of the WBS, and arrives at a sum for the project. It is completed with the project team and can be one of the most time-consuming and most reliable methods to predict project costs.

Brainstorming This approach encourages participants to generate as many ideas as possible about the project requirements. No idea is judged or dismissed during the brainstorming session.

Budget estimate This estimate is somewhat broad and is used early in the planning processes and also in top-down estimates. The range of variance for the estimate can be from −10 percent to +25 percent.

Business risks   These risks may have negative or positive outcomes. Examples include using a less experienced worker to complete a task, allowing phases or activities to overlap, or forgoing the expense of formal training for on-the-job education.

Cardinal scales   A ranking approach to identify the probability and impact by using a numerical value, from .01 (very low) to 1.0 (certain).

Cause-and-effect diagrams   Diagrams that show the relation between the variables within a process and how those relations may contribute to a problem. The diagrams can help organize both the process and team opinions, as well as generate discussion on finding a solution to ensure quality.

Certified Associate in Project Management (CAPM)   A person who has slightly less project management experience than a PMP, but who has qualified for and then passed the CAPM examination.

Change control board (CCB)   A committee that evaluates the worthiness of a proposed change and either approves or rejects the proposed change.

Change control system (CCS)   The change control system communicates the process for controlling changes to the project deliverables. This system works with the configuration management system and seeks to control and document *proposed or requested changes* to the project's product.

Change log   All changes that enter into a project are recorded in the change log. The characteristics of the change, such as the time, cost, risk, and scope details, are also recorded.

Change management plan   This plan details the project procedures for entertaining change requests: how change requests are managed, documented, approved, or declined.

Change request   A documented request to add to or remove from the project scope. A change request may be initiated to change an organizational process asset, such as a template or a form.

Checklist   A simple approach to ensure that work is completed according to policy. Checklists, also known as checksheets, can be used in execution, risk management, quality management, and scope validation.

Choice of media   The best modality to use when communicating that is relevant to the information being communicated.

Claims   These are disagreements between the buyer and the seller, usually centering on a change, who did the change, and even whether a change has occurred. Claims are also called disputes and appeals, and are monitored and controlled through the project in accordance with the contract terms.

Closing process group   The project management process group that contains the activities to close out a project or project phase and project contracts.

Closure processes This final process group of the project management life cycle is responsible for closing the project phase or project. This is where project documentation is archived and project contracts are also closed.

Code of accounts A hierarchical numbering system for each item in the WBS. The PMBOK is a good example of a code of accounts, as each chapter and its subheadings follow a logical numbering scheme. For example, PMBOK 5.3.3.2 identifies an exact paragraph in the PMBOK.

Coercive power The project manager has the authority to discipline the project team members. This is also known as penalty power.

Collective bargaining agreement constraints Contracts and agreements with unions or other employee groups may serve as constraints on the project.

Commercial database A cost-estimating approach that uses a database, typically software driven, to create the cost estimate for a project.

Communication assumptions Anything that the project management team believes to be true but hasn't proven to be true. For example, the project management team may assume that all of the project team can be reached via cell phone, but parts of the world, as of this writing, don't have a cell signal.

Communication barrier Anything that prohibits communication from occurring.

Communication channels formula $N(N - 1)/2$, where N represents the number of identified stakeholders. This formula reveals the total number of communication channels within a project.

Communication constraints Anything that limits the project management team's options. When it comes to communication constraints, geographical locales, incompatible communications software, and even limited communications technology can constrain the project team.

Communications management plan A project management subsidiary plan that defines the stakeholders who need specific information, the person who will supply the information, the schedule for the information to be supplied, and the approved modality to provide the information.

Competency This attribute defines what talents, skills, and capacities are needed to complete the project work.

Composite structure An organization that creates a blend of the functional, matrix, and projectized structures.

Compromising This approach requires that both parties give up something.

Confidentiality A project manager should keep certain aspects of a project confidential; consider contract negotiations, human resource issues, and trade secrets of the organization.

Configuration identification This includes the labeling of the components, how changes are made to the product, and the accountability of the changes.

Configuration management plan This plan is an input to the control scope process. It defines how changes to the features and functions of the project deliverable, the product scope, may enter the project.

Configuration management system This system defines how stakeholders are allowed to submit change requests for the project's product, the conditions for approving a change request, and how approved change requests are validated in the project scope. Configuration management also documents the characteristics and functions of the project's products and any changes to a product's characteristics.

Configuration status accounting The organization of the product materials, details, and prior product documentation.

Configuration verification and auditing The scope validation and completeness auditing of project or phase deliverables to ensure that they are in alignment with the project plan.

Conflict of interest A situation where a project manager may have two competing duties of loyalty. For example, purchasing software from a relative may benefit the relative, but it may do harm to the performing organization.

Constraint A condition, rule, or procedure that restricts a project manager's options. A project deadline is an example of a constraint.

Context diagram These diagrams show the relationship between elements of an environment. For example, a context diagram would illustrate the networks, servers, workstations, and people that interact with the elements of the environment.

Contingency reserve A contingency allowance for risk events. Contingency allowances are used to respond to risk events.

Contract A contract is a formal agreement between the buyer and the seller. Contracts can be oral or written—though written is preferred.

Contract change control system This defines the procedures for how the contract may be changed. The process for changing the contract includes the forms; documented communications; tracking; conditions within the project, business, or marketplace that justify the needed change; dispute resolution procedures; and the procedures for getting the changes approved within the performing organization.

Contract closure The formal verification of the contract completeness by the vendor and the performing organization.

Contract statement of work (CSOW) This document requires that the buyer fully describe the work to be completed and/or the product to be supplied. The SOW becomes part of the contract between the buyer and the seller.

Control account A WBS entry that considers the time, cost, and scope measurements for that deliverable within the WBS. The estimated performance is compared against the actual performance to measure overall performance for the deliverables within that control account. The specifics of a control account are documented in a control account plan.

Control chart   A quality control chart that maps the performance of project work over time.

Control threshold   A predetermined range of acceptable variances, such as +/–10 percent off schedule. Should the variance exceed the threshold, then project control processes and corrective actions will be enacted.

Corrective action   A corrective action brings project work back into alignment with the project plan. A corrective action may also address a process that is producing errors.

Cost aggregation   Costs are parallel to each WBS work package. The costs of each work package are aggregated to their corresponding control accounts. Each control account then is aggregated to the sum of the project costs.

Cost baseline   A time-phased exposure of when the project monies are to be spent in relation to cumulative values of the work completed in the project. It is an aggregation of the project deliverables and their associated costs. The difference between the cost estimates and the actual cost of the project identifies the cost variance.

Cost-benefit analysis   A process to study the trade-offs between costs and the benefits realized from those costs.

Cost budgeting   The cost aggregation achieved by assigning specific dollar amounts for each of the scheduled activities or, more likely, for each of the work packages in the WBS. Cost budgeting applies the cost estimates over time.

Cost change control system   A system that examines any changes associated with scope changes, the cost of materials, and the cost of any other resources, and the associated impact on the overall project cost.

Cost management plan   This plan details how the project costs will be planned for, estimated, budgeted, and then monitored and controlled.

Cost of conformance   This is the cost associated with the monies spent to attain the expected level of quality. This is also known as failure costs.

Cost of nonconformance to quality   This is the cost associated with not satisfying the quality expectations. This is a component of the cost of quality.

Cost of poor quality   The monies spent to recover from not adhering to the expected level of quality. Examples may include rework, defect repair, loss of life or limb because safety precautions were not taken, loss of sales, and loss of customers. This is also known as the cost of nonconformance to quality.

Cost of quality   The monies spent to attain the expected level of quality within a project. Examples include training, testing, and safety precautions.

Cost performance index (CPI)   Measures the project based on its financial performance. The formula is CPI = EV/AC.

Cost plus fixed fee contract   A contract that requires the buyer to pay for the cost of the goods and services procured plus a fixed fee for the contracted work. The buyer assumes the risk of a cost overrun.

Cost plus incentive fee   A contract type that requires the buyer to pay a cost for the procured work, plus an incentive fee, or a bonus, for the work if terms and conditions are met.

Cost plus percentage of costs   A contract that requires the buyer to pay for the costs of the goods and services procured, plus a percentage of the costs. The buyer assumes all of the risks for cost overruns.

Cost reporting system   A system to record the actual costs of the project activities.

Cost variance (CV)   The difference of the earned value amount and the cumulative actual costs of the project. The formula is $CV = EV - AC$.

Crashing   A schedule compression approach that adds more resources to activities on the critical path to complete the project earlier. When crashing a project, costs are added, as the associated labor and sometimes resources such as faster equipment cause costs to increase.

Critical chain method   A network analysis approach where the deadlines associated with individual tasks are removed and the only date that matters is the promised due date of the project deliverable. CCM works to modify the project schedule based on the availability of project resources rather than on the pure sequence of events, as in the critical path method.

Critical path   The path in the project network diagram that cannot be delayed, or the project completion date will be late. There can be more than one critical path. Activities in the critical path have no float.

Cultural and social environment   Defines how a project affects people and how those people may affect the project. Cultural and social environments include the economic, educational, ethical, religious, demographic, and ethnic composition of the people affected by the project.

Culture shock   The initial reaction a person experiences when in a foreign environment.

Customer/user   The person(s) who will pay for and use the project's deliverables.

Data precision   The consideration of the risk ranking scores that takes into account any bias, the accuracy of the data submitted, and the reliability of the nature of the data submitted.

Decision tree   A method to determine which of two or more decisions is the best one. The model examines the cost and benefits of each decision's outcome and weighs the probability of success for each of the decisions.

Decoder   The device that decodes a message as it is being received.

Defect repair   The activity to repair a defect within the project.

Definitive estimate   This estimate type is one of the most accurate. It's used late in the planning processes and is associated with bottom-up estimating. You need the WBS in order to create the definitive estimate. The range of variance for the estimate can be from –5 percent to +10 percent.

Deliverable   A product, service, or result created by a project. Projects can have multiple deliverables.

Delphi Technique   An anonymous method of querying experts about various factors, such as requirements, estimates and risks within a project, phase, or component of a project. The results of the survey are analyzed by a third party, organized, and then circulated to the experts. Because the surveys are anonymous, participants are more likely to be honest with their requirements, opinions, and statements. The project manager organizes these comments and inputs and then sends them back to the participants for another round of anonymous input. There can be several rounds of anonymous discussion with the Delphi Technique, without fear of backlash or offending other participants in the process.

Deming's PDCA cycle   Standard project management is based on Deming's plan-do-check-act cycle, which describes the logical progression of project management duties.

Design of experiments   An approach that relies on statistical scenarios to determine what variables within a project will result in the best outcome.

Dictatorship   A decision method where only one individual makes the decision for the group.

Direct costs   These are costs incurred by the project in order for the project to exist. Examples include equipment needed to complete the project work, salaries of the project team, and other expenses tied directly to the project's existence.

Discretionary dependencies   These dependencies are the preferred order of activities. Project managers should use these relationships at their discretion and should document the logic behind the decision. Discretionary dependencies allow activities to happen in a preferred order because of best practices, conditions unique to the project work, or because of external events.

Duty of loyalty   A project manager's responsibility to be loyal to another person, organization, or vendor. For example, a project manager has a duty of loyalty to promote the best interests of an employer rather than the best interests of a vendor.

Early finish   The earliest a project activity can finish. Used in the forward pass procedure to discover the critical path and the project float.

Early start   The earliest a project activity can begin. Used in the forward pass procedure to discover the critical path and the project float.

Earned value (EV)   Earned value is the physical work completed to date and the authorized budget for that work. It is the percentage of the BAC that represents the actual work completed in the project.

Effective listening   The receiver is involved in the listening experience by paying attention to visual cues from the speaker and paralingual characteristics, and by asking relevant questions.

Encoder   The device that encodes the message being sent.

Enhancing   A risk response that attempts to enhance the conditions to ensure that a positive risk event will likely happen.

Enterprise environmental factors   Any external or internal organizational factors that can affect project success. Enterprise environmental factors include the culture, organizational structure, resources, commercial databases the project will use, market conditions, and your project management software.

Estimate at completion (EAC)   These forecasting formulas predict the likely completed costs of the project based on current scenarios within the project. Three variations of this formula are based on conditions the project may be experiencing.

Estimate to complete (ETC)   An earned value management formula that predicts how much funding the project will require to be completed.

Ethics   Describes the personal, cultural, and organizational interpretation of right and wrong; project managers are to operate ethically and fairly.

Ethnocentrism   Happens when individuals measure and compare a foreigner's actions against their own local culture. The locals typically believe their own culture is superior to the foreigner's culture.

Executing process group   The project management process group that provides the activities to carry out the project management plan to complete the project work.

Expectancy Theory   This theory states that people will behave based on what they expect as a result of their behavior. In other words, people will work in relation to the expected reward.

Expected monetary value (EMV)   The monetary value of a risk exposure based on the risk's probability and impact in the risk matrix. This approach is typically used in quantitative risk analysis because it quantifies the risk exposure.

Expert power   The project manager's authority comes both from experience with the technology the project focuses on and from expertise in managing projects.

Exploit   A risk response that takes advantage of the positive risks within a project.

External dependencies   As the name implies, these are dependencies outside of the project's control. Examples include the delivery of equipment from a vendor, the deliverable of another project, or the decision of a committee, lawsuit, or expected new law.

External QA   Assurance provided to the external customers of the project.

External risks   These risks are outside of the project, but directly affect it—for example, legal issues, labor issues, a shift in project priorities, or weather. "Force majeure" risks call for disaster recovery rather than project management. These are risks caused by earthquakes, tornados, floods, civil unrest, and other disasters.

Fast tracking A schedule compression method that changes the relationship of activities. With fast tracking, activities that would normally be done in sequence are allowed to be done in parallel or with some overlap. Fast tracking can be accomplished by changing the relation of activities from FS to SS or even FF or by adding lead time to downstream activities. However, fast tracking does add risk to the project.

Feedback The sender confirms that the receiver understands the message by directly asking for a response, questions for clarification, or other confirmation.

Finish-to-finish An activity relationship type that requires the current activity be finished before its successor can finish.

Finish-to-start An activity relationship type that requires the current activity be finished before its successor can start.

Fixed costs Costs that remain constant throughout the life of the project (the cost of a piece of rented equipment for the project, the cost of a consultant brought on to the project, and so on).

Fixed-price contracts Also known as firm fixed-price and lump-sum contracts, these are agreements that define a total price for the product the seller is to provide.

Fixed-price with economic price adjustments A fixed-price contract with a special allowance for price changes based on economic reasons such as inflation or the cost of raw materials.

Flowchart A diagram illustrating how components within a system are related. Flowcharts show the relation between components, as well as help the project team determine where quality issues may be present and, once done, plan accordingly. System or process flowcharts show the relationship between components and how the overall process works. These are useful for identifying risks between system components.

Focus groups A moderator-led requirements collection method to elicit requirements from stakeholders.

Force majeure An "act of God" that may have a negative impact on the project; consider fire, hurricanes, tornados, and earthquakes.

Forcing power The person with the power makes the decision.

Formal power The project manager has been assigned the role of project manager by senior management and is in charge of the project.

Forming The project team meets and learns about their roles and responsibilities on the project. Little interaction among the project team happens in this stage because the team is learning about the project and project manager.

Fragnet A representation of a project network diagram that is often used for outsourced portions of a project, repetitive work within a project, or a subproject. Also called a subnet.

Free float   This is the total time a single activity can be delayed without affecting the early start of its immediately following successor activities.

Functional analysis   This is the study of the functions within a system, project, or, what's more likely in the project scope statement, the product the project will be creating. Functional analysis studies the goals of the product, how the product will be used, and the expectations the customer has of the product once it leaves the project and moves into operations. Functional analysis may also consider the cost of the product in operations, which is known as life cycle costing.

Functional structure   An organization that is divided into functions, and each employee has one clear functional manager. Each department acts independently of the other departments. A project manager in this structure has little to no power and may function as a project coordinator, project expeditor, or project administrator.

Funding limit   Most projects have a determined budget in relation to the project scope. There may be a qualifier on this budget, such as plus or minus 10 percent based on the type of cost estimate created.

Funding limit reconciliation   An organization's approach to managing cash flow against the project deliverables based on a schedule, milestone accomplishment, or data constraints.

Future value   A benefit comparison model to determine a future value of money. The formula to calculate future value is $FV = PV(1 + I)^n$, where PV is present value, I is the given interest rate, and n is the number of periods.

General management skills   These include the application of accounting, procurement, sales and marketing, contracting, manufacturing, logistics, strategic planning, human resource management, standards and regulations, and information technology.

A Guide to the Project Management Body of Knowledge (PMBOK)   A PMI publication that defines widely accepted project management practices. The CAPM and the PMP exam are based on this book.

Hard logic   Logic that describes activities that must happen in a particular order. For example, the dirt must be excavated before the foundation can be built. The foundation must be in place before the framing can begin. This is also referred to as mandatory dependencies.

Herzberg's Theory of Motivation   Frederick Herzberg's theory of the motivating agents and hygiene agents that affect a person's willingness to excel in his career.

Hierarchical organizational chart   A chart showing the relationship between superior and subordinate employees, groups, disciplines, and even departments.

Human resource plan   This plan defines how project team members will be brought onto the project team, managed, and released from the project team. It also defines team training, safety issues, roles and responsibilities, and how the project's reward and recognition system will operate. Chapter 9 defines the human resource plan in detail.

Inappropriate compensation   The project manager is to avoid inappropriate compensation, such as bribes. The project manager is to act in the best interest of the project and the organization.

Independent estimates   These estimates are often referred to as "should cost" estimates. They are created by the performing organization or outside experts to predict what the cost of the procured product should be.

Indirect costs   Costs that are representative of more than one project (for example, utilities for the performing organization, access to a training room, project management software license, and so on).

Influence diagrams   An influence diagram charts out a decision problem. It identifies all of the elements, variables, decisions, and objectives and also how each factor may influence another.

Influence/impact grid   Stakeholders are mapped on a grid based on their influence over the project in relation to their influence over the project execution.

Influencers   Persons who can positively or negatively influence a project's ongoing activities and/or the project's likelihood of success.

Information presentation tools   A software package that allows the project management team to present the project's health through graphics, spreadsheets, and text. (Think of Microsoft Project.)

Information retrieval system   A system to quickly and effectively store, archive, and access project information.

Initial project organization   The project scope statement identifies the project team and the key stakeholders. In some organizations, especially on larger projects, the team organization and structure are also documented.

Initiating process group   The project management process group that allows a project to be chartered and authorized.

Integrated change control   A process to consider and control the impact of a proposed change on the project's knowledge areas.

Interactive communications   This is the most common and most effective approach to communication. It's where two or more people exchange information. Meetings, videoconferences, phone conferences, even ad-hoc conversations are all examples of interactive communications—the participants are actively communicating with one another to ensure that all participants receive the correct message and conclusions.

Internal dependencies   Internal relationships to the project or the organization. For example, the project team must create the software as part of the project's deliverable before the software can be tested for quality control.

Internal QA   Assurance provided to management and the project team.

International and political environment   The consideration of the local and international laws, languages, communication challenges, time zone differences, and other non-collocated issues that affect a project's ability to progress.

Interpersonal interfaces   This organizational interface considers the formal and informal reporting relationships that may exist among the project team members. The interpersonal interface also considers the job descriptions of the project team members, existing reporting structures between supervisors and subordinates, and existing relationships, if any, that may affect the project work. This interface also considers any cultural or language differences among the project team that may need to be addressed.

Interpersonal skills   The ability to interact, lead, motivate, and manage people.

Interrelationship diagraphs   Used for complex solutions where the causes and effects of problems and benefits are intertwined with one another.

Interviews   A requirements collection method used to elicit requirements from stakeholders in a one-on-one conversation.

Invitation for Bid (IFB)   From buyer to seller. Requests the seller to provide a price for the procured product or service.

Iron Triangle of Project Management   A triangle with the characteristics of time, cost, and scope. Time, cost, and scope each constitute one side of the triangle; if any side of the Iron Triangle is not in balance with the other sides, the project will suffer. The Iron Triangle of Project Management is also known as the Triple Constraints of Project Management because all projects are constrained by time, cost, and scope.

Ishikawa diagrams   These cause-and-effect diagrams are also called fishbone diagrams and are used to find the root cause of factors that are causing risks within the project.

ISO   The abbreviation for the International Organization for Standardization. ISO is Greek for "equal," while "International Organization for Standardization" in a different language would be abbreviated differently. The organization elected to use "ISO" for all languages.

Issue log   A logbook of the issues the project team has identified and dates as to when the issues must be resolved by. The issue log may also include team members or stakeholders who are responsible for finding a solution to the identified issues. All identified issues are documented in the issue log, along with an issue owner and a deadline to resolve the issue. The outcome of the issue is also recorded.

Kill point   The review of a phase to determine if it accomplished its requirements. A kill point signals an opportunity to kill the project if it should not continue.

Known unknown   An event that will likely happen within the project, but when it will happen and to what degree is unknown. These events, such as delays, are usually risk related.

Lag time   Positive time, or waiting time, that moves two or more activities further apart.

Late finish   The latest a project activity can finish. Used in the backward pass procedure to discover the critical path and the project float.

Late start   The latest a project activity can begin. Used in the backward pass procedure to discover the critical path and the project float.

Leading stakeholder status   The stakeholder is aware of your project, they want the project to succeed, and they're leading the charge to make certain the project outcome is positive.

Lead time   Negative time that allows two or more activities to overlap where ordinarily these activities would be sequential.

Learning curve   An approach that assumes the cost per unit decreases the more units workers complete, because workers learn as they complete the required work.

Lessons learned   This is documentation of what did and did not work in the project implementation. Lessons learned documentation is created throughout the project by the entire project team. When lessons learned sessions are completed, they're available to be used and applied by the entire organization. They are now part of the organizational process assets.

Letter contract   A letter contract allows the vendor to begin working on the project immediately. It is often used as a stopgap solution.

Letter of intent   A letter of intent is not a contract, but a letter stating that the buyer is intending to create a contractual relationship with the seller.

Logistical interfaces   The logistics of the team locale, time zones, geographical boundaries, and travel requirements within a project.

Low-priority risk watch list   Low-priority risks are identified and assigned to a watch list for periodic monitoring.

Majority   A group decision method where more than 50 percent of the group must be in agreement.

Make-or-buy decision   A process in which the project management team determines the cost-effectiveness, benefits, and feasibility of making a product or buying it from a vendor.

Management reserve   A percentage of the project duration to combat Parkinson's Law. When project activities become late, their lateness is subtracted from the management reserve. This can be a financial amount, not just time, to pay for the associated labor expenses.

Manage project team   The project manager must, according to enterprise environmental factors, manage the project team to ensure that they are completing their work assignments with quality and according to plan.

Manage stakeholder engagement This process is based on what the stakeholders expect from the project and on project communications from the project manager.

Mandatory dependencies These dependencies are the natural order of activities. For example, you can't begin building your house until your foundation is in place. These relationships are called hard logic.

Maslow's Hierarchy of Needs Abraham Maslow's theory of the five needs all humans have and work toward.

Mathematical model A project selection method to determine the likelihood of success. These models include linear programming, nonlinear programming, dynamic programming, integer programming, and multi-objective programming.

Matrix diagrams A data analysis table that shows the strength between variables and relationships in the matrix.

McClelland's Theory of Needs David McClelland developed this theory, which states that our needs are acquired and developed by our experiences over time. All people are, according to this theory, driven by one of three needs: achievement, affiliation, or power.

McGregor's Theory of X and Y Douglas McGregor's theory that states management views workers in the Y category as competent and self-led and workers in the X category as incompetent and needing to be micromanaged.

Medium The device or technology that transports a message.

Milestone Milestones are timeless events in the project's progress that represent accomplishment in the project. Projects usually create milestones as the result of completing phases within the project.

Milestone list This list details the project milestones and their attributes. It is used for several areas of project planning, but also helps determine how quickly the project may be achieving its objectives.

Mind mapping This approach maps ideas to show the relationship among requirements and the differences between requirements. The map can be reviewed to identify new solutions or to rank the identified requirements.

Mitigation A risk response effort to reduce the probability and/or impact of an identified risk in the project.

Monitoring and controlling process group The project management process group oversees, measures, and tracks project performance.

Monte Carlo analysis A project simulation approach named after the world-famous gambling district in Monaco. This predicts how scenarios may work out, given any number of variables. The process doesn't actually churn out a specific answer, but a range of possible answers. When Monte Carlo analysis is applied to a schedule, it can examine, for example, the optimistic completion date, the pessimistic completion date, and the most likely completion date for each activity in the project and then predict a mean for the project schedule.

Monte Carlo technique A simulation technique that got its name from the casinos of Monte Carlo, Monaco. The simulation is completed using a computer software program that can simulate a project, using values for all possible variables, to predict the most likely model.

Multicriteria Decision Analysis A method to rate potential project team members based on criteria such as education, experience, skills, knowledge, and more.

Murder boards These are committees that ask every conceivable negative question about the proposed project. Their goals are to expose the project's strengths and weaknesses, and to kill the project if it's deemed unworthy for the organization to commit to. Also known as project steering committees or project selection committees.

Negative stakeholders Stakeholders that are opposed to the project's existence. These stakeholders do not want the project to succeed because they do not see or agree with the project's benefits that the project may bring about for the organization.

Net present value Evaluates the monies returned on a project for each period the project lasts.

Neutral stakeholders Stakeholders that are not affected by the project's success or failure. Examples may include inspectors, procurement officers, and some end users.

Neutral stakeholder status The stakeholder is aware of your project and doesn't care if the project succeeds or fails.

Noise Anything that interferes with or disrupts a message.

Nominal group technique As with brainstorming, participants are encouraged to generate as many ideas as possible, but the suggested ideas are ranked by a voting process.

Nonverbal Facial expressions, hand gestures, and body language are nonverbal cues that contribute to a message. Approximately 55 percent of communication is nonverbal.

Norming Project team members go about getting the project work, begin to rely on one another, and generally complete their project assignments.

Oligopoly A market condition where the market is so tight that the actions of one vendor affect the actions of all the others.

Opportunity cost The total cost of the opportunity that is refused to realize an opposing opportunity.

Ordinal scales A ranking approach that identifies and ranks the risks from very high to very unlikely or to some other value.

Organization chart Traditional chart that depicts how the organization is broken down by department and disciplines. This chart is sometimes called the organizational breakdown structure (OBS) and is arranged by departments, units, or teams.

Organizational interfaces The project management team needs to identify which departments are going to be involved in the project.

Organizational process assets The methodology an organization uses to perform its business, as well as the guidelines, procedures, and knowledge bases, such as the lessons learned documentation from past projects and any relevant historical information.

Organizational risks The performing organization can contribute to the project's risks through unreasonable cost, time, and scope expectations; poor project prioritization; inadequate funding or the disruption of funding; and competition with other projects for internal resources.

Organizational structure constraint The structure of the organization has a direct correlation to the amount of power a project manager has within a project.

Ouchi's Theory Z William Ouchi's theory is based on the participative management style of the Japanese. This theory states that workers are motivated by a sense of commitment, opportunity, and advancement.

Paralingual The pitch, tone, and inflections in the sender's voice affecting the message being sent.

Parametric estimate A quantitatively based duration estimate that uses mathematical formulas to predict how long an activity will take based on the quantities of work to be completed. This approach may also use a parametric model to extrapolate the costs for a project (for example, cost per hour and cost per unit). It can include variables and points based on conditions.

Pareto diagram A histogram that illustrates categories of failure within a project.

Parkinson's Law A theory that states: "Work expands so as to fill the time available for its completion." It is considered with time estimating, because bloated or padded activity estimates will fill the amount of time allotted to the activity.

Passive observation The observer records information about the work being completed without interrupting the process; sometimes called the invisible observer.

Payback period An estimate to predict how long it will take a project to pay back an organization for the project's investment of capital.

Performance report A report that depicts how well a project is performing. Often, the performance report is based on earned value management and may include cost or schedule variance reports.

Performing If a project team can reach the performing stage of team development, they trust one another, work well together, and issues and problems get resolved quickly and effectively.

Performing organization The organization whose employees or members are most directly involved in the project work.

Phase The logical division of a project based on the work or deliverable completed within that phase. Common examples include the phases within construction, software development, or manufacturing.

Phase-end review The review of a phase to determine if it accomplished its requirements. A phase-end review is also called a phase exit, a phase gate, and a kill point.

Phase exit The review of a phase to determine if it accomplished its requirements. This is also known as a phase gate.

Physical environment The physical structure and surroundings that affect a project's work.

Planned value (PV) Planned value is the work scheduled and the budget authorized to accomplish that work. It is the percentage of the BAC that reflects where the project should be at this point in time.

Planning package A WBS entry located below a control account and above the work packages. A planning package signifies that there is more planning that needs to be completed for this specific deliverable.

Planning process group The project management process group that creates the project management plan to execute, monitor and control, and close the project.

Plurality A group-decision method where the largest part of the group makes the decision even if it's not more than 50 percent of the total. (Consider three or four factions within the stakeholders.)

PMI Code of Ethics and Professional Conduct A PMI document that defines the expectations of its members to act responsibly, respectfully, fairly, and honestly in their leadership of projects and programs.

PMI member Anyone, certified as a project manager or not, who has joined the Project Management Institute.

Political interfaces The hidden goals, personal agendas, and alliances among the project team members and the stakeholders.

Positive stakeholders Stakeholders that want the project to succeed. Positive stakeholders are often the people that have the most to gain from the project's success and/or the most to lose if the project fails.

Power/influence grid Stakeholders are mapped on a grid based on their power and influence over the project.

Power/interest grid Stakeholders are mapped on a grid based on their power over the project in relation to their interest on the project.

Practitioner A person who is serving in the capacity of a project manager or contributing to the management of a project, portfolio of projects, or program. For example, a program manager is considered to be a project practitioner under this definition.

Precedence diagramming method A network diagram that shows activities in nodes and the relationship between each activity. Predecessors come before the current activity, and successors come after the current activity.

Predictive life cycle   A predictive life cycle, also called a plan-driven or waterfall approach, is a life cycle that "predicts" the work that will happen in each phase of the project.

Present value   A benefit comparison model to determine the present value of a future amount of money. The formula to calculate present value is $PV = FV \div (1 + I)^n$, where FV is future value, I is the given interest rate, and n is the number of periods.

Preventive action   A risk-related action that avoids risk within the project. A workaround to a problem within your project is an example of a preventive action.

Prioritization matrices   A table to rank and score project decisions and alternatives to determine the best solution for the project.

Privity   The contractual relationship between the buyer and the seller is often considered confidential and secret.

Probability and impact matrix   A matrix that ranks the probability of a risk event occurring and its impact on the project if the event does happen; used in qualitative and quantitative risk analyses.

Problem solving   This approach confronts the problem head-on and is the preferred method of conflict resolution. This is also known as confronting.

Process   A set of integrated activities to create a product, result, or service. Project management processes allow the project to move toward completion.

Process decision program chart (PDPC)   Helps the project team define all of the steps to get from the current state to a desired goal. It facilitates a conversation about what must be completed to reach the goal.

Process improvement plan   A project management subsidiary plan that aims to improve the project, not just the end result of the project. It strives to identify and eliminate waste and non-value-added activities.

Procurement management plan   The procurement management plan controls how the project will be allowed to contract goods and services.

Procurement planning   A process to identify which parts of the project warrant procurement from a vendor by the buyer.

Product acceptance criteria   This project scope statement component works with the project requirements, but focuses specifically on the product and what the conditions and processes are for formal acceptance of the product.

Product breakdown   A scope definition technique that breaks down a product into a hierarchical structure, much like a WBS breaks down a project scope.

Product life cycle   The life cycle of the product a project creates. For example, a project can create a piece of software; the software then has its own life cycle until it becomes defunct.

Product process A process that is unique to the type of work creating the product of the project. Product processes can also be unique to the performing organization of the project.

Product scope Defines the product or service that will come about as a result of completing the project.

Product scope description This is a narrative on what the project is creating as a deliverable for the project customer.

Profile analysis meeting A profile analysis meeting examines each of the roles in the project and documents that role's interests, concerns, influence, knowledge about the project, and the attitude that role will likely have toward the project.

Program A collection of related projects working in unison toward a common deliverable.

Progressive elaboration The process of gathering project details in steady, uniform steps. This process uses deductive reasoning, logic, and a series of information-gathering techniques to identify details about a project, product, or solution.

Project A temporary endeavor to create a unique product, service, or result. The end result of a project is also called a deliverable.

Project assumptions A project assumption is anything that is held to be true but not proven to be true.

Project boundaries A project boundary clearly states what is included with the project and what's excluded from the project. This helps to eliminate assumptions between the project management team and the project customer.

Project calendar The calendar that documents when the project work can occur.

Project charter This document authorizes the project. It defines the initial requirements of the project stakeholders. The project charter is endorsed by an entity outside of the project boundaries.

Project constraints A constraint is anything that limits the project manager's options. Consider a predetermined budget, deadline, resources, or materials the project manager must use within the project—these are all examples of project constraints.

Project deliverable The output of the project.

Project environment The location and culture of the environment where the project work will reside. The project environment includes the social, economic, and environmental variables the project must work with or around.

Project float This is the total time the project can be delayed without passing the customer-expected completion date.

Project life cycle The collection of phases from the start of a project to its completion.

Project Management Institute (PMI)   An organization of project management professionals from around the world, supporting and promoting the careers, values, and concerns of project managers.

Project management office (PMO)   A business unit that centralizes the operations and procedures of all projects within the organization. The PMO supports the project manager through software, templates, and administrative support. A PMO can exist in any organizational structure, but it is most common in matrix and projectized structures.

Project management plan   The documented approach of how a project will be planned, executed, monitored and controlled, and then closed. This document is a collection of subsidiary project management plans and related documents.

Project Management Professional (PMP)   A person who has proven project management experience and has qualified for and then passed the PMP examination.

Project management risks   These risks deal with faults in the management of the project: the unsuccessful allocation of time, resources, and scheduling; unacceptable work results; and poor project management.

Project management system   The defined set of rules, policies, and procedures that a project manager follows and utilizes to complete the project.

Project network diagram   A diagram that visualizes the flow of the project activities and their relationships to other project activities.

Project objectives   These are the measurable goals that determine a project's acceptability to the project customer and the overall success of the project. Objectives often include the cost, schedule, technical requirements, and quality demands.

Project portfolio management   The management and selection of projects that support an organization's vision and mission. It is the balance of project priority, risk, reward, and return on investment. This is a senior management process.

Project presentations   Presentations are useful in providing information to customers, management, the project team, and other stakeholders.

Project records   All the business of the project communications is also part of the organizational process assets. This includes e-mails, memos, letters, and faxes.

Project reports   Reports are formal communications on project activities, their status, and conditions.

Project requirements   These are the demands set by the customer, regulations, or the performing organization that must exist for the project deliverables to be acceptable. Requirements are often prioritized in a number of ways, from "must have" to "should have" to "would like to have."

Project scope management plan   This project management subsidiary plan controls how the scope will be defined, how the project scope statement will be created, how the WBS will be created, how scope validation will proceed, and how the project scope will be controlled throughout the project.

Project scope   This defines all of the work, and only the required work, to complete the project objectives.

Project scope statement   The project scope defines the project, the project deliverables, product requirements, project boundaries, acceptance procedures, and scope control.

Project stakeholder   Anyone who has a vested interest in a project's operation and/or its outcome.

Project statement of work (SOW)   This document defines all the products and services the project will provide.

Project variance   The final variance, which is discovered only at the project's completion. The formula is VAR = BAC − AC.

Projectized structure   An organization that assigns a project team to one project for the duration of the project life cycle. The project manager has high-to-almost-complete project power.

Proposal   A document the seller provides to the buyer. The proposal includes more than just a fee for the proposed work; it also includes information on the vendor's skills, the vendor's reputation, and ideas on how the vendor can complete the contracted work for the buyer.

Prototype   A model of the finished deliverable that allows the stakeholder to see how the final project deliverable may operate.

Pull communications   The central repository of information allows stakeholders to pull the information from the central source when they want—this is an example of pull communication. Pull communication means that the audience retrieves the information as they desire rather than the information being sent, or pushed, to them.

Purchase order (PO)   A purchase order is a form of a unilateral contract that the buyer provides to the vendor showing that the purchase has been approved by the buyer's organization.

Pure risks   These risks have only a negative outcome. Examples include loss of life or limb, fire, theft, natural disasters, and the like.

Push communications   If you created a report about your project and you sent it to five specific stakeholders, that would be an example of push communications. Push communications means that the sender pushes the same message to multiple people. Think of memos, faxes, press releases, broadcast e-mails: These are all pushed from one source to multiple recipients.

Qualitative risk analysis   This approach "qualifies" the risks that have been identified in the project. Specifically, qualitative risk analysis examines and prioritizes risks based on their probability of occurring and their impact on the project should they occur.

Quality   According to ASQ, the degree to which a set of inherent characteristics fulfills requirements.

Quality assurance   A management process that defines the quality system or quality policy that a project must adhere to. QA aims to plan quality into the project rather than to inspect quality into a deliverable.

Quality baseline   Documents the quality objectives for the project, including the metrics for stakeholder acceptance of the project deliverable.

Quality control   An inspection-driven process that measures work results to confirm that the project is meeting the relevant quality standards.

Quality management plan   This plan defines what quality means for the project, how the project will achieve quality, and how the project will map to organizational procedures pertaining to quality.

Quality metrics   The operational definitions that specify the measurements within a project and the expected targets for quality and performance.

Quality planning   The process of first determining which quality standards are relevant to your project and then finding out the best methods of adhering to those quality standards.

Quantitative risk analysis   This approach attempts to numerically assess the probability and impact of the identified risks. It also creates an overall risk score for the project. This method is more in-depth than qualitative risk analysis and relies on several different tools to accomplish its goal.

Quotation   From seller to buyer. Price is the determining factor in the decision-making process.

RACI chart   A RACI chart is a matrix chart that only uses the activities of responsible, accountable, consult, and inform.

RAG rating   An ordinal scale that uses red, amber, and green (RAG) to capture the probability, impact, and risk score.

Receiver   The person who receives the message.

Referent   The project team personally knows the project manager. Referent can also mean that the project manager refers to the person who assigned him the position.

Refinement   An update to the work breakdown structure.

Regression analysis   This is a statistical approach to predicting what future values may be, based on historical values. Regression analysis creates quantitative predictions based on variables within one value to predict variables in another. This form of estimating relies solely on pure statistical math to reveal relationships between variables and to predict future values.

Reporting system   A reporting system is usually a software program that can capture, store, and provide data analysis on the project. A good reporting tool allows the project manager to take project information, such as percentage of work complete, run the data through some earned value analysis, and then create reports to share with the stakeholders.

Request for Proposal (RFP)   From buyer to seller. Requests the seller to provide a proposal to complete the procured work or to provide the procured product.

Request for Quote (RFQ)   From buyer to seller. Requests the seller to provide a price for the procured product or service.

Requirements documentation   This documentation of what the stakeholders expected in the project defines all of the requirements that must be present for the work to be accepted by the stakeholders.

Requirements management plan   This subsidiary plan defines how changes to the project requirements will be permitted, how requirements will be tracked, and how changes to the requirements will be approved.

Requirements traceability matrix (RTM)   This is a table that maps the requirements throughout the project all the way to their completion.

Reserve analysis   Cost reserves are for unknown unknowns within a project. The contingency reserve is part of the project cost baseline, and is included as part of the project budget.

Residual risks   Risks that are expected to remain after a risk response.

Resistant stakeholder status   The stakeholder is aware of your project, but they aren't keen to the changes your project will create

Resource breakdown structure (RBS)   This is a hierarchical breakdown of the project resources by category and resource type. For example, you could have a category of equipment, a category of human resources, and a category of materials. Within each category, you could identify the types of equipment your project will use, the types of human resources, and the types of materials.

Resource calendar   The calendar that documents which project resources are available for the project work and when they are available.

Resource-leveling heuristic   A method to flatten the schedule when resources are overallocated. Resource leveling can be applied using different methods to accomplish different goals. One of the most common methods is to ensure that workers are not overextended on activities.

Responsibility   A responsibility is the work that a role performs.

Responsibility assignment matrix (RAM)   A RAM chart shows the correlation between project team members and the work they've been assigned to complete.

Reward   The project manager has the authority to reward the project team.

Risk   A project risk is an uncertain event or condition that can have a positive or negative effect on the project.

Risk identification   The systematic process of combing through the project, the project plan, the work breakdown structure, and all supporting documentation to identify as many risks that may affect the project as possible.

Risk management plan   A project management subsidiary plan that defines how risks will be identified, analyzed, responded to, and monitored within the project. The plan also defines the iterative risk management process that the project is expected to adhere to.

Risk management planning   The agreed-upon approach to the management of the project risk processes.

Risk owners   The individuals or entities that are responsible for monitoring and responding to an identified risk within the project.

Risk register   The risk register is a centralized database consisting of the outcome of all the other risk management processes, such as the outcome of risk identification, qualitative analysis, and quantitative analysis.

Risk-related contractual agreements   When the project management team decides to use transference to respond to a risk, a risk-related contractual agreement is created between the buyer and the seller.

Risk response audit   An audit to test the validity of the established risk responses.

Risk response plan   This subsidiary plan defines the risk responses that are to be used in the project for both positive and negative risks.

Risk responsibilities   The level of ownership an individual or entity has over a project risk.

Risk score   The calculated score based on each risk's probability and impact. The approach can be used in both qualitative and quantitative risk matrixes.

Role   This person is responsible for a specific portion of the project. Roles are usually tied to job titles, such as network engineer, mechanical engineer, and electrician.

Rolling wave planning   The imminent work is planned in detail, while the work in the future is planned at a high level. This is a form of progressive elaboration.

Root cause identification   Root cause identification aims to find out why a risk event may be occurring, the causal factors for the risk events, and then, eventually, how the events can be mitigated or eliminated.

Rough order of magnitude   This rough estimate is used during the initiating processes and in top-down estimates. The range of variance for the estimate can be from −25 percent to +75 percent.

Rule of Seven   A component of a control chart that illustrates the results of seven measurements on one side of the mean, which is considered "out of control" in the project.

Run chart   A quality control tool that shows the results of inspection in the order in which they've occurred. The goal of a run chart is first to demonstrate the results of a process over time and then to use trend analysis to predict when certain trends may reemerge.

Salience model   Groups of stakeholders are mapped on a grid where their power, urgency, and legitimacy are in relation to one another.

Sapir-Whorf hypothesis   A theory that suggests there's a link between the language a person (or culture) speaks and how that person or culture behaves in the world.

Scatter diagram   A quality control tool that tracks the relationship between two variables. The two variables are considered related the closer they track against a diagonal line.

Schedule baseline   The expected timeline of the project. The difference between the planned schedule and the experience schedule reveals schedule variances within the project.

Schedule management plan   A subsidiary plan in the project management plan. It defines how the project schedule will be created, estimated, controlled, and managed.

Schedule milestones   The project customer may have specific dates when phases of the project should be completed. These milestones are often treated as project constraints.

Schedule performance index (SPI)   Measures the project based on its schedule performance. The formula is $SPI = EV/PV$.

Schedule variance (SV)   The difference between the earned value and the planned value. The formula is $SV = EV - PV$.

Scope baseline   The scope baseline is a combination of three project documents: the project scope statement, the work breakdown structure, and the WBS dictionary. The creation of the project deliverable will be measured against the scope baseline to show any variances from what was expected and what the project team has created.

Scope creep   Undocumented, unapproved changes to the project scope.

Scope validation   The formal inspection of the project deliverables, which leads to project acceptance.

Scoring models   These models use a common set of values for all of the projects up for selection. For example, values can be profitability, complexity, customer demand, and so on.

Screening system   A tool that filters or screens out vendors that don't qualify for the contract.

Secondary risks   New risks that are created as a result of a risk response.

Seller rating systems   These are used by organizations to rate prior experience with each vendor they have worked with in the past. The seller rating system can track performance, quality ratings, delivery, and even contract compliance.

Sender   The person who is sending the message.

Sender-receiver models   Feedback loops and barriers to communications.

Sensitivity analysis A quantitative risk analysis tool that examines each risk to determine which one has the largest impact on the project's success.

Sharing A risk response that shares the advantages of a positive risk within a project.

Single source Many vendors can provide what your project needs to purchase, but you prefer to work with a specific vendor.

Smoothing This approach smooths out the conflict by minimizing the perceived size of the problem. It is a temporary solution, but can calm team relations and boisterous discussions.

Soft logic The order of the activities doesn't necessarily have to happen in a specific order. For example, you could install the light fixtures first, then the carpet, and then paint the room. The project manager could use soft logic to change the order of the activities if so desired. This is also known as discretionary dependency or preferential logic.

Sole source Only one vendor can provide what your project needs to purchase. Examples include a specific consultant, specialized service, or unique type of material.

Staffing management plan This is a subsidiary plan of the human resource management plan. It specifically addresses how the human resource requirements will be met in the project. It can address internal staffing, procurement of resources, or negotiations with other projects for shared resources.

Stakeholder A person or group that is affected by the project or that may affect the group. Stakeholders can be positive, negative, neutral in their attitude toward the project success.

Stakeholder analysis Stakeholder analysis is a process that considers and ranks project stakeholders based on their influence, interests, and expectations of the project. This process uses a systematic approach to identify all of the project stakeholders, ranking the stakeholders by varying factors, and then addressing stakeholders' needs, requirements, and expectations.

Stakeholder classification models Grids that rank their stakeholders influence in relation to their interest in the project. There are several types of these models that are used as part of stakeholder analysis. The most common models are the power/interest grid, the power/influence grid, the influence/impact grid, and the salience model.

Stakeholder engagement The project manager and the project team aims to keep the project stakeholders engaged and involved in the project to ensure that decisions, approvals, and communications are maintained as defined in the stakeholder management plan and the stakeholder management strategy.

Stakeholder identification Stakeholder identification is the process of ensuring that all of the stakeholders have been identified as early as possible in the project. Stakeholder identification ensures that all of the stakeholders are identified and represented, and their needs, expectations, and concerns are addressed.

Stakeholder management   Stakeholder management is a project management knowledge area that focuses on four activities: identifying the project stakeholder, planning on how to manage the stakeholders, managing the stakeholders, and controlling the stakeholder engagement.

Stakeholder management plan   The stakeholder management plan helps the project manager and the project team define a strategy for managing the project stakeholders. It helps to establish stakeholder engagement at the launch of the project, over the project life cycle, and how to improve upon the level of engagement identified.

Stakeholder management planning   Stakeholder management planning is the process of creating a strategy to manage the stakeholders in the project. It's the analysis of what the stakeholders want the project to do, how the stakeholders' wants align with that of other stakeholders, and the prioritization of the stakeholders within the project.

Stakeholder notifications   Notices to the stakeholders about resolved issues, approved changes, and the overall health of the project.

Stakeholder register   The stakeholder register documents all of the stakeholders' information, positions, concerns, interests, and attitudes toward the project. The stakeholder register should be updated as new stakeholders are identified or as stakeholders leave the project.

Start-to-finish   An activity relationship that requires an activity to start so that its successor can finish. This is the most unusual of all the activity relationship types.

Start-to-start   An activity relationship type that requires the current activity to start before its successor can start.

Statistical sampling   A process of choosing a percentage of results at random. For example, a project creating a medical device may have 20 percent of all units randomly selected to check for quality.

Status review meeting   A regularly scheduled meeting to discuss the status of the project and its progress toward completing the project scope statement.

Storming   The project team struggles for project positions, leadership, and project direction. The project team can become hostile toward the project leader, challenge ideas, and try to establish and claim positions about the project work. The amount of debate and fury can vary depending on if the project team is willing to work together, the nature of the project, and the control of the project manager.

Strong matrix structure   An organization where organizational resources are pooled into one project team, but the functional managers have less project power than the project manager.

Subnet   A representation of a project network diagram that is often used for outsourced portions of projects, repetitive work within a project, or a subproject. Also called a fragnet.

Subprojects A smaller project managed within a larger, parent project. Subprojects are often contracted work whose deliverable allows the larger project to progress.

Sunk costs Monies that have already been invested in a project.

Supportive stakeholder status The stakeholder is aware of your project, is happy about the project, and hopes that your project is successful

SWOT analysis SWOT analysis is the process of examining the project from the perspective of each characteristic: strengths, weaknesses, opportunities, and threats.

System or process flowcharts Flowcharts that illustrate the flow of a process through a system, such as a project change request through the change control system, or work authorization through a quality control process.

Systems analysis A scope definition approach that studies and analyzes a system, its components, and the relationship of the components within the system.

Systems engineering This project scope statement–creation process studies how a system should work, designs and creates a system model, and then enacts the working system based on the project's goals and the customer's expectations. Systems engineering aims to balance the time and cost of the project in relation to the scope of the project.

Technical interfaces The project team identifies the disciplines and specialties that the project will require to complete the project scope statement. The technical interfaces are the resources that will be doing the project work.

Technical, quality, or performance risks Technical risks are associated with new, unproven, or complex technologies being used on the project. Changes to the technology during the project implementation can also be a risk. Quality risks are the levels set for expectations of impractical quality and performance.

Template A previous project or a methodology that can be adapted for the current project.

Three-point estimate An estimating technique for each activity that requires optimistic, most likely, and pessimistic estimates to be created. Based on these three estimates, an average can be created to predict how long the activity should take.

Time and materials contract A contract type in which the buyer pays for the time and materials for the procured work. This is a simple contract, usually for smaller procurement conditions. These contract types may contain a not-to-exceed clause, or the buyer assumes the risk for cost overruns.

Time reporting system A system to record the actual time to complete project activities.

To-Complete Performance Index A formula to forecast the likelihood of a project to achieve its goals based on what's happening in the project right now. There are two different flavors for the TCPI, depending on what you want to accomplish. If you want to see if your project can meet the budget at completion, you'll use this formula: TCPI = (BAC – EV)/(BAC – AC). If you want to see if your project can meet the newly created estimate at completion, you'll use this version of the formula: TCPI = (BAC – EV)/(EAC – AC).

Total float   This is the total time an activity can be delayed without delaying project completion.

Transference   A risk response that transfers the ownership of the risk to another party. Insurance, licensed contractors, or other project teams are good examples of transference. A fee and contractual relationships are typically involved with the transference of a risk.

Tree diagram   Tree diagrams show hierarchies and decomposition of a solution, an organization, or a project team. The WBS and an org chart are examples of tree diagrams.

Trend analysis   The science of using past results to predict future performance.

Triple Constraints of Project Management   Also known as the Iron Triangle. This theory posits that time, cost, and scope are three constraints that every project has.

Unanimity   A group decision method where everyone must be in agreement.

Unaware stakeholder status   The stakeholder doesn't know about the project, nor how it might affect the stakeholder.

Value analysis   As with value engineering, this approach examines the functions of the project's product in relation to the cost of the features and functions. This is where, to some extent, the grade of the product is in relationship to the cost of the product.

Value engineering   This approach to project scope statement creation attempts to find the correct level of quality in relation to a reasonable budget for the project deliverable while still achieving an acceptable level of performance from the product.

Variable costs   Costs that change based on the conditions applied in the project (the number of meeting participants, the supply of and demand for materials, and so on).

Variance   The difference between what was expected and what was experienced.

Variance at completion (VAC)   A forecasting formula that predicts how much of a variance the project will likely have based on current conditions within the project. The formula is VAC = BAC – EAC.

WBS dictionary   A WBS companion document that defines all of the characteristics of each element within the WBS.

WBS template   A prepopulated WBS for repetitive projects. Previous projects' WBSs are often used as templates for current similar projects.

Weak matrix structure   An organization where organizational resources are pooled into one project team, but the functional managers have more project power than the project manager.

Weighting system   This takes out the personal preferences of the decision maker in the organization to ensure that the best seller is awarded the contract. Weights are assigned to the values of the proposals, and each proposal is scored.

Withdrawal   This conflict resolution method sees one side of the argument walking away from the problem, usually in disgust.

Work-around   An unplanned response to a negative risk within the project. This is an example of a corrective action.

Work breakdown structure (WBS)   A deliverables-oriented breakdown of the project scope.

Work package   The smallest item in the work breakdown structure.

Work performance information   The results of the project work as needed. This includes technical performance measures, project status, information on what the project has created to date, corrective actions, and performance reports.

INDEX

preparing for inspection, 186
project team management and,
356–357
quality control and, 314, 321
risk monitoring/control and,
436
scope control and, 188

stakeholder engagement and,
508, 510
writing style, 380

X

X and Y Theory, 361–362

Z

zero-sum awards, 347, 355
Z Theory, 362